KU-749-480

EG29434

Penguin Reference Books

THE PENGUIN ATLAS OF WORLD HISTORY

Vol. 2: From the French Revolution to the Present

Herman Kinder and
Werner Hilgemann

The Penguin Atlas of World History

Translated by
Ernest A. Menze
with maps designed by
Harald and Ruth Bukor

Volume II: From the French Revolution to the Present

Updated Edition

Penguin Books

PENGUIN BOOKS

Published by the Penguin Group
Penguin Books Ltd, 27 Wrights Lane, London w8 5tz, England
Penguin Putnam Inc., 375 Hudson Street, New York, New York 10014, USA
Penguin Books Australia Ltd, Ringwood, Victoria, Australia
Penguin Books Canada Ltd, 10 Alcorn Avenue, Toronto, Ontario, Canada M4V 3B2
Penguin Books (NZ) Ltd, Private Bag 102902, NSMC Auckland, New Zealand

Penguin Books Ltd, Registered Offices: Harmondsworth, Middlesex, England

dtv-Atlas zur Weltgeschichte, Vol 2 first published by
Deutscher Taschenbuch Verlag 1966

This translation first published 1978
This updated edition published 1995
3

Typeset in Monophoto Times
Typeset by Fyldetype Limited, Kirkham, Preston, Lancashire PR4 3BJ

Printed in Singapore by Kyodo Printing Co plc

Contents

List of Abbreviations

Abys.	Abyssinian
acc.	according
addit.	additional
admin.	administration
Afr.	African
agricult.	agricultural
Alger.	Algerian
Alp.	Alpine
Amer.	American
anon.	anonymous
approx.	approximately
Argen.	Argentinian
Arab.	Arabic
archbp.	archbishop
Armen.	Armenian
Aust.	Austrian
auton.	autonomous
b.	battle
Balk.	Balkan
Balt.	Baltic
Bav.	Bavarian
Belg.	Belgian
bib.	biblical
Boh.	Bohemian
bp	bishop
bpc	bishopric
B.R.D.	German Federal Republic
Brit.	British
Bulg.	Bulgarian
Byz.	Byzantine
c.	*circa*
cal.	called
cap.	capital (city)
Calv.	Calvinistic
Can.	Canadian
capit.	capitalist
Carol.	Carolingian
Cath.	Catholic
cen.	central
cent.	century
cf.	compare
Chil.	Chilean
Chin.	Chinese
christ.	christian
c.-in-c.	commander-in-chief
colon.	colonial
Com.	Communist
con.	conservative
concl.	concluded
confed.	confederation
const.	constitutional
ctr(s).	culture(s)
cult.	cultural
d.	died
Dan.	Danish
D.D.R.	German Democratic Republic (East Germany)
dem.	democratic
dest.	destroyed
dom.	domestic
Domin.	Dominican
dyn.	dynastic
E.	east
eccles.	ecclesiastical
econ.	economic
educ.	educational
Egypt.	Egyptian
elect.	electoral
Eng.	English
esp.	especially
est.	established
Est.	Estonian
Eur.	European
exc.	except
excl.	excluding
exec.	executive
extraterrit.	extraterritorial
fed.	federal
Fin.	Finnish
finan.	financial
for.	foreign
Fr.	French
Ger.	German
Germ.	Germanic
Gk	Greek
gov.-gen.	governor-general
gvt	government
gvtl	governmental
Heb.	Hebrew
hered.	hereditary
hr(s)	hour(s)
Hung.	Hungarian
imp.	imperial
incl.	including
incorp.	incorporated
ind.	independent
Ind.	Indian
indust.	industrial
infl.	influence
int.	international
Ion.	Ionian
Iran.	Iranian
Isl.	Islamic
Ital.	Italian
Jap.	Japanese
Jes.	Jesuit
Jew.	Jewish

kdm	kingdom
km	kilometre
Kor.	Korean
Lab.	Labour
Latv.	Latvian
leg.	legislative
lib.	liberal
Lith.	Lithuanian
Liv.	Livonian
loc.	located
m	metre
mar.	married
Medit.	Mediterranean
Mex.	Mexican
mi.	miles
mil.	million
milit.	military
minist.	ministerial
miss.	missionary
mod.	modern
Mongol.	Mongolian
mt(s)	mountain(s)
N.	north
nat.	national
NE.	north-east
Nor.	Norwegian
Nord.	Nordic
nr	near
N.T.	New Testament
NW.	north-west
obt.	obtained
Orth.	Orthodox
O.T.	Old Testament
Ott.	Ottoman
Pac.	Pacific
Pak.	Pakistani
Palest.	Palestinian
parl.	parliamentary
Pers.	Persian
Pol.	Polish
polit.	political
pop.	population
Port.	Portuguese
posn	position
P.O.W.s	prisoners of war
pres.	presidential
prob.	probably
Prot.	Protestant
prov.	provincial
provis.	provisional
Prus.	Prussian
pty	principality
rad.	radical
relig.	religious
repub.	republican
rest.	restoration
Rom.	Roman
roy.	royal
Roum.	Roumanian
Rus.	Russian
s.	south
sc.	scientific
Scand.	Scandinavian
SE.	south-east
sec.	secular
sep.	separate
Serb.	Serbian
Slav.	Slavonic
Slovak.	Slovakian
soc.	social
Sp.	Spanish
sq.	square
subj.	subjugate(d)
subs.	subsequently
SW.	south-west
Swed.	Swedish
Syr.	Syrian
tech.	technological
territ.	territorial
Tib.	Tibetan
trad.	traditional
Turk.	Turkish
Ukr.	Ukrainian
unconst.	unconstitutional
var.	various
vict(s).	victory(ies)
W.	west
yr(s)	year(s)

During the **19th cent.**–the transitional and final period of Eur. or Occidental dominance–there were great advances in learning. These had been made possible by man's conviction that all things may be encompassed by reason (rationalism) while aiming for the exact determination and exploration of facts (positivism) and acting on theories of their practical application (pragmatism). The **tech. cent.** fostered a materialistic viewpoint, belief in progress and utilitarianism. Accompanied by an increasing loss of cult. style, it developed bourgeois modes of life which, containing modern bureaucratic elements, made possible the creation of large imperialistic states and the Europeanization of the world. After the Enlightenment, the face of the world was shaped by revolutions:

1. **Polit. revolutions** overcame the absolutist system and est. forms of gvt based on Natural Law and sec. reason to safeguard personal liberty and polit. equality. They replaced the feudal state with a dem. **class society** and reached their highest stage with the development of the principle of popular sovereignty. This new concept of the state was first realized in N. America; after the Fr. Revolution it asserted itself in Europe, where it unleashed polit. nationalism as a result of the struggles against the forces of the *Ancien Régime* and the rule of NAPOLEON (p. 41).
2. **The Indust. Revolution** proceeded from England. It replaced existing methods of production (the crafts, the putting-out system, manufactures), and made possible, through the utilization of machines, entrepreneurs (the owners of private capital) and wage earners, mass production for a world-wide market. Tech. and sc. advances, the legal and soc. emancipation of the individual, capitalistic industrialization and the sudden increase of pop. changed the material, soc., and intellectual conditions of life fundamentally and found specific expression in Socialism (p. 66).

New Polit. and Econ. Theories

Stimulated by the examples of Rom. antiquity and an idealized image of England, **Montesquieu** (1689–1755) published

1721 the *Lettres Persanes* (*Persian Letters*), which presented an ironic critique of Fr. absolutism, and, his major work,

1748 *De l'esprit des lois* (*The Spirit of the Laws*), which further developed LOCKE's concept of the separation of powers (I, p. 269). Acc. to MONTESQUIEU, personal liberty could be guaranteed only by a 'moderate state' such as a **const. monarchy,** in which each branch of power placed checks and balances on the others. **Exec. power** (the admin.) rested with the king; he determined the leg. periods and held veto power over the **legislative.** Leg. power was exercised by representatives elected directly by the people **(the representational system)** and was divided into two chambers: the aristocratic, hered. upper chamber and the elected bourgeois lower chamber; it controlled the executive and had the right to approve taxation. Of less importance was the ind. **judicature** (courts of law).

Significance: great infl. on const. developments during the 19th cent. (cf. U.S., pp 13–15; Fr. Revolution, pp. 18–21).

Jean-Jacques Rousseau (1712–78; I, p. 257) conceived an idealized dem. image of society in his

1762 Contrat Social (The Social Contract). Since it is people who join in the state to protect their liberty and equality, sovereignty rests with them; those who govern are the people's functionaries; laws need universal consent, popular sovereignty being absolute, indivisible, inalienable and manifesting itself in the **volonté général** ('general will'), which always aims at the best interest of all; which is therefore always right and always identical with the will of the individual. Liberty exists only in this **equality,** i.e. in the acceptance of the general will. It is not identical with the *volonté des tous* (the sum of self-centred individual wills); it may, moreover, be represented by a minority on behalf of all.

Significance: the Utopian concept influenced the Fr. Revolution as well as the dem. and nationalistic movements of the 19th cent. The question of its infl. on the 20th cent.'s totalitarian systems remains controversial.

The transfer of Enlightenment ideas into econ. and soc. life led to **econ. liberalism.** Under the motto **'Laissez faire,** laissez passer' it called for a 'natural order' free from the infl. of the state, in which the freedom of property and the crafts, free competition and trade would guarantee econ. progress and wealth.

François Quesnay (1694–1774), was a representative of **physiocratic** thinking (Gk for the supremacy of nature) who reacted against mercantilism (I, p. 261); the personal physician of LOUIS XV, QUESNAY considered the soil to be the only source of wealth. Agriculture was to him the one productive force; trade and the crafts he considered 'sterile'.

Adam Smith (1723–90) considered labour to be the true source of wealth. Natural self-interest promotes the production of goods for the market; they receive their (exchange-)value in accordance with the 'natural law' of supply and demand, expressed in the **market price.** Free competition and free trade will lead to soc. harmony and justice. The state's only task remains to protect the country against enemies from without and to provide for order at home (the law; the maintenance and admin. of public institutions).

Significance: published in 1776, ADAM SMITH's epoch-making work, **The Wealth of Nations** (full title: *Inquiry into the Nature and Causes of the Wealth of Nations*; sometimes called 'The Bible of capitalism') developed for the first time the concept of a comprehensive econ. system and laid the foundations for the so-called Classical School of Economics, which became the guiding force of the 19th cent.

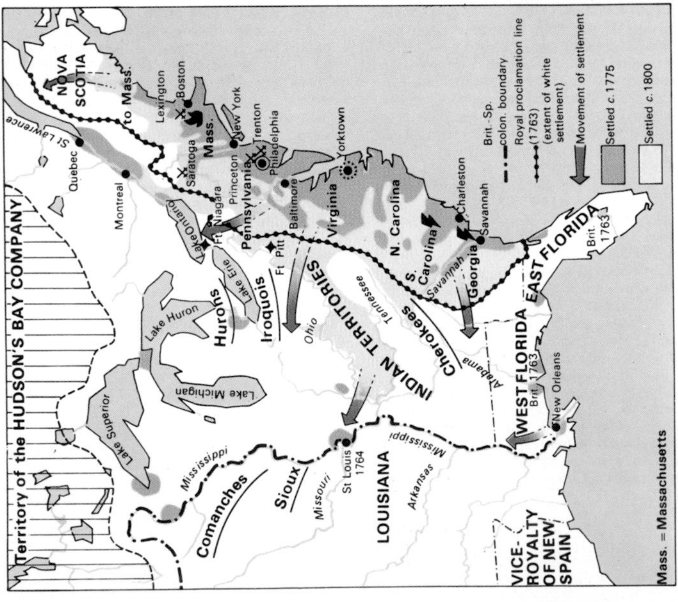

European settlement of North America in the 18th cent.

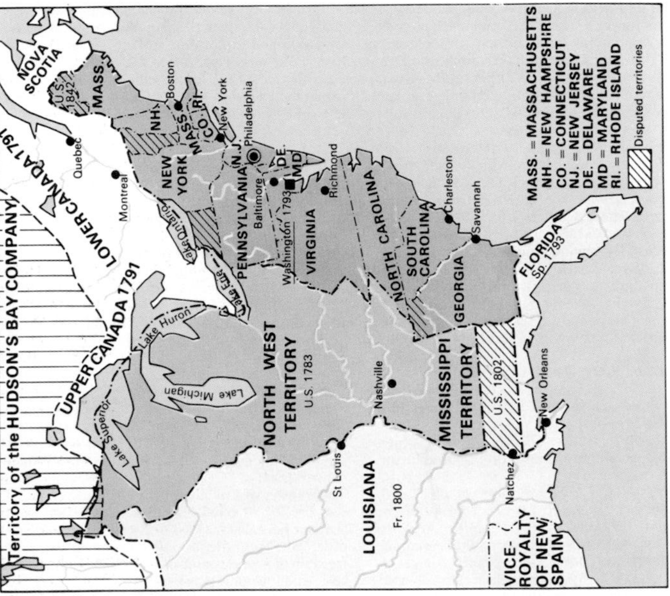

The United States, 1783

The Road to Independence

The Peace of Paris (1763, cf. I, p. 283) removed for the Brit. settlers the danger of Fr. encirclement and enhanced their polit. self-esteem. This was, however, violated by the imp. policies of the 'King's friends', a group of parliamentarians dependent on GEORGE III [1760–1820]. Tensions between the mother country and the colonies increased (prohibition of settlement w. of the Appalachians, limitations of colon. trade, the levying of direct taxes to help to pay Brit. war debts, etc.).

1765 The Stamp Act was passed, placing a tax on documents, newspapers, books. The elder PITT (I, p. 283) and BURKE (p. 31) stood up for the interests of the colonists, but were only partially successful. In 1766 the Stamp Act was repealed; but in its stead new import duties were introduced (the Townshend Act); after 1770, this led to unrest in Boston, Mass., and a boycott of Brit. goods. Radicals like SAMUEL ADAMS (1722–1803) and THOMAS JEFFERSON est. 'corresponding societies' to organize separation movements, which later received extra momentum through THOMAS PAINE's (p. 31) pamphlet *Common Sense* (1776).

Demands for representation in Parliament ('no taxation without representation') were not met by the Brit. gvt, though the special taxes, with the exception of the tea duty, which safeguarded the E. India Company's monopoly on tea, were eliminated. Open conflict was unleashed by the

1773 Boston Tea Party: the cargoes from three tea ships were thrown into Boston Harbour. The gvt closed the harbour and declared martial law.

1774 1st Continental Congress at Philadelphia: delegates of the 13 colonies (Massachusetts, New Jersey, New York, Rhode Island, Connecticut, New Hampshire, Pennsylvania, Delaware, Virginia, Maryland, N. Carolina, S. Carolina, Georgia) decided to suspend trade with Britain until the pre-1763 legal *status quo* was restored.

The first armed clash between Amer. militia and Brit. troops came on

18 Apr. 1775 at Lexington. It developed into the

1775–83 **Amer. War of Independence.** The settlers, numbering *c.* 3 mil., lacked trained troops, money, war materials or consistent leadership. **George Washington** (1732–99), a Virginia planter (Mt Vernon), was made c.-in-c. by the 2nd Continental Congress. His opponents were, first, the Brit. colon. army (among them 17,000 partly unreliable mercenaries from Hesse and Brunswick, who had been sold by their princes); secondly, the 'loyalists', Americans who remained faithful to England; and thirdly, Ind. tribes allied with England.

4 Jul. 1776 Declaration of Independence of the 13 United States (symbolized by the 13 stripes of the Amer. flag): first formulation of **human rights** (life, liberty and the pursuit of happiness), which became guiding forces for the U.S., and of the **right to polit. opposition** derived from them. The document attesting to the birth of the new nation and present world power was the work of **Thomas Jefferson** (1743–1826). The '4th of July' became a nat. holiday for the U.S.A.

1776 Brit. defeats along the Delaware at Trenton and Princeton. Logistics problems and the unorthodox guerrilla tactics of the settlers made the struggle more difficult for the British.

1777 Amer. vict. at Saratoga.

Benjamin Franklin (1706–90) represented the Amer. cause in Paris as the first U.S. ambassador. Aristocratic volunteers fought under WASHINGTON (among them the Marquis DE LAFAYETTE (p. 19), the Pol. nat. hero THADDEUS KOSCIUSZKO (I, p. 285), and the Prus. general and organizer of the Amer. army Baron VON STEUBEN). 'Midwives of the Amer. Republic', the absolutist powers France and Spain entered the war against England; 1779–82 unsuccessful siege of Gibraltar, but conquest of Minorca by Spain; Brit. naval victs. in the w. Indies (RODNEY) at St Vincent, 1781, and Santo Domingo, 1782.

To combat Brit. naval raiding

1780 Russia, France, Spain, the Netherlands, Sweden, Denmark, Austria and Prussia est. 'armed neutrality at sea'. The principle that the 'neutral flag protects enemy goods with the exception of war materials' became part of mod. int. maritime law. Under ROCHAMBEAU's command, Fr. troops landed in Rhode Island.

1781 After the siege of Yorktown by the Americans, the British surrendered (GNEISENAU (p. 33) was among the 7,200 P.O.W.s).

1783 Peace of Paris: Britain recognized Amer. Independence; Tobago in the w. Indies and Senegambia fell to France; Spain received Minorca and Florida.

Significance (for Britain): most important defeat since the 100 Years War (I, p. 191); injury to the Brit. Transatlantic empire;

(for France): addit. war debts burdened the already run-down public finances (p. 16); the Fr. volunteers were acclaimed as freedom fighters, criticism of the *Ançien Régime* increased;

(for N. America): independence attained after great sacrifices (70,000 dead); 'loyalists' emigrated to Canada; const. problems remained unresolved, the loose confederation threatening to fall apart.

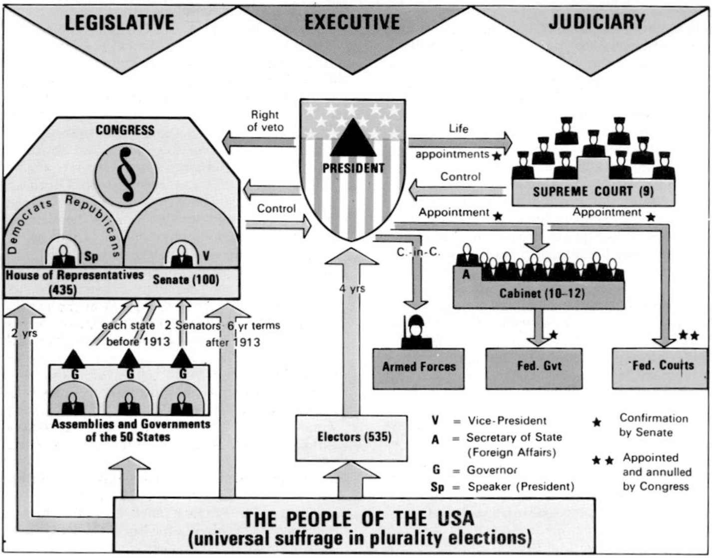

LEGISLATIVE
EXECUTIVE
JUDICIARY
CONGRESS
§
Democrats Republicans
Sp
V
House of Representatives (435)
Senate (100)
Right of veto
Control
PRESIDENT
Life appointments ★
Control
SUPREME COURT (9)
Appointment ★
Appointment ★
C.-in-C.
A
Cabinet (10–12)
4 yrs
2 yrs
each state before 1913
2 Senators
6 yr terms after 1913
G G G
Assemblies and Governments of the 50 States
Armed Forces
Fed. Gvt
Fed. Courts
★
★★
Electors (535)
V = Vice-President
A = Secretary of State (Foreign Affairs)
G = Governor
Sp = Speaker (President)
★ Confirmation by Senate
★★ Appointed and annulled by Congress
THE PEOPLE OF THE USA
(universal suffrage in plurality elections)

The Constitution of the United States of America

to Gt Britain 1818
Missouri
to U.S. 1818
CANADA
Great Lakes area
Quebec
U.S. 1842
MISSOURI TERRITORY
Mississippi
MINNESOTA TERRITORY
MICHIGAN TERR
V. 1791
Boston
Comanches
Border treaty 1819
Sioux
New York
NEW MEXICO
LOUISIANA
Purchased from France 1803
ILLINOIS 1818
INDIANA 1816
OHIO 1803
Pittsburgh
Baltimore
Washington
1776–89
Indianapolis
Danville
Richmond
Arkansas
St Louis
Ohio
VICE-ROYALTY OF NEW SPAIN
from 1821 Emp. of Mexico
ARKANSAS TERRITORY
KENTUCKY 1792
Nashville
TENNESSEE 1796
13 ORIGINAL STATES
Kansas
MISSISSIPPI 1817
ALABAMA 1819
TEXAS
1812 LOUISIANA
Natchez
New Orleans
FLORIDA
Purchased from Spain 1819
Extent of settlement 1830
Brit. attacks 1813/14
Trails of the settlers
V. = VERMONT

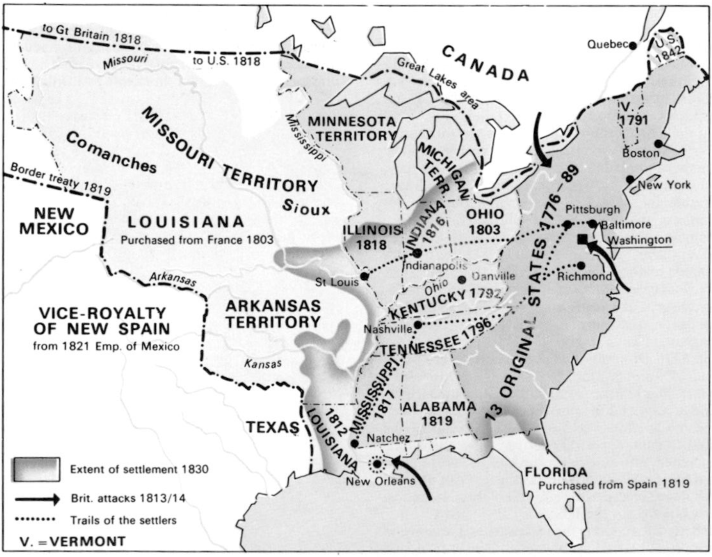

The development of the United States of America to 1820

The Establishment of the United States of America

Following Virginia's example, the individual states replaced their colon. statutes with state constitutions. These guaranteed:

1. Popular sovereignty by means of basic dem. rights: **1776 the Virginia Bill of Rights** (JEFFERSON).
2. The separation of powers and the elective principle for all offices of state;
3. The separation of church and state (1785 Virginia Statute of Relig. Liberty).

Inflation, econ. problems and border conflicts with Indians forced the states to cooperate.

1787 Const. Convention at Philadelphia: BENJAMIN FRANKLIN and JAMES MADISON mediated between the 'Federalists', who advocated a strong cen. gvt (ALEXANDER HAMILTON, JOHN ADAMS, GEORGE WASHINGTON), and the Republicans (later Democrats–JEFFERSON), who stressed the rights of the individual states. The 55 delegates of the 13 original states compromised by establishing a **fed. republic under a president.** The written constitution was ratified by all the individual states only reluctantly, but became law in 1789. The veneration of the 'founding fathers' in the U.S. corresponds to the 'myth of the legitimate ruling house' in Europe.

17 Sep. 1787 The Const. Convention issued the **Constitution of the United States of America,** the constitution of the 1st mod. democracy. Essential characteristics: the **separation of powers** (MONTESQUIEU, p. 11) and a system of checks and balances (a) between the Fed. gvt and the states (double citizenship): the Fed. gvt responsible for defence, currency, for. policy, overseas trade; the individual states for roads, education, law enforcement, police; (b) between the individual states of the Union.

The **President** became head of state and chief administrator. He was later nominated by the parties and indirectly elected for a 4-yr term (re-election possible once; exception ROOSEVELT 1940–44). He appoints the secretaries of state (ministers) and may be removed from office before the expiration of his term only through successfully completed impeachment procedures; politically, however, he is subject to control by Congress, and constitutionally by the Supreme Court.

Congress consists of 2 chambers which may not be dissolved: the House of Representatives (members elected directly for 2-yr terms) and the Senate (one third of the senators elected for 6-yr terms every 2 yrs to represent the individual states). The president, who holds a suspensive veto, and the Supreme Court watch over the legislative process.

The Supreme Court (consisting of 9 ind. members appointed by the president for life terms) exercises the judicial review of const. and leg. problems. The constitution has been amended only 26 times since 1789.

The Period of the Virginia Presidents

1789–97 George Washington. ALEXANDER HAMILTON (1757–1804) proposed a nat. programme to develop industry, commerce and finances. This stabilized the newly created state and laid the foundations for the power of Amer. capitalism. Founded in 1793, the cap. of Washington became in 1800 the seat of the presidents (the White House) and of the Congress (the Capitol). Under

1797–1801 JOHN ADAMS (a Federalist) the first difficulties with the s. (Kentucky)–owing to the Alien and Sedition Acts–set in. Under

1801–9 Thomas Jefferson (Republican) there was a reaction against the centralistic policies of the Fed. gvt, expressed in the maxim 'a minimum of government and governing'. The energies and interests of the nation were directed to the

'Winning of the West': the westward expansion through settlement by Americans and immigration from Western, Cen. and Northern Europe. The pop. increased from 3·9 mil. (1790) to 7·2 mil. (1810), pushing across the Appalachians into the interior. Settlers and land-settlement companies received grants of land against payment of the legally fixed minimum price (approx. $1.00 an acre). Though theoretically equal in the eyes of the law, the Indians were persecuted (Gens. WAYNE, ANDREW JACKSON) and reacted with cruel raids.

After 1787, settlement of the NW. and Mississippi territories led to the establishment of the following states: Kentucky (1792), Tennessee (1796), Ohio (1803), Louisiana (1812), Indiana (1816), Mississippi (1817), Illinois (1818) and Alabama (1819).

For. policy: a tendency to **isolationism** existed from the establishment of the United States.

1793 Declaration of neutrality despite the alliance with France (1778) and the War of the Coalition (p. 23). In his 'farewell address' (1796), WASHINGTON warned against 'lasting entanglements' with Europe.

1803 Louisiana Purchase, sold by NAPOLEON for $15 mil. (p. 31). This, the 'greatest real-estate deal in the history of the U.S.', facilitated the opening of the continent by means of the now unobstructed Mississippi River traffic. The Embargo Act of 1807 was the response of the U.S. to tensions with Britain over Ind. problems, territ. claims, commercial competition.

1809–17 To obtain Canada, JAMES MADISON (Republican) allowed himself to be drawn into war with Britain,

1812–14 ('the 2nd War of Independence'); he was unable to prevent Brit. coastal raids and the destruction of Washington. Gen. ANDREW JACKSON ('Old Hickory', p. 95) defended New Orleans.

1814 Treaty of Ghent: Britain was satisfied with the rest. of the *status quo ante* because of the situation in Europe (p. 37); the Great Lakes were neutralized.

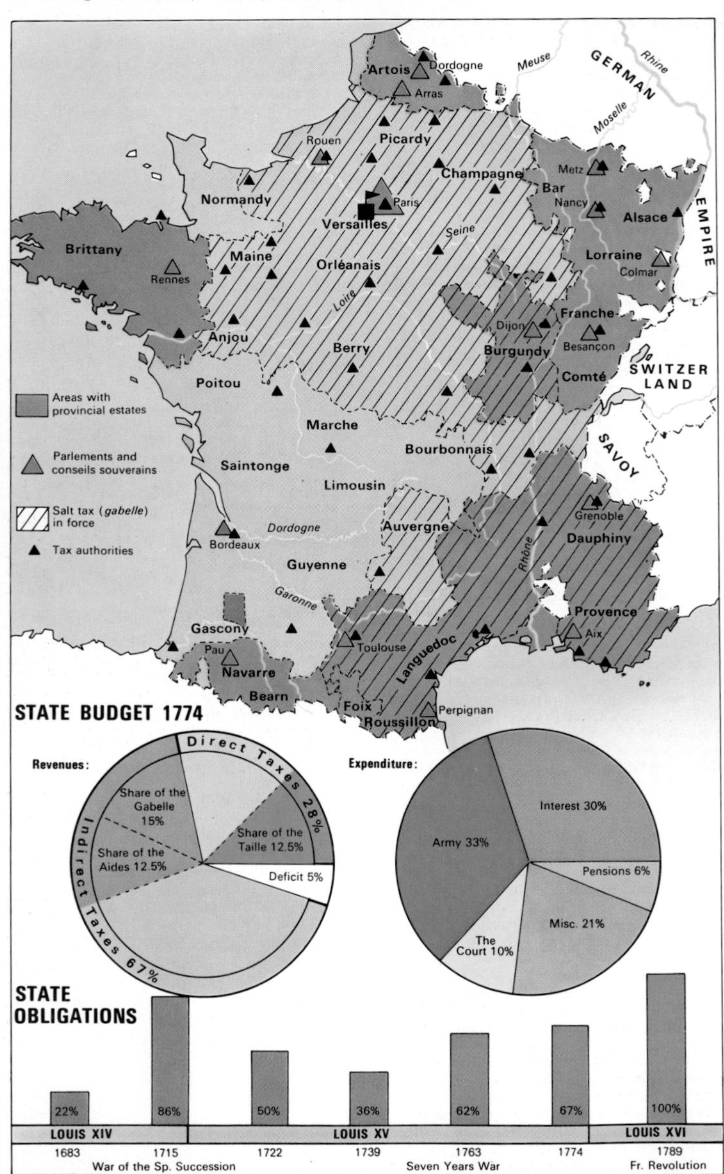

France before the Revolution

France on the Eve of the Revolution

The decay of the **Ancien Régime** resulted from the decadence of the absolutist systems.

The crown: loss of authority and prestige because of the incompetence of LOUIS XV (I, p. 281) and because of costly failures in for. affairs after 1714, which had undermined the Fr. position of power.

The admin.: officialdom (the intendancy) was over-centralized; local powers (prov. estates in the *pays d'états*, parlements as standing courts of law), eccles. and aristocratic privileges remained in existence and the venality of offices continued. The crown conflicted with the **Paris parlement,** which claimed the right to approve royal fiats.

Soc. and econ. life: the outdated feudal order caused dissatisfaction and soc. tensions in all estates.

The nobility had claim to the officers' commissions in the army and the upper echelon of administrative positions; it consisted of the upper nobility (depending on royal offices and pensions and rents from land-holdings), the country nobility in the provinces, and the *noblesse de robe* (bourgeois officials who had purchased titles of nobility). Great differences in standards of living existed in the

Eccles. estate, which consisted of upper and lower clergy.

The **bourgeoisie** (bankers, manufacturers, merchants, lawyers, physicians) as well as the aristocracy were favoured by the mercantilistic system (I, pp. 260f.). The prevailing guild organization of

the crafts was dissolved in the metropolis of Paris (approx. 650,000 inhabitants). The army in particular needed mass-produced goods, which led to the establishment of factories and the beginnings of an indust. proletariat.

The peasantry: though no longer in a condition of serfdom, was socially and legally disadvantaged. Even though they were suffering under the pressures of the 'feudal reaction' (extension of noble titles to land with the aid of the parlements), the free landowning peasants could get along. The hered. tenant farmers and leaseholders also remained relatively ind. despite considerable obligations on their part (payments, corvées, etc.). The increasing class of propertyless **agricultural labourers,** making up more than 50% of the pop., was subject to crises.

Fiscal policy: constant deficits bordering on state bankruptcies were due to extravagant spending. To cover it, loans were taken up at high rates of interest; inflexible admin. of taxation (*aides*= excise taxes, esp. on salt (*gabelle*=salt tax)) by tax farmers, who profited in the process. The nobility defended its exemption from the property tax (*taille*), the clergy contributed only voluntary payments (*dons gratuits*). Thus the burden of taxation fell on the poorest classes: up to 70% of the income of the peasants was taken by taxation. Rising prices further diminished real income.

Opposition to the gvt was prepared by the Enlightenment: rad. criticism of prevailing conditions by the encyclopedists and **Voltaire** (I, p. 257); slogans of liberty and equality influenced public opinion, which was represented by:

1. The privileged upper classes; they insisted on retaining their feudal privileges, but demanded at the same time the limitation of the absolute monarchy and the elimination of the judicial functions of the cabinet.
2. The bourgeoisie, which, as the 3rd Estate (*Tiers état*), demanded soc. equality and polit. representation.

1774–92 Louis XVI, an honest but insignificant man, decided to effect reforms. He appointed the physiocrat **Anne-Robert Turgot** (1727–81) to be minister of finance. After restrictions on the trade in grains had been removed, the workers of Paris rose in protest against the sudden rise in the price of bread. The **reform programme** (abolition of feudal rights and guild restrictions, development of local self-admin., introduction of a general property tax) was defeated by the court party of Queen MARIE ANTOINETTE ('Madame Déficit') and the parlements. Despite TURGOT's warning, volunteers under **Lafayette** (p. 19) were sent to America (p. 13).

1778 Alliance with the U.S. against Britain and involvement in the war. **Jacques Necker** (1732–1804), a Calv. banker of Geneva, attempted in vain to cover the war debts by means of loans. He lost office because he dared to publicize the miserable state of public finance in the

1781 **Compte rendu.**

1783 Peace of Paris. Though it brought the addition of Senegambia and Tobago, it did not ease the finan. burdens but rather added new public debts. The success of the Amer. independence movement reinforced criticism of the régime. Salons, cafés, clubs, masonic lodges became centres of a 'patriotic party' of lib. nobles, ecclesiastics and bourgeois (LAFAYETTE, MIRABEAU, PHILIP D'ORLÉANS, TALLEYRAND, SIEYÈS, *et al.*).

1783–7 The finance minister Charles Alexandre de Calonne (1734–1802) took TURGOT's plans up again; however, an assembly of notables (persons enjoying the royal confidence, meeting for the first time since 1626) was unwilling to approve proposals to cover the deficit without receiving information about finan. policies. CALONNE's successor LOMÉNIE DE BRIENNE (1727–94) failed because of opposition of the Paris parlement, which pushed through the

convocation of the Estates General to effect tax reforms (previous meeting in 1614). After the

1786 commercial treaty with Britain, the domestic situation was aggravated by indust. crises (caused by the effects of Brit. competition), unrest and famines resulting from poor harvests.

1788 Public bankruptcy and recall of NECKER, who made possible the doubling of the representatives of the 3rd Estate. After an intensely fought election, the Estates General were formed. The *cahiers* (a catalogue of desires and complaints) called for a limited monarchy. The pamphlet *What is the Third Estate?* by the **Abbé Emanuel Joseph Sieyès** (1748–1836) demanded the participation of the representatives of the nation in the gvt.

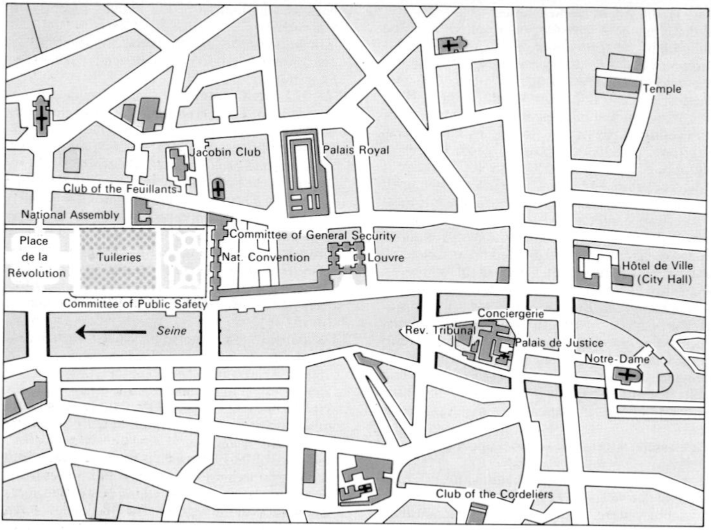

Paris, *c.* 1789

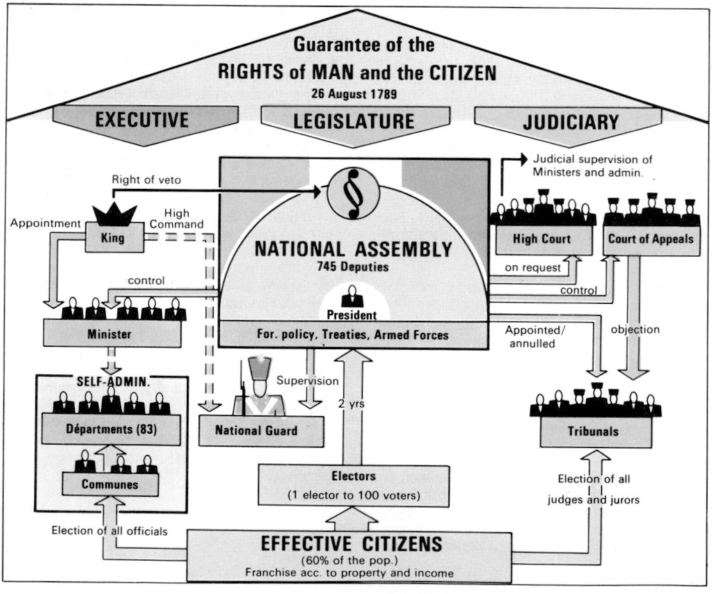

The French Constitution of 1791

The Fr. Revolution (1789–92)

5 May 1789 Convocation of the Estates General (p. 17) at Versailles. The 3rd Estate demanded voting by head instead of by estate. The revolution began with its announcement of the establishment of the Nat. Assembly (17 Jun.) and the 'Tennis Court oath' and its pledge 'not to separate until a constitution had been devised' (BAILLY, president of the National Assembly), and 'to yield only to the force of the bayonet' (MIRABEAU).

The 'Constituante' (1789–91)

The king acknowledged the changes in the situation; but NECKER's (p. 17) dismissal and troop concentrations in the suburbs prompted the masses of Paris to the

14 Jul. 1789 Storming of the Bastille (a polit. prison which stood as a symbol of despotism). The people overcame absolutism and the day became a Fr. nat. holiday; the army dissolved itself. **La Fayette** (1757–1834) est. a Nat. Guard (a militia of citizens wearing the tricolour cockade).

Consequences: peasant risings in all of France; first wave of emigration of the nobility; collapse of public admin.; following the example of Paris, auton. communes were est. Under the impact of the mass uprisings, the Nat. Assembly

4/5 Aug. 1789 abolished the feudal order and freed the peasants. A society differentiated by estates became one of classes free of restrictions in terms of office-holding and trades.

26 Aug. 1789 Declaration of the rights of man (influenced by the Virginia Bill of Rights, p. 15): proclamation of *liberté, égalité, fraternité* (personal liberty, equality before the law, the brotherhood of man). Famine and fear of counter-revolution drove the masses of Paris to further acts of violence.

5 Oct. 1789 Procession of the market women to Versailles. The king and the Nat. Assembly were forced to transfer to Paris (the Tuileries, the royal residence in the city); from this time on they were under the pressure of the 'galleries and the street'. The new dress of the people, the 'Phrygian cap' and the *'sans-culottes'* (long trousers, lit. 'without breeches') and the new address of *'citoyen'* instead of *'monsieur'* were generally accepted. To ease the fiscal difficulties, Bishop **Talleyrand-Périgord** (1754–1838, excommunicated in 1791) proposed the

10 Oct. 1789 confiscation of the property of the Church in exchange for *assignats* (notes issued as paper currency which became legal tender in 1790), which led to inflation; however, the purchase of this nat. property led to the growth of a new class of propertied citizens.

Modelled after the Eng. example, polit. clubs were established in Paris: the moderate **Feuillants** (BAILLY, LAFAYETTE) and the rad. **Cordeliers** (DANTON, DESMOULINS, MARAT). The

Jacobins (named after the dissolved monastery of St Jacob) thought of themselves as the 'holy league against the enemies of liberty' and as the 'watchdogs of the revolution' (ROBESPIERRE, ST-JUST). They met in closed meetings and created an efficient organization extending through all of France.

Jul. 1790 the Civil Constitution of the Clergy: the Church was made into a state church; monasteries and orders were dissolved, priests were to be elected. Most of the ecclesiastics refused the demanded oath to the constitution, leading to a conflict between Church and state. After the death of **Mirabeau** (1749–91), further connection of the royal family with the revolution became impossible.

Jun. 1791 Attempted flight by LOUIS XVI: the king was recognized in Varennes, returned to Paris and deprived of all polit. power. From this time on he was only the 'automaton of the constitution'.

3 Sep. 1791 Proclamation of the new constitution (which became the model of all lib. constitutions of the 19th cent.).

Characteristics: const. monarchy; a weak executive and a popular assembly elected indirectly on the basis of limited suffrage (restricted to 'active' propertied citizens); election of all officials, judges and jurors; open courts; organization of the state in 83 departments with auton. admin. Guarantees of human rights, equality before the law and private property.

The Legislative Assembly (1791–2)

The newly elected 745 deputies to the **Legislative Assembly** (more than 50% of them lawyers) lacked polit. experience. They were grouped in the factions of the loyalist **Feuillants** (*c.* 20 members, dissolved 20 Mar. 1792), the **Girondists** (*c.* 250 members; as representatives of the propertied bourgeoisie they were republicans and opposed centralized power), the **Jacobins** (*c.* 30 members, rad. advocates of centralized power who influenced the masses through agitation and newspapers (MARAT: *'ami du peuple'*, HÉBERT: *'père Duchesne'*) and dominated the Paris Commune), the **indépendents** (who lacked a clear polit. programme). To divert attention from domestic problems, but also in reaction to agitation by émigrées abroad and fear of the Habsburgs

Apr. 1792 Declaration of war on Austria: beginning of the wars of the coalition. Capt. ROUGET DE LISLE composed music and text of the **Marseillaise**, the battle-hymn of the revolution and the Fr. national anthem. Remonstrances of the king ('Monsieur Veto') against decrees persecuting priests refusing the oath to the constitution; milit. failures causing 'peril to the fatherland'. More than anything, it was the

25 Jul. 1792 Brunswick Manifesto (proclamation of the Duke of Brunswick calling for the liberation of the king), composed in the main by émigrées, which brought the revolutionaries to

10 Aug. 1792 the Storming of the Tuileries. The royal family was interned in the 'Temple'; the Girondists demanded the abolition of the monarchy and the election of a repub. **Nat. Convention. Danton** (1756–94), the minister of justice, **Marat** (1743–93), and the Commune caused

2–7 Sep. 1792 the 'September Massacres' (to 'clear out the prisons'). A second wave of noble émigrés left the country (among them LAFAYETTE, who became an Aust. prisoner).

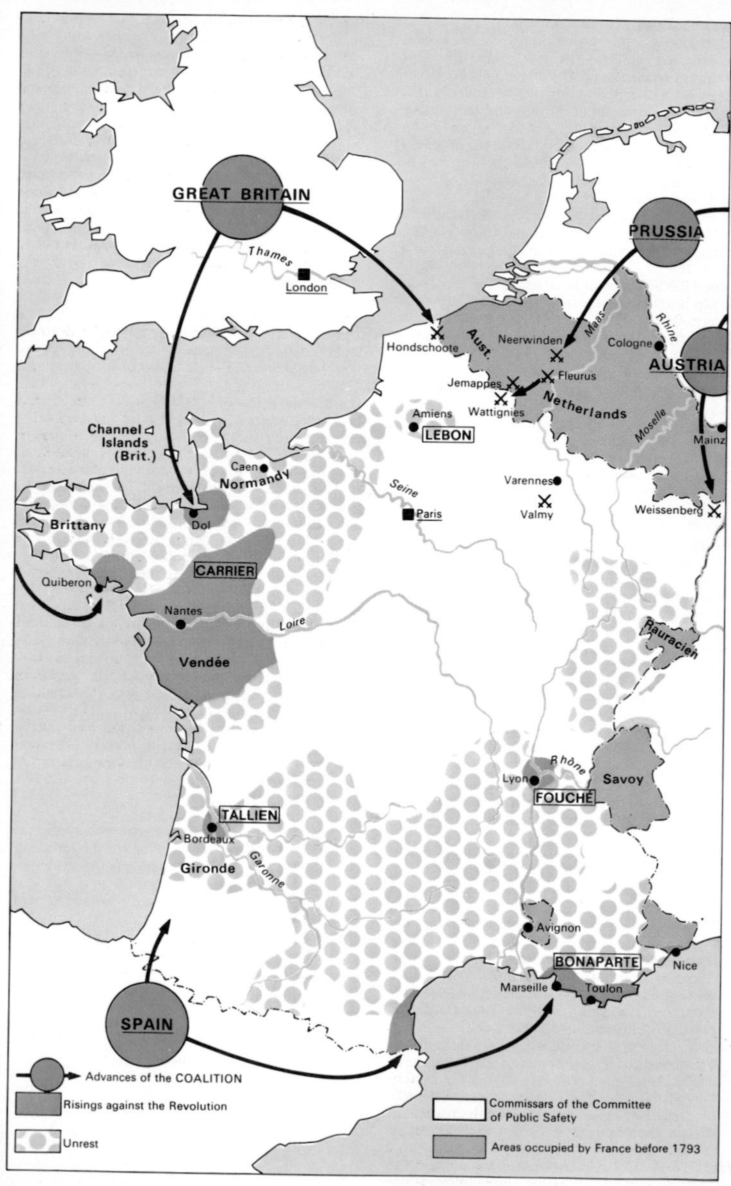

The crisis of the Revolution, 1793

The Nat. Convention (1792–3)

Sep. 1792 France was proclaimed a republic (BRISSOT: 'The people will it'). A new repub. calendar was introduced, 1792 became the Year 1. New parties were formed in the Nat. Convention:

The plain (also *marais*, the morass; the seats on the floor of the convention hall), also cal. the Girondists, who advocated equality before the law, the sanctity of private property, and local autonomy of admin. (BRISSOT, VERGNIAUD, ROLAND).

The mountain (the upper seats in the convention hall; *c.* 110 of 749 deputies) or Jacobins, who demanded a centralized admin. and the power to dispose of private property to ease the burden of the poor (DANTON, ROBESPIERRE, MARAT). In the show trial of 'citizen Capet' (LOUIS XVI)

17 Jan. 1793 the death penalty, proposed by ROBESPIERRE, was accepted by 361 to 360 votes. The king was guillotined on 21 Jan. 1793 (the guillotine was a 'dropping axe' advocated by GUILLOTINE, a physician, to humanize the procedure of executions). Britain and other Eur. powers now entered the war (p. 23). Milit. setbacks, famine, inflation, unrest and royalist peasant uprisings threatened the revolution.

The Reign of Terror (1793–4)

The emergencies in domestic and for. affairs were successfully dealt with by fanaticism and severity.

Jun. 1793 Proclamation of the constitution of the Nat. Convention: absolute popular sovereignty provided plebiscites for every law and eliminated the separation of powers; yet its provisions could not be realized in practice. Under the impact of the milit. setbacks

Jul. 1793 the Girondists were driven from power by the Jacobins. **Robespierre** (1758–94), a lawyer, and his 'sword bearers' (ST-JUST, MARAT–murdered by CHARLOTTE CORDAY and glorified as a martyr) est. a dictatorship. DANTON proposed that the **Committee of Public Safety** (consisting of 9 members elected by the Nat. Convention) be made the provisional gvt with absolute powers.

The Terror in Paris: rad. laws and judicial terror, exercised by the **revolutionary tribunal**, for all practical purposes suspended human rights. By Jul. 1794, 1,251 'suspicious persons' had been guillotined, among them BAILLY, the chemist LAVOISIER, PHILIP OF ORLÉANS ('Citizen Egalité') and Queen MARIE ANTOINETTE.

The Terror in the Departments: commissars of the Committee of Public Safety suppressed uprisings and unrest (mass liquidations); the generals LA HOCHE and KLÉBER conducted a war of extermination against the loyalists under CHARETTE DE LA CONTRIE in the **Vendée** and against the Chouans (named after their leader COTTEREAU) in **Brittany**. The atheism of the so-called Hébertists (named after the Jacobin HÉBERT, 1757–94) intensified at the same time. 'Buildings known as churches' were closed. Notre Dame was proclaimed the 'temple of reason'. ROBESPIERRE, 'the incorruptible', caused the execution of extreme Hébertists (Mar. 1794) as well as moderate 'indulgents' (DANTON and his followers, Apr. 1794).

May 1794 Abolition of Christianity in favour of the **'Cult of Reason',** including adoption of a new chronology (the month to have 3 weeks of 10 days each). ROBESPIERRE celebrated the festival of the 'Supreme Being' (Jun. 1794).

The Terror culminated in the 'great purification' by the Jacobins. The reformation of the revolutionary tribunal ('moral proof' sufficed to cause condemnation) united the opposition in the Nat. Convention and brought about the

27–28 Jul. 1794 fall of Robespierre. With 21 of his adherents (incl. ST-JUST) he was executed.

Sep. 1794 Abolition of the revolutionary tribunal and the polit. clubs; prohibition of the 'Marseilleise'. A youth movement (the Muscadins) cleaned up the Paris Commune; esp. in southern France, the 'White Terror' of the royalists provided an equivalent to the terror of the Jacobins and the sans-culottes.

The Directory

In response to the Terror and 'popular dictatorship',

Sep. 1795 the new constitution provided for a weak executive in a gvt of 5 directors; deputies to the 2 chambers (Council of Elders (250 members) and Council of the 500) were elected indirectly. The views of the propertied bourgeoisie were thereby recognized. Searching for pleasure and indulging in luxury, Paris society in its salons created the classicist *haute couture* of the *Directoire*; meanwhile the Directory was too weak to prevent unrest on the right (the royalists) and the left (early communists, organized in the 'Conspiracy of Equals' of the 'popular tribune'. FRANÇOIS-NOEL BABEUF, b. 1760, executed 1797). Decisively supported by NAPOLEON BONAPARTE (p. 23), BARRAS (1755–1829) was able to suppress

5 Oct. 1795 the rising of the royalists in Paris on the 'Day of the Sections'. Attempts to solve the econ. and fiscal crisis did not prevent public bankruptcy.

4 Sep. 1797 *Coup d'état* of 18 Fructidor by General AUGEREAU to rid the state of royalist corruption. CARNOT (p. 23), the organizer of the revolutionary army, and General PICHEGRU fled the country; the Directory (now a triumvirate under BARRAS) became dependent on NAPOLEON BONAPARTE.

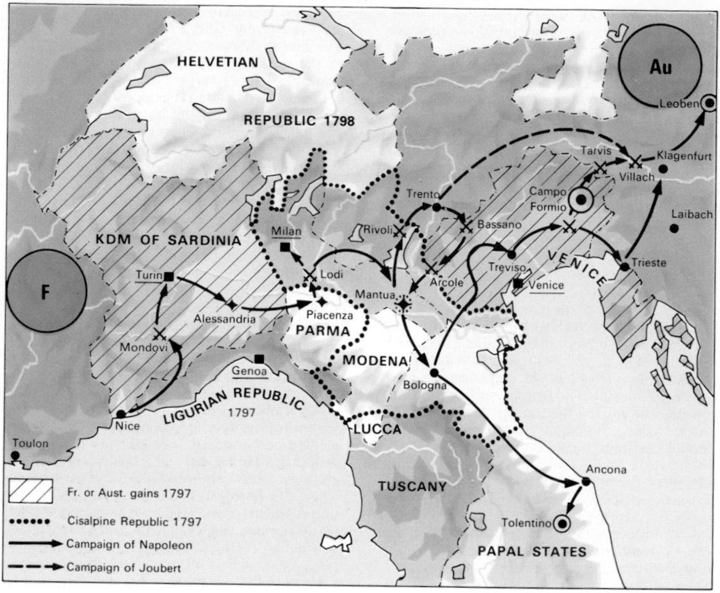

Upper Italy, 1796/7

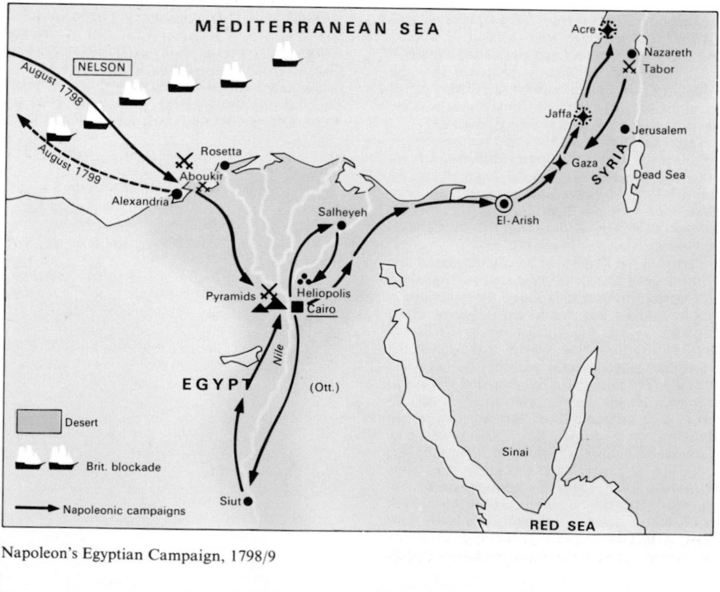

Napoleon's Egyptian Campaign, 1798/9

Apr. 1792 Declaration of war by France against Austria (p. 19) caused by threats of invasion and the conclusion of an Aust.-Prus. protective alliance (Feb.). The French saw themselves as a nation of pioneers in the struggle against absolutism and feudalism; they also demanded their 'natural frontiers, the Alps and the Rhine'.

The 1st War of the Coalition (1792–7)

Advances by the armies of the coalition and the manifesto of their c.-in-c. (p. 19) inflamed Fr. nat. feelings.

20 Sep. 1792 b. of Valmy: turning-point of the war, retreat of the Prus. army. General Dumouriez (1739–1823) was victorious at Jemappes and conquered Belgium; Savoy was annexed.

Feb. 1793 Britain and other Eur. powers entered the war. The domestic crisis (p. 21) of the revolution also affected the Fr. conduct of the war.

Mar. 1793 Defeat at Neerwinden (DUMOURIEZ); Aust. reconquest of Belgium and renewed threat to Paris. The Brit. navy intervened in the Mediterranean. France responded with total mobilization (*levée en masse*). **Carnot** (1753–1823) reformed the army and brought its strength to 1 mil. (4% of the pop.); polit. commissars watched over the officers.

Consequences of reorganization: 2nd conquest of Belgium by Jourdan (victs. at Wattignies, 1793; Fleurus, 1794); the **Batavian Republic** proclaimed in Holland. Brit. invasion attempts at Toulon and Quiberon failed; but the British were able to occupy the Dutch colonies (Ceylon, Capetown).

1795 Peace of Basle: to obtain freedom of action in Poland (I, p. 285), Prussia surrendered its possessions on the left bank of the Rhine in exchange for compensation in the form of territory on the right bank. A line of demarcation secured the neutrality of Northern Germany until 1806. Spain concluded peace and entered the war against Britain by the terms of the

1796 Treaty of Ildefonso; Britain dest. the Sp. fleet at Cape St Vincent. Austria continued to carry on the war with Brit. financial aid. Fr. advances into southern Germany (JOURDAN, MOREAU) were repulsed by the Archduke CHARLES (1771–1847) at Amberg and Würzburg. Logistical problems paralysed the Fr. army in Upper Italy.

The Revolution in Warfare and Milit. Organization

The new ties between people and nation fundamentally changed milit. organization and the conduct of war; it led to the **Age of Nationalism** of the 19th cent.

1. The total war involving all the people with conscription for milit. duty and labour services took the place of the wars of the cabinets and mercenaries.
2. The massing of troops made **decisive offensive battles** possible. The strategy of exhausting the enemy by forcing him to march and thus to tire his soldiers and preserve one's own troops became ineffective.
3. Flexible operations in loosely formed lines **(tirailleur tactics)** were superior to attacks in closed lines (linear tactics used to prevent desertions).
4. Provisioning through storehouses took the place of **requisitioning** by the fighting troops.
5. Promotion based on courage and accomplishment, no longer depending on (noble) birth of the officers.

In the hands of **Napoleon Bonaparte** (1769–1821), the new Fr. nat. army became invincible. Born in Ajaccio, Corsica (Genoese till 1768), the artillery officer (since 1785) and apostle of ROUSSEAU joined the revolution at an early stage. After the siege of Toulon in 1793, he became the youngest revolutionary general; arrested as a Jacobin after the fall of ROBESPIERRE, he was freed later and entrusted with the suppression of the Paris 'Day of the Sections' (p. 21) by BARRAS; subsequently he was made c.-in-c. of the army in Upper Italy.

The Campaign in Upper Italy (1796–7)

NAPOLEON, the 'little corporal', mastered the crisis of the revolutionary army and conquered Lombardy in a lightning campaign.

1797 Capitulation of Mantua; Peace of Tolentino with Pope PIUS VI (Feb.); advance into Carinthia and provisional Peace of Leoben (Apr.). His successes obligated the gvt and the people; contributions of the 'liberated Italians' supported the bankrupt Directory (p. 21) and promoted the **Napoleonic legend** (transfer of Ital. works of art to the Louvre). The 'Saviour of France' dictated

Oct. 1797 the Peace of Campo Formio: Austria had to agree to the surrender of the left bank of the Rhine (63,000 sq. kms. with a pop. of 3·5 mil.); it exchanged Belgium and Milan for Venice (fall of the 1,000-yr republic). Extension of the Fr. system of satellite states through **daughter republics:**

1797 Establishment of the **Cisalpine** (Milan) and **Ligurian** (Genoa) Republics;

1798 Civil war and transformation of Switzerland into the **Helvetian Republic**; the Papal States were made into the **Rom. Republic** after the capture of Rome and the imprisonment of the Pope. Naples became the **Parthenopean Republic** in 1799.

The Campaign in Egypt (1798–9)

NAPOLEON received the supreme command in the war against Britain, which was to be hit indirectly through the Mediterranean. He occupied Malta and landed in Alexandria (with 232 ships, 2,000 cannon, 32,300 soldiers as well as 175 engineers and scholars to explore the country). He defeated the Mamelukes nr the Pyramids and captured Cairo.

1798 Brit. naval vict. at Aboukir (NELSON, p. 31). The Fr. army was cut off from France. An advance to Syria (1799) failed at the gates of Acre (Akko); a victorious land b. at Aboukir failed to save the undertaking. Russia and the Ott. Empire concluded an alliance; Malta and the Mediterranean Sea came under Brit. control. Fr. rule in Egypt lasted until 1802.

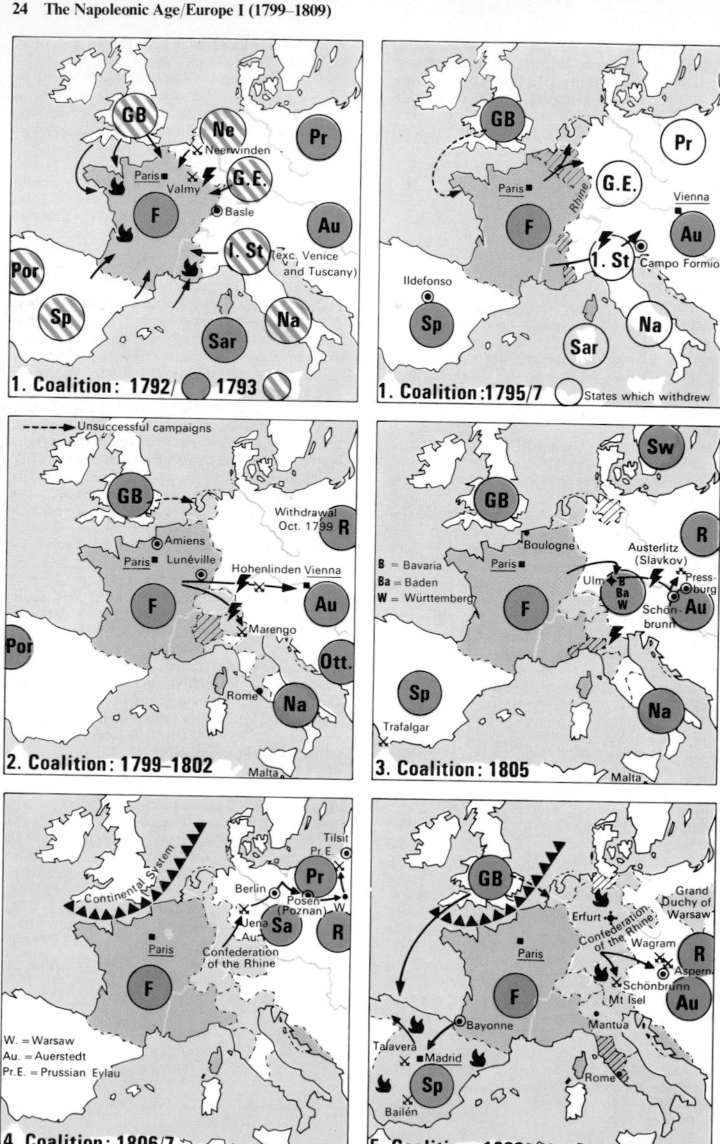

The coalitions against France, 1792–1809

The Wars of the Coalitions

Fighting in var. coalitions, the Eur. powers opposed the spread of the revolutionary ideas and the expansion of the Fr. Republic, under the leadership of NAPOLEON from 1799. The wars altered the polit. balance of power in favour of the Napoleonic domination of the Continent; at the same time, they aroused the nat. resistance of the Eur. peoples and their readiness for reform, thereby laying the foundations of mod. states (p. 33). The centres of resistance were **Austria**, which after 1805 came under the polit. leadership of Count STADION (1763–1824), and **Britain** (PITT the Younger, p. 31), which remained unconquered, extended its naval and colon. dominance and, overcoming the obstacles of econ. warfare (the Continental System, p. 27), rose to become the strongest commercial and indust. nation in the world. After the

1792–7 1st War of the Coalition, under the impact of the Fr. occupation of Malta and the Brit. vict. at Aboukir, PITT the Younger was able to gain the adherence of Austria and of the Grand Master of the Knights of Malta (the Knights of St John or Hospitallers), Tsar PAUL I [1796–1801]. An attack by Naples on the Rom. Republic led to

1799–1802 2nd War of the Coalition. Initial successes of the allies: Archduke CHARLES defeated JOURDAN at Osterach and Stockach (Mar.), MASSENA at Zürich (Jun.); SUROVOV defeated MOREAU at Cassano (Apr.); JOUBERT was defeated by JOVI (Aug.). Rus. operations in Switzerland and a Brit.-Rus. invasion nr Alkmaar in Holland remained unsuccessful. Put out by the Brit. occupation of Malta, PAUL I left the Coalition (Oct.). Meanwhile NAPOLEON had left his army in Egypt (Aug.); he landed in France, overthrew the Directory (p. 27) and est. a milit. dictatorship. After unsuccessful attempts at concluding peace, he assumed command of the army in Italy.

1800 Victs. at Marengo (NAPOLEON) and Hohenlinden (MOREAU).

Feb. 1801 Peace of Lunéville: Austria had to confirm the conditions of Campo Formio (p. 23).

1801 Northern Coalition for the protection of neutral trade (Russia, Sweden, Denmark, Prussia); England retaliated with the raid of Copenhagen (NELSON). After France concluded peace with Russia, England was isolated; PITT fell.

Mar. 1802 Peace of Amiens–NAPOLEON reached the first high point of his power: England surrendered all colon. conquests (exc. Ceylon and Trinidad); the French, in turn, abandoned Egypt.

1802 Reorganization of Italy by NAPOLEON: rest. of the Papal States (without Romagna) and the Bourbon Kdm of Naples. The Grand Duchy of Tuscany became the Kdm of Etruria, the Cisalpine Republic became the Italian Republic (NAPOLEON its president); Piedmont remained under Fr. milit. admin.; renewed Franco-Brit. tensions resulted from attempts to restore the Fr. colon. empire (acquisition of Louisiana from Spain in 1800, Fr. landings on Haiti and Martinique); tensions also resulted from the Fr. occupation of Hanover (1803) in defiance of the terms of the Treaty of Basle (p. 23), Fr. measures introducing protective tariffs, and the

1804 preparations for an invasion in the camp at Boulogne (NAPOLEON: 'Should we be able to control the Eng. Channel for 6 hrs, we will be the masters of the world!'). England did not surrender Malta; the Younger PITT formed a new coalition with Tsar ALEXANDER I [1801–25]; Austria, Sweden and Naples joined it.

1805 3rd War of the Coalition. Encirclement and capitulation of an Aust. army at Ulm; NAPOLEON entered Vienna.

21 Oct. 1805 The naval b. of Trafalgar secured Brit. supremacy at sea. After successes in Upper Italy (Caldiero), the Archduke CHARLES retreated through Hungary to concentrate the armies; previous to this

2 Dec. 1805 the b. of Austerlitz ('3-Emperors' Battle'), had resulted in a brilliant Napoleonic vict. Prus. mediation came too late.

12 Dec. 1805 The Treaty of Schönbrunn granted Prussia the Electorate of Hanover in exchange for Cleves, Neuenburg and Ansbach-Bayreuth. Prussia joined the Napoleonic system through a pact of mutual assistance.

25 Dec. 1805 Peace of Pressburg: Austria lost Venetia and Dalmatia to the **Ital. Republic**; it lost Tyrol, Voralberg and Lindau to **Bavaria** and the Breisgau with Constance to **Baden and Württemberg**. Austria gained Salzburg and acknowledged the elevation of Ger. princes in rank (p. 29). After the defeat of his enemy PITT, NAPOLEON, breaking his treaty with Prussia, offered Hanover to England. Mistaking the nature of its situation, Prussia initiated the

1806–7 4th War of the Coalition (p. 29). Left in isolation, Prussia collapsed completely.

1806 Proclamation of the Continental System in Berlin, 'as England refuses to abide by the principles of inter. law and abuses the laws governing embargo'.

1807 Peace of Tilsit (2nd high point of NAPOLEON's career). The rump of the Prus. state (E. of the Elbe) was preserved only through Rus. intervention. As partner in an alliance with NAPOLEON (division of Europe into Fr. and Rus. spheres of influence) Russia joined the Continental System. The nat. rising of Austria in

1809, the 5th War of the Coalition, failed also. The Peace of Schönbrunn (p. 29) separated the Danubian monarchy from the sea. The successor of Count STADION, Prince METTERNICH (p. 39), successfully effected a reorientation of Aust. policies along Napoleonic lines. Treaties of assistance incorp. Prussia and Austria into the Napoleonic system.

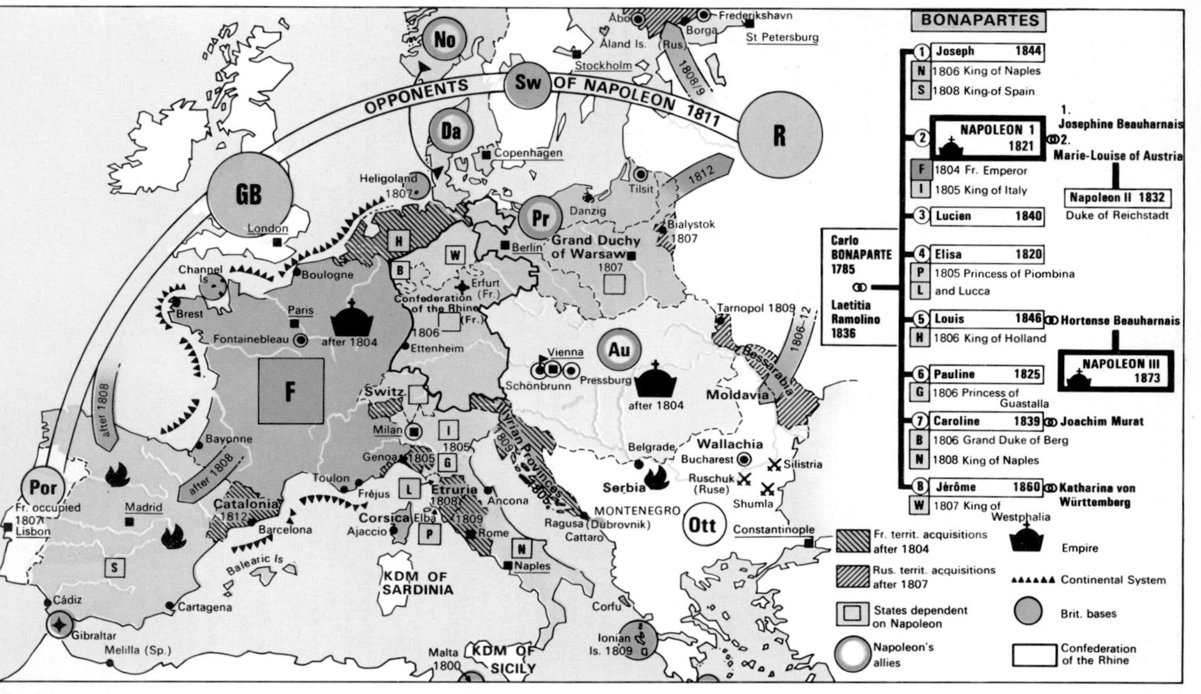

The reorganization of Europe brought about by Napoleon, 1812

The Consulate (1799–1804)

1799 Coup d'état of 18 Brumaire: aided by the military and his brother LUCIEN, NAPOLEON dissolved the incompetent Directory, broke up the Council of 500 and formed a provis. gvt incl. FOUCHÉ (1759–1820) as minister of police and TALLEYRAND as foreign minister. SIEYÈS composed the new

Constitution of the Consulate: counselled by 2 consuls and the **Council of State**, the **1st Consul** (who alone had the power to initiate legislation) appointed all army officers, gvt officials, judges, and the 80 members of the **Senate**. They, indirectly in the name of the people, proposed the notables who elected the candidates for the **Tribunate** (which served as a forum for discussion only) and the **Corps Législatif** (which voted on, but did not discuss, legislation). This milit. dictatorship in democratic wrappings was accepted by a plebiscite (against only 1,562 votes); Napoleon was chosen **1st Consul** for a term of 10 yrs.

Admin.: the bureaucracy was given specialized functions (professional bureaucrats) and the judiciary was coordinated with the administrative apparatus.

Education: the educational system was uniformly organized in primary, secondary and higher schools, controlled and regimented by the state. Emphasis was on formalistic-logical subjects (Latin, mathematics) and applied natural sciences. Administrative and educational centralization characterize France to the present day.

The Church: 'For the sake of peace', PIUS VII renounced claims for the return of Church property (p. 19).

1801 The Concordat (in effect until 1905) tied the clergy and the Cath. pop. to the state (appointment of bps; state salaries for, and loyalty oaths to the state by, the priests).

1811 Nat. Council. Renewed conflicts (closure of eccles. schools and seminaries).

Econ. and judicial affairs: stabilization of public finances through

1800 the establishment of the Bank of France, which also achieved the decline of inflation. Crafts and industry recovered under protective tariffs and the business generated by road construction and the needs of the army. The laws of the revolution were codified in the

1804 Code Civil (Code Napoléon). This guaranteed personal liberty, equality before the law, private property, civil marriage and the right to divorce.

Soc. stratification: the upper bourgeoisie remained the dominant element in society; the émigré nobles were requested to return; careers in gvt or public service were open to all.

1802 Establishment of the Legion of Honour. The régime was backed by censorship of the press, a spy system and a police apparatus (FOUCHÉ). Critics (Mme DE STAËL, CHATEAUBRIAND) were not tolerated.

Milit. organization: conscription (with the possibility of exemptions) raised *c.* 1·3 mil. soldiers between 1806 and 1812 (i.e. 41% of those qualified to serve). Transportation, medical care, supplies and equipment suffered because of business speculations by private creditors.

1802 Under the impact of his successes, another plebiscite extended NAPOLEON's term of office to life.

1804 FOUCHÉ uncovered a royalist conspiracy: although not involved, the Bourbon Duke D'ENGHIEN was abducted from Ettenheim in Baden and became the victim of judicial murder. To secure his position, NAPOLEON caused the Senate to propose a plebiscite on the question of a hered. empire.

The Napoleonic Empire

1804 Coronation of NAPOLEON I as Emperor of the French. Members of his family received the titles of princes; ministers and generals were elevated to the positions of high dignitaries and marshals.

1807 Establishment of a new nobility with the system of primogeniture and hered. titles (by 1814, 31 dukes, 451 counts, 1,500 barons). Continuous annexations extended the territory of the empire (p. 24).

The Imp. System: a rational creation, the **Napoleonic hegemony over Europe** was organized (after 1807) on the basis of states headed by family members, dependent vassal states and allies. The Fr. Marshal BERNADOTTE (CHARLES XIV) was elected heir to the Swed. throne (1810). To justify his policies, NAPOLEON pointed to parallels in history (the Rom. and Carol. Empires). However, personal ambition for power played a large role in them; in addition, the Brit. enemy forced him to ever stricter concentration.
States which refused to obey the

1807 Decree of Milan intensifying the **Continental System** were occupied: Portugal, 1807; Etruria, Rome, 1808/9; northern Germany, 1810.

Consequences for continental Europe:

1. The spread of lib. ideas, the overcoming of feudalism, and the introduction of mod. codes of law (*Code Civil*).
2. Development of states with centralized bureaucracies and public educational systems controlled by the state.
3. Alien Fr. rule and the consolidation of territories which had not been polit. units led to nationalism.
4. Preferential treatment of the Fr. economy; expansion of textile industries; shortages in colon. goods (cotton, cane sugar) because of the Continental System, leading to increases in prices, *ersatz* products (beet sugar), smuggling, black markets, and corruption.
5. As a partner of NAPOLEON, **Russia** gained in importance. It obtained Bialystok in 1807, Tarnopol in 1809, and **Finland** in the

1809 Peace of Fredrikshavn; **Bessarabia** in the

1806–12 Russo-Turk. War.

1808 Congress of Erfurt: meeting of NAPOLEON and ALEXANDER I. To elevate the position of his own dynasty and to oblige Austria,

1810 NAPOLEON mar. MARIE-LOUISE, daughter of FRANCIS I.

1812 Greatest extent of the empire: 152 departments, containing 50 mil. of the 175 mil. inhabitants of Europe.

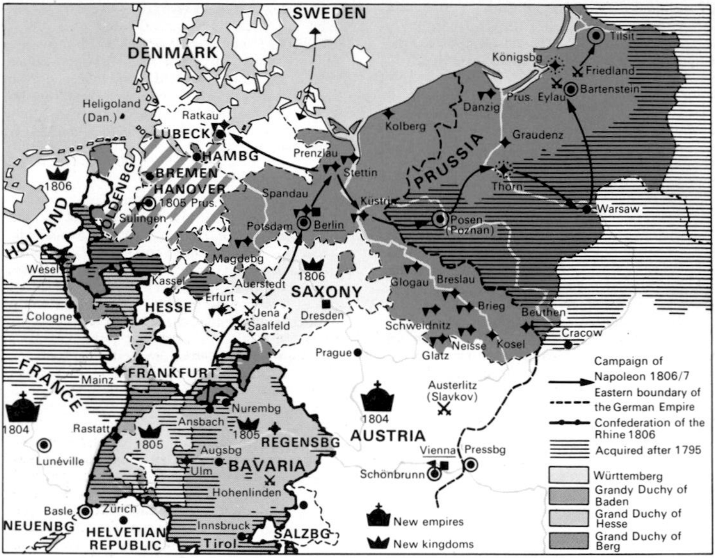

The dissolution of the German Empire, 1804–6

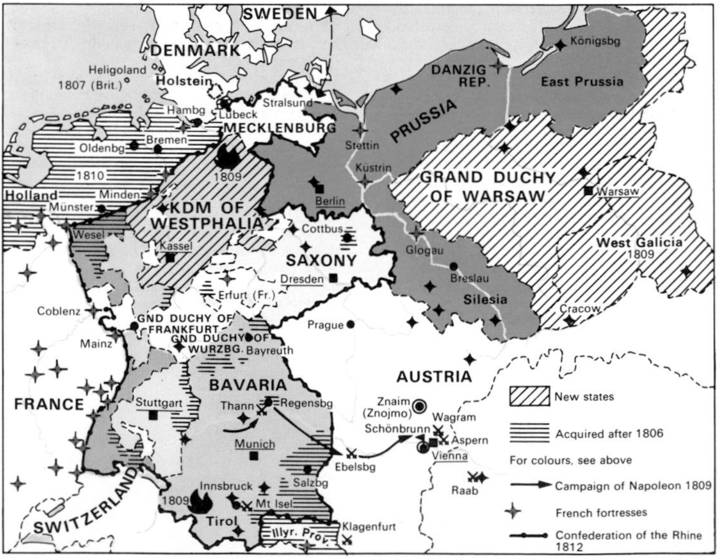

Confederation of the Rhine, 1812

The Dissolution of the Ger. Empire

1797–9 Congress of Rastatt. Attempts to reconstitute Germany in view of the territ. losses of Ger. princes on the left bank of the Rhine failed. NAPOLEON enforced this reconstitution with the Peace of Lunéville (Feb. 1801). NAPOLEON's aims: (a) the dissolution of the empire; (b) the creation of Ger. 'middle' states as a polit. counterweight to Austria; (c) the obligation of Ger. princes to vassal loyalty through the granting of territ. additions. Polit. reorganization took place in 4 stages:

1. Secularization of the eccles. states after the Fr. model (p. 19) through a deputation appointed by the Ger. Reichstag which was bound by Russo-Fr. plans in matters of territ. compensation.

1803 Reichsdeputationshauptschluss: all eccles. territories, exc. Mainz, were divided; as were 45 of the 51 imp. cities, small principalities and counties, totalling 112 imp. states with a pop. of 3 mil. The main beneficiaries were **Baden,** which gained 738% in territory, 948% in pop.; **Prussia** 489%/438%; **Württemberg** 414%/857%; **Bavaria** 144%/142%.

2. Mediatization (loss of their status of being subject to the empire only) of 350 imp. knights (1804).

3. Elevation in rank of Ger. princes with the approval of NAPOLEON, but in violation of Ger. imp. law:

1804 FRANCIS II [1792/1806] assumed the imp. title for Austria (and reigned as FRANCIS I until 1835).

1805 Bavaria and Württemberg became kdms;

1806 Baden, Hesse-Darmstadt and Berg became grand duchies.

4. 16 S. and W. Ger. states committed open treason to the empire by forming the

1806 Confederation of the Rhine under a Napoleonic protectorate. They were obliged to render him milit. assistance. Primate of the princes (*Fürstenprimas*) was KARL THEODOR FREHERR VON DALBERG (1744–1817), the Archbp of Mainz and Grand Duke of Frankfurt after 1810.

6 Aug. 1806 Under the pressure of NAPOLEON, FRANCIS II gave up the Ger. imp. crown: end of the **'Holy Rom. Empire of the Ger. Nation'**, the final result of the dissolution of the empire which began in 1232 (I, p. 173), and was continued in 1356 (I, p. 195), 1555 (I, p. 235) and 1648 (I, p. 255). The territ. adjustments laid the foundations for the establishment of the Ger. nat. state (p. 32). The people were painfully conscious of the humiliation of the nation, but accepted it. The Nuremberg bookseller PALM, executed in 1806 by the French because of his pamphlet 'Germany in its Deepest Humiliation', became the only martyr.

The Collapse of Prussia

Mistaken cabinet policies of Count HAUGWITZ (1752–1832) made Prussia dependent on NAPOLEON. To counteract his arbitrary actions (border and treaty violations), Prussia formed a coalition with Russia and Saxony. An ultimatum demanding the withdrawal of all Fr. troops E. of the Rhine and the dissolution of the Confederation of the Rhine led to the

1806–7 4th War of the Coalition. Following a preliminary engagement at Saalfeld, the obsolete Prus. and Saxon armies suffered a disastrous defeat in the

Oct. 1806 Dual b. of Jena and Auerstedt. Milit. and moral collapse of Prussia: transfer of the royal residence to Königsberg; unopposed occupation of Berlin by NAPOLEON; dissolution of Prus. army groups at Prenzlau and Ratkau (BLÜCHER); only the fortresses of Kolberg (GNEISENAU, NETTELBECK), Graudenz (COURBIÈRE) and Glatz resisted.

Dec. 1806 Peace of Posen with Saxony, which joined the Confederation of the Rhine.

Feb. 1807 b. of Prus. Eylau: SCHARNHORST prevented the French from taking advantage of their vict. FREDERICK WILLIAM III [1797–1840] fled to Memel.

Jun. 1807 Rus. defeat at Friedland.

Jul. 1807 Peace of Tilsit: the dissolution of Prussia was only prevented by Rus. intervention (p. 25); Prussia lost her territories W. of the Elbe and the formerly Pol. territories exc. for W. Prussia; Danzig was made a republic, to be garrisoned by the French. Pending substantial reparations, Prussia was to remain under Fr. occupation, its army reduced to 42,000 men. Newly created states were the **Kdm of Westphalia** under NAPOLEON's brother JÉRÔME and the **Grand Duchy of Warsaw** (in personal union with Saxony).

The Aust. Uprising (1809)

The Sp. upheaval (p. 35) was the signal to nat. resistance for Count STADION. The Archduke CHARLES directed an address to the 'Ger. peoples', but hopes that Ger. states would join the cause were disappointed. Prus. intervention was prevented by the Fr. occupation of the country and the infl. of Tsar ALEXANDER I. NAPOLEON pushed the Aust. army back into Bohemia.

May 1809 b. of Aspern. Incurring heavy losses, NAPOLEON suffered by the Archduke CHARLES his 1st defeat. Subs. the Rus. and Pol. allies advanced to Cracow 'with all due caution'. Unsuccessful single operations in northern Germany **(Freikorps Schill).**

Popular war in Tyrol: under the leadership of ANDREAS HOFER and JOSEPH SPECKBACHER, victorious struggles against Bavarians and French at **Mt Isel**. HOFER was betrayed and executed at Mantua in 1810.

Jul. 1809 Aust. defeat at Wagram. The Archduke CHARLES and STADION resigned.

Oct. Peace of Schönbrunn: Austria cut off from the sea; it lost Salzburg, the Inn district and N. Tyrol to **Bavaria**, S. Tyrol to **Italy**; the province of Illyria to **France**; western Galicia, incl. Cracow, to **Warsaw**; Tarnopol (100,000 sq. kms with a pop. of 3·5 mil.) to **Russia**; the army was limited to 150,000 men.

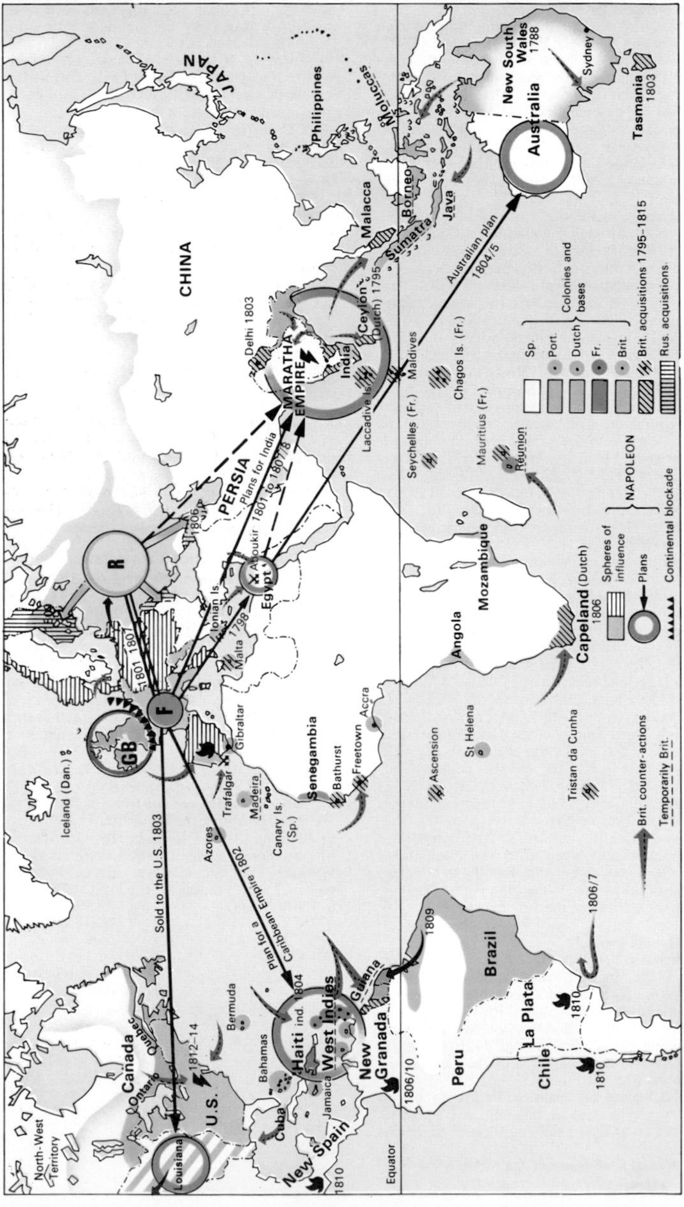

Napoleon's world-wide power struggle with Britain

The Domestic Situation in Britain

The parl. system: under the impact of the Amer. War of Independence, the gvt of Lord NORTH had fallen in 1782. Under the monarchy of GEORGE III [1760–1820], the prime minister was dependent on Parliament to conduct the gvt. Small cliques of a noble oligarchy of landowners–their seats secure because of an elect. system that favoured their class–fought with each other in Parliament. Participation in the gvt was rewarded with well-paid office; the power of patronage passed from the king to the prime minister and remained a source of corruption in the elect. constituencies. The **Tories** relied on the Anglican Established Church; the **Whigs** tended more to represent the *dissenters* (Protestant Nonconformist). Prominent in the economy, they aspired to reform parliament through the abolition of the **'rotten boroughs'** (depopulated older communities with elect. privileges) in favour of the new indust. cities which lacked representation. **Catholics** obtained the repeal of the prohibition to perform public relig. services in 1779, but were not fully emancipated.

Encounter with the ideas of the Fr. Revolution: rad. democratic ideas (popular sovereignty, abolition of the monarchy) were proclaimed by **Thomas Paine** (1737–1809). His *Rights of Man* (1792) was directed against **Edmund Burke** (1729–97), whose conservative critique in the *Reflections on the Revolution in France* (1790) had a powerful influence in England and Europe.

Industrialization and the agricult. revolution: despite domestic problems (abuses of patronage, obsolete criminal justice), England–on the basis of a capitalistic economy and attitude–became the 'workshop of the world' (p. 43). The consolidation of scattered landholdings and an improved rotation of crops raised the yield of the fields. Still, a shortage of foodstuffs developed because of a pop. increase (esp. in the cities) between 1750 and 1820 from 7·8 to 14·3 mil. Machines, indust. cities and wage labour reduced the importance of crafts, small cities and the agricult. sector. New methods of road construction (METCALFE, MACADAM) improved transportation and traffic. The export of indust. products strengthened the Brit. position in world trade. Soc. problems remained unresolved for the time being.

Except for the yrs 1801–4, the gvt was in the hands of

1783–1806 William Pitt the Younger (24 yrs old when he first became prime minister). The state suffered under the burden of debts incurred during the Amer. War.

1785 Reduction of all duties between England and Ireland. But in

1791 WOLFE TONE (1763–98) founded the United Ireland society, which sought alliance with France and in 1798 launched a swiftly defeated rebellion. These events led in

1801 to the **Act of Union** which joined Ireland to the United Kingdom of Great Britain.

Renewed Stabilization of the Brit. Colon. Empire

Canada: attachment of the Fr. settlers was made possible by the

1791 organization of Canada into French-speaking **Lower Canada** (Quebec) and English **Upper Canada**, areas which differed in religion, language, customs and laws.

Australia: starting with Sydney (Botany Bay)

1788 beginning of settlement by Whites (initially convicts).

India: the East India Act of 1784 shifted control of the E. India Co. from Parliament (Regulating Act of 1773) to the gvt (p. 89).

The Struggle for Brit. World Power

PITT's greatest achievement was his leadership in the Brit. struggle for existence against the Fr. Revolution and NAPOLEON.

1793 Britain was forced to intervene in the 1st War of the Coalition (p. 23) because of (a) the Brit.-Fr. colon. conflict; (b) the threat to the Eur. balance of power; (c) the Fr. occupation of the Delta of the Rhine.

CHARLES JAMES FOX (1749–1806), the Whig opposition leader, demanded the termination of the struggle and contributed to the fall of PITT and to the

1802 Peace of Amiens (p. 25).

Napoleon's plans to destroy the Brit. enemy:

1798–9 The Egypt. campaign (p. 23).

1801 1st Ind. plan in alliance with PAUL I. The plan was abandoned following the murder of the Tsar. The eastern coast of India was conquered by RICHARD WELLESLEY in the 2nd Marathan War (1803–5).

1802 The Brit. navy obstructed the plan for the creation of a Caribbean empire. To gain the adherence of the U.S.A.

1803 sale of Louisiana (p. 15).

1804–5 Plans to conquer south-eastern Australia and to invade the Brit. Isles were given up.

1807–8 A 2nd plan to obtain India failed because of the reluctance of the Tsar ALEXANDER I.

1812–14 The Brit.-Amer. War ended without results of consequence (p. 15).

Brit. defence measures: formation of new coalitions (p. 25); contribution of 'few troops and much money'; **naval warfare** under the command of Admiral **Nelson** (1758–1805). His great successes secured Brit. naval supremacy and the sea route to India. The **blockade** of Fr. ports and the seizure of ships (including those of neutral countries) increased the Brit. fleet by *c.* 2,000 vessels a year. NAPOLEON countered with the

1806 Proclamation of the Continental System (p. 25), which was intensified after the

1807 bombardment of Copenhagen and confiscation of the Dan. fleet.

1808 ARTHUR WELLESLEY est. a '2nd front' in Portugal (p. 35).

Consequences for Britain: increases in taxation, subventions to agriculture, loss of Eur. markets; but, also, the opening of new markets in overseas regions (s. America). Increases in indust. production caused marketing crises after 1810 (unemployment, famine).

1811–12 1st anti-indust. riots by machine-breakers **(Luddites)**. The gold reserves of the Brit. banks prevented the collapse of the price structure. Econ. warfare did not bring about a decision; both sides had to rely on licences (regulations governing the import and export of scarce commodities to the enemy).

The Development of Ger. Nat. Consciousness

The Western Eur. peoples who were already united in polit. entities became conscious of their **polit. nationhood**–in England and France because of the Enlightenment conceptions of liberty, in Spain because of common traditions–during the course of the Fr. Revolution. Territ. particularism by the princes, the dissolution of the Holy Rom. Empire and a certain subservient habit of mind made any similar development difficult for the Ger. people. Beginning in the middle of the 18th cent., poets, scholars and the educated in general increasingly thought of themselves as members of a **nation in terms of ctr.**; they became representatives of the initially unpolit. so-called **Ger. Movement: Lessing** (I, p. 257) fought against alien Fr. influence on Ger. literature; JUSTUS MÖSER (1720–94) praised the old Ger. customs and traditions; **Klopstock** (1724–1803) celebrated love of the fatherland. Opposing the Enlightenment, the **Sturm und Drang** ('storm and stress') movement (*c.* 1760–80, so named after a drama by KLINGER, influenced by pietism and ROUSSEAU, I, p. 257) contrasted freedom of emotion with the rationalism of the Enlightenment and evoked SHAKESPEARE, the Ger. past and the creativity of natural or individual **genius**. The movement at first centred in Strasbourg about the young **Goethe** (*Götz von Berlichingen*, 1773). 1770 a decisive encounter with **Johann Gottfried Herder** (1744–1803), who, pursuing humanistic ideals, discovered manifestations of the unconsciously creative **Volksgeist** (spirit of the people) in vernacular tongues and folksongs, the nat. uniqueness of peoples in the *Ideen zur Philosophie der Geschichte der Menschheit* (1784–91). His work stimulated the Ger. *Klassik* (classics), Romanticism and a nat. consciousness, esp. among the Slav. peoples. The Ger. *Klassik* (**Johann Wolfgang von Goethe**, 1749–1832; **Friedrich Schiller**, 1759–1805) represented a cosmopolitan viewpoint. SCHILLER linked the concept of **inner direction** with KANT's **moral imperative** to respect human dignity. The ideal of classical Gk humanity, 'noble simplicity and quiet greatness' (WINCKELMANN), was to be the model for the morally emancipated individual (**Neuhumanismus** = a revival of humanism). Through art, the tensions between 'the ideal and the real' were to be bridged in aesthetic harmony; art thus had moral value. **Ger. idealism,** working in the realm of speculation and attempting to come to conclusions about the world 'as it really is', was also inspired by KANT (I, p. 257). In his *Wissenschaftslehre* (1794), JOHANN GOTTLIEB FICHTE (1762–1814) reduced all existence to an absolute spiritual force (the *Ur-Ich* = primeval self) which manifested itself in free, subjective activity, and to whose level man was able to raise himself intellectually. Nature as spirit manifest and spirit as invisible nature were identical acc. to **Friedrich Wilhelm Schelling** (1775–1854). The artist is superior to the thinker, because his work gives spirit to the world of the senses, and manifests the spiritual to the senses, thereby coming closest to the creations of the 'universal soul'. Both philosophers strongly influenced **Romanticism:** the older, purely lit. school of romanticism (Jena, Berlin, centring around the SCHLEGEL brothers, TIECK, NOVALIS, *et al.*) aspired to dissolve the conflicts between nature and the spiritual, emotion and reason, the finite and the infinite through subjective internalization (phantasy, dream, mystic vision). Romantics were conscious of the fact that the yearned-for 'boundlessness of things' ('the blue flower') could not be achieved (romantic irony). The **Younger School of Romanticism** (Heidelberg, centred on BRENTANO, VON ARNIM, VON EICHENDORFF, *et al.*) turned to the sources of folk ctr. (folk songs, fairy tales, sagas) which were thought to develop in organic fashion, to possess values rooted in historic uniqueness (*Historismus*) and to be beyond all laws of reason. The transfer of Romantic principles to music, art, literature, etc., led to the development of new intellectual disciplines **(Geisteswissenschaften)**: history (NIEBUHR, RANKE); the law (SAVIGNY); literature (the SCHLEGEL brothers); philology (the GRIMM brothers, UHLAND); Romance languages (DIETZ); relig. studies (BACHOFEN); polit. theory (p. 41). The spread of Romantic ideas in Europe (Mme DE STAËL, *De l'Allemagne*, 1813) unfolded to become a general intellectual and artistic current, as in England (BYRON, SHELLEY, KEATS), France (HUGO, LAMARTINE, GEORGE SAND), Italy (LEOPARDI, MANZONI), Denmark (ANDERSEN), Poland (MICKIEWICZ), Russia (LERMONTOV, PUSHKIN).

The Awakening of Ger. Nat. Consciousness

The apolitical conceptions of liberty of the 'Ger. Movement' were applied to the problems of the nation under the impact of Fr. dominance (SCHILLER, *Jungfrau von Orleans*, 1801; *Wilhelm Tell*, 1804). **Friedrich Hölderlin** (1770–1843) glorified the 'free people of the Greeks' and death for the fatherland. FICHTE demanded freedom of thought for the sake of polit. renewal in the *Addresses to the German Nation* (1807–8); in nationalistic exaggeration, he equated 'Germanness' with genuine morality and ctr. Patriotic sermons by the theologian **Schleiermacher** (1768–1834) roused feelings of nat. community; **Heinrich von Kleist**'s (1777–1811) *Hermannsschlacht* (1808) became the model for a nat. uprising. In the *Rheinischer Merkur*, **Joseph Görres** (1776–1848) est. the most aggressive anti-Napoleonic journal. **Ernest Moritz Arndt** (1769–1860) phrased the nat. aim in popular language ('to be one people is the religion of our day'). THEODOR KÖRNER and MAX VON SCHENKENDORF, among others, gave currency to nat. songs. **Friedrich Ludwig Jahn** (1778–1852) est. the nat. gymnastics movement. The meaning of nat. freedom remained obscure. These were the conceptions of the nation:

1. Under the influence of the Ger. *Klassik* and Enlightenment ideas, it was seen as a **cult. community**.
2. Under the influence of the Romantic concept of the folk (*Volk*) and the medieval empire, it was conceived of as a preordained nat. union.
3. Under the influence of the Fr. nat. state, it was conceived of as a polit. community of free men.

Differences between nat. conceptions were for the time being subordinated to the common aim of throwing off Fr. rule. In that sense, NAPOLEON became 'unifier of the Ger. people'. After his death, the polit. differences became apparent.

Domestic Reforms in the Germanies (1807–14)

Prussia: the absolutist system of gvt had already been criticized by leading officials before the collapse of 1806. The reformers sought a 'revolution from above' to create a more popular state, still based on estates, by liberating and educating the subjects to be responsible citizens. The **Reichsfreiherr vom und zum Stein** of NASSAU (1757–1831) played a leading role. A judicial official in the service of Prussia, he encountered elements of self-admin. in the estates as administrator of mines in Westphalia; discharged as a 'Jacobin' in 1807, he was recalled to office after the Peace of Tilsit and discharged again in 1808 (each time on NAPOLEON's urging). As a polit. adviser to the tsar, he worked for Ger. nat. unification until 1815 ('I have one fatherland only, and that is Germany!'). Awareness of traditions combined in him with lib. (Fr.) and dem. conceptions to form a con. system of thought all his own. His plans for reform (*The Nassau Memorandum*, 1807) were realized after

1810 by Chancellor Freiherr **Karl August von Hardenberg** (1750–1822; count in 1778, prince in 1814). The **Riga Memorandum** (1807) of the able diplomat of lib. and rationalistic persuasion cal. for 'dem. reforms within the framework of the monarchical state' without emphasis on self-admin. of the estates.

Soc. reforms to eliminate barriers between the estates:

1807 the edict emancipating the peasants: abolition of serfdom; guarantees of personal liberty; freedom to own property and work in one's chosen occupation; equality before the law.

1808 Municipal organization: self-admin. through the propertied bourgeoisie represented by elected city councillors (magistracy organization).

1810–11 Abolition of the guilds and limited freedom of the exercise of the trades.

1811 Edict regulating the abolition of labour services (*corvées*) in exchange for the surrender of one third of the peasant's land to the noble estate owners (p. 47).

1812 Emancipation of the Jews.

Administrative reforms incl. the separation of the judiciary from the admin.:

1808 establishment of departmental ministries (war, the interior, admin. (finances), justice, for. affairs). HARDENBERG's efforts led to a centralized admin. organized in provinces (each headed by an *Oberpräsident*); then administrative districts (each headed by a president); and finally counties (each headed by an elected *Landrat*; or, after the Gendarmerie Edict of 1812, by county directors appointed by the king). Only parts of the self-admin. of the estates aspired to by STEIN were realized by the county and district assemblies and nat. representation.

The reforms were opposed by con. nobles around VON DER MARWITZ, in association with the 'Christ. Ger. Round Table' (*Christliche Deutsche Tischgesellschaft*) and the *Berliner Abendblätter* (HEINRICH VON KLEIST). They regarded the dissolution of the trad. Prus. patrimonial order as a threat to the state (cf. p. 40).

Reforms of the army to develop a patriotic popular army through the efforts of **Scharnhorst** (1755–1813), **Gneisenau** (1760–1831) and their associates BOYEN (1771–1848), GROLMAN (1777–1843) and **Clausewitz** (1780–1831), the creator of mod. theories of war (*Vom Kriege*, written 1816–30). Despite the limitations on the numbers of the troops of the line imposed by NAPOLEON, reserves were created through the *Krümpersystem* (brief training periods for reservists); promotion on the basis of merit, elimination of humiliating corporal punishment and development of fresh leadership (war academy).

1814 Milit. law, incl. general conscription.

Reform of the educ. system along humanistic principles by the statesman and scholar **Wilhelm von Humboldt** (1767–1835), minister of education 1809–10, with HARDENBERG, Prus. representative to the Congress of Vienna. (HUMBOLDT was one of the first to carry out comparative studies of languages.)

1810 Establishment of **Berlin University** as an institution of 'academic freedom' and the 'unity of research, teaching and learning' in all disciplines. FICHTE, SCHLEIERMACHER, NIEBUHR and SAVIGNY were among those summoned to teach there.

1812 Establishment of the public *Gymnasia*, secondary schools organized to provide for an education in the lib. arts with an emphasis on classical languages and humanistic values; state examinations of philologists and pupils (*Abitur*). Reformation of the elementary schools to develop the natural gifts of the children along the lines of the Swiss educ. pioneer **Johann Heinrich Pestalozzi** (1746–1827): *Wie Gertrud ihre Kinder lehrt* (1803: *How Gertrud Teaches her Children*).

The new Prus. state became the hope of Ger. patriots.

Austria: More severe resistance against reforms under

1805–9 for. minister **Johann Philip Count Stadion** (1763–1824). The problem of multiple nationalities and the unequal state of education and development in the var. parts of the country necessitated preferential treatment of the nobility, which held the state together. Preparations for a nat. rising against NAPOLEON were nevertheless carried out (p. 29).

Reforms of the army under archdukes **Charles** (p. 23) and JOHANN (1782–1859).

1808 Introduction of general conscription.

The Confederation of the Rhine: inspired by the Fr. model, the foundations of the mod. unitary state were created most particularly in **Bavaria** under MONTGELAS (1759–1838) and **Baden** under REITZENSTEIN (1766–1846). They included (a) cen. bureaucracy, departmental ministries and professional bureaucrats; (b) dissolution of self-admin. of the estates in the communities; (c) the guarantee of certain freedoms (trades, choice of occupation, religion), with equal taxation and equality before the law; and (d) public supervision of churches and the educ. system.

Significance: the beginnings of constitutionalism promoted lib. and dem. polit. thought, esp. in southern Germany.

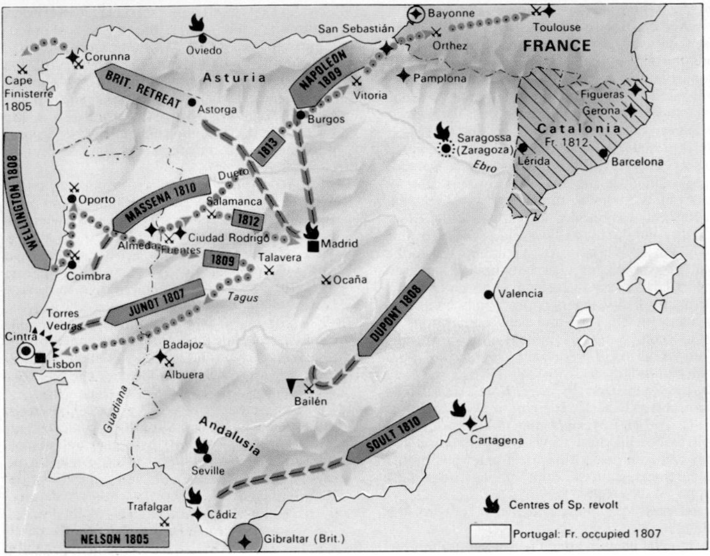

The Spanish uprising against Napoleon, 1808–14

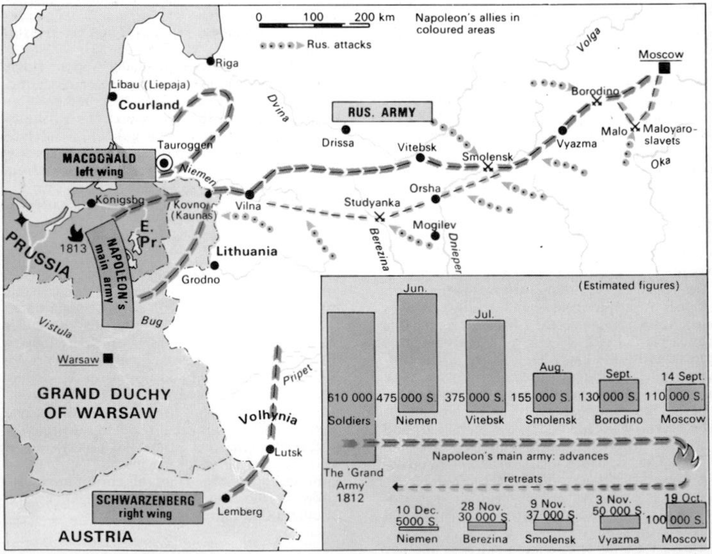

Napoleon's Russian Campaign, 1812/13

Nat. Upheaval in Spain

For his planned attack on Portugal, which still traded with Britain, NAPOLEON secured the right to establish milit. garrisons in and march through Spain in the

Oct. 1807 Treaty of Fontainebleau. **Junot conquered Portugal** (1807) and the royal family (JOHN VI) fled to Brazil.

Feb. 1808 **Marshal Murat** (1767–1815) led the reinforced Fr. troops against Madrid to 'protect the coasts from England'. CHARLES IV was forced to abdicate in favour of his son FERDINAND VII after an uprising in Aranjuez against GODOY, the pro-Fr. favourite of the king. Concerned for the representation of his own interests, NAPOLEON interfered in the family quarrels of the Sp. Bourbons and, in Bayonne, forced both CHARLES IV [1788–1808] and FERDINAND VII [1808–33] to abdicate in favour of his own brother JOSEPH (May); MURAT became King of Naples. The Cortes of Oviedo and Cartagena thereupon called for nat. resistance. Asturia and Andalusia rose and a provis. gvt (Cen. Junta) for FERDINAND was formed in Seville.

Jul. 1808 Capitulation of a Fr. corps of 23,000 men in Bailén; JOSEPH fled and the Brit. general ARTHUR WELLESLEY (1769–1852, Lord in 1809, and **Duke of Wellington** from 1814) landed in Portugal, pushing JUNOT back. The Emperor now intervened personally with 300,000 men.

1808–9 Sp. campaign of Napoleon: Madrid occupied, Saragossa captured and King JOSEPH able to return. The Aust. uprising (p. 29) interrupted the campaign. By order of the Emperor, the Brit. expeditionary corps under MOORE was pushed back by SOULT to Corunna. Nevertheless, the **guerrilla war**, waged by the *guerrilleros* and led by the nobility and clergy, continued to tie up considerable Fr. forces.

1809 The annexation of the Papal States and the arrest of the Pope stiffened the resistance of the Sp. people, who were loyal to the Church. WELLINGTON made some advances and repulsed

1810 MASSÉNA's attack on Lisbon in the fortifications of Torres Vedras. During NAPOLEON's Rus. campaign he was able

1812 to liberate Madrid. In besieged Cádiz, the Cen. Junta proclaimed the **Constitution of Cádiz of 1812**, which retained the monarchy but severely limited the powers of the king.

1813–14 WELLINGTON's vict. at Vitoria during his last offensive finally liberated Spain and led to the capture of Toulouse.

Dec. 1813 Treaty of Valençay. FERDINAND received his crown back from NAPOLEON. He rejected the lib. constitution and reigned as an absolute ruler. His reactionary régime provoked the liberals to resistance, uprisings and civil war (p. 45).

The Rus. Campaign of Napoleon, 1812

Econ. difficulties prompted the Tsar ALEXANDER I to discontinue Russia's role in the **Continental System** (Dec. 1810); preferential tariffs favoured Brit. trade in urgently needed indust. goods. The removal of the DUKE OF OLDENBURG from his throne (he was a relative of the tsar) and the disregard for Rus. interests in Poland and Turkey increased Franco-Rus. tensions.

NAPOLEON intended to assert the 'System of Tilsit' (p. 25) through direct milit. action. Milit. alliances with Prussia (Feb.) and Austria (Mar.) made possible the gathering of the **Grande Armée**, the largest army ever assembled in history. NAPOLEON's support for Denmark placed him at odds with Sweden's BERNADOTTE (p. 27), who wanted to join Norway (heretofore tied to Denmark) to Sweden to make up for the loss of Finland; an alliance between Russia and Sweden was thus made possible (Apr.). Russia terminated her war with Turkey.

The Napoleonic troops crossed the Niemen in Jun. 1812 without a declaration of war. The left wing operated in Courland to secure the flank (Prussians under MACDONALD), the right wing in Volhynia/Lithuania (Saxons and Austrians under SCHWARZENBERG). NAPOLEON advanced with the main army past Vilna in the direction of Moscow, which was occupied without resistance after victs. at **Smolensk** (Aug.) and **Borodino** (Sep.). The leader of the **'great patriotic war'** and the Rus. nat. hero, **Kutuzov** (1745–1813), relied on the vastness of Russia's expanses and decided on a flexible defence avoiding decisive battles. His 'Parthian tactics' became for the Rus. people the symbol of the invincibility of their land. After the **fall of Moscow**, the Freiherr VOM UND ZUM STEIN, the tsar's polit. adviser, and the Rus. nobility urged ALEXANDER to continue the fight. Peace offers by NAPOLEON were rejected. Logistical difficulties, the **burning of Moscow** (incl. the destruction of the Kremlin) and the coming of the winter forced NAPOLEON into a belated retreat (Oct.). The army was constantly pursued by Rus. troops and had to abandon its winter quarters at Smolensk.

The **crossing of the Berezina** nr Studyanka (Nov.) became a catastrophe. Hunger, disease and cold led to the complete dissolution of the *Grande Armée* (30,000 men surviving). NAPOLEON left his troops and appeared unexpectedly in Paris after a hurried journey undertaken to strengthen his shaky régime (attempted *coup* by General MALET in Oct.) and to raise new armies.

By the end of 1812, the remnants of the main army had reached the Prus. border (supposedly 1,000 men with 60 horses and 9 canon). The catastrophe was widely regarded as a divine judgement (*'Mit Mann und Ross und Wagen hat sie der Herr geschlagen'* = 'Man, horse, and wagon train, the Lord has beaten them!').

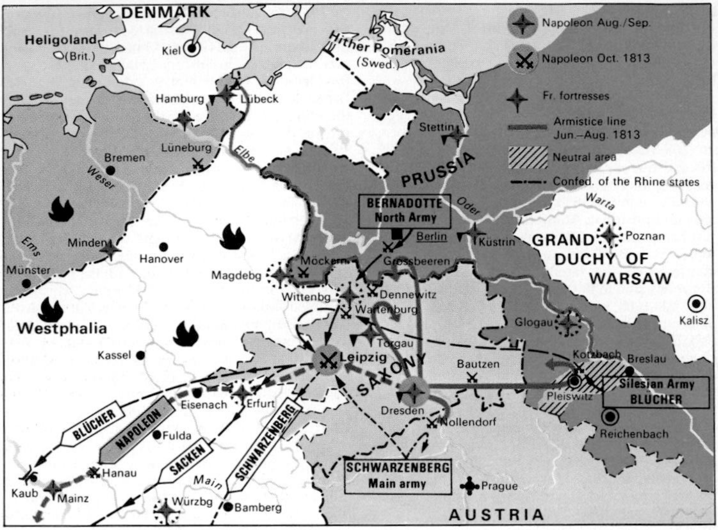

The Autumn Campaign, 1813

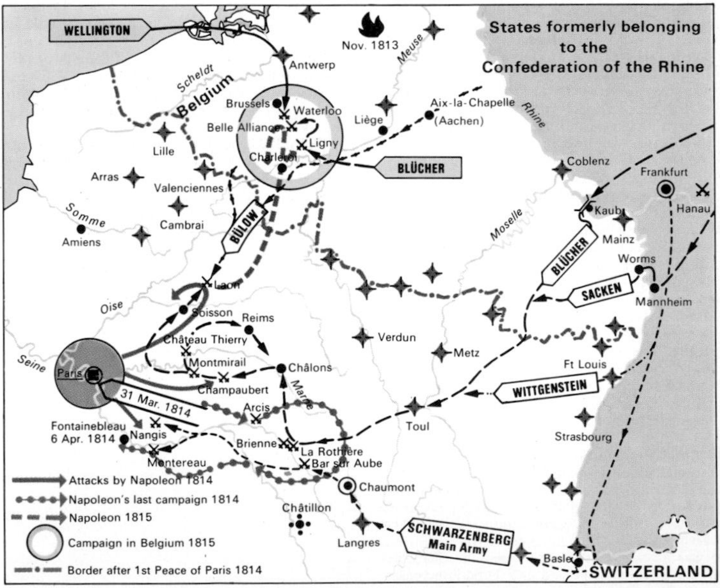

The campaigns against Napoleon, 1814/15

The Wars of Liberation (1813–15)

The catastrophe befalling NAPOLEON's *Grande Armée* kindled the nat. resistance of the Eur. peoples in opposition to alien Fr. rule.

The rising in Prussia: on his own responsibility, General **Yorck** (VON WARTENBURG, 1759–1830) concluded the

Dec. 1812 Convention of Tauroggen, promising neutrality by the Prus. auxiliary troops to the Rus. General DIEBITSCH (who was advised by CLAUSEWITZ–in the service of Russia since 1812) and thereby opening E. Prussia to the Rus. army. At the tsar's request the Freiherr VOM STEIN, YORCK and the E. Prus. estates raised levies of the people's militia (*Landwehr*).

Feb. 1813 Treaty of Kalisz. Russia obtained Poland in exchange for the rest. of Prussia (which incorp. Saxony into her territory). Under pressure from Prus. patriots (SCHARNHORST, HARDENBERG), FREDERICK WILLIAM III declared war on France (Mar. 1813). The establishment of the Iron Cross as a milit. decoration and the king's appeal 'To My People' evoked a spontaneous mood for sacrifice in the populace. Ind. mounted riflemen units were formed (among them the **Freikorps Lützow**, bearing the colours red/black/gold); donations of money and material helped to transform reservists and volunteers into troops of the line. Training of the people's army (SCHARNHORST). Prussia carried the main burden after Russia of the Wars of Liberation (6% of the pop. saw active service in the army).

The improvised Prus. and Fr. 'conscript armies' met during the **spring campaign** at Grossgörschen (fatal wounding of SCHARNHORST) and Bautzen. NAPOLEON drove the allies in the direction of Silesia; but Swed. troops landed in Pomerania (May). Britain joined the coalition (Jun.).

The joining of Austria: the states of the Confederation of the Rhine held back for the time being, even though the Freiherr VOM STEIN had issued the

Mar. 1813 Proclamation of Kalisz calling for a nat. Ger. constitution and support for the forces of liberation. METTERNICH negotiated with both sides and mediated the

Jun. 1813 Armistice of Pleiswitz (NAPOLEON: 'The greatest stupidity of my life!'). Austria entered the war (Aug.) only after peace negotiations in Prague had failed. During the

autumn campaign the 3 coalition armies advanced concentrically while retaining their flexibility. NAPOLEON's vict. at Dresden (Aug.) and other partial successes did not prevent the Fr. army being encircled.

16–19 Oct. 1813 b. of the Nations at Leipzig (more than 100,000 dead and wounded): vict. of the coalition, but orderly retreat by NAPOLEON across the Rhine.

Consequences: collapse of the Napoleonic system; dissolution of the Confederation of the Rhine; liberation of Germany, Holland and Upper Italy; defection of Naples (MURAT) from NAPOLEON's cause; Denmark had to give up Norway to Sweden in the

1814 Peace of Kiel; Prussia obtained Hither Pomerania.

The Campaign in France, 1814

Blücher (1742–1819) and SCHWARZENBERG crossed the Rhine at Kaub and Basle during the winter. NAPOLEON overcame BLÜCHER at Brienne, but was defeated by him at La Rothière; NAPOLEON was, however, able to preserve his freedom of action through energetic offensives (at Champaubert, Montmirail, Montereau among other sites), esp. since the conduct of the war by the coalition was obstructed by polit. problems. The peace congress of Chêtillon, sponsored by METTERNICH, dragged on through Feb. and Mar., and led to no conclusion. The coalition powers agreed anew to joint action in the Treaty of Chaumont (Mar.).

31 Mar. 1814 The allies entered Paris; a provis. gvt (TALLEYRAND) removed NAPOLEON from office.

6 Apr. 1814 The army forced NAPOLEON to abdicate at Fontainebleau. NAPOLEON was granted the island of Elba as a pty, and received the services of a guard of honour of 800 men. In the person of

1814–24 Louis XVIII the Bourbons returned to the throne. The king issued a lib. constitution; but he favoured nobility and clergy.

May 1814 1st Peace of Paris. Moderate peace conditions for France on the basis of the territ. *status quo* of 1792.

The 100 Days

The tensions among the allies at the Congress of Vienna (p. 39) led NAPOLEON to

Mar. 1815 land at Cannes. He assembled the core of the Fr. army, promised rad. dem. reforms, and entered Paris. LOUIS XVIII fled to Ghent. **Murat**, who aspired to the crown of Italy, took NAPOLEON's side; but, he was defeated by the Austrians in the

May 1815 b. of Tolentino (NEIPPERG). FERDINAND I [1816–25] became 'King of the Two Sicilies'. Following the immediate proscription of NAPOLEON, the two main armies of the victors under WELLINGTON and BLÜCHER and GNEISENAU advanced to the s. and w. respectively. NAPOLEON opened the

campaign in Belgium with only 120,000 soldiers. BLÜCHER was beaten at **Ligny**; however, he was able to join his troops to WELLINGTON's army in time during the

Jun. 1815 b. of Waterloo: the last Napoleonic army was dest.; 2nd entry of the coalition into Paris. NAPOLEON placed himself under Brit. protection. He was deported to the Atlantic island of St Helena, where he d. in 1821. His ashes were transferred to Paris in 1840, where they were laid to rest in **Les Invalides**.

Nov. 1815 2nd Peace of Paris: France lost Saarbrücken to Prussia, Landau to Bavaria, and Savoy to Sardinia. It was forced to pay a war-indemnity of 700 mil. francs; 17 fortresses were occupied for a duration of 5 yrs.

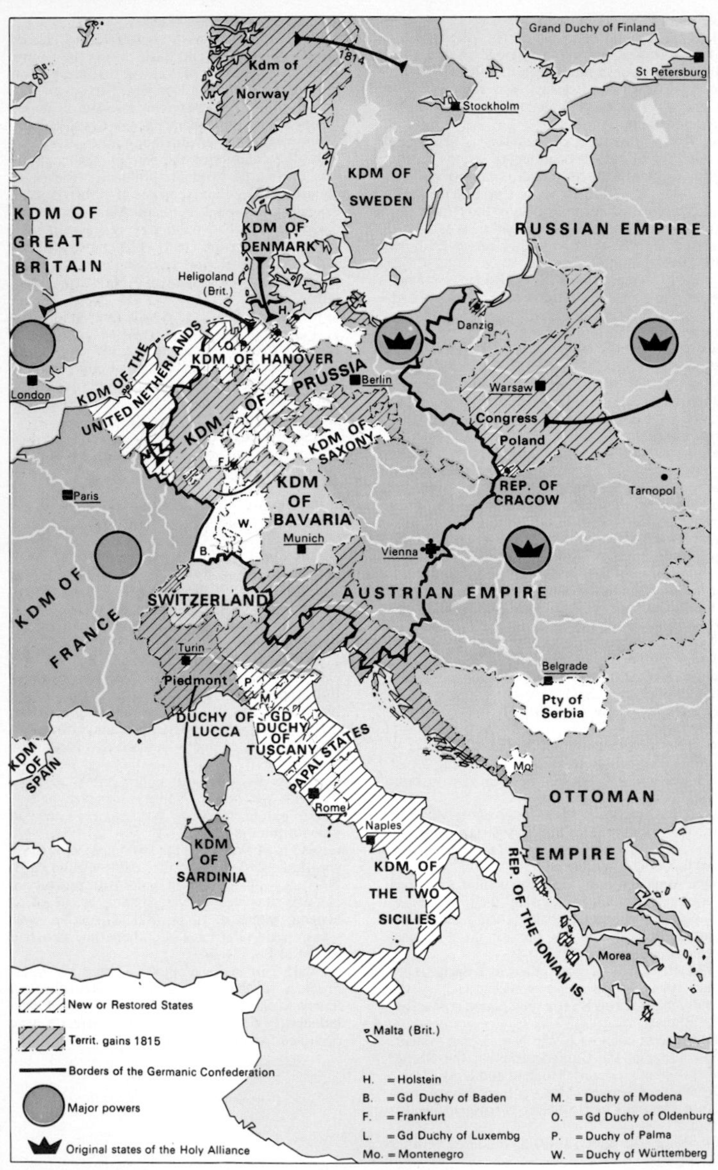

Grand Duchy of Finland
St Petersburg
1814
Kdm of Norway
Stockholm
KDM OF SWEDEN
KDM OF GREAT BRITAIN
RUSSIAN EMPIRE
KDM OF DENMARK
Heligoland (Brit.)
H.
Danzig
London
O.
KDM OF HANOVER
KDM OF THE UNITED NETHERLANDS
KDM OF PRUSSIA
Berlin
Warsaw
Congress Poland
KDM OF SAXONY
F.
Paris
KDM OF BAVARIA
REP. OF CRACOW
Tarnopol
W.
Munich
B.
Vienna
AUSTRIAN EMPIRE
KDM OF FRANCE
SWITZERLAND
Turin
Piedmont
P.
M.
Belgrade
Pty of Serbia
DUCHY OF LUCCA
GD DUCHY OF TUSCANY
PAPAL STATES
KDM OF SPAIN
Mo.
OTTOMAN EMPIRE
Rome
Naples
KDM OF SARDINIA
KDM OF THE TWO SICILIES
REP. OF THE IONIAN IS.
Morea
Malta (Brit.)
New or Restored States
Territ. gains 1815
Borders of the Germanic Confederation
Major powers
Original states of the Holy Alliance
H. = Holstein
B. = Gd Duchy of Baden
F. = Frankfurt
L. = Gd Duchy of Luxembg
Mo. = Montenegro
M. = Duchy of Modena
O. = Gd Duchy of Oldenburg
P. = Duchy of Palma
W. = Duchy of Württemberg

The reorganization of Europe through the Congress of Vienna 1815

The Congress of Vienna (1814–15)

The 3rd great peace congress (cf. I, pp. 255, 269) of mod. history for a **Eur. New Order** was mainly the work of Prince **Metternich** (1773–1859), who as a diplomat of con. persuasion rejected the lib. and nat. ideas of the time as dangerous to the state. Polit. principles of the congress: **rest.** (of the polit. situation of 1792); **legitimacy** (TALLEYRAND's principle to justify the dyn. claims of the *Ançien Régime*); **solidarity** (common policies of the legitimate princes against revolutionary ideas and movements). Representatives of almost all Eur. states and princes took part in the congress; for the 5 great powers: METTERNICH for Austria, CASTLEREAGH (1769–1822) for Britain, the Tsar ALEXANDER I and NESSELRODE (1780–1862) for Russia, HARDENBERG and VON HUMBOLDT (p. 33) for Prussia, TALLEYRAND for France.

Course: the Pol.-Saxon question led to the brink of war. Concerned to preserve the balance of power, METTERNICH and CASTLEREAGH protested at the annexation of Poland by Russia, and of Saxony by Prussia (Treaty of Kalisz, p. 37). **Talleyrand** (p. 19), for. minister under BARRAS, NAPOLEON and LOUIS XVIII, utilized the crisis to improve the int. polit. situation of France; France joined the secret Brit.-Aust. treaty against Russia and Prussia (Jan. 1815). As a result of METTERNICH's mediation, esp. under the impact of NAPOLEON's return from Elba, the powers reached a compromise.

Jun. 1815 Final Act of the Congress of Vienna. The balance of power between the 5 great powers ('pentarchy') was restored.

France retained its territ. possessions of 1792, checked additionally by a 'circle of medium-sized states': Sweden in personal union with Norway; the new Kdm of the United Netherlands; the Kdm of Sardinia-Piedmont, enlarged by Savoy.

The main victor was Britain, which was in personal union with the newly created Kdm of Hanover and received Malta, Ceylon, Cape Colony and Heligoland.

Russia obtained 'Congress Poland' (with its own constitution) and rose to become the leading Continental power.

Austria gave up the Habsburg Netherlands (Belgium) and Hither Austria in exchange for additions in Galicia, Upper Italy and Dalmatia. It exercised polit. primacy over restored Italy; as a multinat. state, it became alienated from Germany, but nevertheless claimed the leadership of the Germ. Confederation.

Prussia was satisfied with the partition of Saxony and was compensated by the Rhenish province and Westphalia; but this led to its separation into two economically and confessionally differing parts. It assumed the *'Wacht am Rhein'* ('Watch on the Rhine') against France and grew closer to the rest of Germany.

Switzerland was guaranteed 'eternal neutrality'. Acc. to the new constitution (Aug. 1815), the confederation consisted of 22 cantons, each with its own (for the moment reactionary) constitution.

The Reorganization of Germany

The patriots in the circle of the Freiherr VOM STEIN, E. M. ARNDT and JOSEPH GÖRRES (p. 32) wished to see a nat. Ger. state. Austro-Prus. dualism and the claims to sovereignty by the princes (particularism) did not allow strong cen. gvt; thus neither was the empire restored, nor the principle of rest. observed; but secularization (p. 29) was confirmed. METTERNICH realized his conceptions in the

Jun. 1815 Act of Confederation: 'to preserve the internal and external security of Germany and the independence and inviolability of the Ger. states' (Art. 2).

1815–66 The Germ. Confederation had 39 members (35 princes, among them the kings of Britain (Hanover), Denmark (Holstein), and the Netherlands (Luxemburg)). Austria and Prussia belonged to the Confederation only with part of their territories. The **Bundestag** at **Frankfurt** (a permanent meeting of ambassadors under the chairmanship of Austria) could be expanded into the **Assembly of the Confederation** for the deliberation of important decisions. It was not a representative popular assembly. Decisions by the confederation (unanimous or with a two-thirds majority) bound the gvts, but not their subjects. In the event of war, the **army of the confederation** (consisting of individual contingents supplied by the member states) was to provide protection. Art. 13, providing for local assemblies and constitutions, was one concession to liberalism. HUMBOLDT's plan uniformly to regulate finances, the law, traffic and the economy (coinage, measures and weights) was dropped.

Solidarity of the Powers

Influenced by pietistic-romantic circles, the Tsar ALEXANDER I designed a programme to protect religion, peace and justice.

Sep. 1815 Establishment of the Holy Alliance: the rulers of Gk. Orth. Russia, Cath. Austria, and Prot. Prussia bound themselves to govern at home in a Christ. patriarchal spirit – 'in accordance with Holy Writ' (Art. 1), and to practice solidarity in for. affairs. They derived their **right of intervention** against all lib. and nat. movements from their responsibility to God **(gvt by divine right).** All Eur. monarchs, exc. the Pope and the Sultan, joined the alliance.

Significance: formulated unclearly in polit. terms, the **'alliance of throne and altar'** est. the first supranational organization to preserve peace in mod. history. METTERNICH used the Holy Alliance as an effective weapon to enforce his con. policies. The Brit. Parliament rejected any right of intervention; England became the mainstay of lib. democrats.

Basic Polit. Conceptions after 1815

The overlapping of con., lib., dem. and socialistic ideas was as characteristic of the 19th cent. as the 'intermediate' form of gvt, the **const. monarchy**.

Conservatism (from Lat. *conservare* = to preserve): the polit. counter-currents to the Fr. Revolution (cf. **Edmund Burke**, p. 31) derived from the instinctive inclination to preserve obsolete forms of life out of reverence for est. institutions **(traditionalism)**. In the variety of their historic manifestations, state, society, the law and ctr. were considered to be organically growing institutions which could not be altered by the imposition of ideas, theories or constitutions. Institutions and authorities which safeguard the traditional, God-given order (the 'alliance of throne and altar') were defended: the monarchy, the churches, the occupational structure, the family and property. The individual was seen as belonging to a hierarchical community, which was subject to legitimate authority as much as the estates and associations; centralistic omnipotence by the state was rejected in favour of polit. federations.

Dangers: the tendency of con. principles to ossify led to **reaction** (obstruction of development), the encapsulation of privileged groups (nobility), uncritical submission to authority, relig. orthodoxy, intellectual and cult. sterility.

The nobility, clergy, officialdom and landowners were the supporters of the con. movement, which dominated Cen. Europe (Austria, Prussia) to the mid 19th cent. (the METTERNICH system).

Con. thinkers: motivated by patriotism, **F. L. von der Marwitz** (1777–1837) supported a patriarchal order of society based on estates and rejected the Prus. reforms (p. 33) as tending to give licence to egotistical striving for profits and dissolve the community of the body politic. The Prussian **Friedrich Gentz** (1764–1832) translated the writings of BURKE into German and became a mouthpiece for con. ideas as alone guaranteeing the Eur. balance of power. As a confidant of METTERNICH, he supported his policies of restoration. Revolutionary ideas were also abandoned by the politician and poet **René Chateaubriand** (1768–1848, *Essai sur les révolutions*, 1797), who found his way to a subjectively corrupted form of Christianity. So did the romanticist FRIEDRICH VON HARDENBERG, cal. **Novalis** (1772–1801), who in his *Christianity or Europe* (*Christenheit oder Europe*, 1799) conceived of an idealized image of a medieval world order. In his *Elements of Statecraft* (*Elemente der Staatskunst*, 1808–9), **Adam Müller** (1779–1829) formulated the **polit. theory of Romanticism:** God-given, the organically grown Christ. state of estates incorporates all human concerns. Its authority is neither bound by natural law, nor is it divisible. Its manifold historical manifestations are entitled to preserve their existence. *The Restoration of the Science of the State* (*Restauration der Staatswissenschaften*, 1816–34) of the Swiss **Karl Ludwig von Haller** (1768–1854) gave the age its name: magnifying reactionary impulses, he considered the state to be the property (*patrimonium*) of the prince (responsible to God only) on a basis of civil law; the subject had no rights except those of submission. Supported in its authority by the Church, it was the task of the **patrimonial state** to preserve the est. order. **Legitimism** was generated by DE BONALD and **de Maistre** (1753–1821), who emphasized the **divine right** of the dynasties to rule independently of the will of the people, justified the aims of the Holy Alliance (p. 39) and, in the *Du Pape* (*Of the Pope*), described the Cath. faith and papal primacy as the foundations of polit. order **(ultramontanism)**. Together with HALLER's ideas, the Christ. polit. and legal school of thought of **Friedrich Julius Stahl** (1802–61) influenced con. circles in Prussia (the GERLACH brothers, FREDERICK WILLIAM IV, p. 47): const. rights of the estates and the separation of powers were necessary checks of arbitrary rule, but law and moral order call for legitimacy and monarchy.

Liberalism: intellectually rooted in Enlightenment conceptions of the Social Contract and natural law (LOCKE, MONTESQUEIU), it gained momentum during the Fr. Revolution. Confident in the **progress** of reason, it aimed at the realization of **individual freedom**, conceiving it as:

1. **Freedom of the individual,** protected by basic **const.** or **human rights**: freedom of conscience, the press and thought; equality before the law, but not of property and education.
2. A **const. state,** its powers limited by the **separation of powers** and constitutions: a state of laws which protects the citizen and abstains from power politics.
3. Participation of the politically emancipated citizen through the **election** of representatives to a **parliament**, which decides on legislation and controls the gvt.
4. **A free economy** with freedom of occupation, trade, entrepreneurial activity, coalition, competition and movement.

Represented by the bourgeoisie of property and education, liberalism succeeded above all in England and flourished in the mid 19th cent.

Drawbacks: a tendency to anarchy (in Gk = absence of gvt), also to the dissolution of public authority in favour of individual liberty. Complete systems of polit. thought were therefore not developed; rather, frequent shifts of party positions occurred.

Lib. thinkers: polit. liberalism was described in the *Staatslexikon* (1834–48) of the Baden professors, VON ROTTECK and WELCKER. **Jeremy Bentham's** (1748–1832) *Introduction to the Principles of Morals and Legislation* (1780), and **John Stuart Mill's** (1806–73) *On Liberty* (1859) were influential, as was **Herbert Spencer** (1820–1903), who concerned himself with the course of progress; these represented the principles of experience and utility (Utilitarianism), which would bring the 'greatest happiness for the greatest number' through lib. reforms and a policy of laissez-faire (p. 11).

The attempt to reach a compromise between liberalism and eccles. authority–**freedom of Church from state**–by LACORDAIRE, MONTALEMBERT and LAMENNAIS (1782–1854) was rejected by the reactionary Pope GREGORY XVI [1831–46] as indifferentism (laicism).

Dem. endeavours: by their emphasis on **equality** and **popular sovereignty** (ROUSSEAU), the democrats (radicals, republicans) set themselves apart from the liberals. The **rights of man** ranked to them above the rights of the individual; the state, the union of the governing and the governed, was to protect them. As a precondition for a dem. order they demanded **universal suffrage**; under the influence of early Fr. socialist thought, they also urged a more equitable distribution of property, the elimination of class differences and privileges in education. The movement gained adherents among the *petite bourgeoisie* and the workers (proletariat). It achieved the extension of suffrage in the indust. states during the 19th cent. and **mass democracy** in the 20th.

Drawbacks: deterioration of majority rule into the **dictatorship of the majority**, which could be turned into the dictatorship of individuals, parties or groups through popular leaders (cf. ROBESPIERRE, the Jacobins, p. 21) and claim total power (totalitarian democracy).

Nationalism: generated during the Fr. Revolution, mod. nationalism or patriotism became one of the strongest polit. currents of the 19th cent. The aim was the sovereign **nat. state** through the right of self-determination of the **nation** (Lat. for people, from *nasci*=to be born), a concept which cannot be defined unambiguously. Nat. characteristics were found in natural conditions (common area and descent), cult. factors (language, religion, traditions, morals, customs) or subjective irrational attitudes (awareness of destiny, emotions, will). Preconditions for the mod. conception of the nation were the rational as well as the irrational teachings of the age: among them that of popular sovereignty, the conception of autonomy through freedom and the romantic notion of the race. Because of its heterogeneity, nationalism appealed to all polit. persuasions and developed most forcefully in those regions where the polit. unity of complete nations had not yet been realized: in Germany, Italy, Poland, Hungary; in the Balkans, in Belgium and in Ireland. It disrupted the supranational states (the Sp. colon. empire, the Ott. Empire, and the Danubian monarchy); in the 20th cent. it spread to the Afro-Asian peoples (p. 261). On the other hand, it helped to consolidate new polit. entities into nations (U.S.A.).

Drawbacks: an overrating of the individual and nat. aspirations for power were exaggerated in **nationalism** and led to a feeling of superiority over other 'inferior' peoples or nationalities, which were aggressively suppressed as nat. minorities or incorp. in nat. colon. empires **(chauvinism, imperialism).**

Basic Conceptions of the Philosophy of History

The fundamental thinker of the age, who brought together Enlightenment, Romantic and Neoclassical thought in a system that sought to fathom the universe and rounded out Ger. idealism, was **Georg Wilhelm Friedrich Hegel** (1770–1831): reason (intellect, thought) and reality (being) are identical with the 'absolute spirit'. The 'absolute world spirit' manifests itself in history through the **dialectical** cancelling out of conflicting tensions (thesis and antithesis) into higher forms of reason and freedom (synthesis). Every historical event occupies an ascertainable position in the scale of values of the historical process. Great personalities believe themselves to be acting in their own interest, but are really only tools of the 'cunning of reason'. The 'objective spirit' (reality) reaches its highest stage in the timeless state, which alone makes freedom, justice and ctr. possible. In the moral order, it is superior to the individual and raises it to realize its essence. The most complete form of the state is the **const. monarchy**, in which the objective will of the state is manifested in the person of the monarch, who guarantees the freedom of the individual, property, and society and a lawful admin.

Significance: HEGEL's idealistic conception of the state and the meaning of history in the realization of freedom, justice and reason strongly infl. his contemporaries, had an impact on the revolutionary thinkers of Russia (p. 69) and turned into rad. criticism of existing conditions in the 'Young Hegelians', BRUNO BAUER, LUDWIG FEUERBACH and **Karl Marx** (p. 64).

Historicism (*Historismus*), a concept developed by FRIEDRICH MEINECKE (1862–1954), gives expression to the consciousness that all of life and reality are historically conditioned. Acc. to MEINECKE, historicism culminated in the work of **Leopold von Ranke** (1795–1886), who, proceeding from the singular and unique, sought to understand universal ideas. RANKE expressed the essence of historicism by saying that each epoch is 'immediate to God', that each historical event must be understood and described in its own terms.

Following on the failure of the revolution of 1848, the pessimism of **Arthur Schopenhauer** (1788–1860) gained ground among the Ger. bourgeoisie, which became politically withdrawn. In *The World as Will and Idea* (*Welt als Wille und Vorstellung*, 1819, vol. II, 1844), he no longer saw a purposeful meaning in history; rather, he saw the blindness of the will as the unreal first cause of the world, a 'playground of passions' turning aimlessly in circles. Among other critics of historicism was FRIEDRICH NIETZSCHE (p. 64), who in his *Untimely Reflections* (*Unzeitgemässe Betrachtungen*, 1873–6), considered history to be dangerous because it paralyses the capacity to act.

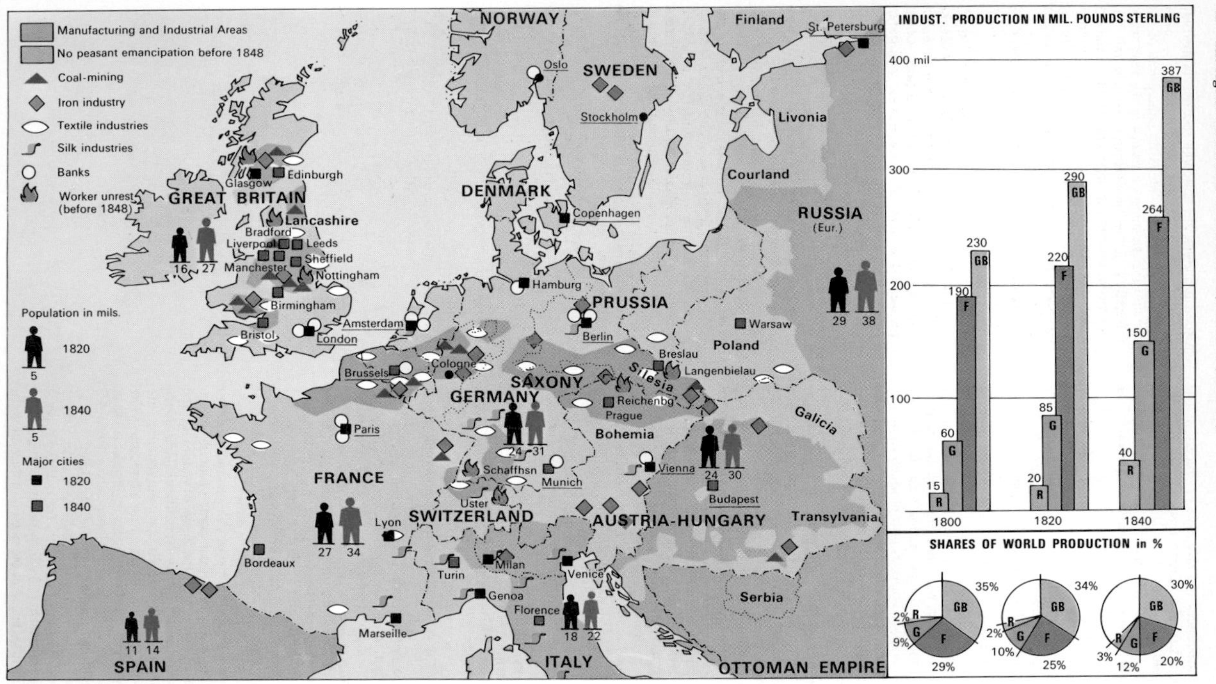

Manufacturing and industry in Europe, 1820–40

The Industrialization of England

Econ. and soc. conditions changed during the 18th cent. so that the preconditions for the

Indust. Revolution (a term introduced by BLANQUI in 1837 and ENGELS in 1845) were created. A number of factors, contingent on each other, brought it about: ever since the Test Act (1673) had barred those outside the Anglican confession from polit. life, Calv. ethics (I, p. 238) had helped to bring out a new

conception of work. Diligence, frugality and the sober striving for profits beyond the satisfaction of individual needs had created **private capital** for investment in the expansion of productive capacities in large-scale enterprises; limitations on these practically disappeared during the 18th cent. (limitations on the exercise of trades were eliminated in 1814). The theoretical foundations of

capitalism were laid by ADAM SMITH (p. 11) and the classical school of economics (DAVID RICARDO, 1772–1823), which conceived of economic

liberalism as proceeding from the basic factors of labour, the striving for personal profits and liberty; economic liberalism found its most convinced advocates in the **Manchester School**, a group of textile manufacturers around RICHARD COBDEN (1804–65). BACON's view (I, p. 256) that empirical knowledge applied in observation and experiment increases wealth was widely spread by Eng. Enlightenment thought.

The sciences found their practical application. Yet, also, craftsmen without formal education accomplished basic

technical innovations (cf. I, p. 279): the flying shuttle –KAY (1733); the coking process in the production of iron–DARBY (1735); the steam engine–WATT (1775); the 'Mule Jenny'–CROMPTON (1779); the power-driven loom–CARTWRIGHT (1786).

1789 propulsion of a manufacturing machine by a power-engine: beginning of the **mechanization of work** and thus of the Indust. Revolution. In terms of economics, Britain had since 1707 (union of Scotland and England) had the largest Eur.

Free Trade Area with an est. system of finan. credits (Bank of England, 1694), active coastal traffic, a strong fleet and a profitable trade. The wealth of capital brought about an

agrarian revolution (p. 31): redistribution of open fields, dispossession of small farmers, enclosures of common lands by large aristocratic landowners aided by Act of Parliament. Rising yields of the soil and early breakthroughs in medicine (hygiene and the fight against contagious diseases) led to a sudden increase in pop., or even to

over-population. The economist **Thomas Robert Malthus** (1766–1834) considered the privation and misery of the masses to be the consequence of natural law, because, he thought, pop. increases geometrically, whereas yields of the soil increase only arithmetically. **Emigration** (N. America, Australia, later New Zealand), **flight from the countryside** and the development of the proletariat in big cities were consequences of this over-population. Also, the

growth of industry was stimulated: the new

factory system required self-confident initiative, capital for machines and raw materials, a labour supply and markets for goods mass-produced by machines. The **new classes** came from all levels of society: **entrepreneurs** (the owners of private capital) and unskilled **proletarians**. Both groups were opposed to the gentry and the large merchants; at the same time, they were opposed to each other. An over-supply of workers and draconic measures (long working hours at starvation wages, female and child labour) brought about the new, still unfamiliar toil of factory labour. The starvation wages justified RICARDO's theory of wages, which holds that labour and its products underly the same law of supply and demand. Favourable conditions for industrialization were found in the

processing of cotton (centring on Manchester, Lancs.). Spinning mills (after 1790) and weaving mills (after 1815) called for relatively little initial capital and secured high profits because of an already established cycle: the transport of slaves (until 1807) to Amer. cotton plantations, import of raw cotton, export of cotton goods to Africa and the plantation countries. Imports rose between 1785 and 1840 from £11 mil. to £366 mil. as prices of yarns dropped by 95%. The Continental System led to the establishment of new markets for the

textile industry in s. America and India. Downward business trends between 1815–20 increased the 'reserve army of industry' and depressed wages. The enormous gains in capital laid the foundations for new capital-intensive branches of industry: **mining** and **heavy industry**. These industries *c.* 1840 advanced because of the

revolution of transport through the steamship (FULTON, 1807) and the railway **locomotive** (STEPHENSON, 1814).

1830 1st railway Liverpool–Manchester; by 1848 the rail network extended 5,000 mi.

Consequences: to the end of the 19th cent., England remained the leading indust. nation. Following the Eng. model, but with local variations, other Eur. indust. states developed: Belgium, Holland, Switzerland, France (after 1825), Germany (after 1850), Sweden (after 1880). Industrialization led to concentration in **indust. areas** (urbanization), the development of dem. class societies, the raising of nat. incomes and the general standard of living and the establishment of **world markets**–an epoch of tech. civilization which is not yet over. The crafts and the small peasantry were reduced in importance, class differences intensified and the **soc. question** became the most urgent problem of the indust. nations.

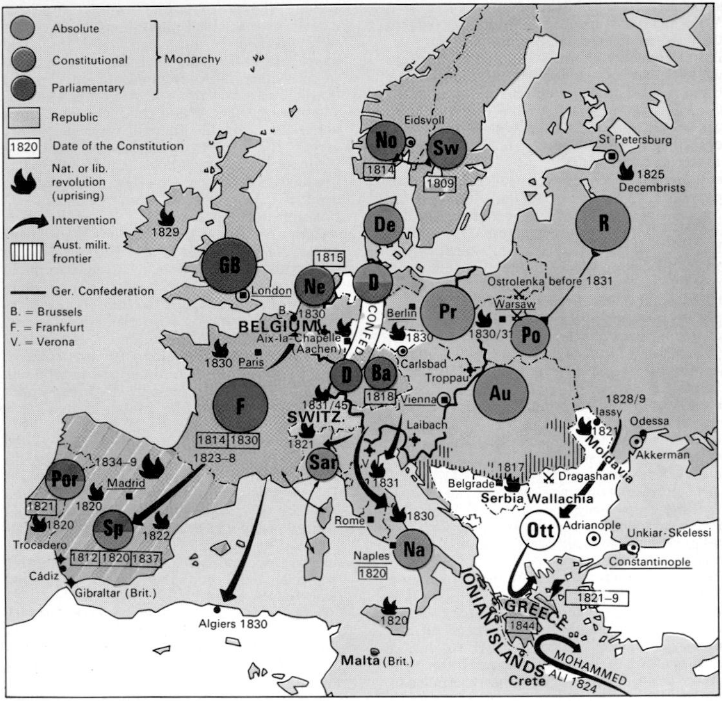

Reaction and reform in Europe, 1815–48

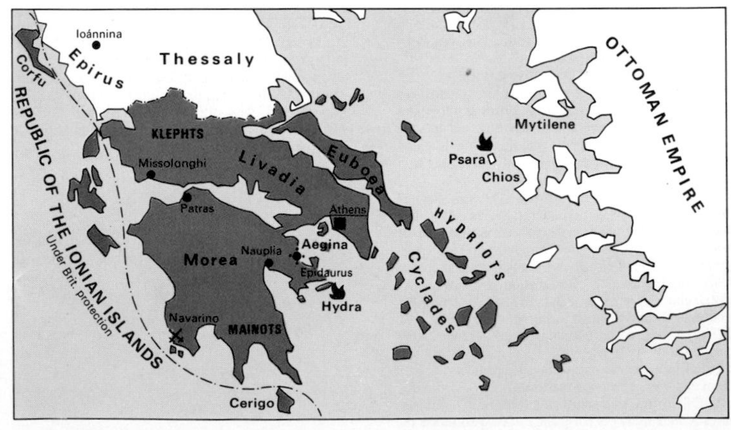

Greece, 1829

The Congress System (1815–22)

METTERNICH and ALEXANDER I of Russia attempted to establish cooperation between the great Eur. powers on the basis of congresses to safeguard the settlement of Vienna (p. 39). This balance-of-power policy was supported by CASTLEREAGH, even though the British proceeded with caution. The 'concert of the powers' was expanded at the

1818 Congress of Aix-la-Chapelle (Aachen) by the admission of France into the Holy Alliance. The principle of intervention (p. 39) was secured by METTERNICH at the

1820 Congress of Troppau over the objections of Britain. Gradually Britain freed herself from polit. ties to Europe ('splendid isolation') and–as the protector of the small nations–supported their lib. movements during CANNING's period in the For. Office (1822–7). Solidarity of the powers was discontinued as they split into a lib. western bloc (Britain and France) and a con. eastern bloc (Russia, Austria and Prussia).

Nat. and Lib. Uprisings in Southern Europe

Spain: uprising of troops at Cádiz and

1820 revolution of the liberals. The 'serviles' (the supporters of the absolute monarchy) were defeated. The victors split into the *'exaltados'* and *'moderatos'*. A decision of the

1822 Congress of Verona–despite Brit. objections (WELLINGTON)–authorized Fr. milit. intervention: Madrid and the fortress of Trocadero were taken in 1823. Severe retribution was exacted by FERDINAND VII under the guns of Fr. occupation. Renewed conflicts broke out after his death and resulted in the

1834–9 Carlist Wars.

Portugal: proclaimed by the Cortes in

1821, the constitution was recognized by JOHN VI after his return from Brazil (p. 35). CANNING prevented unrest when he supported the succession of JOHN's grandchild, MARIA II DA GLORIA, against that of Dom MIGUEL, the candidate of the reactionaries. MARIA was accepted as queen in 1834, but was unable to prevent continued unrest until 1847. Since that time England has been regarded as the champion of lib. causes.

Naples: the secret society of the **Carbonari** (after *c.* 1796) worked towards a nat. revolution.

1820 The revolt in Nola forced FERDINAND I to grant a constitution. While Sicily (secret society of the Mafia) attempted to leave the kdm, the Ital. nat. movement spread to Sardinia-Piedmont and Upper Italy.

1821 The Congress of Laibach authorized Aust. intervention. The uprising collapsed; its leaders were convicted and sentenced to confinement in polit. trials; or left the country. All Ital. patriots were united in their hatred of the Habsburgs.

Serbia: based on memories of the Greater Serb. Kdm (I, pp. 204f.), which had been preserved by the Orth. Church and popular writings, and strengthened by the guerrilla wars of the Hajdukes, mod. Serb. nationalism also related to modern conceptions of freedom.

1804–12 1st popular uprising against the Ott. Empire under KARA GEORG PETROVIĆ, cal. KARADJORDJE ('Black George'). A distinct polit. organization composed of a senate and the Skupshtina (popular assembly) was est.

1815–17 The 2nd uprising under MILOŠ OBRENOVIĆ (1780–1860). Domestic autonomy was achieved. Still obliged to pay tributes to the Porte, the pty was able to retain independence by manoeuvring between Russia and Turkey, even though the competing peasant dynasties of the Karadjordjević and the Obrenović were constantly involved in power struggles.

Greece: conscious of their classical heritage, Gk patriots formed **Hetairai** (secret societies) in 1814 at Athens (Count KAPODISTRIAS) and Odessa (Prince YPSILANTI) to liberate the nation from the infidel. Supported by Gk merchants in Constantinople (Fanariots) and the Orth. Church, they organized popular uprisings on the mainland (Klephts, Mainots) and in the Aegean Islands (Hydriots).

1821–9 Gk War of Liberation. Led by the Gk general Prince ALEXANDER YPSILANTI (1792–1828), who was in the service of Russia,

1821 the uprising in Moldavia and Wallachia failed (b. of Dragashan). Even so,

1822 the Nat. Congress of Epidauros proclaimed Gk independence, celebrated enthusiastically by con. and lib. 'Philhellenes' alike (LOUIS I of Bavaria, CHATEAUBRIAND, JEAN PAUL, HÖLDERLIN, among others). Eur. volunteers (BYRON) assembled at Geneva. But reprisals (Turk. atrocities on Chios) threatened to extinguish the uprising.

1824 Intervention of the Egypt. Fleet of MOHAMMED ALI (p. 97);

1826 Missolonghi fell after determined resistance. While METTERNICH condemned the insurrection as a revolution, even the 'policeman of reaction', the Tsar NICHOLAS I, supported the Gk uprising because of his Orth. faith, his enmity towards Turkey and polit. considerations (the Straits).

1827 Treaty of London. England, France and Russia supported Gk autonomy.

1827 Destruction of the Turk.–Egypt. fleet at **Navarino** by the combined naval forces of England, France and Russia. Count KAPODISTRIAS was chosen regent and est. Gk admin. from Nauplia. A Fr. auxiliary corps liberated the Morea.

1828–9 The Russo–Turk. War was observed with suspicion by Britain.

1829 Peace of Adrianople (through Prus. mediation): Russia received the mouth of the Danube and the right to protect Greece. Gk independence was recognized by the

1830 London Conference. After the murder of KAPODISTRIAS

1832 OTTO I of Wittelsbach was chosen king. His absolutist 'Bav. reign' was terminated in 1862 by his removal from the throne, despite the

1844 granting of a constitution.

Results: discontinuation of the Holy Alliance because of Austro-Rus. conflicts over the 'Eastern Question'. The Eur. revolutionary movements received renewed momentum through the Fr. July Revolution (p. 51).

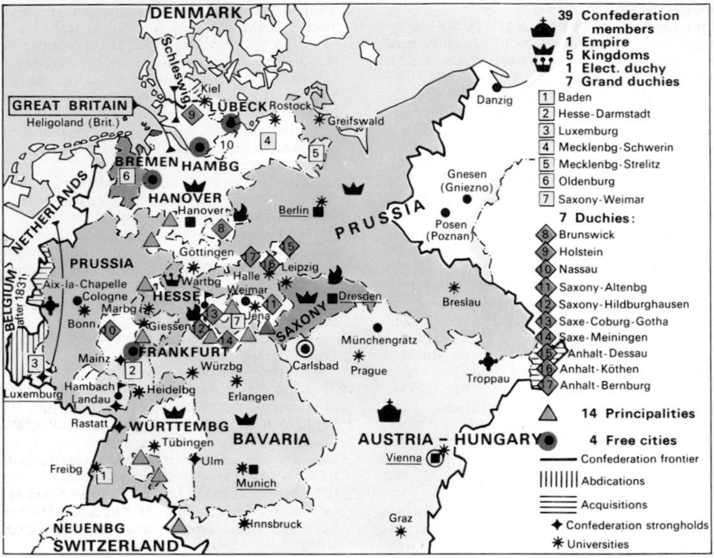

The German Confederation, 1815–48

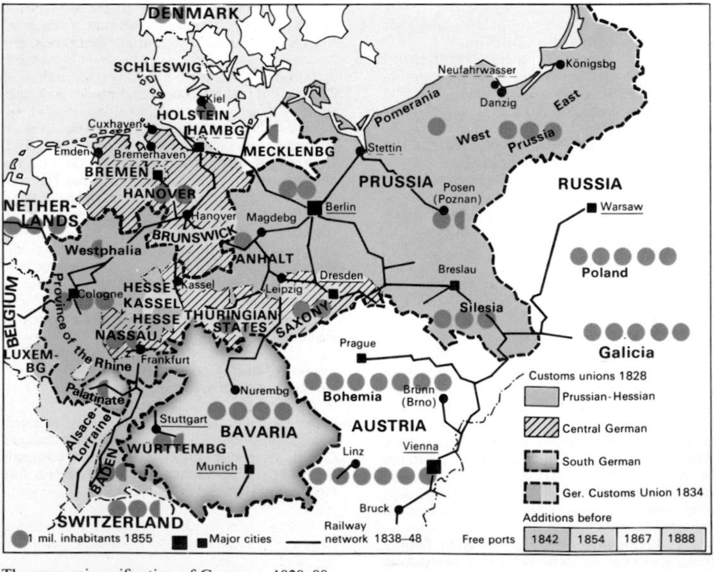

The economic unification of Germany, 1828–88

Reaction and Nat. Opposition

The policy of rest. pursued by the Assembly of the Confederation and the (35) princes ensured a period of outward calm (*Biedermeier* period). The nobility and con. officialdom and bourgeoisie rejected lib. ideas. Participation in the polit. process by the 'limited understanding of the common herd' was considered to be superfluous.

1815 Establishment of the Ger. Burschenschaft at Jena in response to the 'Metternich system' (it was an association of students wearing the 'imp. colours' of black, red and gold and adhering to the motto 'Honour, freedom and fatherland').

1817 The Wartburg Festival, celebrated to commemorate the b. of the Nations at Leipzig, was concluded with the burning of the constitution of the Confederation and reactionary writings and symbols. Rad. groups (KARL FOLLEN) urged action.

1819 After murdering the poet KOTZEBUE, believed to be an agent of the tsar, the student K. L. SAND was executed. Prompted by METTERNICH, a conference of ministers of state reacted with the

1819 Karlsbad Decrees: a cen. commission of investigation was est. at Mainz; prohibition of the Burschenschaft; persecution of the 'demagogues'; control over the press and the universities. These decisions became part of the

1820 Final Act of the Congress of Vienna, and thereby part of the constitution of the Confederation. The nat. movement was suppressed by police-state methods.

The Development of Mod. Polit. Trends

Princes of the former Confed. of the Rhine granted **constitutions** after the Fr. model (emphasis of the monarchical principle, popular representation in 2 chambers); Nassau, 1814; Saxony-Weimar, 1816; Bavaria, Baden, 1818; Württemberg, 1819; Hesse-Darmstadt, 1820. Limited polit. participation of the people–esp. in **Baden**–led to

S. Ger. liberalism: pacifistic and nationalistic conceptions (WELCKER) joined with demands for self-admin., trial by jury, a popular militia and a nat. system of economics (FRIEDRICH LIST). Exposed to stronger pressures by reactionary gvt,

N. Ger. liberalism developed more slowly; it was modelled more after the Eng. example and pre-eminently stressed nat. union (DAHLMANN). The historian JOHANN GUSTAV DROYSEN as well as the s. Ger. PAUL PFIZER pleaded for Prus. leadership in Germany. Influenced in part by Romanticism, the first centres of

polit. Catholicism developed in Munich (LOUIS I, GÖRRES), Frankfurt and the Rhineland. Under the impact of the arrest of high ecclesiastics (Archbp DROSTE ZU VISCHERING, 1837) during the

1836–40 Cologne disorders (troubles with the Prus. state over mixed marriages), they joined more closely. Early

conservatism found its strongest support in the circle around the Prus. crown prince and the brothers GERLACH. After 1848, its organ of publication was the *Kreuzzeitung*.

Prussia and the Ger. Customs Union (Zollverein)

1797–1840 FREDERICK WILLIAM III clung inflexibly to the principles of the Holy Alliance. 'Demagogues' were persecuted; such men as STEIN, GNEISENAU and SCHLEIERMACHER were held under suspicion. Domestic reforms were interrupted; self-admin. in the country was not put into effect; the emancipation of the peasantry was impeded. The

1816 edict regulating the compensation of estate owners created new **large landholdings** with rationalized admin., but also a kind of agrarian **proletariat** (day labourers), leading to an increased flight from the land and emigration.

1817 Union of the Luth. and reformed Churches. Const. projects by WILHELM VON HUMBOLDT and BOYEN failed; only

1822 prov. assemblies (*'Landtage'* of the 8 provinces, domination by the milit., office-holding and land-owning nobility). The fusion of the old Prot. and con. agrarian regions with the recently added Cath., commercial and lib. regions (the Rhineland, Westphalia) remained the major task of gvt. The exchange of goods was promoted by the new law regulating

1818 taxation and customs (MAASSEN): border customs duties and consumer taxes took the place of the *'Akzise'*. To overcome the 38 Ger. customs systems the Swabian **Friedrich List** (1789–1846) founded the

1819 Commerical and Crafts Union (Handels- und Gewerbeverein).

1828 Establishment of limited customs unions against the objections of METTERNICH. On the initiative of the Prus. finance minister MOTZ (1775–1830), they joined to form

1834 the Ger. Customs Union (Zollverein), led by Prussia. It became the first step in the polit. unification and industrialization of Germany (p. 60). The development of the railway system, as planned by LIST, began with the

1837–9 construction of the Leipzig–Dresden line.

Prelude to Revolution (1830–48)

1834 After the **Vienna meetings of ministers**–under the impact of the Jul. Revolution (p. 51)–reactionary policies intensified with renewed persecutions of demagogues and press censorship. Emigrants congregated in Paris (KARL MARX, HEINE) and in Switzerland (HERWEGH, FREILIGRATH). After the dissolution of the personal union with England, King ERNST AUGUST of Hanover broke the constitution:

1837 protest and removal from office of the **'Göttingen Seven'** (among them Prof. DAHLMANN, JACOB and WILHELM GRIMM).

1840 Fr. demands for the border along the Rhine (p. 49) evoked storms of protest all over Germany. Patriotic songs were composed (*'Die Wacht am Rhein', 'Deutschlandlied'*). The expectations of the nationalists fastened on

1840–61 FREDERICK WILLIAM IV of Prussia, who granted amnesties to the 'demagogues', terminated the 'Cologne disorders' and created nat. symbols with the celebration of the construction of Cologne Cathedral in 1842 and the 'Thousand Year Anniversary of the Empire' in 1843. But he refused to grant a constitution. Reluctantly he consented to the

1847 Convocation of the united prov. assemblies (*Vereinigte Landtage*) as a consultative representation of the estates.

Brit. domestic policy focused on 4 basic problems: (a) adjustment of the parl. system (p. 31) to the new soc. conditions; (b) putting into effect econ. liberalism; (c) the demands of the workers for soc. security and polit. recognition; (d) the solution of the Irish problem.

The Con. Period (1815–30)

Respect for the crown declined because of the marital scandals of the 'dandy'

1820–30 GEORGE IV, regent after 1811. After the termination of the Napoleonic Wars, severe econ. depressions, incl. the fall of prices and unemployment as a result of overproduction. The landowners, to counteract the influx of cheap overseas grains, were able to obtain the passage of the

1815 Corn Laws through the

1812–27 Tory cabinet of LIVERPOOL. Severely affected, the working people found a spokesman in the pamphleteer **William Cobbett** (1762–1835) and cal. attention to his rad. demands through demonstrations.

1819 Unrest in Manchester (the **'Peterloo Massacre'**) was met by the 'Ultra Tories' with the '6 Acts': laws limiting freedom of the press and assembly; but the moderate Young Tories around **Robert Peel** (1788–1850) gained in infl. Under

1822 CANNING (1770–1827) as for. minister, England turned from the policies of rest. (p. 45) to mitigation of penal laws and the granting of the freedom of workers' alliances.

1824 Legal recognition of trades unions (localized unions). Owing to the efforts of PEEL and the 'Irish Cath. Association', of **O'Connell** (1775–1847), the WELLINGTON cabinet passed

1829 Cath. emancipation. O'CONNELL forced an amelioration of the Irish tax burden through Parliament and demanded the dissolution of the 1801 union of England and Ireland.

The Period of Lib. Reforms (1830–48)

1830–37 WILLIAM IV; the elections at the beginning of WILLIAM's reign were affected by the impact of the Jul. Revolution in France and brought

1830 the Whig cabinet of GREY to power. It successfully pushed through the reform plans of Lord **John Russell** (1792–1878), broadly favouring the middle classes.

1832 1st Reform Bill: 143 of 200 seats of the 'rotten boroughs' came to new urban elect. districts; the extension of the franchise to those paying a certain annual rental enlarged the electorate by about one half.

Consequences: concern for public opinion, dependence of the gvt on parl. majorities, change of the names of the parties to **Conservatives** and **Liberals**.

1833 1st Factory Act: limitation of child labour to 8 hrs, gvt inspections.

1833 Abolition of slavery; new Poor Laws, incl. forced labour for paupers in workhouses; a municipal code with increased self-admin. (1835). **Charles Dickens** (1812–70) served with his novels (*Oliver Twist*, 1838–9) as a soc. critic.

1837–1901 Queen Victoria. Popular, like her consort Prince ALBERT of Saxe-Coburg (1819–61), VICTORIA loyally honoured the constitution, raised respect for the crown and became the symbol of the **'Victorian era'** (p. 104).

Disappointed by the failure in 1834 of the Grand National Consolidated Trades Union of **Robert Owen** (p. 67) and his associates, the cabinet-maker **William Lovett** (1800–77) founded

1836 the London Working Men's Association. Referring to the Magna Carta of 1215, he formulated his popular demands in the 'People's Charter': universal male suffrage, finan. allowances for M.P.s, annual elections, etc.

1838 After rejection by the Parliament, the petition became the programme of the **Chartists**, the first polit. workers' movement. The rad. O'CONNOR ousted LOVETT from the leadership and cal. for demonstrations. Chartist agitation led (1839) to disturbances in Birmingham and an uprising in Newport. Because of a common interest in **free trade**, the Manchester School (p. 43) joined the workers. RICHARD COBDEN and JOHN BRIGHT (1811–89), while opposing the Chartists, created

1838 the Anti-Corn Law League and advocated public education, pacifism, tolerance and elect. reform; but they strictly rejected all soc. legislation (the principle of laissez faire). Their agitation among the masses was successful.

1842 first attempt at a general strike. The b. for econ. improvement was carried on with peaceful means by the

1844 1st consumers' cooperative, the 'Rochdale Pioneers', inspired by OWEN. The soc. crisis was intensified by the

1845–6 great famine in Ireland caused by the potato blight. About 1 mil. d. of starvation; the pop. of 8·3 mil. had decreased by 1851 to 6·6 mil., over 1 mil. emigrating, mostly to N. America. The wave of terror by the 'Young Ireland' movement was beaten down in 1848.

At the eleventh hour the Con. cabinet of PEEL acted against the right wing of its own party (DISRAELI) and

1846 repealed the Corn Laws, thereby turning to a free trade policy. The vict. of the 'Free Trade' School split the Con. party and removed the last obstacles in the way to the development of the purely indust. and commercial state. Brit. arable agriculture became severely depressed after 1875.

1847 Transition to the 10-hr day in the factories; the Chartist movement decreased in intensity. But in 1848 the 'Young Ireland' movement, led by SMITH O'BRIEN, attempted an unsuccessful insurrection in Ireland.

The Rest. of the Bourbons (1814–30)

1814–24 Louis XVIII. Returning from exile (Verona) 'with the white flag in his baggage', he granted the

1814 Charte Constitutionelle: a 2-chamber legislature modelled after the Brit. example (hered. peers and a chamber of deputies chosen on the basis of an extremely limited suffrage); leg. initiative rested with the executive alone; it was exercised by ministers responsible to the king. The revolutionary land settlement, equality before the law (*Code Civil*) and civil rights were acknowledged. The propertied bourgeoisie became the most powerful polit. element in society.

Parties: the **Ultra-royalists** (CHARLES X, POLIGNAC, VILLÈLE) worked for the rest. of the traditional privileges of the nobility;
the **Independents** (CONSTANT DE REBEQUE) worked for the 'lib. principles of 1789';
the **Doctrinaires** (GUIZOT) worked for a const. monarchy. After the interlude of the '100 Days' (p. 37),

1815 the 2nd Rest.: 'White terror' against Jacobins and Bonapartists; election of the Ultra-royalist 'Chambre introuvable' (dissolved 1816); 'cleansing' of the admin. (70,000 arrests); execution of Napoleonic generals (Marshall NEY). The king endeavoured to balance the forces of rest. and revolution and sought the support of moderate royalists. The cabinets of RICHELIEU (1815) and DECAZES (1818) brought about the removal of the occupation forces and the polit. readmission of France into the concert of the great powers in the

1818 Congress of Aix-la-Chapelle. After the

1820 murder of the Duc DE BERRY (son of CHARLES X), reaction intensified; revision of the elec. laws (doubling of the votes for the highest tax brackets strengthened the Ultras). The lib. opposition organized itself after the Ital. model in the secret societies of the **Charbonnerie** (LAFAYETTE); the **Bonapartist movement** propagated songs (BÉRANGER) and the veneration of NAPOLEON's veterans (their old leader dying in 1821). To divert attention from domestic problems,

1823 intervention in Spain (p. 45). The intervention was engineered by the for. minister CHATEAUBRIAND, the Fr. romantic poet and politician of the rest. in the spirit of the Holy Alliance.

1824–30 CHARLES X ruled in cooperation with the Church and the Ultras (the VILLÈLE cabinet, 1821–8). Laws prohibiting sacrilege and controlling the press, the eccles. supervision of schools, return of the Jesuits, dissolution of the nat. guard and compensation of the émigrés (the 'billion to the emigrants') angered the opposition. After 1828, the liberals had a majority in the Chamber of Deputies.

1830 The conquest of Algiers could not avert the state crisis which had been developing since 1829, when the moderate cabinet of MARTIGNAC was replaced by the reactionary cabinet of POLIGNAC. The **Jul. ordinances** (dissolution of the chamber, censorship of the press, changes in the elect. law) brought about the

1830 Jul. Revolution, which had been prepared by the historian and editor of the *National*, **Adolphe Thiers** (1797–1877). Following fighting on the barricades, CHARLES X abdicated and fled to England.

The Jul. Monarchy (1830–48)

Politically more powerful than the Republicans, the party of the bourgeoisie (LAFAYETTE, LAFITTE, THIERS, GUIZOT) proclaimed

1830–48 LOUIS PHILIPPE I, Duke of Orléans (57 yrs old), who accepted the *Tricolore* as the Fr. flag, 'King of the French'. The revision of the constitution (minist. responsibility, broadening of the suffrage) initiated the 'golden age' of the propertied bourgeoisie; capitalism and industrialization (mining and railways) gained ground. The 'bourgeois monarch' manoeuvred between the parties of *mouvement* (lib.) and *résistance* (con.) and was able to maintain his position against uprisings on the right and left (1831/4 Lyon, 1832/4 Paris), and had by 1840 stabilized it through authoritarian cabinets (the banker PÉRIER). With the aid of the historian **François-Pierre Guillaume Guizot** (1787–1874), he was able to establish a con.-personal régime. The propertied bourgeoisie (*pays légal*) was won over by the slogan *'Enrichissez vous!'* ('Enrich yourselves!'). The gvt resembled (in the words of DE TOCQUEVILLE) a corrupt corporation which bribed its voters with material advantages (transfer of the railway system into private hands 1842).

For. policy: at first, jointly with England (TALLEYRAND–PALMERSTON: Entente Cordiale, 1830), support of lib. movements in Portugal, Spain, Belgium. During the Near Eastern crisis, which caused his fall, in

1840 the prime minister, THIERS, sought to gain prestige by advances in Egypt and along the Rhine, which evoked a storm of nat. protest in Germany (p. 47).

1840–47 As for. minister, GUIZOT again attempted to establish an alliance with England.

1843 State visit of Queen VICTORIA; Marshal BUGEAUD completed the conquest of Algeria (p. 107). After 1846, approximation to the policies of the Eastern powers (METTERNICH). The opposition (intellectuals and students) grew stronger. More dangerous than the **Legitimists** (landed nobility) were the **Republicans**, under LEDRU ROLLIN (1802–74), and the **Bonapartists**.

1840 Solemn transfer of NAPOLEON's remains to Les Invalides; attempted *coups* by the pretender LOUIS NAPOLEON, 1836 from Strasbourg, 1840 from Boulogne. He escaped from jail to England in 1846.

1846–7 Econ. crisis (the potato blight, overproduction and its consequences) radicalized the new proletariat. Split into factions, the *petite bourgeoisie* and workers (cf. early socialism, p. 66) were united and politicized by **Louis Blanc** and his demands for job security through nat. workshops.

1847 Banquets at which reforms of the elect. laws and parliament were advocated (LAMARTINE) were banned by GUIZOT. This was the cause of the outbreak of the Feb. Revolution (p. 55).

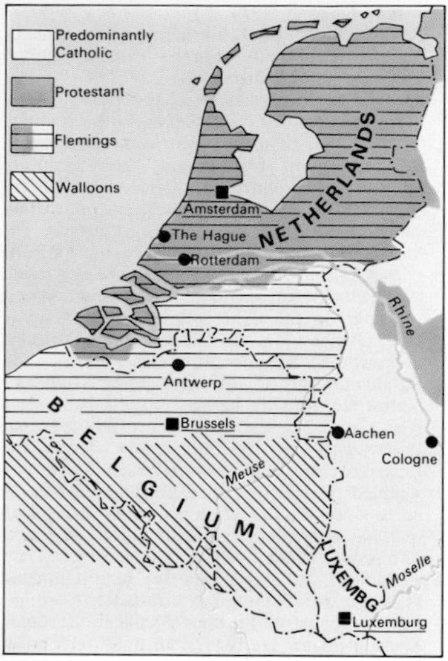

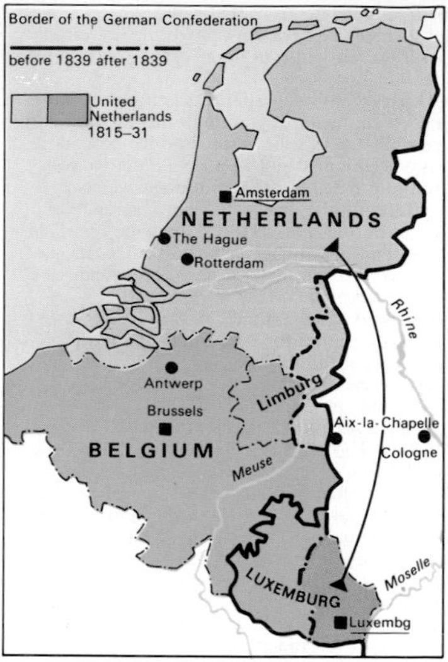

The creation of Belgium, 1831–9

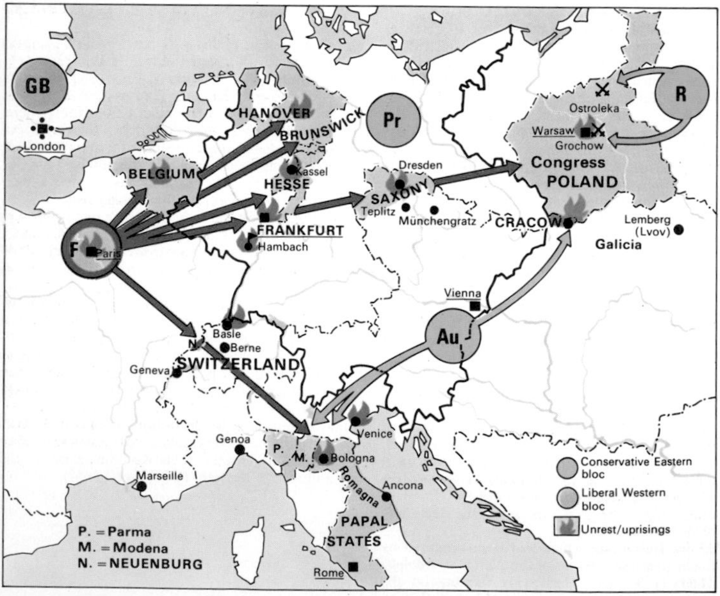

The effects of the July Revolution in Europe

The Effects of the Jul. Revolution

The period of bourgeois predominance in the form of const. monarchies in **Western Europe** was initiated by the Jul. Revolution (p. 49). The nat.-lib. movements in **Cen.** and **Southern Europe** received new momentum. A resulting conflict between the great powers was prevented by Prus. mediation, through the preoccupation of Russia in Poland and the coming to terms of France and England over the Belg. question. The split of the powers into a reactionary, con. eastern bloc (renewal of the Holy Alliance: meeting of the monarchs at Münchengrätz and Teplitz, 1833) and a lib. western bloc (Quadruple Alliance, 1834) deepened.

Belgium: Cath. and lib. opposition to the United Netherlands was the expression of confessional, historical, polit. and econ. differences in the state founded in 1815 (p. 39). Also, Belgium was under the tutelage of the N.: Prot. educ. policies and introduction of Dutch as the official language.

1830 After petitions proved in vain, an uprising took place in Brussels; bombardment of Antwerp. A provis. gvt and nat. assembly declared the **independence of Belgium** (Nov.). The great Eur. powers guaranteed autonomy and eternal neutrality (cf. Switzerland, p. 39) to the new state in the

1831 London Protocol. The Brit.–Fr. compromise candidate

1831–65 Prince LEOPOLD I of Saxe-Coburg (41 yrs old) became king. He respected the

1831 Belg. **Constitution** (popular sovereignty, civil rights, a parl. system).

1831–2 Attack by the Netherlands. It was repelled with Fr. help (fall of Antwerp). Partition of Luxemburg in the

1839 Treaty of London: the major part fell to Belgium. Limburg remained in part Dutch. The Netherlands recognized Belgium.

Switzerland: the dem. movement ('regeneration') in this refuge of the polit. fugitives of Europe grew. After

1830 replacement of the aristocratic constitutions in the 10 cantons through a dem. (indirect) elect. system.

1831 Repub. uprisings in the pty of Neuenburg failed.

Italy: a wave of revolutions spread to Modena, Parma, Romagna in 1831, but, exc. for the

1831–8 occupation of Ancona, hoped-for Fr. aid did not arrive. Aust. troops suppressed the second major centre of the Eur. crisis. While in exile (Marseilles), the Genoese **Giuseppe Mazzini** (1805–72)

1832 est. the secret society **'Giovane Italia' (Young Italy)** to bring about the nat. unification and internal renewal of Italy. Under the battle-cry *'Italia fara da se'* ('Italy liberates herself'), he pursued three aims: (a) to rouse the masses from nat. inertia; (b) to renew the concept of the state; (c) the cooperation of all nations in a dem. league of nations; to this end

1834 establishment of the 'Young Europe' movement in Bern. Proceeding from Piedmont, a network of conspirators was est. to prepare uprisings and assassinations.

Germany: unrest caused the establishment of

1830–31 constitutions in Saxony, Hanover, Brunswick and Hesse-Kassel. The pressure of public opinion (the press) grew in pace with the polit. interest of the people. The poets of the **'Young Germany'** movement, BÖRNE, **Heinrich Heine** (1797–1856), GUTZKOW, *et al.*, proclaimed their dem. ideals in the new manner of polit. journalism (Feuilletonism). The revolutionary spirit expressed itself in demonstrations during the

1832 Hambach Festival and the

1833 storm of the Frankfurt guardhouse. Incited by students, the attempted putsch again caused the intensification of reaction (p. 47).

Poland: econ. rise under the finance minister Prince LUBECKI. After the accession of NICHOLAS I (p. 69), Rus. violations of the constitution (drawn up by CZARTORYSKI) increased. The Tsar's intention to use the Pol. army against the Fr. and Belg. revolutions led to the

1830 Warsaw uprising; the Rus. Grand Duke CONSTANTINE fled. Prince **Czartoryski** (1770–1861) est. a nat. gvt; the nat. diet ousted the Rus. dynasty. Europe in general sided with the Pol. cause, but no assistance was rendered.

1831 Defeats at Grochow (by the Rus. general DIEBITSCH) and Ostroleka. **Paskievich** (1782–1856) took Warsaw. After his appointment as governor and severe punishment of the insurgents, he carried out an uncompromising programme of Russification.

1832 The 'Organic Statute' gave Poland the status of a Rus. province. Thousands of Pol. freedom fighters fled into exile. Paris became the centre of the 'Great Emigration', but the exiled Poles split into the aristocratic 'Whites' (CZARTORYSKI) and the democratic 'Reds' (LELEWEL), who took part in all revolutionary struggles.

1846 Uprising in Cracow, which led to the Aust. annexation of the 'free city'. Count ZAMOYSKI endeavoured to promote a peasant uprising in Poland; under the Tsar ALEXANDER II (p. 69), the Marquis **Wielopolski** re-established Pol. autonomy. The nat. movement (TRAUGUTT) rejected his renunciation of nat. independence. Left once more in the lurch by Europe (NAPOLEON III), the renewed

1863 Pol. uprising, caused by resentment at Rus. milit. levies, ended in nat. catastrophe. The anticipated popular upheaval did not materialize; 'Whites' and 'Reds' fought with one another. Brit., Fr. and Aust. notes of protest in the face of Russo-Prus. cooperation in the suppression of the uprising (p. 75) were ineffective. Execution of the nat. leaders; forced labour; deportations; confiscation of estates. At the same time

1864 generous land reforms, supervised by Count MILYUTIN, were carried out. Reorganization of the Vistula region into 10 *gouvernements* (total Russification: discharge of 14,000 Pol. officials, prohibition of the Pol. language). Galicia remained the final refuge of the Pol. nat. movement (the Universities of Cracow and Lemberg).

LATIN AMERICA (SOUTH)
Caracas
Trinidad (Brit.)
Panama
Angostura
Carabobo
VENEZUELA
Georgetown
Paramaribo
Cayenne
Boyacá
1811
Guiana
Bogotá
Dutch
Fr.
COLOMBIA
Bomboná
Pichincha
Quito
ECUADOR
Equator
Rio
Amazon
Pará
Negro
Madeira
Marañon
Ceará
EMPIRE OF BRAZIL
Junin
PERU
1822
Bahia
Cailao
Lima
Mato
Ayacucho
Goiaz
1821
BOLIVIA
Grosso
La Paz
Minas
Gerais
1825
Paraña
São Paulo
PARAGUAY
1811
Rio de Janeiro
Asunción
Tucumán
CHILE
ARGENTINA
URUGUAY
1810/18
1810/16
Chacabuco
Valparaiso
Santiago
1828
Buenos Aires
Montevideo
Valdivia
Ancud
United Rep. of Colombia 1819–30
Disputed border areas
1811 Year of Independence
Campaign of Bolivar 1821–4
Campaign of San Martin 1817–22
Sp. bases up to 1826
Explored or developed regions in area colours

CENTRAL AMERICA
Texas
ind. 1836
U.S.A.
New Orleans
Florida
Sp. to 1819
Bahamas (Brit.)
MEXICO
Tampico
1821
Cuba (Sp.)
Mexico City
Vera Cruz
YUCATÁN
1821–68
REP. of HAITI
1822–44
Puerto Rico
(Sp.)
Guadeloupe
(Fr.)
Belize (Brit.)
Jamaica
Martinique
(Fr.)
GUATEMALA
HONDURAS
EL SALVADOR
NICARAGUA
Barbados
(Brit.)
Curaçao (Dutch)
COSTA RICA
UNITED PROVINCES OF
NEW GRANADA
1811–19
Panama
Caracas
VENEZUELA
Angostura
United Provinces of Central America 1823–39

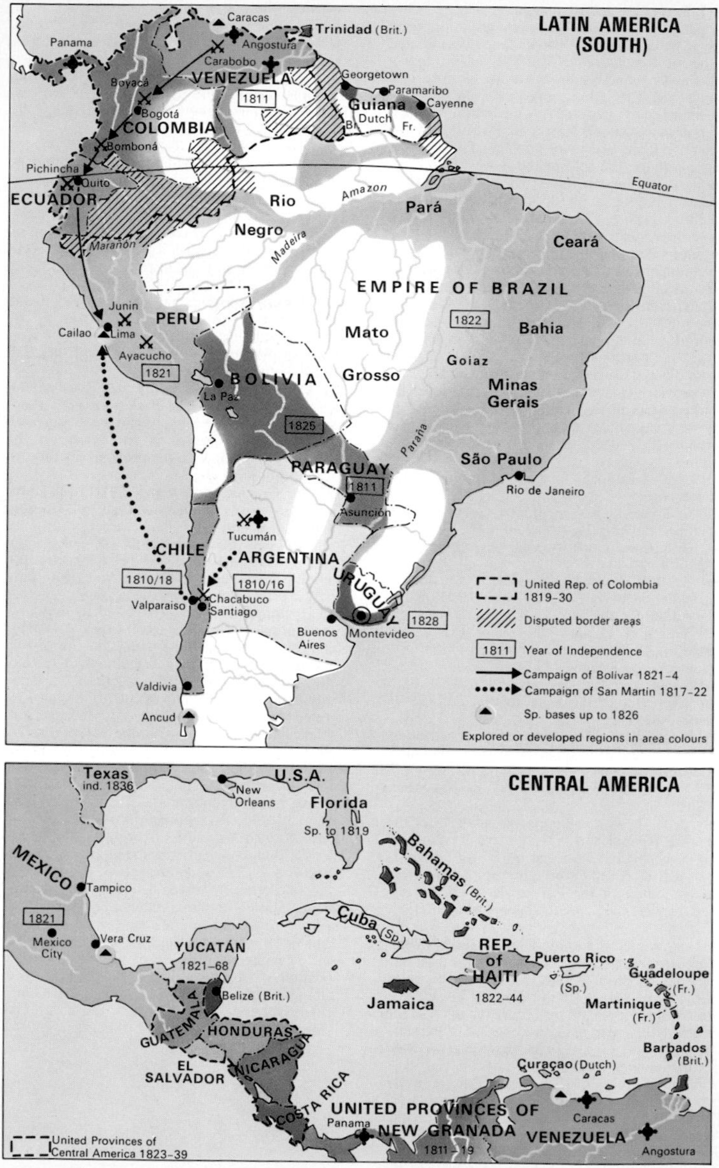

The establishment of new states in South and Central America

The End of the Sp. and Port. Colon. Empires

The 'spiritual mother of the revolution' was the freemasonry movement, originating in the Enlightenment. Founded by the Venezuelan FRANCISCO DE MIRANDA (1754–1816), the freemasonry lodges (*Lautaros*) spread over the Continent. The struggle was at first directed only against colon. exploitation (I, p. 277); for commercial reasons, it was supported by England and mainly carried on by **Creoles** (*criollos*, colon. Spanish, *naturaes*, colon. Portuguese, making up 10–40% of the pop.). The examples of N. America and the Fr. Revolution strengthened a desire for freedom. During the Napoleonic domination of the Sp. mother-country, municipal councils and assemblies (juntas) formed aut. gvts. Milit. action by FERDINAND VII (p. 45) to restore the old system radicalized the moderate desires of the lib. white upper class (*Blancos*), uniting them with the dem. demands for independence of the coloured proletariat (*colorados*: mestizos, mulattos, i.e. half-breeds). Helped by the int. polit. situation, leaders of the liberation movement, such as **Simón Bolívar** (1783–1830) and **San Martín** (1778–1850), were able to effect the separation of the colonies. The

1823 Monroe Doctrine of the U.S. president JAMES MONROE warned against intervention on the part of the Holy Alliance ('America to the Americans'). Burdened by racial problems, lack of public education and econ. development, the new republics, controlled by milit. or polit. leaders (*caudillos*), enjoyed little stability. The U.S. and Britain recognized the new states immediately. (CANNING: 'I called the new world into existence to restore the balance of the old'.)

1826 Panama Congress: BOLÍVAR's 'S. American Union' did not come to pass.

The Vice-Royalty of New Spain (est. 1535): after initial attempts (uprisings of the priests HIDALGO Y COSTILLO 1810 and MORELOS 1815) independence was obtained by Colonel AUGUSTÍN DE ITURBIDE (1783–1824).

1821 Declaration of Independence of **Mexico**: ITURBIDE proclaimed himself emperor, but was sent into exile by General SANTA ANA (1797–1876) and later executed.

1823 A republic was est. under General VICTORIA (1768–1843); the **'United Provinces of Cen. America'** separated from Mexico. Despite domestic struggles between 'federalists' and 'centralists', **Santa Ana** was able to defeat a Sp. army of invasion in 1829; he est. a dictatorial régime in 1833, which lasted until 1855.

The Vice-Royalty of New Granada (est. 1718):

1811 The Congress of Caracas proclaimed the independence of **Venezuela.** FRANCISCO DE MIRANDA received the supreme command; but he was defeated by Sp. troops and capitulated (1812). BOLÍVAR, named dictator in 1813, failed also, but organized a new army in Haiti, consisting of horsemen and Brit. and Ger. legionaries. With this army he (1817–20) liberated Venezuela and Colombia.

1819 Congress of Angostura: Proclamation of **Gran Colombia**, BOLÍVAR became president. After difficult marches through the Andes, he defeated the Spanish in Ecuador with his friend SUCRE.

1830 Disintegration of Gran Colombia into the republics of **Ecuador**, **Venezuela**, and the United States of New Granada (after 1861 **Colombia**).

The Vice-Royalty of La Plata (est. 1776): during the liberation struggles, which began *c.* 1810, juntas proclaimed the independence of

1811 **Paraguay** under JOSÉ FRANCIA (dictator 1814–40), and in Tucumán

1816 the United States of the Rio de la Plata **(Argentina).** SAN MARTÍN abandoned his milit. career in Madrid and was already in

1814 supreme commander of the Argen. liberation forces, forming an army to liberate Peru.

The Vice-Royalty of Peru (est. 1542): the commander of the patriotic forces of Chile, BERNARDO O'HIGGINS, and his rival CARRERA were defeated by the Spanish in 1814. O'HIGGINS fled to SAN MARTIN, who in

1817–18 crossed the Andes during the winter and liberated Chile. The Brit. adventurer Lord COCHRANE used his private fleet to transship the liberation army in 1820 to Callao.

1821 Peru was the last state to gain independence under its protector SAN MARTÍN, who joined his troops with those of BOLÍVAR.

1824 The victs. of Junin and Ayacucho broke the remaining Sp. resistance in S. America. SAN MARTÍN resigned because of differences with BOLÍVAR and d. in exile in Europe. S. Peru est. its independence as the

1825 Republic of **Bolivia** under its president, ANTONIO JOSÉ DE SUCRE (1795–1830).

Brazil was the only Lat. American state to separate from the mother country (Portugal) without struggle. Raised in the country, PEDRO, the Port. heir to the throne, did not return with his family to Portugal after NAPOLEON's downfall. A nat. assembly convoked by PEDRO

1822 proclaimed the independent Empire of Brazil under PEDRO I. A war with Argentina over **Uruguay**, annexed in 1817, ended with the

1828 Peace of Montevideo. **Uruguay** gained its independence. The emperor abdicated in 1831 in favour of his son PEDRO II.

The West Indies: French since 1697, **Haiti** liberated itself in 1804 under the black emperor JEAN-JACQUES DESSALINES (p. 30) and est. a republic in 1806. Following uprising of Sp. settlers, the eastern part of the island separated in 1808 and again came under Sp. rule.

1821 Declaration of Independence of the **Dominican Republic** (occupied 1822–44 by Haiti).

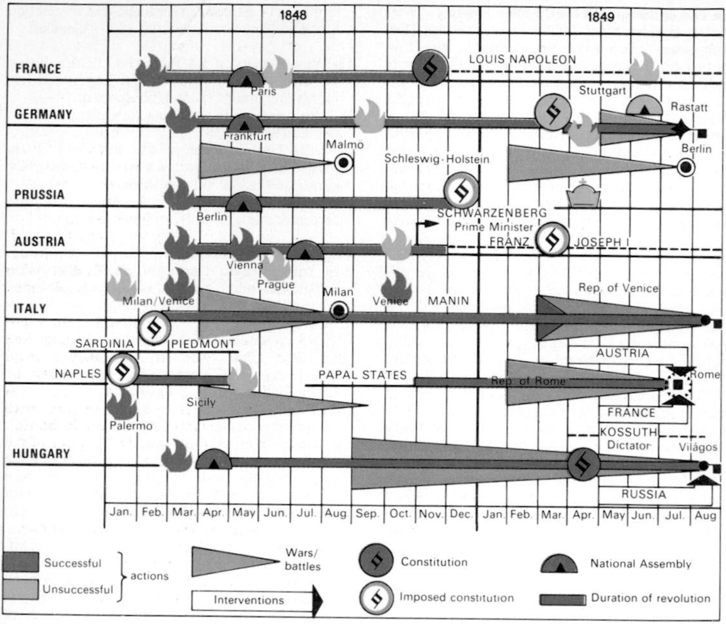

The European revolutions, 1848–9

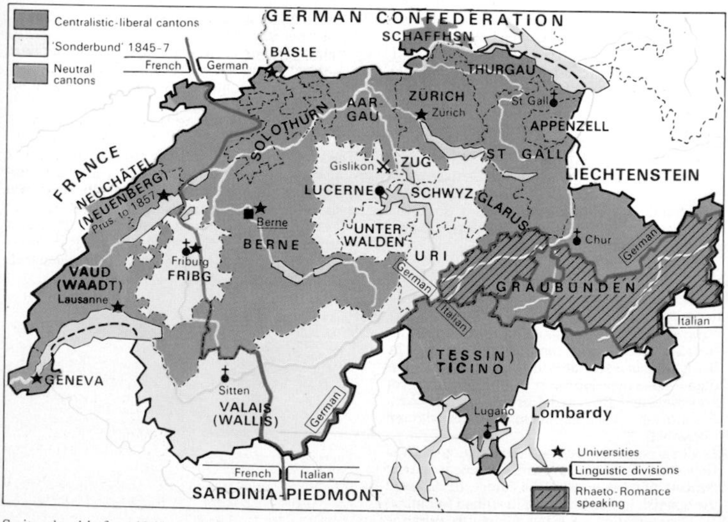

Switzerland before 1848

The Revolution of 1848 spread to all the large Eur. states, exc. Britain and Russia. The lib., nat. and soc. struggles ended in failures which shook the faith in the power of ideas over reality (HEGEL) and led to an epoch of realistic power politics.

Prelude to the Revolution: Switzerland (1847–8)

The momentum of the dem. movement increased after 1838 (revision of the constitutions of the cantons); this led to a sharp conflict between the lib. cantons, which aspired to being a unitary fed. state, and the con.–Cath. cantons, which wanted to retain a confederation with freedom of action for individual cantons.

1844–5 Groups of rad. irregulars campaigned against Lucerne.

1845 Formation of a 'protective association' (*Sonderbund*), the dissolution of which was called for by the *'Tagsatzung'* (general order of the assembly of the confederation).

1847 The Sonderbund War: quick vict. of the army of the confederation (*Tagsatzung* army) under General DUFOUR at Gislikon. PALMERSTON (p. 49) delayed an intervention by the powers protecting Switzerland under the arrangements of 1815.

1848 New constitution of the confederation (on the Amer. model): nat. council (parliament) and council of the estates (representation of the cantons) form the assembly of the confederation (the legislature); the legislature chooses the federal council (7 members) and the president of the confederation, who in turn are under the control of the fed. court. The **confederation** is responsible for for. policy, the militia, customs, the railway system and coinage; the **cantons** are responsible for church affairs, the schools, the courts and the press.

France: The 2nd Republic (1848–52)

The prohibition of a banquet sponsoring reforms (p. 49) unleashed the

22–4 Feb. 1848 Feb. Revolution: battles at the barricades; students, workers and the nat. guard forced the abdication of the 'bourgeois king' and proclaimed the republic. Formation of a provis. gvt: The poet ALPHONSE DE LAMARTINE (1790–1869), serving as for. minister, prevented the acceptance of the 'Red Flag' of the Socialists and thus saved the 'Tricolour' for France. As minister of labour, LOUIS BLANC (p. 49) proclaimed the 'right to work' and est. **'nat. workshops'** to take care of the unemployed.

Apr. The 1st general elections for a nat. assembly, bringing a bourgeois majority, were conducted under the minister of the interior, **Ledru Rollin** (1807–74).

May Massive demonstrations of rad. Socialists (LOUIS-AUGUSTE BLANQUI).

Jun. Closing of the unprofitable nat. workshops. Thereupon the **Jun. uprising of the Paris workers** ('June Days'). The minister of war, **Eugene Cavaignac** (1802–57), received dictatorial powers: he ordered open fire against the 'red peril' (*c.* 10,000 killed).

Nov. Constitution of the 2nd Republic, providing for 1 chamber and direct election of the president (to head the executive for a 4-yr term without provision for re-election). Virtually ignoring CAVAIGNAC and LEDRU-ROLLIN, the bourgeoisie, worried about security, gave NAPOLEON's nephew a 75% vote:

Dec. 1848 Louis Napoleon (40 yrs old) became president. Master of the bureaucracy and army, he ruled in opposition to parliament, but gained the confidence of the people and the Church.

1849 Rom. expedition to preserve the Papal States, carried out against the opposition of the Republicans, who were outmanoeuvred with the aid of the monarchists (two thirds of the chamber). A Rep. uprising (LEDRU-ROLLIN) failed in Jun. NAPOLEON used the

1850 law limiting suffrage to stimulate opposition to the chamber, which rejected a const. amendment making NAPOLEON's re-election possible.

Dec. 1851 Coup d'état: dissolution of the chamber and arrests (THIERS, CAVAIGNAC). A plebiscite approved the new

Jan. 1852 constitution. (10-yr term for the presidency, a senate, a council of state with leg. powers (cf. p. 27)–the legislature could only approve or reject legislation, not initiate or amend it; control of the press and the nat. guard.) A decision of the senate and another plebiscite (with 97% votes approving) brought about the hered.

Dec. 1852 Empire of Napoleon III, 'emperor of the French by the grace of God and the will of the nation'.

The Revolution in Italy (1848–9)

The patriotic movement (MAZZINI, GIOBERTI) had hopes in

1846–78 PIUS IX, the presumably lib. pope. His amnesty of polit. crimes and his reforms became exemplary for other princes. CHARLES ALBERT of Sardinia [1831–49] discharged reactionary ministers. The writer **Massimo d'Azeglio** (1798–1866) proclaimed the 'principle of open conspiracy'.

1847 Uprisings in Messina and Reggio; Aust. occupation of Ferrara.

1848 Unrest in Palermo, Milan, Venice. Naples (under Brit. pressure), Sardinia, Tuscany and the Papal States received constitutions modelled after Belgium.

Mar.-Aug. 1848 'Guerra Santa' (Holy War) of CHARLES ALBERT and Ital. volunteers (p. 59); after initial successes, disunity of the princes over polit. reorganization. Capitulation of papal troops nr Vicenza (Jun.). Ital. defeat. **Garibaldi** (p. 73) escaped to Switzerland.

Mar. 1849 Resumption of the war.

Naples: FERDINAND II [1830–59], 'King Bomba', suppressed lib. uprisings and reconquered Sicily (by Sep.).

Papal States: PIUS IX fled the popular uprising to Gaeta;

Feb. 1849 Proclamation of the **Rom. Republic**. **Mazzini** designed a programme of renewal 'from the ideal centre of the nation', while the pope appealed for help to Austria, Naples and France. **Garibaldi** caused Fr. intervention to be delayed and defeated Naples at Velletri.

July 1849 Entrance of Fr. troops into Rome; after an adventurous march, GARIBALDI reached San Marino. The

Aug. 1849 capitulation of Venice, after heroic resistance (MANIN, p. 59), terminated the unsuccessful revolution.

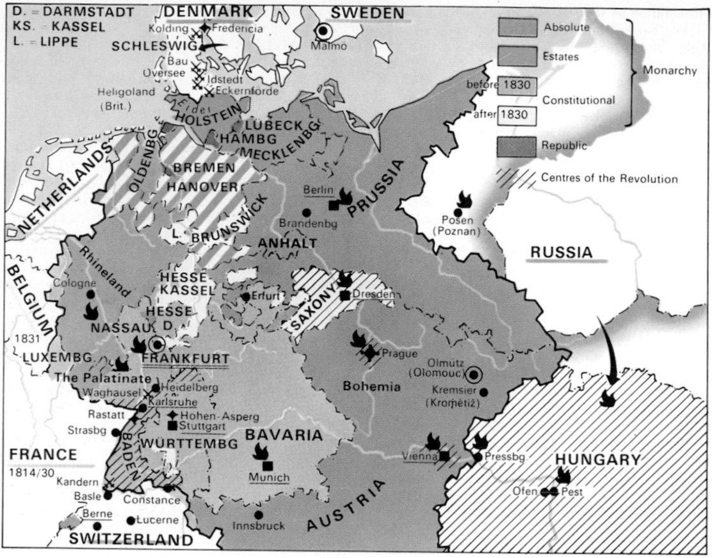

The German Confederation, 1848

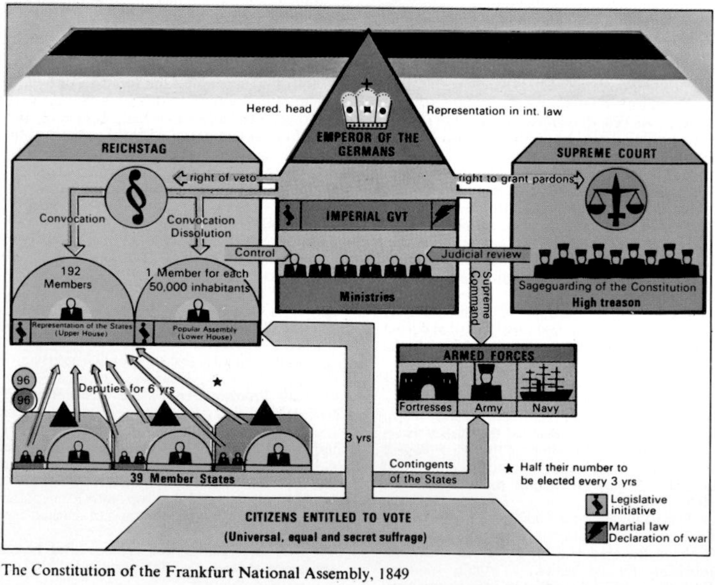

The Constitution of the Frankfurt National Assembly, 1849

The Mar. Revolution (1848)

The Feb. uprising in France (p. 55) spread to Germany. Demonstrations demanding freedom of assembly and of the press, trial by jury and a people's militia. While the **radicals** (*petit bourgeoisie* and peasants along the Rhine, in **Baden**, Saxony and Silesia) aspired to a dem. republic, the lib. bourgeoisie of property and ctr. limited its aims to moderate petitions; but they had in common the wish for nat. unification. The princes gave in to the 'demands of Mar.' and est. the lib. 'ministries of Mar.'; the assembly of the Ger. Confederation abolished censorship, but its plans for reform came too late. The revolution spread to the larger states of **Prussia** and **Austria**. Students unleashed

13 Mar. the first uprising in Vienna (p. 59); this prompted the Prus. king to make lib. concessions. When, during a demonstration of thanksgiving, the palace guard fired two shots, the people suspected treachery.

18 Mar. Confrontations on the barricades in Berlin: FREDERICK WILLIAM IV withdrew the troops from Berlin, est. a lib. ministry (CAMPHAUSEN), under public pressure paid tribute to the 230 'victims of Mar.', and promised a nat. assembly to debate the draft for a constitution (p. 61) and the solution to the nat. question. Prussia was to become part of a larger Germany.

20 Mar. Munich: LOUIS I abdicated in favour of his son MAXIMILIAN II (scandal over the dancer LOLA MONTEZ).

The Attempt at Ger. Unification

Feb. Motions in the Baden assembly (*Landtag*) for the convocation of a Ger. parliament.

5 Mar. Heidelberg assembly: 53 members of s. Ger. assemblies invited representatives from all Germany to make preparations for a nat. assembly.

31 Mar.–4 Apr. The Frankfurt **Vorparlament** (preliminary parliament) (*c.* 500 members) decided to admit Schleswig and E. and W. Prussia, and to call for general and free elections (1 representative to every 50,000 inhabitants). A motion by the radicals (STRUVE) to make the preliminary parliament a permanent assembly was rejected (H. VON GAGERN). **Hecker** (1811–81) thereupon proclaimed the republic in Constance. Troops of the Confederation (F. VON GAGERN) choked off the

Apr. uprisings of dem. irregulars in Baden (skirmish at Kandern) and in Alsace (HERWEGH). The assembly of the Confederation approved the election of a nat. assembly; non-Ger. nationalities in Austria refused to take part (PALACKY).

18 May Opening of the Constituent Nat. Assembly in St Paul's Cathedral, Frankfurt. Among the 586 representatives (223 members of the legal profession, 106 professors, 46 industrialists, 4 craftsmen, no peasants) were ARNDT, JAHN, J. GRIMM, UHLAND, DÖLLINGER, Bp KETTELER. **Heinrich von Gagern** (1799–1880), the Hessian 'Mar. minister', was chosen president. 'Acting boldly', without consulting the princes, he took care of the election as *Reichsverweser* (regent) of the popular Archduke JOHN, who formed a provis. *Reich* gvt (Jun.).

The 'parliament of the professors' began its work with the

Jul.–Oct. deliberation of **basic rights** (BESELER), which were proclaimed in Dec. (to become the model for all dem. Ger. constitutions). Polit. factions developed which were named after their meeting places:

The Con. Right (Café Milani, Steinernes Haus: Count SCHWERIN, Prince LICHNOWSKY, VON RADOWITZ; for a federation);

The Lib. Centre, split into the **Right Centre** (Kasino, Landsberg: DAHLMANN, DROYSEN; for a const. federation) and the **Left Centre** (Württemberger or Augsburger Hof, Westendhall: VON MOHL; formation of the first working-men's associations

The Dem. Left (Deutscher Hof, Donnersberg: ROBERT BLUM, RUGE; for a centralized republic). Socialist-revolutionary stirrings (MARX, ENGELS), formation of the first workingmen's associations (STEPHAN BORN), increased Aust. and Prus. resistance (p. 59); the pressure by for. powers over the Schleswig-Holstein question made polit. progress more difficult.

Schleswig-Holstein: while the 'Danes of the Eider' promoted the annexation of Schleswig to Denmark, the Ger. party insisted on the 'real union' of Schleswig and Holstein (in effect since 1460, I, p. 199).

Mar. Incorporation of Schleswig into Denmark; uprising in Schleswig-Holstein.

May At the request of the Germ. Confederation, Prussia launched a campaign into Denmark; but Russia, Britain and France compelled the combatants to conclude the

Aug. Armistice of Malmö. The Nat. Assembly in Frankfurt (on a motion by DAHLMANN) joined in the general nat. protest, but was later forced to accede to the armistice. This 'treason' caused the radicals

Sep. to rise in Frankfurt against the Nat. Assembly, which was forced to summon armed assistance. The ensuing catastrophe strengthened the reactionary forces (p. 61). After the 'Jun. Days' in Paris (p. 55) the lib. centre and the bourgeoisie tended rather to side with traditional 'authority and gvt' than make common cause with the dem. revolutionaries.

Oct. 1848–Mar. 1849 Deliberation of the constitution: a synthesis of tradition (the **Reich**, monarchy, states rights) and progress (universal male suffrage, popular representation) was attempted. The

const. problem was settled through the division of powers between the **Reichstag** and the **hered. empire** (Mar. 1849, 267:263 votes). The solution to the

problem of fed. union emphasized cen. authority (for. policy, armed forces, legislation), but with consideration for the fed. states.

The nat. problem split the Nat. Assembly into **'Great Germans'**, incl. (a) those favouring a federation (incl. all Austria under a (Cath.) Habsburg dynasty); and (b) those favouring a unitary-dem. state (a republic, incl. only Ger. Austria; and the **'Small Germans'** (a nat. state under a (Prot.) Prus. dynasty, excl. Austria).

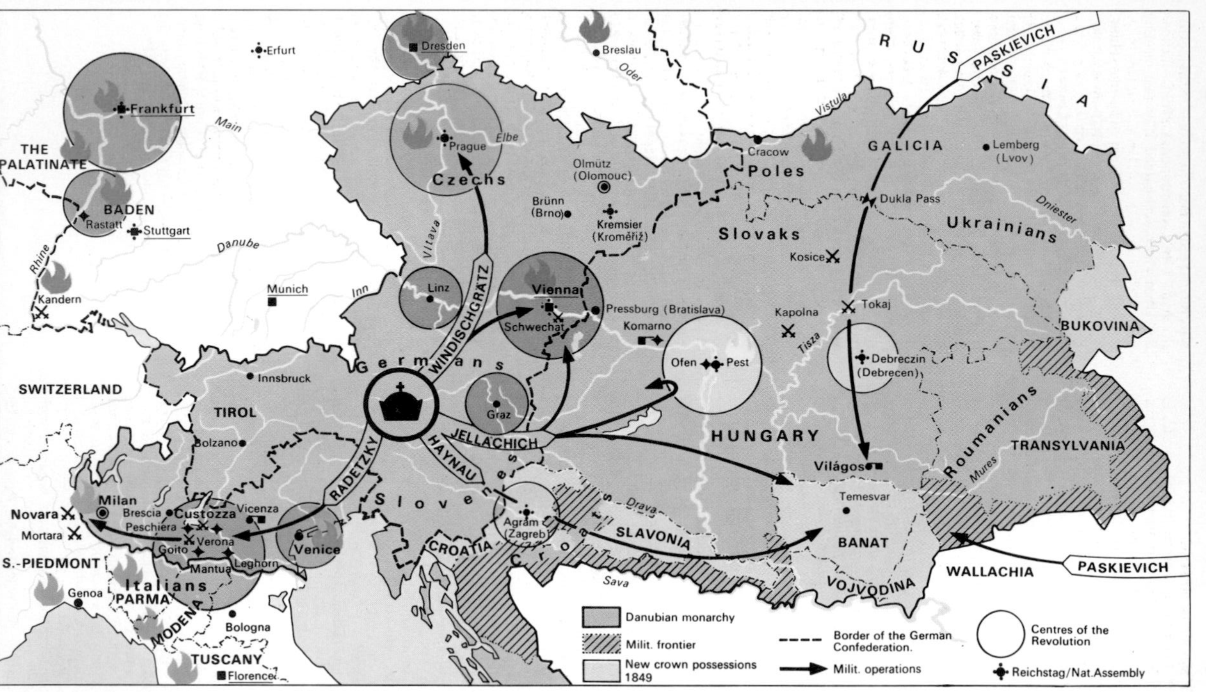

The Danubian monarchy, 1848/9

The Danubian Monarchy (1848–9)

Mar. 1848 1st uprising in Vienna (students, municipal militia): METTERNICH fled to England. His fall stimulated nat. uprisings in all parts of the empire; the court's promise of a constitution, however, met general rejection.

May 2nd uprising: convocation of a constituent **Reichstag** which decided the definitive emancipation of the peasantry (HANS KUDLICH, 1823–1917).

Oct. 3rd uprising carried out by mutinous troops meant to fight in Hungary: barricade fighting, pillage of the arsenal and arming of the proletariat; murder of the minister of war, LATOUR. The court fled to Olmütz; the troops vacated Vienna (AUERSPERG); but the for. minister, **Alfred Prince of Windischgrätz** (1787–1862), was able to break the resistance of the nat. guard. Their leaders, incl. ROBERT BLUM (p. 57), were, as representatives of the assembly at Frankfurt, executed. JOSEPH JELLACHICH (1801–59), Viceroy of Croatia, defeated Hung. auxiliary contingents at Schwechat.

Nov. Transfer of the *Reichstag* to Kremsier (Kroměřiž). The new prime minister, **Felix Prince Schwarzenberg** (1800–52), strove for the

Dec. abdication of FERDINAND I, who was mentally unbalanced, in favour of

1848–1916 Francis Joseph I, his nephew.

Mar. 1849 Imposition of a centralist constitution. Milit. and Rus. aid saved the monarchy.

Bohemia: under the leadership of the historian **František Palacky** (1798–1876),

Jun. 1848 the Pan Slav Congress of Prague advocated the equality of all nationalities within the Danubian monarchy (Austro-Slavism). The leaders of the Czech movement (PALACKY, RIEGER) were opposed to the Pentecost uprising, which was overthrown by WINDISCHGRÄTZ.

Croatia: the Croatian assembly at Agram under Hung. pressure gave up plans for a s. Slavic state. JELLACHICH was named Ban and used his troops to support the monarchy.

Upper Italy: Mar. uprisings in Milan and Venice aiming at nat. liberation via Piedmont (*'Italia fara da se!'*).

Mar.–Aug. 1848 'Guerra Santa' against Austria (p. 55): the for. minister **Radetzky** (1766–1858) retreated, but defeated CHARLES ALBERT at Custozza (Jul.), took Milan, and concluded an armistice. Venice proclaimed itself a republic and chose **Daniele Manin** (1804–57) dictator. After addit. defeats at Mortara and Novara,

Mar. 1849 abdication of the king. **Victor Emanuel II** [1849–78] concl.

Aug. the Peace of Milan; Venice capitulated. Austria retained Lombardo-Venetia and hegemony over Italy.

Hungary: uprisings led to the establishment of a nat. gvt (Prime Minister BATTYÁNY) in personal union with the Habsburg dynasty in the person of the 'Palatin' (deputy) Archduke STEPHAN. The conservatives gave way to the liberals (EÖTVÖS, 1813–71; **Louis Kossuth**, 1802–94; **Francis Deák**, 1803–76): peasant emancipation and abolition of the privileges of the nobility; development of the **Honvéd** (voluntary troops).

Sep. 1848 Murder of the royal commissioner LAMBERG in Pest. The dissolution of the assembly, demanded by Vienna, was not carried out; FRANCIS JOSEPH I was not recognized (Dec.). The imposition of a constitution led to the

Apr. 1849 removal of the Habsburgs from the Hung. throne and the elevation of KOSSUTH as regent. Struggles with nat. minorities took place (Serbs). Generals GÖRGEY and BEM repulsed the Aust. army.

May 1849 Meeting of the emperors at Warsaw: the Tsar NICHOLAS I promised aid. Two Rus. armies under PASKIEVICH defeated the Hungarians in the E.; Generals HAYNAU and JELLACHICH attacked from the W. (Temesvar). **Sándor Petöfi** (1823–49), the creator of the poetry of liberation, fell in battle. KOSSUTH fled to Turkey and was interned there until 1851.

Aug. Capitulation of Világos (General GÖRGEY); the fortress of Komárno resisted until Oct. Punitive Aust. trial (General HAYNAU): execution of Hung. freedom fighters (BATTYÁNY); BEM and ANDRASSY (p. 83) escaped. Organization of Hungary into 5 provinces under milit. admin.

The End of the Nat. Assembly (1849)

SCHWARZENBERG rejected the proposal for a 'closer federation within a broader federation' (GAGERN) and demanded the admission of all of the Habsburg monarchy; the **'Small Ger.' school** of thought thereupon prevailed.

Mar. 1849 Election of the Prus. king as hered. emperor by 290 to 248 votes. FREDERICK WILLIAM IV rejected the honour (which he considered 'affected by the smell of the gutter'). Resignation of GAGERN, recall of the Aust. and Prus. deputies; dissolution of the assembly in Frankfurt; formation of the Stuttgart rump parliament (May), which was, however, forced to dissolve by the military in Jun. Rad. **popular uprisings** along the Rhine, in Berlin, **Dresden** (RICHARD WAGNER, BAKUNIN), and esp. in **Baden** and the **Palatinate**. The Grand Duke of Baden asked for Prus. milit. assistance. WILLIAM, the 'grapeshot prince', defeated Badensian troops and irregulars. After the fall of the fortress of Rastatt (Jul.), courts martial and mass executions.

Dec. 1849 Abdication of Archduke JOHN as regent.

Results: the revolution faltered on the bourgeoisie's fear of revolutionary radicalism, on lack of polit. experience (underestimation of Ger. and Eur. power relationships), on the loyalty of army and bureaucracy to established authority and on for. intervention (in Hungary and Schleswig-Holstein).

Consequences: the nat. desire for unification remained alive; but the bourgeoisie, politically disappointed, turned their attention to econ. endeavours (p. 61). **Massive emigration** (among the emigrants CARL SCHURZ, KINKEL, FREILIGRATH, HECKER; from Baden alone, 80,000 people emigrated) weakened the dem. movement.

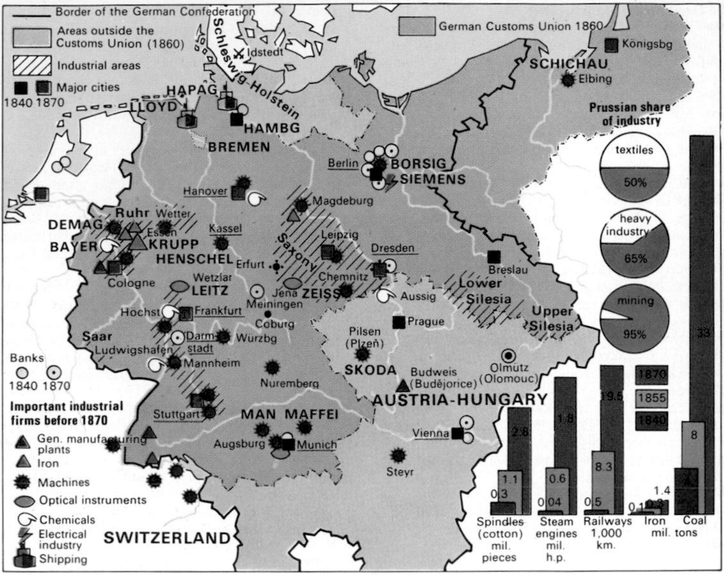

The industrialization of Germany, 1840–70

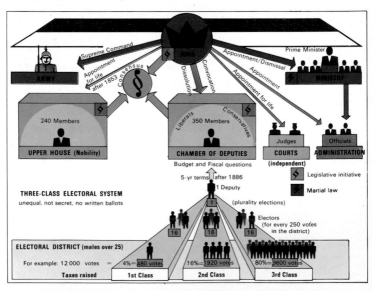

The revised Prussian Constitution of 31 January 1850

Prussia: the revolutionary period and attempts to establish a union of princes (1848–50)

May 1848 Nat. assembly in Berlin: during the struggle between the leftist majority (advocating popular sovereignty) and the crown, the **Con. party** developed (the (GERLACH brothers, BISMARCK); it aimed at preserving class privileges and royal authority. The storming of Vienna (Oct., p. 59) reinforced reactionary attitudes: the nat. assembly was transferred to Brandenburg and dissolved by General WRANGEL (1789–1877).

Dec. 1848 the *'Oktroyierte'* (imposed) constitution: the lib. draft of WALDECK was altered to meet con. demands (the **3-class elect. system**).

Apr. 1848 Rejection of the imp. crown (p. 59); to solve the nat. question, the king planned a union of princes.

1849 Alliance of the 3 kings of Prussia, Saxony and Hanover;

1850 the Erfurt Union parliament deliberated the draft of a constitution. SCHWARZENBERG (p. 59) was able to win the 'middle states' (among them Bavaria, Saxony) against the **policy of union** (VON RADOWITZ). Open Austro-Prus. conflict threatened over the disputed Prus. right to march through elect. Hesse. When appealed to as arbitrator, the Tsar NICHOLAS I (p. 69) decided in favour of Austria.

1850 Treaty of Olmütz: rest. of the Germ. Confederation in Frankfurt under Aust. leadership.

Schleswig-Holstein: the Danes renewed the war (Feb. 1849). Although victorious (at Idstedt), Prussia – under Russo-Fr. pressure – surrendered the duchies in the

1850 Peace of Berlin.

1852 London Protocol: personal union of the auton. duchies with Denmark.

The Period of Reaction (1850–62)

1850–51 Dresden conferences to reform the assembly of the Confederation: establishment of a reactionary committee to control such lib. states as **Baden** (the 'model of a lib. state' under Grandduke FREDERICK [1856–1907]). Alongside Austria and Prussia, **Saxony** (Prime Minister BEUST) and **Bavaria** under

1848–64 Maximilian II (Prime Minister VON DER PFORDTEN, 1811–80) pursued an ind. 'triad policy'.

Econ. life: lib. entrepreneurs of substance and corporate enterprises developed mining, the railways and machine industry. Banking, insurance, transport, communication, the electrical and optical industries were expanded.

1847 Establishment of Hapag, 1851 the Disconto Co. (D. HANSEMANN), 1853 the Darmstädter Bank, 1857 the N. Ger. Lloyd. Developed by **Justus Liebig** (1803–73), the process of synthetic fertilization increased agricultural yields; the production of synthetic dyes laid the foundation of large-scale chemical industries (Farbwerke Hoechst, Badische Anilin and Sodafabrik). Notwithstanding the first

1857 econ. crisis, overpopulation (despite emigration) pushed econ. expansion forward; Prussia gained most (see map, p. 60). Business interests demanded increased polit. privileges and nat. unification. Politically engaged historians like GUSTAV DROYSEN (1808–84), HEINRICH VON SYBEL (1817–85) and THEODOR MOMMSEN (1817–1903), the singing, gymnastic, and shooting societies, SCHILLER memorial celebrations (1859), and also some of the nobility (ERNST VON COBURG-GOTHA, the 'prince of sharpshooters') promoted patriotism. Founded in 1859, the **Nationalverein** (National Club) (BENNIGSEN, SCHULZE-DELITZSCH) found its 'Great-Ger.' counterpart in 1862 in Austria and southern Germany in the *Reformverein* (Reform Club).

Prussia: the large landowners, the Prot. Church and the bureaucracy supported the police system of the MANTEUFFEL ministry. Appointed in

1850 to the post of top eccles. official (*Oberkirchenrat*), F. J. STAHL (p. 40) was given control of elementary education in 1854.

1852 The Cath. party in parliament (REICHENSPERGER), named **'Centre party'** after 1859, opposed the Prot. policies in ctr. and education (RAUMER).

1852–4 During the crisis of the customs union (admission of the Hanoverian *Steuerverein*; 'Great Ger.' customs policies of Austria) it was RICHARD VON DELBRÜCK (1817–1903) who preserved Prus. leadership. In for. policy there was uncertainty: the *Kamarilla* (a clique of courtiers around the king) and the party of the *Kreuzzeitung* prevented a closer relationship with the Western powers. As ambassador to the Germ. Confederation, **Bismarck** (p. 75) strove to attain equal rank with the presiding Aust. ambassadors (THUN, RECHBERG); 1859 he became ambassador to St Petersburg, 1862 to Paris.

Austria: after the victorious rest. of the dynasty,

1851 abolition of the constitution; **neo-absolutism** of the BACH ministry; centralized bureaucracy, milit. dictatorship in Hungary and Italy.

1855 The concordat secured for the Church supervision of education, cult. life and the regulations governing marriage. Successful econ. policies of the minister of commerce, **Bruck** (1798–1860): industry, railway construction, trade in the Adriatic (Trieste) and credit expansion were promoted. His customs policies failed because of the econ. backwardness of the Danubian monarchy. The country was beset by a permanent finan. crisis, milit. weakness, lib. and nationalist opposition; nevertheless, Austria demanded a leading position in Germany and Italy.

1859 Collapse of hegemony over Italy (p. 73); discontinuation of neo-absolutism. Conflicts between cen. authority, the imp. lands and the var. nationalities made the establishment of a constitution more difficult. Hungarians and Germans rejected the federalist

1860 Oct. Diploma. As prime minister, SCHMERLING (1805–93) drafted the

1862 Feb. Patent: division of control over the leg. branch of gvt between the crown and the **Imp. Council** (House of Peers and House of Deputies), which was boycotted by the Hungarians, Croats, Czechs and Tyroleans.

The emancipation of the Jews in the 19th cent. (in some German states before 1871)

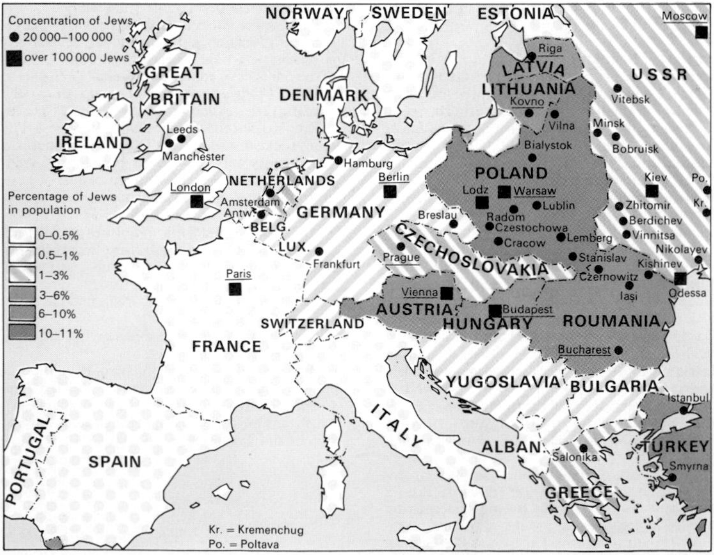

The Jewish population of Europe, 1930

Emancipation

The emancipation of the Jews – the transition from a merely tolerated element of the pop., exposed to legal discrimination, into citizens with equal rights – was prepared by the type of puritanism of N. America, which was strongly shaped by O.T. influences and by the Enlightenment (I, p. 257). The **intellectual pioneers of emancipation** in Germany were GOTTHOLD EPHRAIM LESSING (*The Jews*, 1749, *Nathan der Weise*, 1779; cf. I, p. 257); also, *Kriegsrat* (milit. counsellor) CHRISTIAN W. DOHM, whose book *Über die bürgerliche Verbesserung der Juden* (*On the Improvement of the Jews' Status as Citizens*) (1781) advocated the thesis that the supposed Jew. imperfections were the result of legal inequity, whereas the granting of equal rights would make them into good citizens; and MOSES MENDELSSOHN (I, p. 257), who in his work *Jerusalem, or On Religious Power and Judaism* (1783) differentiated between the intellectual content of the Jew. religion (a religion of reason without dogma) and Judaism as the incarnation of certain commandments and laws which derive from revelation (the giving of the laws on Mt Sinai: nat. foundation). 'The Virginia Bill of Rights' (p. 15) and the 'Declaration of the Rights of Man' (p. 19) initiated the granting of equal rights to the Jews. The first high point was reached

1791 in the granting by the Fr. Nat. Assembly of citizen's rights to Jews who took the loyalty oath of citizens: the Jew. religion was recognized as one of the confessions and the Jews lost the character of a 'nation'. A setback was caused by the

1807 establishment of the **'great Sanhedrin'** as the highest Jew. authority in the state by NAPOLEON I: it did not mean autonomy, but the creation of centralized organization.

The decree of 1808 **('Décret infâme')** again limited the freedom of movement of the Jews within the Fr. realm of power; it was later repealed by the Bourbons. In **Western Europe** the Jews – with few exceptions – received full equality during the course of the 19th cent. (in Portugal only in 1910).

In **Eastern Europe** (Poland, Russia) the Jew. population was often under oppression (pogroms). In Russia, the Jews were not allowed to engage in agriculture while their freedom to obtain an education was limited.

In **South-eastern Europe**, exc. Roumania toleration prevailed. In 1917 the Jews were granted equality in the Soviet Union, later in the new states of eastern Europe. The abolition of the external ghetto was followed by the disappearance of the 'internal' ghetto; this manifested itself in **assimilation** (the surrender of traditions and the adoption of the cult. values of the host people) and the **reform movement** (relig. liberalism). The encounter of Western Eur. lib. Judaism with the Jews of the formerly western parts of Russia brought about a revival of trad. Jew. forms (MARTIN BUBER, 1878–1965; FRANZ ROSENZWEIG, 1886–1929).

Antisemitism

Antisemitism was directed against the Jews, not the Semites, and was based on relig., polit. and econ. motives (I, p. 155).

During the 19th cent. racial antisemitism was added. Its path was prepared by the Fr. Count DE GOBINEAU (p. 65), whose work about the inequality of the human races (*Essay sur l'inégalité des races humaines*, 1853–5) advocated the superiority of the 'Arian' race and interpreted the history of the world in racial terms; and by the native Englishman and German by adoption, HOUSTON STEWART CHAMBERLAIN (p. 65). Their imitators then equated 'Arian' with Germanic and finally German. Racial teachings (primarily a zoological concept) and the conceptions of Soc. Darwinism (p. 64), derived from perversions of DARWIN's teachings, formed the foundation of the 'biological naturalism' of the **3rd Reich** in Germany.

Zionism

As a consequence of the **pogroms in Russia** (1881–82), the Odessa physician LEO PINSKER demanded in his work *Autoemancipation* (1882) a home for oppressed Jewry. Founded after 1882, the **Associations of 'Hoveve Zion'** (Friends of Zion, joined by PINSKER), aspired to the colonization of Palestine by the Jews. Under the impact of the 'Dreyfus Affair' (beginning in 1894, p. 105), **Theodore Herzl** (1860–1904) composed his work *Der Judenstaat* (*The Jewish State*) (1896) and, independently of the movements of eastern Jewry, est. the **Zionist movement**. The Jew. question became a nat. question to be solved by the Jews. At the 1st Zionist World Congress at Basle (1897), a strong polit. organization was created; the **Basle programme** defined as the aim of Zionism 'the establishment for the Jew. people of a home in Palestine, to be secured by int. law'. **Cult. Zionism** aspired to make Palestine an intellectual centre; this was to be done through detailed polit., cult. and colonizing work. Its radiating influence was to lead the Jews of the world to internal unity. Unlike polit. Zionism, cult. Zionism was able to wait for the realization of statehood. CHAIM WEIZMANN (1874–1952) endeavoured to establish a synthesis of both Zionist schools of thought. It found practical realization in the establishment of the Zionist Palestine office in Jaffa (1907) and of the Heb. University (1918). In reaction against the Zionist movement,

1905 the *Protocols of the Elders of Zion* appeared. Published in Germany by the former army captain MÜLLER VON HAUSEN (a friend of LUDENDORFF, p. 125), this forgery intensified antisemitism.

1917 Pledge of Lord Balfour for the establishment of a nat. home for the Jews in Palestine (p. 258).

Intellectual currents in Europe during the 19th cent.
A faith in **progress** and (natural) **science** was prevalent; it was complemented by **relativism**, which denied all ethical values and made cognition dependent on the state of research or the historical situation (historicism, p. 41), on the state of mind of the individual, on society, or on the class to which one belonged. A sc. attitude (unprejudiced, critical thought) was considered the ideal of the emancipated man (intellectual liberalism); sc. findings and theories were made the substance of ideologies which claimed to take the place of religion.
Positivism: acc. to **Auguste Comte** (1798–1857), progress follows the 'law of 3 stages': (a) the theological stage interpreted the world supernaturally; (b) the philosophical stage with the aid of abstract ideas and forces; only (c), the positive stage, makes possible the consolidation of phenomena into laws. Scientists and industrialists were to unite sc. theory and practice to guide the world. *'Savoir pour prévoir, prévoir pour prévenir'* ('Know to see the future, see the future to prevent'). The 'Cours de philosophie positive' (1832–42) contained a sc. system in which each discipline built upon the preceding one: mathematics—astronomy—physics—chemistry—biology—**sociology**. Through a religion of humanity–with humanity as its subject–'soc. engineers' would secure a happy life for society.
MILL and SPENCER among others were influenced by this school of thought (p. 40); laws of history were sought through precise factual research by H. THOMAS BUCKLE (1821–62); HIPPOLYTE TAINE est. the **theory of the milieu** (the shaping of man through environment); E. RENAN (1823–92) represented the *Life of Jesus* ((1863) on the level of human and natural phenomena. In Germany, **D. F. Strauss**'s (1808–74) *Life of Jesus* (1835–6, trans. into English by GEORGE ELIOT, 1846) interpreted the gospels of the evangelists as myths; B. BAUER (1809–82) disputed the historical existence of JESUS; in his *Wesen des Christentums* (*The Essence of Christianity*) (1841, trans. into English by GEORGE ELIOT, 1854), **Ludwig Feuerbach** interpreted religion as an illusion of man, whose ideas he saw as mere reflections of reality, and whose immortality was to be found only in his works or offspring.
Materialism: LUDWIG BÜCHNER (1824–99) formulated the vulgarization of faith in his doctrine that all phenomena are derived from *Energy and Matter* (1855); MOLESCHOTT (1822–93) reduced the function of thought to chemical processes. A development of the greatest importance began with the **historical materialism** of **Karl Marx** (1818–83), outlined in his *Critique of Political Economy* (1859): the historical process goes on in accordance with exact laws (determinism). The ideological superstructure of man and history (consciousness, i.e. art, science, religion, law, the state) depends on the 'substructure' (*Unterbau*) of man and history (being, i.e., econ. and soc. conditions). On this basis (see HEGEL, p. 41) the **forces of production** (tools, human skills) and the **relations of production** develop dialectically. Increased production depends on the accumulation of property and the division of labour; but, at the same time, this leads to the alienation of man from his labour and himself. The reactionary propertied class always clings to the **status quo**, the exploited class seeks constantly to alter it. Class struggles are the moving forces of history and lead necessarily to **revolutions**, which ease the basic tensions, alter the superstructure and introduce periods of qualitatively greater value. History extends from initial communism to ultimate communism, when the exploitation and self-alienation of man will be eliminated (cf. p. 67).
Evolution: acc. to LAMARCK (1744–1829), adjustments to the environment and the heredity of acquired traits are factors of biological development. The theory of descent was expanded by **Charles Darwin** (1809–82) in his work *The Origin of Species through Natural Selection* (1859). On the basis of material collected in the Pacific area (1831–6), he recognized the principles of evolution: variation, heredity and the surplus production of offspring. The latter leads to the 'struggle for survival' and the selection of strong individuals and species fit to live, not subject to any form of teleology (planned purpose). ERNST HAECKEL (1834–1919) contributed to the dissemination of the theory. His *Natürliche Schöpfungsgeschichte* (*Natural History of Creation*) reduced all life to a 'bio-genetic principle' as the first cause. Biological monism was given general application in the so-called *Welträtsel* (1899, *Enigma of the World*) which, as (soc.) **Darwinism**, affected society and politics.
Critics of the age: the thoughts of the historian **Alexis de Tocqueville** (1805–59) on the dangers of egalitarian mass democracy were untouched by faith in progress; these dangers were evaluated as a new barbarism of civilization by the cult. historian **Jacob Burckhardt** (1818–97). The Dan. theologian **Sören Kierkegaard** (1813–55) attacked self-satisfied churches and Christian conformism and demanded the scrupulous acceptance of faith to the point of martyrdom. Dialectical theology and existential philosophy refer back to his thought. Intellectual crisis and cultural decay were uncovered by **Friedrich Nietzsche** (1844–1900, cf. p. 41) in his *Untimely Reflections (Unzeitgemässe Betrachtungen*, 1873–6) with equal radicalism and genius. His hatred was directed at Christianity (the 'shame of humanity'), at the biologically weak with their 'Christ. slave morality', at the 'cultured philistines' and at the glutted bourgeoisie. Not his warning, but his philosophy of life was heard, which, in *Thus Spake Zarathustra* (1883–5), confronted the meaninglessness of life, pessimism and nihilism with the superman as the incarnation of the 'will to power' and a morality *Beyond Good and Evil* (*Jenseits von Gut und Böse*, 1886).

Sc. and tech. progress
Sci. research and the tech. utilization of its results were inter-dependent. They could for the most part hardly be kept distinct any longer.

Physics:

1808 Polarization of light	MALUS
1815 Theory of the frequency of light	FRESNELL
1827 Ohm's Law	OHM
1831 Law of electrical induction	FARADAY
1833 Electrolysis	FARADAY
1859 Spectral analysis	KIRCHHOFF/BUNSEN
1888 Electromagnetic waves	HERTZ
1895 X-rays	RÖNTGEN
1895 Electron theory	LORENTZ
1896 Uranium radiation	BECQUEREL
1900 Quantum theory	PLANCK
1903 Radioactivity	RUTHERFORD

1905 Theory of relativity	EINSTEIN
1911 Atomic structure	RUTHERFORD
1913 Atomic structure	BOHR
Biology:	
1841 Spermatozoons	KÖLLIKER
1842 Periodic fertility of ova	BISCHOFF
1852 Segmentation of cells	REMAK
1865f. Laws of heredity	MENDEL
1901 Law of mutation	DE VRIES
1904 Chromosomes	BOVERI
Chemistry:	
1818 Atomic weights	BERZELIUS
1828 Synthesis of urea	WÖHLER
1831 Analysis of elements	LIEBIG
1833 Derivation of phenol, anilin from coal	RUNGE
1841 Agricultural chemistry	LIEBIG
1856 Tar-based dye	PERLIN
1865 Structural formula of benzene ('ring')	KEKULÉ
1869 Perodic system of elements	MEYER/MENDELEYEV
1878 Synthesis of indigo	BAYER
1898 Radium	CURIE
1909 Synthetic rubber	HOFMANN
1913 Synthesis of ammoniac	HABER/BOSCH
Medicine:	
1846 Ether anaesthesia	MORTON
1848 Appendix operation	HAUCOCK
1858 Cellular pathology	VIRCHOW
1861 Puerperal fever	SEMMELWEIS
1867 Antiseptic treatment of wounds	LISTER
1882 Tuberculosis bacillus	KOCH
1883f. Diphtheria bacillus	KREBS/LÖFFLER
1885 Asepsis	BERGMAN
1893 Diphtheria serum	BEHRING
1894 Cause of plague	KITASATO
1909 Salvarsan	EHRLICH/HATA
Transportation technology:	
1834 Electric motor	JACOBI
1867 Dynamo	SIEMENS
1876 4-cycle gas engine	OTTO
1879 Electric locomotive	SIEMENS
1884 Petrol engine	DAIMLER/MAYBACH
1885 Motor car	DAIMLER/BENZ
1893 Diesel engine	DIESEL
1900 Dirigible	ZEPPELIN
1903 Motorized aeroplane	WRIGHT BROTHERS
Communications technology:	
1837 Telegraph	MORSE
1861 Telephone	REIS
1876 Telephone	BELL/GRAY
1877 Phonograph	EDISON
1897 Wireless	MARCONI
1902 Telegraphy of pictures	KORN
Printing:	
1812 Cylinder press	KOENIG/BAUER
1869 Collotype	ALBERT
1881 Half-tone engraving	MEISENBACH
1884 Linotype	MERGENTHALER
Optics, photography:	
1839 Photography	DAGUERRE
1871 Bromide print	MADDOX/EASTMAN
1895 Cinematograph	LUMIÈRE
War technology:	
1835 Revolver	COLT
1836 Needle gun	DREYSE
1850 Submarine	BAUER
1866 Torpedo	WHITEHEAD
1867 Dynamite	NOBEL
1883 Machine-gun	MAXIM
1911 Tank	BURSTYN
Technological processes:	
1867 Reinforced concrete	MONIER
1885 Seamless pipes	MANNESMANN
1907 Cast concrete	EDISON

Prevailing modes of thought determined the development of new **sc. disciplines.**

Sociology: while SPENCER (p. 40) looked at society as an organism, Count DE GOBINEAU (1816–82) and HOUSTON STEWART CHAMBERLAIN (1855–1927) saw the **racial struggle**, KARL MARX and his school the **class struggle**, as being its driving forces. Sociology as a sc. discipline was developed by LORENZ VON STEIN (1850–90), FERDINAND TÖNNIES (1855–1936), ÉMILE DURKHEIM (1858–1917) and others; **Max Weber** (1864–1920) sought to arrive at basic sociological structures through the concept of the 'ideal type'.

Psychology: by introducing sc. methods, JOHANN FRIEDRICH HERBART prepared the way for 'psycho-physics', which was represented by GUSTAV THEODOR FECHNER (1801–87), HERMANN VON HELMHOLTZ (1821–94) and others; it was expanded into 'experimental' psychology by WILHELM WUNDT (1832–1920) and THÉODULE RIBOT (1839–1916). At this stage of development, complex and delicate psychic functions could not yet be discerned. **Wilhelm Dilthey** (1833–1911) contrasted functional psychology with structural psychology and thereby established the latter and other dimensions of intellectual analysis as auton. disciplines. Behavioural psychology was revitalized by LUDWIG KLAGES (1872–1956); **Gustave Le Bon** (1841–1931) examined the psychology of the masses. **Sigmund Freud's** (1856–1939) psychoanalysis set new trends.

Theology: FERDINAND CHRISTIAN BAUR (1792–1860) and the Tübingen school carried on bib. research with historical-critical methods. ALBRECHT RITSCHL (1822–89) continued this work, but emphasized the autonomy of relig. studies. In *Wesen des Christentums* (*The Essence of Christianity*, 1900) ADOLF VON HARNACK (1851–1930) separated the religion of JESUS from the dogma of the old church. The Cath. Church and Prot. orthodoxy took up defensive postures to this lib. theology; in 1910, PIUS X obliged the Cath. clergy to pledge themselves against modernism. Miss. activity abroad intensified, but the masses in Europe became increasingly alienated from the churches. Founded in 1878 by WILLIAM BOOTH, the **Salvation Army** sought new ways of proclaiming the gospel.

Socialism during the 19th cent.

Socialism (Lat. *socius* = companion; the term appeared *c.* 1832 in France; into the 20th cent. it remained synonymous with Communism), the counter-movement to liberalism and capitalism, aims at a just distribution of property and a just soc. order, equal rights and well-being for the subordinate classes (the **proletarians**), universal peace and the reconciliation of peoples. These aims were to be attained through **soc. reforms**, **class struggle** or **revolution**. Before the 19th cent., Socialist concepts were found in the **Utopias** of Sir THOMAS MORE (I, p. 212), CAMPANELLA (I, p. 256), HARRINGTON (*Oceana*, 1656), MORELLI and others.

Utopian (early) Socialism: ideal conceptions of soc. reform were proposed, to be realized through appeals to the insight and the conscience of the propertied. ÉTIENNE CABET (1788–1856) and WILHELM WEITLING (1808–71) called for a communist order, the realization of which by force had already been advocated during the Fr. Revolution by **Babeuf** (p. 21). Count **Claude Henri de Saint-Simon** (1760–1825), like COMTE (p. 64), considered econ. progress to be the driving force of history; industrialization, capitalism and labour were to be aligned in technocratic organization and advanced by a new relig. spirit. The soc. problem lay in the involvement of the 'idlers' (nobles, the military, the clergy) in the process of production (the 'producers' were the entrepreneurs, the workers, farmers, scholars and artists). SAINT-SIMON's pupils, ENFANTIN and BASARD, expected the abolition of the right of inheritance to lead to the transfer of capital into the hands of the state. Goods were to be distributed with the interest of all in mind, each one receiving in accordance to his capacity and performance; man was to be guided by a religion of the 'here'. **Charles Fourier** (1772–1837) believed in the liberation of labour from coercion, misery and exploitation through *phalanstères*: voluntary cooperatives incl. agriculture, industry and joint participation in admin., production and distribution. Acc. to **Louis Blanc** (p. 49), the full yield of the efforts of labour was to be guaranteed through 'producers' cooperatives' (nat. workshops, p. 55). In dem. self-admin. the workers were to control production and profits, which again were to be distributed in the form of dividends, soc. benefits and investments. The first to see the power of the future in the proletariat was **Moses Hess** (1812–75).

Anarchism (Gk = absence of gvt): MAX STIRNER (1806–56) and **Pierre-Joseph Proudhon** (1809–65) anticipated the abolition of every manner of coercive order (the state, laws) through peaceful means to lead to a communal, socially just existence for all (mutualism). 'Property', gained without work or through exploitation, is acc. to PROUDHON 'theft'. **Bakunin** (p. 113) wanted to attain anarchy through assassinations, **Georges Sorel** (1847–1922) through 'direct action' by an élite of the proletariat (the general strike).

Sc. Socialism: in the **Communist Manifesto** (1847), **Karl Marx** (principal work **Das Kapital**, 1867f.) and **Friedrich Engels** (1820–95) proclaimed the principles of **dialectical materialism** (p. 64) and their effects on economy and society; they demonstrated the structural laws governing the development of capitalism: the exploitation of the wage-earner brings the owner of the means of production **surplus value** (profit), which leads to the **accumulation** of capital and makes technological-industrial progress possible. But this again brings about (a) an excess of labourers who increase the 'indust. reserve army', increase the pressure on wages and worsen the general misery; (b) through competition, a lessening of the number of capitalists and an increase of the number of proletarians who are becoming class-conscious, and with that (c) a **concentration of capital** (the formation of monopolies); and (d) crises of over-production caused by the desire to raise the rate of profits or by lessening purchasing power (because of the increasing general misery). Internal contradictions drive the capitalistic system into the Socialist **revolution**: seizure of power by and **dictatorship of the proletariat** through the 'expropriation of the expropriators'. The **socialization** of the means of production will eliminate class differences. In the final stage of **Communism**, the planning and distribution of production by the producers will guarantee justice, freedom and humanity.

Significance: Marxism became the 'substitute religion' for the masses of the workers, who as a result of urbanization had withdrawn from the churches, in so far as they had ever attended them; it also became the polit. ideology of Socialist parties (p. 101); it changed the **'Lumpenproletariat'** into a self-aware working class.

Christ. Socialism: esp. in England – influenced by Socialist theories – theologians like MAURICE (1805–72) and writers like **Kingsley** (1819–75), CARLYLE (p. 103) and others appealed to the propertied and educated to help ease the misery of the masses. In France, Christian Socialist ideas were represented by LAMENNAIS (p. 40) and LEROUX (1791–1871), in Germany **Adolf Wagner** (1835–1917), STOECKER (p. 77) and FRIEDRICH NAUMANN (p. 110). **Cath. soc. thought**, proclaimed for all Catholics in LEO XIII's [1878–1903] encyclical **Rerum novarum** (1891), stressed the right of private property, **solidarity** (the responsibility of all for the individual and of the individual for all), and **subsidiariness** (private initiative to receive the assistance of larger communities or the state in case the individual or the smaller soc. units were unable to manage). **Wilhelm Emanuel von Ketteler** (1811–77), Bp of Mainz, advocated soc. reforms by the state on the basis of Christian responsibility. State interference to solve soc. problems was also demanded by the so-called 'Socialists of the Chair' (*Kathedersozialisten*), undogmatic lib. polit. economists around **Gustav von Schmoller** (1838–1917). Their thought was linked to the state-Socialist ideas of the Genevan SISMONDI (1773–1841), to **Karl Rodbertus** (1805–75), and to the teaching of the soc. monarchy of LORENZ VON STEIN (p. 65).

The Beginnings of the Labour Movement

Lacking ownership in the means of production, the working class (the '4th estate') was, as part of the indust. free market economy, obliged to sell its labour (wage-labour) and–as the socially least powerful group–was exploited in the process (the **'soc. question'**). The insecurity of existence and increasing misery fostered a feeling of solidarity. The workers joined (MARX: 'Working men of all countries, unite!') in the struggle for polit. and econ. power ('United, the weak are strong too!'). Organizational form and relative strength of the labour movement in the individual indust. states depended on their structure and stage of development. Britain was leading (p. 43).

Trade unions (Fr. = **syndicats;** Ger. = **Gewerkschaften**): organized acc. to crafts, local unions used econ. weapons (negotiations, strikes) to obtain better working conditions and wages through **collective agreements** covering wages, working hours and conditions (discontinuation of employment, holidays). Joint funds for mutual aid in case of emergencies and associations for **continuing worker education** were est. They fought for the **right to organize**–1824 in Britain, 1864 in France, 1869 in Germany –did away with the prohibition of unions: they developed regional and nat. organizations and were, by the end of the 19th cent., recognized by state and entrepreneurs as partners in the soc. system. Following the example of the indust. labourers, white-collar workers, state employees, agricultural and domestic workers organized also.

Cooperatives: Robert Owen (1771–1858), the champion of the establishment of institutions of **self-help** to compete with large-scale business, introduced trend-setting social reforms in his exemplary company in New Lanark ($10\frac{1}{2}$-hr working day, sickness and old-age insurance). Experiments with communistic **producers' cooperatives** (1825–9, New Harmony, U.S.A.) failed, as did Fr. attempts to establish *phalanstères* (p. 66) and nat. workshops (p. 55); and, after 1844, also Amer. groups. Following OWEN's suggestions, a real econ. factor was created in the **Consumers' cooperatives** (p. 48) with low prices (by-passing the wholesale and intermediate trade), discounts, rebates and dividends. In Germany they spread slowly at first because the solution of the soc. question was expected to be achieved through producers' cooperatives, a view held by the labour leader **Ferdinand Lassalle** (p. 100). He opposed **Hermann Schulze-Delitzsch** (1808–93), the lib. founder of commercial cooperatives (wholesale, retail and loan associations for craftsmen), and **Friedrich Wilhelm Raiffeisen** (1818–88), who initiated agricultural cooperative association; after 1854, savings and loan associations to finance seed, machinery, etc. (strong impact abroad).

Consequences: associations and their functionaries increasingly represented the interests of the individual, who in this form of **'representative' democracy** gave up or lost his own initiative to **'pressure groups'** (affecting the state and legislation).

The Soc. Activity of the Churches

Britain: Christ. Socialism (p. 66), also the Oxford Movement (EDWARD PUSEY, 1800–82) transformed 'Sunday-morning Christianity', though the movement later developed into 'ritualism'. Establishment of (female) orders for the care of the sick.

1844 The Young Men's Christian Association (Y.M.C.A.) performed services in the slums. Establishment of workers' homes. After

1865 William Booth (p. 65, 1829–1912) carried on his work in East London.

Germany: THEODOR FLIEDNER (1800–64) opened the first Prot. deaconate institution (Diakonissenanstalt, 1836) in Kaiserwerth, **Johann Hinrich Wichern** (1808–81) a home for wayward youth (Rauhes Haus, 1833) and a fraternal association of male lay-deacons (Diakonie, 1843). Jointly they founded the

1848–9 Innere Mission (miss. work within the country) to aid youth, the aged, the sick and those under duress. **Friedrich von Bodelschwingh** (1831–1910) took over the

1872 Bethel Institutes (hospital, charitable work, workers' settlements).

1877 **Zentralverein für Sozialreform** (WAGNER, p. 66, 'cen. association for soc. reform), continued by STOECKER (p. 77) after 1890 as the Evangelical Soc. Congress. After

1882 Evangelical workers' associations were est. LEO XIII (p. 66) recommended

1884 the establishment of Cath. workers' associations, modelled after the

1846 Cath. Journeymen's Associations of the priest **Adolf Kolping** (1813–65).

Public Soc. Policy

Britain: the 'home of classical liberalism' (p. 43) was forced by the soc. grievances in the textile industry to pass protective legislation:

1833 1st Factory Act (p. 48); 1842 prohibition of female labour in the mines; 1847 10-hr-day for women and minors (general application after 1850).

France: leading in soc. policy on the Continent: 1813 prohibition of child labour in mines.

Prussia: concerned over the physical fitness of recruits, the milit. authorities advocated protective legislation from 1828.

1839 Prohibition of child labour, at first under the age of 9, after 1854 12 yrs.

After 1871 **Germany** took the lead in soc. legislation.

1872 The **Verein für Sozialpolitik** (Association for Social Policy) of the 'socialists of the chair' (*Kathedersozialisten*, p. 66) was est.; jointly with the politicians of the Centre party active in soc. questions (GEORG VON HERTLING, Fr. HITZE), they influenced the

1883 legislation on soc. insurance (p. 77); which became the model for France after 1894, for Britain after 1908 (p. 104).

1891 Continuation of the work of soc. legislation (Sunday rest, protection of wages) by the minister of commerce, HANS FREIHERR VON BERLEPSCH (1843–1926).

Consequences: soc. policies and welfare programmes transformed the lib. state so that, in the 20th cent., it became the **Welfare State**. An anon. **bureaucracy** administered the steadily increasing taxes, soc. levies and contributions.

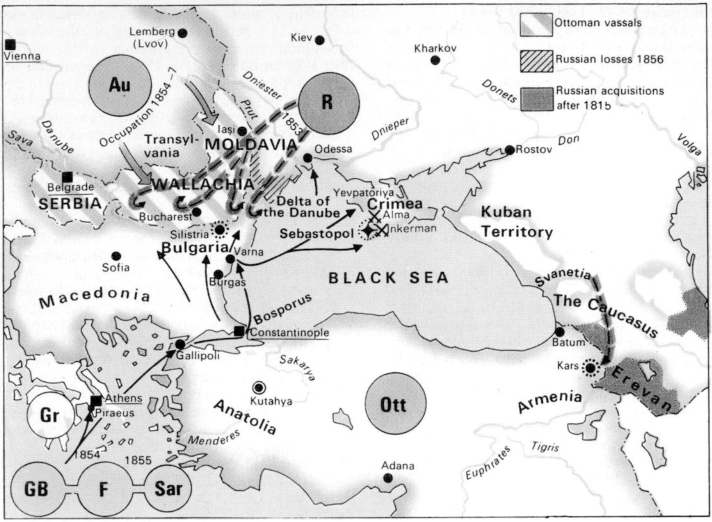

The Crimean War, 1853–6

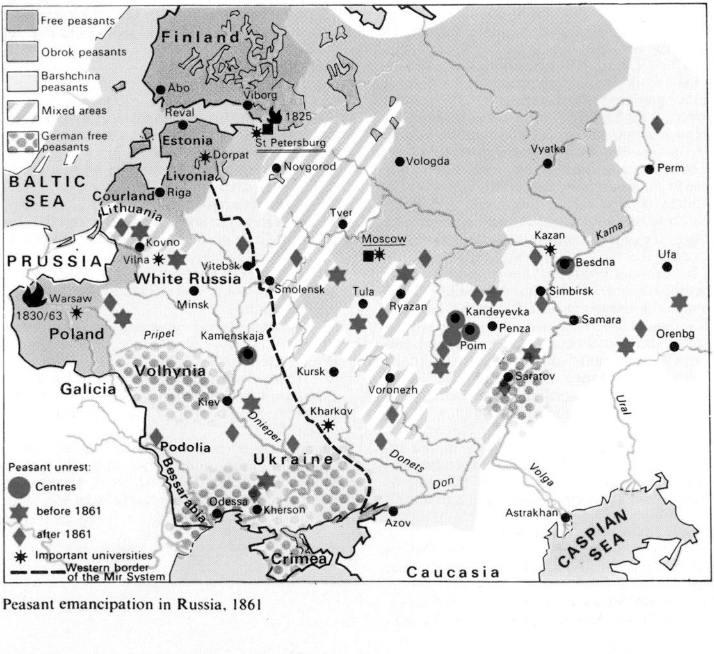

Peasant emancipation in Russia, 1861

The Period of Reaction (1815–55)

1801–25 Alexander I began his reign with lib. reforms of the admin. and the laws.

1802 Establishment of departmental ministries, responsible to the council of state after 1811. At the tsar's request, SPERANSKY (1772–1839), a secretary of state, drafted a

1808–9 constitution incl. the separation of powers, an imp. council and an elected imp. duma (parliament). SPERANSKY was removed from office in 1812. Victorious over NAPOLEON (p. 35), ALEXANDER embraced mystical Christ. and con. ideas (METTERNICH). Under the impact of revolutionary movements (p. 45), he became the champion of reaction. Domestic policies were dominated by his favourite ARAKCHEYEV; his bureaucratic form of despotism culminated in the establishment of milit. settlements resembling penal colonies.

Cult. life: after the Napoleonic Wars the Europeanization of the nobility (the officer corps) increased. Ger. idealism (HEGEL, SCHELLING) and Fr. Utopian Socialism influenced Rus. intellectuals, romanticism affected young poets and writers (PUSHKIN, 1799–1837; GOGOL, 1809–52, LERMONTOV, 1814–41); GLINKA (1804–57) composed the Rus. nat. anthem. Motivated partly by admiration for Europe, partly by Slav. patriotism, **secret societies** strove (after 1816) for a constitution, serf emancipation and the distribution of land to a free Rus. people. The moderate Northern Society (MURAVYEV) and the rad. Southern Society (PESTEL) took advantage of the tsar's death to stage the

1825 **Decembrist Uprising,** which was rigorously suppressed; nevertheless it became the ideal of revolutionary youth. 'Europe's liberator' was succeeded to the throne by 'Europe's policeman',

1825–55 Nicholas I, whose autocracy was supported by the Rus. Orth. Church and Great Rus. nationalism.

1826 By organizing the '3rd Department' to control schools, universities, the press and public opinion, Count BENCKENDORFF est. the state secret police.

For. policy: aimed at the **suppression** of revolutionary movements in Europe (Poland, p. 51; Hungary, p. 59; Germany, p. 61); **expansion** in the Middle East (p. 113), and the disintegration of the Ott. Empire. This led at first to a successful balancing of interests between the major con. powers and the lib. w.; nevertheless, the Holy Alliance broke up (support of Gk independence).

1829 Peace of Adrianople (p. 45). Compromise with Prussia and Austria. A split between the Western powers during the

1839–41 Near Eastern crisis (p. 87) and the subjugation of Austria with Rus. help (p. 59) were outweighed by the

1853–6 Crimean War. Cause: dispute of Gk Orth. and Rom. Cath. monks over the Holy Places in Jerusalem; interference by NICHOLAS I and NAPOLEON III. Supported by England, the Porte rejected Russia's ultimatum (Prince MENSHIKOV), which demanded a Rus. protectorate over Orth. Christians.

1853 Invasion of **the Danubian principalities by Rus. troops.**

Oct. 1853 Declaration of war by Turkey and

1854 entry of the Western powers into the war (Sardinia, Jan. 1855). Austria occupied the Danubian principalities of Moldavia and Wallachia.

Sep. 1854 Brit.–Fr. landing in the Crimea; **siege of Sebastopol** (first instance of mod. trench warfare). Allied victs. on the River Alma and at Inkerman; but losses of 118,000 men suffered owing to cholera and the winter cold. **Florence Nightingale** (1820–1910) laid the foundations for modern care of the wounded.

1855–81 Alexander II continued the war until the fall of Sebastopol in

Sep. 1855. The Russians conquered Kars (Nov.).

1856 Peace of Paris: Russia lost the delta of the Danube; neutralization of the Black Sea; 'Eur. protectorate' over Turk. Christians, with a guarantee of the integrity of the Ott. Empire and the Danubian principalities. The Paris declaration regulating the law of the high seas est. int. rules of naval warfare.

Consequences: reorganization of the Eur. system of states through the transfer of Rus. hegemony to France (p. 71); beginning of the Austro-Rus. tensions in the Balkans; opening of the way for the unification of Italy (p. 73).

The Reform Period (1856–74)

The defeat revealed the backwardness of the admin., army and economy. Serfdom obstructed any form of progress, whether in the moderate form of a head tax (Obrok peasants), or the often arbitrary form of corvées (Barshchina peasants). ALEXANDER II decided on an autocratic 'revolution from above' to eliminate the 'powder keg within the state'.

1856 Dissolution of the milit. settlements. After repeated unrest and prolonged preparations by a commission,

1861 the abolition of serfdom for more than 40 mil. peasants; the **system of the mir** was retained (collective ownership of fields and collective responsibility for the individual in the community). At the same time, promotion of secondary and primary public education and a university statute granting academic autonomy (GOLOVNIN, 1863); also easing of press censorship (1865).

1864 Self-admin. **(Zemstov)** for 'gouvernements' and districts; **judicial reforms,** ind. judges, public trials, easing of penal code.

1870 Municipal organization: self-admin. through elected city councillors from the ranks of the bourgeoisie.

1874 Introduction of general conscription with 6-yr terms (MILYUTIN).

Results: the hoped-for easing of soc. tensions did not come about. The peasantry, increasing in numbers, suffered because of insufficient landholdings and high levels of debt to the landlords; the peasantry was not trained in the ind. admin. of their holdings, which led to relatively low yields at a time of increasing tax burdens; unrest resulted.

1863 Pol. uprising (p. 51).

1866 An assassination attempt on the tsar intensified the autocratic reaction as well as the revolutionary movement of the intelligentsia (p. 111).

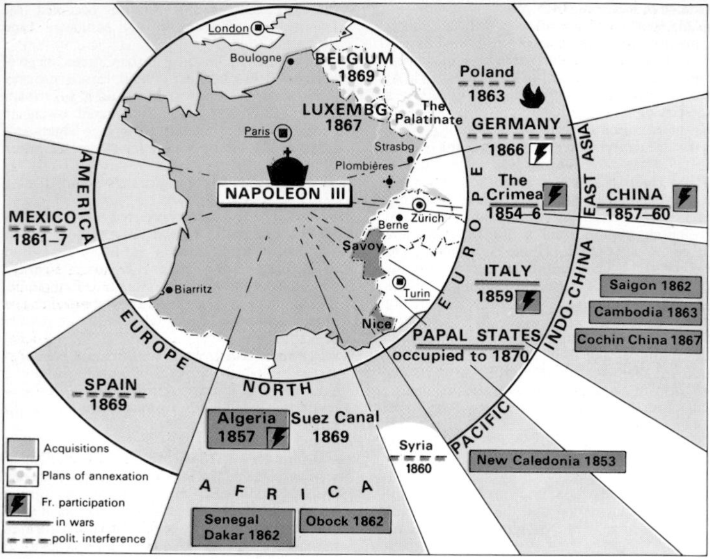

The policies of Napoleon III, 1852–70

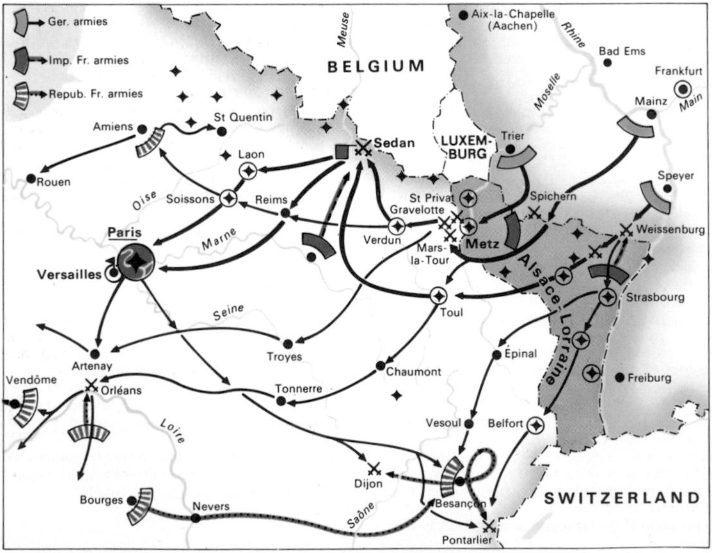

The Franco-Prussian War, 1870–71

The 2nd Empire (1852–70)

Napoleon III (1808–73, mar. to the Sp. Countess EUGÉNIE DE MONTIJO) thought of himself as embodying the nation. His dem. caesarism (plebiscitary dictatorship) aimed at the reconciliation of class conflicts. Fearful of renewed Socialist unrest, the people submitted to his authoritarian régime, which became more severe

1858 after the assassination attempt on the emperor's life by ORSINI (p. 73).

Soc. policies: increased employment through generous building programme (railways, roads, canals, harbours). Between

1852 and 1865, rebuilding of Paris acc. to the plans of the Prefect Baron DE HAUSSMAN to make it the 'cap. of the world': *c.* 60,000 new buildings, boulevards, fortifications. Although there were welfare programmes for workers (public funds for aid, the construction of workers' dwellings and public libraries), the working day still lasted 12 hrs, strikes were prohibited and, until 1864, workers were forbidden to form unions.

Econ. life: fin. capitalism (banking and credit: the PÉREIRE Brothers) and the expansion of major industries brought about the increase of commerce by 300% within 12 yrs. The export of capital made France into a land of creditors and *rentiers*. The

1855 and 1867 Paris World Exhibitions became symbols of prosperity.

Colon. policy: Algeria was the granary and heart of 'France beyond the sea'; immigration of Fr. settlers.

1854–65 Governor FAIDHERBE enlarged Senegal and founded Dakar. Interference in China (Lorcha War, p. 91) and Syria (landing in Beirut, 1860) to 'protect the faith'; development of the colon. empire in Indo-China (p. 107).

1857 Conquest of the Kabyles (Berbers in Algeria).

1859–69 Construction of the Suez Canal under the direction of FERDINAND DE LESSEPS, promoted and aided by France; to this end, Obock was acquired (1862)

For. policy: by supporting nationalist movements (the Balkans, Italy, Germany) NAPOLEON III sought to achieve the revision of the treaties of 1815. By taking advantage of Anglo-Rus. tensions, France gained a new position of power in the

1854–6 Crimean War (p. 69). The emperor served as mediator at the

1856 Paris peace congress. After the

1858 meeting with CAVOUR at Plombières, the solution to the **Ital. question** was planned.

1859 War of Ital. Unification (p. 73): NAPOLEON III pressed for a quick reconciliation with Austria. Peace of Zürich; France acquired Lombardy, but the territory was exchanged for **Nice** and **Savoy** by the

1860 Treaty of Turin.

1861 Mexican expedition (p. 93) under BAZAINE (1811–88). Loss of prestige because of the **Ger. problem**.

1865 Meeting at Biarritz: BISMARCK outfoxed the 'impenetrable', whose confused demands for compensation in Belgium, Luxemburg and the Palatinate in exchange for Prus. power expansion (*'pourboire* politics') in a conflict between Austria and Prussia (p. 75) failed because of the

1866 Aust. defeat at Sadowa. 1867, the 'yr of misfortune', brought neither the expected compensations nor the addition of Luxemburg (which NAPOLEON now hoped to purchase from Holland); the 'Mexican adventure' failed because of opposition by the U.S.; insistence on the continued milit. protection of the Papal States (in consideration of Cath. polit. opposition at home) clouded friendship with Italy.

The transition to the 'Lib. Empire' was brought about by increasing criticism of the régime (conflicts between a policy of support for lib. causes abroad and dictatorship at home), failures in for. policy, and doubts about the

1860 Cobden Treaty with England (introducing a policy of free trade).

1864 Physically ill, the emperor was forced to grant the 'necessary freedoms' (of person, press, parliament and minist. responsibility) demanded as lib. concessions by THIERS.

1869 Elect. vict. of the opposition: polit. amnesty and formation of the OLIVIER Cabinet to work out a lib. constitution.

1870 Plebiscite: 83% of the votes were cast for a lib. empire.

The Franco-Prus. War (1870–71)

Causes: Fr. aspirations for prestige and fear of Prus.-Ger. striving for hegemony (for. minister, GRAMONT).

Immediate cause: the candidacy for the Sp. throne and the 'Ems dispatch' (p. 75); declaration of war against Prussia (19 Jul.). BISMARCK succeeded in securing the neutrality of England (by revealing the Fr. demands for compensation in Belgium in 1866), of Austria (through Rus. and Hung. pressure) and of Italy (because of the Rom. question).

Course of the war: offensive by the superior Ger. troops (Chief of General Staff, HELMUTH VON MOLTKE); following severe fighting encirclement and capitulation of BAZAINE's army in **Metz**.

1 Sep. 1870 b. of Sedan: capitulation of MACMAHON's army; NAPOLEON III was taken prisoner. As a result of the initiative of the mod. republicans **Favre** (1809–80) and **Gambetta** (1838–82),

4 Sep. 1870 the 3rd Republic was proclaimed and a provis. gvt of nat. defence was formed.

Sep. Siege of Paris: GAMBETTA escaped in a balloon and organized the **war of the people** with *franctireurs* (armed civilians). The newly formed armies were beaten or pushed across the Swiss frontier. Paris capitulated (Jan. 1871).

Feb. 1871 The Nat. Assembly at Bordeaux elected THIERS (p. 105) 'Chief Executive'. Preliminary Peace of Versailles: France lost **Alsace-Lorraine**; a war indemnity of 5,000 mil. francs was set, eastern France to be occupied until final payment.

10 May 1871 Peace of Frankurt.

Results: expansion of the Eur. system of states by the addition of **Italy** and **Germany**, which assumed the Fr. position of pre-eminence; deepening of the Franco-Ger. conflict.

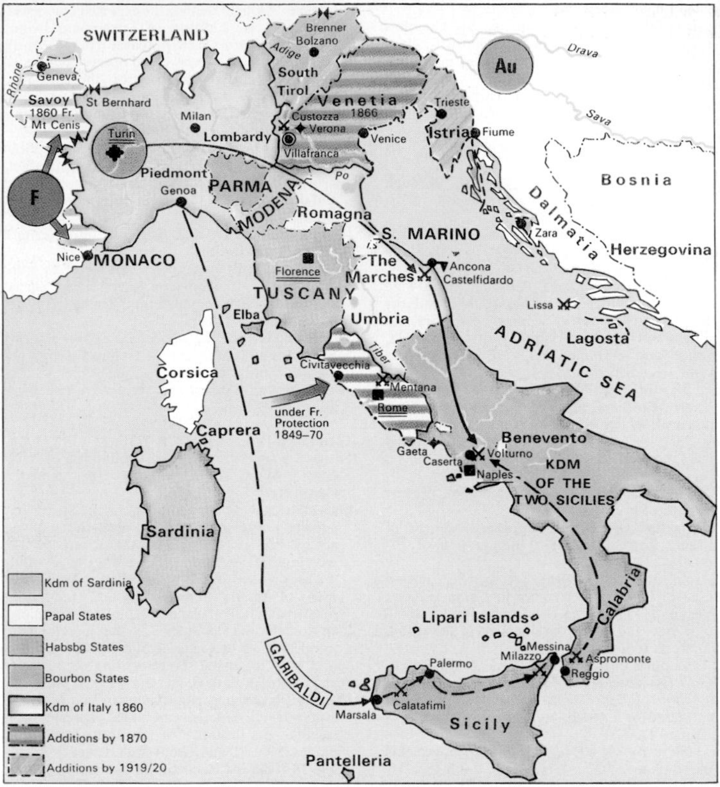

SWITZERLAND
Brenner
Bolzano
Adige
South Tirol
Venetia 1866
Au
Drava
Sava
Geneva
Rhône
Savoy 1860 Fr.
Mt Cenis
St Bernhard
Milan
Lombardy
Custozza
Verona
Villafranca
Venice
Trieste
Istria
Fiume
Turin
Piedmont
Genoa
PARMA
MODENA
Po
Romagna
F
Bosnia
Dalmatia
Zara
S. MARINO
Herzegovina
Nice
MONACO
Florence
TUSCANY
The Marches
Ancona
Castelfidardo
Elba
Umbria
Lissa
Lagosta
ADRIATIC SEA
Corsica
Civitavecchia
Tiber
Mentana
Rome
under Fr. Protection 1849–70
Caprera
Gaeta
Benevento
Caserta
Volturno
Naples
KDM OF THE TWO SICILIES
Sardinia
Calabria
Kdm of Sardinia
Papal States
Habsbg States
Bourbon States
Kdm of Italy 1860
Additions by 1870
Additions by 1919/20
Lipari Islands
Messina
Milazzo
Aspromonte
Reggio
Palermo
GARIBALDI
Calatafimi
Marsala
Sicily
Pantelleria
Italy since 1860

SWITZERLAND
Au
Geneva
Savoy
Lombardy
Venetia
Novara
Milan
Magenta
Verona
Villafranca
Trieste
Turin
Solferino
Venice
Montebello
Mantua
F
Sar
Alessandria
PARMA
Bologna
Genoa
MODENA
Romagna
ADRIATIC SEA
French Fleet
TUSCANY
Florence
S. MARINO
Nice
MONACO
The Italian War of Unification, 1859

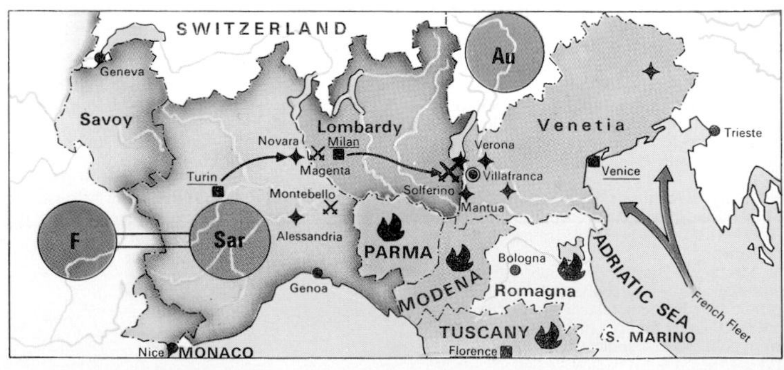

Nat. Unification (1850–71)

Camillo Count Benso di Cavour (1810–61) accepted the consequences of the failure of 1848–9 (p. 55); 'Anglo-Saxon in ideas and Gallic in language' (GIOBERTI)–he was a sober realist and modern agriculturalist (model estate at Leri) whose mind was open to the new age. He was co-editor of the newspaper **Il Risorgimento** (1847), after which the epoch was named. A member of D'AZEGLIO's cabinet since 1850,

1852 CAVOUR became prime minister of Sardinia-Piedmont; through a policy of free trade, judicial reform and eccles. legislation ('a free church in a free state'), he made it into a model state of mod. liberalism. To unite Italy under the leadership of Sardinia-Piedmont, his programme involved the following: (a) surrender of intentions of revolutionary upheaval and liberation on her own (MAZZINI); (b) gradual abolition of absolutism through lib. evolution and liberation of Italy with aid from abroad; (c) the joining of all patriots in the cause against Austria. (1857 foundation of the 'Società nazionale Italiana', Nat. Association of Italy.)

1855–6 Participation of Italy in the Crimean War to put the Ital. question on the map of Eur. politics. CAVOUR gained the support of the Western powers. He used great skill in taking advantage of the assassination attempt on NAPOLEON III's life by the Ital. nationalist ORSINI.

1858 Meeting of Plombières: the emperor promised milit. aid against Austria to make the establishment of an Ital. federation of states under the leadership of the pope possible ('Italy free to the Adriatic Sea'). Milit. preparations on the part of Sardinia-Piedmont and the refusal to meet an ultimatum provoked Vienna to declare war.

1859 Franco-Sardinian War against Austria: victs. of the allies at Magenta and Solferino (Jun.). Uprisings in Cen. Italy and fear of Prus. interference along the Rhine prompted NAPOLEON to conclude the armistice of Villafranca (Jul.).

Nov. 1859 Peace of Zürich: despite the Fr. promise of Ital. unification, Austria was allowed to retain Venetia, but **Lombardy** fell to France. CAVOUR resigned in protest (till Jan. 1860). In opposition to the formation of an Ital. confederation, plebiscites in favour of joining Sardinia were concluded in Bologna, Tuscany, Parma and Modena. NAPOLEON capitulated. In the

1860 Treaty of Turin he gained **Nice** and **Savoy** in exchange for Lombardy.

Lower Italy: followers of MAZZINI who belonged to the Democratic Action party (for e.g. CRISPI, 1819–1901) organized uprisings.

1860 After an unsuccessful uprising in Palermo, armed volunteers (the 'Red Shirts') under **Giuseppe Garibaldi** (1807–82) landed at Marsala.

May–Sep. 1860 'Campaign of the 1,000' through Sicily and Calabria. To prevent anarchy and an attack on Rome, which was (since 1849) under the protection of France, Sardinia intervened and defeated the papal troops at Castelfidardo; they capitulated at Ancona in Sep. Defeat of the Bourbon army at the Volturno and at Caserta by GARIBALDI. Meeting of VICTOR EMANUEL II and GARIBALDI (Oct.); after plebiscites in Umbria, the Marches and the Two Sicilies, which were in favour of joining with Sardinia, GARIBALDI resigned his dictatorial position.

1861 Capitulation of Gaeta (Feb.): fall of the Bourbons; FRANCIS II of Naples escaped to Rome. The all-Ital. parliament at Turin proclaimed Rome the cap. and confirmed

Mar. 1861 Victor Emanuel II (to 1878) as King of Italy. Lack of funds, debts, differences in cult. and econ. development between the N. and S. (the S. had 75% illiterates and was troubled by bandits), resistance to centralized gvt and the polit. dominance of Piedmont ('piedmontesimo') burdened the new state. To bring about the liberation of Venetia,

1866 a milit. alliance with Prussia was concluded; during the **war with Austria** Italy suffered defeats at Custozza and Lissa (p. 75). As a result of Fr. support and Prus. victs. in Bohemia, **Venetia** fell to Italy

Oct. 1866 in the Peace of Vienna; Italy gave up (for the time) its claims to S. Tyrol (Trentino), and Istria, which became the main objectives of the **Irredenta**, (the nat. movement to reclaim the 'unredeemed territories of Ital. ethnic composition'). Over the Rome question, the **'Consorteria'** (the court party of the king), unlike the opposition (Republicans, Mazzinians), and public opinion, hoped for a solution in agreement with France.

The Papal States: the reactionary wing of the Curia (secretary of state, ANTONELLI), the Cath. party in France, and FRANCIS II of Naples undercut attempts at lib. reform and reconciliation with the new monarchy. GARIBALDI assembled armed volunteers; his attack ('Rome or death'), however, ended, having got no further than Calabria, with the

1862 Defeat of Aspromonte.

1864 Sep. convention between Piedmont and France: withdrawal of Fr. troops in exchange for a pledge of defence of the Papal States. Unrest broke out when the cap. was transferred from Turin to Florence (the LA MARMORA cabinet), a move interpreted as the surrender of the claim to Rome as cap.

1864 In the *Syllabus errorum*, PIUS IX [1846–78] condemned 'erroneous' lib. teachings and demanded the subordination of the state and science to the Church's authority.

1867 3rd march of GARIBALDI on Rome, which was given up after fighting at Mentana with newly landed Fr. troops.

1869 1st Vatican Council with the proclamation of the

1870 Dogma of Papal Infallibility in matters of faith and morals (*ex cathedra*).

After the Fr. capitulation in the Franco-Prus. War (p. 71)

Sep. 1870 Ital. occupation of the Papal States (General CADORNA);

1871 PIUS IX rejected the 'guarantee of papal independence'. The pope retained sovereignty over the **Vatican State**. **Rome** became cap. of Italy.

Prussia's wars with Denmark and Austria, 1864 and 1866

The 'New Era' in Prussia (1859–62)

1861–88 William I (61 yrs old), regent for the mentally ill FREDERICK WILLIAM IV, from 1858, appointed a lib. ministry.

1859 Army reform by the minister of war, **von Roon**, intended to increase the **troops of the line** and the **reserves** to correspond to the increase in pop. since 1814. The lib. majority of the Landtag considered the reform measure (3-yr terms of service) to add unduly to the power of the crown and rejected the proposed legislation.

1861 Foundation of the **Progressive party** (*Fortschrittspartei*, WALDECK); dissolution of the Landtag followed by another elect. vict. of the liberals. During the ensuing

1862 const. conflict, the king, following a suggestion of VON ROON, appointed **Otto von Bismarck** (1815–98) **prime minister**. BISMARCK forestalled the abdication of the king and showed his readiness to govern even in opposition to the constitution and the Landtag (theory of the 'gap', i.e. in the absence of a clear definition of a disputed point in the constitution, the interest of the state (as interpreted by him) must prevail). The army was reinforced and received a privileged position in society (beginnings of Prus.-Ger. militarism).

The Struggle for Prus. Hegemony (1862–6)

Objectives of Bismarck's 'Realpolitik' (giving precedence to for. policy, incl. the use of war as the *ultima ratio* of politics): stabilization of the monarchy to strengthen Prussia; Prus. leadership in the Germ. Confederation, even if it meant in opposition to Austria. During the uprising in Poland (p. 51), BISMARCK supported the Rus. measures through the conclusion of the

1863 Milit. Convention of Alvensleben: renewal of friendship with Russia. Austria (minister, SCHMERLING) intended to take advantage of the anti-Prus. sentiments within the confederation to revise its constitution (a directory of princes and a consultative parliament). The plan failed at the

1863 Fürstentag (assembly of the princes) of Frankfurt (presided over by the Emperor FRANCIS JOSEPH), because WILLIAM I, urged by BISMARCK, stayed away. On the other hand, BISMARCK compelled Austria to cooperate in the **conflict with Denmark**, caused by the Dan. 'Nov. Constitution' (1863): annexation of Schleswig and its separation from Holstein (see I, p. 199; II, pp. 57, 61). The nat. movement demanded independence for the duchies; BISMARCK confined himself to emphasizing the violation of the London Protocol (p. 61), and thereby assured the neutrality of the Great Powers.

1864 Ger.-Dan. War: storming of the *'Düppeler Schanzen'* (Dan. fortifications). After the occupation of Alsen, Denmark ceded Schleswig-Holstein and Lauenburg to Prussia and Austria in the Peace of Vienna (Oct.). Problems of the joint admin. of the condominium intensified the problems between Austria and Prussia; they were temporarily settled by the

1865 Convention of Gastein: Aust. admin. of Holstein, Prus. admin. of Schleswig. Serving as mediator, NAPOLEON III (p. 71) hoped for compensation along the Rhine (hinted at by BISMARCK and the Austrians). NAPOLEON favoured the Prus. alliance with Italy.

The Prus. proposal for the reform of the Germ. Confederation through an elected parliament offended the Austrians, who appealed to the Assembly of the Confederation to decide the Schleswig-Holstein question. Prussia responded to this violation of the Convention of Gastein by invading Holstein and leaving the Germ. Confederation; the confederation mobilized against Prussia.

1866 War in Germany: capitulation of the Hanoverian army at Langensalza; decisive vict. of the Prussians (Chief of the General Staff: **Helmuth von Moltke,** 1800–91) at **Sadowa.** BISMARCK implored the king not to take milit. advantage of the vict. and pressed for the conclusion of the preliminary **Peace of Nikolsburg** to forestall Fr. intervention. Territ. demands prompted the s. Ger. states to conclude treaties of mutual protection and alliance with Prussia.

1866 Ital.-Aust. War (p. 73). Peace of Prague (with Prussia), Peace of Vienna (with Italy): Austria lost only **Venetia**. Dissolution of the Germ. Confederation; Prussia annexed all the opposing states N. of the River Main, exc. Saxony and Hesse Darmstadt.

1866–7 Formation of the N. Ger. Confederation.

Nat. Unification (1866–71)

Settlement of the Prus. const. conflict through the Landtag:

Sep. 1866 Acceptance of the **indemnity proposal** (retroactive approval of BISMARCK's unconst. measures by 250 to 75 votes). This violation of dem. principles split the liberals. While the Progressive party remained in opposition, the new

1867 Nat. Lib. party (VON BENNINGSEN, MIGUEL) paid tribute to polit. success and cooperated with BISMARCK and the

1867 Free Conservative party (the left wing of the Old Conservatives).

1867 Constitution of the N. Ger. Confederation: **presidency** (WILLIAM I), **fed. chancellor** BISMARCK), **fed. council** (appointive upper house), elected **Reichstag** (lower house of parliament). Renewal of the customs union through the Ger. *Zollparlament* (Customs Parliament). NAPOLEON III considered himself defrauded having received no compensation (p. 71).

1867 The Treaty of London guaranteed the neutrality of Luxemburg. France (for. minister GRAMONT) feared Prus. hegemony over Europe. The crisis was brought about by the candidacy of a Hohenzollern prince for the Sp. throne, even though he, LEOPOLD VON HOHENZOLLERN-SIGMARINGEN, abandoned it: for reasons of prestige, NAPOLEON III demanded a guarantee that the candidacy would not be renewed (conversation of the ambassador BENEDETTI with WILLIAM I at Bad Ems). The French declared war after BISMARCK shortened and published the record of this conversation as the 'Ems dispatch'.

1870–71 Franco-Prus. War (p. 71) involving also the s. Ger. states, a development unexpected by France. BISMARCK took advantage of the nat. enthusiasm for the war and brought about the

1871 Foundation of the (2nd) Ger. Reich after concluding treaties with the individual states. Proclaimed by LUDWIG II of Bavaria [1864–86] in the Hall of Mirrors at the Palace of Versailles

18 Jan. 1871 WILLIAM I became Ger. Emperor.

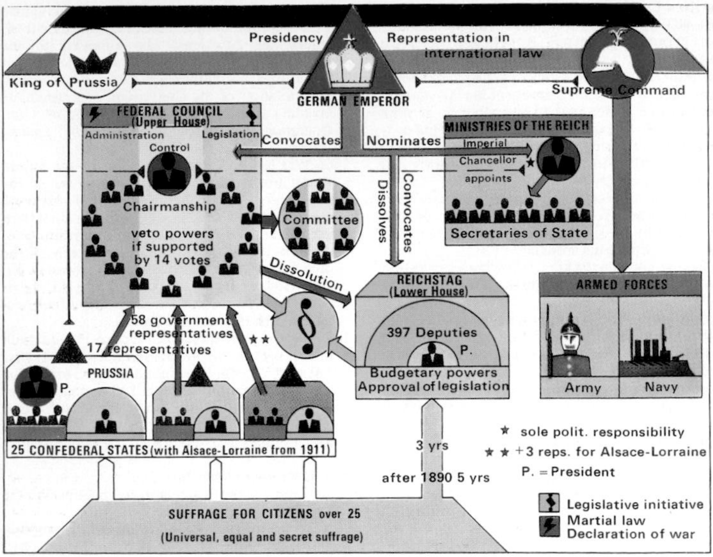

The Constitution of the German Reich of 16 April 1871

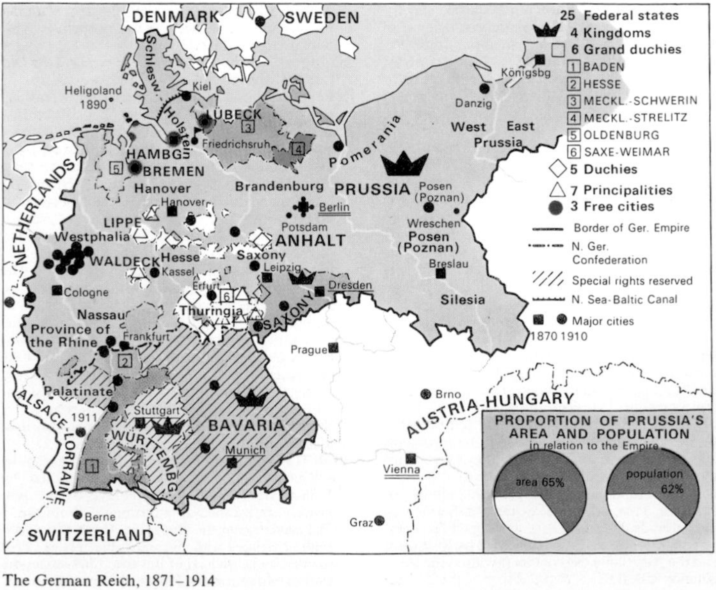

The German Reich, 1871–1914

The Ger. Empire (1871–90)

The constitution: the empire was a confederation of states under Prus. hegemony (modelled after the N. Ger. Confederation, p. 75).

The empire was in control of the armed forces, customs, commerce, transport and the postal services; contributions corresponding to the need to increase the income of the imp. treasury were required of the fed. states.

The fed. states were in control of their own admin., judiciary and cult. life.

The fed. council (Bundesrat) was the most important imp. institution, possessing legislative as well as decree and supervisory powers; the 17 Prus. representatives could collectively veto any cont. measure they opposed.

The hered. **presidency** was vested in the Prus. crown with the title 'Ger. Emperor' and represented the empire in int. affairs, conducted the milit. supreme command and appointed and dismissed

the imp. chancellor, who usually was also Prus. prime minister, chairman of the fed. council and superior of the secretaries of state and the imp. bureaucracy.

The Reichstag was a concession to democracy: it voted on legislation and approved the annual imp. budget (budgetary powers).

Polit. parties in the Reichstag: opposed to the authoritarian gvt of BISMARCK, they did not fully utilize their parl. weapons. The budgetary powers were reduced during the struggle over the

1874 'Iron Budget' for the armed forces, when a compromise, the **Septennium** (each milit. budget to cover 7 yrs), was reached. Up to 1878, BISMARCK received cooperation from the strongest polit. faction in parliament, **the Nat. Liberals** (p. 75), and the **Free Conservatives** (Deutsche Reichspartei). After the policy changes of 1878, he received the support of the Ger. Con. Party (est. 1876): at times also of **The Centre party**, led by **Ludwig Windhorst** (1812–91). Opposition to BISMARCK was represented by the **Old Conservatives**: the lib. democratic **Progressive party** (Fortschrittspartei, after 1884 the Freisinnige) under EUGEN RICHTER (1838–1906); **The Soc. Democrats**, united after 1875 through the Gotha Programme (**Bebel, Liebknecht,** p. 100); the nat. minorities (Poles, Danes, the inhabitants of Alsace-Lorraine and in addition, the Hanoverin Guelphs).

Interior development: standardization of law and economy on the basis of lib. principles (R. VON DELBRÜCK, p. 61).

1872 Penal Code.

1873 laws regulating measures, weights and coinage; 1875 the imp. bank; improvement of the postal services under H. VON STEPHAN (1831–97).

By 1878, standardized judicial practice and organization of the courts had been introduced.

1900 The Code of Civil Law (*Bürgerliches Gesetzbuch*).

The Kulturkampf: The conflict between the Prus. state (FALK, minister of cult. affairs to 1879) and the Cath. Church reflected the antagonism between the state and its claims (BISMARCK), supported by lib. ideology (R. VIRCHOW, 1821–1902) and polit. Catholicism **(Ultramontanism)**. It had its beginnings with the

1870 declaration of Papal Infallibility of the Vatican Council (p. 73). An attempt to subordinate clerics to the state (by considering them as part of the bureaucracy) and to disrupt their connection with the Rom. Curia and the 'Pol. enemy of the empire' failed because of the passive resistance of the clergy, the Centre party and the Cath. pop.

1872 Law regulating the supervision of schools; outlawing of the Jes. Order.

1873–4 The May Laws: gvtl regulations controlling the education of priests and eccles. discipline.

1874–5 Civil marriage; 'restrictive laws' (*Sperrgesetze*: the withholding of salaries, etc.). When regimentation did not bring about the hoped for success, BISMARCK broke off police actions. Steps towards a compromise were undertaken under

1878–1903 Leo XIII. By 1886, gradual elimination of the restrictive legislation; but Cath. mistrust of the Prot. empire was not alleviated.

The policy of protective tariffs: during the 'founder yrs' (the yrs following nat. unification), industry, commerce and the great banks developed rapidly; Fr. war reparations (p. 71) heated up the 'fever of the founder yrs' (between 1870–73, 1,018 new corporations were founded); but the boom ended with the stock market collapse of Vienna and turned into an

1873 econ. crisis. Criticism of free trade, Brit. indust. competition and Rus. and Amer. pressure on the price of domestic grains led to demands for protective laws for the economy. The Conservatives and the Centre party supported the

1878 transition to protective tariffs. BISMARCK expected to obtain finan. independence from the Reichstag through the

1879 tax and customs law. The Nat. Liberals split and the 'alliance of heavy industry and the large land-owning interests' was forged.

Soc. Policy: responsibility for assassination attemps on the life of the emperor was attributed by BISMARCK to the Soc. Democratic party (S.P.D.).

1878 the Anti-Socialist Law: prohibition of the party press and organization. The S.P.D. defended itself against arrest, exile and siege by strict party discipline, party conventions in London and Switzerland and clandestine newspapers.

1878 The Christ. Socialist Workers party (opposed to liberalism, antisemitic) of the court preacher ADOLF STOECKER (1835–1909) was not successful. Positive measures against the Socialists were attempted with the

Soc. legislation introducing sickness (1883), accident (1884), and old-age and disablement insurance (1889): the greatest domestic accomplishment of BISMARCK in cooperation with THEODORE LOHMANN (1831–1905). But the S.P.D. grew in numbers from election to election.

1888 FREDERICK III (56 yrs old), the lib. hope, d. after a brief reign.

1888–1918 William II. Increasing differences of opinion between the emperor (29 yrs old) and BISMARCK (75 yrs old) ended with

1890 Bismarck's dismissal (he died in 1898).

Reasons: ambition and overestimation of his own capacities by the emperor, who introduced the 'personal régime'; adherence by the chancellor to his anti-socialist policies and insistence on the renewal of the Reinsurance Treaty with Russia.

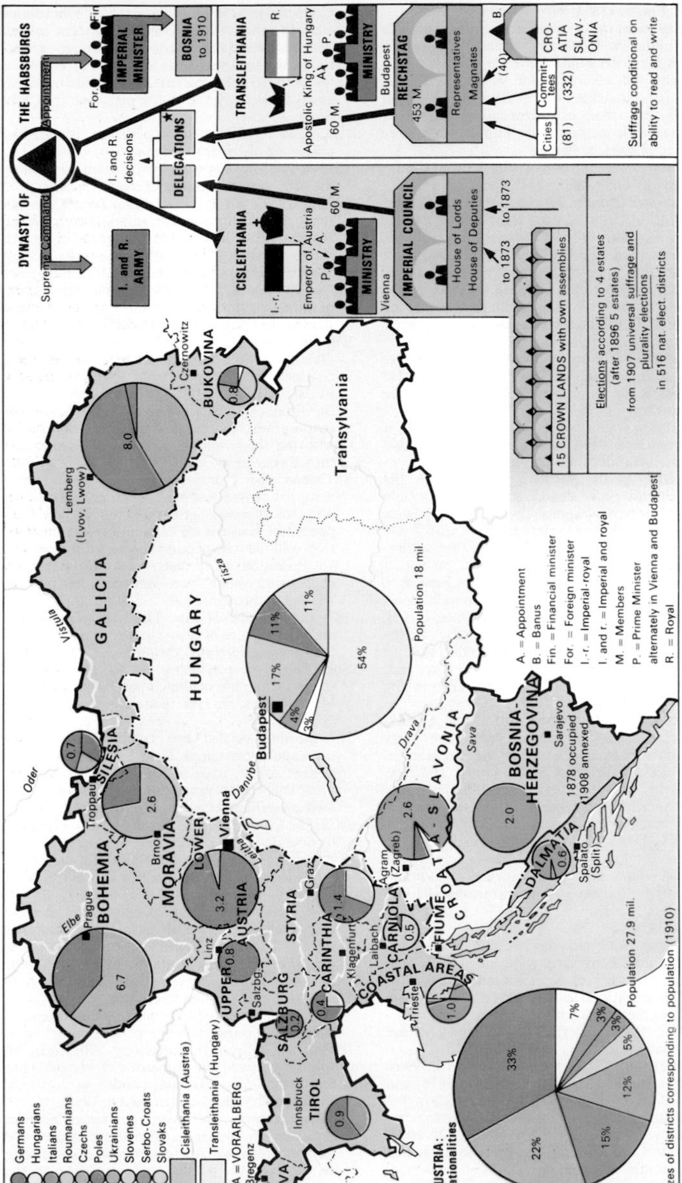

DYNASTY OF THE HABSBURGS
Supreme Command
Appointment
I. and R. ARMY
For. Fin.
IMPERIAL MINISTER
BOSNIA to 1910
I. and R. decisions
DELEGATIONS
CISLEITHANIA
I.-r.
Emperor of Austria
P. A.
60 M.
MINISTRY
Vienna
IMPERIAL COUNCIL
House of Lords
House of Deputies
to 1873
to 1873
15 CROWN LANDS with own assemblies
Elections according to 4 estates (after 1896 5 estates) from 1907 universal suffrage and plurality elections in 516 nat. elect. districts
TRANSLEITHANIA
R.
Apostolic King of Hungary
A. P.
60 M.
MINISTRY
Budapest
REICHSTAG
453 M.
Representatives
Magnates
(40)
B.
Cities (81)
Committees (332)
CROATIA SLAVONIA
Suffrage conditional on ability to read and write

Germans
Hungarians
Italians
Roumanians
Czechs
Poles
Ukrainians
Slovenes
Serbo-Croats
Slovaks
Cisleithania (Austria)
Transleithania (Hungary)
VA = VORARLBERG

Oder
Elbe
Vistula
Danube
Leitha
Tisza
Drava
Sava
Prague
BOHEMIA
6.7
Troppau
SILESIA
0.7
GALICIA
Lemberg (Lvov, Lwow)
8.0
Brno
MORAVIA
2.6
LOWER AUSTRIA
3.2
Vienna
Linz
UPPER AUSTRIA
0.8
HUNGARY
Czernowitz
BUKOVINA
0.8
Bregenz
VA
Salzbg.
SALZBURG
0.2
Innsbruck
TIROL
0.9
STYRIA
Graz
1.4
CARINTHIA
0.4
Klagenfurt
Laibach
CARNIOLA
0.5
COASTAL AREAS
Trieste
1.0
FIUME
Agram (Zagreb)
CROATIA - SLAVONIA
2.6
Budapest
17%
11%
11%
4%
3%
54%
Population 18 mil.
Transylvania
BOSNIA-HERZEGOVINA
2.0
Sarajevo
1878 occupied
1908 annexed
DALMATIA
0.6
Spalato (Split)

AUSTRIA: Nationalities
33%
22%
15%
12%
5%
3%
3%
7%
Population 27.9 mil.
Sizes of districts corresponding to population (1910)

A. = Appointment
B. = Banus
Fin. = Financial minister
For. = Foreign minister
I.-r. = Imperial-royal
I. and r. = Imperial and royal
M. = Members
P. = Prime Minister
alternately in Vienna and Budapest
R. = Royal

The multi-national Austro-Hungarian state, *c.* 1910

The Crisis of the Danubian Monarchy (1867–1914)

The defeat of 1866 brought about the

1867 Compromise (Ausgleich) of 1867, demanded by Hungary: establishment of the Austro-Hung. **dual monarchy** (Austria-Hungary), incl. joint (imp. and roy.) for. policy, finances and milit. affairs, but retaining separate constitutions, admins. and legislatures as well as a distinct Aust. (imp.-roy.) militia and the Hung. (roy.) Honved. Agreements covering questions of trade, taxation, currency and transport were to be renewed every 10 yrs. Mutual expenses were to be covered by customs duties and contributions, of which Austria supplied *c.* 70%.

1867 Coronation of Francis Joseph I (p. 59) as king of Hungary. With the army and the bureaucracy, he held the multinational state together; but he did not effect any reforms. The emperor suffered a number of personal blows: his brother MAXIMILIAN was shot in Mexico (p. 93); RUDOLF, heir to the throne, committed suicide in 1889; his empress ELISABETH was assassinated in 1898, as was his nephew FRANCIS FERDINAND, next in line to the throne, in 1914 (p. 122). **For. policy** (see pp. 83, 121).

Austria (Cisleithania: 8 nat. components, 15 crownlands, 17 parliaments) suffered under increasing **frictions between its different nationalities**.

1867 Constitution of Dec., incl. decree powers of the gvt after the dissolution of the Imp. Council.

1867–78 The lib. era (high finance and the Ger. Lib. Const. party, under PLENER, dominated the era).

1868 The May Laws terminated the concordat with the Church (p. 61); 1869 general conscription and a law setting up elementary schools throughout the empire was enacted. The con. 'Old Czechs' (PALACKY, RIEGER, p. 59) linked with Rus. Pan-Slavism. Fearful of a strengthening of the Slav. element, the Ger. Liberals rejected the

1871 'fundamental articles' of the Boh. assembly which envisaged the establishment of an auton. const. structure; at the same time they rejected the Balk. policies of the monarchy (Bosnia, p. 81).

1879–93 The 'Imp. Minister' EDUARD TAFFE (1833–95) reigned with the aid of the 'iron circle', a Cath.-con.-Slav. coalition. Police-state methods and a policy of 'muddling through' undermined the const. structure. Through gvt cooperation, the **Poles** received a measure of autonomy in Galicia, Polish being recognized as the official language. The conflict between the Poles (landowners and urban citizens) and the Pan-Slavist, peasant Ukrainians (Ruthenians) was not resolved. The **Irredentist** movement in the s. aimed at union with Italy or autonomy for the s. Tyrol and Trieste. The **Czechs** gained in their struggle to assert their nat. ctr. (growth of the Czech bourgeoisie in the cities). 1880 Official recognition of both languages; 1882 establishment of the Czech university at Prague; after 1883, a Czech majority in the assembly.

1882 Elect. reform (the '5-guilder elect. law'). It galvanized the petit bourgeoisie into action: expansion of the Young Czechs (GREGR), the Ger. Populists (Deutsch-Völkisch under SCHÖNERER) and the antisemitic Christ.-Socialist movement (VOGELSANG). The **Ger.-Nat. Union**, issuing the

1882 'Linz Programme', demanded the reconstruction of Galicia, Bukovina and Dalmatia to retain a Ger. majority in Austria. The **Socialist movement** was obstructed by

1884 restrictive laws. After its groups united

1889 establishment of the Soc. Dem. party, a party with strong nationalist overtones (p. 101).

1890 Ger.-Czech compromise, disrupted by the **Pan-Slavist Young Czechs** (KRAMAR, MASARYK). Permanent crisis after the

1897 language decree of the prime minister for Bohemia and Moravia, Count BADENI. The obstructionist policies of Ger. extremists paralysed the Imp. Council. The **Pan-Ger. party** of GEORG VON SCHÖNERER (1842–1921) unleashed the

1897 'Away-from-Rome movement', calling for closer ties with Germany, while the **Christ. Socialist** party of the Lord Mayor of Vienna, **Karl Lueger** (1844–1910), fought for the interests of the dynasty.

1899 Nat. Whitsuntide programme of all Ger. parties. Revocation of the language decree, now followed by Czech obstruction.

1900–8 The cabinets of KOERBER and BECK tried in vain to divert attention from the problems by concentrating all energies on econ. matters. A compromise with Moravia was reached in 1905. Then, in

1907, the introduction of universal manhood suffrage assured a Slav. majority in the Imp. Council (233 Ger., 265 Slav. representatives from a total of 28 polit. factions), but it was unable to function. After 1909 the gvt ruled in authoritarian style by decree. The Boh. assembly was dissolved in 1913.

1914 Adjournment of the Imp. Council.

Hungary (Transleithania) obtained hegemony over the for. policy of the entire empire through

1867–71 the prime minister (for. minister until 1879), **Count Gyula Andrássy** (1823–90).

1868 Croatia granted autonomy. The 'historical classes' retained power in Hungary (the nobility and the clergy). In opposition to the tolerant

1868 'Law of Nationalities', the determined opposition of the Independence party (1874) under

1875–90 the prime minister **Kálmán Tisza** (1830–1902) pursued a policy of consistent **Magyarization.**

1876 Elimination of auton. admin. in Transylvania. Supported by the secret Roum. Nat. Committee (1869), the Roumanians reduced the influence of Hung. and Ger. landowners in Transylvania. In the face of obstruction in the Imp. Council, the opposition of the s. Slav movement and Hung. extremism, the prime minister, **István Tisza** [1903–5, 1913–17], was able to assert a 'policy of the iron hand': coercion of the opposition and rejection of universal manhood suffrage.

The S. Slav. question: Magyarization and anti-Serb. commercial policies (p. 81) transformed Serbo-Croatian differences after 1904 into 'Yugoslavian solidarity'. To counteract Hung. and Gt Serb. claims, plans were made to extend Austro-Hung. dualism by a further Slav. dimension (**Trialism**, represented by the Archduke FRANCIS FERDINAND).

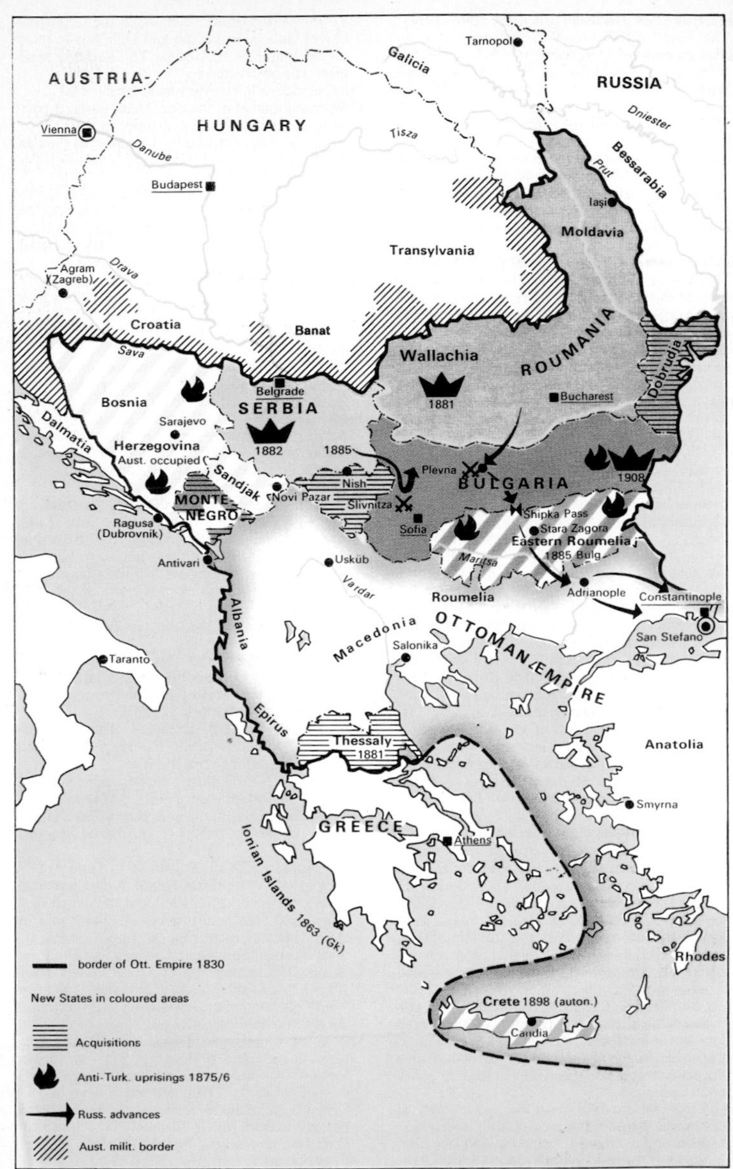
AUSTRIA-
HUNGARY
RUSSIA
Galicia
Tarnopol
Dniester
Bessarabia
Prut
Iaşi
Moldavia
Vienna
Danube
Tisza
Budapest
Transylvania
Agram
(Zagreb)
Drava
Croatia
Banat
Sava
ROUMANIA
Wallachia
1881
Dobrudja
Bucharest
Belgrade
SERBIA
1882
Bosnia
Sarajevo
Dalmatia
Herzegovina
Aust. occupied
1885
Plevna
BULGARIA
1908
Sandjak
Novi Pazar
Nish
Slivnitza
MONTE-
NEGRO
Shipka Pass
Stara Zagora
Eastern Roumelia
1885 Bulg.
Ragusa
(Dubrovnik)
Sofia
Maritsa
Antivari
Usküb
Vardar
Roumelia
Adrianople
Constantinople
San Stefano
Albania
Macedonia
OTTOMAN EMPIRE
Salonika
Taranto
Epirus
Thessaly
1881
Anatolia
Smyrna
GREECE
Athens
Ionian Islands 1863 (Gk)
Rhodes
Crete 1898 (auton.)
Candia
border of Ott. Empire 1830
New States in coloured areas
Acquisitions
Anti-Turk. uprisings 1875/6
Russ. advances
Aust. milit. border

The political reorganization of the Balkans through the Congress of Berlin, 1878

The Balk. Crisis (1875–8)

During the course of the Franco-Prus. War (p. 71) Russia repudiated the conditions of the Peace of Paris of 1856 (p. 69). Supported by BISMARCK, it received the right to free passage through the Dardanelles at the

1871 'Pontus' Conference of London.

1875–6 Uprisings of Turk. vassals aggravated the situation and led to the Serbo-Turk. War. The Porte refused to carry out internal reforms. To free the Christians of the Balkans, Russia initiated the

1877–8 Russo-Turk. War (1st polit. success of Pan-Slavism, p. 113). After fighting over and occupation of the Shipka Pass and the seizure of Plevna, the Russians advanced on Constantinople and into the Caucasus.

Mar. 1878 Peace of San Stefano: enlargement of the Balk. states (Bulgaria) at the expense of Eur. Turkey. Austria and England opposed increasing Rus. influence. BISMARCK mediated as the 'honest broker' at the

Jun.–Jul. 1878 Congress of Berlin: Roumania, Serbia and **Montenegro** became ind.; an auton. pty, **Bulgaria** remained tributary and lost **Macedonia** and **Eastern Roumelia** to **Turkey**, **Eastern Roumelia** receiving internal autonomy. **Russia** obtained **Bessarabia** and parts of Armenia (Kars); England received **Cyprus**; Austria was given administrative rights over **Bosnia** and **Herzegovina**.

Consequences: preservation of the peace, but Rus. annoyance; Russo-Ger. estrangement and aggravation of the Austro-Rus. Balk. conflict, leading to closer Austro-Ger. relations. The nationality problems of the Balkans remained unresolved.

The Balk. States (to 1908)

Bulgaria: closely orientated towards Russia, artisans, Hajduks (irregulars) and priests fought alien Turk. rule and the regimentation of the Gk Orth. Church.

1870 The establishment of a Bulg. Exarchate was not recognized by the Patriarch of Constantinople (to 1945). Soc. revolutionaries like ROKOVSKI and **Christo Botev** (1848–76) carried on the polit. struggle.

1872 The Cen. Bulg. Revolutionary Committee in Bucharest planned general popular uprisings; these were

1875–6 suppressed with much bloodshed. The 'Turk. atrocities' caused the Rus. attack (see above). Against Russia's wishes, the Bulg. Nat. Assembly introduced a lib. constitution modelled after that of Belgium; but it chose the nephew of the tsarina

1879–86 ALEXANDER VON BATTENBERG (of the Hesse-Darmstadt dynasty) to be reigning prince. This underdeveloped agrarian state was ruled by him with the help of Rus. advisers. Brit. and Aust. imports ruined the artisans and indebtedness increased. The prince was only able to gain the support of the nation after the

1885 acquisition of Eastern Roumelia, carried out despite protests of Russia and Serbia. The Rus. advisers withdrew. Without for. milit. aid, Bulgaria was victorious over Serbia in the

1885 b. of Slivnitsa. Rus. intrigues forced ALEXANDER to abdicate.

1887–1918 FERDINAND I (Saxe-Coburg dynasty). Against the opposition of Russophil efforts, the 'Bulg. Bismarck', **Stambulov** (1854–95), the prime minister, europeanized the admin., the economy and the army. After his dismissal, FERDINAND became reconciled to Russia.

Greece: the Nat. Assembly chose

1863–1913 GEORGE I (Glücksburg dynasty), 'King of the Hellenes'. After the

1863 Brit. hand-over of the Ion. Islands, the **Enosis** movement (union of all Greeks) took precedence over attempts at econ. development. An uprising on Crete failed (1866). After the acquisition of Thessaly, **Macedonia** became the object of dispute between Greece and Bulgaria. A 2nd uprising on Crete led to the

1897 Greco-Turk. War with Gk defeats in Thessaly. Nevertheless, **Crete** gained polit. autonomy under Turk. sovereignty because of the interference of the great powers. The leader of Enosis, **Venizelos** (1864–1936), proclaimed the annexation of Crete in 1905.

1908 Formal union of Crete and Greece.

Roumania: the principalities of Moldavia and Wallachia united in 1858 under the Moldavian Bojar CUZA (1820–73).

1861 Proclamation of the establishment of the Roumanian state. Secularization of eccles. property, peasant emancipation and legal reforms. A putsch overthrew CUZA; following a suggestion of NAPOLEON III,

1866–1914 Carol I (Hohenzollern-Sigmaringen dynasty) was chosen king.

1881 From this date on, establishment of an army modelled after that of Prussia; construction of railways, improvement of the educational system; and development of means to utilize the petroleum resources.

1883 Joining of the Dual Alliance (p. 83).

Serbia: increase of pop. without the chance of emigration led to the parcelling of land. Consequences: impoverishment of the peasantry, break-up of large family units.

1860–68 MICHAEL OBRENOVIĆ based his efforts to unite all s. Slavs on the Great-Serb. Omladina movement, represented in Croatia by Bp STROSSMAYER of Diakovar (1815–1905).

1862 Withdrawal of the last Turk. garrisons.

1868–89 MILAN OBRENOVIĆ (14 yrs old) ruled autocratically, even though

1869 a lib. constitution had been introduced. In opposition to the efforts of the Rad. party, led by **Nikola Pasić** (1846–1926), the régime sought close cooperation with Austria.

1882 Proclamation of a Serb. kingdom; unsuccessful war against Bulgaria (1885). After the

1903 assassination of ALEXANDER I by nationalist officers, the s. Slav. movement (Yugoslavism) grew.

1903–18 PETER I KARADJORDJEVIĆ led the Rad. party with PASIĆ as his prime minister. Vienna responded to his anti-Aust. policies in 1906 with a ban on the import of Serb. animals (83% of Serb. exports). Serbia survived the 'pig war' with the aid of Fr. capital, used to build up domestic industry to process agricultural products.

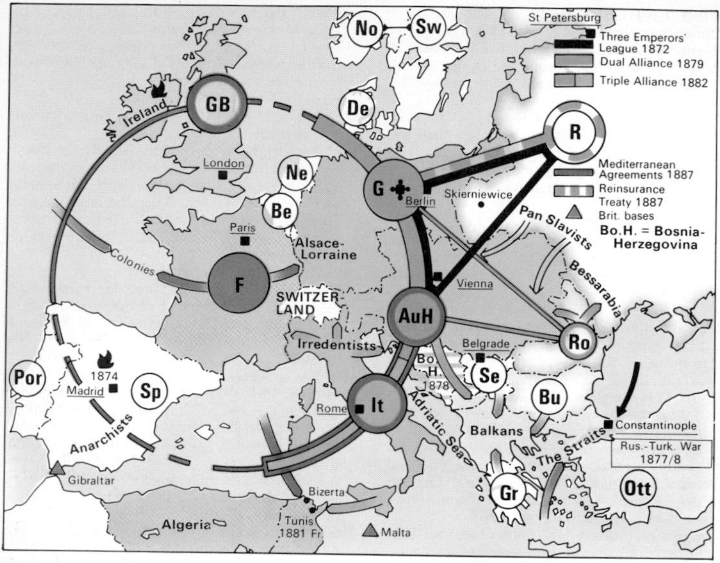

Bismarck's alliance system

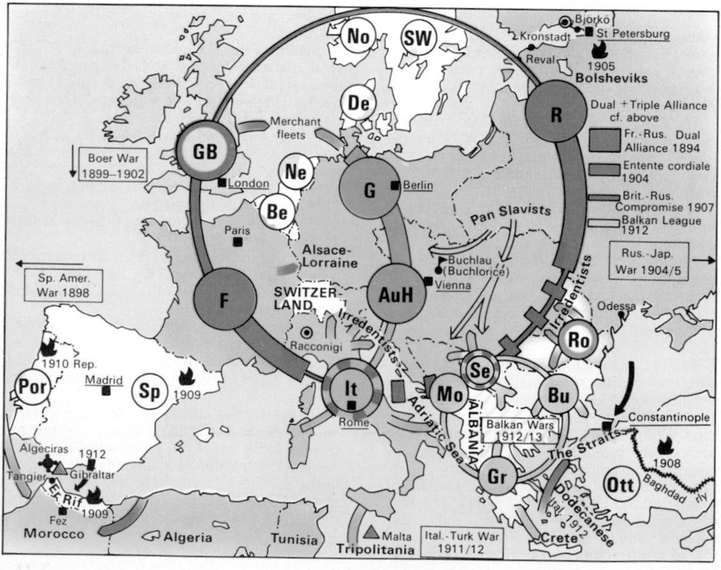

The European alliance system before the First World War

Bismarck's Alliance System (1871–90)

Considering the Ger. Empire to be 'saturated' in terms of territ. expansion, BISMARCK secured its position by alleviating Eur. tensions and concluding defensive alliances. He countered expected Fr. policies of retribution by (a) the isolation of France and (b) encouraging the Fr. republic (unlikely to find allies in monarchical Europe) and Fr. colon. amibitions.

1872 The League of the 3 Emperors (Germany, Austria-Hungary and Russia) for defence against France's wish for revenge.

1875 The 'War-in-sight crisis': Due to the supposed intentions of waging a preventive war by the Germans, the French armed and the British and Russians (for. minister GORTSHAKOV, to 1882) intervened; Austria, on the other hand, moved closer to the Ger. position (for. minister ANDRASSY, to 1879).

1878 After the Congress of Berlin (p. 81), Germany and Austria-Hungary concluded the

1879 Dual Alliance. Following Rus. conciliatory moves,

1881 the League of the 3 Emperors was renewed: it stipulated neutrality of the partners in case of attack by a 4th power. Italy (Crispi) expedited the conclusion of the

1882 Triple Alliance (Germany, Austria-Hungary and Italy); however, the tensions between Italy and Austria-Hungary (p. 119) remained.

1883 Roumania joined the Triple Alliance.

1884 The league met at Skierniewice. It failed to reach a compromise in the Balk. conflict between Russia and Austria-Hungary (p. 121).

1885–7 BISMARCK attempted to overcome the crisis in the treaty system (the Bulg. conflict, p. 81; the Fr. BOULANGER affair, p. 105 through

1887 the Reinsurance Treaty with Russia (the secret supplementary protocol promised Ger. support for Rus. policies relating to the Dardanelles).

1887 The Medit. Agreements were supported by BISMARCK; they consisted of agreements of the powers interested in maintaining the status quo in the Medit. esp. with regard to Turkey; England declined a direct alliance with Berlin in 1887–9 (SALISBURY).

Germany's 'New Course' (1890–1914)

After the fall of BISMARCK (p. 77), the int. situation was aggravated by (a) imperialistic power politics; (b) impulsive actions of WILLIAM II; and (c) the Ger. 'policy of the free hand' based on an over-estimation of the Ger. power position (VON HOLSTEIN, the 'grey eminence' of the Ger. For. office till 1906). Because of the

1890 non-renewal of the Reinsurance Treaty, the French made approaches to Russia (naval visit at Kronstadt).

1894 Franco-Rus. Dual Alliance: development of Rus. industry and a rail system with the help of Fr. capital; initiation of Rus. Far Eastern policies. Simultaneously, relations between England and Germany cooled owing to misguided Ger. 'continental-block policies', commercial competition, the emperor's telegram to KRUGER (1896) and Ger. Far Eastern policies (Tsingtao);

1898 The naval construction programme (TIRPITZ); options obtained to construct the Baghdad railway (1899). Because of Fr. expansion in Africa and the

1898 Fashoda Crisis (p. 107), the British decided to **abandon their policy of 'splendid isolation'.**

1898–1901 Germany rejected Brit. proposals for an alliance, it being presumed impossible for Britain to reach an understanding with France or Russia. The Boer War, (1899–1902), the Boxer Rising (1900) in China, the Brit. compromise with the U.S. (Panama, p. 117) all reinforced the impression of Brit. isolation.

1902 the Brit.-Jap. alliance and the

1904–5 Russo-Jap. War initiated a reversal of Rus. policies from eastern expansion to emphasis on European problems (the Balkans). The tensions between France (for. minister DELCASSÉ) and England over Morocco and Egypt were lessened.

The Policies of the Entente (1904–14)

The division of Europe into two power blocs was slowed down neither by crisis nor by attempts to relieve tensions; the Ger. Empire stood at the side of Austria, Britain at the side of France and Russia. The Franco-Brit.

1904 Entente Cordiale passed its 1st test during the

1905–6 1st Moroccan crisis: Germany had protested (visit of the Kaiser WILLIAM to Tangiers) against the 'peaceful penetration' of the country by France. The meeting of the Ger. and Prus. emperors at Björkö had no effect on int. relations. The Morocco question was decided by the

1906 Algeciras Conference: confirmation of the 'policy of the open door' (from 1880); Germany gained prestige, but was increasingly isolated while the partners of the Entente Cordiale were brought closer together.

1907 Brit.-Rus. conciliation of interests at the expense of Persia (p. 87), which was aided by the

1907 2nd Convention of The Hague: the rules of land warfare were clarified; Germany's rejection of disarmament increased general mistrust.

1908 Futile attempts to solve the problems over naval armaments between Germany (BÜLOW) and Britain; new proposals to strengthen the Ger. navy came forward. Official visit of EDWARD VII to Reval, formation of the Triple Entente. During the

1908 Bosnian Crisis (p. 121) Russia felt deceived (for. minister ISVOLSKI).

1909 Secret Russo-Ital. Treaty of Racconigi to keep the status quo in the Balkans.

1911 2nd Moroccan Crisis (after the Fr. occupation of Fez, the Ger. warship *Panther* was dispatched to Agadir, 'the leap of the panther', p. 109). The crisis was alleviated by an agreement over a Fr. protectorate in Morocco and Ger. compensations in the Cameroons. Italy occupied Tripolitania and the Dodecanese.

1912 Negotiations over the naval question between Berlin (KIDERLEN-WÄCHTER) and London (Lord HALDANE) failed again. Franco-Brit. agreement over naval dispositions in the Channel and the Mediterranean. State visit of the Fr. prime minister, POINCARÉ, to St Petersburg and conclusion of a naval agreement.

1912–13 Balk. crisis resulting from the division of the Eur. territory of Turkey (p. 121).

1913 Strengthening of the Ger. and Rus. armies; 3 yr military service introduced in France.

1914 The Assassination at Sarajevo (p. 122) precipitated the outbreak of the First World War.

Scandinavia in the 19th Cent.
At first a cult., lat., under the leadership of the Eider Danes, a polit. unification movement, **Scandinavianism**, for all practical purposes, failed over the Schleswig-Hostein question (p. 75).

Denmark (pop. in 1800, 900,000: in 1900, 2.5 mil.: an increase of 177%.
1814 Peace of Kiel. Loss of **Norway**; Heligoland became Brit. Even though the state was bankrupt and agriculture in crisis, a lib. opposition arose only after 1830. The 'Eider Danes' wished for a constitution incl. a provision separating Schleswig from Hostein.
1844 The level of popular education was raised by the university extensions of the theologian GRUNDTVIG (1783–1872).
1848–63 The 'Eider-Dan.' Cabinet, appointed by FREDERICK VII, gave rise to a popular uprising in Schleswig-Holstein and caused the
1848–50 1st Ger.-Dan. War (p. 61).
1852 London Protocol: rest. of the state *in toto*.
1849 Jun. constitution (universal manhood suffrage, elimination of guild restrictions). The dominant nat.-liberals renewed the Eider policies.
1863 Nov. constitution and Ger.-Dan. dyn. struggle centring on the person of
1863–1906 CHRISTIAN IX. Solution of the Schleswig-Holstein question in
1864 the 2nd Ger.-Dan. War (p. 75).
1875–94 Con. reaction under the ESTRUP Cabinet; the majority in the Folkething (lower chamber), led by **Bajer** (1837–1922), consisted of liberals and agrarians.
1879 BISMARCK refused to grant the pop. of Northern Schleswig their promised autonomy; Dan. ctr. was, however, sustained through nat. associations. Farmers' cooperatives increased the export of agricult. products.
1901 Change of polit. systems: the CHRISTENSEN Cabinet forced the adoption of an agrarian reform programme.
1903 Const. autonomy for **Iceland**.
Radicals and Socialists were able to introduce
1915 const. parl. reform under CHRISTIAN X (1912–47).

Sweden pop. in 1800 2.3 mil.; in 1900 5.1 mil.: an increase of 122%.
1818–44 CHARLES XIV (BERNADOTTE, p. 27)
1844–59 Orientating his policies towards Britain, OSCAR I supported 'Scandinavianism'.
1855 Franco-Brit. guarantee of the frontiers.
1859–72 CHARLES XV left the business of gvt to his prime minister, DE GEER, (1818–96), who eliminated the polit. privileges of nobility and Church through the
1866 parl. reform. The new 'Landmann party' gained a majority but did not supply the Cabinet. A pro-Ger. policy of neutrality was followed under
1872–1907 OSCAR II. The rich resources of lumber and iron ores were exploited by water power; but agrarian crises caused **mass emigration** to the U.S. and necessitated the transition of agriculture to animal husbandry.
1888 Protective tariffs for grains; 1892 for indust. products.
1901 Universal conscription. After the dissolution of the union with Norway, the party system was reorganized. Parliamentarism carried the day
1907–50 under GUSTAVUS V. The Socialists (1889) and the Lib. Coalition party, against the opposition of the con. Progressive party (1906) forced the introduction of
1909 universal suffrage.

Norway (pop. in 1800, 900,000; in 1900 2.2 mil.: an increase of 144%.
1814 Convention of Moss: **personal union with Sweden**: but the Storting (popular assembly) opposed the Veto power of the Swed. king.
This opposition weakened gradually as a result of common 'Scandinavianism'. Increased econ. development after 1850.
1884–19 The SVENDRUP ministry of the agrarian left introduced, for all practical purposes, the first parl. system; universal suffrage had existed from 1898. To take care of Nor. shipping interests, the Storting demanded an ind. for. policy. A law granting the right to establish Nor. consulates was vetoed by OSCAR II. This led to the
1905 dissolution of the union. Proclamation of Prince CHARLES of Denmark as
1905–57 King HAAKON VII. The great Eur. powers recognized the new kdm in 1907. The Dan. language was replaced by the native landsmal (New Norwegian), developed by IVAR AASEN (1813–96).

Finland (pop. in 1800=800,000; in 1900=2.6 mil.: an increase of 225%.
1809 Assembly of Borga: the aut. grand duchy, subject to Rus. sovereignty, was granted confirmation of the basic Fin. rights enacted in 1772–89. Election of the Senate under participation of the popular assembly; the Tsar was represented by a governor-general; a committee to put Fin. questions to the Tsar was appointed. The popular assembly was never convoked under NICHOLAS I (p. 69); however, Fin. nat. consciousness developed. By reinterpretihg traditional Fin. ballads, ELIAS LONNROT (1802–84) created the nat. epic *Kalevala*. JOHAN VILHELM SNELLMAN (1806–81) founded a movement to prepare for the establishment of an ind. state, even though 'Swed. Finns' (the upper classes) and 'peoples' Finns' were at odds. Conscription was introduced and
1878 a Fin. army organized. The Fin. movement suffered a setback because of the
1899 Feb. Manifesto of NICHOLAS II. The popular assembly lost its leg. powers.
1899–1904 Governor-General BOBRIKOV dissolved the army and introduced Russian as official language. The 'Old Finns' attempted to preserve their special privileges by capitulating; the 'Young Finns' continued passive resistance.
1905 Revocation of the Tsarist decree during the Rus. revolution of 1905. The MECHELIN Cabinet democratized the popular assembly. STOLYPIN (p. 111) again aggravated the conflict: readiness to separate from Russia intensified.

The Iberian States (1840–1914)
Liberals, republicans and Socialists fought in Spain and Portugal against monarchists (*moderatos*) and Catholics. Continued possession of the colonies was endangered by econ. backwardness and polit. and fiscal instability.

Spain (pop. in 1800 = 11.5 mil.; in 1900 = 18.6 mil.: an increase of 62%):
1843 ISABELLA (1830–1904) was declared of age. *Coups* took place.
1847 The 2nd Carlist War and repub. uprisings weakened the lib. system. As prime minister, O'DONNELL (1858–63) sought to divert public attention to for. affairs through the
1859–60 war against Morocco and participation in the Mex. expedition (p. 93).
1868 Fall of ISABELLA; Generals SERRANO and PRIM cultivated the candidacy of LEOPOLD of Hohenzollern (p. 75).
1872–6 3rd Carlist War against AMEDEUS of Savoy, who had been proclaimed king; simultaneous Socialist unrest.
1873 Proclamation of the 1st republic; but also rest. of Bourbon rule through MARTÍNEZ DE CAMPOS (1831–1900).
1874–85 ALFONSO XII.
1876 New constitution: freedom of press and association, but abolition of civil marriage and strengthening of the Cath. Church. Repub. assassinations, milit. mutinies, an autonomy movement in Catalonia, and tensions between capit. circles and rad. trade unions (see syndicates, p. 100).
1886–1931 ALFONSO XIII, to 1902 under the regency of the king's widow MARIA CHRISTINA of Austria. The uprising in Cuba (1895), supported by the U.S.A., developed into the
1898 Sp. Amer. War (p. 117), which ended with the dissolution or sale of the Sp. colon. empire, exc. for Spain's Afr. possessions. A period of critical self-appraisal followed in the field of literature with MIGUEL DE UNAMUNO (1864–1936), MARTÍNEZ RUIZ and later **Ortega y Gasset** (1883–1955) and others.
1904 Morocco Treaty with France.
1909 Campaign against the Riffs tribes in Morocco. Lib. cult. policies under
1910–12 CANALEJAS; yet no soc. or econ. reforms carried out. Substantial emigration to America.

Portugal (pop. in 1800 2.9 mil.; in 1900 5.4 mil.: an increase of 86%.)
1834–53 MARIA II DA GLORIA. Continual party struggles between con. and lib. groups; and, after 1848, republicans. Under PEDRO V (1853–61) power was in the hands of the dictator SALDANHA, overthrown in
1857 by DE LOULE (1805–75).
1890 Substantial loss of polit. prestige: a Brit. ultimatum demanded discontinuation of attempts to expand colon, possessions by connecting Angola and Mozambique. In exchange, Britain guaranteed existing colon. possessions in the
1899 Treaty of Windsor.
1906–8 Dictatorship of JOÃO FRANCO.
1910 Proclamation of the republic. The 1st anti-clerical prime minister, BRAGA (1843–1924), was not able, however, to establish the rule of law.

The Smaller States of Cen. Europe (1848–1914)
Switzerland (pop. in 1800 = 1.7 mil.; in 1900 = 3.3 mil.: an increase of 94%).
1859 Prohibition of mercenary milit. service. The b. of Solferino (p. 73) moved the Genevan **Henri Dunant** (1823–1910) to
1864 found the Red Cross: inviolability of hospital services and care of all wounded in time of war.
1874 Establishment of the Universal Postal Union in Berne.
1874 Revisions of the constitution in favour of the fed. gvt: provision for the referendum to make leg. decisions; a unified milit. and public education system was introduced, leading to cult. dissension which lasted to 1884. Highly developed, Swiss industry was dependent on the world market and therefore subject to recurring monetary crises. The Social Democrats (1887) and the Peasants' League (1897) increased in membership.

The Netherlands (pop. in 1800 = 2.1 mil.; in 1900 = 5.2 mil.: an increase of 148%). Struggles in the Dutch E. Indies notwithstanding, domestic politics dominated. Lib. and con. Christ. parties struggled for power.
1848 A parl. constitution with minist. responsibility, budgetary powers and control of the colon. admin. through the Estates General was introduced by **Thorbecke** (1798–1872), the Lib. leader; it was he to whom the state owed its lib. development during the reign of
1849–90 WILLIAM III. During the
1866–8 conflict with the crown over the sale of Luxemburg to NAPOLEON III (p. 75), parliament carried the day.
1890 Independence of **Luxemburg**.
1890–1948 **Queen Wilhelmina** loyally adhered to the constitution, adopted in 1887. The work of soc. legislation was continued under alternating lit. and con. Cath. ministries. Struggles with Atjeh in Sumatra were followed by the 'ethnic' period of col. policy, which saw the natives gain a measure of polit. influence.

Belgium (pop. in 1800 = 3.0 mil.; in 1900 = 6.7 mil.: an increase of 123%): the lib.-clerical tensions were compounded by the conflict between Flemings and Walloons. Trade and industry prospered
1865–1909 LEOPOLD II. NAPOLEON III's plans of annexation constituted a threat to the country. Disputes over education led to a break of relations with Rome in 1880. The king acquired the
1885 Congo Free State as his private possession and deeded it to the state.
1885 Congress of Brussels: establishment of the Marxist Workers' party. As the '3rd power', it gained voting strength through the introduction of
1894 universal suffrage. After 1898, the Flem. and Fr. languages were given equal rank. Brit. complaints over colon. exploitation (the 'Congo Atrocities') quickened the
1908 takeover of the Congo through the state.
1909–34 ALBERT I wished for peaceful relations in int. affairs; but, once the Ger. Schlieffen Plan (1906) became known (p. 125), he sought support from Britain.

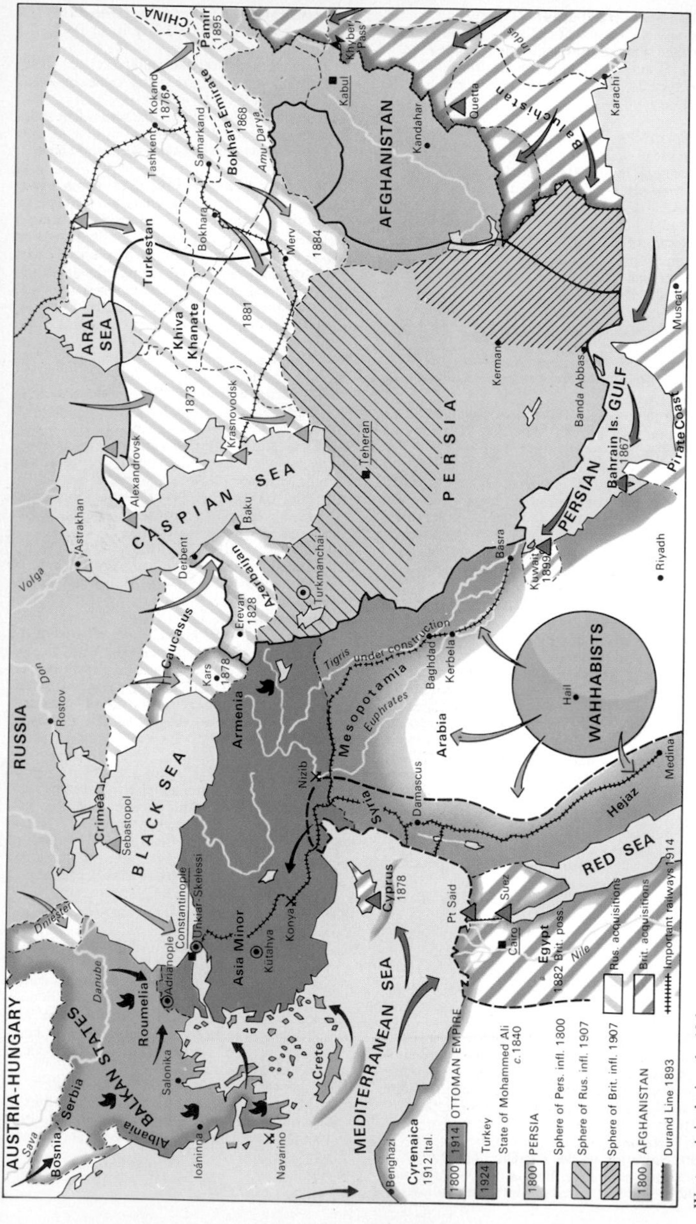

Western Asia during the 19th cent.

The Decay of the Ott. Empire (1788–1914)
Obsolete **state organization** (e.g. the vilayets were centrally administered districts which existed side by side with auton. vassal states and semi-official tribal confederations), corrupt **administrative practices** (arbitrary rule and power ambitions of the pashas, 'tax-farming' and bribery), a weak army of Janissaries and a **soc. order** based on relig. distinctions characterized the Ott. Empire. After the Russo-Turk. wars (I, p. 285), **permanent crisis** set in accompanied by the secession of parts of the empire, interference in the affairs of, or intentions of dividing up, the empire by Eur. powers (the Eastern question), nat. movements in the Balkans and revolts in Arabia by the **Wahhabists** (an orth. sect attempting to preserve the 'purity of Islam').

1789–1807 SELIM III. Attempts at reform were cut off by the

1798–1801 Egyp. war against NAPOLEON (p. 23). After the

1803 withdrawal of the French (General KLÉBER) the Albanian **Mohammed Ali** (1769–1849) usurped power in Egypt (p. 97).

1803–39 MAHMUD II (24 yrs old) subj. the Dere-beys (lit. the 'princes of the valleys' of Asia Minor and Roumelia); however, he subsequently suffered severe losses in Russia in 1812 (p. 27) and during the Gk uprising (p. 45). IBRAHIM PASHA, stepson and general of MOHAMMED ALI, waged

1813–15 war against the Wahhabists in Mecca and Medina on behalf of the Porte. Their new state of Riyadh (1820) was overcome by the tribal princes of Hail.

1826 Army reform and elimination of disobedient janissaries.

1831 Attack by MOHAMMED ALI: he was victorious at Konya and obtained **Syria** through the

1833 Treaty of Kütahya. His

1839 advance on Nizib brought about the

1839–41 Eastern crisis: a Brit.-Rus.-Prus. convention forced France (THIERS) to cease supporting Egypt; MOHAMMED ALI became hered. governor of Egypt; Russia was displeased over the

1841 Dardanelles Treaty of London, which **closed the Straits** to non-Turk. warships.

1839–61 ABDUL MEJID I, urged by the Western powers, issued 'useful decrees' (*Tanzimat*) to reform judiciary and admin.; but he was unable to eliminate the prerogatives of the Eur. consulates.

1853–6 The Crimean War (p. 69) and the

1856 Peace of Paris exposed Turkey to 'conquest by Western capital'. Trade agreements specifying low import duties (reducing the amount of domestic production) were concluded. Mortgaging of state income, increasing indebtedness to for. countries,

1875 public bankruptcy, after 1881 int. admin. of the public debt. Addit. reforms (abolition of torture) culminated in the

1876 'basic law of the state', the 1st decreed constitution, which placed relig. creeds and nationalities on an even footing. Yet

1876–1909 ABDUL HAMID II laid the constitution aside and ruled despotically.

1878 The Congress of Berlin (p. 81).

1890–97 Uprisings by and atrocities against the Christians of Armenia discredited the régime. Germany rejected the Brit. plan to

1895 divide Turkey (SALISBURY), and received in turn concessions for the construction of railways **(Anatolia and Baghdad railway).**

1896–7 Turkey was victorious in the Greco-Turk. war over Crete.

The Young Turk Movement: opposition to autocracy and the privileges of foreigners consolidated after 1860 (students and army officers). Groups of officers, such as the 'Freedom and Progress' Committee (1891) and the secret association of **Mustafa Kemal** (ATATÜRK, p. 167), founded in Damascus in 1905, combined to form the **Young Turk party.** Concern over the possible partition of the empire and the constitution of 1876 brought about the

1908 Milit. uprising of Salonika, led by **Enver Pasha** (1881–1922). Crises (p. 121), uprisings (Albania, Arabia), counter-revolution and removal of the Sultan from the throne. Under

1909–18 MOHAMMED V, the Young Turks obtained power during the

1911–13 Tripolitanian War (p. 119) and the Balkan Wars (p. 121).

1913 Army reform under Ger. guidance, naval development with Brit. aid.

1914 Ger.-Turk. defensive alliance (Aug.). Nov.: Allied declaration of war.

Persia, Afghanistan (1736–1909)

1736 Persia was conquered by the Turkoman NADIR; subsequent struggles led to the rise of the **Kajar dynasty** and the

1747 founding of Afghanistan through AHMAD KHAN DURANI.

1797–1834 Persia was ruled by FATH ALI SHAH: losses to Russia were terminated by the conclusion of the

1828 Peace of Turkmanchai.

1838 Revolt and escape of the leader of the Ismaili sect, AGA KHAN, to India. The Shi'ites infl. the people. Beginnings of Eur. reforms under

1848–96 NASIR UD-DIN. The Westernized press and schools spread lib. ideas. A popular uprising led to the

1906 proclamation of a constitution which was, however, abrogated by Shah MOHAMMED ALI [1907–9]. Uprisings and unrest caused Britain and Russia to conclude the

1907 Treaty of St Petersburg: division of Persia into spheres of interest accompanied by an agreement not to expand in Afghanistan and Tibet. After rejecting the Brit.-Rus. demands,

1909 Brit.-Rus. occupation of the country and reinstatement of the constitution.

Afghanistan: during the 19th cent. Britain made futile efforts to obtain the 'turnstile of Asia's fate' (the Afghan Wars, p. 89).

1818–34 Loss of the eastern Indus territories. The rulers took advantage of Rus.-Brit. rivalry to retain their autonomy.

1880–1901 ABDURRAHMAN granted Britain protective and controlling powers. As a means of defence against India, in

1893 the Durand line was fixed.

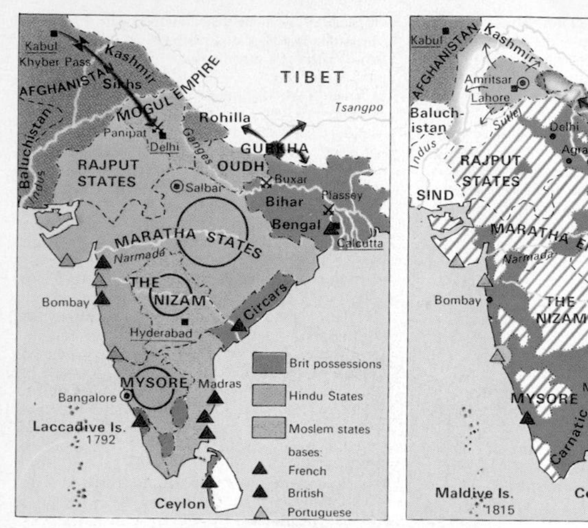

India, *c.* 1795

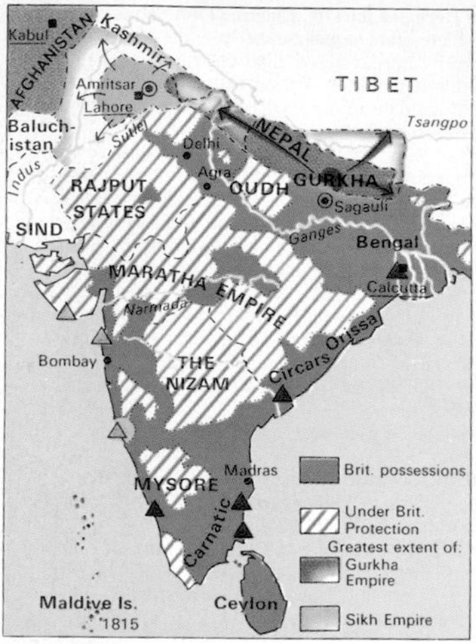

India, *c.* 1818

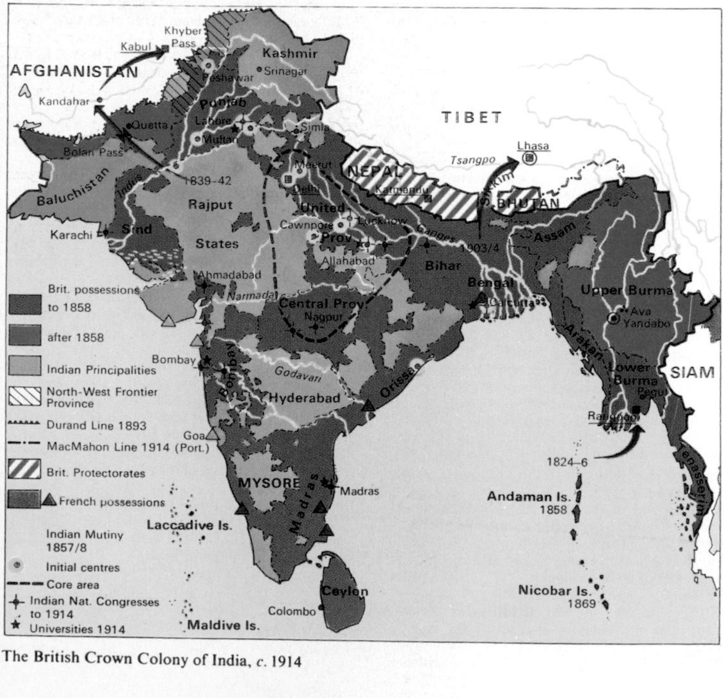

The British Crown Colony of India, *c.* 1914

Brit. Rule 1750–1858

The **E. India Co.** (I, p. 275) to safeguard its trading interests interfered in the power struggles of the Ind. princes. Bribery, the granting of pensions and milit. aid were rewarded with administrative rights (*Diwani*) and the power to levy taxes in the provinces or polit. control through 'residents' or 'agents'. Brit. domination was established by **Robert Clive** I, p. 283).

1757 Vict. at Plassey, then at Buxar (1764): the Nawab of Bengal and the Nawab of Oudh were rendered powerless. The Grand Mogul surrendered

1765 the 'Diwani' over Bengal and Bihar.

1773 The Regulating Act (p. 31): transformation of the E. India Company into a Brit. administrative agency. The first Brit. governor-general appointed.

1773–85 Warren Hastings reorganized the legal system and admin. and overcame the coalition of Britain's 3 most important enemies: the **Maratha League**, the **Nizam of Hyderabad** and **Hyder Ali**, the usurper of **Mysore**.

1795–1815 Conquest of Dutch Ceylon.

1798–1805 Governor-General Lord Wellesley strove for hegemony: he disarmed the Nizam (1798); Mysore became a vassal state (1799); annexation of the Carnatic (1801). The Maratha League disintegrated because of internal disorders.

1803 Seizure of Delhi and Agra.

Nepal: the **Gurkhas**, a mountain people, expanded after 1768. The

1814–16 Gurkha War ended with the Treaty of Sagauli: Nepal became a protectorate of Britain, which was allowed to hire Gurkha warrior (exceptionally able Ind. soldiers and fighters).

Cen. India: civil wars, highwaymen and raids by bandits made intervention necessary.

1817–18 3rd Marathan War: subjugation of the Marathan and Rajput states.

Burma: the rivalry between upper (Ava) and lower (Pegu) Burma was overcome by King ALAUNGPAYA [1753–60]. His successors expanded the newly founded empire. Incursions into Bengal (1813) and Assam (1822) caused the

1824–6 1st Burmese War: Brit. landing in Rangoon. By the Treaty of Yandabo, Brit. India obtained Tenasserim, Arakan and Assam.

1852 During the 2nd Burmese War, lower Burma was annexed.

1885–6 3rd Burmese War: incorporation of the remainder of Burma into Brit. India (1891).

Afghanistan: concern over Rus. expansion in Cen. Asia (p. 113) prompted Britain to interfere in the struggles over the throne during the

1839–42 1st Afghan War. After the raid on the Brit. garrison in Kabul, the British left the country.

The Sikh State (cf. I, p. 229): expansion of the milit. state under

1799–1839 RANJIT SINGH.

1809 Treaty of Amritsar: the Sutlej river was to form the border with Brit. India.

1849 Brit. annexation of the Punjab.

Expansion of the colon. empire: heirless Ind. principalities were confiscated.

1835 Introduction of the Brit. university system; popular Ind. education and languages were neglected. Dislike of alien influences exploded in the

1857–8 Ind. Mutiny: mutinies, massacres and initial successes of the Sepoys (Ind. troops): proclamation of the last Mogul BAHADUR SHAH II as 'Emperor of India' in Delhi. Brit. reinforcements, Sikhs and Gurkhas put down the rebels.

1858 Dissolution of the E. India Co.; India became a Brit. viceroyalty.

The Brit. Crown Colony (1858–1914)

1877 Queen VICTORIA (p. 103) assumed the title 'Empress of India'. To safeguard the Ind. possessions, dependent buffer states were created: **Nepal** 1816; **Bhutan** 1865; **Sikkim** 1890.

1876–87 Incorporation of **Baluchistan**. Afghan border tribes were reconciled by

1898–1905 Viceroy Lord Curzon: the North-west Province was created (1901).

1903–4 Expedition to **Tibet**.

1904 Trade agreement of Lhasa; the Conference of Simla strove for Tib. autonomy from China.

Econ. life: development of the country (railways, irrigation projects, harbours). Import of Brit. indust. products dest. the self-supporting village economies and Ind. cotton production. Unemployment and over-population. Development of extensive jute, tea and indigo plantations with Brit. capital.

The Ind. Nat. movement: a Europeanized Ind. élite crystallized in the colleges and universities. Its conscious fostering of nat. traditions, running counter to prevailing soc. disadvantages and a feeling of cult. despondency, did not at first have any broad effect because of polit. apathy and relig. and class prejudices (the caste system). Relig. reforms were the precondition for internal renewal: RAM MOHAN ROY (1772–1833) taught the

1828 Brahma Samaj (the fusion of Ind. and Christ. religions). DAYANAND SARASVATI (1828–83), in the *Arya Samaj* (1875), cal. for a return to the ancient teachings (Veda). The village guru **Ramkrishna** (1836–86) combined Western learning with Hindu piety.

1885 Founding of the Ind. Nat. Congress to participate in the gvt. The British reacted uncertainly: they fostered internal Ind. conflicts; but afterwards, in

1892, they granted conditional suffrage for the cen. parliament and allowed the employment of Indians as higher officials in the municipal or prov. admin. and the council of the viceroy. Famines and epidemics of plague (1896/7), but esp. the Jap. vict. over Russia (p. 115), strengthened the 'New Party' of the extremists under TILAK (1856–1920). Nat. dissatisfaction over the partition of

1905 Bengal (creation of a new province with a Moslem majority): boycott of Brit. textiles, bombings. The Isl. minority advanced its claims through the **Moslem League** (est. 1906). Nevertheless, the partition was undone; but

1911 the site of the cen. gvt was transferred to the city of the Moguls, Delhi.

1916 Pact of Lucknow: Hindus and Moslems jointly called for autonomy.

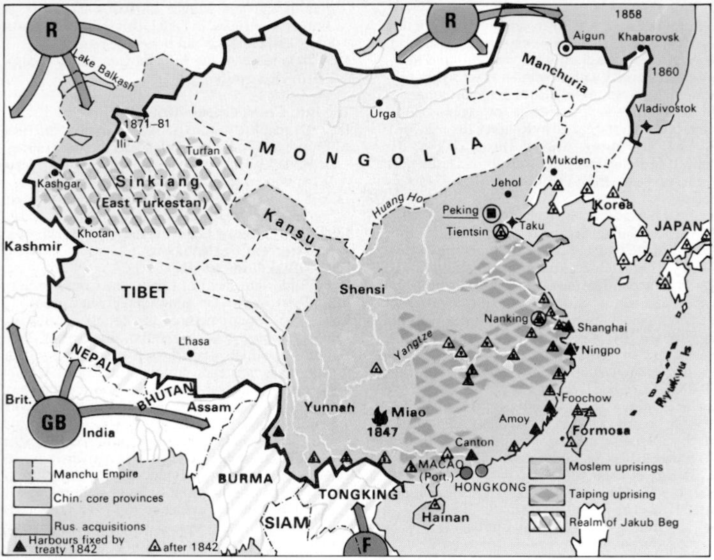

China, *c.* 1860

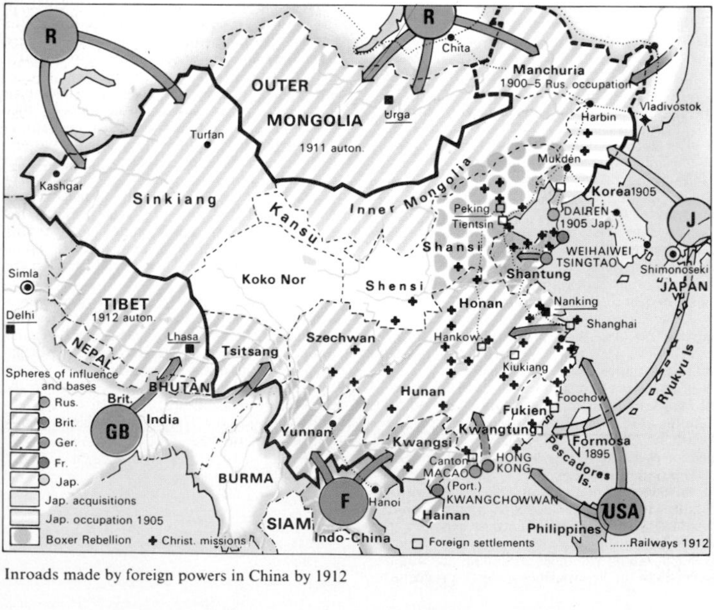

Inroads made by foreign powers in China by 1912

Japan: the Tokugawa Shogunate

Strictly secluding Japan from the outside world, the Shogun buttressed his power by police-state methods and by depriving the Tenno, who was to be revered only as the relig. head, of polit. power. The feudal soc. order found the court nobility (*Kuge*) at the top, followed by the feudal lords required to reside at court (*Daimyo*), officials and vassals (*samurai*), the people (*Heimin*) and the pariah (*eta*; *hinin*). Under the 'dog-Shogun'

1680–1709 TSUNAYOSHI, lyrical poetry and the theatre, and later also art (coloured woodcuts), flowered.

1716–45 YOSHIMUNE improved the lot of the peasantry and taxed the luxuries of the samurai caste. After 1720, admission of Eur. books. Rapid decline of the shogunate with the reign of

1761–86 IEHARU: increasing indebtedness and sinking morale of the daimyos and samurai, suffering of the peasants and natural catastrophes. Prepared by the 'romantic' KAMO MABUCHI (1697–1769), the '4 great men' (AZUMA MARO, 1768–1830, and his pupils) revived the nat. **Shinto movement:** elevation of the Tenno cult and de-emphasis of the Shogunate.

1853–4 Opening of Japan to for. powers (p. 115).

The Intrusion of Eur. Powers into China

Up to the first half of the 19th cent., governmentally controlled for. trade through the Hong merchants (I, p. 275). Waged against the illegal Brit. importation of opium, the

1840–42 Opium War demonstrated the superiority of Eur. weapons.

1842 Peace of Nanking: cession of Hongkong; trade concessions for 5 specified harbours. After 1844, similar 'lopsided treaties' were concluded, regulating the establishment of extraterrit. settlements with auton. admins., courts, police and customs. Subs. a general quest for privileges set in; China's milit. weakness tempted the Eur. powers to pursue aggressive intentions. Because of the misuse of the Brit. flag by a Chin. junk (Lorcha), the Brit.-Fr.-Chin.

1856–8 Lorcha War broke out: Fort Taku was taken. After the violation of the Treaty of Tientsin (1858), Peking was occupied.

1860 Treaty of Peking: establishment of Eur. embassies; liberalization of trade and Christ. miss. activity. Fixing of the Russo-Chin. border in the

1858 Treaty of Aigun; cession of the coastal provinces in 1860.

1870 Rising in Tientsin: murder of the Fr. consul and Eur. retaliatory expedition; 1885 recognition of the Fr. protectorate over Tongking; 1886 cession of Burma to Britain. During the

1894 Sino-Jap. War (p. 115), loss of Formosa. In retaliation for the murder of two missionaries, Ger. occupation of Tsingtao (1897); Germany was granted a concession for the Shantung railway and,

1898, in a leasing agreement obtained Kiaochow for 99 yrs. Similar agreements were concluded with Russia (Dairen), Britain (Weihaiwei), and France (Kwangchowwan). Hatred for the 'for. devils' found expression in the

1900 Boxer Rising: massacre of Christians, murder of the Ger. ambassador; punitive expedition under Ger. command (Count WALDERSEE).

1901 The Boxer protocol provided for Chin. atonement. Mutual suspicion prevented a partition of China; the colon. powers agreed to an **'open door policy'** (a common market for the 'econ. development' of China).

The Decline of the Manchu Empire

The Opium War opened China to the Western world. Because of its connection with commerce and politics, Christ. miss. activity had little success. On the other hand, Christ. charitable work had significant results (orphanages, hospitals). Miss. schools spread the knowledge of Eur. science and civilization. The trad. structure of China was thereby upset and altered, a process accompanied by revolutionary upheavals.

1850–64 The Taiping Rebellion: carried out by a millennialist sect endeavouring to establish a Christ.-Taoist 'Heavenly kdm'; agrarian reforms. 1853 conquest of Nanking. Originating in Yunnan,

1864–78 Moslem uprisings gained ground.

1865–77 JAKUB BEG, Khan of Kashgar, est. a Turk. state to unite all Moslems. Relying in part on Eur. aid, Chancellor **Li Hung-chang** (1823–1901) restored the imp. order (a group of adventurers under Major GORDON playing a role). The regency council, carrying out the affairs of the Emperors T'UNG CHIH [1861–74] and KUANG HSU [1875–1908], was deprived of power by the widow of the Emperor HSIEN FENG

1881–9 Tzu Hsi, who as Dowager Empress governed to all practical purposes as sole ruler.

Intrusion of Western capitalism: cheap imports of indust. goods dest. crafts and trades as soc. conditions and the standard of life decayed in the densely settled rural areas. A proletariat and a revolutionary intelligentsia developed in the ports. Translators (YEN-FU, 1853–1921) provided them with the works of Western thinkers. Reformers like K'ANG YU-WEI (1858–1927) influenced the emperor. His reforms were met by a

1898 *coup d'état* of the reactionaries (TZU-HSI): internment of the emperor, execution of the reformer, aid to the 'Boxers'. For. pressure and domestic powerlessness made necessary the

1905 abolition of the old examination system (I, p. 177) and the reform of the army (General **Yuan Shih-kai**, 1859–1916).

1905 Founding of the Kuomintang (Nat. People's party) by the physician **Sun Yat-sen** (1866–1925). His programme of the '3 principles' (auton. nat. life, democracy, a guaranteed income for all) was spread by students and pupils of the missions.

1911 Revolution of the Young Chinese for the rad. renewal of China; abdication of the Manchu dynasty in 1912; SUN YAT-SEN proclaimed the republic in Nanking; but he handed the presidency to YUAN SHIH-KAI so as to be free to win the army for the task of preserving the unity of the empire. **Mongolia** and **Tibet** declared their independence.

Havana
CUBA 1898
DOMINICAN REP.
Guantánamo
HAITI
Puerto Rico 1898 to USA
Under Protection of
USA
Caracas
Panama Canal
Panama
PANAMA 1903
VENEZUELA
Orinoco
Georgetown
Paramaribo
Cayenne
Guiana
Brit.
Dutch
Fr.
Bogotá
COLOMBIA
Equator
ECUADOR
Oriente
Rio Negro
Border adjustments 1900–10
Amazon
Xingu
Acre 1899–1903 (Free State)
Madeira
Marañón
Yungay
PERU
BRAZIL
Empire to 1889
Ancón
Lima
Callao
Miraflores
São Francisco
La Paz
BOLIVIA
Tacna
Arica
1879–83
Atacama
Antofagasta
Paraná
Petrópolis
PARAGUAY
1865–70
Asunción
Rio de Janeiro
Uruguay
CHILE
ARGENTINA
URUGUAY
Pavon
Valparaiso
Santiago
Montevideo
Buenos Aires
ind. 1852–9
Patagonia
1899–1902
Falkland Is. 1833 Brit.
Tierra del Fuego
Cape Horn
1831–61 REP. NEW GRANADA
Conflicts (Circles in colours of states involved)
Temporarily independent
Disputed territory
Border revisions

South America in the 19th cent.

The introduction of mod. constitutions did not lead to stability in the new states. Class, party and racial conflicts, the differences between advocates of unitary and fed. forms of gvt found expression in constantly alternating revolutions and counter-revolutions, anarchy and milit. dictatorships. Caudillos (strong leaders), who came to power through *pronunciamientos* (milit. revolutions accompanied by a statement of intention) developed a style of authoritarian democracy. In the tropical areas, the old Creole aristocracy was substantially weakened and, in part, migrated back to Europe. Coloured and racially mixed people evolved their own strata of leadership. A white upper bourgeoisie retained its position in the climatically moderate regions. Of the new states:

- Argentina and Uruguay were predominantly white;
- Brazil, Chile, the W. Ind. and Cen. Amer. states were of predominantly mixed stock;
- Bolivia, Venezuela, Colombia, Peru, Ecuador and Paraguay had a predominantly Ind. pop.

The influx of Brit. and N. Amer. capital gave rise to a new phase of development by the end of the 19th cent.: increase of Eur. immigration, railway building, the development of large-scale grain production and cattle raising in a plantation economy, and the production of raw materials (saltpetre, tin, copper). A white petit bourgeoisie and a working class developed in Argentina, southern Brazil and Chile. Territ. claims along the borders led to tensions and wars.

Brazil: during the lib. reign of

1831–89 PEDRO II the economy was stabilized by the colonization of the interior, Eur. immigration and the export of coffee and rubber.

1888 The abolition of slavery caused planters and liberals to unite to overthrow the monarchy (1889). Expedient treaties expanded the territory of the **Republic of the United States of Brazil** by 1910.

Paraguay lost over 70% of its pop. as a result of the

1865–70 Paraguayan War with Brazil, Argentina and Uruguay, a war which had been caused by the excessive expansionist ambitions of the dictator F. SOLANO LÓPEZ [1862–70].

Argentina: President **Juan Manuel de Rosas** [1829–52] terminated internal upheavals.

1833 Britain compelled Argentina to cede the Falkland Islands. The 'educator of the nation',

1868–74 President SARMIENTO promoted schools and universities, immigration, railways and communication. The struggle with the Pampas Indians was decided by

1880–86, 1898–1904 President ROCA, who obtained

1902 Patagonia as a result of arbitration. Argentina developed to become the foremost econ. power of Lat. America.

Peru: dictatorial powers were assumed by Marshall RAMÓN CASTILLA (1797–1867) after the

1842–5 civil war. Peru was defeated by Chile in the

1879–83 'Nitrate War', precipitated by the discovery of the value of the saltpetre deposits as agricultural nitrate fertilizer; subs. it was ruled by successive milit. régimes.

Bolivia: as a result of the 'Nitrate War', Bolivia lost the province of Atacama, and with it access to the sea; but, because of its rich resources of tin, the econ. loss was slight.

Chile: gained naval supremacy in the 'Nitrate War' and retained its conquests in the Peace of Ancón.

1891 Congressional revolution. Subs. parl. gvt.

Colombia (New Granada): constant civil wars between advocates of a unitary form of gvt and the federalists, liberals and clericals. After the formation of the confederation of 8 states (1858)

1861 proclamation of the United States of Colombia. As a result of U.S. efforts,

1903 Panama separated (p. 117).

Venezuela: the federalist constitution was defended during the

1861–8 Federalist War; yet the country remained under dictatorial rule.

1902 A naval blockade by Eur. powers was launched in protest against the violation of the rights of for. nationals by President CASTROS [1899–1908].

Ecuador: the gvt of President MORENO [1860–65, 69–75] emphasized friendly relations with the Church. After his assassination, liberals and clericals came into conflict.

Cen. America: attempts at unifying the 5 states failed; increasing finan. dependence on the U.S. developed into polit. tutelage.

Mexico: owing to the secession of Texas (1836) and the

1846–8 war with the U.S., the country underwent a severe crisis.

1853 The sale of Southern Arizona brought northern Mexico to the U.S. In reaction against the clerical régime of the dictator SANTA ANA (p. 53), overthrown in 1855,

1858–72 Benito Juárez brought the immense clerical possessions into the public domain and abolished clerical and milit. privileges.

1858–61 Civil war between the clerical and lib. parties, incl. intervention by Brit., Fr. and Sp. troops.

1863 Fr. conquest of Puebla and entry into Mexico City. Following efforts by NAPOLEON III (p. 71), an assembly of notables proclaimed the empire and offered the throne to the Archduke MAXIMILIAN of Austria. Because of protests by the U.S. (violation of the Monroe Doctrine, p. 53) France was forced to withdraw her troops.

1867 Seizure of Queretaro by the republicans; MAXIMILIAN shot on orders from JUÁREZ.

1877–80, 1884–1911 Presidency of PORFIRIO DIAZ, who orientated his for. policy towards Japan and England. After his abdication, renewed unrest.

The W. Indies: the main transit ports for the slave trade lost in importance following the prohibition of slavery (1833 in the Brit. colonies, as late as 1883 in those of Spain). The Negroes became day-labourers on the plantations or swelled the urban proletariat.

1844 Re-establishment of the Domin. Republic, which, from 1861, was under Sp. protection; after 1865, U.S. influence increased (1905–7 control of the finances).

Cuba: supported by the U.S.A., Cuba rebelled against Spain in 1895, leading to the

1898 Sp.-Amer. War (p. 117). As protector of the new Cuban Republic, the U.S. took leases on naval stations (Guantánamo).

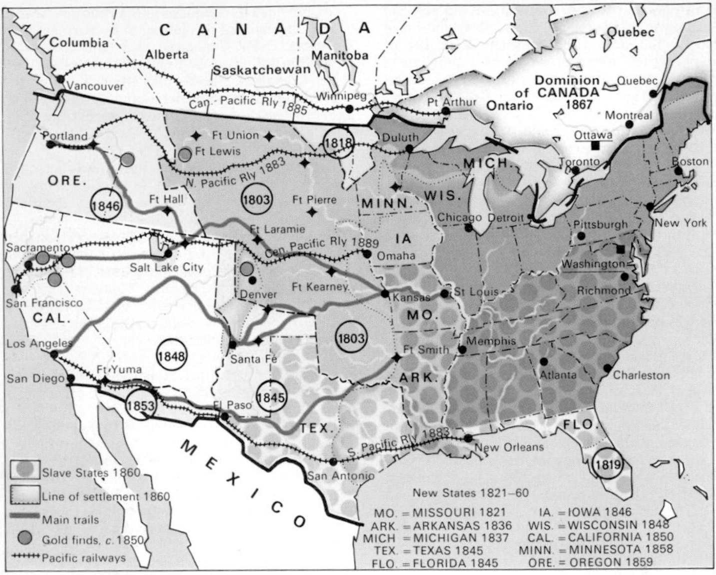

The United States, *c.* 1850

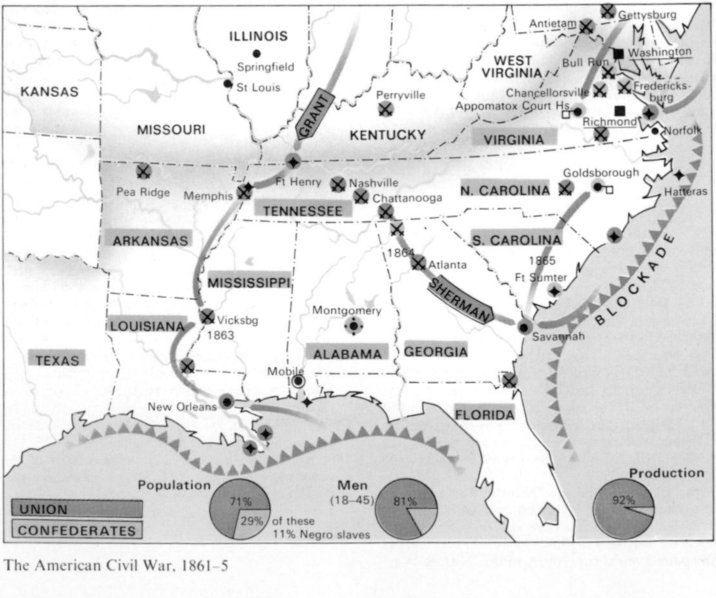

The American Civil War, 1861–5

The Opening of the West

The pop. increased from 9·6 mil. in 1820 (in 23 states) to 31·3 mil. in 1860 (in 33 states), a growth of 226%. The advance to the w. brought territ. gains to the U.S.

1819 Purchase of Florida from Spain.

1823 Monroe Doctrine (p. 53): proscription of any interference in Amer. affairs by Eur. states.

1845 Admission of Texas into the Union.

1848 Peace of Guadalupe-Hidalgo: Mexico lost all territory N. of the Rio Grande. The U.S. became a transcontinental power. After the

1846 Oregon Treaty, the 49th parallel of latitude became the border with Canada.

Between 1830 and 1860 immigration increased and amounted to 4·6 mil. The 'Prot. British' among the immigrants remained politically dominant. In terms of numbers it was the Irish (39%) and the Germans (30%), among them disappointed democrats like CARL SCHURZ (1829–1906), who led. The frontier shifted to the w. Regulated by the Homestead Law (1862), the free land was claimed in 3 waves: squatters, pioneers and trappers followed by farmers, who were again followed by merchants, speculators and craftsmen. The Indians were fought and forced into reservations. The discovery of minerals and gold accelerated the westward movement (esp. the California Gold Rush of 1848–9). The land was exploited unscrupulously; scarcity of labour brought an increased production of agricultural machinery and created new indust. markets. Overland trails and railroads spanned enormous distances (1862–9 construction of the first transcontinental railroad). The **West**, the concept of the 'land of the unlimited possibilities' and the 'melting-pot' for all immigrants, shaped the 'Amer. way of life' for the 'little man'. The polit. leadership of the **Democratic party** was given new direction through the presidency of General **Andrew Jackson** [1829–37]. This 'self-made man' and 'hero of New Orleans' (p. 15) united farmers and workers against the capital of the E.; he eliminated all restrictions on suffrage and introduced the 'spoils system' ('to the victor the spoils': appointment of the party faithful to office). The Whigs, his opponents, also adopted the methods of 'Jacksonian democracy'.

The Civil War (1861–5)

The differences between E. and W. came to be overshadowed by the tensions between N. and S., indust. states and plantation states, dem. **Yankees** and aristocratic planters, protective tariffs and free trade. Appealing to human rights, the N. demanded the abolition of slavery; the S. feared the threat to its worldwide monopoly in 'King Cotton'.

1820 The Missouri Compromise drew the line between slaving and non-slaving states, but did not bring lasting settlement. Using the **Liberator** as his forum, W. GARRISON led the press campaign against slavery from 1831; the 'Amer. Anti-Slavery Society' helped Negroes to escape from the S.

1847 Establishment of the Afr. Free State of Liberia for the settlement of Amer. Negroes. To prevent secession, the

1850 Compromise of 1850 (CLAY Compromise) left the question of slavery to individual states. However, among other things, the worldwide success of HARRIET BEECHER STOWE's *Uncle Tom's Cabin* (1852) strengthened the hand of the abolitionists. The conflict over the

1854 Kansas-Nebraska Act and the introduction of slavery in the western territories led to the establishment of the **Republican party**. Its electoral vict. split the Union. S. Carolina and 10 addit. states formed

1861 the Confederate States of America (Richmond as cap.) under President JEFFERSON DAVIS (1808–89). His opponent was the Republican

1861–5 Abraham Lincoln. Born in 1809 in Kentucky, formerly a backwoodsman, he became a lawyer, a Whig member of the House of Representatives from Illinois and the 16th president of the U.S.A. A moderate on the question of slavery, he fought with determination for the preservation of the Union in the

1861–5 Civil War. Initially the struggle was carried on with volunteers equipped with modern arms (cannon mounted on rail wagons, repeating rifles and armoured naval vessels). A naval blockade limited shipments of war materials to the S.; the S. was recognized as a belligerent force if not as an independent gvt by Britain and France (see Mexico, p. 93), while Russia tended to side with the N. The Confederates resisted stubbornly, even though they lacked the finan. and indust. resources of the N. Led by the finest strategist of the war, General ROBERT E. LEE (1807–70), they were victorious at Bull Run 1861 and 1862, Fredericksburg 1862 and Chancellorsville 1863; however, the S. was unable to break the supremacy in men and materials of the N. (rapidly accelerating production of war materials).

Jan. 1863 Emancipation proclamation of LINCOLN.

Jul. 1863 The struggle at Gettysburg was decisive: General LEE was forced to retreat. General SHERMAN's 'scorched earth' campaigns through Georgia and Carolina caused famine and unrule.

Apr. 1865 LEE surrendered unconditionally to General GRANT at the Appomatox Courthouse. Shortly thereafter LINCOLN was assassinated by JOHN WILKES BOOTH, an actor of Southern extremist views, in Ford's Theatre, Washington.

The Civil War brought heavy losses to both sides (over 600,000 dead, many through epidemics in hospitals and prison camps); the war cost more than $8,000 mil.; the S. was ruined.

Significance: the Union was preserved; under the leadership of the N. the U.S. became an industrialized econ. power. The infl. and econ. importance of the S. gave way to some extent in face of the increase of cotton production in Egypt and India, though production continued to increase up to the First World War. The slavery question turned into a socially and politically unresolved racial problem.

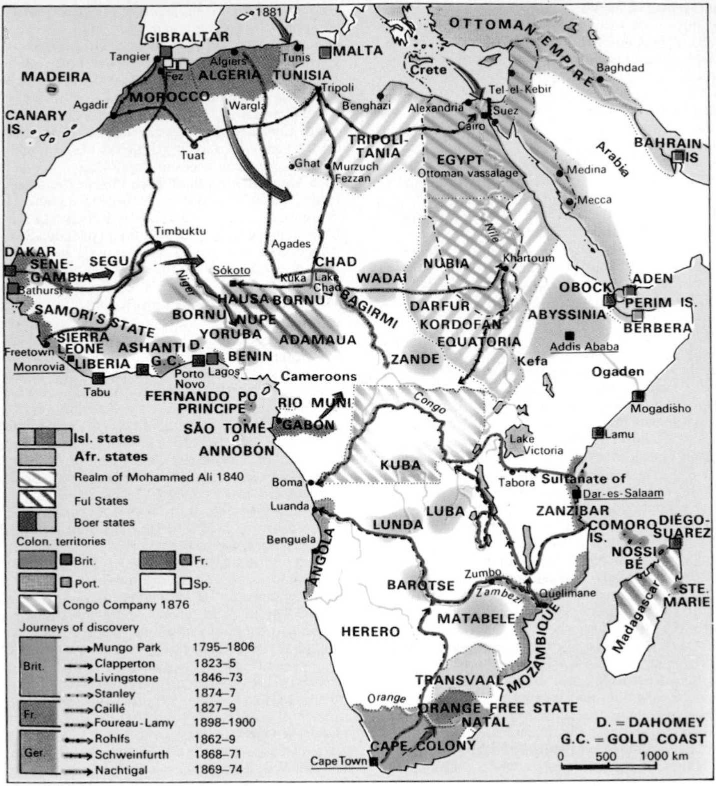

1881
GIBRALTAR
Tangier
Fez
Algiers
ALGERIA
Tunis
TUNISIA
MALTA
OTTOMAN EMPIRE
Crete
Baghdad
MADEIRA
MOROCCO
Agadir
CANARY IS.
Wargla
Tripoli
Benghazi
Alexandria
Tel-el-Kebir
Suez
Cairo
Tuat
TRIPOLITANIA
EGYPT
Ottoman vassalage
Arabia
BAHRAIN IS
Ghat
Murzuch
Fezzan
Medina
Mecca
Nile
Timbuktu
Agades
DAKAR
SENEGAMBIA
SEGU
Bathurst
Niger
Sókoto
Kuka
Lake Chad
CHAD
WADAI
NUBIA
Khartoum
ADEN
OBOCK
PERIM IS.
BERBERA
HAUSA
BORNU
BAGIRMI
DARFUR
KORDOFAN
ABYSSINIA
SAMORI'S STATE
BORNU
NUPE
YORUBA
ADAMAUA
EQUATORIA
Addis Ababa
SIERRA LEONE
Freetown
Monrovia
LIBERIA
ASHANTI
D.
G.C.
BENIN
ZANDE
Kefa
Porto Novo
Lagos
Cameroons
Ogaden
Tabu
FERNANDO PO
PRINCIPE
RIO MUNI
Congo
Mogadisho
SÃO TOMÉ
GABON
ANNOBÓN
Lake Victoria
Lamu
KUBA
Boma
Tabora
Sultanate of
Dar-es-Salaam
ZANZIBAR
Luanda
LUBA
LUNDA
COMORO IS.
DIÉGO-SUAREZ
Benguela
ANGOLA
NOSSI BÉ
BAROTSE
Zumbo
Zambezi
Quelimane
STE. MARIE
Madagascar
MATABELE
HERERO
MOZAMBIQUE
TRANSVAAL
Orange
ORANGE FREE STATE
NATAL
CAPE COLONY
Cape Town
D. = DAHOMEY
G.C. = GOLD COAST
0 500 1000 km

Isl. states
Afr. states
Realm of Mohammed Ali 1840
Ful States
Boer states
Colon. territories
Brit.
Fr.
Port.
Sp.
Congo Company 1876
Journeys of discovery

Brit.	Mungo Park	1795–1806
	Clapperton	1823–5
	Livingstone	1846–73
	Stanley	1874–7
Fr.	Caillé	1827–9
	Foureau-Lamy	1898–1900
Ger.	Rohlfs	1862–9
	Schweinfurth	1868–71
	Nachtigal	1869–74

Africa before the colonial partition, *c.* 1870

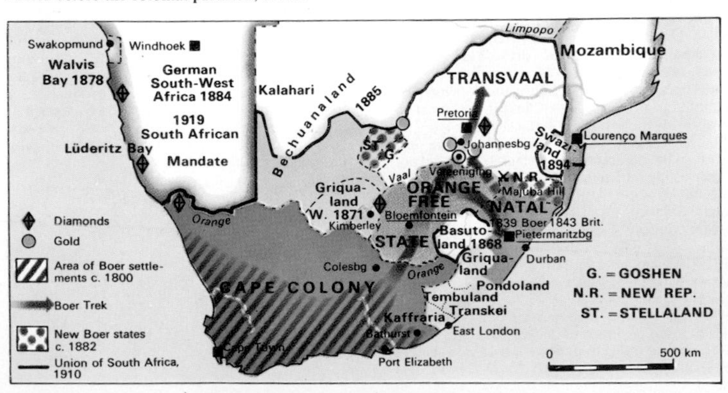

South Africa in the 19th cent.

The Dissolution of Ott. Rule

Egypt:

1811 After the elimination of the Mamelukes MOHAMMED ALI (p. 87) consolidated his power: development of the country with Fr. aid; however, the tax burden was heavy.

1820–22 Subjugation of Nubia, foundation of Khartoum in 1823. Eur. intervention made it impossible for Egypt to cut the ties of Ott. sovereignty.

1859–69 Construction of the Suez Canal (p. 71).

1863–79 ISMAIL PASHA conquered Darfur (1874), fought against Abyssinia, but also wasted funds for the construction of buildings and railways and in the effort to effect reforms. This led to the

1875 sale of the Egypt. shares in the Suez Canal Co. to Britain.

1881 Nat. uprising (under the minister of war, ARABI PASHA) in Alexandria and **Brit. intervention.**

1882 Establishment of a Brit. protectorate over Egypt (p. 103).

The Eastern Sudan (p. 118): MOHAMMED AHMED (1840–85), the **Mahdi** (Arab. for 'the Guided One'), preached a holy war against Egypt.

1882–5 The Mahdi uprising.

1885 The 10-month siege of Khartoum, culminating in its fall and the death of its defender, General CHARLES GORDON (1833–85). EMIN PASHA (EDUARD SCHNITZER), governor-general of Equatoria, held out until freed by STANLEY in 1888. Brit. power was re-established in the Sudan under Lord **Kitchener** (1850–1916) by the

1898 vict. over the Mahdists at Omdurman.

1899 The Sudan became an Anglo-Egypt. condominium.

The Berber States: Ott. governors, janissaries, corsairs and the consuls of Eur. states competed for power. After 1830 France conquered

Algeria (p. 107).

1880 The Madrid Convention settled the rights of Eur. states in relation to the Sultanate of **Morocco** (the Alid Dynasty).

Africa before the Imperialistic Partition

The Isl. States: feudal arrangements dominated the confederations of local tribes.

El Hadj Omar (d. 1864) established a theocracy in the Western Sudan. In

1854 he clashed with Fr. interests expanding along the Upper Niger;

1861 seizure of Segu, which OMAR's son AHMANDU (d. 1898) was able to retain.

Samori Turé (d. 1900) administered justice severely.

1887 Treaty placing the state under Fr. protection.

The Ful States (Fulani States): of unknown origin, the Ful nomads conquered the city states of the Hausa, exc. Bornu and Kahem, under **Usman dan Fodio** (1754–*c.* 1815). MOHAMMED BELLO (d. 1837), the Master of Sokoto, gained sovereignty over the Ful States. Once the Brit. protectorate had been est., the power of the emirs was secured.

Rabeh (d. 1900), the 'Afr. Napoleon', expanded his rule (p. 118) over Bornu and Bagirmi; he was defeated by Fr. troops in 1900.

Eastern Africa: the Sultanate of Zanzibar was the centre of the slave trade. As a defence against Arab. slavers, native chiefs concluded protective treaties with Brit. (JACKSON) and Ger. (PETERS) representatives.

Afr. states: feudal despotisms (such as that of the Ashanti) exploited Afr. tribes to benefit from the slave trade. King **Geso of Dahomey** (1818–58) raised regiments of female soldiers and attacked **Yoruba**, the 'land of the big cities'. Highly developed art (cast bronze) and admin. were also found in **Benin**.

Liberia: founded in 1822, the settlement of freed and returned slaves from the U.S. became an ind. republic in 1847.

Abyssinia: the usurper RAS KASA united the Coptic-Christ. empire

1853 taking the name THEODORUS II.

1867–8 Brit. punitive expedition (Lord NAPIER).

1872–89 The Brit. pretender JOHN IV repulsed Egypt. attacks (1875–9).

1889–1910 Aided by Italy, MENELIK II proclaimed himself **Negus Negesti** (p. 119).

S. Africa: Chaka (the 's. Afr. Attila'), developed a new technique of combat at close quarters and transformed his Bantu followers into the warrior state of the **Zulus**. His advance into Natal displaced all the s. Afr. Bantu peoples.

The Eur. Colon. Powers: Brit. prohibitions of the slave trade (1807), slavery (1833) and the exportation of slaves (1841) had paralysed the trade. Dan. and Dutch trading posts were given up. Only France continued to build up its colon. empire, proceeding from Algeria, Senegambia and Gabon, from the mid 19th cent. (p. 107). **Christ. missionaries** est. mission stations, hospitals and schools. With the exploration of the interior the interest of the colon. powers increased. LEOPOLD II of Belgium (p. 85) was the first to recognize possibilities of exploitation. In the employ of the Congo Co., est. by LEOPOLD, **Henry Morton Stanley** (1841–1904), who had won fame as the journalist who had made contact with the great miss.-explorer DAVID LIVINGSTONE in 1871, explored the Congo region. It was granted to LEOPOLD at the

1884–5 Congress of Berlin over Brit.-Port. claims.

The S. Afr. Boer States (1842–1902)

Internal conflicts and the freeing of the slaves in the Brit. Cape Colony (after 1806 and 1814) prompted *c.* 10,000 con. Boers to undertake

1836–44 the 'Great Trek' into the interior. After struggles with the Zulus and the Brit. annexation of Natal, they est.

1842 the Orange Free State (Brit. till 1854) and the

1853 Transvaal (the s. Afr. Republic). The discovery of gold attracted immigrants (*Uitlanders*).

1877 Brit. annexation of the Transvaal, leading to a

1880–81 Boer uprising and defeat for the British.

1883–1902 President 'Ohm' Kruger led the ind. republic. Gold deposits nr Johannesburg (est. 1886) aroused Brit. interest. The area was ringed by Brit. colonies (Bechuanaland, Swaziland, Rhodesia). RHODES (p. 103) supported the futile 'Jameson Raid' (1895–6), intended to lead to the fall of KRUGER.

1899–1902 The Boer War: the Boers scored initial successes under Generals **Smuts** (1870–1950), BOTHA and HERZOG; but Brit. milit. superiority (KITCHENER) and the tough Brit. conduct of the war (concentration camps) broke the Boers.

1902 Peace of Vereeniging. The Boer republics lost their independence (p. 103).

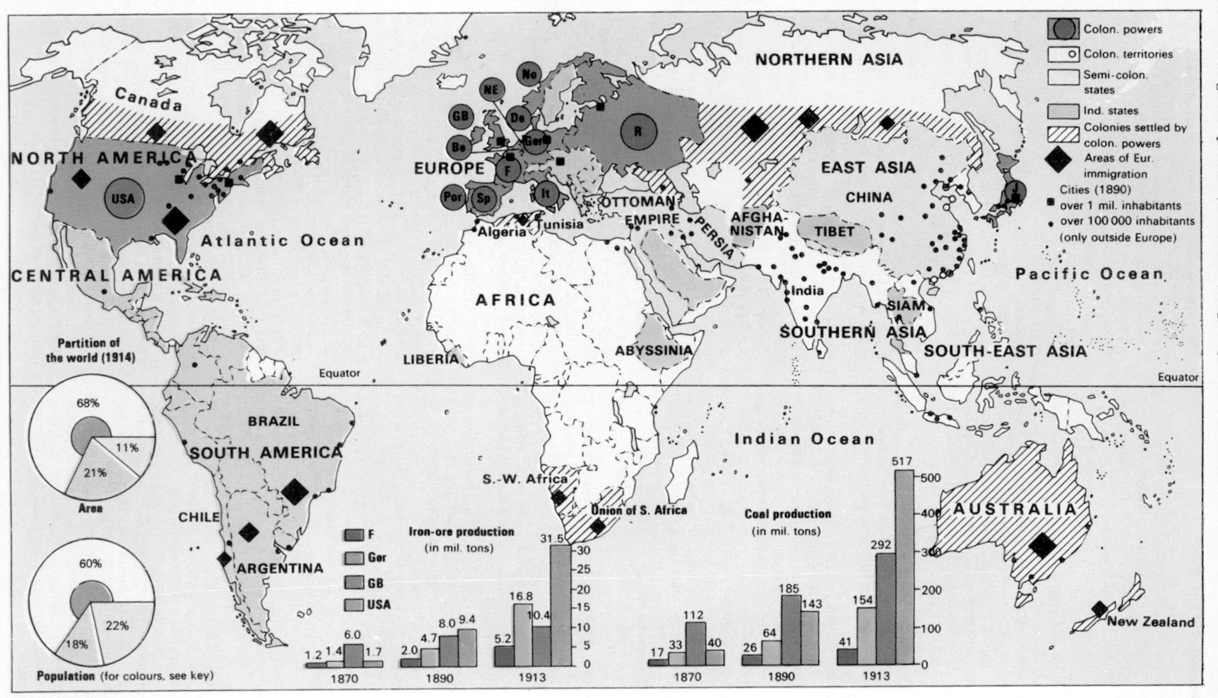

The colonial distribution of the world, 1914

Mod. Imperialism
(Lat. *imperium* = power of command). Continuing the colon. policies of the 16th–18th cents. (I, pp. 225, 275f.), the great powers after 1880 competed with one another in the econ. and polit. **partition of the world**. They were governed by the conviction that the balance of power as well as the wealth and power of the nations would thereby be determined. As the 19th cent. advanced two types of colony developed: (a) **settlement colonies**, est. by emigrants who left their homes for relig. or polit. reasons, or because their econ. survival was threatened (overpopulation); (b) **commercial colonies** (in part for. bases with trading concessions), used as sources of raw materials (India, Africa). The beneficiaries were private trading companies (chartered companies), which appealed to the state for the protection of their interests. The formation of **colon. empires** or econ. spheres of interest ('dollar imperialism', p. 117) had a variety of causes (see below).

High Capitalism
Rapid econ. rise of the indust. states: the U.S.A., Britain, Germany; followed by France and Japan; Italy and Russia were slowly developing. **Technical and sc. advances** (p. 65) opened up new sources of **energy** (electricity, oil) and **branches of industry** (electrical and chemical); **transportation and communications** (telegraph, telephone) created the preconditions for world-wide trade and economic connections. **Increasing capital investments** for new methods of production, large urban construction projects, railways, canals and harbours altered econ. structures.
Monopoly capitalism (the fusion of companies in large enterprises): **stock-issuing corporations**, concerns rationalizing purchases of raw materials and distribution; they were structured horizontally (firms of the same branch) or vertically (uniting companies engaged in various stages of production, such as mines, foundries and machine factories); **cartels** agreeing to limit production and fix prices developed; **syndicates** with joint marketing organizations to influence the market were formed; **trusts** attempted to control the market through monopoly.
Finan. capitalism: development of large **banking institutions** to supply credits (purchase and sale of stocks, mortgages, etc.). The export of capital and the int. cooperation of capital increased the power of **high finance**, which gained polit. influence.
Consequences: production and the soc. product increased, the general standard of living, including that of the workers, was raised. Migration from the countryside into the cities, large urban areas and new occupations (white-collar workers) altered soc. structures and ways of life. Unions and polit. parties promoted the **democratization** of the masses. **Increasing entanglement of the state and the economics of finance** because of the state-ownership of transport facilities and public utilities (railways, postal services, water and gas supplies) and public control of finan. affairs (**cen. banks** to regulate the circulation of money and control the currency). Econ. problems (int. competition over raw materials, markets, capital investments) became polit. problems.
Colon. policies: the colonies, the importance of which were overestimated, were expected to render states economically self-sufficient (**autarchy**), which meant independence from world-wide competition and econ. crises through the opening of new sources of raw materials and the preservation of the standard of living, imperilled because of **overpopulation** (see medical progress, p. 65) and increasing mass demands. The thought of the period was dominated by conceptions of 'people without space to expand' joined to Malthusian theories (p. 43). Emigration of an increased domestic market through expanding purchasing power was not yet recognized. Econ. and colon. expansion was therefore demanded for the sake of sustaining the nation.
Protective tariffs (neo-mercantilism) began to be introduced and bilateral trade agreements and tariffs were used as weapons to secure autarchy; these measures led to further concentration of large enterprises at home. HOBSON emphasized the econ. character of imperialism in his interpretation (*Imperialism*, 1902); **Lenin** considered 'imperialism the highest stage of capitalism' (1915, p. 140).

Intellectual Origins of Imperialism
Nationalism: the gains obtained through realistic power politics (**Realpolitik**) in the process of nat. unification (Germany, Italy) gave impetus to the conviction that only great powers–those with the will to possess power (NIETZSCHE, p. 64) and to carry through the struggle for existence (soc. Darwinism, p. 64)–were fit to rule over 'inferior' (coloured) peoples (racism, p. 65). Nat. prestige and self-preservation called for policies of a world-wide scope, which were based on the use of power and war **(militaristic thinking)** and therefore made **armaments** necessary; this meant esp. the construction of naval vessels, because control of the seas meant control of the world (**navalism:** Mahan: *The Influence of Sea Power on History*, 1890). The **'sense of mission'** (p. 103), acc. to which the white race, the nation or the larger ethnic unit (Panslavism, p. 113; Pan-Germanism) were called to **Europeanize the world**, was an ideological variant of nationalism.
Supported by the milit., econ. interests, the upper and petit bourgeoisie, imperialism spread Western civilization (morals, ideology, customs and fashions) across the world; it developed **infrastructures** (railways, admin., harbours, schools, hospitals) and developed the economies of the colonies (plantations, industries, markets) by exploiting the colon. peoples or exterminating them (colon. atrocities) and destroying their traditions (India, China).
New needs were aroused in the colon. peoples, but also resentment and feelings of hatred, which led to the **'awakening of the coloured nations'** and to internal, often religiously inspired, revitalization movements, to the discovery of native history (nat. consciousness), and, esp. after the 2nd World War, to struggles for emancipation (p. 261).

The Labour Movement (1860–1914)

Trade unions: industrialization brought about the organization of the trade unions and their great **period of development**: nat. unions with autonomous fiscal organization, admin., headquarters, press and officers. Ideological-polit. differences led to the development of various schools of thought: free (i.e. socialist), revolutionary-syndicalist, pacifist ('yellow', rejecting the strike as a weapon), lib. and Christ. unions. They sought int. contacts. After

1901 int. conferences were held and a permanent secretariat under **Carl Legien** (1861–1920) est. in Berlin.

1908 Establishment of the General Christ. International (1st secretary ADAM STEGERWALD).

1913 Int. Federation of Trade Unions (Amsterdam). Even though the unions obtained advantages for the workers, the viewpoint that capitalism can only be overcome through polit. struggle broadened its appeal (MARX).

Polit. parties of the labour movement: the issue of polit. tactics led to the formation of groups and parties: **revolutionaries** (orth. Marxists), anarchists (p. 66), mutualists (Proudhonists, who aspired to a soc. order based on cooperatives) and reformists (who advocated polit. and soc. activity within the polit. process). Proposed by **Karl Marx** (p. 66), founded in London

1864–76 the 1st International (1st Int. Working-men's Association) failed because of internal struggles (Marxists *v.* Anarchists), personal animosities between MARX and BAKUNIN (p. 113) and the alienation of leftist dem. elements in England, Italy and Switzerland after the

1871 Uprising of the Paris Commune (p. 105). On the occasion of the centennial of the Fr. Revolution,

1889 the 2nd International was est. in Paris (permanent secretariat in Brussels).

1890 Initiation of **May Day** celebrations. The Anarchists were expelled in 1896, reformism was rejected in 1904 and the general strike was declared the weapon to combat war and to demonstrate for peace (Basle 1912). Yet, with the outbreak of the 1st World War, the 2nd International disintegrated.

England: here the local syndicates of the non-polit. trade unions (p. 67) remained predominant.

1868 Establishment of the **Trades Union Congress** (T.U.C.) as their umbrella organization; further developed by 1895. To help to bring members of the Lib. party favourable to their cause into Parliament, the trade unionists formed the

1869 Labour Representation Committee.

1881 The Soc. Democratic Federation, founded by MARX's translator HYNDMAN, gained little support. Partyless intellectuals around SIDNEY WEBB (1859–1947) and GEORGE BERNARD SHAW (1856–1950) joined to form the

1884 Fabian Society (p. 104). Their conception of State Socialism, which was to be realized gradually, was adopted by the

1893 Independent Labour Party (I.L.P.), founded by **Keir Hardie** (1856–1915).

1906 The **Labour party** grew out of the Labour Representation Committee; initially it supported the Lib. party. The Labour parties of Australia and New Zealand, est. after 1910, were modelled on the Brit. Labour party.

U.S.A.: the struggle against capitalism was led by the unions, at first by the

1869 Knights of Labor, an association attempting to organize all workers; then in agriculture by the

1873 National Farmers' Alliance. Founded in

1877 the Socialist Labor party, however, dissolved after internal dissension and splits; the programme of the People's party (1891) was taken over by the Democrats.

1886 The Amer. Federation of Labor (A.F.L.) was led by **Samuel Gompers** (1850–1924); it gained extensive support. In contrast to Europe, it was supported by skilled workers (it advocated protection against the competition of unskilled immigrants and the maintainance of high levels of wages).

Germany: Ferdinand Lassalle (1825–64) founded the

1863 General Association of Ger. Workers (Leipzig) as the 1st Socialist party. His nat. programme expected the solution of the soc. question through the effects of universal, equal suffrage and producers' cooperatives supported by the state (p. 66). While BISMARCK was sympathetic to LASSALLE's programme, its 'State Socialism' was rejected categorically by KARL MARX.

1869 The Soc. Democratic Workers' Party of Germany was founded by Marx's followers **Wilhelm Liebknecht** (1826–1900) and **August Bebel** (1840–1913) in Eisenach. The **Gotha Programme**, a compromise, led to the fusion of both parties in the

1875 Socialist Workers' Party. Its suppression through the

1878 Anti-Socialist Law (p. 77), incl. the dissolution of the unions, the expulsion of officers and the prohibition of its press, was in the long run unsuccessful. Underground activity made strict discipline and organization necessary, to become characteristics of the

1890 **Soc. Dem. Party of Germany (S.P.D.).** Its purely Marxist programme was devised by **Karl Kautsky** (1854–1938), who defended it against radicals on the left like LEDEBOUR (1850–1947) and **Rosa Luxemburg** (p. 149), and revisionists on the right. Beginning in

1890 rebuilding of the unions: the **free Socialist unions** organized by industries.

1892 Congress of Halberstadt: election of a general commission. Under CARL LEGIEN it proved its worth during the

1896–7 Hamburg docker's strike and in the rejection of the

1899 'penitentiary bill' (p. 110).

1905 Congress of Cologne: emphasis of neutrality in party politics. **Christ. trade unions** developed out of workers' associations of the churches (p. 67).

1900 Union in an overall federation (after 1902 under general-secretary **Adam Stegerwald** (1847–1945).

1905 'Yellow' unions, modelled after Fr. examples (in part supported by business), were est. Inspired by Eng. practices, the older workers' associations of Hirsch-Duncker (est. 1869, of lib. persuasion), appealed esp. to skilled tradesmen.

Revisionism: successes of the trade unions, the rise in the general standard of living, and the ideas of the Eng. Fabians caused **Eduard Bernstein** (1850–1932) critically to re-examine the Marxist theories of increasing impoverization and revolution (p. 66). Although officially rejected by the party, the revisionist movement gained in importance in the realm of practical affairs.

1914 Approval of the war credits.

France: Anarchist leadership of the labour struggle. The position of the **syndicalists** was apolitical, opposed to the state and to militarism. Hoping to bring about the classless society by spontaneous 'direct action' (p. 66), it rejected contracts with employers, soc. reforms and parliaments. *'Bourses du Travail'* (local labour exchanges), formed after 1882, and countrywide trades associations fused in

1895 Confédération Générale du Travail (C.G.T.); Léon Jouhaux (1879–1954) assumed its leadership in 1909. In addition, Christ. dem. and yellow syndicates (*c.* 1899 in the Schneider-Creusot plants) were formed.

1879 The Fédération du Parti des Travailleurs Socialistes was led by the Marxist **Jules Guesde** (1845–1922). In 1882 the moderate 'possibilists' split away from it, in 1890 the 'Allemanists'.

1890 The Parti Ouvrier Socialiste Révolutionnaire was founded by the followers of **Blanqui** (1805–81), the former editor of *Ni dieu ni Maître* and a moving force behind the Commune of 1871. Attempts by **Jaurès** to bring the factions together failed because, among other things, of

1899 MILLERAND's participation in the gvt as a Cabinet member (p. 147), which was opposed by the extremists (Blanquists, Marxists, Allemanists) under GUESDE.

1904 Amsterdam Congress: under pressure of the 2nd International (following a motion by Germany's AUGUST BEBEL), the united

1905 Section Française de l'Internationale Ouvrière (S.F.I.O.) was formed. It normalized its relationship with the syndicalists (Amiens Charter of 1906), but was unable to bring about any rad. alteration in the soc. structure; however, it gained influence over soc. policy.

Italy: cooperatives and syndicates joined in the

1889 Milan Confederation of Labour. Other organizations were modelled after it, but the trade union movement remained splintered.

1891 The papal encyclical *Rerum novarum*, dealing with soc. questions, was proclaimed by LEO XIII (p. 66): Cath. unions joined in the Confederazione Italiana dei Lavoratori; Anarchist-syndicalist groups were also formed at this time. After initial stirrings (such as those by the Fasci operai in Bologna and others), and splits in the Marxist Workers' party

1892 the Partite Sozialista Italiane (P.S.I.) was formed, 'Integralists' and reformists (BISSOLA) (united since the

1906 Rome Party Convention), asserted themselves over the Marxists under **Labriola** (1843–1904). They gained the adherence of 20% of voters.

1906 The Confederazione Generale del Lavore achieved a loose organization of indust. unions and trade associations.

Austria: the 'Imp. Counsellor of the revolution', **Victor Adler** (1852–1918), united the various Socialist groups.

1889 The Soc. Dem. Party of Austria (S.P.O.), following a Marxist programme (KAUTSKY), as early as 1897 obtained 14 seats in the Imp. Council; it was, however, divided in special groups based on nat. origins. VICTOR ADLER was able to hold them together through the

1899 Brünn Programme: a demand for a dem. federalist state of auton. peoples. Aided by MAX ADLER (1873–1937), **Otto Bauer** (1882–1932) formulated **'Austromarxism,'** a programme recognizing the right to nat. self-determination. After 1913 he pleaded for union with Germany and the dissolution of the Aust. Empire. With the introduction of universal manhood suffrage in 1907, the S.P.O. grew to become the 2nd largest party in the state. Hampered by the lack of industrialization and conflicts between the nationalities, the Ger. nat. trade associations, Socialist and Christ. trade unions remained relatively small.

Poland: dominated by the Socialist groups of **Galicia**

1892 the Pol. Socialist party (P.P.S.) under **Pilsudski** (p. 155), because of its role in the struggle for Poland's nat. freedom, assumed leadership. After

1908 a Pol. army (its units concealed as sharp-shooting clubs) was built up. Up to 1897 the 'Soc. Dem. Party of Congress Poland' was led by ROSA LUXEMBURG (p. 149).

Russia: the revolutionary movement (Nihilists, Narodniks, p. 111), which developed *c.* 1860, was introduced to Marxism by **Plekhanov**. Founded in

1898 the Soc. Dem. Workers' Party split into

1903 **Mensheviks** and **Bolsheviks**; led by **Lenin** (p. 111), the Bolsheviks formed their own party at the

1912 Party Convention of Prague; they asserted themselves in the

1917 Oct. Revolution and assumed the leadership of world communism (the 3rd International, p. 141).

Pacifism

(Lat. *pacificus* = peace-loving). Because of ethical and relig. considerations, the rad.-idealist movement rejected the use of all manner of force, incl. the milit. safeguarding of peace and defensive war. Pacifism was fostered by **organizations for the preservation of peace** (such as England's Peace Society, 1816, and one in Geneva, founded in 1830), which held int. congresses after 1848.

1869 Society of the Friends of Peace.

1891 The Peace Bureau in Berne est. Leading representatives: **Elihu Burrit** (1810–79), **Cobden** (p. 48), **Bertha von Suttner** (1843–1914; 'Lay down your arms'), A. H. FRIED, the pedagogue F. W. FOERSTER, the Socialist **Jaurès** (p. 105), the physician **H. Dunant** (p. 85). Pacifism gained considerable infl. over the politics of the day at the time of the

1899 and 1907 Peace Conferences of The Hague on questions of disarmament, the arbitration of int. conflicts and the conduct of land warfare (p. 83). A major role was played by **Professor Lammasch** (1853–1920) at the

1901 Int. Court of The Hague. Neither the pacifist movement nor the 2nd International were able to temper imp. policies and war politics (p. 99).

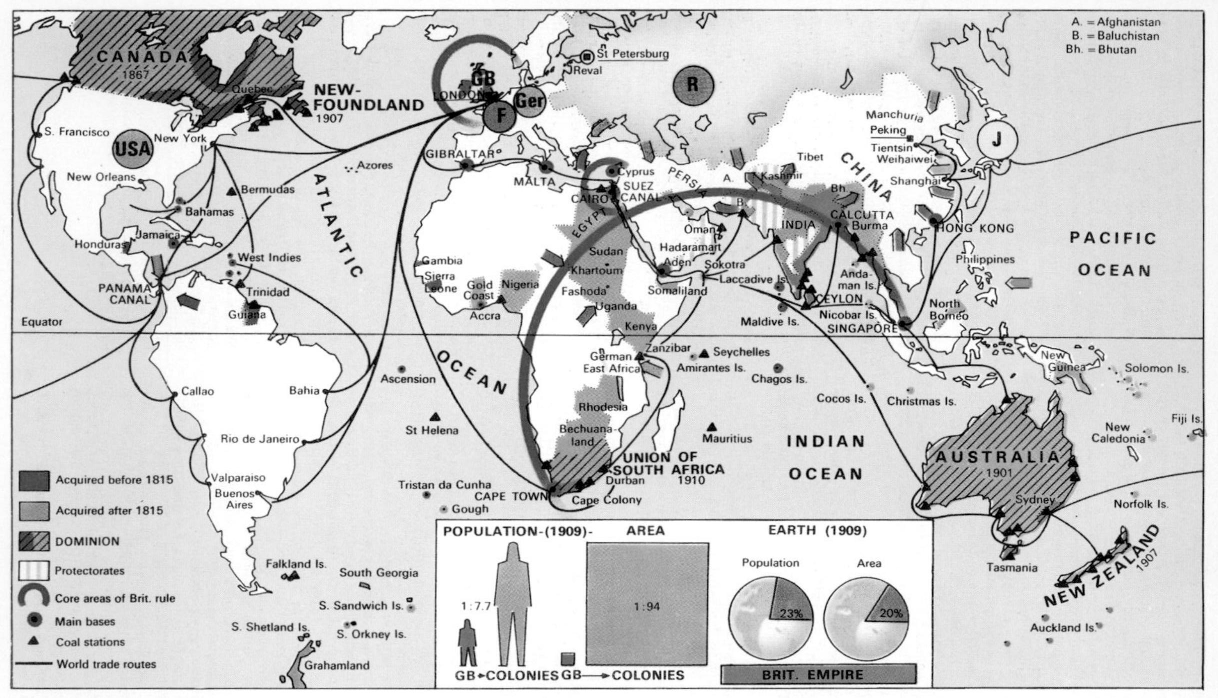

The British Empire to 1914

The Brit. Colon. Empire (1814–75)

After the prohibition of the slave trade, the interest in Afr. colonies lessened; *c.* 1865 Britain went so far as to consider giving them up altogether. Commerce and industry sought markets in s. America, India and China. The largely incidental new acquisitions served to safeguard the trade-lanes at sea (Singapore 1819, the Falkland Islands in 1833, Aden in 1839), to facilitate the opening of new markets (Hongkong 1841), or, after the loss of New England, to receive Brit. immigrants: 1806–14 Cape Colony; after 1824 the Straits Settlements (map, p. 106); after 1829 Western Australia; 1814–40 New Zealand. Propositions of self-admin. for the 'white' settlement colonies were entertained by 'progressives' like WAKEFIELD (1796–1862) in New Zealand and Lord DURHAM (1792–1840), whose

1839 'Report on the Affairs of Brit. N. America' initiated the process leading to the union and self-admin. for the Canad. provinces. The conception of trusteeship by the mother country over the colonies up to the time of their polit. self-sufficiency became a guiding principle of Brit. colon. policy. **Canada**, the 1st

1867 Dominion, received complete polit. autonomy by the N. America Act.

The Brit. Empire (1875–1914)

Economic life: the increase in pop., the flight of people from agrarian areas and urbanization continued. Despite increasing competition (by the U.S.A., Germany and Japan), Britain continued to adhere to the principle of free trade; by 1880 Brit. shipping made up 46% of world-wide tonnage, and had by 1913 doubled its for. trade with an unfavourable balance of active trade but a favourable balance of passive trade owing to int. banking and insurance business earnings ('invisible exports'). Investment capital in the empire increased and Brit. leadership in the world market was secured by the further development of imp. institutions.

The Brit. sense of mission: influenced by puritanism (I, p. 267), the conviction of an obligation to promote progress and civilization in the world, reinforced econ. and power-polit. interests. **Thomas Carlyle** (1795–1881) justified the Brit. mission in the world (the chosen nation) and **Sir Charles Dilke** (1843–1911) conceived the image of

1868 'Greater Britain' in a 'world that was growing more English every day'; **Robert Seeley** (1834–95) called for a planned

1883 'expansion of England'; **Rudyard Kipling** (1865–1936) proclaimed the 'white man's burden' and the mission of Britain. Propagated by associations and in journals, imperialism encompassed all classes.

Imperialist policy: in his Crystal Palace speech

1872 **Benjamin Disraeli** (p. 104) attacked the indifference of the Liberals (GLADSTONE) in colon. matters. To secure the sea route to India, he

1875 purchased the Egypt. Suez Canal shares. Queen VICTORIA, after

1877 Empress of India, supported DISRAELI's policies.

1878 Acquisition of Cyprus (p. 81).

1882 Occupation of Egypt. Under Brit. protection (it was declared a protectorate officially in 1914) the country recovered.

Africa: in the race for the partition of Africa (p. 97), Brit. imperialism gained direction and purpose as a result of the **Cape-to-Cairo plan**. While CROMER (1841–1917) advanced from the N. into the Sudan and encountered the opposition of the Mahdists (p. 97), **Cecil Rhodes** (1853–1902) in the s. used power and wealth, gained through the monopoly over the gold and diamond fields of s. Africa, to the end of Brit. expansion once the

1879 Zulu War was over. The s. Africa Co., headed by RHODES, obtained Bechuanaland in 1885 and

1888–91 Rhodesia. Britain also obtained Somaliland (1884), Uganda (1895), Kenya (1886) and, after the Fashoda Crisis (p. 107),

1899 the Anglo-Egypt. condominium of the Sudan.

1890–96 RHODES became prime minister of Cape Colony. He prepared for the conquest of the Boer states, which after the Jameson Raid into the Transvaal (1895–96), was completed during the

1899–1902 Boer War (p. 97). After the Brit. vict., the Boers were granted self-admin. and Dutch was made the official language (Afrikaans after 1923).

Asia: the fringe areas of India (p. 89) were developed, still ind. parts of islands and other islands in the Pacific were occupied.

1885–92, 1895–1902 Orientating his policy towards the Triple Alliance (the Medit. Agreements, p. 83) the Brit. prime minister, **Salisbury**, consequently pursued the policy of 'splendid isolation' (colon. tensions with France in Africa and Russia in Asia). A dominant figure was the 'Pan-Ger.' **Secretary of Colon. Affairs**,

1895–1903 Joseph Chamberlain (1836–1914). He attempted to stem the danger of competition for the Brit. Empire by **expansion** into still unoccupied areas; naval armaments were brought to a level of superiority over the two next strongest naval powers in the world (2-power standard), the empire was cemented by the restriction of free trade in favour of an imp. federation of the 'white' colonies united by the Crown, a common language and econ. privileges (preferred tariffs and the sterling gold rate); **compromise with the U.S.** over the Panama question (p. 117), and in an attempt to give up the policy of splendid isolation,

1898–1901 negotiations over a possible alliance with the Ger. Empire (p. 109). CHAMBERLAIN's plan for a Brit. defensive and econ. union, though resulting in his resignation (1903), advanced the conception of the Commonwealth and the politics of the Entente Cordiale.

1886 Colon. exhibition in London.

1887 The Trademark Law: products must be marked by the name of the country of their origin ('Made in Germany'). This law, designed to counteract Ger. competition, did not have the wished-for results. After

1887 Colon. Conferences (after 1907: Imp. Conferences). Dominion status was granted to

1901 the Commonwealth of Australia; 1907 New Zealand and **Newfoundland,** and, with the former Boer general BOTHA, as prime minister,

1910 the Union of S. Africa.

The Victorian Era (1848–86)

Manchester liberalism limited the tasks of the state to the protection of the laws and internal security. Cen. and municipal admin., the bureaucracy, the police and the postal services were modernized.

1840 Introduction of the postage stamp (Sir ROWLAND HILL), later also of the postcard and parcel post.

For. policy: under **Henry John Temple, Lord Palmerston** (prime minister, 1855–65), Britain was ready to support lib. forces in Italy. Denmark and Poland. Apart from the Crimean War (p. 69) and the Sepoy Rebellion in India (p. 89), this was an extended period of peace ('Pax Britannica').

1851 The 1st World Fair, an exhibition of Brit. industry at London's 'Crystal Palace' in Hyde Park.

The growth of the soc. product had raised the standard of living, broadened the middleclass temper of society and lessened class conflicts. Movements motivated by relig. and moral considerations (KINGSLEY) supported the **reform programmes** of the polit. unions: reform of the admin. of the Poor Laws and penal institutions; public health and factory regulations. Transformation of the aristocratic polit. parties into dem. parties with mass membership by the leading polit. figures of the era: **Benjamin Disraeli** (1804–81) and **William Ewart Gladstone** (1809–98), who changed from a supporter of PEEL (p. 48) into a lib. reformist and stressed domestic politics: the reform of fiscal policy and the admin.

1860 The Cobden Treaty with France: extension of free trade. DISRAELI, who had as an opponent of PEEL risen to leadership in the Con. party with his programme of 'Tory democracy'.

1867 2nd Reform Bill: enfranchising of petit bourgeoisie and skilled workers. GLADSTONE was the beneficiary of this Bill (to 1894 he headed 4 Cabinets).

1884 3rd Reform Bill: agricultural workers with fixed abodes were enfranchised, swelling the electorate to more than 4 mil. active voters.

1874–80 2nd DISRAELI Cabinet: initiation of imp. policies (p. 103); GLADSTONE, on the other hand, attempted to find a solution for the

Irish Question: emigrants to the U.S. founded there the secret society of the

1858 Fenians to establish an auton. Irish republic. Without much success, GLADSTONE passed

1869 Disestablishment of the Irish Church and Land Acts to aid Irish renters and to counteract terrorism and peasant unrest. Using legal means, the Irish representatives in Parliament under CHARLES STEWART PARNELL (1846–91) strove for **Home Rule**. To this end they formed the

1879 Irish Land League. They used passive resistance against Captain **Boycott**, an Eng. land agent, whose name became a familiar word in the Eng. language.

1882 Murder of the Irish secretaries, CAVENDISH and BURKE, in Phoenix Park, Dublin. Obstructionist tactics were used by the Irish in Parliament, GLADSTONE's

1886 Home Rule Bill divided the Lib. party and brought about the fall of his Cabinet. His Home Rule Bill for 1893 had his party's general support.

The struggle for freedom was continued by the 1900 United Irish League.

Domestic Crises (1886–1914)

Weakening of the Lib. party and almost uninterrupted rule by the Conservatives for a period of 20 yrs were the outcome of changes in the soc. structure:

1. Reacting to Home Rule policies, the lib. 'Unionists' (JOSEPH CHAMBERLAIN, p. 103) joined the Conservatives and supported their imperialistic policies.
2. Members of the impoverished rural aristocracy intermarried with members of indust. families; lib. circles belonging to 'society' changed over to the Con. party.
3. 'Great Depression' in agriculture and partial decline in industry (caused by competition from such protectionist countries as the U.S.A., Germany and also Japan) and large capitalist enterprises (p. 99) forced the labour movement to take account of its polit. fortunes. This led to the creation of industry-wide unions. Unlike the

1883 Fabian Society (p. 100), the

1881 Marxist Soc. Dem. Federation gained little influence. Collaborating with the

1893 Independent Labour Party, the Fabian Society and the Marxist Soc. Dem. Federation founded the Labour Representation Committee, out of which grew the

1906 Labour Party (Chairman: **James Ramsay MacDonald**, p. 146).

1901–10 EDWARD VII (60 yrs old) showed interest in for. policy.

1905 Lib. party victorious at the polls as a result of their opposition to CHAMBERLAIN's tariff reform scheme. Soc. measures (old-age pensions, 1908; sick and unemployment insurance, 1911) and army reforms under

1905–11 Secretary of War, **Richard Burdon Viscount Haldane** (1865–1928), burdened the budget. The House of Lords rejected the 'Budget of 1909' of the Chancellor of the Exchequer **David Lloyd George** (1863–1945) in ASQUITH's Cabinet [1908–16]. During the **const. conflict**

1910–36 GEORGE V endeavoured to arbitrate.

1911 The Parliament Act: the House of Lords lost its permanent veto power. The domestic crisis continued: **suffragettes** under **Emmeline Pankhurst** (1858–1928) demonstrated for the emancipation of women and female suffrage. Railway, docks and miners' strikes disrupted the economy and the domestic order.

Ireland: a nat. uprising was prepared by the Sinn Féin ('Ourselves Alone') party, founded in 1905, even though the Land Act of 1903 gave the right to own land also to Irish renters.

1912 The proposed Home Rule Act was opposed by the Conservatives, Protestant Ulster, the House of Lords and the army. The danger of civil war was concealed solely by the outbreak of the 1st World War.

The 3rd Republic (1870–1914)

Even before the conclusion of the peace treaty with Germany (p. 71)

Mar.–May 1871 the rising of the Paris Commune took place. After their rad. seizure of power, the communards were savagely suppressed by MACMAHON in the 'bloody week' with 30,000 fatalities.

1871–3 President THIERS (p. 49) brought about the withdrawal of the Ger. occupation troops ahead of schedule after the war indemnity had been paid in full; but the con. majority (split into Legitimists, Orléanists and Bonapartists) elected

1873–9 Marshall MacMahon (1808–93) as president of the republic, to serve as 'guardian of the monarchy'. The attempts to restore the monarchy failed owing to the refusal of the Comte DE CHAMBORD, the last Bourbon pretender, to recognize the *Tricolore* as the Fr. flag.

1875 Proclamation of the 3rd Republic (353 to 352 votes).

Constitution: universal manhood suffrage was instituted for elections to the **Chamber of Deputies**. With the **Senate**, it formed the **Nat. Assembly** (the legislature), which elected the **President** (the executive) for a 7-yr term, controlled the Cabinet, and was empowered to alter the constitution. Because of the division of the chamber into parties based on personal loyalties and lacking firm programmes, majorities were wavering and gvts unstable (by 1914 there had been 50 Cabinets). Thanks to an apolit. and stable bureaucracy, the 'republic of the comrades' (DE JOUVENEL) slowly took firm root. In its relations abroad, the 'state of lawyers, writers and professors' quickly gained acceptance.

1876 Repub. elect. successes of the **Opportunists** (GAMBETTA, FERRY, p. 107), who drew their support from the upper bourgeoisie and were opposed by the petit bourgeois **Radicals** under **Georges Clemenceau** (1841–1929). Because of the conflict over the president's free hand in appointing gvt ministers, the chamber was dissolved; however, MACMAHON's abortive

1877 *coup d'état* ('the *seize mai* crisis') only strengthened the republicans; from this point on, Cabinets were formed in accordance with the prevailing majorities in the chamber.

1879–87 President JULES GRÉVY (1807–91), pursued a policy of domestic polit. consolidation by sec. and anti-clerical reforms:

1880 amnesty for the communards, restrictions on eccles. Orders (the Jesuits);

1881 freedom of assembly and the press; 1882 all elementary schools became public schools; 1884 civil marriage, a lib. municipal code. Anger over corrupt politicians, increasing demands for a 'strong gvt' and calls for 'revenge' on Germany by

1882 the League of Patriots, founded by DÉROULÈDE (1846–1914), led to

1885 elect. gains by the monarchists. The minister of war, **Georges Boulanger** (1837–91), rallied conservatives, radicals and Bonapartists in the authoritarian-nationalist

1886–9 Boulangist Movement. A repub. elect. vict. averted dictatorship; flight of BOULANGER and suicide in Brussels.

1889 The Paris World Fair (construction of the Eiffel Tower, 300 m. high).

1892 Policy of protective tariffs; LEO XIII advised Fr. Catholics to support the Republic.

1892–3 The Panama Canal scandal: bankruptcy of the corporation founded by FERDINAND DE LESSEPS (p. 117), termination of construction work on the canal begun in 1881.

1894 Assassination attempt by Anarchists on President CARNOT, who had become President in 1887; Socialists organized in syndicates (p. 100) and also formed

1895 the Confédération Générale du Travail (C.G.T.), the Parti Ouvrier Socialiste Révolutionnaire (1890) and the party of the Rad. Socialists (1893). The struggle between leftist and rightist parties during the

1894–1906 Dreyfus Affair divided the nation. In protest against the condemnation of the Jew, officer ALFRED DREYFUS (1859–1935) by a milit. tribunal on the basis of forged documents,

1898 the Bloc Républicain was formed: **Émile Zola** (*J'accuse*, 1898), CLEMENCEAU, and the Socialist JEAN JAURÈS (1859–1914 (assassinated)) demanded the resumption of the trial. CHARLES MAURRAS (1868–1952) preached 'integral nationalism' against Germans, Protestants, Jews, romanticism (ROUSSEAU), human rights and the Republic. With LÉON DAUDET (1867–1942), he founded the nationalistic

1898 Action Française and thereby spurred on the anti-clericalism of the left-rad. opponents. Under the gvt of

1902–5 ÉMILE COMBES, relig. orders, monasteries and schools were dissolved, Church property was confiscated and relations with the Vatican were broken off.

1905 Separation of Church and state, carried out by the Ind. Socialist **Aristide Briand** (1862–1932), who was a member of

1906–9 CLEMENCEAU's Cabinet. With the rehabilitation of DREYFUS civil power remained victorious over the army. Soc. legislation was extended, but authoritarian measures were taken against strikes.

1909 BRIAND's Cabinet promised the easing of tensions and reconciliation; however, the Rad. Socialists asserted themselves. Under

1911–12 CAILLAUX as prime minister, the Franco-Ger. Morocco Treaty was concluded (p. 83); still, anti-Ger. nationalism (BARRÈS) and the division of the Socialists into *'ministeriels'* (BRIAND) and the Unity Party (Section Française de l'Internationale Ouvrière (S.F.I.O.), founded 1905 by JAURÈS) brought advantages to the conservatives and made possible the

1912 Ministry of **Raymond Poincaré** (1860–1934) (President of the Republic, 1913–20). CLEMENCEAU approved of the retribution-seeking policy of 'war-preparedness', while as a pacifist JAURÈS advocated Franco-Ger. reconciliation.

1913 Strengthening of the armed forces through the introduction of the 3-yr service law (Cabinet BARTHOU), which was opposed by the Socialists.

1914 Elect. vict. of the S.F.I.O.; after the outbreak of the war, the prime minister, VIVIANI, and POINCARÉ endeavoured to bring about a *Union sacrée* of all parties.

Indo-China before 1914

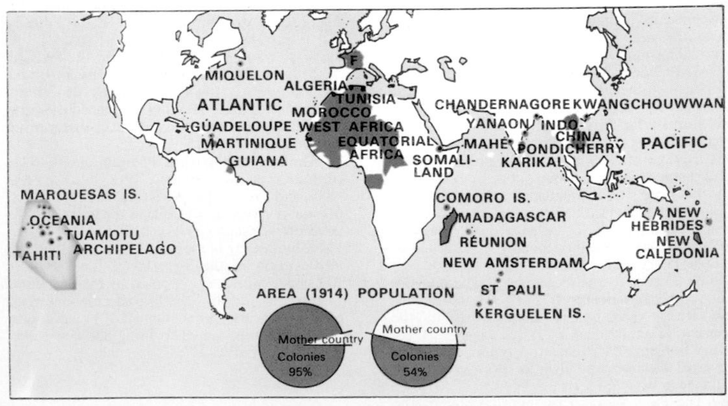

The French Colonial Empire before 1914

The Foundation of the 2nd Colon. Empire (1830–70)
Although colon. policies at this time enjoyed little popularity, the nation had – ever since the Enlightenment and the Fr. Revolution – conceived of itself as the champion of Eur. ctr. and civilization. Assimilation of the élite of the coloured pop. in the remaining colon. possessions: Senegambia, Réunion, Miquelon, Guadeloupe, Guiana (1818) and the Ind. bases. To divert attention from domestic difficulties,

1830 Algiers was occupied, to be secured by the For. Legion, founded in 1831 and composed of emigrants, deserters and adventurers. Berber tribes under the Emir ABD EL-KADER (1807–83) fought the Fr. advance. The policy aiming at prestige in Egypt (THIERS) failed during the

1839–41 Eastern Crisis (p. 87). Haphazard acquisitions in Africa (Gabon, 1843–4), and Oceania (Marquesas Islands, Tahiti, 1842). Despotic rule prevailed in **Algeria**.

1840–47 Governor-General BUGEAUD (1784–1849).

1844 Vict. over the Sultan of Morocco at the Isly river; ABD EL-KADER capitualted in 1847. 'France beyond the seas' became the nation's granary; by 1906 the proportion of Eur. settlers rose to 13% of the pop. General **Faidherbe** (1818–89) reorganized the admin. of

1854–65 Senegal; he founded Dakar in 1857 and trained Afr. (Senegalese) troops for expeditions into the interior. Care was taken to foster the relations with **Egypt**, which, after the construction of the Suez Canal (p. 97), was considered a Fr. protectorate.

Annam: the emperor, nominally under Chin. suzerainty, was the object of relig. veneration. Polit. power was in the hands of the administrators of Tongking (the Trinh dynasty) and Cochin China (the Nguyen dynasty).

1787 With the Treaty of Tourane, NGUYEN ANH obt. Fr. aid against the Island of Pulo Condor; following these developments he was able to ascend the imp. throne of Vietnam as the Emperor

1802–20 Gia Long (residence in Hué). Because of the persecution of Christians, a naval show of force and

1858–9 occupation of Tourane and Saigon. 1862 annexation of the eastern, 1867 of the western, province of Cochin China.

Cambodia: Siam and Annam fought over the remnant of the Khmer Empire. NORODON (1859–1904) asked for Fr. protection from Siam (1863).

The 'Empire Français' (1871–1914)
Deeply hurt by the defeat of 1871 (p. 71), the Fr. gvt, milit. command and finan. circles pursued a purposeful imp. policy to safeguard Fr. prestige and power in Europe. A centralized colon. bureaucracy strove for cult. assimilation and the milit. enlistment of the 'coloured Frenchmen'. BISMARCK encouraged Fr. colon. expansion, which was opposed by the petit bourgeoisie and the Radicals (CLEMENCEAU).

Econ. life: protective tariffs (1892) brought advantages to the agrarians and heavy industry (Briey, Nancy, Longwy). Owing to the stagnant birth-rate and limited coal production, the Fr. share in the world production of steel and iron fell. On the other hand, because of the savings accumulated by its people (rentier capitalism) France became the 'banker of the world'. Capital investments abroad (in the colonies, Russia) were controlled by the large banks. The new colon. policy was guided after

1880 by the prime minister Jules Ferry (1832–93). Following BISMARCK's dismissal (p. 110), the polit. isolation of France lessened. Colon. expansion was continued under President FAURE (1895–9).

Africa: formation of a large colon. empire. The establishment of

1881 the protectorate over Tunisia displeased Italy (p. 119); Egypt was lost to England (p. 103). Proceeding from Algeria and Senegal, the Sahara was penetrated and the western Sudan 'pacified'.

1904 Establishment of the Gouvernement Générale **W. Africa** (A.O.F.). The bloodless acquisition of **Equatorial Africa** (Gouvernement Générale A.E.F., 1910) was owed to the accomplishment of **Brazza** (1852–1905), who explored the Fr. Congo, concluded treaties with Afr. chiefs and resisted the exploitation of these areas through private companies.

1895–6 Subjugation and annexation of **Madagascar**: General GALLIÉNI fitted the colon. régime to the character of the country. The plan to encircle Egypt or to establish an E.-W. connection in the Sudan led to the

1898 Fashoda Crisis with Britain (p. 83). General KITCHENER demanded the withdrawal of the Fr. expedition under MARCHAND. Injured Fr. nat. pride demanded satisfaction; but

1898–1905 For. Minister Delcassé recalled MARCHAND and sought a compromise solution.

1902 Secret treaty with Italy concerning Tripoli (p. 83). Sudan treaty (1899, accommodation over Morocco and Egypt, leading to the

1904 Entente Cordiale with Britain (p. 83). During the 1st Moroccan crisis the prime minister ROUVIER dropped DELCASSÉ.

1906 Algeciras Conference: Ger. recognition of France's 'special' position in **Morocco**. Occupation of Fez and

1911 2nd Moroccan crisis, overcome by the Franco-Ger. **Congo agreement**. Governing the Sultanate in almost absolutist fashion, General **Lyautey** (1854–1934) did not alter the polit. and soc. structure.

Indo-China: the 2nd centre of the empire grew during the

1873–86 struggles with the 'Black Flags' (remnants of the Chinese Taiping rebels) and with China over **Tongking**.

1883 Establishment of a protectorate over Annam (Treaty of Hué), which had to be acknowledged by China in the

1885 Peace of Tientsin.

1887 Formation of the Union of Indo-China. The territories were rounded out at the expense of

Siam, which, by introducing Eur. reforms, after 1880 transformed itself into a mod. state.

1868–1910 King CHULALONGKORN. In the

1893 Treaty of Bangkok he recognized the Fr. protectorate over **Laos**.

1896 England and France guaranteed the neutrality of Siam. Its borders with Fr. Indo-China were fixed in 1907.

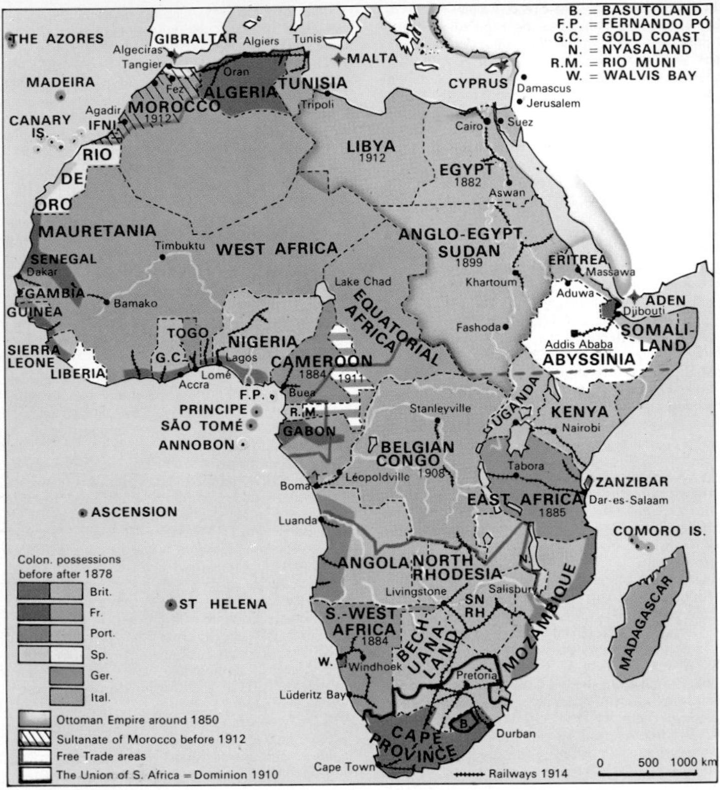

B. = BASUTOLAND
F.P. = FERNANDO PÓ
G.C. = GOLD COAST
N. = NYASALAND
R.M. = RIO MUNI
W. = WALVIS BAY

THE AZORES
GIBRALTAR
Algeciras
Tangier
Algiers
Tunis
MALTA
Oran
MADEIRA
Fez
ALGERIA
TUNISIA
CYPRUS
Damascus
Jerusalem
Agadir
MOROCCO
1912
Tripoli
CANARY IS.
IFNI
Cairo
Suez
RIO DE ORO
LIBYA
1912
EGYPT
1882
Aswan
MAURETANIA
Timbuktu
WEST AFRICA
ANGLO-EGYPT. SUDAN
1899
SENEGAL
Dakar
ERITREA
Massawa
Lake Chad
Khartoum
GAMBIA
Bamako
Aduwa
ADEN
GUINEA
EQUATORIAL AFRICA
Djibouti
TOGO
NIGERIA
Fashoda
SOMALI-LAND
SIERRA LEONE
G.C.
Lagos
Addis Ababa
ABYSSINIA
LIBERIA
Lomé
Accra
CAMEROON
1884
1911
F.P.
Buea
UGANDA
PRINCIPE
R.M.
Stanleyville
KENYA
SÃO TOMÉ
Nairobi
ANNOBON
GABON
BELGIAN CONGO
1908
Léopoldville
Tabora
Boma
ZANZIBAR
EAST AFRICA
1885
Dar-es-Salaam
ASCENSION
Luanda
COMORO IS.
ANGOLA
NORTH RHODESIA
N.
Livingstone
Salisbury
MOZAMBIQUE
MADAGASCAR
ST HELENA
S.-WEST AFRICA
1884
SN RH
BECHUANA-LAND
W.
Windhoek
Pretoria
Lüderitz Bay
B.
Durban
CAPE PROVINCE
Cape Town

Colon. possessions before after 1878
Brit.
Fr.
Port.
Sp.
Ger.
Ital.
Ottoman Empire around 1850
Sultanate of Morocco before 1912
Free Trade areas
The Union of S. Africa = Dominion 1910
Railways 1914
0 500 1000 km

The colonial partition of Africa before 1914

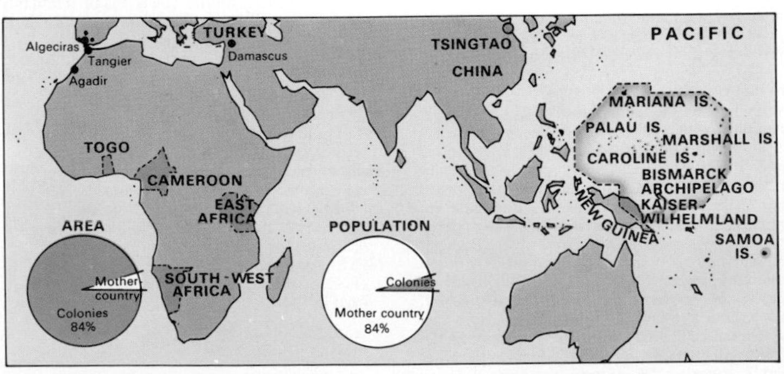

The German colonies before 1914

The Colon. Policy of Bismarck (1871–90)

1882 Establishment of the Colon. League (BENNIGSEN, ROHLFS) and

1884 the Society for Ger. Colonization by **Carl Peters** (1856–1918), the 'inventor of Ger. imperialism'. Conclusion of private treaties with natives in s. (LÜDERITZ), w. (WOERMANN) and E. Africa (PETERS, Count PFEIL), in the s. Seas (the Godefroy Company). BISMARCK wished to avoid risks which might pose dangers to Eur. politics. At the

1884–5 Congo Conference he mediated the formation of a neutral Congo state under the sovereignty of LEOPOLD II of Belgium (p. 85) with freedom of trade for all nations. Utilizing the favourable polit. situation (Fr. and Brit. preoccupation with Egypt, friendship with Austria, Italy and Russia; agreement with France), BISMARCK reluctantly let 'the flag follow trade'. The following Ger. protectorates were est.:

1884 Ger. S.-W. Africa: treaties fixing the borders with Angola in 1886, with Cape Province in 1890. Native troop contingents, est. in 1889, combated

1889–1906 Herero and Hottentot uprisings. The most important of the settlement colonies was granted self-admin. in 1907.

1884 Cameroons, Togo: the imp. commissioner, **Nachtigal**, obtained Brit. recognition for Ger. claims by giving up Ger. demands relating to Nigeria.

1884–5 Ger. colonies in the S. Seas: Kaiser Wilhelm Land, acquired from the New Guinea Co. in 1880; the Marshall Islands, the Bismarck Archipelago.

1885 Ger. E. Africa: establishment of a protective force consisting of Africans (Askari) to serve against rebellious Arabs (1889–90).

The Striving for World Power (1890–1914)

William II (p. 110) claimed a 'place in the sun' for Germany in the race for colonies. The maxim, 'a global policy the task, world-wide power the aim, the navy the means', was welcomed by the nation and stridently represented by the

1891 Pan-Ger. League (HUGENBERG, p. 151) and influenced by the chief of the polit. section of the Ger. For. Office, **Friedrich von Holstein (1837–1909)**. Overestimating their strength, the Germans initiated an ad hoc, vacillating for. policy ('zig-zag course').

Econ. life: rise to the rank of strongest Eur. nation in terms of industrialization; Germany's for. trade and merchant marine (Hamburg-America Line: ALBERT BALLIN, 1857–1918) competed with England. Heavy industry, electrical industry and chemical industry were concentrated in large **corporations**: **Stinnes**, **Krupp**, **Stumm**, **Siemens**, **AEG**, **IG-Farben**. The conviction grew that industry, trade, the need for food and supplies for the pop. made imperialist power politics necessary.

1890–94 The imp. chancellor Leo von Caprivi (1831–99) and ADOLF MARSCHALL VON BIEBERSTEIN, the head of the For. Office 1890–97, viewed this policy sceptically.

1890 The Zanzibar Treaty: the exchange with Britain of Zanzibar for Heligoland, incl. the surrender of claims to Uganda, was severely criticized.

1890 The cancellation of the Reinsurance Treaty against Russia's wishes paved the way for Franco-Rus. understanding.

1895 Ger.-Rus. measures against Japan, and esp. the Kruger telegram (p. 83), soured the British. Still, **Bernhard von Bülow** (1849–1929), secretary of state from 1897, imp. chancellor 1900–9, felt that he had a 'free hand' as the guide of Ger. for. policy. Admiral **Alfred von Tirpitz** (1849–1930) gained enthusiastic support from the Kaiser and from the public for his **naval policy.**

1898 He justified the naval building programme in terms of the risk it created for potential aggressors.

1898 The Naval League (*Flottenverein*) popularized the Ger. 'interests at sea'. The risk theory and the view of Germany's 'fleet as luxury' (CHURCHILL) increasingly affected Anglo-Ger. relations.

Near Eastern policy: visits by the Kaiser to the Near E. and his

1898 Damascus speech roused Brit and Rus. suspicions. The Deutsche Bank acquired railway concessions in Turkey. After

1903 construction of the Baghdad railway.

Colon. policy: in terms of energy expended, little achieved.

1897–8 Occupation of Tsingtao, a treaty leasing it concluded with China (p. 91).

1899 Purchase of the Carolines, Marianas and Palau Islands from Spain. Partition of the Samoa Islands between the U.S.A. and Germany. After the Boxer Rising (p. 91), the Yangtse Treaty concluded with Britain to safeguard the 'open door' to China; however,

1898–1901 negotiations aiming at an alliance failed because of Brit. hesitation (SALISBURY) and a false estimate of the polit. situation (HOLSTEIN). BÜLOW insisted that Britain join the Triple Alliance in the belief that Germany still faced a choice between the 'Rus. Bear' and the 'Brit. Whale'. During the **1st Moroccan Crisis** he attempted to break up the Franco-Brit. Entente.

1905 The Kaiser went ashore at Tangier and declared the sultan a free sovereign.

1906 The Algeciras Conference revealed the extent of Ger. isolation. The intensification in Ger.-Brit. naval rivalry, owing to the development of the 'Dreadnoughts', aided Brit. conciliation with Russia (p. 113). A forceful appearance was made and prestige was gained during the

1908 Bosnian crisis. However, the 'loyalty of the Nibelungen' to Austria limited Germany's freedom of polit. action. **Theobald von Bethmann-Hollweg** (chancellor from 1909) and the For. Office (KIDERLEN-WÄCHTER) sought an understanding with Britain (Sir EDWARD GREY); but after

1911 the dispatch of the frigate *Panther* ('the leap of the panther') to Agadir during the **2nd Moroccan Crisis**, England took the side of France. Germany gave up its claims in Morocco in exchange for the Fr. cession of New Cameroons. Germany co-operated with Britain during the Balk. crises (p. 121); but in Berlin in

1912 TIRPITZ scuppered negotiations for a compromise solution with Lord HALDANE by making concessions to Britain on the question of naval armaments dependent on a Brit. declaration of neutrality.

The 'Wilhelminische' Era (1890–1914)

The Kaiser William II (1859–1941), fond of pomp, vain, inconsistent and unbalanced, was convinced that, in a mystical sense, he ruled by God's grace. Influenced by such confidants as PHILIPP ZU EULENBURG (1847–1921), he determined the **'new course'**, after BISMARCK's dismissal (p. 77), in semi-authoritarian fashion. Although imp. bureaucrats (HOLSTEIN), politicians loyal to the state, historians (OTTO HINTZE, H. DELBRÜCK, F. MEINECKE *et al.*) criticized the personal régime of the Kaiser, they did not touch on the principle of the 'strong monarchy' considered the 'wholesome heritage of BISMARCK'. Difficult domestic polit. problems were concealed by the continuous upward development of the economy:

1. **Finan. dependence** of the empire on the fed. states.
2. **Paralysis of imp. policy** because of const. conflicts, esp. with Prussia. While Prussia was secure in a reactionary-con. policy because of the 3-class elect. system, the Ger. empire had to be increasingly concerned with non-con. forces (the Centre party, liberals, socialists) because here universal manhood suffrage prevailed.
3. **The lack of parl. const. reforms:** deprived of real polit. responsibility, the parties tended to split up (like the liberals), to follow a doctrinaire line (as with the socialists) or to become opportunistic in character (as with the conservatives).
4. **Militaristic tendencies,** promoted by the structure of the bureaucracy, stressed the importance of obedience even in the realm of civilian life.
5. **Prevention of democratization:** the alliance of agrarians, industrialists and bourgeois propertied interests led to the failure of the revisionist movement within the Soc. Dem. party (p. 101) as well as of the Nat. Soc. Union founded by **Friedrich Naumann** (1860–1919) and other attempts (MAX WEBER) to integrate the workers into the state.
6. **Clumsy Prus. policies towards Poland (the 'Eastern Marches'):** suppression of Pol. protests and school strikes (1906), pro-Ger. settlement and land confiscation decrees.

1890–94 Imp. Chancellor Leo von Caprivi (p. 109), Prus. prime minister to 1892, sought for a 'correct' course 'above the parties'; however, he encountered difficulties.

1890 Repeal of the Anti-Socialist Laws.

1890–91 Workers' protective legislation. Disappointed by the negative reaction of the S.P.D. (BEBEL), the Kaiser turned his back on the 'ruffians without fatherland'.

1891–4 Lowering of tariffs by means of commercial treaties, esp. with Russia, against opposition from the agrarians. The

1893 Agrarian League (Bund der Landwirte) transformed the Conservatives into a party representing the interests of the large E.-Elbian landowners (OLDENBURG, JANUSCHAU). The Progressives (Freisinnige), the Centre, and the S.P.D. rejected the army proposals in the Reichstag. However, after the dissolution of the Reichstag

1893 the army was even so increased by 83,000 men. Criticism by BISMARCK. His

1894 (apparent) reconciliation with WILLIAM II offended CAPRIVI, who fell from power over the issue of repressive policies against the S.P.D. desired by the Kaiser. Stagnation continued under

1894–1900 Chlodwig Fürst zu Hohenlohe-Schillingfürst (75 yrs old), Bav. prime minister, 1866–70, after 1885 imp. stadtholder of Alsace-Lorraine. Proposed tough legislation against revolutionary activity (*Umsturzvorlage*) (1894) and the Penitentiary Bill (1899) were rejected by the Reichstag.

1895 Opening of the canal linking the N. Sea and the Baltic. A new phase in the development of soc. policy was opened with the reform of the insurance system (1899).

1900 Introduction of the Civil Code of Laws (*Bürgerliches Gesetzbuch*, B.G.B.). A protégé of EULENBURG and HOLSTEIN,

1900–9 Reichskanzler Bernhard von Bülow (1849–1929) won the sympathy of the Kaiser and the conservatives through the

1902 revision of Ger. commercial policy, which included new protective tariffs; but the 'speculation in bread' again won voters to the ranks of the S.P.D. After the rejection of colon. policy by the Centre party and the S.P.D.,

1906 the con.-lib. bloc politics were developed. However, tensions were in the air after the liberals demanded the reform of the Prus. elect. law.

1908 The 'Daily Telegraph' Affair (caused by an unauthorized interview of the Kaiser discussing Anglo-Ger., relations), roused waves of protest from all parties. The chancellor, who shared responsibility for the incident, exposed the Kaiser to his critics. He did so at a time when the Kaiser's polit. self-esteem had already suffered from revelations by the journalist MAXIMILIAN VON HARDEN of intimate details concerning his circle of friends. BÜLOW failed to take advantage of the opportunity to bring about const. change; he fell from power because of a

1909 defeat in the effort to reform the imp. finances.

1909–17 Imp. Chancellor Theobald von Bethmann-Hollweg (1856–1921), Prus. secretary of the interior from 1905, recognized the problems inherent in the imp. policies, but he lacked the energy to bring about change.

1910 The attempt to reform the Prus. elect. law failed because of the inflexible position taken by the conservatives. The new

1911 Constitution of Alsace-Lorraine, which provided for internal autonomy, came too late.

1911 The Imp. Insurance Legislation (*Reichs-Versicherungsordnung*, R.V.O.) extended soc. security to the middle classes. But no honourable compromise reconciling the soc. structure with the antiquated polit. organization could be found.

1912 Although it lacked polit. influence, the S.P.D. grew to become the strongest party in the Ger. parliament; meanwhile, the Centre party, under the leadership of **Matthias Erzberger** (1875–1921 (assassinated)), experienced a shift to the left.

1913 The 'Zabern Incident' demonstrated the limitations of civil power: the popular uproar over the ridiculing of Alsatians by an officer of the army was suppressed by milit. force; an interpellation in the Reichstag remained without effect.

1913 Reinforcement of the army to the level of 780,000 men because of the generally prevailing feverish arms race (p. 83). The internal dissolution of the empire was temporarily halted after the outbreak of the war owing to the

1914 *Burgfrieden* (agreement to cease party-polit. hostilities for the duration of the conflict).

The Decline of Tsardom (1874–1914)

The disruptions of the reform era (p. 69), industrialization, land hunger and the impoverishment of the peasantry created permanent **revolutionary ferment**. Imbued, much like HERZEN (p. 113) and Count **Leo Tolstoy** (1828–1910), with a mystical faith in the 'simple peasant', the

Narodniks went as teachers, 'soc. workers' and scribes among the people; however, their attempts to enlighten them politically were mistrusted by the people, who held to the Church's teaching of an autocratic tsardom willed by God.

The **Nihilists** (so named after a term used by TURGENEV in his novel *Fathers and Sons*, 1862) expected an effective struggle against tsardom and soc. injustice to lead from BAKUNIN's Anarchism (p. 113). CHERNYSHEVSKY, in

1863 *What To Do?*, TKACHEV (1844–85), and others, developed the theory and tactics of the overthrow of gvts by active revolution (adopted by LENIN), secret societies like 'Land and Freedom' (1877) and 'The Will of the People' (1879) distributed propaganda, organized militant groups and carried out sabotage and assassinations.

1877–81 The Nihilist trials: banishment and death penalties intensified radicalism and distrust in the judicial system.

1878 Attempted assassination of the tsar and acquittal of VERA ZASULICH (1851–1910).

1881 Murder of ALEXANDER II.

Socialists: Plekhanov (1856–1918), who introduced Marxism into Russia and

1883 founded the 1st Soc. Dem. group 'Liberation of Labour', objected to terroristic methods.

1881–94 Alexander III was under the influence of his teacher POBEDONOSTSEV (1827–1907), who brought about the establishment of absolute autocracy. Founded in

1881 the **Okhrana** (polit. police), aided by a network of agents and informers, controlled the schools, universities, the press and the judiciary. Peasants and workers remained at the mercy of the large landowners and industrialists. An energetic policy of Russification was carried out in the border areas.

1881–2 general dissatisfactions found vent in anti-semitic pogroms (p. 63).

1894–1917 Nicholas II continued to rule with the support of the alliance of autocracy and orthodoxy, backed in his policy by his hysterical and bigotted wife ALEXANDRA (formerly a princess of Hesse-Darmstadt). Their Moscow coronation ended with the death of more than 1,000 during the

1896 catastrophe of Khodynka Meadow. The empire was kept in a state of permanent crisis by unrest over Russification in Finland, Poland, the Ukraine and the Baltic area, strikes, soc. and agrarian revolts. The police broke up the

1898 Soc. Dem. Workers' party, founded in Minsk, which reorganized itself abroad. **Vladimir Ilyich Ulyanov**, cal. **Lenin** (1870–1924) spread his revolutionary ideas (p. 129) by his writings and the expatriate newspaper *Iskra* (*The Spark*, 1900). Born in Simbirsk and educated in the law, he agitated for the liberation of the working class; banished to Siberia, he studied Marxism; from 1900 to 1905 he lived in exile in London, Munich and Geneva.

1902 As minister of the interior, PLEHVE (1846–1904) eliminated the last remnants of local self-gvt; he penetrated the

1902 Soc. Revolutionary party (S.R.), led by CHERNOV (1876–1952) and SAVINKOV (1879–1922), with informers (ASEF), and sought to counteract their revolutionary tendencies with workers' associations organized 'from above', like that of the priest GAPON (1873–1906 (murdered)), a policy known as 'police socialism'.

1903 Antisemitic pogroms (Kishinev).

1903 The bourgeoisie organized itself in the 'Liberation League' (Const. Democrats = KD = **'Cadets'**).

1903 2nd Congress of the Soc. Dem. Workers' Party of Russia at Brussels and London: split into **Mensheviks** (the 'minority') who, as the 'legal Marxists' wanted to await the evolution of capitalism and the proletariat (MARTOV, PLEKHANOV and **Leo Bronstein**, cal. **Trotsky** (1879–1940, murdered)); and the **Bolsheviks** (the 'majority') under **Lenin**, who cal. for a dictatorship of the proletariat to be brought about by an élitist party that was to be effective even in the predominantly agrarian society of Russia.

1904–5 The 'little war against the Jap. dwarf' (p. 113) precipitated the

1905 1st Russian Revolution: on

9 [22] Jan. 1905, 'Bloody Sunday', the military fired on a peaceful demonstration led by Fr GAPON carrying a petition to the Tsar; strikes and revolts followed throughout Russia; mutinies broke out on the armoured cruiser *Potemkin* in Odessa and in the Kronstadt garrison. The Bolsheviks in London decided on the armed overthrow of the gvt and the formation of workers' soviets (carried out, among others, by LENIN and TROTSKY); nat. uprisings took place in Finland and Poland. In Aug. the tsar promised the convocation of the **Duma** (parliament) and, in the

Oct. Manifesto, issued a constitution worked out by WITTE (p. 113). A general strike and the Dec. uprising in Moscow were beaten down by milit. force. During the

1906–17 era of pseudo-constitutionalism there were reactionary policies, the police again gaining the upper hand

1906 under the prime minister **Stolypin** (1862–1911 (murdered)). An Imp. Council was placed alongside the first lib. 'Duma of popular hopes'. To help to build an agrarian middle class (kulaks) and to increase purchasing power

1906–10 agrarian reforms were carried through. The dissolution of the Mir system, adjustments in the distribution of land, and settlement projects (Siberia) increased the numbers of the agrarian proletariat. The influence of the Socialist parties grew during the period of the

1907 2nd 'Duma of popular anger'. After alterations in the elect. laws, the

1907–12 3rd 'Duma of the masters, priests and lackeys' led to continued waves of strikes and unrest, increased emigration overseas (by Poles) and to Germany (by Baltic peoples). The tsar's court was dominated by the Siberian peasant 'holy man' **Rasputin** (1872–1916 (murdered)), reputed to be a performer of miracles from his healing influence on the haemophiliac tsarevich.

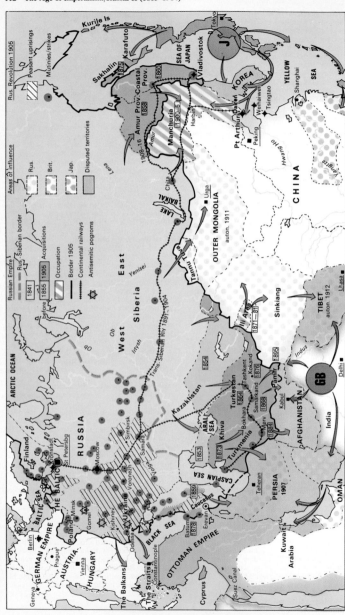

Russia before 1914

Russia's Expansion in Asia (19th cent.)

Motivation for expansion rested in the tsar's striving for power, the 'search for a border' in the geographically uncharted expanse of Cen. Asia and, since the days of PETER THE GREAT, the wish to find entry to the oceans of the world through ice-free harbours (warm-water ports).

The Near E.: the ambition to **control the Straits** (the Dardanelles) combined with a relig. sense of mission to free Constantinople and the Gk-Orth. 'brethren' of the Balkans from Turk.-Isl. rule. The nat. aim was not reached: 3 attempts (1828–9, p. 45; during the Crimean War, p. 69; in 1877–8, p. 81) failed because of Brit. or Aust. opposition.

1878 Congress of Berlin (p. 81): nation-wide Rus. disappointment and cooling-off of Russo-Ger. friendship.

The Middle E.: with the accession of NICHOLAS I (p. 69) the border moved southward and eastward towards Persia, India and China.

1830–59 Minor wars with mt peoples of the Caucasus. The good relationship with Prussia provided Russia with reassurance in Europe as her for. policy was steered by Prince **Gorchakov** (1789–1883);

1864 The annexation of Turkestan intensified Brit.-Rus. rivalry.

The Far E.: treaties were concluded with China related to China's

1858 cession of the Amur region and 1860 the coastal provinces resulting

1860 in the establishment of the port of **Vladivostok**.

1867 The sale of Alaska to the U.S.A. (p. 117) was a measure directed against Britain.

1875 Acquisition of Sakhalin in exchange for the cession of the Kuriles to Japan.

Imperialism and Balk. Policy (1878–1914)

Econ. life: industrialization began after 1881; the railway network was expanded for milit. considerations:

1883–6 the Trans-Caspian Railway; 1891–1904 the **Trans-Siberian Railway**.

1892–1903 As minister of finance, Count **Witte** (1849–1915) transformed Russia into a 'hotbed of capitalism'. Concentrated in large concerns, heavy industry developed with a speed comparable to the U.S. following the influx of esp. Fr. capital (the 'revenge loans'). Limited purchasing power at home and the public debt made exports necessary (e.g., in 1891, of grains, even though famine prevailed at home); profits found their way abroad; orders for armaments alleviated impending crises (1899–1903). The enormous fortune of the Church was unproductive; the emancipated peasants were in debt to the point of despair. The insufficient allotment of land, interest on leaseholds, taxes, substantial increase in the pop. (98 mil. in 1880; 175 mil. in 1914) contributed to the formation of the **Proletariat**.

Rus. Messianism: in the literary circles of Moscow University the destiny and mission of Russia was discussed (p. 69); a Rus. form of messianism developed:

Westerners: CHAADYEV, BELINSKY, SOLOVYEV cal. for the adoption of Western technology, polit. institutions, and lib. and socialist ideas. The anarchist **Michael Bakunin** (1814–76) believed in a better future to follow the destruction of the authority of Church and state. He fled from banishment in Siberia, and in London met KARL MARX and the Rus. exile **Alexander Herzen** (1812–70), whose paper *Kolokol*, founded in 1857, had a strong impact on public opinion in Russia. Disappointed by Eur. 'huckster religiosity' and greed for profits, he saw seeds of moral regeneration in the Mir system (p. 69).

Slavophiles: KHOMYAKOV, **Constantine Aksakov (1817–60)** and others expected to find a state of grace and salvation from Western selfishness in the Rus. soul's righteous faith, intuition and capacity for suffering.

Pan-slavists: MICHAEL POGODIN (1800–75) fused Slavophilism and Western thought in the conception of the polit. unification of all Slavs.

1867 At the 2nd Pan-slavist Congress in Moscow this conviction was also represented by the novelist **F. M. Dostoyevsky (1821–81)**. In his book

1871 *Russia and Europe*, **Nikolai Danilevsky** (1822–85) proclaimed a new evangelism, incl. the downfall of a decadent Europe, the leadership of which was to fall to a morally superior Russia. In the *Moscow News*, **Michael Katkov** (1818–87) propagated an autocratic **Pan-Russianism** which appealed to public opinion. In int. affairs, the for. minister NIKOLAI GIERS (1882–95) nevertheless stood by the

1881 '3 Emperors' League'. An understanding with France was reached only after

1890 the non-renewal of the Reinsurance Treaty by Germany (see Dual Alliance, p. 83).

East Asia: WITTE pressed for imperialistic expansion through econ. measures, but he warned the minister of war, KUROPATKIN (1898–1904), against polit. adventures involving Japan.

1896 Intervention in favour of China, which granted railway concessions in exchange.

1898 Lease treaty obtaining **Port Arthur**;

1900 Occupation of Manchuria (on the occasion of the Boxer Rising). Over-estimating their own strength, the Russians provoked Japan in Korea.

1904–5 The Russo-Jap. War (p. 115) disrupted the internal structure of tsardom (p. 111).

1905 Peace of Portsmouth (U.S.). WITTE obtained moderate peace conditions (surrender of claims to Korea, Port Arthur, s. Sakhalin). Russia retained her leading position in E. Asia.

1905 The defensive treaty of Björkö between WILLIAM II and NICHOLAS II remained without effect. For. minister IZVOLSKY terminated Russo-Brit. rivalry through the

1907 agreement relating to Persia (p. 87); he returned to a for. policy concentrating on the **Balkans** and **the Straits**, supported Serb. Panslavism (p. 81); however, he encountered intensified Austro-Hung. activity in the Balkans (for. minister AEHRENTHAL) and suffered a defeat during the

1908 Bosnian Crisis (p. 121). For. minister SAZONOV lost control of affairs abroad during the

1912–13 Balk. Wars. He was unable to stem the 'escape of Pan-slavist and milit. circles from revolution into war'. Armament was increased and, in

1912, a naval convention was concluded with France.

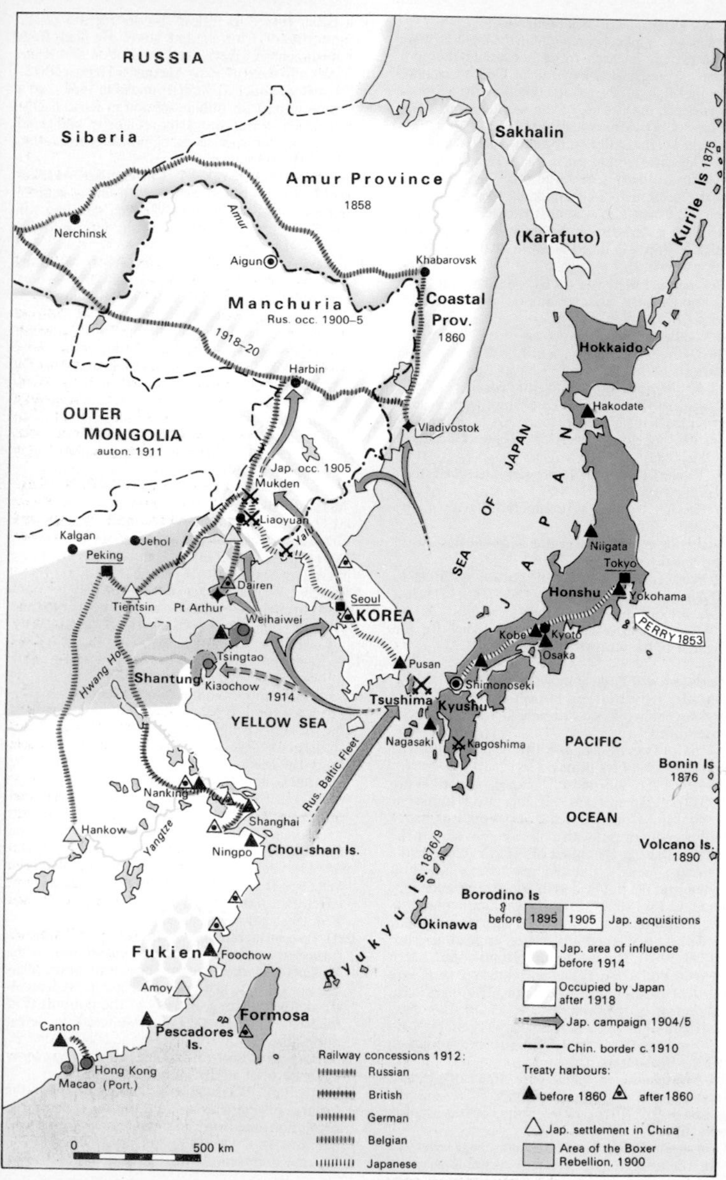
RUSSIA
Siberia
Amur Province
1858
Sakhalin
(Karafuto)
Kurile Is 1875
Nerchinsk
Amur
Aigun
Khabarovsk
Manchuria
Rus. occ. 1900–5
Coastal
Prov.
1860
1918–20
Hokkaido
Harbin
Hakodate
OUTER
MONGOLIA
auton. 1911
Vladivostok
SEA OF JAPAN
Jap. occ. 1905
Mukden
Liaoyuan
Yalu
Kalgan
Jehol
Niigata
Peking
Tokyo
Dairen
Honshu
Yokohama
Tientsin
Pt Arthur
Seoul
Weihaiwei
KOREA
PERRY 1853
Kobe
Kyoto
Osaka
Tsingtao
Pusan
Hwang Ho
Shantung
Kiaochow
Shimonoseki
1914
Tsushima
Kyushu
YELLOW SEA
Nagasaki
Kagoshima
PACIFIC
Rus. Baltic Fleet
Bonin Is
1876
Nanking
Shanghai
OCEAN
Hankow
Yangtze
Ningpo
Chou-shan Is.
Volcano Is.
1890
Ryukyu Is. 1876/9
Borodino Is
Okinawa
before
1895
1905
Jap. acquisitions
Fukien
Foochow
Jap. area of influence before 1914
Amoy
Occupied by Japan after 1918
Formosa
Jap. campaign 1904/5
Canton
Pescadores Is.
Chin. border c. 1910
Hong Kong
Macao (Port.)
Railway concessions 1912:
Russian
British
German
Belgian
Japanese
Treaty harbours:
before 1860
after 1860
Jap. settlement in China
Area of the Boxer Rebellion, 1900
0
500 km

Japanese expansionist policies from 1875

Eur. interest in Japan was aroused by ENGELBERT KAEMPER's account of his journey to Japan (1690–92). Whalers sought coaling and freshwater stations in Jap. ports; beginning in 1804 Rus. and Amer. attempts to obtain these remained unsuccessful, until in

1854, Japan was opened to the world by Commodore PERRY. PERRY appeared before Tokyo and compelled Japan to accept the

1854 Treaty of Kanagawa (nr Yokohama) with the U.S.A., incl. concessions in two ports (relating to customs duties, extraterrit. judicial privileges, and administrators). Trade agreements with Eur. powers followed; reaction hostile to foreigners led to humiliation (the bombardment of Jap. ports). The Shogunate lost prestige.

1867 Abdication of the last Shogun, KEITI.

The Meiji Era (1868–1912)

1867–1912 MUTSUHITO. Mod. Japan developed during the 'illumined reign of the emperor' **(Meiji Tenno)**. Japan became aware of the fact that its existence was in danger unless it adopted Eur. ways. The transformation took place in 3 stages:

1. The overcoming of the ancient feudal structures: the southern Damyos voluntarily transferred their power to the emperor; this enabled him to implement the 'programme of the new era'; it was officially proclaimed in 1869, and enforced in an absolutist manner.

1871 abolition of the feudal order; fiefs were replaced by new administrative districts; the state provided pensions to compensate the nobility. The prohibition of for. travel was lifted; the gvt promoted for. study; Eur. advisers were called to Japan.

1872 Introduction of general conscription and reorganization of the army after Fr. and Prus. models. In rapid succession the following institutions were formed or adopted from Europe: mandatory public schooling; the police, press, the judicial system, the post office, the railways, public health and finance (the Yen currency was modelled after the Amer. system of coinage); establishment of the Bank of Japan. The abolition of pensions to the Samurai and of the ancient code of the sword drove the opposition to the last

1877 uprising under SAIGO TAKAMORI. Following the defeat at Kagoshima, the Samurai caste disintegrated.

2. The domestic application of the reforms: factions (clans) developed in the new bureaucracy: after the rest. of imp. power, the con. milit. party rejected Eur. influence; it considered expansion to the continent of Asia more urgent than soc. and econ. reforms. The Progressive party (Kaishinto), although it also pursued a policy of expanding the econ. area, wanted to effect Western reforms first. The Rad. party (Siyute) cal. for a parl. system which was not, however, directed against the 'council of the elder statesmen' (Genro: the 'invisible power behind the throne'), nor against the divine absolutism of the Tenno.

1878 Establishment of prov. parliaments.

1884 Establishment of an Upper House composed of members of the court nobility (**Kuge**) and the Damyo families, who received new titles of nobility in a hierarchy of 5 ranks (from prince to baron).

1885 Convocation of the 1st Cabinet appointed by the emperor, 1888 convocation of the Secret Council of State (Sumitsuin). Prince **Ito Hirobumi** (1841–1909) designed the new

1889 constitution (of a const. hered. monarchy), in which the emperor represented the highest power in the state, who could not be removed; the Upper House and the Chamber of Deputies had 300 members each; the municipalities and communities were given a form of self-admin. modelled after the Prus. system. The great clans retained polit. power. *c.* 1900 the Seiyukai party was founded (ITO), as was the Kenseihonto party; both were shaped by the great clans.

3. The rise of the empire to world power status: industrialization was promoted by a significant rise in pop. (1867: 26 mil.; 1913: 52 mil.). The Japanese, because of their eagerness to learn, their capacity to adapt, their discipline and their frugality, caught up with the world economy more quickly than expected. Family trusts (among them the Mitsui, the Yasuda, the Sumitomo) controlled industry, trade and the banks. They were concerned with obtaining raw materials (coal) and markets abroad. Imperialistic aims were pursued by the Choshu clan (the army) and the Satsuma clan (the navy); the gvt suffered from their rivalry.

1875 Agreement with Russia over Sakhalin (Rus.) and the Kuriles; 1876 occupation of the Bonin and Ryukyu Islands. Interference by Jap. and Chin. troops in the Kor. Tonglak uprising caused the

1894–5 Sino-Jap. War. The superior Jap. forces conquered Dairen, Weihaiwei, Shantung, Seoul.

1895 Peace of Shimonoseki: China ceded Formosa and the Pescadores Islands; it was obliged to pay a war indemnity and to recognize the independence of Korea (which became an empire under Rus. protection in 1897).

1895 Establishment of a battleship fleet, consisting of 4 heavy armoured cruisers and 8 battleships; participation in the suppression of the Boxer Rising (p. 91). Rus. advances in E. Asia were met by the

1902 defensive alliance with Britain. Attempts to limit spheres of infl. in Korea and Manchuria resulted in the raid on Port Arthur: destruction of the Rus. E. Asia naval squadron.

1904–5 Russo-Jap. War: incompetent leadership and domestic polit. problems undermined the Rus. conduct of the war. The Jap. armies forced Port Arthur to capitulate; they occupied Korea and advanced into Manchuria.

1905 Vict. on land at **Mukden**, at sea at **Tsushima**: Admiral TOGO dest. the obsolete Rus. Balt. squadron after its journey half-way around the globe.

1905 Peace of Portsmouth (U.S.): Japan gained S. Sakhalin (Karafuto), Port Arthur and, in addition, a protectorate over Korea and S. Manchuria. Internationally it was recognized as a new **great power**.

1907 Treaties of friendship with France and Russia; the U.S. restricted Jap. immigration.

1910 Annexation of Korea (Chosen).

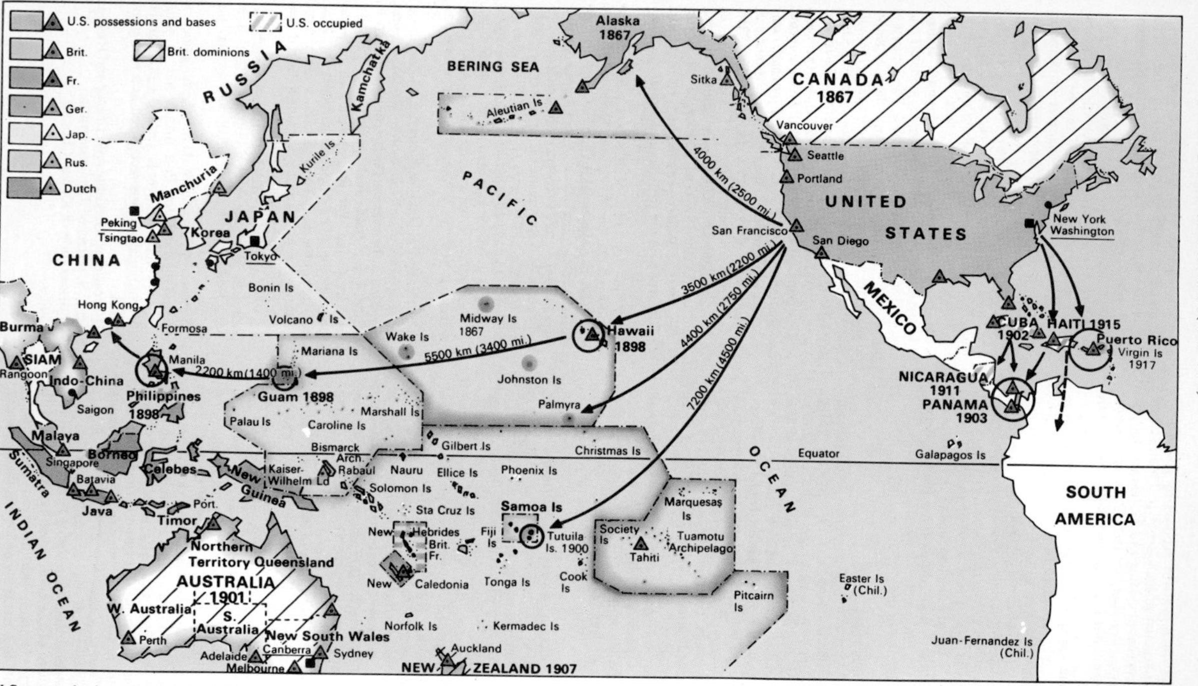

U.S. expansionist policies from 1867

'Reconstruction'

1865–9 Andrew Johnson continued the moderate policies of ABRAHAM LINCOLN; however, the rad. Republicans forced him into a power struggle which led to impeachment proceedings. In 1868 black Americans were granted citizenship, in 1870 the right to vote.

1869–77 President Grant considered the state an institution to provide for the needs of war veterans. During his tenure the U.S. experienced its darkest period of corruption. A milit. dictatorship over the Southern rebels (to 1877) protected the agents of the N. ('carpet-baggers'), who fostered the formation of questionable local admins., incited the coloured population and wasted public funds. The planters suffered under a burden of taxation and debts. To stem anarchy they resorted to self-help (secret societies: the Ku Klux Klan; lynchings). Elect. restrictions (literacy tests) and racial segregation continued the degradation of the Negroes to the level of a socially inferior class. Although the lib. Republicans (CARL SCHURZ), who split away from the main body, turned against the mixing of business and politics, Presidents HAYES, GARFIELD, ARTHUR and CLEVELAND

1877–89 made only slow progress in breaking down the 'spoils' system. With the Civil Service Act of 1883, examinations for officials were introduced.

Econ. Growth

Although the impotence of the state fostered the greed for profits and gangsterism, it also actuated the courage to take risks, energy and private initiative. Despite econ. crises (1873, 1907), industry, technology, business and capital expanded. Between 1860 and 1914 the pop. increased from 31·3 mil. to 91·9 mil. incl. 21 mil. immigrants. The number of workers grew by 700%, the rate of production by 2000%, that of investment capital by 4,000%. The U.S. was first in the production of iron, coal, oil, copper and silver; steam power gave way to electricity; protective tariffs facilitated the formation of monopolies. Often rising from small beginnings, trusts and the giant corporations of the 'tycoons of big business', ASTOR (fur trade), **John Rockefeller** (Standard Oil), CARNEGIE (steel), **Morgan**, VANDERBILT (railroads) and others developed. In 1913, 2% of the Amer. people earned 60% of the nat. income; MORGAN and ROCKEFELLER alone controlled 20% of the wealth of the nation (341 large corporations with $22,000 mil. in capital).

The general progress of democratization continued even though there was a threat to equality (from racial discrimination) and to liberty (from the concentration of capital in the N.). Mass production raised prosperity; indust. magnates provided funds for the foundation of universities, sc. institutes, museums, soc. welfare institutions. Union organizations (the Amer. Federation of Labor (A.F.L.) 1886; the Indust. Workers of the World (I.W.W. or 'Wobblies' 1905) carried on bitter struggles to increase wages (over 1,000 strikes annually). The gvt began the struggle against monopolies and exploitation.

1901–9 Theodore Roosevelt reformed the admin. and the tariff structure of the railroads.

1909–13 Taft pushed through anti-trust legislation.

1913–21 Woodrow Wilson proclaimed a programme of the 'New Freedom', restricted protective tariffs, introduced progressive taxation and further reduced the power of the trusts.

America Enters the Polit. World Stage

1891 Repeal of the Preemption Act of 1841; internal expansion slowed down. Finan. and business circles infl. for. policy. To appease public opinion, the new imperialistic form of power-politics was justified on moral grounds and carried out mainly by econ. means **(dollar imperialism).**

1867 The purchase of Alaska from Russia for $7·2 mil. still met critical opposition (by 1913 the fur trade and gold yields were bringing profits of $81 mil.).

1895 During the Cuban uprising against Spain, which was supported by Amer. volunteers, the Pulitzer and Hearst press influenced public opinion strongly; the Maine incident in Havana harbour (explosion of an Amer. warship) and the accompanying public uproar then unleashed

1898 the Sp.-Amer. War (occupation of Cuba). At the Peace of Paris, America obtained Guam and Puerto Rico. The conflict between the imperialists and their opponents (CARL SCHURZ) over Hawaii and the Philippines was reluctantly decided in favour of annexation by MCKINLEY (1897–1901), who pointed to similar intentions on the part of Japan, Russia and Germany. **Theodore Roosevelt**, **Taft** and **Wilson**, on the other hand, were not reluctant in pursuing an imperialist policy. Under the threat of intervention, capital investments were turned into finan. protectorates over Cen. and S. America (the policy of the 'big stick'). After 1889 the Pan-Amer. conferences served similar objectives. They were supposed to safeguard the unity of the continent (domination by the U.S.A.).

1910 Establishment of the Pan-Amer. Union.

Cordial relations with Germany cooled (1889 dispute over Samoa, partition in 1899; commercial competition), as did those with Russia (emphasis on the policy of the 'open door' in E. Asia, p. 91; mediation during the Russo-Jap. War, p. 115). The relationship with the trad. enemy, Britain, developed along another tack. In the struggle over the **Panama Canal** question

1850 the Clayton-Bulwer Treaty continued to call for the construction of the canal on an int. basis. Founded by DE LESSEPS in 1879 (p. 105), the Panama Canal Co. ended because of scandals.

1895–7 During the border dispute between Venezuela and Brit. Guiana, Britain bowed to America's demand for mediation. Beginning of Brit.-Amer. rapprochement. The construction of the canal was left to the U.S. (1901); the Canadian-Alaskan frontier was fixed (1903).

1903 A revolution, provoked by the U.S. in Panama, separated the country from Colombia.

1914 Opening of the Panama Canal after 10 yrs of construction.

The Italian colonial empire, 1914

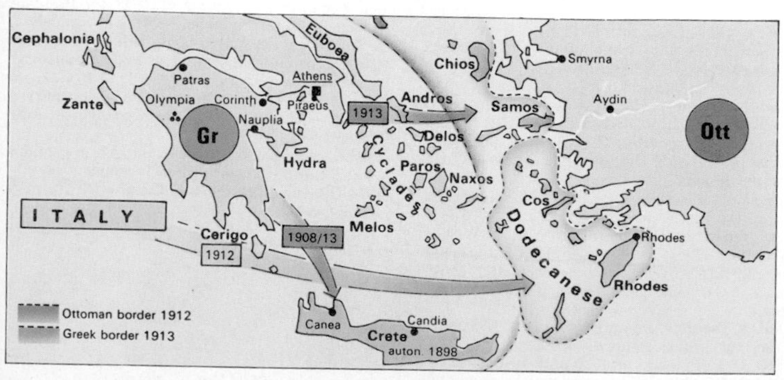

The Aegean Sea before 1914

The unification of Italy was followed by a period of exhaustion. Traditions and personalities of the bourgeois parties (Radicals, Left and Right Liberals) were more important than polit. programmes, which were blurred by the polit. system cal. *'Trasformismo'* (the transformation of the opposition through co-operation, bribery and coercion). After

1876 Italy was ruled by rad. lib. Cabinets (e.g. that of DEPRETIS). The fostering of agriculture, industry, the army and the navy necessitated sacrifices, leading to continuous budget deficits and a tendency to divert attention from domestic difficulties by resorting to the politics of irredentism (p. 73).

1878 Establishment of the 'Italia Irredenta' League.

1879 Mandatory schooling for elementary school children introduced (ages 6–9).

1882 Extension of suffrage (making approx. 20% of the male pop. eligible to vote, the right to vote being still linked with school matriculation).

The Era of 'Grandiose Politics' (1882–1900)

1878–1900 HUMBERT I.

Disconcerted and concerned over the Fr. occupation of Tunis (p. 107),

1882 Italy joined the Triple Alliance (p. 83), which was, however, troubled by Italy's irredentist claims on Austria (s. Tyrol, Istria, the Adriatic). Fr. advances in N. Africa after

1887 prompted the prime minister, **Crispi** (p. 73), to pursue an expansionist colon. policy, relying on the Triple Alliance for support and suppressing nat. ambitions to obtain the unredeemed territories still under Aust. rule.

1887–90 Despite Abyss. opposition, Massawa was expanded (1885) and became the colon. possession of **Eritrea**.

1889 Treaty of Uccialli: **Abyssinia** became a protectorate, MENELIK II was recognized as Negus (p. 97).

1889 Annexation of **Ital. Somaliland**. After the cancellation of the protectorate agreement by MENELIK II, CRISPI, over-estimating Italy's power, began the

1894 war with Abyssinia.

1896 Defeat of Aduwa: a severe crisis resulted; CRISPI fell from power. In the Treaty of Addis Ababa Italy abandoned the plan to establish an Abyss. colon. empire. Her policy now concentrated on creating a balance between the Eur. power blocs by mitigating Fr.-Ital. differences.

1900 Secret agreement delimiting spheres of interest in N. Africa (France: Morocco; Italy: Libya).

Domestic affairs: pop. increased, despite a rising rate of **emigration** (by 1914 every 4th Italian lived abroad).

1887 Protective tariffs promoted the industrialization of the N. (aided by for. capital investments). In the S., econ. and finan. crises, scandals in banking and corruption in other areas.

1888–98 Tariff war with France. Economy measures and increased taxation by the 'strong' CRISPI Cabinets were not enough to balance the increased expenses of admin. and armaments: a sharp rise in prices, distress among (agricultural) workers, child labour, lower wages and longer hours of work than in other industrialized nations.

1882–3 Establishment of the Socialist party (BISSOLATI, TURATI, and others). Associations of cooperative self-help and local trade unions developed.

1894 Dissolution of the Socialist Leagues. Assassinations by Anarchists, secret societies in the s. (the Mafia, Camorra) undermined the authority of the state.

1893–4 Famine caused upheavals by the 'Fasce' workers' leagues in Sicily.

The Giolitti Era (1900–15)

1900–46 VICTOR EMANUEL III.

1903–5/6–9/11–14 The Cabinets of Giolitti (the 'strong man' of the liberals), who as prime minister played off parties and factions against each other and won the support of both Cath. 'Popolari' party and moderate Socialists for reforms.

1905–6 The railways taken over by the state; workers' compensation and soc. insurance; recognition of trade unions.

1906 Establishment of a 'Cen. Council of Labour'. The econ. and finan. situation improved and Italy caught up with the rest of Europe. Even so, 'Giolottism' lost power in favour of a new, 'integral' **nationalism**. **Gabriele d'Annunzio** (1863–1938), the poet and admirer of NIETZSCHE, believed that 'a people wishing to take part in the conquest of the world' could do 'without freedom'. He inspired

1910 the Nationalist party, which cal. for the 'struggle of the nations' in place of the class struggle and advocated irredentist policies.

1912 The introduction of universal manhood suffrage put an end to the bourgeois-lib. polit. system.

1912 Split-up of the Socialists: the 'reformists' (BISSOLATI) were defeated by the 'revolutionaries' under **Benito Mussolini** (p. 182), from 1909 Secretary of the Chamber of Labour in Trento, and from

1912 editor of *Avanti!* He roused the dissatisfied masses of workers and peasants, esp. during the

Jun. 1914 'Red Week', to participate in strikes.

For. policy: compromise with France in the

1902 Agreement of Neutrality; the crises over Morocco (p. 109) and Bosnia (p. 121) weakened the Triple Alliance. Nationalist agitation and the success of the French in Morocco brought about a revival in the irredentist tradition (calling for the fortification of the Alp. frontier) and of colon. expansionist policies.

1911 Annexation of **Tripolitania**, leading to

1911–12 war with Turkey, which was complicated militarily by the resistance of the Senussi; politically by the Ital. advance into the Aegean (the Dodecanese).

1912 Peace of Lausanne: Libya became auton. and, *de facto*, came to Italy; the question of the **Dodecanese** remained unsolved.

1912 Promise of neutrality to France. At the outbreak of war in

1914 Declaration of Neutrality (3 Aug.). In the struggle between the neutralists (GIOLITTI) and the interventionists (D'ANNUNZIO, MUSSOLINI), the prime minister **Salandra**, represented *'Sacro egoismo per Italia'*. As for. minister SONNINO presented territ. claims to Austria.

1915 In the **Treaty of London** SONNINO was able to obtain greater concessions from the Entente powers. The Triple Alliance was cancelled by Italy on 3 May.

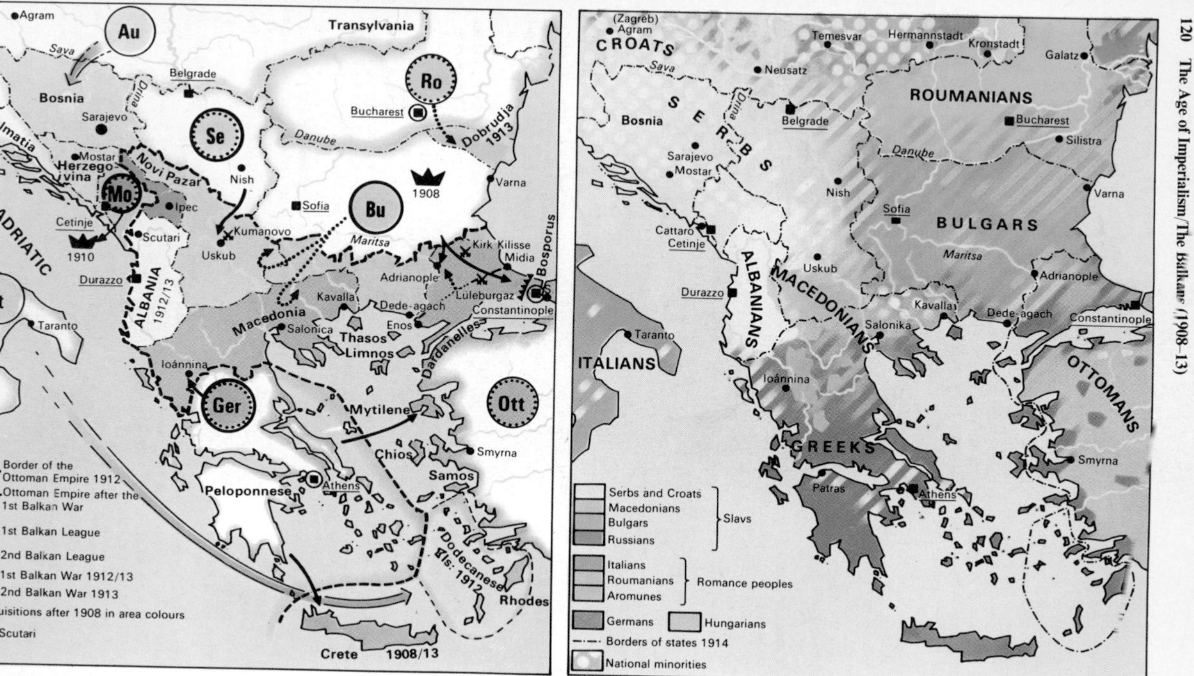

The partition of European Turkey, 1908–13

The Balkan peoples before 1914

The Balk. Crises (1908–13)

The decay of the Ott. Empire and the far-reaching nat. ambitions of the new nat. states with their manifold ethnic, cult. and relig. divisions (causing minorities and *'irredenta'* problems), kept the Balkans in constant unrest. It became the high-tension area of world politics, directly (Austria-Hungary, Italy, Russia) or indirectly (Germany, France, Britain) involving the great powers.

1908–9 The Bosnian Crisis was caused by the

1908 revolt of the Young Turks (p. 87), who endeavoured to transform the Ott. Empire into a const. state with equal rights and suffrage for all subjects.

Sep. Union of Crete with Greece. As leader of the Lib. party, VENIZELOS (p. 81) gave momentum to the 'Greater Greece Movement'.

Oct. FERDINAND I (p. 81) proclaimed himself tsar of the ind. kdm of **Bulgaria**. **Austria-Hungary** feared demands for a return of those parts of the Ott. Empire administered by her since the Congress of Berlin (1878). After Austro-Rus. Balk. agreements had been reached during the

Sep. meeting of for. ministers at Buchlau (between the Aust. for. minister, AEHRENTHAL, and his Rus. counterpart IZVOLSKY) Austria decided on the

Oct. 1908 annexation of Bosnia and Herzegovina, which was objected to by the Turks; the annexation caused indignation in Serbia, which, seeing its plans for a Greater Serb. State disrupted, mobilized. Over the question of the **Straits** (the opening of the Bosporus and the Dardanelles), **Russia** met Brit. opposition; convinced of having been outmanoeuvred by the Austrians, Russia backed Serbia. **Britain** (under the for. minister SIR EDWARD GREY) backed the Rus. position and cal. for an int. conference to clear the Bosnian question; fearful of being outvoted, Austria rejected the call for a conference. Italy did not wish to see further expansion of Aust. power; to maintain the *status quo* in the Balkans,

1909 the secret Treaty of Racconigi was concluded with Russia (p. 83). **France** used restraint during the crisis because her gvt did not yet feel up to a test of milit. power. Acting in accordance with the proverbial 'loyalty of the Nibelungen', **Germany** (under Imp. Chancellor VON BÜLOW) stood by Austria. Germany opposed the intentions of the Aust. chief of the General Staff, **Franz Count Conrad von Hötzendorf** (1852–1925), for a preventive war to 'settle accounts' with Serbia, but did allow an Aust. ultimatum to Serbia and, in the

Mar. Petersburg Dispatch (considered to be a humiliation), warned Russia not to support Serbia. IZVOLSKY resigned and, as Russia's ambassador in Paris, became a determined opponent of the Cen. Powers.

Consequences: success of Ger. policies, making a compromise between Austria and the Porte possible: evacuation of the Sandjak Novi Pazar (a Turk. administrative district) and finan. compensation. Since Austria-Hungary was Germany's only reliable ally, her dependence on her Danubian partner increased. The ties between the Entente powers did not loosen; tensions in the Balkans were not eased:

1910 NIKITA I of Montenegro assumed the title of king;

1911 Establishment of the secret Greater Serbian association 'Union or Death' (the 'Black Hand') by Colonel DIMITRIJEVIĆ-APIS.

1912–13 Crisis in the Balkans. Unrest in Albania (ESSAD PASHA); internal upheavals and weakening of the Turk. position because of the

1911–12 Tripoli War with Italy (p. 119) caused Serbia and Bulgaria to join forces. Encouraged by Rus. diplomacy, the 2 states joined in the

Mar. 1912 1st Balkan League (directed against Aust. expansion in case of the expected partition of Eur. Turkey). Greece and Montenegro joined the alliance.

Oct. 1912 1st Balkan War: the 4 members of the alliance declared war on Turkey. Severe defeats of the Turks at Kirk Kilisse, Lüleburgaz and nr Adrianople (by Bulgaria), at Kumanovo (by Serbia). In consequence, a **critical int. situation** developed: supported by Russia, **Serbia** demanded access to the Adriatic; **Italy** opposed this. Italy wished to annex Albania and cal. for the renewal of the Triple Alliance. **Greece** protested against the occupation of the Dodecanese by Italy (1912). **Austria-Hungary** objected to any kind of increased power for Serbia or Italy while it backed **Bulgaria**. **Russia** (for. minister, SAZONOV), concerned for the last of her Balk. allies and for her policies towards the Straits, looked with apprehension at the pressure exerted by Bulgaria on Serbia and Turkey. At the

Dec. London Conference of Ambassadors, **Germany** (guided by Imp. Chancellor VON BETHMANN-HOLLWEG) and **Britain** (GREY) jointly endeavoured to bring about the

May 1913 Peace of London: cession of all Turk. territories w. of the Enos–Midia line and of all Aegean islands. During the conflict over the spoils, **Bulgaria**, overestimating her strength, attacked Serbia.

Jun. 1913 2nd Balkan War: the intervention of **Roumania**, **Greece**, **Montenegro** and **Turkey** on the side of Serbia confused the situation completely. Relations between Austria-Hungary and Roumania (already burdened by the presence of a Roumanian minority in Transylvania) cooled because of Austria's threat to interfere to save Bulgaria; Germany and Italy, however, prevented her from doing so.

Aug. 1913 Peace of Bucharest: Bulgaria lost Macedonia and Dobruja; Crete finally united with Greece; **Albania** became an auton. pty (under Prince WILHELM ZU WIED, who was outmanoeuvred by ESSAD PASHA).

Consequences: overall disappointment, esp. in **Serbia**, which had been prevented by Austria from reaching the Adriatic Sea. Prevailing friendships and alliances were reinforced; the situation in the Balkans, the 'powder-keg' of Europe, remained unstable, and in the

Jul. Crisis of 1914, ignited the 1st World War (p. 122).

Causes of the War

Conflicts generated by power politics within the Eur. state system (Germany/Britain, Germany/France); **armament race of the great powers** (Ger. and Fr. army budgets of 1913, pp. 105, 110); **Anglo-Ger. naval rivalry** (Franco-Brit. naval agreement of 1912); **difficulties of the multi-national Austro-Hung. state** (striving for autonomy by the Czechs, the Slav. problem); **the Eur. alliances lost their defensive character**; **Russia's Balk. policy** (p. 121); hasty mobilizations and ultimatums (caused by preconceived plans of milit. operations). Of less importance were Fr. ('revenge policy') and Ger. (the 'Pan-Ger. League') nationalism and Anglo-Ger. trade rivalry.

The Question of Responsibility

The war was unleashed because of mutual distrust; because of the belief that a limited Eur. war could not be avoided (a belief esp. fateful on the Ger. side); because of the limited freedom of decision on the part of the leading statesmen; and because of the peoples' willingness to arm to ensure their security. None of the states was willing to abandon its aims to preserve the peace:

1. **Austria-Hungary** held on to the conception of a supra-nat. empire.
2. **Serbia** sought to realize the idea of a nat. state.
3. **Russia** feared another failure of its Balk. policy and faced the alternative of war abroad or revolution at home.
4. **Britain** wavered between neutrality and partisanship (indecisiveness of the Cabinet, fear of Rus. policy of offence);
5. **France,** delivered from polit. isolation by its alliance with Russia, saw this alliance as a means of bringing pressure to bear on Germany.
6. **Germany,** to escape from increasing polit. isolation and to help the domestically and internationally troubled Danubian monarchy to gain prestige, stood by its alliance with Austria-Hungary. The Ger. General Staff urged the initiation of the war in 1914, since otherwise the preconditions for a quick subjugation of France would no longer be present (Schlieffen Plan, p. 125);
7. **France and Germany** failed to exert any moderating influence on their alliance partners, Russia and Austria-Hungary.

The Jul. Crisis, 1914

28 Jun. Assassination of the heir to the Aust. throne, the Archduke FRANCIS FERDINAND (b. 1863), and his wife in Sarajevo by the Bosnian student PRINCIP, who was under orders from the secret 'Black Hand' organization (no direct involvement by the Serb. gvt).

6 Jul. Assurance of unconditional Ger. loyalty to the alliance (*'carte blanche'*).

20–23 Jul. Visit of the Fr. president, POINCARÉ, and prime minister, VIVIANI, to St Petersburg. Reassurance of the alliance. After their departure, Austria-Hungary presented

23 Jul. an ultimatum to Serbia that was to be acted on within 48 hrs; it demanded action with Aust. participation against the anti-Aust. movements in Serbia and the punishment of the guilty.

25 Jul. Serbia voiced objections regarding possible violations of its rights of sovereignty; Serbia ordered partial mobilization.

25 Jul. Imp. Council of Krasnoye Selo: Russia decided to support Serbia. Regardless of Brit. and Ger. attempts to mediate (proposal of a conference of ambassadors and direct negotiations between Russia and Austria-Hungary),

28 Jul. Austria-Hungary declared war on Serbia.

29 Jul. Partial mobilization of Russia.

30 Jul. General mobilization of Russia. The Ger. chief of the General Staff, HELMUTH VON MOLTKE (p. 125), urged his Aust. colleague FRANZ CONRAD VON HÖTZENDORF to effect general mobilization; he advised against attempts at mediation, which were undertaken once more by the Ger. Imp. Chancellor VON BETHMANN-HOLLWEG (p. 110) because of the threat of Brit. intervention: **there was no coordination between the milit. and the polit. leadership in Germany**.

31 Jul. General mobilization of Austria-Hungary. Germany proclaimed a 'state of impending hostilities' and presented Russia with a 12-hr ultimatum, demanding the discontinuation of mobilization; in an 18-hr ultimatum to France, Germany asked for a declaration of neutrality in the event of a Russo-Ger. conflict. The Ger. ambassador in Paris was instructed to ask in the event of a forthcoming declaration of neutrality by France for the surrender of the fortresses of Toul and Verdun as pledges. Russia did not respond. Thereupon

1 Aug. Ger. mobilization and declaration of war against Russia. France declared it would act 'in accordance with its own interests'. Therefore

3 Aug. Ger. declaration of war on France. The right of free passage demanded of Belgium by Germany on 2 Aug, was refused. Nevertheless

2–3 Aug. Ger. troops invaded Belgium and so challenged the Allies' guarantee of Belg. neutrality. Britain, which mobilized its fleet on 1 Aug. and assured France of protection on the N. Sea coast on 2 Aug, thereupon presented

4 Aug. an ultimatum to Germany, demanding respect for Belg. neutrality; this amounted to a declaration of war. Declarations of war by Serbia on Germany (6 Aug.), Austria-Hungary on Russia (6 Aug.), France on Austria-Hungary (11 Aug.) and Britain on Austria-Hungary (12 Aug.) followed.

Involving other Nations

Japan hoped to avoid open disagreement with the Entente powers and the U.S.A.; she also wanted to establish herself in Kiaochow; **Japan** wished to **extend her sphere of influence from northern China down to the Yangtze.**

23 Aug. 1914 Declaration of war on Germany. After the occupation of Ger. possessions (p. 109) Japan responded to the Chin. demand for the return of the Ger. territories with the

1915 '21 demands,' which China was forced to accept: N. China became a Jap. sphere of interest.

1916 Secret Russo-Jap. Treaty: both powers committed themselves to protecting China.

After the conclusion of a treaty with Germany, directed against Russia, **Turkey** proclaimed its armed neutrality (3 Aug. 1914).

Oct. 1914 Bombardment of Rus. coastal cities by the Ger. warships *Göben* and *Breslau*, which had officially become part of the Turk. navy, leading to

2–5 Nov. 1914 Rus., Brit. and Fr. declarations of war on Turkey.

Italy's decision to side with the Entente powers was dictated by her interests and her opposition to Austria-Hungary on the 'Irredenta' and 'Adria' questions (p. 119).

26 Apr. 1915 Secret Treaty of London. In exchange for entering the war, Italy received the promise of territ. concessions: the Alp. frontier was to be moved to the Brenner Pass and she was to receive Istria, the largest part of Dalmatia, Libya, Eritrea and parts of Asia Minor.

23 May 1915 Declaration of war by Italy on Austria-Hungary;

25 Aug. 1915 on Turkey; and

26 Aug. 1916 on Germany.

6 Sep. 1915 **Bulgaria** concluded a friendship and alliance treaty with Germany: as reward for entering the war (14 Oct. 1915) it received Serb. Macedonia. In the event of the entry into the war of Greece and Roumania on the side of the Entente powers, Bulgaria declared its intention to claim Gk Macedonia and Dobruja.

3 Aug. 1914 **Roumania** proclaimed its neutrality; however, in

1916 it concluded a treaty with the Entente powers which granted her Banat, Transylvania and Bukovina.

27 Aug. 1916 Declaration of war by Roumania on Austria-Hungary; followed by declarations of war by the Cen. Powers on Roumania.

Greece for the time being remained neutral.

1916 Blockade of the Gk coast by the Entente Powers. Supplies to the pop. were endangered; Greece was forced to make concessions. After the ultimatum of the Fr. High Commissioner JONNART

Jun. 1917 abdication of CONSTANTINE, the Gk king, and formation of a new gvt under the prime minister VENIZELOS.

27 Jun. 1917 Gk entry into the war on the side of the Entente Powers.

War aims and secret treaties:

1. The Entente Powers: in the

Sep. 1914 Treaty of London, Britain, France and Russia agreed not to conclude a separate peace (the treaty was endorsed by Italy in 1915, by Japan in 1917). Milit. cooperation was agreed on at several conferences.

1915 Britain and France assured Russia of the future possession of Constantinople and the Straits.

1915 Conference of Chantilly: coordinated offensives and the clearing of the Dardanelles were agreed on. Britain strove to obtain possession of the greater part of the Ger. colonies (Africa). France wished to regain Alsace-Lorraine.

1916 Sykes–Picot Agreement: agreement over the partition of Asiatic Turkey between France and Britain. The agreement conflicted with promises that T. E. LAWRENCE had made to the Arabs on Britain's behalf.

1917 Secret Franco-Rus. agreement: France was granted expansion 'to the extent of the boundaries of the former Duchy of Lorraine, incl. the Saar basin'. A neutral state (the Republic of the Rhine) was to be formed from the Ger. territories on the left bank of the Rhine. Russia was 'to fix her western frontier in full freedom and in accordance with her wishes'. These concessions were made out of fear of a separate peace between Russia and Germany.

2. The Cen. Powers: overestimation of initial milit. successes, an exaggerated feeling of nat. importance and the striving for a 'lasting peace' secured by pledges and guarantees for the future were the reasons for the immoderate and unrealistic Ger. war-aims policies, which were represented not only by the Pan-Germans and the quartermaster-general, **Erich von Ludendorff** (p. 125), but also by a polit. spectrum reaching from the Conservatives to the right-wing Soc. Democrats. These were the aims of the Ger. Empire:

1. The milit., polit. and econ. domination of Belgium (Reichstag speech of the imp. chancellor, VON BETHMANN-HOLLWEG, 5 Apr. 1916), through the annexation of Liège, Antwerp, the Flanders coast, and the iron-ore basin of Briey.
2. The econ. unity of 'Cen. Europe', incl. buffer states (such as Poland) and areas of econ. influence (such as in Roumania).
3. The enlargement of Ger. colon. possessions.
4. By means of uprisings, the elimination of Brit. rule and influence in the regions stretching from Morocco to India (proclamation of the 'Holy War').
5. A separate peace with Russia, which did not come about. For this reason

1916 the **auton. Congress Poland was proclaimed,** exclusive, however, of Poznan and Galicia. Germany now promoted the revolutionizing of Russia, enlisting the aid of the rad. left, hoping to bring about the establishment of buffer states from the Caucasus to Finland.

Austria-Hungary abandoned claims to Poland; but sought territ. expansion in the SE.: Serbia, Montenegro, Roumania.

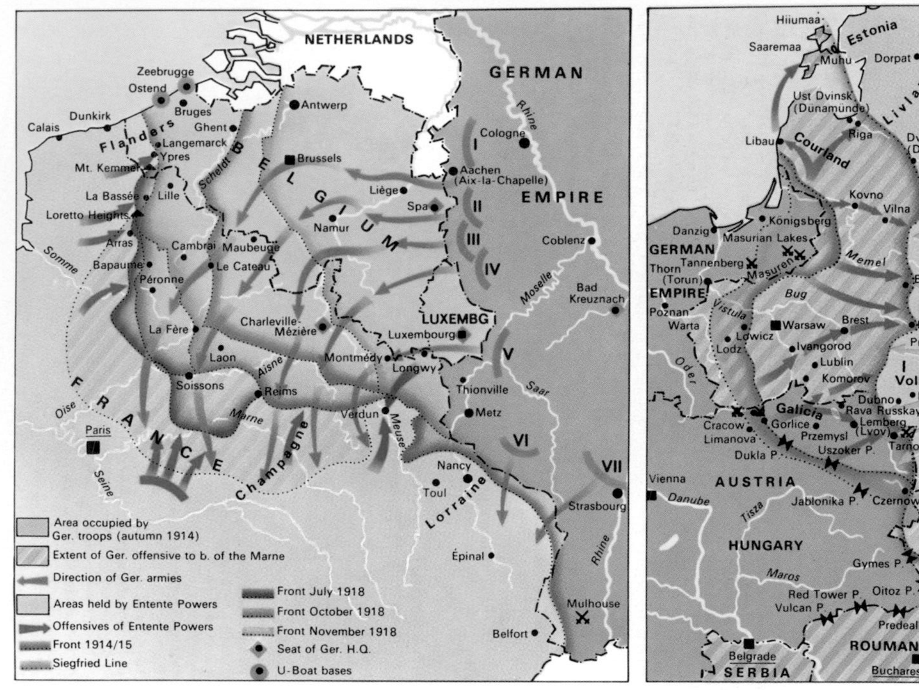

The course of the war in the west, 1914–18

The eastern theatre of war, 1914–17

The War in the W. (1914–17)

Ger. plans for the conduct of the war were based on the memorandum of the former chief of the General Staff, Count ALFRED VON SCHLIEFFEN (1833–1913), on how to handle a 2-front war (the 'Schlieffen Plan', 1905–6): the war was to be conducted defensively in the E., while a quick decision was to be sought in the W. through the encirclement of the Fr. army by a strong **'right wing'**. In anticipation of Fr. advances through Alsace-Lorraine, the plan was altered by HELMUTH VON MOLTKE (1848–1916), a nephew of the great 19th-cent. general: the right wing was weakened. Because of the entry of Belgium and Britain into the war, a **milit. risk** materialized: 80 Ger. divisions were confronted by 104 Allied divisions.

The war of movement in 1914: the 5 Fr. armies under General JOFFRE were drawn up and the Brit. Expenditionary Force under Field-Marshal Sir JOHN FRENCH was positioned at Le Cateau; the Fr. offensive began.

Aug. 1914 b. of Mulhouse. The Fr. attack failed.

Aug. 1914 Fighting in Lorraine. The Southern Fr. army group was forced back across the border. After the deployment of 7 Ger. armies under the command of MOLTKE,

18 Aug. 1914 the offensive of the pivotal right wing began.

Sep. 1914 5 Ger. armies stood between Verdun and Paris.

6–9 Sep. 1914 b. of the Marne: a Fr. counter-offensive halted the Ger. advance. A 40-km. gap developed between the 1st and 2nd Ger. Armies. The Germans thereupon retreated to the Aisne.

14 Sep. 1914 Gen. ERICH VON FALKENHAYN (1861–1922) was appointed Chief of the Ger. Gen. Staff.

Oct.–Nov. 1914 'The race to the sea': Anglo-Fr. attempts to turn the flank of the Germans failed. Their offensive stalled at the Yser Canal and before Ypres: **the mobile war turned into trench warfare.**

Feb.–Mar. 1915 Winter offensive in Champagne: Fr. attempts to break through failed.

Apr.–May 1915 b. of Ypres (use of poison gas): the Germans obtained minor territ. gains. The Allies attacked in vain in the

May–Jul. 1915 offensives around Loreto.

Sep.–Nov. 1915 Autumn b. of Champagne: the outcome remained indecisive.

21 Feb.–26 Nov. 1916 The struggle for Verdun ('the hell of Verdun'). After initial Ger. successes (at 'Dead Man's Hill', Height 304, Forts Douaumont and Vaux) excessive casualties made the discontinuation of the struggle essential.

24 Jun.–26 Nov. 1916 b. of the Somme: the Brit.-Fr. attempt to break through the Ger. lines failed.

24 Oct.–16 Dec. 1916 Recapture of the fortifications of Verdun by the French. Failures on both sides brought about changes of command:

Aug. 1916 HINDENBURG and LUDENDORFF assumed the supreme command of the Ger. armies;

Nov. 1916 Gen. NIVELLE took JOFFRE's place as generalissimo.

Feb.–Mar. 1917 Retreat of the Germans to the **'Siegfried Line'**, prepared between Arras and Soissons. A Brit. offensive at Arras was unsuccessful, as were Fr. attempts to advance along the Aisne and in Champagne (Apr.–May 1917).

May 1917 Following a mutiny (p. 129), General NIVELLE was replaced by General PÉTAIN. Brit. attempts to break through in Flanders (May–Dec. 1917) failed.

The War in the E. (1914–17)

After the b. of Gumbinnen (Aug. 1914) and the evacuation of E. Prussia by Ger. troops, the Russians were beaten by Colonel-General PAUL VON HINDENBURG (1847–1934; his Chief of Staff was Major-General ERICH LUDENDORFF, 1865–1937).

26–30 Aug. 1914 b. of Tannenberg. Encirclement of the Rus. Narev Army.

6–15 Sep. 1914 b. of the Masurian Lakes. The Russians left E. Prussia.

The 1st and 4th Aust. Armies in Galicia advanced on Lublin and passed Lemberg; however, after the **2 bs. of Lemberg** (Aug./Sep. 1914) they were forced to break off the b. at Rawa Russkaya because of Rus. superiority in numbers (5 armies). **Austria lost E. Galicia;** there was **fighting in the Carpathian passes**. The 9th Ger. Army advanced from Cracow; but was pulled back when its flank was threatened.

1 Nov. 1914 HINDENBURG was appointed supreme commander in the E. The Rus. offensive (the 'Rus. steamroller') was countered

Nov. 1914 by the offensive of the Ger. 9th Army. Fighting took place at Lodz and Lowicz; the Austrians were victorious at Limanova.

Feb. 1915 Winter campaign in Masuria; E. Prussia freed at last.

Dec. 1914–Apr. 1915 Winter campaign in the Carpathians. Repulsion of the Russians, who were pushing into Hungary.

May 1915 b. of Tarnow and Gorlice. Galicia and Bukovina were obtained.

Apr. 1915 Ger. advance into Lithuania and Courland.

From 1 Jul. 1915 Austro-Ger. offensive from the Baltic to the San river. Warsaw (8 Aug.), Kovno (18 Aug.), Brest-Litovsk (25 Aug.) and Vilna were taken. The offensive stalled in Eastern Galicia, in the

Sep. 1915 b. of Tarnopol, lat. also in other sectors of the front.

Sep. 1915 the Tsar NICHOLAS II took over the supreme command in place of the Grand Duke NICHOLAS NIKOLAYEVICH.

Jun.–Aug. 1916 1st Brusilov Offensive. Russia obtained territ. gains in Volhynia and Galicia, but at the cost of great casualties; beginning of the demoralization of the Rus. Army. The 2nd (Sep./Oct.) and 3rd (Oct.–Dec.) Brusilov Offensives were not crowned by success, neither was the 4th Brusilov Offensive or the Kerensky Offensive.

From Jul. 1917 the Germans and Austrians staged counter-offensives. They recaptured almost all of Galicia and Bukovina.

Sep. The Germans took Riga and

Oct. 1917 the islands of Saaremaa, Hiiumaa and Muhu.

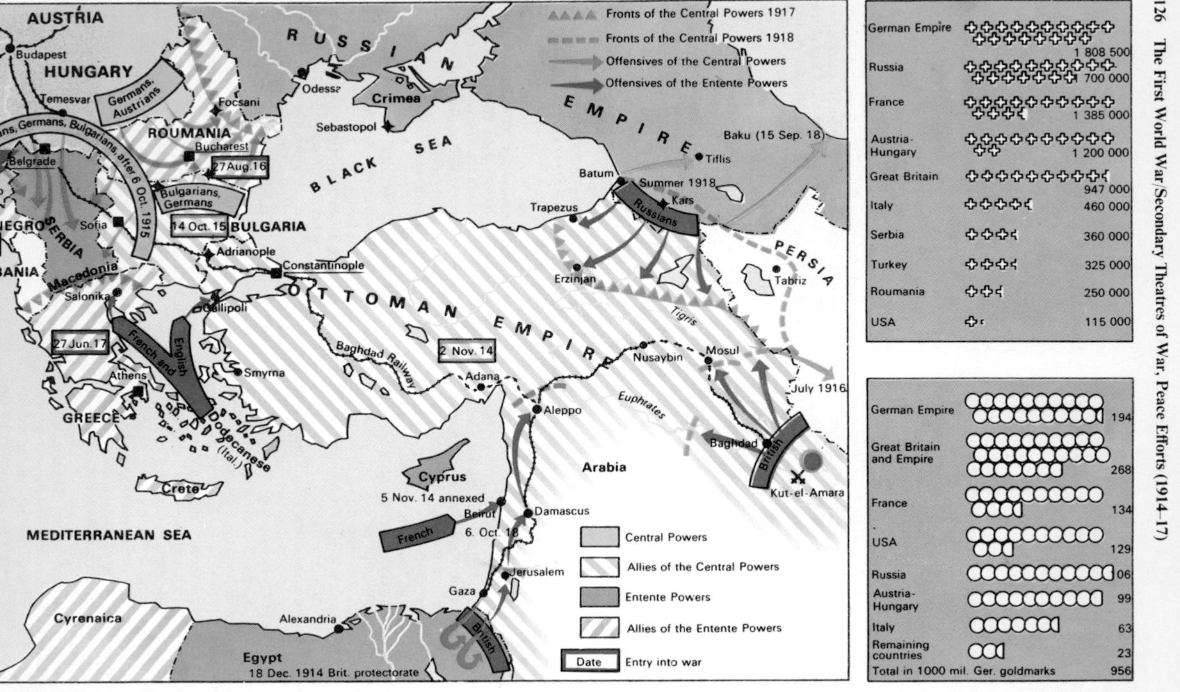

Secondary theatres of war, casualties and cost of the war

The War at Sea

The N. Sea: in 1914 and 1915 naval encounters took place at **Heligoland** and the **Dogger Bank**.

31 May–1 Jun. 1916 b. of Jutland (Skagerrak), which ended in a draw when the Brit. fleet withdrew. Subs. mine and submarine warfare was waged.

The Balt. Sea: the risk of losses meant only isolated naval actions were undertaken.

Overseas actions: after initial successes (at the encounter before Coronel, 1914), Ger. cruiser warfare was ended by the Ger. defeat in the

8 Dec. 1914 b. of the Falkland Islands and the loss of the cruisers *Karlsruhe*, *Emden* and *Königsberg*. From now on auxiliary cruisers were used.

Submarine warfare: after the

Sep. 1914 sinking of 3 Brit. cruisers, Britain

Nov. 1914 declared the N. Sea and,

Feb. 1915, Germany the waters around the Brit. Isles as a war zone and Germany initiated submarine **(U-boat)** attacks without prior warning on shipping in these waters. The Ger. order to initiate this type of warfare was given on

22 Feb. 1915. The sinking of the liners *Lusitania* (7 May 1915) and *Arabic* (19 Aug. 1915) led to Amer. protests. Germany gave assurances that she would carry on the U-boat war in accordance with the rules of int. law.

After Feb. 1916 Ger. submarine warfare against armed merchant vessels intensified.

4 May 1916 Germany presented the U.S. with a note committing itself to observing the rules of int. law governing the conduct of cruiser warfare provided Britain assumed the same obligation.

1 Feb. 1917 Ger. declaration of unlimited submarine warfare.

The War in the Air

From Jul. 1916 (b. of the Somme), **France and Britain** enjoyed **superiority in the air**. The war in the air was not, however, of decisive importance.

The War in the Colonies

Few in numbers, the Ger. protective forces in the colonies surrendered in the face of considerable Allied superiority. Only the troops in Ger. E. Africa, under the command of General PAUL VON LETTOW-VORBECK (1870–1964), held out until the Armistice.

Secondary Theatres of War

Turkey:

Nov. 1914 Britain annexed Cyprus.

Dec. 1914 Egypt became a Brit. protectorate. After futile attempts by the Allies to take them (landings at **Gallipoli** on 25 Apr. 1915, evacuation on 9 Jan. 1916), the **Dardanelles** remained in Turk. hands. After the failure of a Turk. offensive against the **Suez Canal**, the canal's eastern bank was occupied by the British in 1916. Following Rus. advances into **Armenia** and **Persia** (Jan.–Apr. 1916), Turk. Armenia was regained (Aug. 1916). The 1st Brit. offensive in **Mesopotamia** ended in a Brit. surrender at Kut el-Amara (Apr. 1916); their 2nd offensive resulted in the seizure of Baghdad (Mar. 1917). Following the outbreak of the Rus. Revolution, Britain occupied Persia.

The Balkans:

Oct. 1915 Offensive by the Cen. Powers against Serbia and capture of Belgrade.

Nov. 1915 b. of the Field of the Blackbirds. Conquest of Montenegro (Dec.); invasion of Albania (Jan. 1916). The front in Macedonia was maintained until 1918. The campaign against Roumania (initiated 28 Aug. 1916) ended with the

Dec. 1916 occupation of Bucharest.

Italy:

Jun. 1915–Mar. 1916 In the 5 bs. of the Isonzo, the Italians vainly attempted to break through.

After May 1916 the Austrians launched a counter-offensive. It was halted, after initial successes, because of the commencement of the 1st Rus. Brusilov Offensive (p. 125).

Aug. 1916 6th b. of the Isonzo: the Italians gained Gorizia (Görz). The 7th, 8th and 9th (Sep.–Nov. 1916) and the 10th and 11th (May–Aug. 1917) bs. of the Isonzo remained indecisive.

Oct. 1917 Breakthrough of the Cen. Powers at the Isonzo and retreat of the Italians behind the Piave.

Peace Efforts

As representative of the U.S. president **Woodrow Wilson** (1856–1924), Colonel HOUSE visited Paris, London and Berlin (1914–16). After its vict. over Roumania, Germany, via the U.S.A., addressed a

12 Dec. 1916 peace proposal to the Allies, which was rejected (30 Dec.).

21 Dec. 1916 WILSON sent a note to the belligerent powers, asking them to make their conditions for peace public.

26 Dec. 1916 The Ger. gvt presented no concrete conditions, but showed willingness to participate in a peace conference.

10 Jan. 1917 In its response, the Entente demanded the return of Alsace-Lorraine, the rest. of Belgium, Serbia and Montenegro; the realization of the principle of nationality; the separation of Italians, Czechs, Slovaks, Roumanians and s. Slavs from Austria-Hungary; the removal of the Turks from Europe and the liberation of the peoples under Turk. rule; the autonomy of Poland within Russia.

22 Jan. 1917 Wilson called for **'Peace without vict.'**.

29 Jan. 1917 Presentation of the Ger. conception of peace in Washington by the ambassador Count BERNSTORFF: guarantee of Ger. security and border revisions in Belgium and France to that end; the incorporation of Poland into the Ger. sphere of power; colonies to be retained and compensation paid for damages caused by the war. But whereas the **Entente Powers** were in agreement over their demands, only Germany of the **Cen. Powers** responded to WILSON's efforts to mediate. Austro-Hung. efforts to bring about peace (Prince SIXTUS of Bourbon-Parma, Count CZERNIN, 1917) and offers by Pope BENEDICT XV (Jun./Aug. 1917) remained unsuccessful.

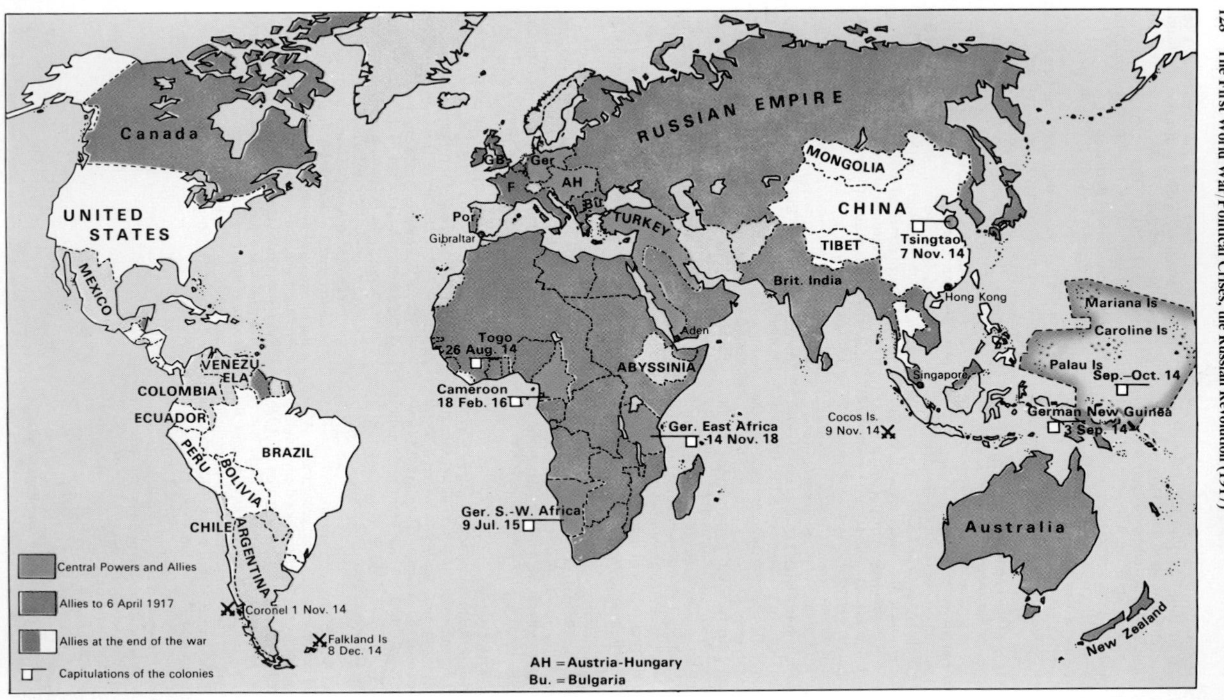
Canada
UNITED STATES
MEXICO
VENEZUELA
COLOMBIA
ECUADOR
PERU
BRAZIL
BOLIVIA
CHILE
ARGENTINA
Coronel 1 Nov. 14
Falkland Is
8 Dec. 14
GB
Ger
F
AH
Bu
Por
Gibraltar
TURKEY
RUSSIAN EMPIRE
MONGOLIA
CHINA
TIBET
Tsingtao
7 Nov. 14
Brit. India
Hong Kong
Aden
ABYSSINIA
Togo
26 Aug. 14
Cameroon
18 Feb. 16
Ger. East Africa
14 Nov. 18
Ger. S.-W. Africa
9 Jul. 15
Cocos Is.
9 Nov. 14
Singapore
Mariana Is
Caroline Is
Palau Is
Sep.–Oct. 14
German New Guinea
3 Sep. 14
Australia
New Zealand
Central Powers and Allies
Allies to 6 April 1917
Allies at the end of the war
Capitulations of the colonies
AH = Austria-Hungary
Bu. = Bulgaria

Power blocs during the First World War

The Entry of the U.S.A. into the War

Ever since the beginning of the war the U.S.A. had largely sided with the Allies. The incidents at sea and the proclamation of unlimited submarine warfare by Germany led to the

Feb. 1917 break of diplomatic relations. After the publication of the 'Zimmermann Telegram' (sent on 19 Jan. 1917 and constituting a Ger. attempt to induce Mexico to enter the war on the side of Germany) by the Brit. gvt, WILSON sent a message to the U.S. Senate (2 Apr. 1917), and, on

6 Apr. 1917, the U.S. declared war on Germany; on 7 Dec. 1917 on Austria-Hungary.

Domestic Polit. Crises in the Belligerent States

The balance of forces on the battlefield, est. by the end of 1916, lessened hopes for a quick end to the war and led to war-weariness in the armies and dissatisfaction in the civilian populations. Parliaments criticized leadership in the var. states.

Britain: the Lib. gvt of ASQUITH was toppled by **David Lloyd George** (1863–1945), the mouthpiece for the rad. wing of the Lib. party, in alliance with the Conservative BONAR LAW.

6 Dec. 1916 Formation of a War Cabinet under LLOYD GEORGE, stressing the concentration of nat. energies and the tightening of leadership.

France: the failure of NIVELLE's spring offensive and the epidemic of mutinies–influenced by the strike movement of the metal-workers in Paris and other indust. centres, and spreading to 16 Fr. army corps before being brought under control by Marshall PÉTAIN (1856–1951) – led to the

16 Nov. 1917 formation of a Cabinet under Georges Clemenceau (1841–1929), who combated defeatism and est. the conditions for Fr. vict.

Austria-Hungary was ruled with the help of emergency legislation and martial law. After the

21 Nov. 1916 death of the Emperor Francis Joseph, his grand-nephew CHARLES (I) succeeded to the throne. Count CZERNIN was the new for. minister.

May 1917 Convocation of the Austro-Hung. Parliament after a suspension of 3 yrs. CHARLES's policies of reconciliation failed because of the demands for autonomy on the part of the Czechs and s. Slavs.

Germany: the conflict over dem. reforms of the imp. constitution led to embittered domestic polit. struggles.

7 Apr. 1917 Easter Message of the Kaiser William II: reform of the Prus. 3-Class Elect. Law.

Apr. 1917 Formation of the Ind. Soc. Dem. party (U.S.P.D.): opposition to the continuation of the war and strikes of munitions workers. The deputy of the Centre party, MATTHIAS ERZBERGER, cal. for a

Jul. 1917 peace of reconciliation without victors or vanquished.

14 Jul. 1917 Dismissal of the imp. chancellor, VON BETHMANN-HOLLWEG.

Jul. 1917 Peace resolution of the majority parties in the Ger. Reichstag (S.P.D., Centre, Progressives). Under the new chancellor, MICHAELIS, the differences between the gvt, the supreme command of the army and the Reichstag increased. The domestic polit. crises ended when the majority parties yielded; it resulted in the weakening of gvtl authority: the polit. influence of the supreme command of the army became dominant.

The Rus. Revolution: revolutionary unrest developed after the failure of the 1st Brusilov Offensive (p. 125) and because of mass dissatisfaction (the length of the war, difficulties in food supply).

23 Feb. (8 Mar.) 1917 Outbreak of the Feb. Revolution in St Petersburg (Petrograd): some troops went over to the side of the revolutionaries, a **Provis. Executive Committee of the Soviet of Workers' Deputies** was created.

Feb. (Mar.) 1917 Formation of a provis. gvt under Prince LVOV.

Mar. 1917 Abdication of the Tsar NICHOLAS II. Dual gvt by the Provis. Gvt, which worked for the continuation of the war, and the Petrograd Soviet of Workers' and Soldiers' Deputies, which exercised control over the army under the power of its 'Order No. 1' (1 (14) Mar. 1917).

3 (16) Mar. 1917 Return of Lenin and his entourage from Switzerland, initiated by the Ger. For. Office in agreement with the supreme command of the army.

4 (17) Apr. 1917 Theses of 4 April: call for the Socialist Revolution ('All power to the Soviets'), the establishment of a Soviet Republic, the nationalization of the banks and landed estates.

3(16)–4(17) Jul. 1917 The Petrograd *coup* of the Bolsheviks failed because of intervention by the milit. LENIN fled to Finland. **Alexander Fyodorovich Kerensky** (1881–1970) became prime minister (21 Jul. [3 Aug.] 1917). After the abortive *coup* of General KORNILOV (Sep. 1917), a 'Politburo was founded, its 7 members included LENIN, TROTSKY, STALIN, ZINOVIEV (p. 189), KAMENEV (p. 189), to promote armed revolution.

24 Oct.(6 Nov.)–25 Oct.(7 Nov.) 1917 The Oct. Revolution in Petrograd, arrest of the members of the Provis. Gvt, flight of KERENSKY. The **Provis. Gvt had failed.** (Causes of failure: continuation of the war, refusal to redistribute land, postponement of elections for the constituent assembly.)

26 Oct. (8 Nov.) 1917 2nd All-Rus. Congress of Soviets: the **Council of People's Commissars** was created as the governing organ and the **Decree of the termination of the war** and the **Land Decree** were proclaimed: confiscation of the property of large landowners without compensation (150 mil. hectares).

2 (15) Nov. 1917 Proclamation of the right of self-determination of all the peoples of Russia. Elections to the constituent assembly (25 Nov. (8 Dec.) 1917): LENIN's party received only 9 mil. of 36 mil. votes cast.

5 (18) Jan. 1918 Opening of the Constituent Assembly: proclamation of Russia as a dem., fed. republic.

6 (19) Jan. 1918 Dissolution of the Constituent Assembly by the Council of People's Commissars with the aid of Red troops.

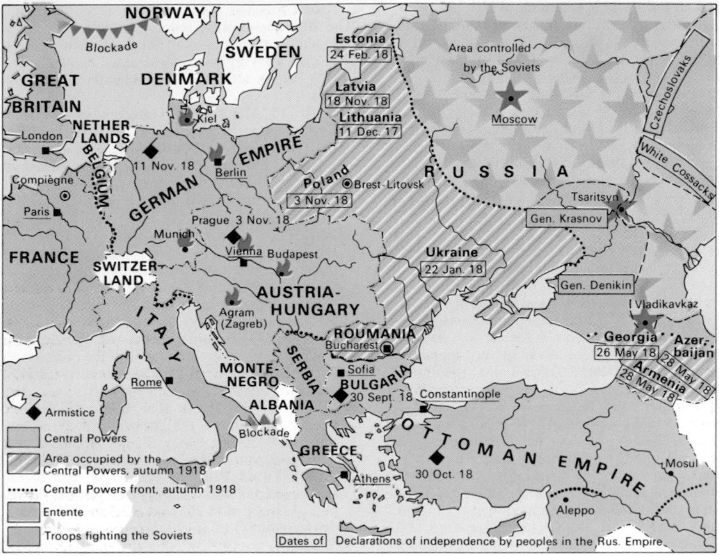

The war year of 1918

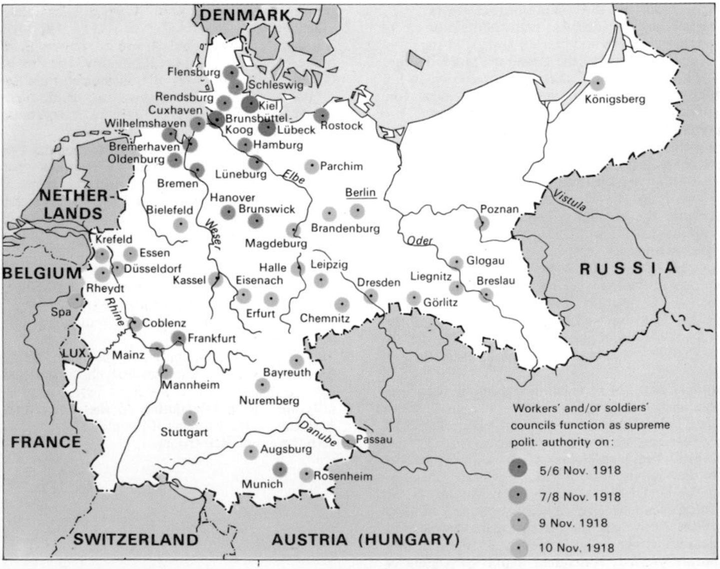

The revolution in Germany

Wilson's Peace Policies

8 Jan. 1918 Proclamation of the '14 Points' by the Amer. president, WOODROW WILSON: open covenants to be openly arrived at; freedom of the seas; removal of econ. barriers in the world; limitation of armaments; adjustments of colon. claims; evacuation of Russia by the Cen. Powers; rest. of Belgium; return of Alsace-Lorraine; readjustment of the borders of Italy in accordance with the principle of nationality; free aut. development of the peoples of the Danubian monarchy; evacuation of Roumania, Serbia and Montenegro; independence of Turkey, the opening of the Straits and autonomy for the non-Turk. peoples of the Ott. Empire; establishment of an ind. Pol. state with free and secure access to the sea; establishment of a League of Nations.

9 Feb. 1918 'The Peace of Bread', concluded by Germany, Austria-Hungary and Turkey with the Ukraine: recognition of the Ukr. state, Ukr. autonomy in Eastern Galicia (in exchange for the delivery of grain supplies to the Cen. Powers). TROTSKY (p. 111), who conducted the peace negotiations at Brest-Litovsk (beginning on 22 Dec. 1917) as the representative of Russia, declared an end to the state of war without accepting the Ger. conditions; he broke off negotiations (10 Feb. 1918). Resuming the war (with the 'rail offensive'), the Cen. Powers enforced the conclusion of the

3 Mar. 1918 Treaty of Brest-Litovsk: Russia surrendered Livonia, Courland, Lithuania, Estonia and Poland; it recognized Finland and the Ukraine as ind. states; Russia was to pay reparations.

7 May 1918 Peace of Bucharest between the Cen. Powers and Roumania; cession of Dobruja to Bulgaria; Roumania's oil resources to be exploited by Germany.

The Collapse of the Cen. Powers

Germany: although the Ger. spring offensives along the Western Front (Mar.–Jul. 1918) brought limited territ. gains, no decisive breakthrough was accomplished. The Allies, under Marshal **Ferdinand Foch** (1851–1929), forced the Germans, through their counter-offensive

Jul.–Aug. 1918 between the Marne and Aisne rivers, and the

8 Aug. 1918 tank offensive of Amiens ('the black day of the Ger. army'),

Aug./Sep. 1918 to pull back their troops to the 'Siegfried Line'.

14 Aug. 1918 Conference in the H.Q. at Spa: the supreme command of the Ger. Army declared the continuation of the war to be without prospect of success. The emperor, CHARLES I, and his for. minister, BURIAN, and the Ger. leadership could come to no agreement on the terms for an armistice.

Sep. 1918 After the collapse of Bulgaria (see below), HINDENBURG and LUDENDORFF cal. for an offer of an armistice.

Oct. 1918 Prince MAX VON BADEN (1867–1929) became imp. chancellor.

3–4 Oct. 1918 Offer of an armistice from the Ger. gvt to Wilson (based on the 14 Points). The Amer. notes in reply (8, 14 and 23 Oct. 1918) cal. for an end to submarine warfare, the evacuation of occupied territories and dem. representatives as authorized negotiators.

29 Oct. 1918 Mutiny on board the Ger. fleet in Wilhelmshaven. The revolution spread and soviets of workers and soldiers were formed.

7 Nov. 1918 Revolution in Munich.

9 Nov. 1918 Revolution in Berlin: announcement of the abdication of WILLIAM II and the crown prince; **proclamation of the Republic** by the Soc. Democrat PHILIPP SCHEIDEMANN (1865–1939), transfer of the powers of gvt to the chairman of the S.P.D., **Friedrich Ebert** (p. 149).

10 Nov. 1918 WILLIAM II went into exile to Holland. Formation of a new gvt: a 'council of people's deputies' (3 members of the Majority Socialists, 3 members of the Ind. Socialist party); alongside the gvt an **'executive council of the workers' and soldiers' deputies'** was formed.

8–11 Nov. 1918 Armistice negotiations (representative for the Allies: Marshal FOCH; for Germany: MATTHIAS ERZBERGER (p. 110)).

11 Nov. 1918 Armistice on the basis of the 14 Points: evacuation of the occupied western territories and the left bank of the Rhine, nullification of the peace treaties of Brest-Litovsk and Bucharest. Surrender, among other things, of heavy war materials and U-boats. Reparations in the occupied territories.

Austria-Hungary: after the failure of the last Austro-Hung. offensive at the mouth of the Piave (Jun. 1918) and the refusal of a peace conference by WILSON (14 Sep. 1918), Austria-Hungary agreed to the same armistice conditions offered to Germany by the Allies (4 Oct. 1918).

17 Oct. 1918 CHARLES I promised a fed. structure of the state to the peoples of the Danubian monarchy.

20 Oct. 1918 WILSON cal. for the recognition of the claims for independence by the peoples of Austria-Hungary. After the outbreak of revolution in Vienna and the opening of a Ger.-Aust. Nat. Assembly (21 Oct. 1918), the Danubian monarchy dissolved itself.

28 Oct. 1918 Proclamation of Czechoslovakia.

29 Oct. 1918 Separation of the Yugoslavic peoples from the Austro-Hung. system of states.

1 Nov. 1918 Formation of an ind. Hung. gvt under Count KÁROLYI.

3 Nov. 1918 Armistice.

11 Nov. 1918 CHARLES I abandoned all claims to participation in the gvt.

Bulgaria: after the successful breakthrough of the Allied offensive in Macedonia (Sep. 1918), the Bulg. army fell apart.

30 Sep. 1918 Armistice

Turkey: following the breakthrough on the Turk. front achieved by the Allies in the fighting in Palestine (Sep. 1918), the Turk. Cabinet directed a request for an armistice to WILSON (14–15 Oct. 1918).

30 Oct. 1918 Armistice.

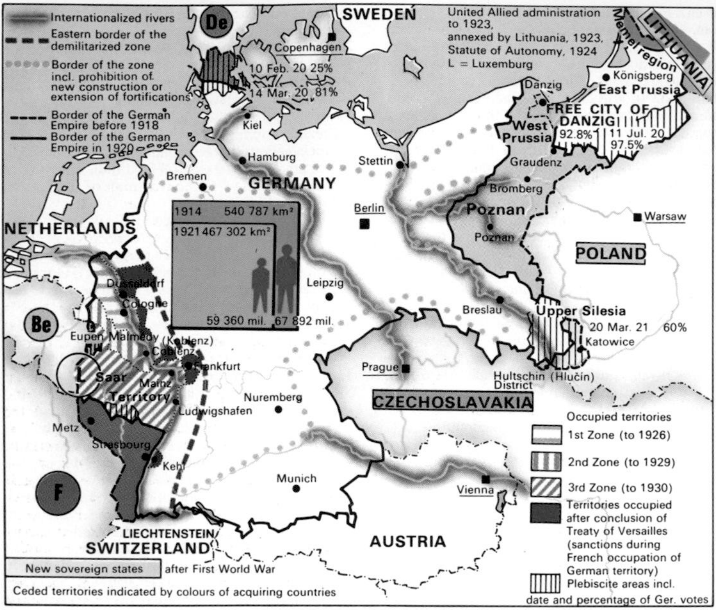

Germany after the Peace of Versailles

South-East Europe and Asia Minor after 1918

The Peace Treaties (1919–20)

18 Jan. 1919 Opening of the peace conference in the For. Ministry at Paris in the presence of 70 delegates of the 27 victorious powers, under the chairmanship of the Fr. prime minister, CLEMENCEAU; the defeated powers were not represented. During the negotiations – esp. those of the supreme council of the 'Big 10' (U.S.A.: **Wilson**, LANSING; Britain: **Lloyd George**, BALFOUR; France: **Clemenceau**, PICHON; Italy: **Orlando**, SONNINO; Japan: **Saionjii**, MAKINO), later of the **'Big 4', (Wilson, Lloyd George, Clemenceau, Orlando)** – the '14 Points', proclaimed by WILSON as the basis for negotiations, increasingly lost ground to the war aims of the Entente Powers as est. in secret treaties.

7 May 1919 Presentation of the peace conditions to the Ger. delegation (for. minister, Count BROCKDORFF-RANTZAU); their plea for verbal negotiation was rejected. Written notes by the Ger. negotiators brought only a few alterations (such as provision for a plebiscite in Upper Silesia) to the proposed treaty.

16 Jun. 1919 The Allies, in the form of an ultimatum, demanded the signing of the treaty, which contained only a few changes. Because of the threat of an invasion of Ger. territory, the Ger. Nat. Assembly assented – under protest – to the signing of the treaty (by 237 to 138 votes, the negative votes coming from the Democrats, the Ger. People's party and the German Nat. party). BROCKDORFF-RANTZAU resigned.

28 Jun. 1919 HERMANN MÜLLER (for. minister) and JOHANNES BELL (min. of colon. affairs and transport) **signed the treaty** for Germany in the Hall of Mirrors at the Palace of Versailles.

Contents of the Treaty (440 articles):

Part I: the covenant of the **League of Nations** (p. 135) and provisions for the admin. of the Ger. colonies by the 'developed countries' under the mandate of the League of Nations. Parts II and III: fixing of the **new frontiers**. Germany surrendered the following areas: Alsace-Lorraine, Posen (Poznan) w. Prussia, the Hultschin (Hlučín) district and the Memel district. Danzig became a Free City. Plebiscites were to be held in Eupen-Malmédy, Northern Schleswig, parts of E. Prussia and Upper Silesia. The Saar Basin was placed under the admin. of the League of Nations for 15 yrs; the yield of the coal mines was to fall to France. Parts IV and V: Germany surrendered its **rights in for. countries** and its **colonies**. Disarmament was to be supervised by joint Allied commissions: Germany was to hand over all its war materials. It was to establish a professional army of 100,000 men, the General Staff was to be dissolved, all fortifications to a line 30 mi. E. of the Rhine were to be razed. The confiscation of weapons and the supervision of the process was to be carried out by joint Allied commissions. Part VI: stipulations relating to P.O.W.s and soldiers' cemeteries. Part VII: surrender of war criminals (WILLIAM II was to be put on trial). Part VIII: justification of **reparations on the basis of the determination of war guilt**. (Art. 231: 'The Allied and associated gvts declare, and Germany accepts the responsibility for, all the loss and damage suffered by the Allied and associated gvts as a consequence of the war imposed upon them by the aggression of Germany and her allies.') The amount of reparations was to be fixed by a special commission. Germany also was to surrender all of her merchant marine ships over 1,600 tons and a quarter of her fishing fleet and to provide livestock, coal, benzol, locomotives, railway wagons, machinery, ocean cables, *et al.* The amount of the Ger. debts was fixed at the Boulogne Conference (21 Jun. 1920), but later revised: 269,000 mil. Ger. Goldmarks, to be paid in 42 annual instalments. Parts IX–XIV: stipulations relating to finan. affairs, econ. life, civil aviation, the navigation of rivers, railways and the int. organization of labour; as security, the Ger. territory on the left bank of the Rhine was divided into 3 zones which, upon fulfilment of the conditions of the treaty, were to be evacuated after 5, 10 and 15 yrs respectively.

10 Jan. 1920 The Versailles Peace Treaty became effective.

10 Sep. 1919 Signing of the peace treaty with Austria at St Germain-en-Laye: cession of s. Tirol to the Brenner Pass; in addition, Trieste, Istria, Dalmatia and parts of Carinthia and Carniola were to be given up; Austria was to recognize the independence of Hungary, Czechoslovakia, Poland and Yugoslavia; prohibition of the use of the name 'Ger.-Austria' by the new Aust. state as well as *'Anschluss'* to Germany; Austria was allowed to maintain a professional army of 30,000 men.

27 Nov. 1919 Signing of the peace treaty with Bulgaria at Neuilly: cession of the south-western areas of Thrace along the Medit. coast to Greece; however, Bulgaria retained access to the sea (at Dede-Agach, which was renamed Alexandroupolis). Strength of the army: 20,000 men.

4 Jun. 1920 Signature of the peace treaty with Hungary at Trianon: as a 'successor' to the Danubian monarchy, Hungary was considered to be one of the powers responsible for the outbreak of war: cession of Slovakia and Carparto-Ukraine to Czechoslovakia; of Croatia-Slavonia to Yugoslavia; of Banat to Yugoslavia and Roumania; of Transylvania to Roumania; of the **Burgenland** to Austria. Strength of the army: 35,000 men.

10 Aug. 1920 Signature of the Peace Treaty of Sèvres by the Turk. gvt (not ratified by the Turk. parliament, p. 167): internationalization of the Straits, cession of eastern Thrace (incl. Gallipoli), the Aegean islands (exc. Rhodes) and Smyrna (with adjacent area) to Greece; Syria and Cilicia went to France; Iraq and Palestine to Britain, which also assumed the protectorate over Arabia (the Hejaz Kdm). The Dodecanese and Rhodes fell to Italy. Armenia became aut. As spheres of interest, the coastal region from Adramyttium to Adalia fell to Italy; Cyprus and Egypt to Britain. Kurdistan became aut. The strength of the army was fixed at a limit of 50,000 men.

Major Problems of the Post-war Period in Europe

1. Intensification of nat. feeling owing to the ideal of polit. self-determination. Consequences: the problem of nat. minorities and border problems remained largely unsolved; the masses of the people gave way to primitive emotions and the infl. of demagogues.

2. Disputes over the peace treaties: France was concerned to preserve the new order through conferences (see below) and to stabilize it through alliances (p. 165); revisionist aspirations of the defeated powers influenced Eur. int. affairs.

3. The delay of the econ. recovery of Europe as a result of reparations being linked to the question of war guilt by the victors (see below).

4. The problem of the polit. structure of the states: because of the lack of polit. experience and judgement on the part of the new democracies, the vict. of democracy remained precarious. Dangers: the over-simplification of polit. problems and the swaying of the masses by propaganda, which became a polit. weapon (radio from 1920).

5. The ambiguous position taken by the Eur. powers in the face of the Rus. Revolution and the establishment of the U.S.S.R.

6. The failure of the League of Nations (p. 137).

7. Social changes: the working classes gained in influence (assumption of gvtl functions, improvement of the econ. situation).

8. The end of Europe's dominant position in the world: the foundations were laid for the U.S. and the U.S.S.R. to become the dominant nations. Selfish policies, governed by nat. interests and rivalry between peoples, hastened Europe's disintegration:

Germany (pp. 149ff.) strove for the revision of the peace treaty, which was considered unjust and unrealistic.

France (p. 147). The need for security, the extent of the damage she had suffered in the war, and the wish for hegemony were important factors in her rigid position over the question of reparations and disarmament.

Britain (p. 146) attempted to preserve a Eur. 'balance of power' through a policy of 'limited counter-balance': however, problems connected with the British Empire tied down her freedom of action in for. policy.

Italy (p. 159) was the rival of Britain and France in the Mediterranean.

Poland (p. 155) and **Czechoslovakia** (p. 157), which, in terms of Fr. policy, were meant to be the cornerstones in the *'cordon sanitaire'* against the U.S.S.R., became enemies following the dispute over the Cieszyn (Těšin or Teschen) territory (p. 155); the suppression of nat. minorities led to internal polit. crises.

Soviet Russia (p. 143) became a nat. Communist state; the concept of world revolution was promoted by the Comintern.

The Balk. States separated into two groups: Yugoslavia, Roumania and Greece insisted on the status quo; Hungary and Bulgaria called for revision of the treaties concluded on the outskirts of Paris. No common course of polit. action on the Balkans was possible.

9. General disarmament was not achieved because of the conception of nat. sovereignty that governed the peoples.

10. The expansionist for. policy of Fascist Italy (p. 159) and Nat. Socialist (Nazi) Germany (p. 197) increased the danger of war.

Problems in the World beyond Europe

1. Towards Europe the **U.S.A.** followed a policy of isolation; its relations with Cen. and s. America vacillated between 'dollar imperialism' motivated by econ. interests (p. 177) and the realization of Pan-Amer. solidarity. The desire for the latter found expression in the

1923 Gondra Treaty (which provided for cooperation between the individual states regardless of existing tensions), and later in the 'good neighbour policy' of ROOSEVELT (p. 187). The pronounced engagement of the U.S.A. in the Pacific area led to the

1921–2 Washington Conference and 4 treaties: 1. **The Naval Agreement**: determination of the naval strength of the 5 powers: the U.S.A. and Britain were each limited to 525,000 tons, Japan to 315,000 tons, France and Italy to 175,000 tons each. 2. The **4-Power Agreement** (the U.S.A., Britain, France and Japan) guaranteed a status quo of possessions in the Pacific area. Britain's 1902 treaty with Japan was cancelled under pressure from Canada, Australia and New Zealand. 3. The **9-Power Agreement** guaranteed Chin. independence and made the 'policy of the open door' obligatory in China. 4. The **Shantung Treaty**: return of Shantung and Kiaochow by Japan to China. Withdrawal of Jap. troops from Siberia.

1932 Proclamation of the Stimson Doctrine by the U.S. secretary of state, STIMSON: the U.S.A. pledged to deny recognition under int. law to any changes brought about by force.

2. Japan: the attempt to gain acceptance for the principle of racial equality and unhampered emigration failed owing to the resistance by the U.S.A. and the Brit. Dominions of New Zealand, Australia and s. Africa. After the

1930 London Naval Conference (disappointing for Japan, since it maintained the distribution of naval strength between the U.S.A., Britain and Japan at the level of 5:5:3), Japan began her expansion, making, within a few years, enemies of the U.S.S.R. (Manchuria), Britain (India, Burma, the Malay States and Singapore), Australia and New Zealand (the s. Sea islands), the U.S.A. (the Aleutian Islands, Guam, Wake, the Philippines), France (Fr. Indo-China) and the Netherlands (the Dutch E. Indies).

1934 The Cancellation of the Washington Naval Agreement by Japan initiated the armaments race.

3. Revolutionary activity in China (p. 173).

4. The acceleration in the process of emancipation of the oppressed peoples of Asia (infl. of the Rus. and Chin. revolutions) by an intellectual élite, whose nationalism was supported by the Comintern (p. 141; establishment of Communist parties).

5. After the assumption of power in the Near E. by Britain and France (they received mandates from the League of Nations, p. 168), their rivalry (over the oilfields of Mosul) was settled by a compromise at the

1920 San Remo Conference, which provided a share for France. The matter was fully cleared up in the

1926 Treaty of Mosul: the shares of the Iraq Petroleum Co. were divided between Brit. (52·5%), Amer. (21·25%) and Fr. (21·25%) oil companies. C. S. GULBENKIAN received 5% commission for his services as mediator.

The Question of Reparations and Int. Conferences (1920–23)

Before the Depression (p. 185) the **question of reparations** preoccupied all int. conferences. Since the U.S.A. rejected the Brit. and Fr. proposal to cancel all war debts, the obligations of the Cen. Powers to pay reparations and the war debts of the Allies remained linked for all practical purposes. After several conferences during 1920, the

1921 Paris Conference fixed the reparations to be paid by Germany at 269,000 mil. Goldmarks, payable in 42 annual instalments.

1921 The London Conference rejected the Ger. counter-proposals. The negotiations were broken off (for sanctions, see p. 149). The

1921 London Ultimatum demanded the prompt fulfilment of the Peace Treaty (trial of the war criminals, disarmament) and fixed the conditions of payment of the reparations, reduced once more to 132,000 mil. Goldmarks; should the amount of 1,000 mil. Goldmarks not be paid within 25 days, the Ruhr area was to be occupied. Germany accepted the ultimatum (5 May).

1922 2nd London Conference: another set of proposals by Germany was rejected.

1923 The Reparations Commission asserted that Germany had failed to fulfil her obligations in the delivery of timber and coal:

Jan. 1923 Fr. invasion of the Ruhr (p. 149). After the failure of POINCARÉ's Ruhr policy (p. 147), a period of less strained relations was initiated by the conciliatory attitude of Britain and the efforts at mediation (econ. and finan. interests) by the U.S.A. Following a message from President COOLIDGE to Congress, an int. commission of experts prepared the

1924 Dawes Plan: the schedule of reparation payments was modified, but no agreement on the duration was reached. By 1928, Germany was to have paid 5,400 mil. Goldmarks; from 1929 it was to pay 2,500 mil. Goldmarks annually; to secure this end, the incomes of the Ger. state (customs duties, indirect taxes, the profits of the Ger. railway system, which had been placed under for. supervision) were to be bonded. A loan of 800 mil. Ger. Goldmarks was granted to facilitate the return to the gold standard and the payment of the first instalment. The plan was ratified by the London Conference.

1925 The Locarno Conference–initiated by the Ger. for. minister GUSTAV STRESEMANN–contributed to the easing of tensions and the signing of the following agreements:

1. The Treaty of Mutual Guarantee (also Rhine or Western Treaty) between France, Britain, Italy, Belgium and Germany: Germany guaranteed the inviolability of the western border.

2. The Treaty of Arbitration between Germany and Belgium and

3. The Treaty of Arbitration between Germany and France.

4. The Treaty of Arbitration between Germany and Poland and

5. the Treaty of Arbitration between Germany and Czechoslovakia: all conflicts were to be settled peaceably, Germany was to undertake to make no alterations of the borders in the E. by force and to recognize the defensive treaties of France with Poland and Czechoslovakia; Germany did not, however, bind herself contractually to the acceptance of the eastern frontiers.

1929 BRIAND (p. 147) presented the General Assembly of the League of Nations with a plan for the creation of a **'United States of Europe'** (customs and econ. union). Negotiations over the revision of the Dawes Plan led to the signing of the

1930 Young Plan in The Hague: within the next 59 yrs, Germany was to pay 34,500 mil. Goldmarks (by 1988); Germany was given the right to control the transfer of the sums herself and to postpone the payments up to 2 yrs; one third of each annuity had to be paid annually. The creditors agreed to lower the burdens of reparation so that the payment of war debts could be eased (this constituted the first official acknowledgement of the linking of war debts and reparations). This final settlement of the reparations question was of no consequence owing to the onset of the Depression.

1932 The Lausanne Conference terminated the reparations problem: Germany was to make one final payment of 3,000 mil. Reichmarks. Acc. to Ger. calculations, *c.* 53,000 mil. Goldmarks, acc. to the Allied calculations, 20,000 mil. Goldmarks, were paid. It is certain that Germany received more in for., mostly Amer., loans than she paid in reparations ('circulation' of U.S. funds).

The Problem of Disarmament

1932 1st Int. Conference on Disarmament. It failed because of the demands of France (for guarantees of security and an armed force for the League of Nations) and Germany (for equality).

1933 2nd Int. Conference on Disarmament. The Brit. proposal (reduction of the strength of the armies, increase of the Ger. army to 200,000 men) was not accepted. The Brit. for. minister, Sir JOHN SIMON, prevented a quick solution of the question of balanced levels of armaments. Germany left the conference (Oct.), having to all intents and purposes been denied equal rights.

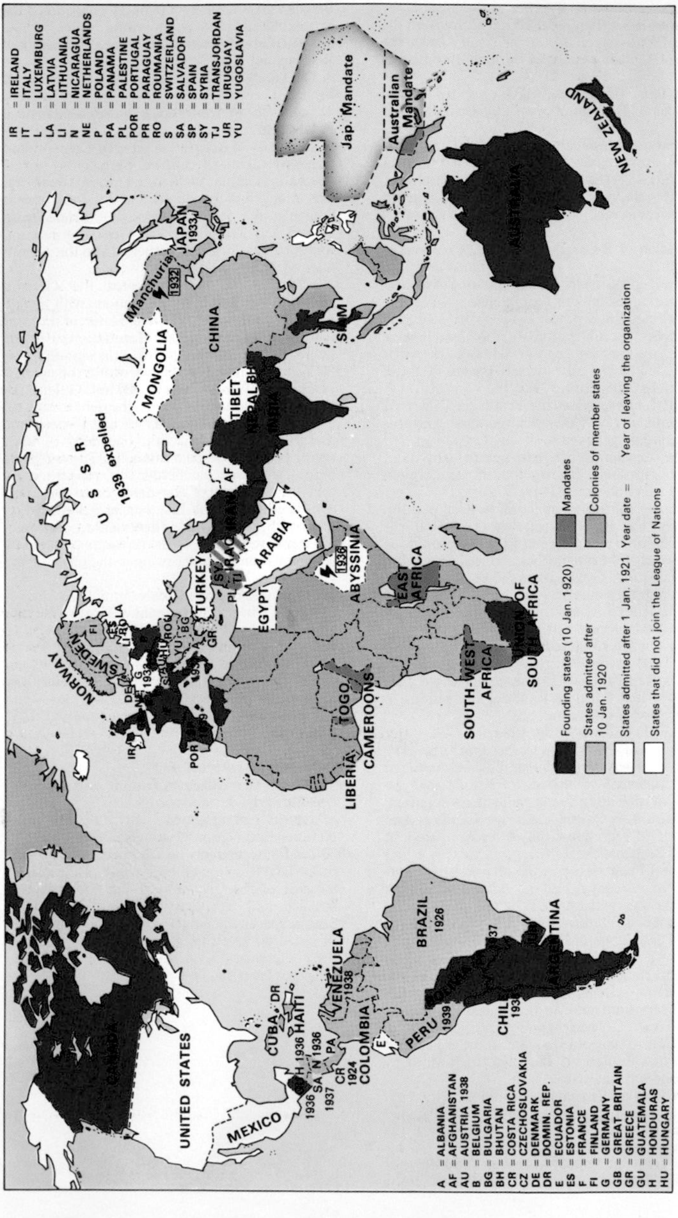

A = ALBANIA
AF = AFGHANISTAN
AU = AUSTRIA 1938
B = BELGIUM
BG = BULGARIA
BH = BHUTAN
CR = COSTA RICA
CZ = CZECHOSLOVAKIA
DE = DENMARK
DR = DOMIN. REP.
E = ECUADOR
ES = ESTONIA
F = FRANCE
FI = FINLAND
G = GERMANY
GB = GREAT BRITAIN
GR = GREECE
GU = GUATEMALA
H = HONDURAS
HU = HUNGARY

IR = IRELAND
IT = ITALY
L = LUXEMBURG
LA = LATVIA
LI = LITHUANIA
N = NICARAGUA
NE = NETHERLANDS
P = POLAND
PA = PANAMA
PL = PALESTINE
POR = PORTUGAL
PR = PARAGUAY
RO = ROUMANIA
S = SWITZERLAND
SA = SALVADOR
SP = SPAIN
SY = SYRIA
TJ = TRANSJORDAN
UR = URUGUAY
YU = YUGOSLAVIA

CANADA
UNITED STATES
MEXICO
CUBA
DR
HAITI
GU H 1936
1936 SA
N 1936
1937 CR
PA
1924
VENEZUELA 1938
COLOMBIA
E
PERU 1939
BRAZIL 1926
CHILE
ARGENTINA
NORWAY
SWEDEN
FI
ES
LA
LI
IR
DE
NE
G 1933
P
AU
HU
RO
YU
BG
A
GR
POR
SP 1939
TURKEY
SY
PL
TJ
IRAQ
IRAN
AF
EGYPT
ARABIA
ABYSSINIA 1936
LIBERIA
TOGO
CAMEROONS
EAST AFRICA
SOUTH-WEST AFRICA
UNION OF SOUTH AFRICA
U S S R
1939 expelled
MONGOLIA
Manchuria 1932
JAPAN 1933
CHINA
TIBET
NEPAL
BH
INDIA
SIAM
Jap. Mandate
Australian Mandate
AUSTRALIA
NEW ZEALAND

Founding states (10 Jan. 1920)
States admitted after 10 Jan. 1920
States admitted after 1 Jan. 1921
States that did not join the League of Nations
Mandates
Colonies of member states
Year date = Year of leaving the organization

The League of Nations

Pre-History and Establishment

Reacting to the 'soc. revolution' of the Bolsheviks (p. 129), WILSON, on

8 Jan. 1918, announced the '14 Points' (the 'democratic world revolution'), elaborating on them in his address to Congress (11 Feb.), in Mt Vernon (4 Jul.), and New York (27 Sep.). Among other things, WILSON cal. for the establishment of a League of Nations to maintain world peace and secure the territ. inviolability and polit. independence of all states. Hegemony by one state should no longer be averted through the balance of power – the principle of int. order which had governed the Eur. states from the Peace of Westphalia to the First World War – but rather through the establishment of a League of Nations (a union of states), which was to declare future wars injust in int. law. During the peace conference, the plans and proposals of MILLER-HUT, WILSON, SMUTS and Lord PHILLIMORE were used as a basis for discussion.

28 Apr. 1919 Acceptance of the Covenant of the League of Nations by the plenary assembly of the Versailles Peace Conference.

28 Jun. 1919 Signing of the covenant, consisting of 26 articles, by the founding states, which were also the signatory powers to the peace treaty. The covenant became **an integral part of the Versailles Treaty**.

Jan. 1920 The League of Nations began its activities (Geneva), though the U.S. voted against joining.

Nov. 1920 1st meeting of the General Assembly.

1928 The Briand–Kellogg Pact (banning war as a means to settle conflicts between states), was signed in Paris by 15 nations (STRESEMANN signing for Germany, p. 149) and joined – by the end of 1929 – by 54 states. The initiative for concluding the treaty to ban war came from the Amer. secretary of state, KELLOGG; it was supported by the Fr. for. minister, ARISTIDE BRIAND.

Organization

The General Assembly of the League of Nations, meeting once a year, with each member receiving one vote, consisted of the representatives of all members of the League; the **Council of the League of Nations** consisted of 4–6 permanent members and, later, 9 non-permanent members, chosen by the General Assembly. Among the permanent members were the representatives of Britain, France, Italy and Japan, and later also Germany; after Germany left the League (1933), its seat fell to the U.S.S.R. (1934). Both organs had competence in the same fields (arbitration, mediation); but the Council pursued the more active polit. role and met several times a year. The Council had to arrive at unanimous decisions; so did the General Assembly, with few exceptions. Parties involved in disputes had to abstain. These two organs were supplemented by the **permanent secretariat** under a secretary-general with a seat at Geneva. The **Permanent Int. Court at The Hague** (arbitration in case of disputes) and the Int. Chamber of Labour (int. laws relating to labour) were affiliated to the League of Nations.

Talks and Purpose

The League of Nations, as a world-wide organization of free peoples, served to promote peace and international cooperation by placing limits on the trad. power politics pursued by individual states as well as secret diplomacy; to do so, it replaced these policies with the collective use of force by all states (econ. and milit. sanctions) against the aggressor (two thirds of all members were empowered to decide on sanctions) and free discussion by statesmen before a world forum. But, because of its link with the Paris Treaties, the League of Nations was responsible not least for the preservation of the new polit. system which had been created in 1919–20 and which, because of the principle of unanimity, could hardly be altered peacefully. The member states obliged themselves to settle all conflicts peaceably and to appeal, in case of disagreement, to the League and were bound to accept the unanimous decision of all members (without the votes of the parties in question). The League of Nations was involved in the implementation of the peace treaties (securing of borders, disarmament, the supervision of Danzig, control over the mandated territories, admin. of the Saar basin), in the protection of nat. minorities, in the distribution of econ. assistance to some countries (among them Austria), and in the care of fugitives. The work of the League was successful in the mediation of the dispute over Vilna (1920), in the conflicts over Corfu (1923) and Mosul (1924); but it failed in its efforts to safeguard overall peace (the Geneva Protocol, 1924, which was not signed by Britain), and over the disarmament question (1932–8). Positive results were achieved by the League of Nations on questions of econ. and technological cooperation; its subsidiary organs also worked with success.

The Failure of the League of Nations

The League of Nations was weakened by the absence of the U.S.A. and other major powers. Of the 63 member states, 14 had left by 1939, 2 were eliminated because of annexation, and 1 was expelled (the U.S.S.R. because of its attack on Finland). The League of Nations failed at the time of the

1931 Jap. invasion of Manchuria and the

1935 Ital. assault on Abyssinia. The League declared Italy the aggressor.

Nov. 1935 Application of econ. sanctions against Italy; but the U.S.A. continued to deliver oil; and Germany to deliver coal.

1937 Italy left the League.

The League of Nations undertook no measures to deal with the expansionist policies of the Nat. Socialist gvt in Germany.

18 Apr. 1946 Dissolution of the League of Nations following a decision by the General Assembly of the League.

Democracy on the defensive, 1919–33

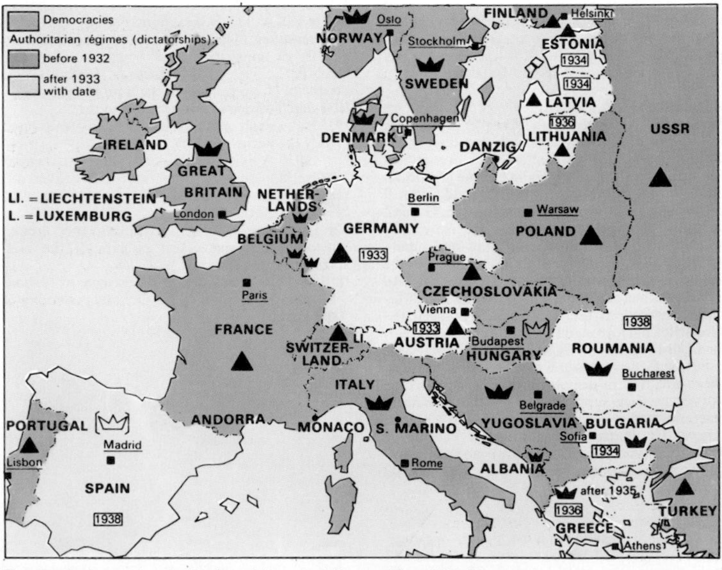

Totalitarianism and authoritarian régimes and dictatorships, 1933–39

Democracy Gains the Ascendancy

During the 1st World War, many of the peoples–even in the Western democracies–not only became used to the exercise of strong executive powers in the solution of the econ. and polit. problems posed by the war, but were also strengthened in their belief in the efficacy of power in the rapid attainment of polit. aims. After the war, many peoples also expected solutions to post-war problems to be through forceful gvts making quick decisions on such questions as demobilization, provision for jobs, the settling of war debts, reparations, reconstruction, etc. This applied esp. in countries with a lib. and parl. tradition. Initially, however, the vict. of arms was followed by the triumph of democracy. The war aim of the U.S.A. seemed to have been realized in the Europe of 1919: the 'dem. world revolution' appeared to be at hand. The dynasties of the Habsburgs and Romanovs, of the Hohenzollerns and Ottomans, disappeared. Europe, consisting in 1914 of 17 monarchies and 3 republics (Switzerland, France and Portugal), was by 1919 made up of 13 republics and 13 monarchies. In many countries, monarchy was temporarily replaced by the repub. form of gvt (e.g. Greece).

Crises Begin

Crucial in the causation of the post-war crises was the **conflict between democracy and totalitarianism**. The Rus. Revolution and the establishment of a Bolshevik dictatorship (p. 131) diverted attention from the dangers of Fascism during the 1920s, esp. since the dictators in part confined their gvtl activities to the mastery of passing crises and were often aware of the fact that they enjoyed popular support. It took the seizure of power by the Nazi party in Germany to demonstrate the danger threatened by right-wing dictatorships and to render the apparent triumph of democracy in 1918 illusory. By 1939 there were only 12 democratically ruled states left in Europe; 6 of them (7 if Hungary and its 'vacant throne' is counted) were monarchies, 5 republics.

Causes of the Crisis of Democracy

1. **Soc. changes:** acceptance of polit. equality for the masses (universal suffrage, incl. the right of women to vote, though this was still to be won in France and Switzerland among other countries).
2. **Psychological and sociological consequences of the war:** trust in force, soc. changes in the bourgeoisie; organization and cen. leadership of the masses; extensive sections of populations uprooted.
3. **Disappointment over the peace treaties.**
4. **New conflicts:** disruption of the world's economy and currencies; the world-wide Depression (p. 185).
5. **Domestic power struggles:** conflicts between the ruling ethnic groups in the newly established multi-national states (Czechoslovakia, Yugoslavia) with nat. minorities.
6. **Introduction of proportional representation** in elections in many of the states of continental Europe. Consequences are said to include: formation of splinter groups and the hampering of the establishment of clear parl. majorities. Many nations were ready to trust one 'leader' and to accept the one-party state.

Mass democracy was the **precondition for the establishment of dictatorship**. The masses were won over by appeals to a great nat. past, by opportunistic programmes which fused opposing elements of the pop., and by clever propaganda, which hammered home faith in the nation's vict. Dictatorial states were characterized by controlled news media, rigged elections (selection of candidates by the ruling party), elimination of opposition, brutal suppression of resistance, abandonment of the concept of the const. state to 'preserve the nation's fabric', and disregard for the rights of the individual. Ital. Fascism (p. 182) and Ger. Nat. Socialism (p. 183), particularly because of their anti-Marxist slogans and their fanatical nationalism, provided models for right-wing groups in many countries of Europe.

The Eur. Dictatorships (1922–36)

Oct. 1922 BENITO MUSSOLINI's 'March on Rome' in **Italy**.

Jun. 1923 Following a putsch of officers in **Bulgaria**, formation of the ZANKOFF gvt.

Sep. 1923 After a milit. *coup*, a milit. dictatorship was est. in **Spain** by General PRIMO DE RIVERA.

Oct. 1923 GAZI MUSTAF KEMAL PASHA (after 1935 KEMAL ATATÜRK) was elected 1st president of **Turkey**.

Jan. 1925 AHMED ZOGU became president of **Albania** with broad powers.

May 1926 Milit. putsch by PILSUDSKI in **Poland**.

May 1926 Milit. uprising by General GOMEZ DA COSTA in **Portugal**, who was driven from power by General CARMONA.

Dec. 1926 The dictatorial régime of SMETONA/VOLDEMARAS was est. in **Lithuania**.

Jan. 1929 *Coup d'état* of King ALEXANDER in **Yugoslavia**.

Feb. 1930 Personal régime of King CAROL II in **Roumania**, turned into a royal dictatorship in 1938 by a *coup d'état*.

Jul. 1932 Formation of the SALAZAR gvt in **Portugal**.

Dec. 1932 **Lithuania** became an authoritarian one-party state.

Jan. 1933 HITLER's 'seizure of power' in **Germany**.

Mar. 1933 *Coup d'état* of DOLLFUSS in **Austria**: dictatorship by the semi-Fascist 'Fatherland Front'.

Mar. 1934 Dictatorship est. by KONSTANTIN PÄTS in **Estonia**.

May 1934 By the *coup d'état* of K. ULMANIS, presidential dictatorship was est. in **Latvia**.

Aug. 1936 *Coup d'état* of General METAXAS in **Greece**.

Sep. 1936 General FRANCO became *'Caudillo'* of the nationalist insurrection in **Spain**.

Marxism-Leninism

Lenin (p. 111) endeavoured to apply the Socialist theories of MARX and ENGELS (p. 66) to polit. realities in Russia. In this attempt he paid particular attention to the establishment of a strong party organization. The following factors were important in his ideological considerations:

1. **The theory of imperialism,** set forth in his essay **Imperialism – the Highest Stage of Capitalism**, based on J. A. HOBSON's *Imperialism, a Study* (1902) and R. HILFERDING's *Das Finanzkapital.* **Main characteristics of imperialism:** monopolies in econ. and finan. life are concentrated in a few hands; the normal exchange of goods gives way to the export of capital. Imp. policies dominate int. relations and the world is increasingly divided into spheres of interest and colon. territories.
   The polit. consequences as Lenin saw them:
   (a) Imperialistic wars, interrupted by respites of varying duration made possible by alliances.
   (b) A successful proletarian revolution even in a country of relative backwardness in indust. development, a weak link in the 'chain of world capitalism' such as Russia, from where **the world revolution would later spread to the industrialized countries.**
   (c) The danger of the formation of a 'workers' élite' in the imperialist nations, created by the ruling class's bribery, leading to nationalistic and opportunistic thought in the working class and the development of a **'petit bourgeoisie'.**
   (d) Shifting of the class struggle to the int. stage through the alliance of the revolutionary workers with the exploited proletariat of the colon. and semi-colon. areas.
2. **The theory of a 'new type of party'** (advocated first in the essay *What Is to Be Done?* (1902) and then in *One Step Forward, Two Steps Back* (1904)): creation of a well-schooled **cadre party of professional revolutionaries** (the 'avant garde of the proletariat'), an **'officer corps of the army of the civil war'**, to serve the development of polit. class consciousness and the guidance of the proletariat; the party was to be structured in accordance with the principle of **'dem. centralism'**: election of the guiding organs of the party from the lower levels up, strictest party discipline and centralized leadership. **Tasks of the party:** 'the struggle for the purity of Marxist–Leninist ideology', the combating of 'deviations', the formation of class alliances (i.e. the formation of 'united fronts', 'popular fronts', etc.), to bring about the revolution in accordance with the 'teachings of strategy and tactics', practical realization of the overall aims ('general line') of the party for a particular period as they had been developed in sc. analysis. The party was to rule through the domination of the admin. of the state and the mass organization of society.
3. **The teaching of the 'dictatorship of the proletariat'** (advocated in *State and Revolution* (1918)), a 'power which is not bound by any laws'. The 'dictatorship of the proletariat' was to suppress the bourgeoisie in the transition period from capitalism to socialism and was to hasten the advent of a classless society (communism).
4. **The development of historical Marxism (p. 66) into dialectical materialism (Diamat)**, the 'ideology of the Marxist-Leninist party' (advocated in *Materialism and Empirio-Criticism* (1908)). Its major components were:
   (a) Philosophical materialism (epistemological realism), acc. to which the various manifestations of matter move independently of the human will, but are 'reflected' in human consciousness ('the theory of reflection'). Matter forms the only reality of this world.
   (b) The dialectical method: the interconnection and mutual dependence of things, the development of movements out of the 'conflict of opposites' (thesis–antithesis) which exist in each reality as 'internal contradictions' and lead to change (the synthesis).

Stalinism

Stalin (p. 189) added some elements to Marxism-Leninism. His most important ideological theses were challenged in 1956:

1. **The theory of 'Socialism in one country'** (clashing with TROTSKY's teaching of 'permanent revolution'): establishment of a Socialist economy without the aid of the highly developed countries of the W., i.e. on the basis of native energies.
2. **The theory of 'revolution from above',** to be carried out by the 'initiative of the state' (the party) with direct 'support from below' (the proletariat) by means of gradual change. No counter-revolution and 'overthrowing of the existing powers' (1938).
3. **Dogmatic simplifications** of Marxism-Leninism in Ch. 4 of the *Short History of the Communist Party of the Soviet Union* (1938).
4. **Fostering of Rus. patriotism** through the evocation of 'love for the Union of Soviet Republics' as the 'home of the working people', thereby safeguarding and preserving the 'Socialist fatherland'. The U.S.S.R. became a 'family of peoples' under the guidance of the 'great Rus. comrades'. At the same time, it was the 'vehicle of progress'.
5. **The ideological justification of nationalism** in the *Letters of Language* (1950). Language became the symbol of the historical continuity of the Rus. people and the 'creative role' of the Socialist soviet state (justification of the claim to hegemony by the U.S.S.R. over other peoples).

Notwithstanding the emphasis on nationalism during the 'Great Patriotic War' (p. 207), the int. aspirations of Bolshevism were retained.

The Communist International
World-wide Communism aimed at bringing Com. ideology to polit. domination by using the power structure of the **Com. International (Comintern)** in accordance with a specific principle of organization and conduct. The universal aim was the **world revolution** led by the Com. parties in all countries. All Com. parties were to adopt the programme of action of the **Com. Party of the Soviet Union (the Bolsheviks).** On the initiative of LENIN, the formation of a 3rd International was planned. Reasons:

1. Collapse of the 2nd International (est. in 1889), which had a Soc. Dem. orientation, during the 1st World War,
2. Seizure of power by the Bolsheviks in Russia (p. 129). Already in the *Apr. Theses* (p. 129) of 1917, Lenin was calling for the establishment of a new International, to be organized with an emphasis on its opposition to the 2nd International. The 'Open Letters' to the workers of Europe and America were followed by

Jan. 1919 the official invitation to a congress in Moscow.

Mar. 1919 Establishment of the 3rd International in Moscow by delegates of Com. and Socialist parties, to support the Soviet gvt endangered by civil war and for. intervention, and to serve as a 'preliminary step of the Int. Republic of Soviets towards the world-wide vict. of Communism' (LENIN), ZINOVIEV (p. 189) was elected president.

Jul.–Aug. 1920 2nd Congress of the Comintern in Petrograd and Moscow (delegations from 37 countries): deliberations over the method for spreading Com. propaganda; plans for the establishment of secret Com. organizations to prepare proletarian revolutions; at the same time, the legal activity of the official Com. parties was to continue and LENIN's **21 Points** were to be accepted: all Com. parties were to model themselves unconditionally after the Rus. Com. party, the Soviet Union was to be defended, strictest discipline was to be observed, and all were to subordinate themselves to the commands of the cen. organization; continued struggle against Soc. Democracy, now splitting into revolutionary and reformist wings. At the head of the permanent executive committee (with its seat at Moscow), and entrusted with tactical leadership between congresses, were ZINOVIEV, chairman, KARL RADEK (1885–1939), secretary; both were members of the Cen. Committee of the Com. party of the Soviet Union (amounting to 'personal union' of the Comintern and the Soviet gvt). After the 'miracle of the Vistula' (p. 155), the mutiny at Kronstadt (p. 143) and the collapse of the gen. strike in Germany (Mar. 1921),

Jun.–Jul. 1921 the 3rd Congress of the Comintern initiated the discussion of 'unity from above' (cooperation with Soc. Dem. leaders), a policy which was adopted by the Executive Committee as 'general policy'.

Nov.–Dec. 1922 4th Congress of the Comintern: because of the 'defensive position of the revolutionary forces', an attempt was made at polit. cooperation with Socialists; Ger. demands to the Western Allies and nationalist forces were to be supported. Consequences: offer of benevolent Soviet Rus. neutrality in the event of a Franco-Ger. war (presented by RADEK), and counselling of the Ger. Communists to join nat. resistance (ZINOVIEV) during the Ruhr crisis (p. 149). The revolutionary situation in Germany was overcome by STRESEMANN (p. 149). A final attempt to revolutionize Germany failed with the suppression of the uprisings in Saxony and Thuringia (p. 149). This failure, and the attempts at revolution in Bulgaria (1922) and Estonia (1924), forced retrenchment and a transition to more cautious methods.

Feb.–Mar. 1924 5th Congress of the Comintern: formation of a 'united front from below' (cooperation with the Socialist workers) and 'int. solidarity of trade unions'.

Contrary to LENIN and TROTSKY, who conceived of the world revolution as proceeding from the revolutionary movements in the var. countries (dependence of the destiny of the Soviet Union on the world revolution), STALIN saw the history and unfolding of the world revolution in the struggle between a centre of imperialism composed of capitalist countries, and a centre of Socialism (the U.S.S.R.), composed of Soviet states (thus making the destiny of the world revolution dependent on the U.S.S.R.); he therefore called for the consolidation of power in one country ('Socialism in one country', p. 140).

Jul.–Sep. 1928 6th Congress of the Comintern: announcement of binding guidelines: the 'Programme of the Com. International' (domination of the dictatorship of the proletariat of the U.S.S.R., obligation to defend the Soviet Union); 'the resolutions on Communist activity in the dependent colon. territories and the struggle against imperialist war' (support of nat. liberation movements, transformation of imperialist wars into civil wars); 'the task of the Communist'.

Jun.–Aug. 1935 7th Congress of the Comintern: fight of Communists against **Fascism** in alliance with the Socialists (the **'Popular Front'**); collaboration with bourgeois parties. The Popular Front policy failed because Nat. Socialist for. policy was successful, because STALIN liquidated his opponents (the 'show trials' in Moscow, p. 189), and because Spain's Repub. gvt succumbed to the Fascists in the Spanish Civil War (p. 160 f.).

May 1943 Dissolution of the Comintern: the plan to bring about world revolution was apparently abandoned; from this point on, the U.S.S.R. endeavoured to present its position in a less threatening light (to create favourable conditions for the post-war plans of the Soviets).

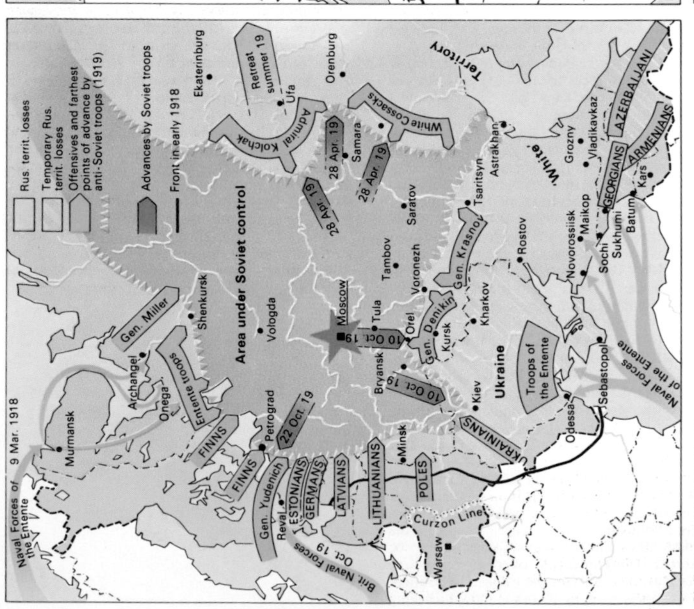

Civil war and interventions

The end of the civil war, 1920/21

The Establishment of the U.S.S.R. (1918–24)

Consequences of the Treaty of Brest-Litovsk (p. 131):

1. **Declaration of independence** by White Russia, Georgia, Armenia and Azerbaijan (1918).
2. **Attempts to seize power by the Soc. Revolutionaries** in some cities. The Soviets responded by suppressing non-Rus. nationalities.

Mar. 1918 7th Party Congress: the Cen. Committee received authority to decide for peace or war in the relationship with the 'bourgeois and imperialist states'.

Jul. 1918 Establishment of the Rus. Socialist Federative Soviet Republic (R.S.F.S.R.). Acceptance of a provis. constitution, based on the principle of soviets and the dictatorship of the proletariat.

Jul. 1918 Assassination of the tsar and his family at Ekaterinburg.

1919 8th Party Congress: the Politburo, the Orgburo and the Secretariat became the party's supreme executive organs.

1918–20 The Rus. Civil War:

1918 Formation of socially and politically diverse anti-Bolshevist groups (the 'Whites'). They fought against the Red Army, organized by TROTSKY (p. 111, commissar for nat. defence from Apr. 1918), in Siberia and the Ural-Volga area (Admiral KOLCHAK, the Czech Legion), in s. Russia Generals DENIKIN, KRASNOV, VRANGEL), in Estonia (General YUDENICH) and N. Russia (General MILLER). To safeguard their interests, the Allies landed troops in Vladivostok, Murmansk, Archangel and the ports of the Black Sea.

1919 The 'Whites' rejected President WILSON's proposal for a conference of all Rus. parties (Feb.). The plan for a 'crusade' by the Fr. Marshal FOCH was rejected by the Allied Supreme Command. For this reason, the Allies withdrew their troops. The threats to Petrograd (YUDENICH), Moscow (DENIKIN) and the Volga (KOLCHAK) were eliminated by the counter-offensives of the Red Army.

1919-20 Russo-Pol. War (p. 155).

1920 Evacuation of the last 'White' troops from the Crimea (Nov.).

Causes for the collapse of the 'Whites':

1. The lack of cooperation and their reactionary-restorative attitudes (absence of an agrarian reform programme);
2. Conflicting Allied views over the question of intervention.

Consequences of the war: Leninist centralism was imperilled by the

1921 Petrograd strike (and the **sailors' mutiny at Kronstadt**, which was suppressed by the assault of the Red Army under General MICHAEL TUKHACHEVSKY (1893–1937 (executed for a presumed anti-STALIN plot)).

1917–21 Collapse of the econ. system of 'war Communism': the socialization (nationalization) of all means of production and cen. planning of the economy led to an econ. crisis. After

1921 the establishment of the 'gvtl planning commission' (GOSPLAN: coordination of the economy), LENIN was forced,

1921, at the 10th Party Congress, to introduce the New Econ. Policy (N.E.P.). It meant the return to capitalistic forms of econ. life ('state capitalism'): peasants taxed by goods in kind; tariff-free domestic trade; admission of private entrepreneurs and for. capital. For. trade, major industries and construction projects remained in the control of the state. However, the R.S.F.S.R. now obtained int. recognition:

1921 Friendship treaty with Persia (p. 168), trade agreements with Britain and Germany;

1922 The Rapallo Treaty (p. 165), followed by *de jure* recognition by Britain, Italy and France (1924).

The dictatorship of the Com. party was strengthened through the

1921 prohibition of all opposing groups within the party. Trade unions were placed under the control of the party and lost their controlling function over the economy.

1922 Transformation of the Cheka into the 'State Polit. Admin.' (G.P.U.) (Feb.). Stalin (p. 189) became secretary-general of the party and was given the task of purging it of opposition elements and of providing for reliable secretaries, i.e. for men agreeable to the Politburo: revolutionaries replaced by functionaries. 'Show trials' of the Soc. Revolutionaries.

Dec. 1922 10th All-Rus. Congress of Soviets (1st All-Union Congress of Soviets): Formation of the Union of Socialist Soviet Republics (U.S.S.R.), consisting of the R(ussian) S(ocialist) F(ederative) S(oviet) R(epublic), the T(ranscaucasian) S.F.S.R., the U(krainian) S.S.R., and the W(hite Rus.) S.S.R.; later joined by the Uzbek, Turkmenian (1924) and Tajikistan (1929) S.S.R.s.

1923 New Constitution of the U.S.S.R., ratified by the 2nd All-Union Congress of Soviets. It differentiated between the powers of the Union (for. policy, for. trade, econ. planning, defence, soc. insurance, etc.) and the powers of the member republics, which officially retained the right to secede. The supreme organ of the state was the All-Union Congress composed of the delegates of the various Soviets; it elected, from its members, the Executive Committee, to function as the gvt under a chairman, the personal representative of the Union (1923–46: M. J. KALININ). The actual work of gvt was carried out by the Council of Peoples' Commissars. No mention of the party was made in the constitution; its centralized organization contrasted, however, with the decentralized admin. of the state.

21 Jan. 1924 Death of Lenin, who had shortly before voiced concern at the amount of power in STALIN's hands.

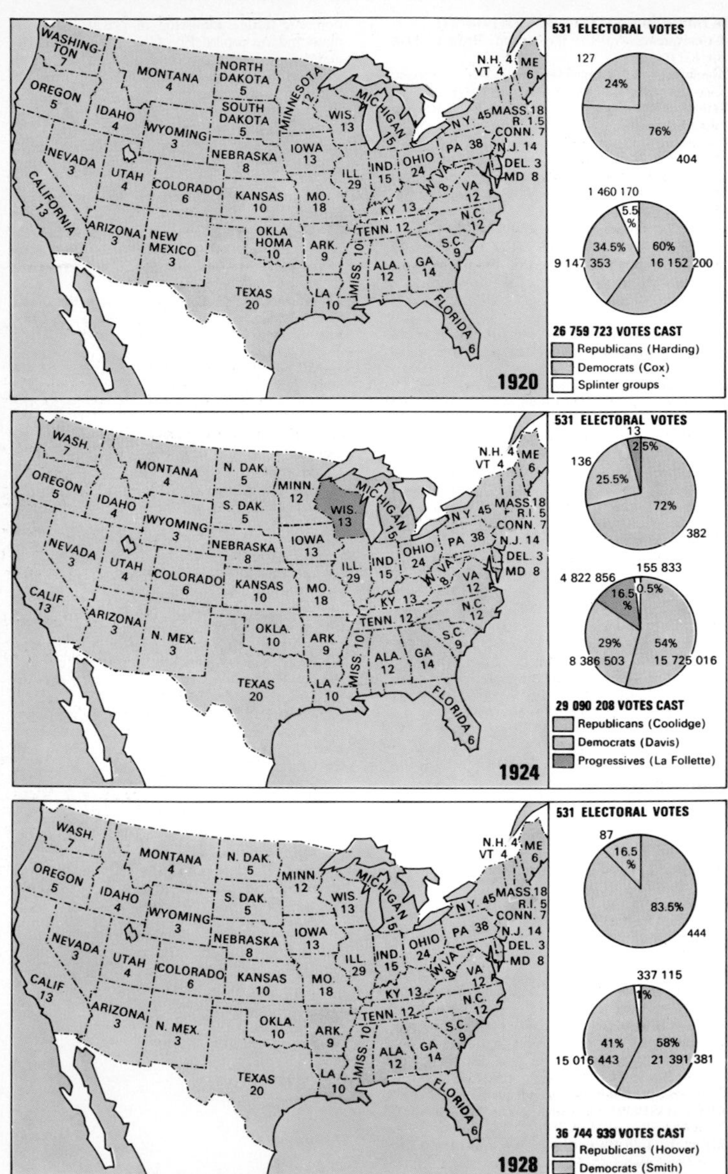

Elections won by the Republicans (the numbers under the names of States indicate the number of elected representatives)

The 'Era of Big Business' (1919–29)

Characteristics of the era's first 2 (Repub.) presidents,

1921–3 Warren G. Harding (1865–1923): election slogan: 'Return to normalcy'; and

1923–9 Calvin Coolidge (1872–1933), were

1. **Reaction** against the policies of the Democrat WILSON, whose reform measures, tinged with moralizing, were rejected.
2. **Isolationism** in for. policy, since it was believed that the Peace of Versailles threatened the well-being of America.
3. **Conflict** between the predominantly Anglo-Saxon–Prot. pop. of the agrarian areas and modern urban-industrial sectors of society dominated by intellectuals, technologists and businessmen. Added to these factors must be the

1919–20 'Red Scare': strikes, bombings, crimes of violence, which led to search and seizures, investigations and deportations of suspect elements.

The policy of the Repub. presidents to govern as little as possible led to scandals over corruption in gvt. The interests of big business were to the fore. Main representative of this 'movement' was the multi-millionaire ANDREW W. MELLON (secretary of the Treasury, 1921–30), who brought advantages to large incomes by limiting gvt activity and taxation. The laws of 1921 and 1924, influenced by 'Nordic' racial theories, curtailed immigration.

1920 Prohibition (to 5 Dec. 1933) (18th Amendment). Prohibition divided the people and the parties into 2 camps ('wet' and 'dry') and fostered smuggling, gangsterism and lawlessness.

1924–26 The Ku Klux Klan, founded in 1915, was rampant in the s. and the Midwest (1924, *c.* 5 mil. members: campaigns, in the name of morality, against Negroes, Catholics, Jews, intellectuals and the critics of prohibition).

From 1920 suffrage for women, reflecting an expression of the changed position of women in Amer. society (equal rights for men and women); the number of working women grew from 2 mil. (1914) to 10 mil. (1930).

Severe tariff legislation (1921, 1922, 1930) reflected trad. Repub. protectionism. **Neglect of farmers' interests,** who became burdened by debts, and, owing to the excessive supply of agricultural goods and soil erosion (the 'dust bowl'), impoverished. At the same time, industry prospered by increased production. Mass-production methods, improvements in the productive process (assembly line); indust. production was doubled between 1921 and 1929 by technological innovations (esp. in consumer goods, the construction and automobile industries: 1913 there was a total of 15 mil. cars in the country; 1929 26 mil.). Productive capacity concentrated in large corporations, esp. in the automobile industry, in food processing, in the banking business and in the retail trade and its chain stores.

The Great Depression (1929–32)

1929–33 Presidency of Herbert C. Hoover (1874–1964). The econ. depression was the consequence of an over-extension of the credit market.

25 Oct. 1929 'Black Friday': the collapse of the New York stock market (23–9 Oct.) highlighted the econ. crisis. Indust. stocks fell from 452 (1929) to 58 (1932), indust. production fell by 54% between 1929 and 1932. HOOVER failed because of a lack of goodwill in the business world. Grain and cotton supplies increased and the acreage under agricultural cultivation dwindled. The gvt raised the protective tariffs and est. the R.F.C. (the **Reconstruction Finance Corporation**), intended to counteract the deflationist policies of the banks but misused in the consolidation of the large banking institutions. The econ. crisis could not be overcome by these measures. The crisis was not confined to America. The number of unemployed in America rose to 15 mil.–meanwhile the soc. welfare of the unemployed was inadequately attended to.

20 Jun. 1931 The Hoover Moratorium: moratorium on all war debts of Eur. gvts to the U.S.A.

Amer. For. Policy (1920–33)

19 Mar. 1920 The Senate refused to ratify the Treaty of Versailles (p. 133).

25 Aug. 1921 Conclusion of a separate peace with Germany which excluded the clause accepting the covenant of the League of Nations and the war-guilt article.

Nov. 1921–Feb. 1922 Washington Disarmament Conference: (a) Fixing of the relative strength of the navies of the 5 great powers, the U.S., Britain, Japan, France and Italy, to the ratio of 5:5:3: 1·75:1·75. (b) The 4-Power Agreement guaranteed the status quo for Pacific possessions. (c) The 9-Power Agreement proclaimed the sovereignty of China and the policy of the 'open door'. (d) Shantung and Kiaochow were returned to China (p. 123).

1924 The Dawes Plan (pp. 135, 151).

Jun.–Jul. 1927 Fruitless 3-Power Conference (U.S.A., Britain, Japan) over naval disarmament.

Aug. 1928 Signing of the Briand–Kellogg Pact (p. 137).

1929 The Young Plan (p. 151): to create the conditions for the payment of the Eur. debt, the U.S. advocated the settlement of the reparations problem.

Jan.–Feb. 1930 London Naval Conference, involving the U.S.A., Britain, Japan, France and Italy; it was called because all powers, exc. Britain, wished for the extension of naval armaments: it was agreed that no new battleships were to be constructed until 1936, and submarine construction was to be limited. The U.S.A., Britain and Japan reached agreement over the construction of warships.

Brit. Politics in the Post-war Period

Brit. politics in the post-war period were marked by 3 characteristics:

1. **The full democratization of elect. law** (suffrage granted to men from age 21, to women from age 30 in 1918; women from age 21 in 1928).
2. **The decline of the Lib. party and the rise of the Lab. party;**
3. **Difficulties in for. affairs** (Fr.-Brit. tensions on the Rhine and in the Near East in the 1920s, conflicts with the for. policy of Fascism and Nat. Socialism in the 1930s). **Basic tenor of Brit. for. policy**: no engagement on the Continent (refusal to go along with plans to give milit. muscle to the League of Nations), but closer relations with the dominions and colonies.

Dec. 1918 The 'Coupon election' leading to the vict. of a coalition of the Liberals (in the minority) under LLOYD GEORGE (p. 104) and the Conservatives under ANDREW BONAR LAW (p. 129).

1919–22 Wave of strikes by the miners; railmen, dockers, and other workers employed in transport also demanded increased wages. They ended because of the moderate attitudes of such union leaders as SMILLIE, HODGES, THOMAS and **Ernest Bevin** (1881–1951), who, in 1922, was able to fuse 32 unions into the Transport and General Workers' Union (T.&.G.W.U.), the largest trade union in the world; the termination of the waves of strikes was also aided by soc. measures of the gvt, such as the 1919 Addison Act and the 1920 Unemployment Law and the Depression.

Discontinuation of the involvement of the gvt in those aspects of econ. life that had been under controls during the war and economies in the ministries ('Geddes's axe'). Lib. econ. policies failed (unemployment rose); the Conservatives pleaded for protective tariffs, the Lab. party for moderate programmes of socialization.

The difficulties in Ireland led to the conclusion of a

1921 compromise treaty (p. 170), which was opposed by the Con. right wing.

1922 The Cannes Conference did not eliminate Franco-Brit. differences in the Near East (p. 135).

1922 The Genoa Conference failed in the attempt to bring the U.S.S.R. back into the world-wide econ. system.

1921–2 Washington Conference (p. 134). Britain, although in theory on a parity with the U.S. as a leading naval power, lost prestige as a world power and had to abandon naval supremacy. After the

1922 discontinuation of the protectorate over Egypt (p. 179) and difficulties in India (p. 169),

Oct. 1922 meeting of the Conservatives in the Carlton Club. The group BONAR LAW, STANLEY BALDWIN (1867–1947) and Lord CURZON (1859–1925), won the decision to leave the coalition by 187 votes against 87 by those around AUSTEN CHAMBERLAIN (1863–1937) and Lord BIRKENHEAD (1872–1930), who wished to continue supporting the gvt.

The Politics of the Conservatives (1922–9)

1922 Formation of a Con. Cabinet under BONAR LAW, which was confirmed in office in the elections of Nov.: Lib. losses and gains for the Lab. party, which became the strongest party in opposition ('His Majesty's Opposition'). After BONAR LAW's retirement (for reasons of health),

1923 STANLEY BALDWIN became prime minister, uniting the Con. party. However, Parliament was dissolved, because BALDWIN had demanded authority to introduce protective tariffs to combat unemployment. The election of Dec. was won by the Conservatives. They won 258, the Lab. party 191, the Liberals 158 seats in the House of Commons. Nevertheless,

1924 the 1st Lab. Cabinet under James Ramsay MacDonald (1866–1937) was formed; it was supported by the Liberals, making innovations in domestic policies difficult. At the London Conference (Dawes Plan, p. 135), MACDONALD contributed to the settlement of the reparations problem and the termination of the conflict in the Ruhr (p. 149). The

Feb. 1924 *de jure* recognition of the U.S.S.R. was followed by trade negotiations which had to be broken off after the **Campbell affair** (an attempt to charge the Communist editor of the *Workers' Weekly* with incitement to mutiny) and the

Oct. 1924 publication of the 'Zinoviev Letter' (purporting a connection between the Comintern and revolutionary movements in Britain). A vote of no confidence led to the dissolution of Parliament.

Oct. 1924 Elect. vict. of the Conservatives.

1924–9 2nd Baldwin Cabinet.

1925 Britain returned to the gold Standard. This attempt to stabilize the pound was made by the Chancellor of the Exchequer, WINSTON CHURCHILL (1874–1965); it was unsuccessful because the pound was over-valued.

1926 A strike of miners led to the General Strike, called in support by the trade unions, but collapsed after 9 days, though the miners stayed out for 7 months. The freedom of the unions was restricted by the 1927 Trade Disputes and Trade Union Act.

1926 Treaty with Iraq: independence was acknowledged. The conflict with France over oil concessions was settled in the Treaty of Mosul (p. 135).

1927 Diplomatic relations with the U.S.S.R. were broken off. Reasons: support for the miners' strike through the Rus. trade-union movement and Communist-inspired agitation in the Ind. Raj. (A raid on the London HQ of the Soviet-Brit. trading Co., Arcos, was a polit. blunder that revealed no evidence.)

1928 Treaty with China: recognition of the Nanking gvt.

Main Problems of the Post-war Period

France's territ. gains from the Paris treaties (Alsace-Lorraine, mandates in Africa and the Near East) gave her a position of hegemony in Europe; Belgium, Denmark, Poland, Roumania, Yugoslavia and Czechoslovakia had an interest in seeing France's position preserved, for they too had received Ger. territories.

Apart from the domestic power struggles, caused by the proportional system of representation, **Fr. domestic politics** came under addit. severe pressures:

1. The areas devastated by war had to be restored (cost: over 100,000 mil. francs).
2. Because of the large war debts owed to the U.S.A. and Britain ($5,000 mil.), the franc lost in value–a development intensified by the rising domestic debt ceiling (by 1925, 300,000 mil. francs). Impressed by the phrase: *'L'Allemagne paiera tout'* ('Germany will pay all'), the French counted on Ger. reparations payments; but these did not materialize in the expected amounts.
3. Impoverishment of the bourgeoisie because of the loss of movable properties, caused by the war, the decline of the currency, and the tax burden.
4. A significant decrease in pop. with the encouragement of immigration (1931: 3 mil.) and increased flight from the countryside to the cities hastened soc. changes.

Problems in for. affairs:

1. The attempt to conclude with Britain and the U.S.A. treaties to safeguard the position of France failed.
2. Tensions developed with Britain over Fr. Rhine policy and the reparations question.

Fr. Politics (1919–31)

1919 Elect. vict. of the 'Bloc National' (CLEMENCEAU, POINCARÉ, p. 105) over the *'Cartel des Gauches'* under **Édouard Herriot** (1822–1957). Defeat of CLEMENCEAU in the presid. election; PAUL DESCHANEL [Feb.–Sep. 1920] became president.

1920 The MILLERAND Cabinet (Jan.–Sep.): support for Poland during the Russo-Pol. war through the delivery of munitions and the dispatch of General WEYGAND. Conclusion of a milit. convention with Belgium.

1920–24 Presidency of ALEXANDER MILLERAND (1859–1943), who strongly influenced the BRIAND Cabinet (1921–2) and the

1922–4 Poincaré gvt, which had replaced the former because of its moderate policies of concession and the reparations question. POINCARÉ incurred strong opposition because of the

1923 occupation of the Ruhr (p. 149), which was carried through despite Brit. disagreement. His approval of the Dawes Plan (p. 135) and his **fiscal policies** (economies to strengthen the franc) increased his unpopularity. These factors, and the fear of excessive power in the presid. office and changes in educ. policy (abolition of secular schools), led to the

1924 elect. vict. of the 'Cartel des Gauches'. MILLERAND was forced to resign. GASTON DOUMERGUE (1924–31) became president.

1924–5 The Herriot Cabinet. Recognition of the U.S.S.R.; acceptance of the Dawes Plan.

1925 The Locarno Pact (p. 135).

The attempt of the anti-clerical HERRIOT gvt to break off relations with the Vatican failed, as did the endeavour to enforce secularizing laws in Alsace-Lorraine, which was still subject to the Napoleonic 'concordat'. The gvt fell over its **fiscal policy**: HERRIOT was forced to resign (Apr. 1925); the subsequent Cabinets of PAINLEVÉ, BRIAND, BRIAND-CAILLAUX and HERRIOT, were, for the same reason, of brief duration. Complicated by the

1925–6 uprisings in Morocco (ABD EL-KRIM, p. 179) and Lebanon (the Druses, p. 168), the domestic polit. situation worsened and a serious crisis threatened (power struggles of the parties and associations, esp. of the Left, the Catholics, and Action Française (p. 105).

1926–9 As prime minister Poincaré at first formed a gvt of 'nat. union' with BRIAND as for. minister; later he formed several coalition Cabinets. The **fiscal crisis was overcome** (the budget balanced and the franc stabilized).

1927 Efforts were made in Alsace and Lorraine to obtain autonomy within the Fr. republic. The Alsace-Lorraine 'Home Rulers' demanded a separate representative body and budget for the provinces. Strict measures against the autonomists were taken. After the

1928 elections for the Chamber of Deputies, the effort to stabilize the economy was crowned by the Currency Law (devaluation of the franc); however, the ministers of the Rad. party left the Cabinet.

Jul. 1929 Following the resignation of POINCARÉ (for reasons of health), France was governed by a number of short-lived Cabinets. When he was not prime minister, **Aristide Briand remained in the For. Office**. His **policies of reconciliation** with Germany, initiated at Locarno, amplified in the talks with STRESEMANN at Thoiry (Sep. 1926) and Lugano (Aug. 1928), failed because of the domestic polit. situation in both countries. The animosity between their respective peoples did not cease even after France had agreed to the evacuation of the Rhineland (1929). The French began the construction of the Maginot Line. In the end, BRIAND was forced to resign from the For. Office (1932). The plan for an Austro-Ger. customs union (p. 193) increased Fr. suspicions of Germany, as did the growth of radicalism on the Right. BRIAND's proposal for the establishment of a **'United States of Europe'** was hardly noticed.

1930 The Fr. occupation troops left the Rhineland (p. 151).

1931–2 Presidency of PAUL DOUMER (assassinated by a Rus. émigré in May 1932).

1931 Beginning of the econ. crisis. (For alliances, see p. 165.)

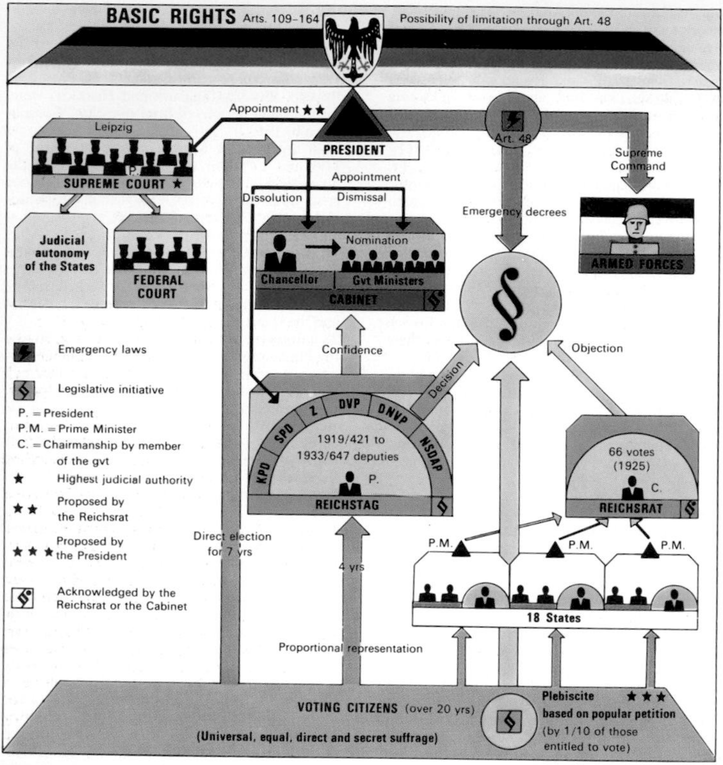

The 'Weimar Constitution', 1919

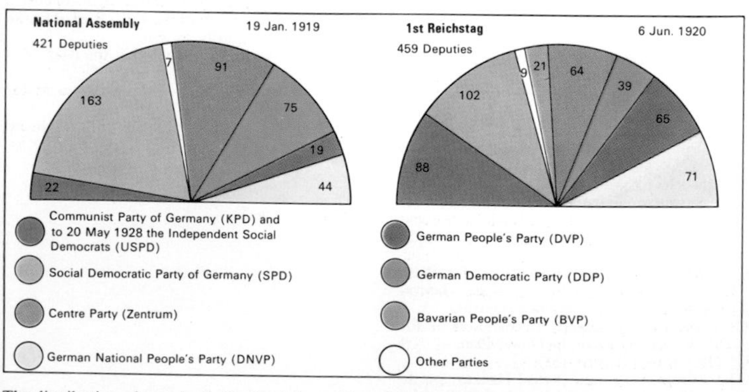

The distribution of seats in the National Assembly and in the first Reichstag

The Establishment of the Republic (1918–19)

The adoption of the Rus. soviet system and the establishment of a dictatorship of the proletariat was prevented by the

Nov. 1918 chairman of the Soc. Dem. party, **Friedrich Ebert** (1871–1925), LUDENDORFF's successor, General WILHELM GRÖNER (1867–1939), and the Stinnes–Legien agreement (providing for cooperation between unions and employers). The Berlin congress of Ger. Workers' and Soldiers' Councils (Dec.) reached a decision to call for elections for a Nat. Assembly. The Ind. Soc. Dem. party (U.S.P.D.) thereupon left the Council of People's Commissars. The extreme left gathered in the K.P.D. (Communist party of Germany, from Nov. 1918 to Jan. 1919 cal. the Spartakus League). It initiated the **Spartakus Uprising** ('Red Guard') in Berlin. The leaders of the K.P.D., **Rosa Luxemburg** (b. 1870) and **Karl Liebknecht** (b. 1871), were murdered by members of the Freikorps (Jan. 1919).

1919 Opening of the Nat. Assembly at Weimar (Feb.).

1919–25 Friedrich Ebert was elected president by the Nat. Assembly. The first prime minister was PHILIPP SCHEIDEMANN (p. 131), who formed the 'Weimar Coalition' of S.P.D., Centre party and D.D.P. (Ger. Dem. party). The peace treaty was signed (p. 133). The constitution, drawn up by HUGO PREUSS (1860–1925), was accepted by the Nat. Assembly (by 262 to 75 votes, Jul.) and signed by the president (11 Aug.).

The Weimar Constitution: Germany, headed by the popularly elected **president**, was to be a **parl., dem. republic**. Parliament consisted of the **Reichstag** (members elected by the people) and the **Reichsrat** (representing the member states). The Reichstag was given considerably more power than in the days of the empire; the president, who also appointed the chancellor, received extensive powers; these were safeguarded by Art. 48 of the constitution (emergency-decree power). But proportional representation (leading to splinter parties), the provision for plebiscites, the emergency-decree power of the president and the limitations on states' rights proved burdensome.

The Years of Crisis (1919–23)

The nationalistic bourgeoisie and the 'apolitical' armed forces (Chief of the Army Command 1920–26: HANS VON SEECKT, 1866–1936) rejected the republic, as did the extreme Right and Left (Communist unrest in the Ruhr, Cen. Germany, Hamburg; a Soviet republic in Munich). The radicalism of disappointed extremists of the Right, who resorted to the 'stab-in-the-back myth', was reflected in the polit. murders of KURT EISNER (1867–1919), MATTHIAS ERZBERGER (p. 110), and For. Minister WALTER RATHENAU (1867–1922); after Rathenau's assassination the president issued the 'decree to protect the republic' (1922); right-wing extremism also found expression in attempted putsches: the Kapp Putsch (1920), and the putsch of the 'Black Army' (Küstrin Putsch, 1923).

The moderate bourgeois parties, esp. **the S.P.D. and the Centre party**, stood by the republic. Constant attacks by the opposing forces weakened the 'Weimar Coalition'. Most criticism was directed against the 'policy of fulfilment' in consequence of the obligations assumed with the signature of the Treaty of Versailles (reparations (yielding to the London ultimatum, 1921), territ. cessions (Northern Schleswig, after a plebiscite, fell to Denmark; Eupen and Malmédy to Belgium, 1920; fixing of the Ger.-Pol. border, 1921)).

1920 Elections to the Reichstag. The 'Weimar Coalition' lost votes. Chancellor FEHRENBACH formed a coalition gvt consisting of members of the Centre, the D.D.P. (Ger. Dem. party), and the D.V.P. (Ger. People's party) (1920–21).

1921–2 Chancellor WIRTH (1879–1956) governed with the Centre, S.P.D. and D.D.P.

1922 Beginning of the disintegration of the currency. Chancellor WIRTH was forced to resign over the reparations question.

1922–3 Chancellor WILHELM CUNO (1876–1933). Inflation reached its climax. The Allies cal. for the fulfilment of Germany's obligations (p. 135).

1923 Invasion of the Ruhr by Fr. and Belg. troops (the 'politics of productive pawns') and occupation of the Memel area by Lithuania. CUNO cal. for passive resistance in the Ruhr: his policy yielded no results.

Aug.–Nov. 1923 The 'Cabinet of the Great Coalition' under Chancellor Gustav Stresemann (1878–1929) discontinued passive resistance. The attacks of the extremists on the republic continued:

1923 Com. uprising in Hamburg (Oct.); elimination of the coalition gvts of K.P.D. and S.P.D. in Saxony and Thuringia through executive action of the cen. gvt. Liquidation of the Hitler putsch (p. 183), in which the tensions between Bavaria and the cen. gvt had to come to a climax: the Bavarian general state commissioner, GUSTAV RITTER VON KAHR (1862–1934 (murdered)), supported the nationalistic forces in Munich and opposed Chancellor STRESEMANN. **Martial Law was proclaimed in Germany** (Sep.). The *Völkischer Beobachter*, the official newspaper of HITLER's N.S.D.A.P. (p. 183), published an article directed against the chancellor and the chief of the army command. KAHR refused to proscribe the newspaper. Only after Hitler's putsch, which was beaten down by the police and the army, was the conflict between Bavaria and the cen. gvt settled (resignation of KAHR, 1924). Attempts to establish a separatist 'Republic of the Rhine' and an 'Auton. Palatinate' failed.

Nov. 1923 Stabilization of the currency. The U.S. dollar had meanwhile reached a value of 4·2 bil. Ger. Marks. After the passage of an enabling law, HELFFERICH, HILFERDING, the minister of finance, LUTHER, and the currency commissioner, **Hjalmar Schacht** (1877–1970), were able to bring order to public finance.

Successes in for. policy:

1921 Peace Treaty with the U.S.A. (p. 145).

1922 Rapallo Treaty (p. 165).

472 Deputies **2nd REICHSTAG** 4 May 1924

62 100 29 16 65 28 45 95 32

493 Deputies **3rd REICHSTAG** 7 Dec. 1924

45 131 29 19 69 32 51 103 14

491 Deputies **4th REICHSTAG** 20 May 1928

54 153 51 16 62 25 45 73 12

577 Deputies **5th REICHSTAG** 14 Sep. 1930

77 143 72 19 68 20 30 41 107

Communist Party of Germany (KPD) and before 20 May 1928 the Independent Social Democrats (USPD)

Social Democratic Party of Germany (SPD)

Centre Party

National Socialist German Workers' Party (NSDAP)

German National People's Party (DNVP)

German People's Party (DVP)

German Democratic Party (DDP, after 1930 German State Party DSP)

Bavarian People's Party (BVP)

Other Parties

Number = number of seats in the Reichstag

Coloured segments of semi-circles = % of votes cast

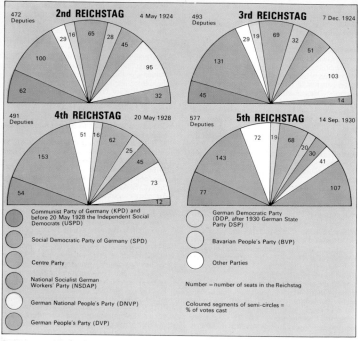

Results of the Reichstag elections, 1924–30

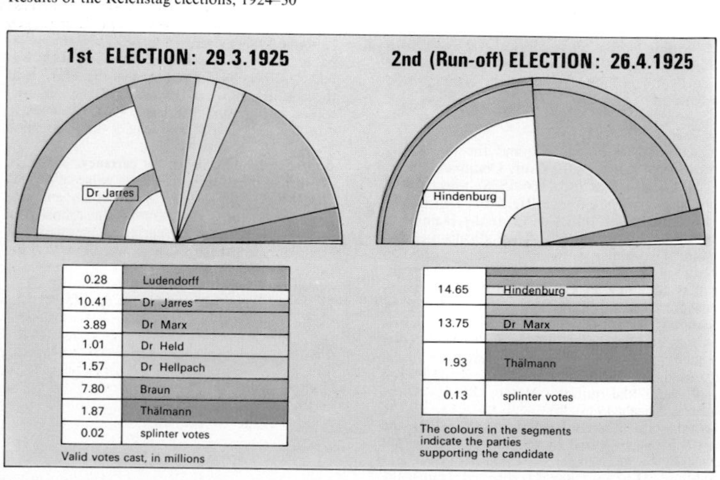

The Presidential election of 1925

Domestic Polit. Developments (1923–30)

Nov. 1923 The STRESEMANN Cabinet was forced to resign because of the vote of 'no confidence' carried by the S.P.D. (provoked by the unequal treatment meted out to radicals of the Left (in Saxony) and radicals of the Right (in Bavaria).

1923–4 A new Cabinet was formed by the Centre politician WILHELM MARX (1863–1946); STRESEMANN occupied the For. Ministry.

May 1924 Reichstag elections. Formation of the 2nd MARX Cabinet. After the vote on the Dawes Plan legislation (p. 135), which was passed, the Reichstag was dissolved (Oct.). To clear up the polit. situation,

Dec. 1924 new Reichstag elections were held. Chancellor MARX resigned, to be replaced by

1925–6 HANS LUTHER (1879–1962), who was without party affiliation. The ruling coalition consisted of the Centre party, the Bav. People's party (B.V.P.), the Ger. People's party (D.V.P.), and the Ger. Nat. People's party (D.N.V.P.); STRESEMANN was again for. minister.

28 Feb. 1925 Death of Friedrich Ebert.

1925–34 President von Hindenburg (p. 125, elected in a run-off election).

Jan.–May 1926 2nd LUTHER Cabinet (STRESEMANN for. minister). It was formed because the ministers of the Ger. Nat. People's party had resigned over the Ger. signature of the Locarno treaties (and the ministers of the Ger. Dem. party had rejoined the gvt). LUTHER's Cabinet fell over the

May 1926 president's flag decree (which provided for the flying of the mercantile flag (black-white-red) next to the nat. flag (black-red-gold) by Ger. consular offices abroad; black-white-red were the colours of the former empire).

May–Dec. 1926 3rd MARX Cabinet (STRESEMANN for. minister). His gvt conducted the

Jun. 1926 plebiscite on the confiscation of the monarchy's property without compensation; the plebiscite did not receive the necessary majority.

Oct. 1926 Resignation of General VON SEECKT (succeeded by General HEYE). The Reichstag deputy SCHEIDEMANN criticized the cooperation of the Ger. army with the Rus. Red Army. The gvt lost a vote of confidence.

1927–8 4th MARX Cabinet (STRESEMANN for. minister). The 'silent coalition' with the S.P.D. was discontinued, the Right dominated.

Jan. 1928 Resignation of the defence minister, GESSLER (1875–1955), because of finan. transactions of the army (he was succeeded by General GROENER, p. 149). Conference of the Ger. states in Berlin to streamline the admin. This attempt at overall reform failed when the interests of the individual states prevailed. The Reichstag passed emergency programmes (to solve the unemployment problem and balance the budget); however, discord set in over the construction of the armoured cruiser 'A'; the Cabinet fell over the Education Bill.

May 1928 Elections to the Reichstag. The S.P.D. and K.P.D. received 42% of all seats.

1928–30 Chancellor HERMANN MÜLLER (1876–1931), S.P.D., formed a Cabinet of the 'Great Coalition'; STRESEMANN remained in the For. Office. The crisis of the state–fragmented by parties–was not overcome.

Jul. 1929 A 'Nat. Committee for the Ger. Plebiscite "against the Young Plan"' was formed: alliance of the chairman of the Ger. Nat. People's party, ALFRED HUGENBERG (1865–1951) with HITLER. The plebiscite (Dec. 1929) did not yield the necessary majority. **Beginning of the econ. crisis** and resignation of the minister of finance, HILFERDING (1929), and the president of the Reichsbank, SCHACHT (1930).

Mar. 1930 The fall of the Müller gvt over the question of the contributions to unemployment insurance marked the **end of the parl. period of the republic.**

Reasons for the Failure of the Republic:

1. **Questionable verdicts of the judiciary** in the trials of opponents of the Weimar Constitution (protection of radicals of the Right).
2. **Shift to the Right by the bourgeoisie:** with the election of HINDENBURG as president in 1925 a monarchist occupied the office. The choice of HUGENBERG as chairman of the Ger. Nat. People's party and of the prelate KAAS as chairman of the Centre party, as well as the gains of the N.S.D.A.P. (p. 183), were indications of the trend to the right, which was strengthened by rad. agitation against the 'system' and the 'fraudulent republic'. By policies of obstruction, the Left pursued the same aims 'in reverse'.
3. The economy was not stabilized by the influx of for. capital; depression.
4. Crises of the gvt and little willingness on the part of the polit. parties to compromise led to the permanent malaise of parl. democracy.
5. The army was increasingly politicized.

For. Policy (1923–9)

Gustav Stresemann (p. 149), as for. minister, conceived his polit. aim as regaining a position of nat. power for Germany through the revision of the Treaty of Versailles by negotiation and conciliation. **The tensions in Franco-Ger. relations were lessened** (Dawes Plan, London Conference, p. 135). HERRIOT (p. 147) agreed to the **evacuation of the Ruhr** (1925). The Fr. desire for security was satisfied by the

1925 Signing of the Locarno treaties (p. 135). Acc. to STRESEMANN, the purpose of the treaties was the 'preservation of the Rhineland'.

1926 Evacuation of the Cologne area. STRESEMANN aspired to the revision of the Ger.-Pol. border; to this end he concluded

1926 the Russo-Ger. Pact of Friendship (Pact of Neutrality, p. 165). **Germany was admitted to the League of Nations** (Sep.).

1927 Dissolution of the Allied Milit. Commission, spelling the **end of the control of disarmament**.

1928 Briand–Kellogg Pact (p. 137). A provisional solution to the reparations problem was reached at the

1929–30 Conferences of The Hague: the Young Plan was accepted. Evacuation of the 2nd zone of the Rhineland (Nov. 1929), leading to the removal of the Allied troops by 30 Jun. 1930. In his last address to the League of Nations (9 Sep. 1929), STRESEMANN supported BRIAND's plan for the polit. union of Europe (with reference also to econ. considerations).

The Papacy

1914–22 During the 1st World War, **Pope Benedict XV** attempted to mediate peace (p. 127). Even though he took issue with the anti-clerical movements of his time,

1922–39 Pope Pius XI concluded the

1929 Lateran Treaties with Italy (wherein the Papacy accepted restriction of its temporal sovereignty to the 'Città del Vaticano' in exchange for compensation of 4,000 mil. lire, etc. and the

1933 Concordat with Germany (p. 197).

1931 The papal position on the soc. question was stated in the encyclical *Quadragesimo anno.*

1939–58 Pope Pius XII maintained strict neutrality during the 2nd World War.

Switzerland

1920 Following the **London Declaration** (Feb.), which took note of Switzerland's status of neutrality, the Confederation entered the League of Nations; Switzerland was therefore not obliged to participate in milit. sanctions.

Dec. 1937 The Rhaeto-Romance idiom was accepted as the 4th language of the Confederation.

May 1938 Recognition of absolute neutrality by the League of Nations.

Luxemburg

Dec. 1918 Vote in the Chamber: 29 to 11 votes decided for the continued existence of the Grand Duchy: the attempt by the Liberals and Socialists to topple the dynasty and bring about union with Belgium failed. Grand Duchess CHARLOTTE became the ruling princess.

1922 Customs union with Belgium.

1925 Withdrawal of Fr. occupation troops.

Belgium

1919 Acquisition of Ruanda and Urundi (Ger. E. Africa). As a result of the Treaty of Versailles, neutrality was abandoned and

1920 a milit. convention with France was concluded. (For the same reason, Belgium took part in the occupation of the Ruhr in 1923.) Following a decision of the League of Nations, Eupen, Malmédy and Moresnet came to Belgium.

Domestic politics were characterized by the coalition gvts of the 3 main parties (Catholics, Socialists and Liberals). The Flemish problem was eased because of the acceptance of the principle of equality for the languages of Flemish and Walloon in public usage (1931–2).

1934–51 Leopold III.

1934–7 Cabinet of nat. concentration of van Zeeland; at this time the Rexists under LÉON DEGRELLE gained in elections (1936).

1936 Cancellation of the milit. convention with France and **return to neutrality**. Germany, France and Britain guaranteed the frontiers and inviolability of Belgium (1937).

The Netherlands

1933–9 Crisis Cabinet of H. Colijn (reaction to econ. crisis and unemployment). Stabilization was achieved through the creation of jobs, successful efforts to combat the finan. crisis, the restriction of rad. polit. movements and protective tariffs. The Guilder was not devalued.

Denmark

During the 1st World War, the mercantile fleet of Denmark had incurred losses of 21·7% (0·3 mil. gross registered tons). After a plebiscite in the 1st zone (1920, with 75% voting in favour of Denmark), **North Schleswig** came to Denmark. Domestic politics were determined by the

1920–42 Soc. Democrats (T. STAUNING). Germany's offer of a

1939 non-aggression treaty was accepted (whereas Norway, Sweden and Finland rejected the offer).

Norway

Despite friendly inclinations towards England, Norway remained neutral during the 1st World War; nevertheless, it lost 49·3% of its mercantile shipping (1·24 mil. gross registered tons). The infl. of the rad. elements in the Workers' party, proceeding from Russia (and leading to the formation of workers' and soldiers' soviets), decreased. The moderate Socialist party was succeeded by

1934–45 the Workers' party (J. NYGAARDSVOLD).

1920 The League of Nations awarded Spitzbergen to Norway.

1931 The coast of Eastern Greenland was occupied; however, the Court of Int. Justice in The Hague decided in favour of Denmark (1933).

Sweden

Despite an appeal from the U.S.A. to Sweden to enter the war, and the call for help by the Fin. gvt against the Bolsheviks, Sweden maintained its neutrality. The Soc. Democrats under H. BRANTING (1920, 1921–3, 1924–6) were succeeded by con. and lib. gvts. After regaining power,

1932 the Soc. Democrats (P. A. HANSSON) fought the world-wide econ. crisis and introduced soc. reforms (from 1936 initiation of the 'Welfare State').

Iceland

1918 Recognition of Iceland as an ind. state in personal union with Denmark. Acc. to the state constitution (1920), for. policy was conducted by Denmark, but the country was pledged to perpetual neutrality (no armed forces); the gvt was in the hands of parliament (the Altinget, with an Upper and a Lower House).

Polit. cooperation between the Scand. states was minimal (neutrality free from alliances); but, with the failure of the League of Nations and the fruitlessness of the conferences on disarmament, the states drew closer together.

1930 The Oslo Pact: preparations for an econ. union of Norway, Sweden, Denmark, the Netherlands, Belgium and Luxemburg (1933 Finland).

Jan. 1932 Meeting of the for. ministers of Denmark, Norway and Sweden in Copenhagen (revival of the conferences of the for. ministers of the Scand. countries).

Finland

1917 Recognition of Fin. autonomy within a Rus. Confederation.

Dec. 1917 Proclamation of Fin. independence.

Jan.–May 1918 War of Liberation and Civil War: struggle of the 'White' forces under the leadership of General **Carl Gustav Baron von Mannerheim** (1867–1951) against the 'Red' forces of the Revolutionary People's Soviet.

Dec. 1918 General Mannerheim became head of state.

1920 Peace Treaty of Dorpat (Tartu) with the Soviet Union: the borders of 1914 were to be retained; the Petsamo region was to be incorp. into Finland. Eastern Karelia to become part of the U.S.S.R.

1921 Recognition of Fin. sovereignty over the Åland Islands by the League of Nations and establishment of their neutral status.

The **domestic polit. struggle** between the Right and the Left led to the formation of an anti-Com. popular movement (the Lappo Movement). The Com. party was outlawed (1930). Coalition gvts enacted soc. reforms, among them the land reform (1922), which expropriated the properties of the landowners, the trad. Swed. upper class.

1931 The former regent Svinhufvud became head of state; he was succeeded by KALLIO, a representative of the Peasants' party (Feb. 1937).

1932 Non-aggression treaty with the Soviet Union.

Estonia

Feb. 1918 Proclamation of Est. independence.

Nov. 1918 The PAETS gvt assumed office. Bolshevik attacks (1918–19) were repulsed and the newly formed army under LAIDONER liberated the country.

1920 Peace Treaty of Dorpat (Tartu) with the U.S.S.R. The formative period of the state came to an end with the completion of the new parl. consitution (Aug. 1920); recognition by the Allies, **rad. land reform** (which eliminated the dominant position of the Ger.-Balt. nobility), and the defeat of Bolshevik attempts to overthrow the gvt further helped to consolidate the state. The right-wing **Movement of Freedom-fighters** forced the acceptance of a

1933 pres. constitution, which weakened the power of parliament; however, the

1934 Coup d'état of Paets ('the Elders of the State'), deprived the Freedom-fighters of influence and initiated an authoritarian form of gvt.

1937 Acceptance of a 3rd Constitution by a Nat. Assembly, which had been elected by questionable methods; the new constitution was characterized by parl. as well as corporative-authoritarian provisions. Non-aggression pacts were concluded with the U.S.S.R. (1932) and Germany (1939).

Latvia

Nov. 1918 Proclamation of Lat. independence by the Ulmanis gvt, leading to conflicts with the Nat. Latvians with Ger. interests, who were concerned with the establishment of a Liv. state dominated by Ger. elements. Riga, which had been seized by the Bolsheviks, was taken with the aid of Ger. *Freikorps* and the Ger. Balt. militia. ULMANIS was able to conquer Latgale with Est. and Pol. assistance.

1922 The final version of the constitution was accepted. After the formation of a gvt by the Peasants' League

1930 KVIESIS became president of the republic.

May 1934 Coup d'état of the prime minister, Ulmanis, who est. an authoritarian gvt with a 'Cabinet of Nat. Union': a new chamber was formed, but the constitution was unrevised.

1936 ULMANIS became president of the republic. Non-aggression pacts with the Soviet Union (1932) and Germany (1939) were concluded.

Lithuania

Proclamation of a Lith. state joined to Germany. Formation of the VOLDEMARAS gvt (1918).

Nov. 1918 Lithuania became an ind. state. After the withdrawal of Ger. troops, a Com. counter-gvt was formed at Dünaburg. However, the Com. threat was eliminated by the Mar. 1919 offensive of Ger. troops and the Pol. advance on Vilna (Apr. 1919), which became Lithuanian in Dec. 1919.

1920 Peace of Moscow with the U.S.S.R., which had occupied Vilna but returned it to Lithuania.

1920 Agreement of Suvalki with Poland; but ZELIGOWSKI's coup led to the loss of Vilna to Poland (1922).

1922 The influence of the old Pol. ruling class was eliminated by land reform.

1922 Acceptance of the constitution establishing a dem. republic.

1926 Rus.-Lith. Treaty of Neutrality.

Dec. 1926 Milit. putsch. SMETONA became president of the republic. His nationalist party (Tautininkai), by-passing parliament, exercised exclusive authority until 1939.

Mar. 1939 The Memel region was ceded to Germany.

The downfall of the Balt. States was a consequence of the Russo-Ger. Non-aggression Pact (p. 197). Mutual-aid treaties forced Estonia, Latvia and Lithuania to make bases available to the Red Army. Cabinets formed under the guidance of Rus. officials and manipulated elections led to the acceptance of the states into the U.S.S.R. on the basis of 'petitions'. In Aug. 1940 they became the 14th, 15th and 16th Socialist Soviet Republics.

The Memel Region

1920 Establishment of a Council of State with Fr. prefects.

1923 Invasion by Lith. irregulars. The conference of ambassadors recognized the annexation by Lithuania (1924).

1924 The Memel statute: autonomy under Lith. sovereignty.

Danzig as Free City

Without the benefit of a plebiscite, Danzig was made a Free City, to be under the control and supervision of the League of Nations.

1933 Elections resulted in an absolute majority for the Nazi party.

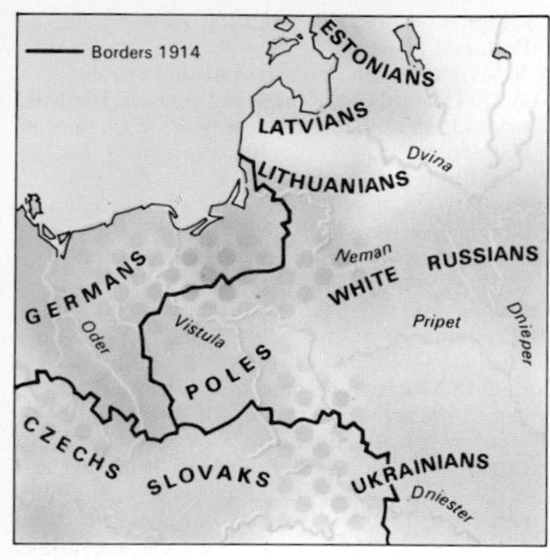

Nationalities, 1914

Republic of Poland, 1918–39

Poland under German occupation, 1941–4

Poland 1916

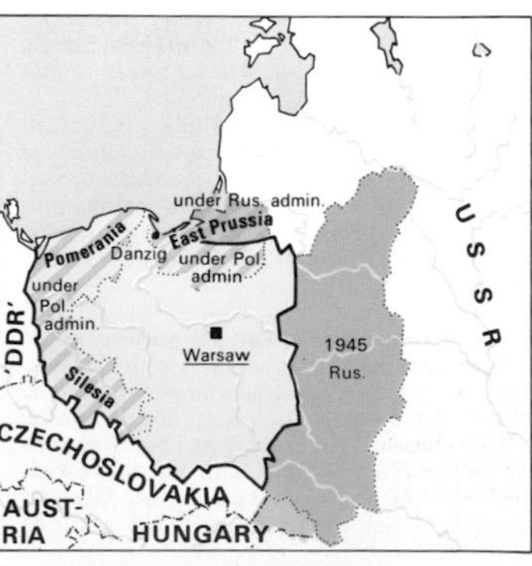

The fourth Polish partition, 1939

People's Republic of Poland after 1945

The Re-establishment of Poland

Aug. 1914 The tsar promised autonomy to the Poles.

1916 Proclamation of Congress Poland by the Cen. Powers (p. 123). In the newly formed Council of State, **Josef Pilsudski** (1867–1935) received a seat; however, after leaving the council (2 Jul. 1917), he was arrested in Magdeburg (detained till Nov. 1918).

Aug. 1917 Formation of a 'Pol. Nat. Committee' in Paris, chaired by the Nat. Democrat, ROMAN DMOWSKI (1864–1939).

1917 Establishment of a 'Council of Regency' as the Pol. gvt subject to Ger. control.

3 Nov. 1918 Proclamation of the Republic of Poland and resignation of the Council of Regency and its chairman, PILSUDSKI.

Domestic Developments (1919–37)

1. **The nationalities question.** The Pol. people had to come to terms with the nat. minorities: there were 100,000 Lithuanians, 1 mil. Germans, 1·5 mil. White Ruthenians, more than 3 mil. Jews, 4 mil. Ukrainians.
2. **The agrarian question.** The land reform (28 Dec. 1925) expropriated above all the large Ger. landowners; Pol. landowners, however, were treated with consideration. The agrarian question was unresolved.
3. **The crisis of the republic.** The conflicts between the 'legionaires' (PILSUDSKI's supporters) and the Nat. Democrats had to be, and were, overcome.

1919 Formation of the PADEREWSKI coalition Cabinet under PILSUDSKI as head of state. After the

1921 ratification of the parl. constitution, and the

1922 elect. vict. of the Nat. Democrats, PILSUDSKI resigned. President G. NARUTOWICZ, assassinated shortly thereafter, was succeeded by

1922–6 STANISLAS WOJCIECHOWSKI (Socialist). Beginning of an econ. and finan. crisis and conflicts with nat. minorities and between, polit. parties.

May 1926 Pilsudski's coup d'ětat.

1926–39 Presidency of Professor Ignaz Mošcicki (1867–1946). Without entirely depriving parliament of power, supported by legionaires, the army and the bureaucracy, PILSUDSKI guided the state, serving as prime minister (1926–8, Aug.–Nov. 1930), minister of defence and chief of the General Staff.

1930 Elect. vict. of the gvt bloc at the elections to the Sejm by terrorist methods.

1935 Acceptance of a new, authoritarian constitution ('guided democracy'), which put an end to the dem. parl. system of gvt. After PILSUDSKI's death, General (later Marshal) **Edward Rydz-Śmigli** (1886–1941) played an important role alongside the president, and in 1936 was made the leading figure of the state. PILSUDSKI's death weakened the 'ruling clique of the colonels'; **Colonel Josef Beck** (1894–1944), serving as for. minister, was a member of it from 1932.

1937 Formation of the 'Camp of Nat. Unity' under Colonel KOC, who intended to strengthen a sense of nat. identity (antisemitism, conservatism).

The For. Policy of Poland (1918–39)

Poland, limited in Nov. 1918 to the area of 'Congress Poland' and Western Galicia, gained

1918 Eastern Galicia (seizure of Lemberg (Lvov)), and, through the Treaty of Versailles (p. 133),

1919 the 'Corridor' (the largest part of the Prus. province of w. Prussia), and the province of Poznan (occupied by Poland after 1918); also,

1920 Poland received part of the indust. region of Teschen (Cieszyn). While PILSUDSKI pleaded for a Lith.-White Rus.-Pol. Confederation under Pol. leadership, and the Nat. Democrats demanded the rest. of the 'borders of 1772' (I, p. 284), the Allies fixed the

1919 'Curzon Line', a line of demarcation corresponding to the situation of the minorities.

Apr.–Oct. 1920 Russo-Pol. War. After concluding an alliance with the anti-Com. gvt of the Ukraine under General SIMON PETLIURA, PILSUDSKI advanced on Kiev. The counter-offensive of the Red Army was halted short of Warsaw ('the miracle of the Vistula') by the Pol. attack from the s., aided by the Fr. general MAXIME WEYGAND (1867–1965). After the conclusion of milit. alliances with France and Roumania (1921), the

18 Mar. 1921 Peace of Riga was signed: the Pol. border was loc. approx. 250 kms. E. of its ethnic frontier.

Oct. 1920 Occupation of Vilna by irregulars under General ZALIGOWSKI. In 1922 the pop. voted for Poland.

1921 Poland received the most important part of the indust. region of Upper Silesia in disregard of the results of the plebiscite (60% for Germany). The relationship between Poland and Germany remained ill at ease. After attempts to carry out preventive measures against Germany (1932–3), the

1934 Non-aggression Pact was concluded between Poland and Germany, followed by econ. and cult. agreements.

1934 The Russo-Pol. Non-aggression Pact of 1932 was renewed. Taking advantage of the crises brought about by HITLER,

Mar. 1938 Poland was able to force the recognition of the Vilna border through an ultimatum to Lithuania.

Oct. 1938 Following the Munich Treaty (p. 197) the Olsa region was annexed.

Mar. 1939 Poland rejected the Ger. demands of Oct. 1938, Jan. and Feb. 1939, which had cal. for the inclusion of Danzig in Germany, an extraterrit. highway and railway track through the Corridor, and closer Ger.-Pol. cooperation. On the other hand, Poland accepted the Franco-Brit. declaration of guarantees for Poland, concluded a milit. agreement with France and a credit agreement with Britain.

Apr. 1939 Cancellation of the Ger.-Pol. Treaty of Friendship by HITLER. Poland's attempt to pursue the policy of an ind. major power, and to steer a middle course between Russia, France and Germany, had thereby failed.

Aug. 1939 Pol.-Brit. Treaty of Mutual Assistance.

The Aust. Republic

1918 The Provis. Nat. Assembly proclaimed **'Ger.-Austria' a republic** and **'part of the Ger. Republic'.** After the elect. vict. of the Soc. Democrats in the elections to the Constituent Assembly (Feb. 1919), K. SEITZ [1919–20] was elected president of the republic (1920–28: MICHAEL HAINISCH). A coalition Cabinet of Soc. Democrats and Christ. Socialists was formed under the 1st Chancellor **Karl Renner** (1870–1950).

1919 Expulsion of the Habsburgs and conclusion of the **Peace Treaty of St-Germain-en-Laye** (p. 133).

1920 The new constitution became operative: a Fed. Council, representing the fed. states, functioned alongside the Nat. Council, which was chosen by direct elections. Together they formed the Fed. Assembly, which elected the president of the republic. Shortages of food, centrifugal forces generated by the particularist ambitions of the fed. states, the peace conditions of the Entente Powers and the claims of the 'successor states' endangered the young republic.

Bourgeois Coalition Gvt (1920–32)

1920 Christ. Socialist elect. vict. Formation of the Cabinet of M. MAYR (to 1921). Austria joined the League of Nations (1920). After the first plebiscites to determine the *Anschluss* (union with Germany) question (Tyrol, 98·8% for Germany; Salzburg 99·3% for Germany), addit. polls were prevented. France threatened to discontinue aid (shortage of foodstuffs).

1921 Following a plebiscite, Ödenburg fell to Hungary.

1922–4 Fed. Chancellor Ignaz Seipel (a prelate and university professor) restored and stabilized finances and the economy.

1922 Int. credits, guaranteed by the League of Nations, were received: Austria was obliged to accept the establishment of a control commission to supervise the enforcement of the Peace Treaty and to abstain from *Anschluss* with Germany for a period of 20 yrs. The **domestic polit. tensions** between the middle class (Christ. Socialists, 'Great Germans', members of the Land League) and the Soc. Dem. party of Austria became a state of latent civil war owing to the interference of paramilit. units (i.e. the Repub. Protective League on the one hand, and the Front-fighters, the Home and Self-defence Association on the other).

1927 Socialist uprising (firing of the Palace of Justice).

1928–38 Presidency of Professor Wilhelm Miklas (1872–1956). The const. reform of 1929 strengthened the powers of the presidency (direct popular election).

1931 Proposal of a customs union with Germany (SCHOBER, CURTIUS, p. 197). For. pressure, esp. on the part of the Fr. gvt, led to the collapse of the Aust. Credit-Anstalt in May 1931. The BURESCH Cabinet (1931–2) attempted to combat the effects of the Depression by a recuperative econ. programme. The deterioration of Austria progressed as a result of the conflicts of the paramilit. units, which received support from abroad (France, Germany).

Sep. 1931 Failure of the putsch by the Home Defence League in the Steiermark (Styria).

The 'Austro-Fascist' Dictatorship (1932–8)

1932–4 Fed. Chancellor Engelbert Dollfuss (1892–1934 (assassinated)) governed democratically, supported by the Christ. Socialist Land League and the Heimatblock (Home Bloc); during the course of a year he was opposed by the Soc. Dem. party of Austria and the 'Great Germans'.

1932 DOLLFUSS forced the conclusion of the Lausanne Agreement: the League of Nations extended its credit, on condition that Austria abstain from *Anschluss* with Germany until 1952.

Mar. 1933 Establishment of an authoritarian régime. Suspension of the parl. constitution and gvt through recourse to the econ. emergency decree of the war year 1917. DOLLFUSS terminated the domestic '2-front war' against the Nat. Socialists and the Soc. Democrats by **outlawing both the Nat. Socialist party and**, after street fighting in Vienna and other cities,

1934 the Soc. Dem. party and all other polit. parties. The single legal polit. party was the **'Fatherland Front'**, a unity movement formed in 1933. A corporative constitution was ratified. During an attempted Nat. Socialist putsch (25 Jul.), DOLLFUSS was murdered. When Italy concentrated troops at the Brenner Pass, Germany officially dissociated itself from the enterprise.

1934–8 Fed. Chancellor Kurt Schuschnigg (b. 1897) failed to stabilize the régime.

1936 Agreement with Germany (a compromise with HITLER). Attempts to restore the Habsburgs encountered the opposition of HITLER and the Little Entente.

1938 SCHUSCHNIGG visited HITLER at Berchtesgaden (12 Feb.): agreement was reached to grant amnesty to Nat. Socialists and to appoint ARTHUR SEYSS-INQUART (1892–1946 (executed)) to the Cabinet. The plebiscite, cal. by SCHUSCHNIGG on 9 Mar., to be held on the 13th, miscarried because of **Germany's ultimatum** (11 Mar.). SCHUSCHNIGG resigned. A Nat. Socialist gvt was formed under SEYSS-INQUART and Ger. troops marched into Austria. **The Anschluss was proclaimed** (13 Mar.).

For. Policy

The Friendship Treaty of 1930 initiated the influence of Fascist Italy on the domestic politics of Austria, further strengthened by the

1934 'Rome Protocols' (p. 165). After the miscarriage of the attempted customs union with Germany, France (TARDIEU) endeavoured to create a politically and economically reorganized Danubian area under Fr. guidance inclusive of Austria; but Austria refused. SCHUSCHNIGG's attempt to link Austria to Italy had been bound to fail because of the improvement of relations between Rome and Berlin. He was therefore compelled to travel the 'Ger. road', which led to Austria's annexation.

Hungary

1918 Proclamation of the Republic (16 Nov.). As prime minister (from 30 Oct.) Count MIHÁLY KÁROLYI (1875–1955) became president of the republic (1919). In protest against the armistice conditions (cession of Croatia, Transylvania, Banat and Slovakia), he resigned and handed over the power of gvt to the

1919 Soviet gvt of **Béla Kun** (1885–*c.* 1937 (prob. liquidated in the U.S.S.R.)) composed of Socialists and Communists. A Hung. 'Red Army' occupied parts of Slovakia. It dissolved after a counter-offensive by the Roumanians. An opposition gvt under the prime minister, PÁL TELEKI VON SZÉK (1920–21; 1939–41), appointed Admiral **Miklós Horthy de Nagybanya** (1868–1957) c.-in-c. of the Hung. army. BÉLA KUN fled (19 Aug.); Budapest was occupied by Roumania (Aug.–Nov.).

1920–44 Miklós Horthy's regency.

1920 Proclamation of Hungary as a monarchy with a vacant throne. In the

1920 Peace Treaty of Trianon (4 Jun.), Hungary lost 67·8% of its territory and 59% of its pop. Since its ethnic frontiers now extended beyond the borders of the state, the latter had become a minor power ethnically Magyar. Two attempts by the Emperor CAROL I to return as king of Hungary (1921) failed following pressure from the Little Entente.

Domestic affairs: the state was burdened by the retention of the trad. feudal system of landholding while agrarian reform measures were inadequate; meanwhile the Jews were suppressed (restrictive laws of 1938 impeded the role of Jews in econ. life) and the nationalist rad. groups, among them the members of the 'Arrow Cross' under Major FERENCZ SZÁLASI (1897–1946 (executed)) greatly increased; SZÁLASI later joined the Hung. Nat. Socialist party (Oct. 1937). As a result of debts incurred in the payment of reparations and the world-wide Depression (p. 185), Hungary experienced a fiscal crisis (1931). A Fr. loan was tied to the condition that revisionist propaganda be discontinued.

For. policy (for alliances, see p. 165): revisionist demands were supported by Italy (from 1927). Fr. plans (consolidation of the Danubian area) were rejected by Hungary. With the improvement of relationships with Germany under the

1932–6 prime minister, Gyula Gömbös (1886–1936), who was a right-wing radical and antisemite, Franco-Hung. relations deteriorated (cooperation with Austria). In the

1938 Agreement of Bled, Hungary renounced the use of force in relationships with the powers of the Little Entente. The Berlin visit of HORTHY and the prime minister, BÉLA VON IMRÉDY (1938–9), in Aug. 1939 sealed the friendship between Hungary and Germany.

1938 1st Arbitration of Vienna (2 Nov.): after the conclusion of the Munich Agreement (see below), Hungary received Slovak. territories (incl. the cities of Neuhäusl (Nové Zámky), Lewenz (Levice), Kaschau (Kosice)).

1939 Occupation of the Carpatho-Ukraine.

Czechoslovakia

Following the Pittsburgh Agreement of 1918 by Czech and Slovak Americans, pledging autonomy to Slovakia,

1918 formation of a gvt in Paris: Tómaš Masaryk (1850–1937) became president, **Edouard Beneš** (1884–1948) for. minister (prime minister 1921–2, president 1935–8, 1945–8). Proclamation of the republic in Prague (Oct.) by the Nat. Committee, which confirmed the KAREL KRAMÁŘ Cabinet (prime minister 1918–19) and MASARYK as president (1918–35). The new state (extending over 930 kms in length) was a politically and confessionally heterogeneous creation with a pop. which, besides Poles and Jews, was composed of 46% Czechs, 13% Slovaks, 28% Germans, 8% Magyars and 3% Ukrainians. The attempt of the Germans to join Ger.-Austria failed (the Allies refused to allow a plebiscite and Czech troops occupied the area (Nov.–Dec. 1918)).

1920 The Constitution was ratified by the expanded Nat. Committee, not by the elected parliament.

Domestic affairs: supported by the Czech bureaucracy, the new state functioned as a parl. democracy until 1939. **The nat. minorities** were integrated, not least because of a land reform law (1919), which expropriated the large landowners. A conflict with the Vatican (terminated in 1927) arose over the **establishment of a Czechoslovak Church free from Rome** (1920) and the proclamation of Hus Day as a national holiday (1925). Measures were taken against the Slovaks, who demanded the promised autonomy (sentencing of the Slovak leader Prof. VOJTĚCH TUKA, 1880–1946, to a term of 15 yrs imprisonment), and the **Sudeten Germans** (esp. after 1933, because of interference from Germany and the strengthening of Nat. Socialism). Backed by HITLER, KONRAD HENLEIN (1898–1945 (suicide)), the leader of the Sudeten Ger. Home Front (after 1935, the 'Sudeten Ger. party'), devised the **'Carlsbad Programme'** (1938): equality, autonomy and reparations for the discrimination suffered after 1918.

1938 The Munich Agreement (29 Sep.): the Sudetenland was joined to Germany. Slovakia and Carpatho-Ukraine became auton. The failure of the Fr. ally to render assistance and the weakness of the Little Entente powers (p. 165) caused the resignation of President Beneš. Under his successor.

1938–45 EMIL HACHA (1872–1945), the **Protectorate of Bohemia and Moravia** was est. (1939).

For. policy: under EDUARD BENEŠ (for. minister to 1935) Czech for. policy was pro-French. It was above all directed against Hungary (because of plans to restore the Habsburgs and revisionist demands) and Germany (because of annexation projects), but also against Poland (p. 155). (For alliances, see p. 165.)

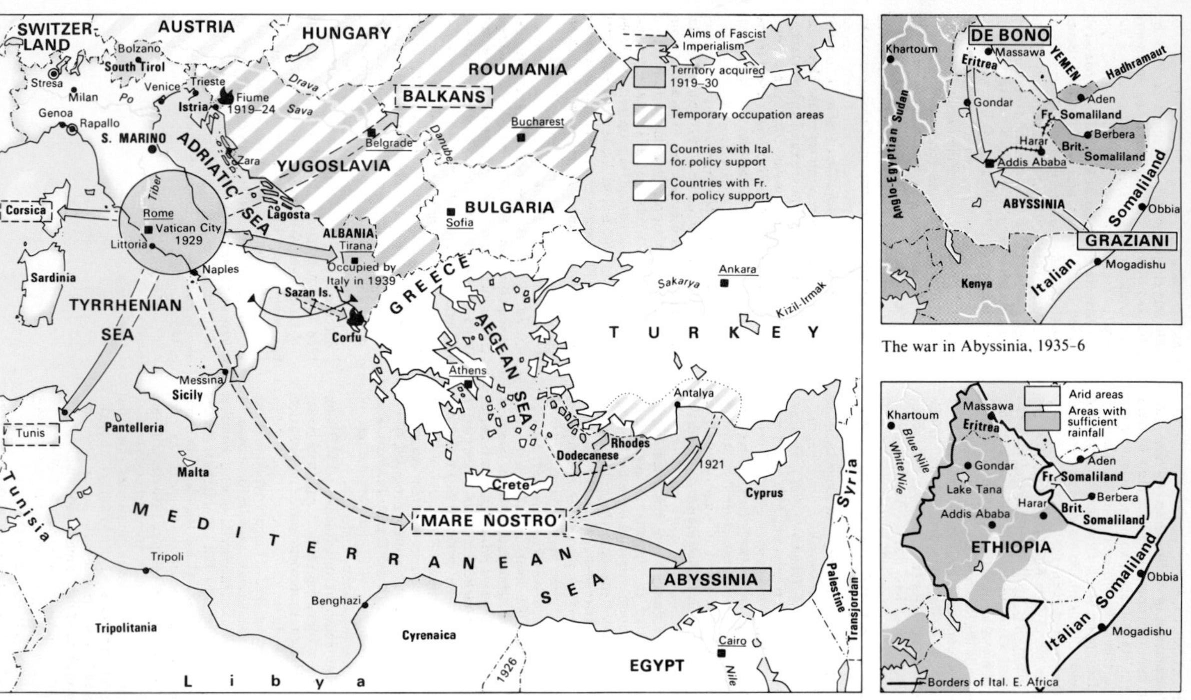

Fascist Imperialism, 1922–39

The war in Abyssinia, 1935–6

Italian possessions in East Africa

The Crisis of Democracy (1919–22)

The disappointment over the outcome of the peace conference (p. 133) split the nation into moderate and nationalistic camps. Spurred on by a sense of lost nat. identity, a tendency to glorify power and a feeling of nat. resentment, **associations of combat and disabled veterans entered the polit. arena**; among them were the first

1919 **'Fasci di combattimento'** (Squadri), who rallied under the leadership of **Benito Mussolini** (p. 182).

1919 Seizure of Fiume by **Gabriele d'Annunzio** (p. 119). Faced by econ. crisis and inflation, the Cabinets of NITTI (Jun. 1919–Jun. 1920) and GIOLITTI (Jun. 1920–Jun. 1921) failed.

1920 Socialist strikes in Milan and Turin. The **Fascists**, having usurped the functions of the ineffective organs of gvt, fought the Socialists by terrorism.

1920 Rapallo Treaty with Yugoslavia: Fiume became a Free City.

1921 Foundation of the Partito Nazionale Fascista (P.N.F.): the revolutionary movement became a polit. party. During the tenure of the powerless BONOMI (1921–2) and FACTA (Feb.–Oct. 1922) Cabinets, it initiated programmes of 'direct action': threats, application of force, and elimination of the prov. bureaucracy in Upper Italy. Industrialists and the armed forces sympathized with Fascist aims. The revolution was proclaimed and a 'committee of 4' (*Quadruumvirat*) was formed: ITALO BALBO (1896–1940), EMILIO DE BONO, CESARE DE VECCHI and MICHELE BIANCHI.

28 Oct. 1922 The 'March on Rome'. The king empowered MUSSOLINI to form a Cabinet; MUSSOLINI's Cabinet was composed of Fascists and members of other parties sympathetic to his cause.

The Consolidation of Fascism (1922–6)

Nov. 1922 Parliament granted unrestricted powers to MUSSOLINI (the authorization to expire in 1924).

1923 Formation of the 'Milizia Volontaria per la Sicurezza Nazionale' (the party militia), composed of Squadri and Fasci, not bound to the king by an oath of loyalty: force was thereby institutionalized. The new elect. law, which favoured the nationalists (two thirds of all seats), made possible the

1924 elect. vict. of the Fascists (65%). After the murder of the Socialist deputy **Giacomo Matteotti** (b. 1885) following his parl. speech on 'the rule of force' (30 May), the opposition deputies carried out their symbolic exodus 'from the Aventine' (15 Jun.).

1925–6 Measures to complete the establishment of the dictatorial régime: struggle against the 'anti-Fascist conspiracy', against freemasons and emigrants; arrests, ostracism, clean-up of the civil service, dissolution of opposition parties and prohibition on the formation of new ones (Nov. 1926).

The Fascist State (1926–38)

1. As head of gvt, the *'Duce del Fascismo'* took a position alongside the king (*'Capo dello stato'*); because of the law 'defining the powers and privileges of the head of the gvt' (1925) and the law 'defining the powers of the executive to fix legal codes', giving **unlimited governing authority to the head of the gvt** (p. 182), MUSSOLINI was more an associate of than subordinate to the king.
2. The development of the syndicalist-corporative system (a hierarchical order (*Gerarchia*) of labour and the professions was made possible by the law governing collective bargaining (strikes and lock-outs), which formed the foundation for the syndicates led by the Fascists (1926); and by the

1927 'Carta del Lavoro', gathering the syndicates in corporate bodies to plan production in accordance with state needs.

1928 New elect. law: establishment of a list of 400 deputies, nominated by the various corporations, selected by the **'Fascist Grand Council'** (*'Gran Consiglio'*).

1930 Law governing the reorganization of the Nat. Council of the Corporations (est. 1929).

1934 Law governing the formation and objectives of the corporations and convocation of the 1st Nat. Assembly.

1938 Establishment of the Chamber of 'Fasci and Corporations'. It was composed of the Duce, the members of the Great Fascist Council, the 150 members of the Nat. Council of the Fascist party, the 500 members of the Nat. Council, and the councils of the 22 corporations.

Fascist Imperialism (1923–39)

MUSSOLINI strove for domination over the Adriatic Sea, hegemony in the Medit. area, and the extension of Ital. colon. possessions in Africa. In the

1923 Peace of Lausanne (p. 167), Italy received the Dodecanese. After the occupation of Corfu (1923), reconciliation with Yugoslavia failed, and Fiume was annexed by Italy (1924). (For treaties with Albania, Roumania and Hungary, see p. 165.)

1929 Lateran Treaties (p. 152).

1934 The 'Rome Protocols' (p. 165). After the first meeting with HITLER in Venice (1934), the Vienna putsch of the same year, and concessions granted by the LAVAL Cabinet in France, Ger. revisionism in the Danubian area brought MUSSOLINI into the

1935 'Stresa Front' against Germany.

Oct. 1935 Ital. invasion of Abyssinia: under the command of Marshal DE BONO (later under BADOGLIO), 2 Ital. armies advanced from Somaliland and Eritrea.

1936 Annexation of Abyssinia. VICTOR EMANUEL becomes 'Emperor of Ethiopia'.

Sympathetic propaganda and econ. assistance by Germany, as well as common policy in the

1936–9 Sp. Civil War (p. 161) prepared the ground for the **'Berlin-Rome Axis'** (p. 197).

1939 Occupation of Albania (p. 163).

1939 Pact of friendship and alliance with Germany (p. 197).

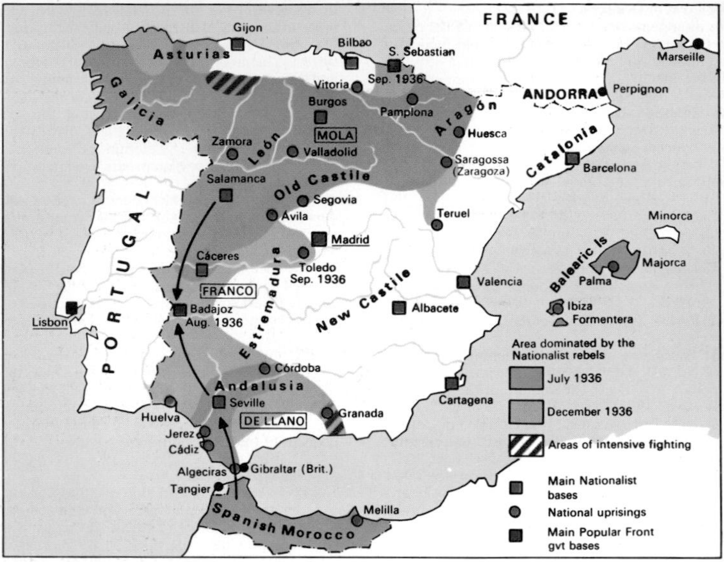

The Nationalist uprising, 1936

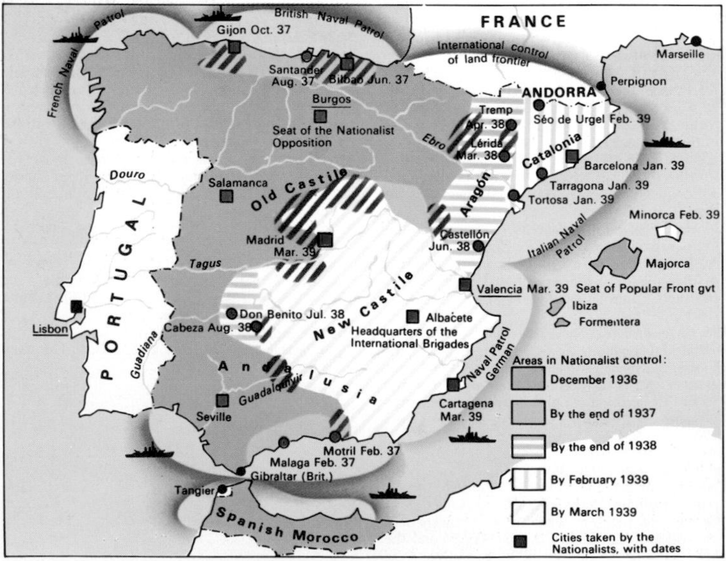

The Spanish Civil War, 1936–9

Spain

During the 1st World War, because of its neutrality, Spain experienced an upswing in its economy; nevertheless, a permanent gvtl crisis enveloped the state. Causes: weakness of the const. monarchy, frequent changes of gvt (between 1917 and 1923 there were 13 Cabinets), movements for autonomy in Catalonia (Barcelona), tensions between a con. upper class (large feudal landowners, supported by the Church and the armed forces) and the radicalized workers, uprising of the Riff tribes in Morocco under ABD EL-KRIM (1880–1962).

1923 Military putsch of the Captain-General of Barcelona, **Miguel Primo de Rivera** (1870–1930), who, in agreement with King ALFONSO XIII (p. 85), est. a milit. directorate (consisting of 8 generals and 1 admiral), suspended the constitution of 1876 and appointed non-polit. specialists to head gvt ministries.

1925 Transformation of the milit. gvt into a civilian Cabinet under PRIMO DE RIVERA as prime minister: extensive leg. activity, reorganization of the admin. (cut-back of the civil service), attempted agrarian reform (1929), policies of soc. reform, econ. rehabilitation through public building projects (roads, railways, irrigation); after a treaty with France (1925), the war in Morocco was terminated (1926). The attempted annexation of Tangier failed; the city was neutralized by the treaty of 1924. Various elements of society dissociated themselves from the dictatorship: the intellectuals opposed it because of its reactionary cult. policies, the nobles because their privileges had been curtailed, the business world because of the soc. reforms and the officer corps because of the army reforms.

1930 Resignation of Primo de Rivera; he died in exile in Paris (16 Mar. 1930).

1931 Communal elections: vict. of the republicans; ALFONSO XIII left the country without surrendering the rights to the throne.

The **2nd Republic** was supported by the lib. bourgeoisie and the Socialist workers (Catalonia, the Basque provinces, Asturia). After elections to a constituent nat. assembly, a lib.-progressive constitution was adopted (Dec. 1931): the republic became a representative democracy; separation of Church and state; a unitary state est.; but Catalonia (1931) and the Basque provinces (1936) were granted autonomy. The coalition of republican parties was challenged by the revolutionary Socialist wing under FRANCISCO LARGO CABALLERO (1869–1946), the 'Sp. Lenin', by the Anarcho-Syndicalists, and, because of the rad. measures against the Church (anticlerical legislation of 1933: civil marriage, nationalization of eccles. property), by con. forces rallying in opposition to the republic (Confederación Española de Derechas Autónomas (C.E.D.A.), founded 1932 by GIL ROBLES).

1933 Vict. of the Right. From this point on until 1936 there were frequent Cabinet crises and severe unrest, causing the dissolution of parliament.

1936 Vict. of the Popular Front (Republicans, Socialists, Communists, syndicalists). MANUEL AZAÑA (1880–1940) became president of the republic. Conditions close to civil war prevailed. After the murder of the monarchist deputy CALVO SOTELO (13 Jul.) the counter-revolution initiated the

1936–9 Sp. Civil War

Jul. 1936 Milit. uprising of the generals SANJURJO, GODED, **Francisco Franco** (1892–1975), MOLA, QUEIPO DE LLANO. It was supported by monarchists, Catholics and the Fascist **Falange**, which had been founded in 1933 by JOSÉ ANTONIO PRIMO DE RIVERA (1903–36), son of the dictator. The rebels were supported militarily by Germany (Condor Legion), Italy and Portugal. The Repub. gvt (Sep. 1936 Popular Front gvt of LARGO CABALLERO, May 1937 Cabinet of JUAN NEGRÍN) received support from the U.S.S.R. and the **International Brigades** of volunteers (60,000 men).

Jul. 1936 Establishment of the supreme milit. command (Junta de Defensa Nacional), which appointed

Sep. 1936 Gen. Franco as head of gvt of the Sp. state and c.-in-c. of the armed forces.

1937 Union of the Falange Española and the traditionalists in the Falange Española Tradicionalista under the **'Caudillo'** FRANCO. The FRANCO gvt was recognized by Germany and Italy in 1936; by France, Britain and the U.S.A. in 1939, after the ultimate defeat of the republic following 3 yrs of bitter fighting. Although Spain joined the Anti-Comintern pact (Apr. 1939), she remained neutral during the 2nd World War.

Portugal

After the abolition of the monarchy (1910), no stable gvt could be formed because the transition to a dem.-parl. form of gvt had been too abrupt. Between 1911 and 1926, Portugal had 8 different presidents and 44 Cabinets, while 20 revolutions and *coups d'état* took place.

1926 Milit. uprising of General Gomes da Costa (May): 'Nat. revolution' without an ideological programme. Dissolution of parliament and suspension of the constitution.

1928 Election of General Carmona to the office of president. Dr Antonio Salazar de Oliveira (1889–1974) became minister of finance of the new gvt. Without assistance from abroad, using draconian measures, SALAZAR was able to impose order on the disrupted finances of the state.

1932 Salazar became prime minister.

1933 Confirmation of the new constitution by plebiscite. The **'New State'** (*Estado Novo*) was a corporatist state after the Fascist model. Retaining friendly relations with Britain and a close relationship with Spain ('the Iberian Bloc'), Portugal remained neutral during the 2nd World War.

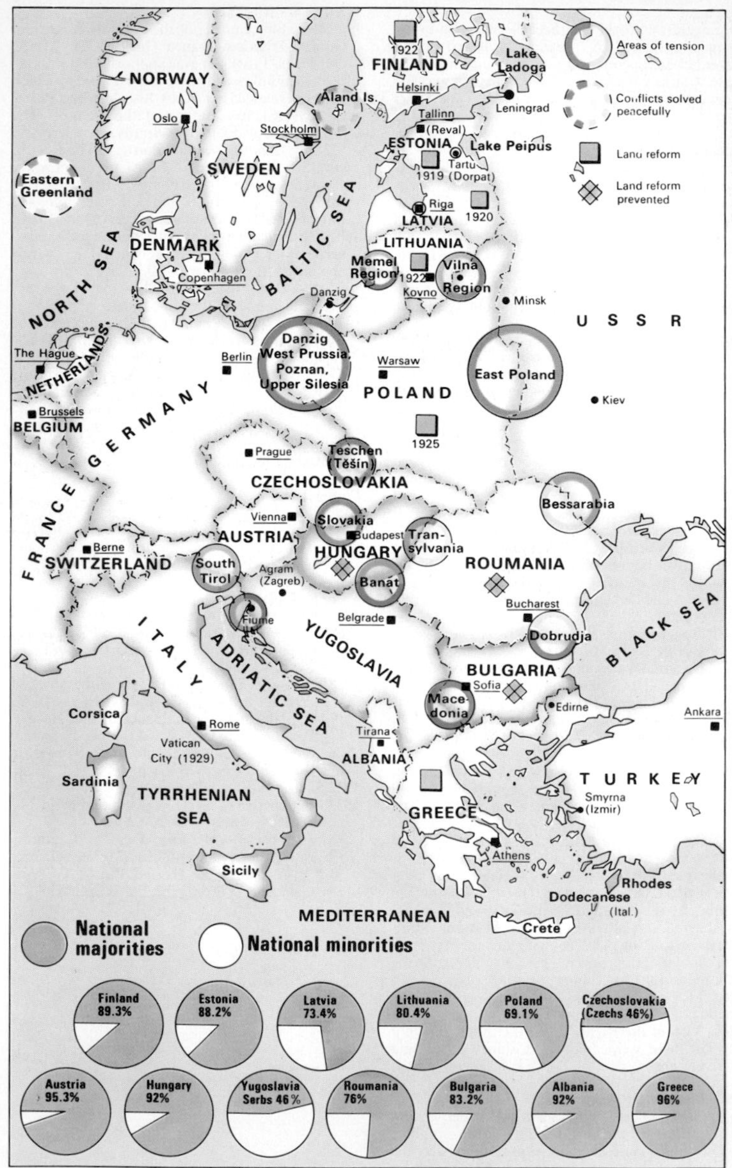
Areas of tension
Conflicts solved peacefully
Land reform
Land reform prevented
FINLAND
1922
Lake Ladoga
NORWAY
Helsinki
Åland Is.
Leningrad
Oslo
Tallinn (Reval)
Stockholm
ESTONIA
Lake Peipus
SWEDEN
Tartu 1919 (Dorpat)
Eastern Greenland
Riga
1920
LATVIA
BALTIC SEA
NORTH SEA
DENMARK
LITHUANIA
Memel Region
1922
Vilna Region
Copenhagen
Kovno
Danzig
Minsk
USSR
The Hague
NETHERLANDS
Berlin
Danzig West Prussia, Poznan, Upper Silesia
Warsaw
East Poland
POLAND
Kiev
Brussels
BELGIUM
GERMANY
1925
Prague
Teschen (Těšín)
CZECHOSLOVAKIA
Bessarabia
FRANCE
Vienna
Slovakia
AUSTRIA
Budapest
Transylvania
Berne
SWITZERLAND
HUNGARY
ROUMANIA
South Tirol
Agram (Zagreb)
Banat
Bucharest
Belgrade
Fiume
YUGOSLAVIA
Dobrudja
BLACK SEA
ITALY
ADRIATIC SEA
BULGARIA
Sofia
Macedonia
Edirne
Corsica
Rome
Tirana
Ankara
Vatican City (1929)
ALBANIA
Sardinia
TYRRHENIAN SEA
TURKEY
Smyrna (Izmir)
GREECE
Athens
Sicily
Rhodes
Dodecanese (Ital.)
MEDITERRANEAN
Crete
National majorities
National minorities
Finland 89.3%
Estonia 88.2%
Latvia 73.4%
Lithuania 80.4%
Poland 69.1%
Czechoslovakia (Czechs 46%)
Austria 95.3%
Hungary 92%
Yugoslavia Serbs 46%
Roumania 76%
Bulgaria 83.2%
Albania 92%
Greece 96%

East European zone of unrest

Roumania

Roumania doubled its territory and pop. by the addition of the Bukovina, Transylvania, Bessarabia (1918), two thirds of the Banat (1919), and, during the struggle against Hungary's 'Red Army', Sathmar, Grosswardein (Oradea) and Arad; however, it also changed from a nat. into a multi-nat. state and became opposed to the U.S.S.R., Hungary and Bulgaria.

Domestic policies were determined by ION BRATIANU (1864–1927), leader of the liberals and creator of Greater Roumania.

1928 After domestic polit. struggles, **Iuliu Maniu** (1873–1951), leader of the Nat. Peasants' party ('Nat. Zaranists'), became prime minister; but the peasants were unpacified (agrarian crisis). After his return, and supported by the liberals,

1930–40 Carol II began his personal régime as **king of Roumania**: he deprived MANIU of power and opposed the antisemitic right-wing groups (the 'Iron Guard' under CORNELIU CODREANU, 1899–1938 (assassinated); the Nat. Christ. party). Although the 'Iron Guard' gained in the elections of 1937, in

1938 the Patriarch Miron Christea (1868–1939) was able to form a Cabinet of 'nat. concentration': **royal dictatorship** was consummated by the suspension of the constitution, the prohibition of all parties, a law to 'maintain order in the state' and the conviction of CODREANU.

Because of the opposition to the U.S.S.R. and Bulgaria (see alliances, p. 165), **for. policy** remained orientated to the w.; however, as a result of increasing nationalist pressure, the for. minister, TITULESCU, was forced to resign in 1936.

1939 Roum. commercial agreement with Germany (p. 197).

Yugoslavia

The policies aiming at the establishment of a s. Slav state were complicated by two addit. objectives: the plan to **build a Greater Serbia** (PAŠIĆ) and that of **creating a S. Slavic confederation** (TRUMBIĆ). The conflict was overcome in the

1917 declaration of Corfu, calling for the creation of a monarchy based on the principle of self-determination.

1918 Establishment of the Kdm of the Serbs, Croats and Slovenes.

1921 Ratification of the 'Vidovdan' Constitution: the minorities within the unitary state did not gain autonomy. As a result of domestic polit. crises (the conflict between Serbs and Croats; the assassination of STEFAN RADIĆ (b. 1871), leader of the Croat Peasants' party, in Jun. 1928, and the opening of a separatist Croat assembly in Agram (Aug. 1928)), King ALEXANDER (1921–34 (assassinated)) proclaimed the establishment of

1929 royal dictatorship: suspension of the constitution, prohibition of polit. parties, dissolution of parliament (Skupština). The new 'Yugoslavia' was organized in 9 banats, without regard for historic or ethnic boundaries.

1931 Suspension of the dictatorial régime. A new constitution providing for 2 chambers and free parl. elections (unity lists of the gvt) was adopted. There was unrest in the Croat peasantry (Ustasha). During the reign of the Regent PAUL (1934–41), and after the resignation of the prime minister, STOJADUNOVIĆ (1935–9),

1939 the new prime minister CVETKOVIĆ admitted 5 Croat ministers to the Cabinet.

Albania

1921 The boundaries of 1913 were affirmed by the conference of ambassadors. Domestic polit. struggles followed.

1925 Ahmed Zogu (1895–1961) became president, and in

1928 king ('King Zog'). The Tirana Treaty (1927) and an interest-free loan (1932) rendered Albania dependent on Italy.

1939 Occupation of Albania by Italy and imposition of a gvt of personal union.

Bulgaria

Domestic politics: the country was troubled by the conditions of the Peace Treaty of Neuilly (p. 133), the problem of settling refugees, its claim to Macedonia, a latent peasant rebellion, and the endeavour of the peasant leader STAMBOLIISKI to create a Greater s. Slav. state. The

1923 army officers' putsch led to the dissolution of the Peasant's party (the prime minister, STAMBOLISKI, being shot) and the Communist party. After a

1934 *coup d'état* by 2 nationalist organizations ('Zveno' and the 'Association of Officers of the Reserve'), an authoritarian régime was introduced, headed by **Colonel Georgieff**. After his resignation (Jan. 1935), **Boris III** continued to rule in authoritarian fashion.

Greece

The policies of the prime minister, **Eleftherios Venizelos** (p. 81), during the 1st World War culminated in the gain of Western and Eastern Thrace in 1919 and Smyrna in 1920. Owing to the

1920–22 Greco-Turk. War (p. 167), Greece lost, in the

1923 Treaty of Lausanne, Eastern Thrace as far as the Maritsa river.

Land reform: large public and private landholdings were expropriated and distributed among the peasants; the Greeks from Turkey were resettled, and the refugees from the Balk. States and the U.S.S.R.

1924–35 The Gk Republic. Domestic polit. struggles took place between the supporters of VENIZELOS and the royalists; but stable gvt was achieved under the new

1928–32 VENIZELOS Cabinet: reconciliation with Turkey was brought about through the Greco-Turk. agreement and the Treaty of Ankara (1930). After an attempted *coup d'état* by VENIZELOS,

1935 the monarchy was proclaimed. King GEORGE II (1922–4; 1935–47) returned.

1936 General Metaxas became prime minister. Parliament was dissolved. Termination of land reform. (For alliances of the Balkan States, see p. 165.)

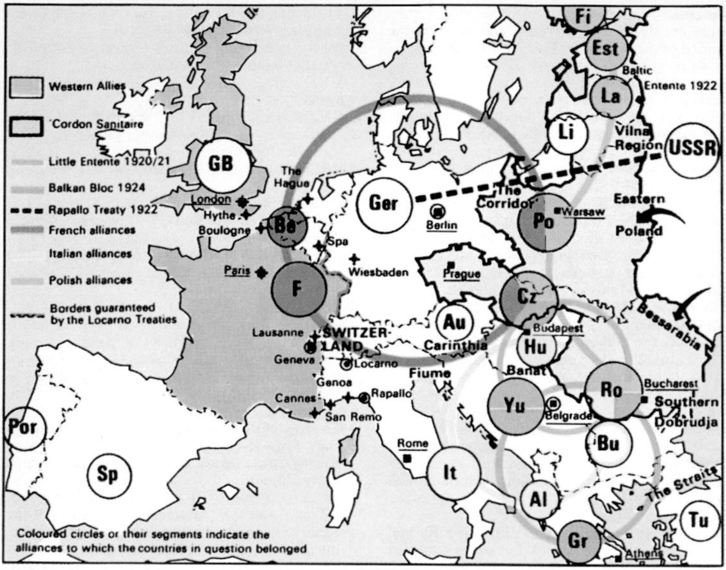

The European alliance system after 1920

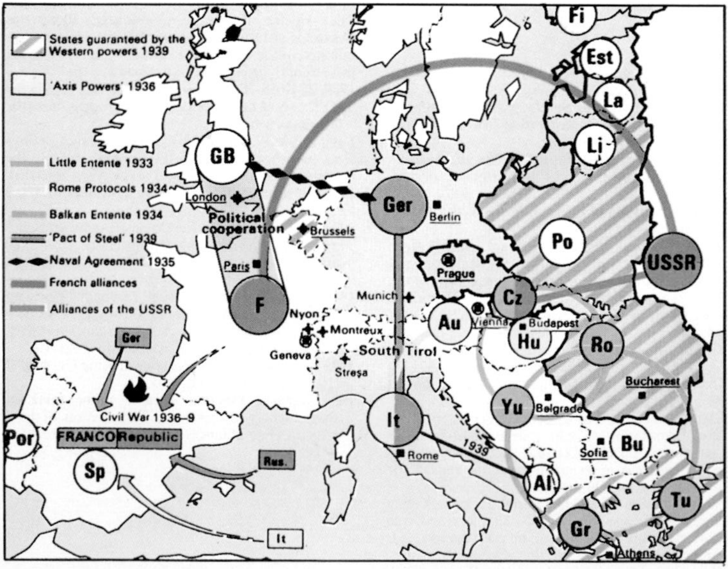

The European alliance system, 1933–9

Eur. Alliances (1918–30)

France: since the conditions of the Peace Treaty of Versailles relating to the left bank of the Rhine did not satisfy Fr. security needs, while Britain had gone back on her promise of assistance (Franco-Brit. Treaty of Defence, 1919), a

1920 Franco-Belg. milit. convention was concluded. When France lost another alliance partner in Russia, it strengthened its position in Eastern Europe through alliances with Poland (1921), Czechoslovakia (1924) and Roumania (1926). The Roum.-Fr. Pact became the keystone of the for. policy of Greater Roumania.

The Little Entente: as a result of fear of the revisionist policies of Hungary and the possible rest. of the Habsburgs, in

1920 a defensive alliance of Czechoslovakia and Yugoslavia was concluded with the support of France. France thereby aimed to stabilize the Versailles system. After the first attempt of the Emperor CAROL to return, Czechoslovakia concluded a

1921 defensive alliance with Roumania, the chief opponent of Hung. revisionism.

1921 Conclusion of an alliance between Roumania and Yugoslavia, directed against Bulgaria.

1921 A treaty between Poland and Roumania promised mutual aid in the event of attack by the U.S.S.R.; the U.S.S.R. had not given up its claims to Bessarabia.

Ger.–Rus. rapprochement: the wish of Germany and the U.S.S.R. to take up polit., milit. and econ. relations formed the background for this development. Germany wished to have *Panzer* officers and pilots trained on Soviet Rus. soil, the U.S.S.R. desired the assistance of Ger. specialists in the development of its armament production. Since the British failed to reach agreement with the Soviet gvt at the

1922 Genoa Econ. Conference, and there was the threat that the U.S.S.R. might be compensated for paying Russia's pre-war debts by association with art. 116 of the Versailles Treaty (reparations), Germany concluded the

1922 Rapallo Treaty with Russia, which regulated Russo-Ger. relations: no war indemnity, resumption of diplomatic relations, a most-favoured-nation clause in trade. The

1926 Berlin Treaty continued the policies initiated at Rapallo: understanding was reached on polit. and econ. questions and the partners promised each other neutrality in the event of attack by any 3rd power.

The Balt. Entente: as a measure of protection from the U.S.S.R., Poland, Estonia, Latvia and Finland concluded a

1922 Non-aggression and Consultation Pact, which was not ratified by the Fin. parliament because of the risk of a Pol.-Rus. conflagration. Lithuania did not join because of the Pol. seizure of Vilna (p. 155). The treaty had insignificant polit. effects; only the Estonia-Latvian treaty (1923) was lasting.

After conclusion of the

1924 Adria Pact, in which MUSSOLINI promised to preserve the status quo, **Italy** concluded treaties of friendship with

1926 Roumania (recognition of the Roumanian possession of Bessarabia);

1927 Albania, which became dependent, and Hungary (directed against Yugoslavia and supporting Hung. revisionism); and

1930 Austria.

The marriage of BORIS III and Princess GIOVANNA led to an improvement in Ital.-Bulg. relations.

Eur. Alliances (1930–39)

France: the alliances of the U.S.S.R. in Eastern Europe – concluded to safeguard its rear in the Far East – and the polit. situation in Germany, formed the preconditions for the

1932 Treaty of Arbitration and the Non-aggression Pact between the U.S.S.R. and France: the partners agreed to assist each other in case of an attack by a 3rd power. Ger.-Rus. relations cooled off. After the failure of the 'Eastern Locarno' the

1935 Franco-Rus. Treaty of Mutual Assistance was concluded, directed against Germany and complemented by a treaty of mutual assistance between the U.S.S.R. and Czechoslovakia, obliging the U.S.S.R. to aid Czechoslovakia pending Fr. action to the same effect.

The Little Entente: the

1933 pact of Organization of the Little Entente powers (Czechoslovakia, Roumania, Yugoslavia) was directed primarily against Hungary.

In the

1934 Triple Alliance of the 'Rome Protocols' (Italy, Hungary, Austria), **Italy** strengthened its infl. in SE. Europe and endorsed a policy of total revisionism, which brought it into conflict with Britain and closer to Nazi Germany.

The Balk. Entente: fear of Rus. ambitions in the Balkans, Nazi policies, the revisionist aspirations of Bulgaria, and the Fr. system of collective security brought about the conclusion of the

1934 Balk. Pact between Yugoslavia, Greece, Roumania and Turkey.

(For Ger. alliances, see p. 197.)

1939 After CHAMBERLAIN's speech (17 Mar.) proclaiming the end of the politics of appeasement, Britain and France issued declarations guaranteeing the integrity of Poland, Roumania, Greece, Turkey and Belgium. After the 'disposal of the rump of Czechoslovakia', the cancellation of the Brit.-Ger. naval agreement and the Ger.-Pol. Non-aggression Pact (p. 197), Britain endeavoured to establish a common line of defence against HITLER. Britain's attempted negotiations with France on the one hand and the U.S.S.R. on the other failed, among other things, because of resistance by Roumania and Poland, who refused to grant the Russians right of passage.

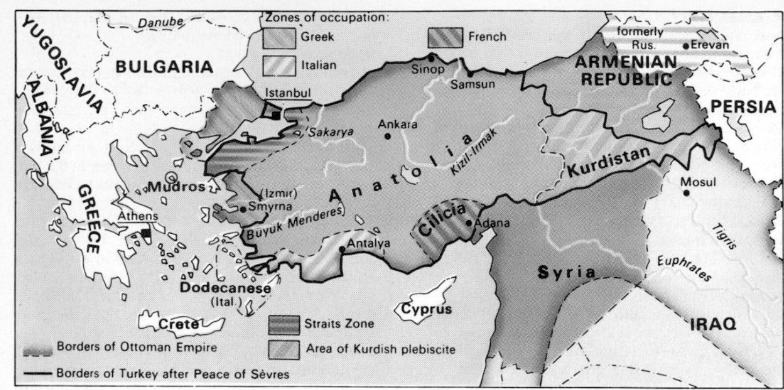

Turkey after the Treaty of Sèvres, 1920

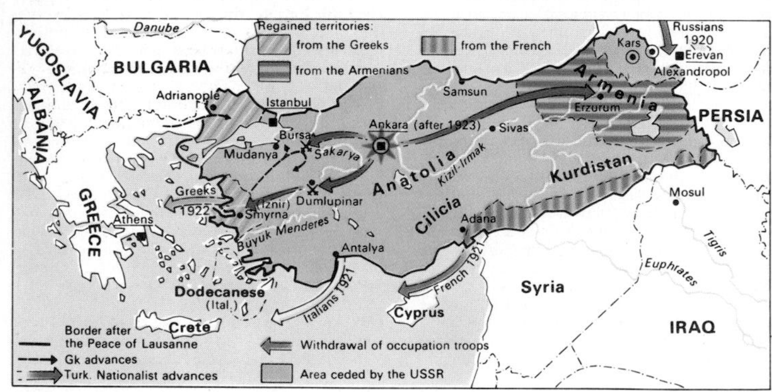

The Turkish-Greek war, 1920–22

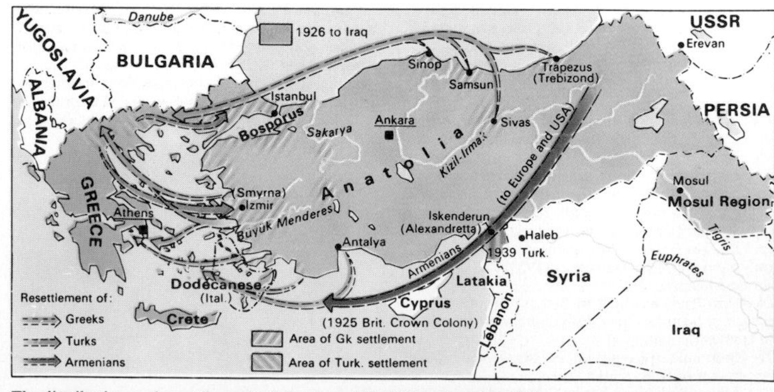

The distribution and resettlement of Greek and Turkish minorities, 1919

The Nat. Uprising (1918–20)

1918 After the Mudros Armistice (p. 131), the 'Grand Fleet' of the Allies entered the Bosporus.

1918–23 **Led by General Mustafa Kemal Pasha (1880–1938), the Turk. Nat. Movement** developed in reaction to the Allied occupation of Istanbul, the occupation of the areas around Antalya and Konya by the Italians (1919), the area around Smyrna by the Greeks (1919), of Cilicia by the French (1919), the danger threatening from the separatist movement of the Kurds and the newly est. state of Armenia.

1919 At the nat. congresses of Erzurum and Sivas, MUSTAFA KEMAL PASHA cal. for the establishment of a Turk. state within the nat. frontiers. A representative committee was elected to 'represent the views of the nation'. Ankara became the seat of the nat. movement. After the signing of the 'Nat. Pact' by the last Ott. parliament (1920) and evidence of resistance, the Allied occupation of Istanbul was reinforced.

Apr. 1920 Convocation of the 'Great Nat. Assembly' in Ankara: the Ott. gvt reacted by imposing the death penalty on MUSTAFA KEMAL and his associates.

Aug. 1920 Peace Treaty of Sèvres (p. 133). MOHAMMED VI (1918–22) and the Nat. Assembly refused 'provis.' ratification.

The Liberation of Turkey (1920–22)

The E.: the vict. of KÂZIM KARABEKIRS forced the Armenians to conclude the

1920 Peace Treaty of Alexandropol. After the Rus. occupation of the Armen. cap. of Erevan, the Rus. part of Armenia went to the U.S.S.R., which concluded a treaty of friendship with Turkey. In

1921 the Treaty of Kars, between Turkey and the Soviet Republics of Azerbaijan, Armenia and Georgia, the Caucasus frontier was recognized.

1920–21 The Turks suppressed the Armenians with terror and cruelty; thousands perished, few were able to emigrate.

The W.: the Supreme Allied War Council gave a 'mandate' to the Gk prime minister VENIZELOS (p. 81) to 'restore order in Anatolia': Bursa (1920) and Adrianople (1920) were occupied and the Gk armies advanced to the Sakarya.

Bs. of Inönü and the Sakarya (collapse of the Gk offensive).

1922 Breakthrough of MUSTAFA KEMAL at Dumlupinar and entry into Smyrna.

Oct. 1922 Armistice of Mudanya: evacuation of Eastern Thrace (Adrianople).

The S.:

1921 Treaty of Ankara: withdrawal of the French.

The Republic (1923–45)

After the abolition of the Sultanate (1 Nov. 1922) the

1923 Peace of Lausanne was concluded: Turkey received back Eastern Thrace as far as the Maritsa, the islands of Imbros and Tenedos, the area around Smyrna and Western Armenia. The Straits were demilitarized (an Int. Straits Commission being appointed). The 'capitulations' were suspended and no reparations were demanded. Occupation troops were withdrawn; *c.* 1·35 mil. Greeks and 430,000 Turks were resettled.

1923–38 Mustafa Kemal (after 1935 Kemal Atatürk) became president of the Republic of Turkey. The seat of gvt was est. at Ankara. Till 1946 the Repub. People's party (founded 1923) was the only polit. party; its members were obliged to pay homage to the repub. form of gvt, nationalism, soc. peace, econ. guidance by the state, the separation of Church and state in polit. life, and a revolutionary cult. policy. Precondition for the efficacy of the reforms was the removal of Isl. relig. law from the admin., the constitution, the judiciary and the educ. system **(laicism).**

1924 Abolition of the Caliphate and elimination of Isl. courts of law.

1925 Dissolution of the Orders of Dervishes.

The legal system was founded on Swiss civil (1926) and fiscal (1926) and Ital. criminal law (1926).

1928 All references relating to relig. life were removed from the constitution.

Education: introduction of the Lat. alphabet and prohibition of Arab. script (1928). Obligatory instruction in Arab. and Pers. was abolished in secondary schools (1929). Establishment of new elementary, middle, professional and agricul. schools and universities (1936: Ankara University).

1934 Introduction of surnames.

1938–50 Ismet Inönü (b. 1884) became 2nd president of the Republic of Turkey. Increased democratization was initiated during his term: new polit. parties were founded; relig. instruction was permitted in the schools.

Econ. life: trade and industry were built up by state aid. The network of roads and railways was extended.

For. policy:

1925 Treaty of Neutrality and Non-aggression with the U.S.S.R.

1926 Mosul Treaty (p. 135).

1930 Treaty of Friendship with Greece.

1934 The Balk. Pact (p. 165).

1936 Int. Straits Conference of Montreux: Turkey received the right to refortify the Straits; increased tension in relations with the U.S.S.R.

1937 The Pact of Saadabad (Turkey, Iran, Afghanistan, Iraq) stabilized the relationship of Turkey with the states in the E. and the SE. Rapprochement with the Western Powers after 1930 led to the

1939 regaining of the Sandjak of Alexandretta (Hatay) and the Franco-Brit.-Turk. Treaty of Mutual Assistance. During the 2nd World War, Turkey remained neutral; but in

1941 concluded a Treaty of Friendship with Germany (which stipulated that its conditions were not to contravene Turkey's obligations to the Western Allies).

1945 Declaration of war on Germany.

The Near East

The adoption of the Eur. conceptions of the nation, freedom and self-determination strengthened **Arab nationalism** and the **striving for nat. independence**. The **heterogeneous obligations assumed by Britain** during the 1st World War complicated any constructive solution to the post-war problems.

1916 Agreement between the Brit. High Commissioner McMahon and Sherif Hussein of Mecca (1853–1931), who joined the Brit. side after receiving the promise of Arabian independence.

1916 Sykes–Picot Note: a secret agreement to partition of the formerly Turk. areas between Britain (Mesopotamia, Palestine, Jordan) and France (Syria). Final settlement was reached at the Conference of San Remo (p. 135).

1917 Balfour Declaration (p. 63).

Syria

1918–20 Emir Feisal (1883–1933), proclaimed king of Syria by the Nat. Congress, was expelled after allocation of the mandate of Syria to France (1919) and bloody uprisings. Syria was organized in the largely auton. districts of Damascus, Aleppo, the Alawite and Druze regions (1925 uprising).

1926 Establishment of the state of Lebanon. Because of

1939 cession of the Sandjak of Alexandretta (p. 167) to Turkey. The relationship with France was made difficult. However, the French did not evacuate Syria.

1941 Conflicts between troops of the Vichy gvt and those of the 'Free French', whose c.-in-c., General CATROUX, promised independence to the areas under mandate to France. **Syria (Apr. 1941) and Lebanon (Dec. 1941) became auton.**

Iraq

1919 The Brit. mandate for Mesopotamia was est. Following the

1921 proclamation of Emir Feisal as king of Iraq violent uprisings were brought to an end. FEISAL, a companion-in-arms of Colonel T. E. LAWRENCE ('Lawrence of Arabia', 1888–1935), est. a const. monarchy in 1925. Through the

1926 Mosul Treaty (p. 135), Iraq received the disputed oil region.

1930 Brit.-Iraqi Treaty: recognition of Iraqi independence, establishment of R.A.F. bases and

1932 admission of Iraq to the League of Nations.

1933–9 King Ghazi I (b. 1912).

1937 Treaty of Saadabad (see below).

Transjordan

1921 Abdullah ibn Hussein (1882–1951 (assassinated)) became **Emir of Transjordan**.

1923 Separation of Transjordan from Palestine. As a buffer state to Cen. Arabia, Transjordan became Britain's closest ally in the Near East. The Arab Legion was formed under the Brit. general GLUBB PASHA (b. 1897).

Palestine (cf. p. 259)

1920 In disregard of the Balfour Declaration, a **Brit. mandate over Palestine was est.** Continuous struggles between Arabs and Jews.

Cen. Arabia

1896–1924 Sherif Hussein of Mecca, the king of the Hejaz (father of King FEISAL and the Emir ABDULLAH) became a rival of the ruler of Nejd,

1902–53 Abd al-Aziz ibn Saud (1880–1969).

1924 Proclamation of HUSSEIN as Caliph. IBN SAUD, the representative of the sect of the Wahhabis, declared war on HUSSEIN. The war ended with IBN SAUD's capture of Mecca and Medina. HUSSEIN was forced to abdicate; his son

1925 ALI abandoned all claims to the land and the crown.

1926 Proclamation of Ibn Saud as king of the Hejaz and Nejd. The countries were joined to form the

1932 Kdm of Saudi Arabia.

1934 War against the Yemen, terminated by the

1936–7 Treaty of Taif.

Persia, from 1935 Iran

After several *coups d'état*, the Cossack leader REZA KHAN became

1925–41 Reza Shah Pahlavi (1878–1944) and hered. Shah of Persia. He introduced educ. reforms, modernized agriculture and restored the state's finances. The plan to settle the nomads and to reconcile the people and the upper classes failed.

For. policy:

1921 Treaty with the R.S.F.S.R., which, in exchange for the promise of Iran. neutrality, gave up all Rus. rights and claims to concessions.

1927 Suspension of the 'capitulations' (special privileges for Europeans).

1933 Agreement with the Anglo-Pers. (after 1935 Anglo-Iran.) Oil Co.: limitation of the concession areas and increase of the share paid to the gvt.

1937 Treaty of Saadabad: reconciliation of Shi'ite Iran with the Sunnite states of Turkey, Iraq and Afghanistan.

1941 Invasion of Rus. and Brit. troops. REZA SHAH abdicated in favour of his son MOHAMMED (b. 1919).

Afghanistan

After the assassination of Emir HABIBULLAH (1901–19), his son proclaimed himself

1919–29 Emir Amanullah. He unleashed the 'Afghan War of Independence' (the 3rd Afghan War) against Brit. India, which was terminated by the

1919 Peace of Rawalpindi.

1921 Treaty of Kabul: recognition of Afghanistan's independence by Britain. Proclamation of AMANULLAH as king (1926). Hastily executed soc. reforms led to soc. unrest, eventually causing the king to be driven from the country. The country was pacified and more moderate reforms were carried out under his successors, MOHAMMED NADIR (1929–33) and MOHAMMED SAHIR (from 1933).

India

The domestic polit. situation in India (p. 89) remained unstable during the 1st World War. A climax of unrest was reached in the

Apr. 1919 Amritsar Massacre; Brit. troops shot into an assembly of people, killing or wounding over 1,000. The

Dec. 1919 Montague–Chelmsford reforms consequently provided for the division of gvtl powers in the provinces ('dyarchy', to 1935): some authorities ('reserved subjects', the police, real-estate taxes, etc.) remained in the hands of the Brit. authorities; others ('transferred subjects': agriculture, industry, education, public health, etc.) were administered by Ind. ministries. The leadership of the nat. movement was assumed by

Mohandas Karamchand Gandhi (1869–1948), the **'Mahatma'** ('the noble-hearted'), who had great infl. over the Nat. Congress (p. 89) and carried on the polit. struggle for self-determination (*Swarai*) in accordance with the ancient Ind. 'Ideal Truth' (*Satya*), the principles of non-violence (*Ahimsa*) and purification through love of neighbour (*Brahmacharya*). The 'Khaddaz' (handspun, white cotton cloth) and salt gained from the sea – to break Britain's monopolies – became the symbols of the striving for independence.

1920–22 The 1st 'Satygraha' campaign (opposition to cooperation with Britain and the constitution) ended with GANDHI's committal to prison for 6 yrs. However, he was pardoned in 1924 and resumed his struggle for econ. and soc. reforms (to 1936). His work benefited the 60 mil. pariahs ('untouchables').

1921–6 The viceroy, Lord READING, governed absolutely without popular representation.

1928 Acceptance of a constitution drafted by MOTILAL NEHRU (1861–1931) by the Congress, and ultimatum to Britain calling for dominion status within the year. The

1930 2nd 'Satygraha' campaign, which saw the arrest of GANDHI and 60,000 nationalists, was interrupted by the

1931 'Delhi Pact' between GANDHI and Lord IRWIN (viceroy from 1926): suspension of 'civil disobedience' in exchange for freedom of the polit. prisoners. After 3 'round-table' conferences in London (1930–32), the campaign was continued (1932–4).

1935 Gvt of India Act: introduction of the dyarchy system into the cen. gvt, autonomy for the prov. gvts, but retention of special privileges for the viceroy and the governors. After the

1937 election, which saw the Congress party victorious in 6 out of 11 provinces, the new constitution became effective. Burma was separated from India and received the status of crown colony.

The rad., anti-Brit. policies of SUBHAS CHANDRA BOSE (1897–1945) during the **2nd World War** ended in failure. While BOSE allied himself with the Nazis, GANDHI, supported by **Jawaharlal Nehru** (1889–1964), carried through the 3rd 'Satygraha' campaign (advocating pacifism).

1940 Conflict over the Pakistan plan of the Moslem League (p. 89) under MOHAMMED ALI JINNAH (1876–1947): establishment of ind. Moslem states.

1942 As Brit. spokesman, SIR STAFFORD CRIPPS (1889–1952) offered **India dominion status after the end of the war.** GANDHI responded with the demand: 'Quit India.'

Outer Mongolia

After the 'Whites' had been expelled by Soviet troops (1921), the Mongol. Revolutionary People's party proclaimed the

1921 independence of Mongolia. The monarchy continued in existence.

1924 Proclamation of the Mongol. People's Republic, the 1st satellite of the U.S.S.R. The NW. gained its independence as the **Urjanchai Republic**, later **Tannu Tuva** (incorp. as an auton. region (Tuva Auton. Republic) into the U.S.S.R. in 1944).

Siam, from 1939 Thailand

1917 Siam entered the 1st World War on the side of the Entente Powers.

1920 Membership of the League of Nations. A **moderate form of nationalism** brought about the suspension of extraterrit. rights for foreigners, the conclusion of new customs agreements safeguarding auton. admin. of duties, and the struggle against the strong Chin. position in Siam's econ. life.

1925–35 King Rama VII Prajadhibok.

1932 Non-violent *coup d'etat*: introduction of const. monarchy. The domestic polit. situation was disrupted by a milit. uprising and a failed counter-revolution of the nobility (1933). RAMA VII abdicated.

1935–46 Rama VIII Ananda Mahidol. Revision of agreements with for. gvts.

Tibet

Following the declaration of independence (p. 91), a Chin. incursion (occurring during the 1st World War) was repulsed (1918).

1920 Armistice with China.

1933 Death of the 13th Dalai Lama.

1940 Inauguration of the 14th Dalai Lama.

Indonesia (Dutch E. Indies)

1918 Convocation of the People's Council of the Dutch-E. Indies parliament (composed of 30 Indonesians, 25 Dutch members, and 5 members of other Asian nationalities). The People's Council became an advisory organ in the leg. process (1925).

1927 Establishment of the Nationalist party of Indonesia (P.N.I.) in Bandung under the chairmanship of ACHMED SUKARNO (p. 263).

1937 Draft of a 10-Year Plan to bring about self-gvt for Indonesia (postponed by the Dutch gvt).

1940–41 Dutch-Jap. negotiations concerning the incorporation of Indonesia into the 'E. Asian Sphere of Prosperity' (p. 174) failed.

1942 Jap. occupation of the Dutch E. Indies.

The 'Brit. Commonwealth of Nations'

The reorganization of the Brit. Empire, the union of Britain and the Dominions as auton. states with equal rights was based on the following causes:

1. **Increasing nat. consciousness** in the Brit. settlement colonies.
2. **Contributions to the conduct of the war.** Consequences: recognition of Canada, Australia, New Zealand and s. Africa as states with equal rights and formation of the Imp. War Cabinet, composed of the Brit. War Cabinet, the prime ministers of the dominions and representatives of India.
3. **Preparation and propagation of the conception of a commonwealth of states** through the journal *Round Table* (founded in 1910 by the members of Lord MILNER's 'Kindergarten', esp. LIONEL CURTIS (1872–1955), who coined the term 'Brit. Commonwealth of Nations').

The fact that the dominions enjoyed equal rights was demonstrated at the peace conference (sep. delegations and signatures), by the fact that they had ind. membership in the League of Nations, and by the granting of mandates by the League of Nations to the Union of s. Africa and to Australia and New Zealand. After the Imp. Conferences of 1921 (discussion of for. policy questions) and 1923 (recognition of the rights of the dominions to conclude state treaties independently), the

1926 Imp. Conference accepted the definition of the status of a dominion (the 'Balfour Formula'): Britain and the dominions (Canada, Australia, New Zealand, the Union of s. Africa, the Irish Free State and Newfoundland) were to be auton. communities within the Brit. Empire, equal in status, in no way subordinate to one another, but united by common allegiance to the crown and freely associated as members of the Brit. Commonwealth of Nations. The

1931 Statute of Westminster confirmed the 'Balfour Formula' and removed restrictive reservation so far held by Britain to leg. autonomy of the dominions. Econ. cooperation, on which the Imp. Conference of 1930 had reached no agreement, was agreed under the pressure of the world-wide Depression (p. 185) at the Imp. Conference in Ottawa (p. 190).

The Commonwealth did not possess an 'Imp. Constitution', but was governed by the will to act in common on the basis of sentiment (the crown) and polit. (deliberations at imp. conferences) and econ. ties (trade and commerce). These were the 7 sovereign states, each possessing a parliament, an independently elected gvt and freedom of decision in for. policy: **Britain**, the **Irish Free State**, **Canada**, **Newfoundland**, **Australia**, the **Union of S. Africa** and **New Zealand**. The Brit. colon. empire remained unchanged; it consisted of the crown colonies and protectorates in Africa, Asia, the w. Indies and the Pacific–all subordinate to the crown and the Brit. parliament.

Ireland

1916 Easter Rising of the Sinn Féin movement, which collapsed after bloody fighting in Dublin, the proclamation of the republic, and the execution of 14 of its leaders. ROGER CASEMENT (1864–1916), who had landed in Ireland from a Ger. U-boat on the eve of the rising, was executed for high treason following his attempts to enlist Germany's aid for the Irish cause.

1918 Parl. elections. Sinn Féin captured 73 of the 106 Irish seats.

1919 Illegal assembly of the members of Sinn Féin in Dublin as the Irish Parliament (Dáil Eireann). Formation of a secret gvt under **Eamonn de Valera** (1882–1975). The climax of the

1919–20/21 warfare between the Irish nationalists (Sinn Féin and the Irish Repub. Army (I.R.A.)) under MICHAEL COLLINS (1890–1922) and the Brit. troops (the 'Black and Tans') was reached on 'Bloody Sunday' (21 Nov. 1920) in Dublin.

1920 Gvt of Ireland Act: Ireland, exc. for Ulster, received, as the **Irish Free State**, a status resembling that of the dominions, with an ind. gvt and its own parliament (Dáil); the deputies of the Dáil were sworn in to the king; Ulster was given up. The rad. wing of Sinn Féin under DE VALERA split away; it aspired to independence for all Ireland.

1922 Ratification of the treaty by the majority of the Dáil and acceptance of the constitution (2-chamber system), which became effective after the **proclamation of the Irish Free State** (6 Dec. 1922). ARTHUR GRIFFITH (1872–1922) became the chairman of the Executive Council; after his death, W. T. COSGRAVE (b. 1880). The civil war between the Radicals and the Moderates, which broke out in Apr. 1922, was terminated in Apr. 1923. The country was reconstructed under COSGRAVE, who pleaded for reconciliation with Britain.

1932–45 Prime Minister de Valera. The treaty of 1921 was undermined by resort to the conditions of the Statute of Westminster. The oath of loyalty to the crown was abolished (1933), annual payments to Britain were terminated. Rad. organizations in opposition to DE VALERA were formed (Fascist 'Blueshirts', the Nat. Guard).

1932–3 Customs war with Britain, which was terminated by the

1936 Brit.-Irish Trade Agreement.

1937 Proclamation of the 'sovereign, ind., democratic state' of Eire under President DOUGLAS HYDE (1938–1945).

1938 Agreement with Britain: regulation of finan. and econ. problems. Surrender of the right to 'treaty ports'. Even so, the country remained unreconciled after the elect. vict. of DE VALERA in Jun. (because of the continued existence of Northern Ireland as a separate entity and the Brit. refusal to grant complete independence to the republic as such). Eire thus remained neutral during the 2nd World War.

Canada

Following the outbreak of the 1st World War, Canada proclaimed its solidarity with the mother country (1914) and, against the opposition of the Fr. Canadians, introduced general conscription (1917): *c.* 450,000 Canadians fought in Europe. Canada signed the Treaty of Versailles and joined the League of Nations.

Domestic affairs: competing with the Con. party (under ARTHUR MEIGHEN) and the Progressive party (under T. A. CREAR), the Lib. party was victorious in the

1921 elections; it was chaired by **William Lyon Mackenzie King** (1874–1950).

1921–30 King Cabinet: with the support of the Progressive party, reforms were carried out (lowering of taxation, amortization of loans, welfare measures for the unemployed).

1926–9 Econ. prosperity: wheat prices rose, mines were expanded, railways were built, more electricity was produced. The tendency towards **particularism in the prov. gvts** increased.

1929 The Great Depression: unemployment, decrease of exports and nat. income (by 50%).

1930–35 Con. Cabinet of Richard Bedford Bennett, which governed with almost dictatorial measures. The raising of import duties to spur domestic production and the reduction of tariffs on Canad. goods granted by the 1932 Ottawa Imp. Conference failed to relieve the situation. Because of dissatisfaction with the cen. gvt, **rad. parties were formed** on regional bases. Most of the laws passed under the

Jan. 1935 Reform Plan of the BENNETT Cabinet (minimum hours of work and minimum wages, unemployment and soc. insurance, agricultural credits) were declared unconst. by the Judicial Committee of the Privy Council in London after the

Oct. 1935 elect. vict. of the Liberals ('King or Chaos') and the formation of the

1935–48 King Cabinet. The invalidation of BENNETT's 'New Deal' legislation placed the fed. system in jeopardy; a plan by the cen. gvt to combat the econ. crisis on a nat. scale was prohibited.

1937 Appointment of the Rowell–Sirois Commission to investigate the relationship of the state and the provinces; an extensive report was presented in 1940. As a result of the Trade Agreement with the U.S.A., active trade between the U.S.A., Canada and Britain (forming the 'North Atlantic Triangle', 1938), and increased armament production (1937–8), **the country recovered slowly.**

For. policy: Canada's main objective was to prevent a break in the relationship between its 2 major trading partners: Britain and the U.S.A.; these were the 2 countries on which Canada, regardless of its nat. independence, had to rely in the event of int. crisis since she herself did not maintain adequate armaments and milit. forces. At the

1917 Imp. Conference, the leader of the Conservatives, **Sir Robert Laird Borden** (1854–1937), like the s. African SMUTS (p. 179), defined the status of the dominions as 'ind. nations of the Imp. Commonwealth with the right to an appropriate voice in for. policy'. For this reason, and also in deference to U.S. policy, Canada, at the

1921 Imp. Conference, opposed the revival of the Brit.-Jap. alliance. At the

1923 Imp. Conference it opposed the centralization of the Commonwealth. The

1923 Agreement between Canada and the U.S.A. (concerning halibut fisheries in the northern Pacific) was a first step towards an **auton. Canad. for. policy**, a policy which was strongly isolationist and which contributed to the paralysis of the League of Nations; but after MUSSOLINI's invasion of Abyssinia (p. 159) and the manifestation of Germany's expansionist policies (p. 197), Canad. isolationism ceased.

1939 Declaration of war on Germany.

Newfoundland

1933 Newfoundland abandoned the status of a dominion because of fiscal difficulties and became a crown colony.

Australia

In 1919 Australia received New Guinea and the Pacific Islands s. of the Equator as mandates of the League of Nations. Under the Con. gvt a planned policy to strengthen the nat. economy was carried out. Exports increased (wheat, butter, meat, wool), and deposits of lead and zinc ores, bauxite and lignite were exploited. The Great Depression put an end to heavy immigration, the establishment of new industries and the expansion of agriculture. Consequences: exports decreased (esp. those of agricultural products), protective tariffs were introduced. During the 1930s Australia's for. policy was strongly dependent on Britain. After the revocation of the Gen. Conscription Bill (1929),

1934 Australia introduced a 3-Yr Plan for rearmament. There were tensions with Japan (over immigration and Japan's 'export offensive'), leading to the

1938 prohibition of the export of iron and manganese ores.

1939 Declaration of war on Germany.

New Zealand

Largely auton. from 1907, New Zealand experienced a period of steady growth after 1919. Agriculture was intensified by the organization of the dairy industry.

1931 New Zealand received dominion status (definitive confirmation in 1947).

1935–45 Soc. reforms were esp. effective under the gvt of the Lab. party. New Zealand's for. policy was strongly dependent on that of Britain.

1939 New Zealand entered the war on the side of the Allies.

Kuomintang (KMT):
Power base of Chiang Kai-shek 1927–37
Capital cities
Milit. obstacles
Communists (CPC):
Area before 1934
Area of concentration from 1935
Capital Cities
Centres of concentration
The Long March (main direction)
Japan:
Annexations
Occupied territories in China 1937–41
Railways
U S S R
(Bayan Tümen) Kerulen
REPUBLIC OF MONGOLIA
1921
Manchuria
MANCHUKUO
1932
Sungari
Harbin
Chahar
1937
Jehol
1933
Shenyang (Mukden)
Paotow
Suiyuan
PEKING
Hopei
Dairen (Talien)
Seoul
Korea
Pusan
Kansu
Taiyuan
Shansi
Chingpien
Yenan
Shensi
Tsinghai
Hwang Ho
Tsinan
Shantung
Yellow Sea
Minhsien
Tsewuchen
Funiushan
Honan
Kiangsu
Nankiang
Anhwei
Nanking
1927
Shanghai
Tsitsang
Lushan
Szechwan
Yangtze
Hankow
1926
Hwangshan
East China Sea
Chungking 1937
Yangtze
Chekiang
Huaiyushan
Weihsin
Maotai
Nanchang
Hunan
Kiangsi
Wenchow
Chiaochetu
Burma Road
Kweiyang
Kinping
Yunghsin
Fukien
Foochow
Ningyuan
Stilwell Road
Kunming
Chenfeng
Kweichow
Juichin
Ichang
Ryukyu Is.
Yunnan
Kwangsi
Amoy
Hsi Chiang
Canton 1921
Swatow
Formosa
Kwangtung
Hong Kong (Brit.)
Macao (Port.)
PACIFIC OCEAN
Kwangchowwan (Fr.)
Hainan
South China Sea
French Indo-China
Mekong
SIAM
Philippines

China, 1918–41

China After the Revolution (1912–21)

After the abdication of the imp. gvt (12 Feb. 1912) and the resignation of the presidency by SUN YAT-SEN (15 Feb.) (p. 91),

1912–16 General Yuan Shih-k'ai (1859–1916) became president of the Republic of China.

1912 Formation of the Kuomintang (National People's party), which grew out of the 'sworn brotherhood' (p. 91) of SUN YAT-SEN. The assassination of SUNG CHAO-YEN led to the **2nd revolution in Nanking** (1913), which was suppressed by YUAN. China was in large measure forced to accept the

1915 '21 demands' of Japan (p. 123).

1916–26 Wars of the 'warlords' for Peking in Northern China: the 'Anfu party' was supported by Japan; the 'Zhili clique' and the 'Fengtien group' were supported by the Western Powers. A gvt was formed at Canton, which chose

1917 SUN YAT-SEN to be generalissimo of the forces of the s.; SUN YAT-SEN, however, resigned (1918) and began the reorganization of the Kuomintang.

1917 China entered the war in the hope of annulling the 'unequal treaties' and Jap. demands; China also expected the return of the territory leased to Germany. China's wishes were unfulfilled at the peace conference.

1919 Demonstration of Peking students against the signing of the peace treaty. Inception of the **'Movement of 4 May'**: abandonment of Confucianism and acceptance of Western ctr.

The Kuomintang and the Com. party (1921–36)

1921–5 Impressed by the Rus. Revolution and LENIN's N.E.P. (p. 143), and also by the fact that Soviet Russia had abandoned all claims and concessions in China (1920), SUN YAT-SEN, then president of the Canton gvt, was ready for

1923 cooperation between the Kuomintang and the Com. party of China.

1924 1st Party Convention of the Kuomintang. Acceptance of the '3 People's Principles' (p. 91) of SUN YAT-SEN as the party's polit. programme: unity of the people (nationalism), rights of the people (democracy), livelihood of the people (Socialism). Admission of the Communists (the Communist party of China had been founded in 1921) into the Kuomintang. Organization of the party with the help of Rus. advisers (BORODIN), and of the army after the Rus. model (General BLÜCHER); also, the Whampao milit. academy was founded (milit. instruction under CHIANG KAI-SHEK, polit. guidance under CHOU EN-LAI).

1925 Death of SUN YAT-SEN; establishment of a nat. gvt in Canton.

1925 Demonstrating students fired on in Shanghai by Brit. police. The **'Movement of 30 May'** unleashed the

1925–7 Nat. Revolution.

1926 Campaign of the revolutionary army under **Chiang Kai-shek** (1887–1975) against the milit. commanders in Cen. and northern China. Seizure of Hankow (Aug.), which became the seat of the nat. gvt (Nov. 1926); of Shanghai and Nanking (Mar. 1927).

1927 CHIANG KAI-SHEK broke with the Com. party and Communists were liquidated in Shanghai (obligations of CHIANG KAI-SHEK to banks, large merchants and anti-Com. members of the Kuomintang).

1927–36 Rule of the Kuomintang.

1927 Formation of a nat. gvt in Nanking: execution of Communists, suppression of peasant rebellions, return of BORODIN and his associates to the U.S.S.R.

1928 Chiang Kai-shek's march to the N. ended with the entry into Peking and the **unification of China**, which became a 1-party state on the basis of the '5 powers' (executive, legislative, judiciary, civil service and censorial). Progress was made during the

1931 'period of educative gvt': for. settlements were brought back under control of the nat. gvt, extraterrit. rights were suspended, interior tariffs were eliminated. The settlements in Shanghai and the admin. of Chin. maritime tariffs remained under the control of the U.S.A. and Britain. There was no land reform. Trad. Confucian ideology was revived (1934) and the transition to milit. dictatorship (under the 'Whampao Officers' Clique') was made.

Supported by the **Peasants' Leagues** (85% of the Chin. pop. were peasants), **Mao Tse-tung** (b. 1893) and CHU TEH were able to **establish Com. bases** in Kiangsi and Fukien provinces (expropriation from landlords, redistribution of the land).

May 1928 Creation of the Red Army in Hunan; after

1930–34 5 unsuccessful campaigns by CHIANG KAI-SHEK to destroy it, the Red Army in the

1934–5 'Long March' removed itself to Yenan.

1936 Establishment of the H.Q. of the Communist party of China under MAO TSE-TUNG in Yenan.

The Sino-Jap. War (1937–45)

After the Mukden incident (p. 175), the separation of Manchuria from China by Japan, the fighting over Shanghai (1932) and the occupation of Jehol province (1922),

1936 CHIANG KAI-SHEK was taken prisoner. An armistice between the Kuomintang and the Com. party of China was agreed on, and CHIANG KAI-SHEK, freed through the good offices of CHOU EN-LAI, was recognized as leader in the struggle against Japan. The

1937 incident at the Marco Polo Bridge, nr Peking, constituted the beginning of the war between China and Japan. A manifesto stipulating the cooperation of the Kuomintang and the Com. party of China was issued (auton. troops and territories). The seat of the nat. gvt was moved to Chungking.

1940 Formation of a pro-Jap. gvt under WANG CHING-WEI in Nanking (p. 175).

1943 The Allies gave up all privileges gained by the 'unequal treaties' to prevent a separate peace of the Kuomintang with Japan.

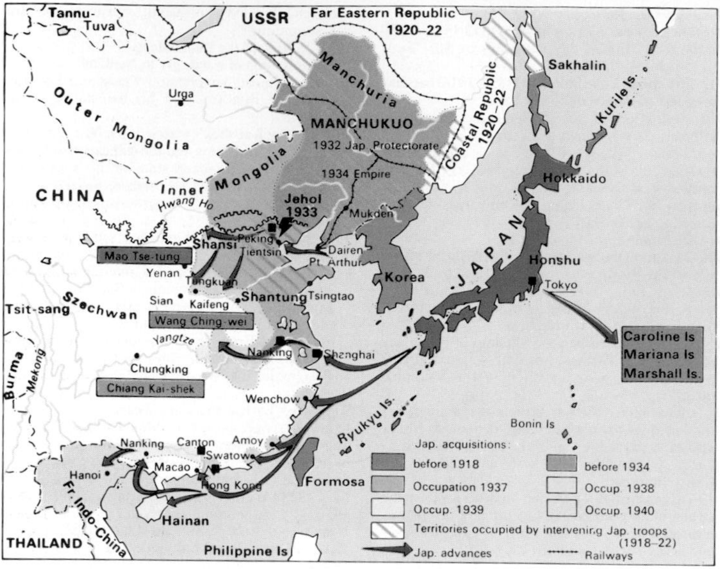

Japanese expansion to 1941

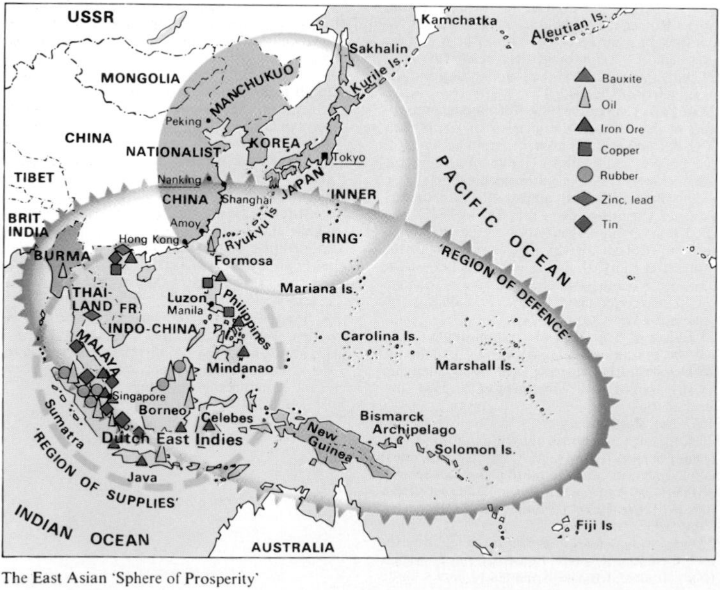

The East Asian 'Sphere of Prosperity'

The Taisho Period (1912–26)

1912–26 Yoshihito (known as the Emperor TAISHO, 1879–1926). During the 1st World War Japan enlarged her navy and its merchant marine: exports rose as Japan moved into int. markets. As a result of the gain of

1919 Tsingtao and Ger. concessions in China, as well as the takeover of the Ger. Pacific Islands N. of the Equator, **Japan became a major power in the Pacific and the 3rd largest naval power in the world.**

1920–22 Econ. crisis: deficient quality of Jap. products led to a loss of for. markets.

For. policy: At the

1921–2 Washington Conference (p. 134) Japan had to suffer a diplomatic defeat. Owing to the

1924 U.S. immigration laws (exclusion of Jap. immigrants), Jap.-Amer. relations cooled. Relations with the U.S.S.R. improved.

1925 Soviet-Jap. Treaty: the Japanese evacuated Northern Sakhalin; the U.S.S.R. recognized the Peace of Portsmouth (p. 113). The policies of SHIDEHARA KIJURO (1872–1951), abandoning the '21 Demands' to China and the policy of force, raised Jap. prestige abroad but roused the resistance of the Jap. army.

Domestic policy: oligarchic domination by the Genro (p. 115) was exchanged for that of the army, the large corporations and the bureaucracy as well as the young generation, which, though powerless, cal. for further liberalization in polit. life and soc. reforms. The domestic polit. situation remained unstable:

1921 assassination of the prime minister HARA TAKASHI (b. 1865).

1923 The great earthquake of Tokyo and Yokohama. The gvt issued the 'decree to preserve the peace'. After the attempted assassination of HIROHITO (see below) and the

1925 introduction of universal male suffrage, domestic tensions increased, leading to the passage of the 'Peace Preservation Law'.

The Showa Period (from 1926)

1926 HIROHITO ascended the throne (imp. name: SHOWA; he had served as regent for the mentally sick YOSHIHITO from 1921).

Domestic affairs: the domestic situation continued tense because of:

1. Apprehension of organized labour and the intellectuals, leading to the combating of 'dangerous ideas' by strict nationalistic education, censorship and police-state methods.
2. Public apathy to polit. parties, which were compromised by finan. scandals, incidents of bribery and ties to capitalistic interests (1940 dissolution of all polit. parties and formation of one 'unity' party).
3. Econ. effects of the world-wide depression (p. 185): Japan's econ. expansion failed (devaluation of the yen, dumping) because of the import restrictions and tariff policies of the countries threatened by the over-supply of Jap. goods; Japan therefore **planned to establish a large sphere of econ. domination** (to provide for raw materials and markets).
4. Increase in pop. (rising birth-rate),
5. Anti-dem. activities by the army and navy (assassinations of lib. politicians and moderate officers of the armed forces); the climax of this development was reached after the elect. vict. of the Liberals in 1936, when a milit. revolt broke out which was, however, suppressed.
6. The increase of nationalism, with Shintoism as its ideological foundation (loyalty of the subjects to the divine and untouchable emperor, a sense of mission).

For. policy: one expression of this nationalism, the so-called

1927 Tanaka Memorandum (of General TANAKA, prime minister 1927–9), cal. for a 'positive' policy of expansion: **the domination of Asia by Japan**. This expansionist policy was supported esp. by the milit., who provoked 'incidents':

1931 the Mukden incident led to the occupation of Manchuria and the

1932 establishment of the state of Manchukuo (empire in 1934).

1933 Acceptance of the Lytton Report by the League of Nations: Japan's actions in Manchuria were found to be in violation of int. law. Japan announced her withdrawal from the League of Nations.

China: after the occupation of the Jehol and Chahar provinces, Japan attempted to introduce auton. gvts into the northern provinces of China.

1936 Japan joined the Anti-Comintern Pact (p. 197).

1937–41 Cabinet of Prince Konoye Fumumaro (1891–1945 (suicide)), whose attempt to control the army failed. The 'incident at the Marco Polo Bridge' (shooting between Jap. and Chin. soldiers) in Peking unleashed the

1937–45 Sino-Jap. War. Even though Japan carried out general mobilization (1938) and achieved many milit. successes, China avoided capitulation.

1938 Proclamation of the New Order in E. Asia by the prime minister Konoye. The **cancellation by the U.S. in**

1939 of **the 1911 trade agreement** (thus restricting the importation of raw materials important for the production of war materials: petrol, scrap-metals, etc.) worsened relations between the 2 states.

1940 Establishment of a pro-Jap. Chin. counter-gvt under WANG CHING-WEI (p. 173) in Nanking.

1940 The 3-Power Pact (p. 197).

1941 Non-aggression Pact with the U.S.S.R. Japan secured her rear in order to carry out her expansion in E. Asia (July 1941: occupation of Fr. Indo-China).

1941–4 Prime Minister Hideki Tojo (1884–1948 (executed)), chief-of-staff of the Kwangtung army and leading exponent of Jap. imperialism. After the resignation of KONOYE, whose policy of reconciliation with the U.S.A. failed, TOJO formed a new, authoritarian cabinet.

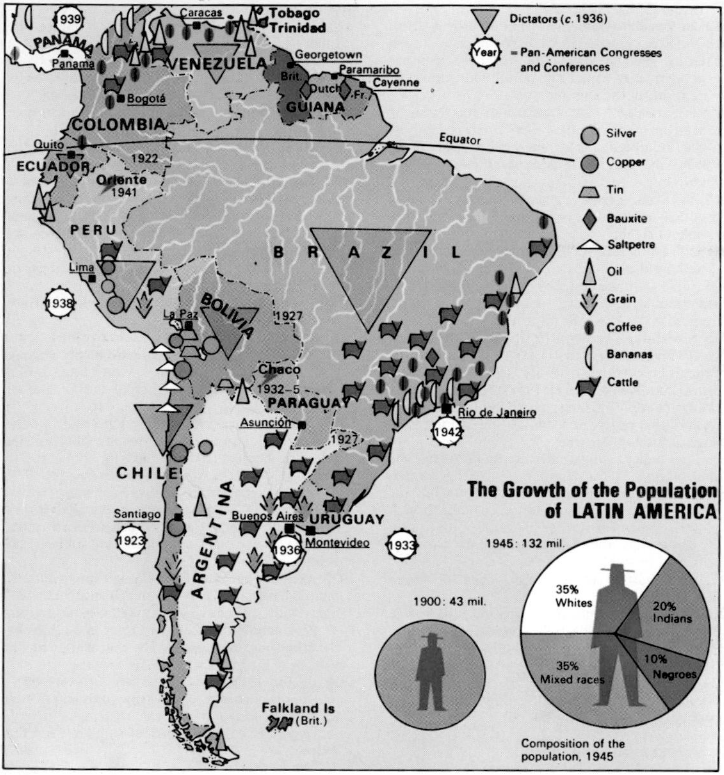

Dictators (c. 1936)
Year = Pan-American Congresses and Conferences

Silver
Copper
Tin
Bauxite
Saltpetre
Oil
Grain
Coffee
Bananas
Cattle

PANAMA
Panama
939
Caracas
Tobago
Trinidad
VENEZUELA
Georgetown
Paramaribo
Cayenne
Brit.
Dutch
Fr.
GUIANA
Bogotá
COLOMBIA
Quito
Equator
ECUADOR
1922
Oriente
1941
PERU
Lima
1938
B R A Z I L
BOLIVIA
La Paz
1927
Chaco
1932–5
PARAGUAY
Asunción
1927
Rio de Janeiro
1942
CHILE
Santiago
1923
ARGENTINA
Buenos Aires
URUGUAY
Montevideo
1936
1933
Falkland Is (Brit.)

The Growth of the Population of LATIN AMERICA

1900: 43 mil.
1945: 132 mil.
35% Whites
20% Indians
10% Negroes
35% Mixed races
Composition of the population, 1945

South America, 1918–45

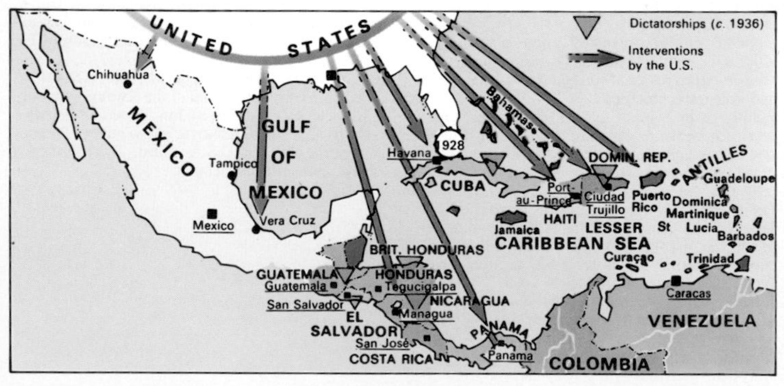

Central America, 1918–45

The steady development of the Lat. Amer. states was disturbed and interrupted by far-reaching changes in soc., econ. and polit. matters.

1. **The soc. structure** was altered by the increase in pop. (the 'demographic revolution'), domestic migration (flight from the countryside to the cities), the settlement of newly opened areas, the racial composition of the pop. and changes of soc. alignment owing to urbanization and industrialization.
2. **The econ. structure** was shaped by the mercantilism of the colon. period and its trad. monocultures (causing dependence on for. trade), the lack of capital for industrialization, the lack of skilled labour (illiteracy), backwardness of agriculture (obsolete methods of cultivation, exploitation of the soil), and the prevention of thorough agrarian reforms.
3. **The polit. structure:** the crisis of democracy (uprisings, *coups d'état*, revolutions) was caused by sharp econ. decline and soc. disintegration, the formation of dem.-revolutionary mass parties (RAUL HAYA DE LA TORRE: 'Auton. Latin Amer. movements free from for. interference and infl.'), the intervention of the milit. in state politics, and the system of pres. democracy (modelled after the U.S.A.), which often served as a preparation for dictatorship.

From 1889 Pan-Amer. congresses and conferences were held to promote polit. unity.

1923 5th Congress at Santiago: signing of the 1st Arbitration Treaty.

1928 6th Congress at Havana: acceptance of the principle making all Amer. states subject to binding arbitration.

1933 7th Congress at Montevideo: participation of the U.S.A.

1936 Inter-Amer. Peace Conference of Buenos Aires: Peace Pact between 21 Amer. states (modelled after the Kellogg-Briand Pact, p. 137). The principles of hemispheric defence were elaborated at the

1938 8th Congress at Lima.

1939 Panama Conference: prohibition of acts of war in a neutral zone 300 mi. deep stretching around the continent, exc. for the coast of Canada.

1942 The Conference of for. ministers at Rio de Janeiro decided the entry into the war against the Axis Powers (with the exception of Argentina (1943) and Chile (1944)).

The policy of direct intervention by the U.S.A. during and after the 1st World War, esp. in Cen. America (Nicaragua, Haiti, the Domin. Republic, Cuba, Panama), was discontinued under FRANKLIN DELANO ROOSEVELT and replaced by the 'good neighbour policy' (p. 187); however, owing to their nationalism, the Lat. Amer. nations proved highly sensitive to the investment of U.S. capital ('dollar imperialism').

Wars:

1932–5 The Chaco War between Bolivia and Paraguay, which, in 1938, received the largest part of the area.

1941 Border conflicts between Ecuador and Peru; but the largest part of the disputed territory was awarded to Peru by the

1942 Rio de Janeiro protocol.

Mexico

After the revolution of 1911 the country pursued a soc.-revolutionary policy. The rights of workers and their welfare were guaranteed, agrarian reforms were carried out, education was secularized, econ. reforms were introduced, the railways and the oil industry were brought under state control and industrialization was promoted.

Cen. America

As a result of the world-wide econ. crisis (p. 185) and its catastrophic consequences (severe drop of the prices of raw materials), unrest and dissatisfaction spread among the people, which again caused the establishment of dictatorships: Cuba (1933–59, FULGENCIO BATISTA), the Dominican Republic (1930–61, RAFAEL LEONIDAS TRUJILLO), Guatemala (1930–44, JORGE UBICO), El Salvador (1932–44, General MAXIMILIANO HERNÁNDEZ MARTÍNEZ), Honduras (1932–49, General TIBURCIO CARIAS ANDINO), and Nicaragua (1936–56, ANASTASIO SOMOZA GARCÍA).

Panama:

1936 Treaty with the U.S.A.: no interference in the internal affairs of the country to maintain order. The annual fee for the lease of the Canal Zone was raised from $250,000 to $430,000.

South America

Venezuela: the dictatorship of JUAN VICENTE GÓMEZ (1908–35) was followed by that of ELAZAR LÓPEZ CONTRERAS (1935–41): the constitution had socialistic features (1936).

Colombia: the rule of the conservatives (to 1930) was followed by that of lib. presidents.

Ecuador: polit. turmoil (1931–48) caused by the Great Depression (p. 185).

Peru: after the dictatorship of AUGUSTO B. LEGUÍA (1919–30) a struggle set in between the dictatorial and the const. order.

Bolivia: alternation of civilian gvt and milit. dictatorship (from 1930).

Chile: supported by the clergy, President ARTURO ALESSANDRI (1920–25, 1932–8) carried out soc. reforms from 1920 (soc. welfare state).

Argentina: after 1916 the old oligarchy was pushed aside by the Rad. party (middle class). In 1930 the conservatives and the milit. toppled the Radicals from power; the milit. in turn put an end to domination by the oligarchy (1943, the 'League of Colonels', providing the background for JUAN DOMINGO PERÓN, p. 271).

Uruguay: a coalition of the 2 strongest parties was able to avert dictatorship.

Paraguay: no stable gvts could be est. because of econ. stagnation.

Brazil: the dictator GETULIO VARGAS (1930–45) outlawed the Communists and Fascist integralists and attempted to win the workers to his side through soc. legislation.

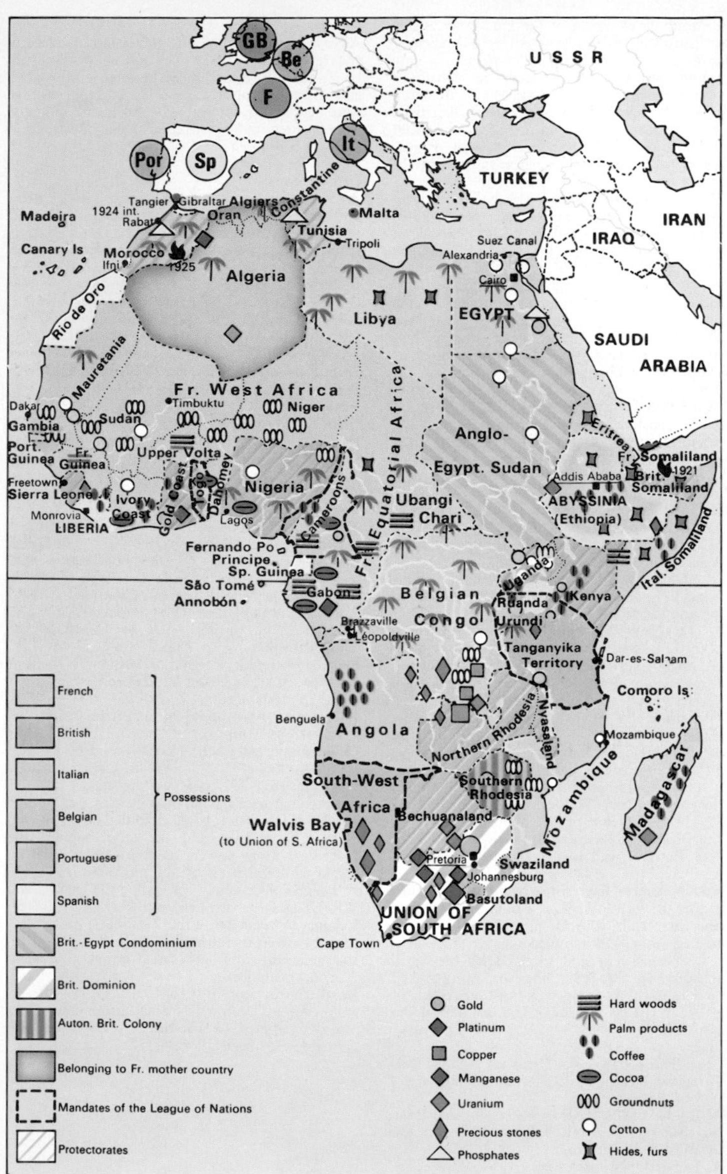
GB
Be
F
Por
Sp
It
USSR
TURKEY
IRAN
IRAQ
SAUDI
ARABIA
Madeira
Canary Is
Tangier
Gibraltar
1924 int.
Rabat
Algiers
Oran
Constantine
Malta
Tunisia
Tripoli
Morocco
Ifni
1925
Algeria
Suez Canal
Alexandria
Cairo
Libya
EGYPT
Rio de Oro
Mauretania
Fr. West Africa
Timbuktu
Niger
Dakar
Gambia
Sudan
Port. Guinea
Fr. Guinea
Upper Volta
Freetown
Sierra Leone
Ivory Coast
Gold Coast
Togo
Dahomey
Nigeria
Monrovia
LIBERIA
Lagos
Cameroons
Fr. Equatorial Africa
Anglo-Egypt. Sudan
Eritrea
Fr. Somaliland
1921
Addis Ababa
Brit. Somaliland
ABYSSINIA (Ethiopia)
Ubangi Chari
Ital. Somaliland
Fernando Po
Principe
Sp. Guinea
São Tomé
Annobón
Gabon
Uganda
Kenya
Belgian Congo
Ruanda
Urundi
Brazzaville
Léopoldville
Tanganyika Territory
Dar-es-Salaam
Comoro Is
Benguela
Angola
Northern Rhodesia
Nyasaland
Mozambique
South-West Africa
Southern Rhodesia
Madagascar
Walvis Bay (to Union of S. Africa)
Bechuanaland
Pretoria
Swaziland
Johannesburg
Basutoland
UNION OF SOUTH AFRICA
Cape Town
French
British
Italian
Belgian
Portuguese
Spanish
Possessions
Brit.-Egypt Condominium
Brit. Dominion
Auton. Brit. Colony
Belonging to Fr. mother country
Mandates of the League of Nations
Protectorates
Gold
Platinum
Copper
Manganese
Uranium
Precious stones
Phosphates
Hard woods
Palm products
Coffee
Cocoa
Groundnuts
Cotton
Hides, furs

Africa, 1939

The Auton. States

Egypt: the **Wafd party,** which grew out of the delegation led in London and at the peace conference by ZAGHLUL PASHA (1860–1927), from 1918 espoused the cause of Egypt. independence.

1922 Britain proclaimed Egypt an auton. monarchy, retaining the following prerogatives: the defence of Egypt, the safeguarding of the Canal Zone, the settlement of the Sudan question, the stationing of troops and the conduct of for. policy.

1917–36 FUAD I (Sultan, after 1922 king) opposed the Wafd party, dissolved parliament (1928) and ruled dictatorially. Negotiations with Britain regarding autonomy failed for the time being.

1936 Rest. of the constitution of 1923.

1936–52 Farouk I.

1936 Brit.-Egypt. Treaty: Egypt became ind., but Brit. troops were to be stationed for 20 yrs in the Canal Zone and the Anglo-Egypt. condominium over the Sudan was to be restored (acc. to the treaty of 1899).

Abyssinia:

1916–30 Empress ZAUDITU. TAFARI MAKONNEN (1892–1975) became regent; after disputes with the empress he assumed the title 'Negus' (1928) and was crowned

1930 Emperor Haile Selassie I.

1935–36 The Italo-Abyss. War began after several border incidents between Ital. and Abyss. troops; it was terminated by the entry of the Italians into Addis Ababa (p. 159).

Liberia:

1925 Agreement of Liberia with the Firestone Rubber Plantation Co.: by 1931 more than half the state's income was used to pay the interest on the loan granted by Firestone.

1930 An investigation commission of the League of Nations est. that forced labour and slavery in fact existed.

1931 Parliament discontinued the amortization of the debt and the economy began to recover.

S. Africa:

s. Africa's politics were influenced by the race question and the conflict between the s. Afr. party under General LOUIS BOTHA (1862–1919) and

1919–24 General Jan Christian Smuts (1870–1950), who was for the establishment of a greater s. Africa within the framework of the Brit. Commonwealth; there was also conflict with the Nat. Party under

1924–33 General James Barry Munnick Hertzog (1866–1942), who wished for the elimination of Britain's polit. influence. After the passage of the Statute of Westminster (p. 170) the aim of polit. independence was realized through the

1934 'Status of the Union Act'. This Act was passed under the

1934–9 HERTZOG–SMUTS coalition gvt, a gvt which brought about the union of the parties in the United s. Afr. Nat. party.

1936 The Representation of Natives Act: a 'native representative council' received advisory functions.

1939 Break of relations with Germany.

The Mandates of the League of Nations

Classified as **'B' Mandates**, to be administered like colon. possessions: Tanganyika, parts of the Cameroons and Western Togoland went to Britain; Eastern Togoland and the Eastern Cameroons to France; and Ruanda-Urundi to Belgium. Classified a **'C' Mandate**, sw. Africa was administered by the Union of s. Africa as part of its nat. territory.

The Colonies

The Brit., Fr., Belg. and Port. colonies were administered by **governors** responsible exclusively to the king or prime minister. The natives did not participate in gvt. 'Indirect rule' (involvement of Africans in the lower levels of (judicial) admin.) prevailed in the Brit. colonies, 'direct rule' (by whites only) in the Belg., Port. and Fr. colonies. The Fr. colonies were characterized by a policy of strong centralization and the attempt to assimilate the natives by the destruction of tribal traditions. Attempts to assimilate the natives were also made in the Port. colonies, which were proclaimed 'part and parcel of Portugal' (1935).

Econ. life, trade and communications: transition or termination of monopoly companies. Roads and other new means of communication were built. Capital investments in the colonies improved the econ. situation of the white settlers, but not of the Afr. peoples (exc. for the inhabitants of the belt stretching from the Sudan to Guinea).

The Africans

Nationalism failed to assert itself after the 1st World War; neither was there any fundamental transformation of public sentiment relating to Europeans and the meaning and purpose of colonialism; however, a return of the educated African to the tribal traditions of the past was made impossible, not least because of the infl. of Christianity. Progress was aided by such educ. endeavours as Afr. seminaries conducted under Christ. auspices, towards the end of the 1920s by secondary schools, and later by colleges est. by the colon. masters. Participation by Afr. intellectuals in the polit. process was rejected. Polit. emancipation was nevertheless advanced by the educ. process, reinforced by aspirations for human dignity and soc. security.

N. Africa

Common to the inhabitants of the N. Afr. countries (the Ital. colony of Libya, the Fr. protectorates of Tunisia and the Moroccan monarchy, and the Fr. Department of Algeria) was a feeling of Isl.-Arab. nat. consciousness and the rejection of Eur. civilization. The **Destur Movement** in Tunisia promoted the right of self-determination and the claim for equal rights. After the

1925 uprising of the Riff Kabyles under ABD EL-KRIM had ended in

1926 unconditional capitulation and the Sp.-Fr. Morocco Treaty had fixed the spheres of interest, the Nat. Moroccan Action Committee–esp. the **Istiqlal party**–espoused the cause of const. gvt and administrative autonomy.

The exploration of Antarctica

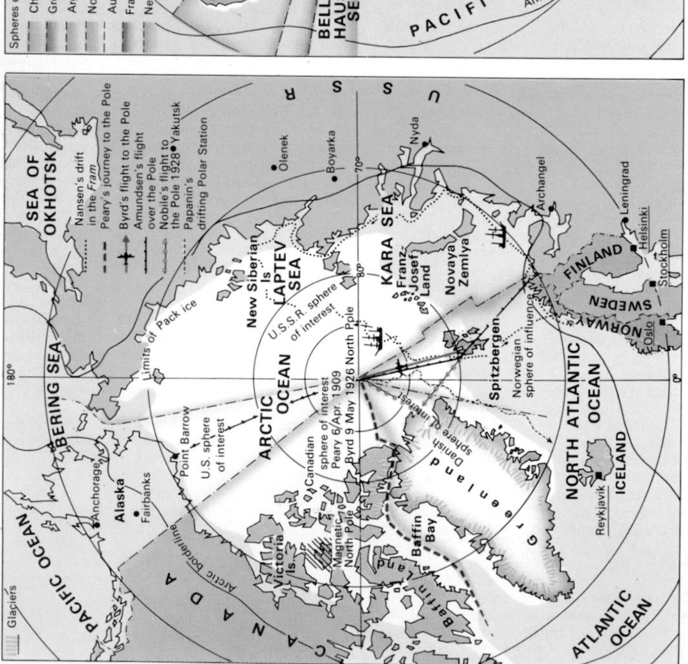

The exploration of the Arctic

Inventions

Physics:

1925 Quantum mechanics — HEISENBERG/BORN/JORDAN
1926 Wave mechanics — SCHRÖDINGER
1928 Geiger-counter — GEIGER/MÜLLER
1932 Positrons — ANDERSON
Neutrons — CHADWICK
Cyclotron — LAWRENCE
1934 Artificial production of radioactive substances — JOLIOT/CURIE
1938 Nuclear fission — HAHN/STRASSMANN

Biology:

1909 Animal psychology — MORGAN
1909 Environmental research — VON UEXKÜLL
1910 Dropsophila genetics — MORGAN
1911 Antidote to Beriberi sickness ('vitamin') — FUNK/TERUUCHI
1912 Human genetics — LENZ
1914 Behaviourism — WATSON
1919 Mapping of chromosomes — MORGAN
1921 Human heredity, eugenics — BAUR/FISCHER/LENZ
Intelligence tests on anthropoid apes — KÖHLER
1927 X-ray genetics — MÜLLER
1928 Genetic theory — MORGAN

Chemistry:

1921 Assimilation of carbonic acid — WARBURG
1922 Production of methyl alcohol from hydrogen — MITTASCH
1925 Macromolecular chemistry — STAUDINGER
Liquefaction of carbon — FISCHER/TROPSCH
1930 Synthetic fibres based on acetylene — REPPE
1932 Heavy hydrogen — LIBEY/BRICKWEDDE/MURPHY
1934 Synthetic vitamin C — REICHSTEIN
1936 Buna (synthetic rubber) — KONRAD
1938 Perlon — SCHLACK
Nylon — CAROTHERS
1939 D.D.T. insecticide — MÜLLER

Medicine:

1909 Transmission of spotted fever by lice — NICOLLE
1910 Typing of blood — MOSS
1917 Sexual pathology — HIRSCHFELD
1921 Insulin — MACKAD/BENTING/BEST
1928 Penicillin — FLEMING
1929 Cardiac catheter — FORSSMANN
1930 Inoculation against yellow fever — THEILER
1932 Sulfonamide — DOMAGK
1935 Corticosteron — KENDALL/REICHSTEIN
1939 Artificial heart — GIBBONS
1940 Rhesus factor — LANDSTEINER/WIEGNER

Transport technology:

1910 Propeller turbine — KAPLAN
1915 All-metal aeroplane — JUNKERS
1918 Light aeroplane — KLEMEN
1922 Helicopter — LA CIERVA
1930 Jet propulsion — SCHMIDT

Communication technology:

1913 Tube transmitter — MEISSNER
1916 Wireless telegraphy — MARCONI
1925 Television experiments (U.S.A., Britain, Germany)
1927 Wireless, transoceanic telephone
1935 Ultra-shortwave transmission — WITZLEBEN

Picture and Sound:

1919 'Talking picture' — VOGT/ENGL/MASOLLE
1928 Magnetophone — PFLEUMER
1929 Television and Tele-cinematography — KARVLUS/TELEFUNKEN
1932 Television — WITZLEBEN

Discoveries

The Arctic:

1893–6 Drift journey of NANSEN in the *Fram.*
1903–6 NW. Passage by AMUNDSEN.
1909 PEARY landed in the vicinity of the Pole on 6 Apr.
1921–4 Thule expedition of RASMUSSEN from Greenland to the Bering Strait.
1926 BYRD flew in 16 hrs from Spitzbergen over the N. Pole and back.
1926 NOBILE flew, with AMUNDSEN and ELLSWORTH, from Spitzbergen across the N. Pole to Alaska.
1928 2 flights of NOBILE to the Pole with the dirigible *Italia.*
1937–8 PAPININ's research expedition on an ice floe E. of Greenland.
1937–40 Drift journey of the icebreaker *Sedow.*

Greenland was explored by MYLIUS-ERICHSEN (1906–8), MIKKELSEN (1910), DE T UERVAIN (1912), KOCH/WEGENER (1913), WEGENER (1929–31), GRONAU/HOVGAARD/WEHREN (1931).

Antarctica:

1901–3 Ger. Antarctic expedition under DRYGALSKI.
1902–4 SCOTT explored Victoria Land.
1902–3 NORDENSKJOLD E. of Louis Philippe Land.
1902–3 BRUCE explored the Weddell Sea.
1909 SHACKLETON came within 200 km of the Pole.
1911 AMUNDSEN reached the Pole.
1911–12 SCOTT reached the Pole in 1912; he perished on the return journey.
1911–12 2nd Ger. Antarctic expedition.
1911–14 MAWSON explored Wilkes Land.
1915 SHACKLETON attempted in vain to traverse Antarctica.
1928–30 Exploratory flights of BYRD, who flew over the Pole in 1929.
1933–6 WILKINS and ELLSWORTH attempted in vain to cross the continent.
1938–9 Ger. 'Swabia' expedition.

Expeditions, carried out with the aid of new means of transportation (ice-breakers, motorized vehicles, aeroplanes) deepened knowledge of Asia (Tibet, Gobi Desert, Arabia), Africa (the Sahara), and S. America (Brazil, Venezuela, Guiana).

The Duce

Benito Mussolini (1883–1945 (shot by partisans)), the son of a blacksmith, became an elementary schoolteacher and was active in Switzerland, France and the Aust. Trentino as a journalist and agitator of rad. Socialist persuasion (1902–10). After his return to Italy he became editor of the newspaper *La Lotta dei Classe* in Forli, later editor-in-chief of the party organ *Avanti!* in Milan and member of the executive committee of the Soc. Democrats. Because of his integral nationalism (p. 119) he was expelled from the party, founded, with for. funds (Fr.?), his own paper, the *Popolo d'Italia*, and formed a *'fascio d'azione rivoluzionaria'*, the initial unit of Fascism, composed of Socialists, syndicalists and his own followers. (Aim: Italy's entry into the war on the side of the Entente Powers.) Actively serving from 1915–17, MUSSOLINI returned from the war after being severely wounded. He was less influenced by Marxist doctrine (class struggle, internationalism), than by NIETZSCHE ('The will to power', 'Superman' (p. 64), HEGEL (p. 41), the vitalism of HENRI BERGSON (1859–1941), GEORGES SOREL (p. 66), from whom he adopted the concept of a 'soc. war' through *'action directe'*, and VILFREDO PARETO (1848–1923) and his theory of the cyclical rise and fall of governing élites.

The Ideology

Fascism (from Lat. *fasces* = a bundle of rods with the arrow as symbol of the power of the Rom. consuls and praetors) was an anti-parliamentarian, anti-dem. and nationalistic revolutionary movement aiming at the establishment of an authoritarian or totalitarian 1-party state. The concept of Fascism, in its Ital. manifestation, has become part of polit. typology. Similar to the development of HITLER's Nat. Socialism (p. 183), Ital. Fascism was shaped by the personality and thought of MUSSOLINI. The 'Saviour of Italy' (*'Salvatore d'Italia'*) developed his conceptions in the *'Dottrina del Fascismo'*: nationalistic and imperialistic tendencies (revival of traditions of Ancient Rome) and Socialist theories were joined to Fascist ideology, which demanded of its followers discipline, will and faith, and glorified the use of force, struggle and danger. Class conflict and internationalism were to be overcome through the nat. community and the nat. state, which the citizen was obliged to serve as his highest value, and which was led by an élite. Pacifism and liberalism were rejected as destructive to the state (expulsion and flight of lib. politicians).

After 1945, Fascist ideology was still represented by a parl. minority, the neo-Fascist Movimento Sociale Italiano (M.S.I.).

The Party

1919 Formation of the first *'Fasci di combattimento'* (polit. combat squads) by MUSSOLINI in Milan. Aims: agrarian reforms, abolition of the Senate, confiscation of eccles. property, support of the demands of war veterans, realization of the war aims. Owing to the failure of parl. democracy, the bourgeoisie, fearful of a Bolshevik revolution, supported the Fascists in their struggle.

1921 Fascist Nat. Congress in Rome: in fulfilment of MUSSOLINI's wish and against the objections of Count DINO GRANDI (b. 1895), the *'movimento'* or revolutionary combat league was transformed into a polit. party: foundation of the **Partito Nazionale Fascista (P.N.F.)**. After the 'March on Rome' (p. 159) MUSSOLINI assumed the powers of gvt.

The Principle of Authority

The Fascist state was an authoritarian, totalitarian, hierarchical, corporative 1-party state (based on the *'legge fascistissime'*); it manifested itself in:

1. The **dictatorship of Mussolini** through his position as **'Capo del governo'** (chief of the ministers) and as **'Duce del Fascismo'**. As such, he was president of the **'Fascist Grand Council'** (p. 159) and appointed to be party secretary, the highest official of the strictly hierarchically organized party. The women's and youth organizations, trade unions, professional organizations and the Milizia Volontaria per la Sicurezza Nazionale (party militia) were affiliated to the P.N.F.
2. The establishment of the 1-party state (1926) with guided plebiscites (from 1928).
3. Reorganization of the body politic through the corporative system: the union of syndicalist conceptions with the totalitarian principle (union of employees, employers, representatives of the state and the party in corporations, p. 159).
4. **Revival of the 'Impero Romano'** through the return to the traditions of public authority of Ancient Rome, the destruction or integration of nat. minorities (s. Tyroleans, Slovenes), the conquest of Abyssinia (p. 159) and of Albania (p. 163), and the proclamation of the Adriatic Sea as the *'Mare nostro'*.

Fascist gvt, an 'enlightened' dictatorship, was moderated by the monarchical principle, the Court, and the officers' corps. The characteristics typical of Nat. Socialism, such as the use of terror and mass arrests to enforce the will of the gvt, were absent, and the secret police had little importance. There was little conflict with the Church because Catholicism was the 'prevailing religion' of Italy (Lateran Treaties, p. 152). But under the impact of Nat. Socialist racist policies (p. 205, from summer 1938) severe legislation was introduced, reflecting fear of *'mestizo'* tendencies in the *'Impero'*.

The Führer

Adolf Hitler (1889–1945 (suicide)) was b. in the Aust. city of Braunau on the Inn river, the son of a customs official. He left high school in Linz prematurely (1905), and lived in Vienna (1909–13), where he attempted in vain to be admitted to the Academy of Art. Lacking funds, HITLER was forced to work at odd jobs, living in hostels and asylums for the homeless and subsisting on the sale of drawings on postcards. His polit. thought was influenced by Pan.-Ger. nationalism and rad. antisemitism (SCHÖNERER, LUEGER, p. 79) shaped his views. In 1913 he moved to Munich, participated in the war as a volunteer, gained the Iron Cross (1st Class) and in 1918 was in hospital after being gassed and nearly blinded. Returning to Munich, he was employed by the Press and Propaganda Department of Group Command IV of the Ger. army. As chairman of the N.S.D.A.P. he came into contact with LUDENDORFF (p. 125), GOTTFRIED FEDER (1883–1941), ERNST RÖHM (1887–1934 (murdered)), and DIETRICH ECKART (1868–1923), whose infl. was reflected in HITLER's thought (FEDER: 'Break the bondage of interest'; RÖHM: the concept of the 'state in arms'; ECKART: antisemitism).

The Ideology

Nat. Socialism developed after 1918 as a countermovement to the Bolshevik revolution and the dem. parl. system. Its intellectual roots were haphazard and to some extent tangled: NIETZSCHE's 'will to power', the racial theories of GOBINEAU and HOUSTON STEWART CHAMBERLAIN (p. 65), the 'faith in destiny' of RICHARD WAGNER, MENDEL's theory of heredity (p. 65), HAUSHOFER's 'geo-politics', or the soc.-Darwinist conceptions of ALFRED PLOETZ (1860–1940) were as much part of Nat. Socialist ideology as the thought of MACHIAVELLI, FICHTE, TREITSCHKE or SPENGLER. Antisemitism became the dominant element: conceiving of Germanness as threatened by gradual disintegration through the Jew. 'race', HITLER cal. for the defence of **'Blood and Soil'**, the annihilation of the Jews (p. 205) and the strengthening of the Nord. race, which was to rule over its 'inferiors' as the **'master race'**. Nat. Socialism emphasized the **element of 'das Volk'** (the people as nation race), demanded unconditional surrender of the individual to the 'community' ('you are nothing, your people is everything'), and preached a charismatic 'faith in the leader' ('Führer, give the command, we shall follow'). It adapted impulses proceeding from the pre-1st World War youth movement (romanticism of communal experience), glorified the comradeship of combat in war, and took on Com. and Fascist characteristics. The 'movement' became a vortex for the discontented, who were disillusioned by parl. democracy and supported the demands of the N.S.D.A.P. for autarchy in econ. life, an expansionist for. policy (*'Volk ohne Raum'* = a people without living-space) liberation from the 'bondage of the Versailles dictate', and the combating of Bolshevik tendencies.

The Party

Jan. 1919 Foundation of the Ger. Workers' Party (D.A.P.) by the railway mechanic ANTON DREXLER (1884–1942).

Sep. 1919 First visit to a D.A.P. meeting by ADOLF HITLER, who was admitted to the party in the same month.

1920 Proclamation of the party programme ('25 Points'): promotion of popular welfare ('the commonweal comes before individual welfare'), the establishment of the right of self-determination for all Germans and equal rights for their state, abrogation of the Paris Treaties, elimination of the Jews, destruction of the 'bondage of interest', etc. **The D.A.P. was renamed the Nat. Socialist Ger. Workers' Party (N.S.D.A.P.).**

Jul. 1921 HITLER became chairman.

1923 Beerhall putsch in Munich ('March on the Feldherrnhalle', p. 149). After the failure of the uprising, HITLER was sentenced to 5 yrs imprisonment at Landsberg. It was here that he wrote the 1st part of his book *Mein Kampf* (the 2nd part was written 1925–7).

1924 HITLER was released prematurely after serving only 8 months. The N.S.D.A.P. was re-established in Munich.

The party was organized acc. to the **'Führer' principle**: it was headed by the **Führer**, his deputy, and the nat. leadership with the 'Reichsleiter' heading nation-wide departments of the party. **The regional polit. organization descended from the prov. level (Gau), to the County (Kreis), local district (Ortsgruppe), and cell (Zelle) to the local bloc (Block).** Party organizations, in part para-milit., such as the S.A. (Brownshirt storm troopers), S.S. (Blackshirt storm troopers), H.J. (Hitler Youth) and B.d.M. (League of Ger. Girls), which were also organized acc. to the *'Führer'* principle, were closely linked to the party, as were the **affiliated associations** (D.A.F. (Ger. Workers' Front), N.S.V. (Nat. Socialist People's Welfare), and the professional organizations of physicians, teachers, lawyers, civil servants, etc.).

Among HITLER's closest associates during the 'time of struggle' were the following: ERNST RÖHM, HEINRICH HIMMLER (1900–45 (suicide)), JOSEPH GOEBBELS (1897–1945 (suicide)), HERMANN GÖRING (1893–1946 (suicide)), ALFRED ROSENBERG (1893–1946 (executed)), RUDOLF HESS (b. 1894), HANS FRANK (1900–46 (executed)), JULIUS STREICHER (1885–1946 (executed)), BALDUR VON SCHIRACH (b. 1907), ROBERT LEY (1890–1945 (suicide)), GREGOR STRASSER (1892–1934 (murdered)), OTTO STRASSER (b. 1897).

HITLER's and GOEBBELS's oratorical gifts and the publications of ROSENBERG (*Der Mythus des 20. Jahrhunderts* = *The Myth of the 20th Century*), assisted by the party newspaper (*Der Völkische Beobachter*), served to spread Nat. Socialist ideology, which was 'drummed' into the consciousness of the people by psychologically effective massed assemblies, rallies, torchlight processions and party conventions. HITLER emphasized that he wished to attain power 'by legal means'. Supported by broad segments of the pop., the N.S.D.A.P. was able steadily to increase its representation in the Reichstag from 1930 (exc. for the election of 6 Nov. 1932, see map, p. 192) and to bring about the establishment of the **3rd Reich**. (For the 'seizure of power', see p. 193.)

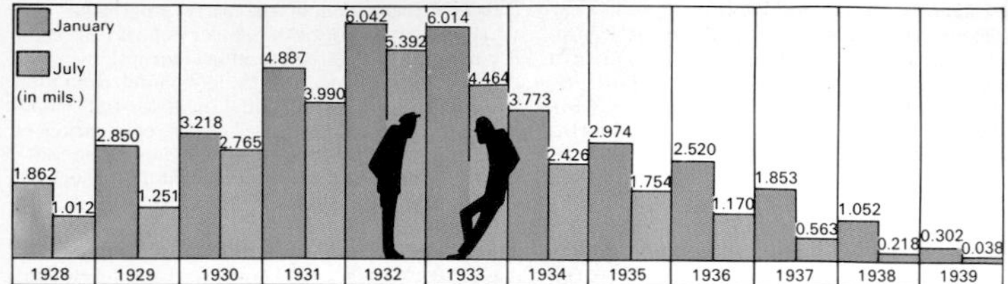

The development of unemployment in Germany, 1918–39

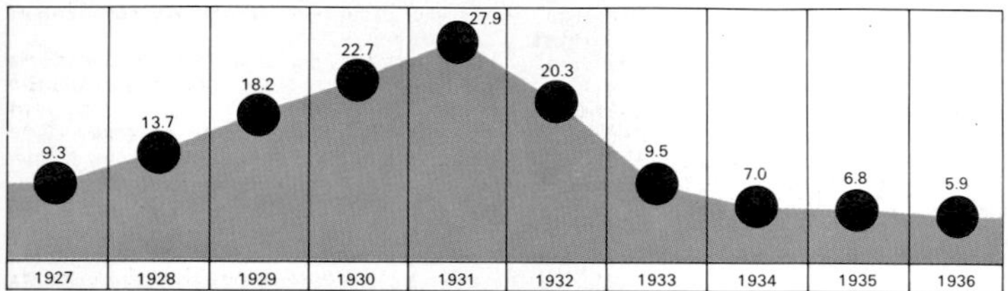

Bankruptcies and voluntary liquidations in Germany (in thousands)

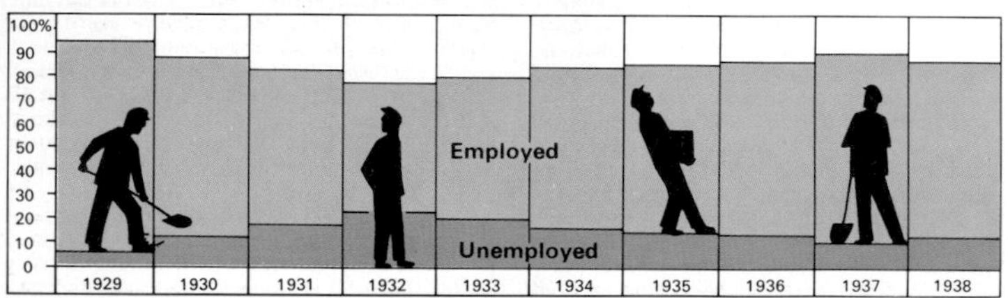

World-wide unemployment patterns, 1929–38

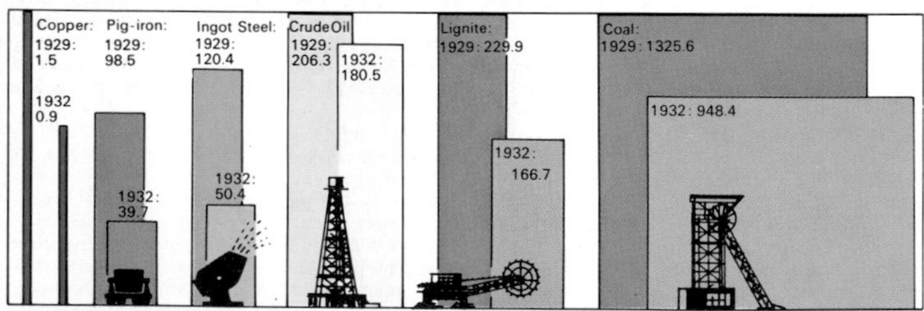

Decline of production in the world economy (millions of tons)

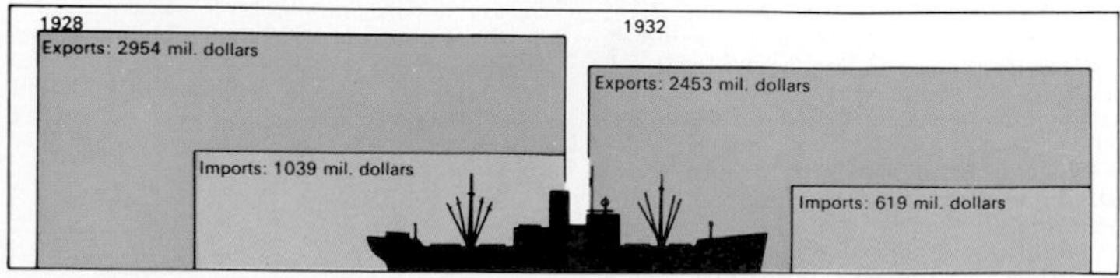

Latin American exports and imports, 1928 and 1932

Econ. Consequences of the World War

Reasons for the crisis of the world economy:

1. Curtailment of int. trade brought about the collapse of the world economy.
2. Restriction of the production of consumer goods and rationing.
3. Expansion of the armament industry.
4. Establishment of industries in the neutral overseas countries to process their own raw materials (e.g. Lat. America).
5. Increase in the productive capacity of the U.S.A.
6. Decrease of holdings abroad and dwindling of the gold reserves of the warring powers (exc. for the U.S.A.).
7. Limitation of the freedom of movement of the workers and increased employment of women.

The quick recovery of world trade and commerce after the war was hampered by the planned economy of the U.S.S.R. (monopolies on for. trade by the state); by protective tariffs benefiting nat. economies; by the transition of the U.S.A. from a debtor to a creditor nation (gold monopoly); by the drawing of new customs frontiers through the establishment of new states (1914 6,000 kms; 1920 12,000 kms); by the attempts of individual states to attain econ. autarchy and thus avoid difficulties of supply; by the disruption of the foundations of law (confiscation of 'enemy property'); by the abandonment of the gold standard; by the chaos of the currencies (inflation and collapse of currencies) caused by the financing of the cost of the war (paper money). At the

1922 World Econ. Conference of Genoa (without the participation of the U.S.A. and Turkey), the abandonment of the unchecked printing of money and the creation of a currency for int. exchange based on gold was proposed as a solution for the econ. and finan. problems. The U.S.A. stopped inflation by deflationary policies, Britain by raising taxes. Inflationary fiscal policies were practised in France, Belgium and the newly created states of Cen. and Eastern Europe. Pressured by the

1921 London Ultimatum (p. 135), Germany was unable to fulfil its reparations payments, even though it reformed its nat. finances in 1919. Steadily accelerating in Germany, inflation was terminated by the

1923 creation of the Ger. Rentenbank: stabilization of the currency by the provision of collateral for the Rentenmark on the basis of a special tax on agriculture and indust. property. After the transition to a peace economy (1922), the

'prosperity' of the 'roaring twenties' (1922–9) began though the phrase is not really applicable to Britain, or to France until the late 1920s. It was based on the rapid development of technology (rationalization and standardization of production), the expansion of large enterprises in the machine, electrical and chemical industries, and increasing econ. concentration, and spurred on by the formation of cartels, trusts, large banking institutions and corporations. Symptoms of impending crisis were overlooked because of the world-wide econ. boom and the increase in nat. incomes. These were the symptoms: widespread unemployment in the industrialized countries of Europe; a development of prices that was, in part, regressive, because its favourable aspects were based on mass-consumption rather than inherent strength, with accompanying low levels of profits ('profitless prosperity'); the rapid rise of the stock market, esp. in the U.S.A.; the decrease of textile production; and the low profit margins of agricult. products.

Owing to the lasting impact of gvtl guidance of the war economies, socialistic conceptions of econ. life, econ. advances of Australia and New Zealand, econ. plans of the U.S.S.R. and rising dictatorships, the concept of a **planned economy** (except in the U.K.) gained acceptance. Because of the increasing interlocking of gvtl power and econ. life, the int. economy of the world, with its unhampered exchange of goods (free trade), was replaced by nat. economies striving for autarchy. The lagging of purchasing power behind production led to the

24 Oct. 1929 collapse of the New York Stock Market, followed by

Summer 1930 an econ. depression in almost all the countries of Europe. Bankruptcies, the rapid disintegration of the price system, unemployment and the collapse of banks were the consequence of the failure of Amer. credits to materialize, and the absence of liquid capital and the fall of prices of raw materials and agricult. products not under the control of cartels.

May 1931 Collapse of the Aust. Credit-Anstalt.

Jul. 1931 The Darmstädter und Nat. Bank was the first Ger. bank to discontinue payments.

Sep. 1931 Britain went off the gold standard.

Apr. 1933 The U.S.A. and (by 1936) all other states modified or went off the gold standard.

After the failure of classical deflationary policies, the gvts intervened to overcome the crisis: public works projects (U.S.A., Germany), partnership of the state in business enterprises or socialization (Britain, France), subsidized purchases of raw materials that could not be marketed, credits for business enterprises and controls of prices and wages. Although recovery of the nat. economies was achieved by a general rise in tariffs, the manipulation of customs duties and currencies, control and rationing of for. exchange, and bilateral trade agreements, int. econ. relations were made more difficult. Despite the rise of indust. production, which reached the level of 1913 in 1936, aspirations to autarchy (esp. by the dictatorships) and int. tensions, prevented the recovery of the world economy before the outbreak of the 2nd World War. The

1937 recession in the U.S.A. (p. 187), esp. in the textile and coal industries, had no effect on Europe because of rearmament.

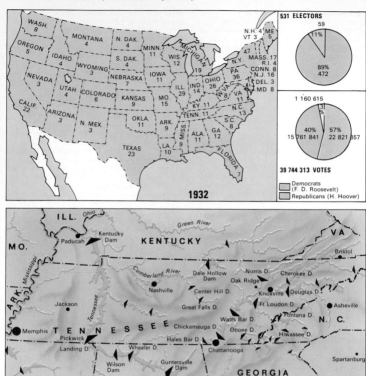

Roosevelt's electoral victory and the Tennessee Valley

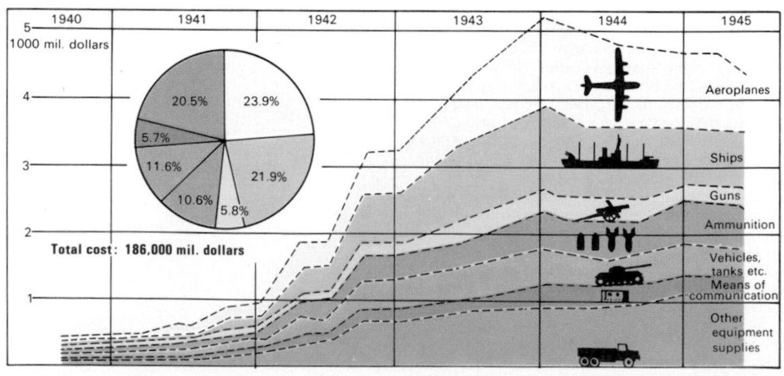

U.S. armaments production, 1940–45

The Roosevelt Era (1933–45)

1933–45 Franklin D. Roosevelt (1882–1945) proclaimed a nat. emergency and introduced extensive reforms to overcome the econ. crisis: the **New Deal**. The measures were planned by a staff of intellectuals (the 'Brains Trust'); private enterprise was not abandoned.

1933 The '100 Days' (9 Mar.–16 Jun.). This 1st phase of reform was intended to ease immediate suffering and, by achieving quick recovery, bring the wheels of econ. life into gear: the banks were closed and only the 'sound' institutions–those associated with the Fed. Reserve System (75%)–were allowed to open again; prohibition of the export and hoarding of gold and currency; devaluation of the dollar (to 50%); legislation to ease the burden of indebted farmers and householders. Key measures of the New Deal:

Agricult. reform (A.A.A.: Agricult. Adjustments Act, declared unconst. in 1936): curtailment of production of major staples (cotton, tobacco) through the payment of premiums.

Tennessee Valley Authority (T.V.A.), under the direction of DAVID E. LILIENTHAL: most extensive regional planning (construction of hydroelectric power plants, indust. plants, river adjustments, irrigation systems; soil erosion was counteracted by reafforestation).

Reconstruction of industry (N.I.R.A.: Nat. Indust. Recovery Act): the interests of employers (limitations of production, price-fixing, etc.) and employees (maximum hours and minimum wages) were to be observed. Declared unconst. in 1935, the legislation was not renewed. A voluntary workers' service, the Civilian Conservation Corps (C.C.C.), was created.

1935 Beginning of the 2nd phase of the New Deal; the measures passed during this period were intended to strengthen the position of the workers and farmers and deprive the opponents of the New Deal, some of whom demanded even more rad. innovations, of influence.

Elimination of the unemployment problem through publicly financed construction projects (W.P.A.: Works Progress Admin., directed by HARRY L. HOPKINS, 1890–1946);

Regulation of the relations between employers and employees (Nat. Labor Relations Act) through the establishment of a Nat. Labor Relations Board, to arbitrate disputes: workers were granted the right to organize, to bargain collectively and to strike;

Establishment of unemployment compensation, old-age and dependent survivor insurance (Soc. Security Act). Addit. legislation promoted housing construction and safeguarded fair conditions of work. After ROOSEVELT's 1st re-election to the presidency (Nov. 1936), he aspired to reform the Supreme Court (Judiciary Reorganization Bill) and to eliminate opposing forces within his own party. These measures, and the econ. recession, which began in Aug. 1937, caused the Republicans to gain 80 seats in Congress and 7 in the Senate in the mid-term elections of 1938.

For. Policy:

In spite of the strong opposition of the isolationists, who consented to the U.S.A. joining the Int. Labour Organization (1934), but objected to U.S. participation in the Int. Court of Justice (1935), ROOSEVELT's policy aimed at int. cooperation.

1934 Resumption of diplomatic relations with the U.S.S.R., as a result of Jap. expansion in the Far East. The 'Good Neighbour Policy' took the place of interventions in Lat. America: the U.S.A. gave up its prerogatives in Cuba and its protectorate over Haiti. Consequences of this policy: at the 8th Pan-Amer. Conference in Lima, the states of the Americas proclaimed their solidarity (1938). The Philippines received assurances that they would be granted independence within 10 yrs.

1935 Neutrality legislation (Neutrality Act): prohibition of the sale and delivery of armaments to belligerent states.

1937 Another Neutrality Act made the delivery of armaments to belligerents possible on a 'cash-and-carry' basis. ROOSEVELT envisaged a struggle for survival between the forces of democracy and dictatorship: a 'reign of terror and lawlessness' which threatened to engulf the world.

1937 The 'Quarantine speech' of Chicago (5 Oct.): neutrality in the face of an epidemic of lawlessness is impossible.

From 1938 (for the Munich Agreement, see p. 157), Amer. rearmament.

From 1939 reinterpretation of neutrality legislation in favour of Britain and its allies.

1940 After his 2nd re-election to the presidency, ROOSEVELT est. the Defense Advisory Commission and proclaimed the

Jan. 1941 '4 Freedoms': freedom of speech and expression, freedom of worship, freedom from want, freedom from fear.

Mar. 1941 The Lend-Lease Act empowered the President to supply war materials to 'any country whose defense the President deems vital to the defense of the United States', and without immediate payment. After the

7 Dec. 1941 Jap. attack on Pearl Harbor, a majority of the Amer. people was ready to enter the war: **declaration of war on Japan** (8 Dec.), followed by **the declarations of war by Germany and Italy** (11 Dec.). The level of troop strength was raised from 2 to 12 mil. (1946). Between 1940 and 1946, *c.* $370,000 mil. were made available for the conduct of the war. **Conditions that made the vict. of the U.S.A. possible:** strict planning, leadership and control; coordination of production, consumption and research; expansion of agricult. production.

1945 Death of Franklin D. Roosevelt (12 Apr.), who had been re-elected for a 4th term in Nov. 1944.

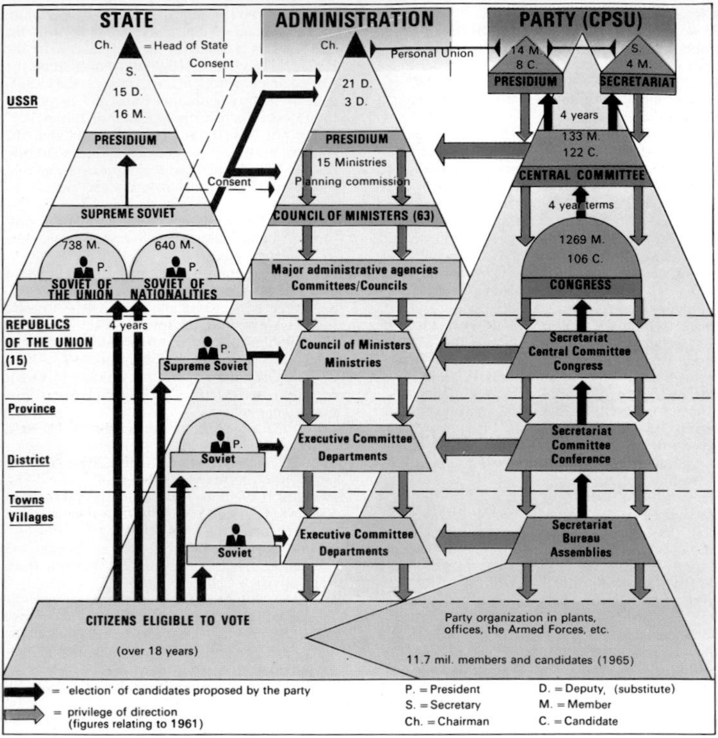

STATE
Ch. = Head of State
S.
15 D.
16 M.
PRESIDIUM
SUPREME SOVIET
738 M. P. SOVIET OF THE UNION
640 M. P. SOVIET OF NATIONALITIES
Consent
Consent

ADMINISTRATION
Ch.
Personal Union
21 D.
3 D.
PRESIDIUM
15 Ministries
Planning commission
COUNCIL OF MINISTERS (63)
Major administrative agencies Committees/Councils

PARTY (CPSU)
14 M. 8 C. PRESIDIUM
S. 4 M. SECRETARIAT
4 years
133 M. 122 C.
CENTRAL COMMITTEE
4 year terms
1269 M. 106 C.
CONGRESS

USSR
REPUBLICS OF THE UNION (15)
4 years
P. Supreme Soviet
Council of Ministers Ministries
Secretariat Central Committee Congress

Province
District
P. Soviet
Executive Committee Departments
Secretariat Committee Conference

Towns Villages
Soviet
Executive Committee Departments
Secretariat Bureau Assemblies

CITIZENS ELIGIBLE TO VOTE
(over 18 years)
Party organization in plants, offices, the Armed Forces, etc.
11.7 mil. members and candidates (1965)

= 'election' of candidates proposed by the party
= privilege of direction
(figures relating to 1961)
P. = President
S. = Secretary
Ch. = Chairman
D. = Deputy, (substitute)
M. = Member
C. = Candidate

The political structure of the U.S.S.R., 1936

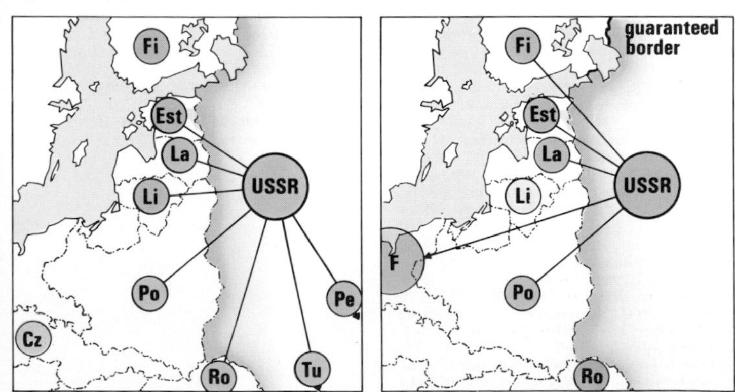

The Moscow Treaty of 1929

Non-aggression treaties of the U.S.S.R., 1932

Stalin's Dictatorship

1924–29 The rise of Joseph Vissarionovich Djugashvili Stalin (1879–1953) to exclusive dominance and leadership of the U.S.S.R. was accomplished by the elimination of all opposition. The troika of STALIN, L. B. KAMENEV (1883–1936 (executed)) and G. ZINOVIEV (1883–1936 (executed)) was able to

1925 remove Trotsky (p. 111) from office as Commissar of War; TROTSKY's thesis of **'permanent revolution'** conflicted with the thesis of **'Socialism in one country'** represented by STALIN and endorsed by the 14th Party Congress. Formation of a right wing, opting for STALIN and incl. A. J. RYKOV (1881–1938 (executed)), N. J. BUKHARIN (1888–1938 (executed)) and M. P. TOMSKY (1880–1936 (suicide)), the leader of the trade unions; and of an ideological left wing (KAMENEV).

1927 Expulsion of Trotsky and Zinoviev from the party and banishment of TROTSKY. From

1929 TROTSKY was forced into exile (to be assassinated in Mexico in 1940). After the rigorous introduction of collectivization was completed, STALIN settled accounts with his rivals on the right. BUKHARIN, TOMSKY and RYKOV lost office (1929).

Nov. 1929 Ejection of Bukharin from the Politburo.

Dec. 1929 STALIN's 50th birthday: initiation of autocratic dictatorship. Beginning in 1928, the

5-Yr Plans transformed the U.S.S.R. into a mod. indust. state. The collectivization of the peasantry became the most extensive agrarian revolution, claiming 60% of all holdings and affecting 11 mil. people ('liquidation of the kulaks', 1932); **Kolkhoz** (village-based agricult. cooperatives) and **Sovkhoz** (state farms) were est. Heavy industry was developed by the opening of new coal and ore mines in the Ural mts, in Siberia and in Cen. Asia. Indust. combinations were formed to rationalize econ. life. Electrification. Autarchy in coal and oil was attained. Human labour was exploited through the application of the 'Stakhanov' system (from 1935). As a privileged class, the new 'technocratic intellectuals' became the mainstay of the régime.

The Stalin Constitution (1936)

A fed. state, consisting of 11 Soviet republics (the Rus., Ukr., White Rus., Georgian, Armen., Azerbaijan, Kazakh, Kirghiz, Uzbek, Turkmen and Tajik Socialist Soviet Republics, constitutionally empowered to leave the union), the U.S.S.R. controlled questions of war and peace, defence, banking, postal services and transportation, for. policy and econ. planning. The component nationalities were protected. The highest public authority was given to the **Supreme Soviet of the U.S.S.R.** (bicameral: Soviet of the Union and Soviet of Nationalities); it was empowered to elect the **Presidium**, the chairman of which fulfilled the function of head of state, the **Soviet of People's Commissars** (the Cabinet) and the **Supreme Court** (5-yr terms), and to appoint the Attorney-General (7-yr terms). Separation of powers did not exist in practice. Nominated by the Com. party and its organizations, the members of the Soviets, from village to Union level, were elected in universal, secret and equal elections by all citizens who had completed their 17th year, to serve 4-yr terms. The citizens were guaranteed basic dem. rights; these rights, however, were to 'conform to the interests of the workers'. The claim to leadership by the Com. party of the Soviet Union and its guiding function were enshrined in the constitution.

The Great Purge (1936–8)

The **Chistka** was STALIN's final settlement of accounts with his opponents of the 1920s. The elimination of the 'Old Bolsheviks' in party and army, for which STALIN and his closer collaborators – such *apparatchiki* as L. M. KAGANOVICH (b. 1893), A. A. ANDREYEV, V. M. MOLOTOV (b. 1890), A. A. ZHDANOV (1896–1948) – were responsible, was the precondition for the establishment of the dictatorship. 8 mil. people were arrested; the camps of northern Russia and Siberia contained 5–6 mil.; their numbers doubled in 1940–42. Arrests, interrogations and executions were carried out with the assistance of the N.K.V.D. (All-Union Commissariat of Internal Affairs) under YAGODA, from 1936 YEZHOV, from 1938 BERIA (p. 227). The great purge trials were high points of the process:

1936 'The Trial of the 16': ZINOVIEV, KAMENEV, *et al.*

1937 'The Trial of the 17': RADEK, MURALOV, PYATAKOV, *et al.*

1938 'The Trial of the 21': BUKHARIN, RYKOV, KRESTINSKY, *et al.* The purge of the Red Army, which claimed 3 marshals, 13 commanding generals and 62 corps commanders as its victims, was initiated by the trial of Marshal TUKHACHEVSKY.

For. policy:

1926 Berlin Treaty (p. 165)

1929 Treaty of Moscow: establishment of an E. Eur. treaty system, to forestall a possible formation of an anti-Soviet front by the Kellogg Pact states (p. 137). Because of the uncertain situation in the Far East, the U.S.S.R., to protect its Western frontier, concluded

1932 non-aggression pacts with W. and E. Eur. states. During the tenure of

1930–39 M. M. LITVINOV as People's Commissar for For. Affairs, esp. after the conclusion of the Ger.-Pol. Non-aggression Pact (p. 197), the U.S.S.R. turned towards the Western Powers.

1933 Recognition of the U.S.S.R. by the U.S.A. (reason: Japan's rise in the Far East).

1934 Admission to the League of Nations.

1935 Soviet-Fr. Mutual Assistance and Non-aggression Pact. (For the policies of the 'Popular Front', see p. 141.)

Depression and Rearmament (1929–35)

As a result of the business recession and increased unemployment, the Lab. party won the

1929 election, obtaining 287 seats against 260 to the Conservatives and 59 to the Liberals, who did not use their votes to prevent the formation of the

1929–31 2nd MacDonald Cabinet (p. 146). Econ. considerations prompted the resumption of relations with the U.S.S.R.: Brit.-Soviet trade had suffered at the expense of Ger.-Soviet trade; Amer. oil firms were competing in the Eur. market. After settlement of the naval question with the U.S.A. (the 'cruiser dispute'), the

1930 Naval Conference of London was convoked (p. 134). The consequences of the world-wide depression (p. 185), the rumours over the grisly state of the public finances (the May Report), the burdening of the budget because of the support given to the unemployed (the 'dole'), but esp. unemployment itself (reaching 2·5 mil. in Dec. 1930), led to a Cabinet crisis.

1931 Resignation of the gvt and formation of a 'Nat.' MacDonald Cabinet, supported by Conservatives and Liberals; a majority of the Lab. party under ARTHUR HENDERSON (1863–1935) and GEORGE LANSBURY (1859–1940) went into opposition. Parliament passed an emergency budget (economy measures and increase in taxation). The gold standard was abandoned. The devaluation of the pound improved the competitive position of Brit. goods in world markets.

Oct. 1931 The result of the elections endorsed the policies of the 'Nat. Gvt': 554 Nat. gvt members faced 52 Lab. members.

1931–5 Nat. gvt (MacDonald prime minister). It was based on Con., Lib. and 13 'Nat.' Lab. members. Of the Conservatives, the most powerful were STANLEY BALDWIN and **Neville Chamberlain** (1869–1940). The gvt abandoned the trad. policy of free trade, but did not pursue a planned programme to fight the crisis. Statute of Westminster (p. 170).

1932 Ottawa Imp. Conference (granting of preferential tariffs (the 'preferential system') in the trade between Britain and the Commonwealth countries). Split of the Liberals; the Lib. for. secretary, Sir JOHN SIMON (1873–1954) remained in the Cabinet. The depression was overcome by the import of low-priced primary goods from the primary-goods-producing countries and finan. gvt measures. Loans were granted, interest was guaranteed, interest rates reduced; war loans were converted from 5% to 3½% and the currency was stabilized through the Exchange Equalization Fund. Nevertheless, there still were 1·6 mil. unemployed. The attempt to bring about an int. monetary agreement failed at the

1933 World Econ. Conference of London.

For. policy in relation to Germany and Japan remained ambiguous.

1934 Beginning of rearmament (the R.A.F.); and, because of Ger. rearmament, demands were made for

1935 an extensive armaments programme.

At the Stresa Conference (p. 159), Britain was briefly able to gain MUSSOLINI as an ally against Germany.

The Politics of Appeasement (1935–9)

1935–7 The 'Nat. Gvt' of Baldwin pursued a policy of **appeasement**. It attempted to avoid war through negotiations, since it shied away from the costs of armament and was sympathetic to the moderate revisionist claims of the defeated powers. Consequences:

1935 Ger.-Brit. naval agreement (p. 197). Under pressure of public opinion the gvt changed its position in relation to Italy: it supported the econ. sanctions decided on by the League of Nations (p. 137). The subsequent election was won (Oct. 1935). The for. secretary Sir SAMUEL HOARE, who had agreed to LAVAL's plan for the partition of Abyssinia (p. 191), was forced to resign from the Cabinet. The policy of 'collective security' was abandoned under the for. secretary, **Anthony Eden** (b. 1897). But Britain returned to the politics of appeasement and therefore held back during the

1936 occupation by Germany of the Rhineland (p. 197). The Brit.-Ital. agreement stipulating the maintainance of the status quo in the Mediterranean (the 'Gentlemen's Agreement', 1937), was also a consequence of the ambiguous policy of appeasement.

1936 Death of King GEORGE V (monarch since 1910). EDWARD VIII (later Duke of Windsor, 1894–1972) was forced to abdicate when the Brit. and Dominion gvts found his intention of marrying the Amer. divorcee Mrs W. W. SIMPSON incompatible with his position as monarch.

1936–52 GEORGE VI. Following the coronation, BALDWIN resigned from the Cabinet.

1937–40 The gvt of Neville Chamberlain. Continuation of the politics of appeasement. EDEN resigned as for. secretary because of the concessions made to Italy. Lord HALIFAX (1881–1959) became his successor.

Apr. 1938 Brit.-Ital. Agreement: recognition of Ital. rule in Abyssinia; withdrawal of Ital. volunteers from Spain after the termination of the war.

Sep. 1938 Munich Agreement (p. 197). After the joint Ger.-Brit. declaration and the occupation of the 'rump' of Czechoslovakia, the politics of appeasement were abandoned.

1939 Introduction of gen. conscription. Checks to the aggressive for. policy of the Nat. Socialists were contrived by the proclamation of guarantees; but owing to the improvement of relations between Germany and the U.S.S.R., a Brit.-Fr.-Soviet Mutual Assistance Pact (Aug. 1939) failed to materialize. (For the outbreak of the war, see p. 197.)

1940 Winston Churchill (1874–1965) formed a coalition Cabinet. CHAMBERLAIN remained in the Cabinet as Lord President of the Council for the last 6 months of his life.

The Crisis Years (1931–40)

1932–40 Presidency of Albert Lebrun (1871–1950). Elect. vict. of the parties of the Left and formation of the

Jun.–Dec. 1932 Herriot Cabinet (p. 147), which contained a majority of ministers from the Rad. party; it fell because of the continued payment of debts to the U.S.A. The period was marked by frequent changes of gvt (PAUL-BONCOUR, DALADIER, SARRAUT, CHAUTEMPS) and a persistent fiscal crisis, resulting from the Fr. parliament's refusal to grant gvts the power to introduce rad. economies. Anti-parl. movements grew (the so-called Leagues ('Croix de Feu'); the Communists) As a result of the STAVISKY scandal (finan. corruption)

1934 the Leagues stormed the Palais Bourbon: the gvt of **Édouard Daladier** (1884–1970) resigned, even though it received a vote of confidence. The new

Feb.–Nov. 1934 gvt of 'nat. union' under the prime minister Gaston Doumergue failed because of its attempt to revise the constitution (strengthening of the executive, dissolution of the Chamber by the prime minister without consent of the Senate).

Nov. 1934–May 1935 Pierre-Étienne Flandin's (1889–1958) gvt of 'peace-at-home' abandoned the project of const. reform, but was also refused the necessary powers to overcome the fiscal crisis.

Jun. 1935–Jan. 1936 Cabinet of Pierre Laval (1883–1945 (executed)). Opposing REYNAUD's proposal to devalue the franc, LAVAL pursued deflationary policies (emergency decrees reducing the salaries of civil servants, lowering of wages and rents). The anticipated quickening of econ. life and a balanced budget failed to materialize. The ministers of the Rad. party left the Cabinet and a new gvt was formed under

Jan.–Jun. 1936 Prime Minister Albert Sarraut (1872–1962). To overcome the danger of Fascism, the Com. leader **Maurice Thorez** (1900–64) proposed the formation of a **'Popular Front'**, to be composed of the Socialist Repub. Union (est. 1935), the Communists and Socialists:

1936 vict. of the 'Popular Front' in the elections to the Chamber.

1936–7 The 'Popular Front' gvt under Prime Minister Léon Blum (1872–1950). Although the Com. party refused to cooperate in the gvt and staged strikes and sit-downs to support its demands, BLUM pushed through the **Malignar agreements**: the 40-hr week, holidays with pay, collective bargaining, increased wages (a minimum of 15%), binding arbitration, recognition of the right to unionize, workers' participation in the running of the factories, nationalization of the Banc de France and armament factories. The Leagues were dissolved, but continued their Fascist activities in organizations concealing their identity. The devaluation of the franc failed to lead to a revival of econ. life or the elimination of unemployment.

1937 Refusal of the Senate to grant BLUM the requested authority to eliminate the fiscal crisis. The Cabinet resigned. The subsequent Popular Front Cabinets of CHAUTEMPS (1937–8) and BLUM (Mar.–Apr. 1938) saw the gradual dissolution of the Popular Front.

1938–40 Daladier Cabinet. Worked to overcome the domestic crisis by emergency decrees, to lessen soc. and polit. conflicts; introduced the enabling law to restore the economy. Following the break with the Popular Front, a

Nov. 1938 general strike was called. It was broken off without achieving its objectives. During the remaining months of peace, family welfare and housing construction laws were passed. Industries were shifted to the provinces.

1939 General mobilization and declaration of war against Germany (2 and 3 Sep.).

1940 Fall of DALADIER (21 Mar.). **Paul Reynaud** (1878–1966) became prime minister. After the invasion by Germany, Marshal PÉTAIN (p. 129) was included in the Cabinet. Requests for aid to the U.S.A. yielded no results. The gvt resigned on 16 Jun.

For. policy (1931–40): France continued the attempt to isolate Nazi Germany by a system of 'collective security'. Individual treaties were signed. After the conclusion of the Geneva 5-Power Agreement (p. 193) and the hardening of Fr. attitudes, Fr. diplomacy under the for. minister LOUIS BARTHOU (1862–1934 (assassinated)) supported the conclusion of the Balk. Pact (p. 165) to aid the Little Entente and denounced Ger. rearmament in a verbal diplomatic protest (Apr. 1934).

1934 HITLER rejected the Fr. proposal for an 'Eastern Locarno' agreement. As a result, France supported the admission of the U.S.S.R. to the League of Nations.

1935 Colon. agreement with Italy and Mutual Aid Pact with the U.S.S.R.

During the **Abys. conflict,** the prime minister, LAVAL, took up an ambiguous position: France participated in the sanctions of the League of Nations, but also submitted a proposal to mediate (the HOARE–LAVAL agreement). For all practical purposes, Franco-Ital. relations were finished by the conclusion of the Ger.-Ital. Pact (p. 197). Although disillusioned by Britain's hesitation during the Ger. occupation of the Rhineland (p. 197) and the annexation of Austria (p. 197), France moved closer to Britain. The improvement of relations between Poland and Germany (p. 197) and between Yugoslavia and Italy (1937) weakened the Fr. alliance system in Eastern Europe.

1938 Visit of the Brit. royal couple to Paris (emphasis on Brit.-Fr. friendship). After the visit of the prime minister, DALADIER, and the for. minister, BONNET, to London (peaceful settlement of the Sudeten crisis), France took part in the Munich Conference (p. 197). A Ger.-Fr. declaration of non-aggression followed in Dec. Tense relations with Italy prevailed because of Ital. annexationist intentions in Tunisia and Corsica and cancellation of the Franco-Ital. colon. agreement (Dec.). Close polit. cooperation with Britain (proclamations of guarantees, p. 190).

LÜBECK
MECKLENBURG 13 Jul. 32
HAMBURG
OLDENBURG 16 Jun. 32
BREMEN
MECKLENBURG-STRELITZ 6 Apr. 32
BRUNSWICK 15 Sep. 31
Berlin
Danzig
Harzburg Front 11 Oct. 31
ANHALT 21 May 32
PRUSSIA
THURINGIA 26 Jul. 32
SAXONY
HESSE
to Oldenburg
THE PALATINATE
BADEN
WÜRTTEMBG.
BAVARIA
HOHENZOLLERN

NSDAP state gvts
State gvts with NSDAP participation

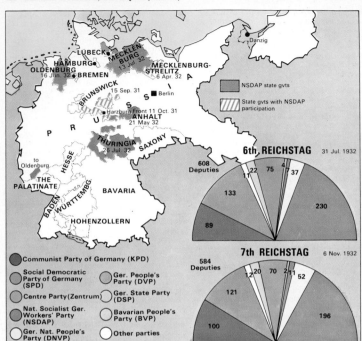

6th REICHSTAG 31 Jul. 1932
608 Deputies
89, 133, 11, 22, 75, 4, 7, 37, 230

7th REICHSTAG 6 Nov. 1932
584 Deputies
100, 121, 12, 20, 70, 2, 11, 52, 196

Communist Party of Germany (KPD)
Social Democratic Party of Germany (SPD)
Centre Party (Zentrum)
Nat. Socialist Ger. Workers' Party (NSDAP)
Ger. Nat. People's Party (DNVP)
Ger. People's Party (DVP)
Ger. State Party (DSP)
Bavarian People's Party (BVP)
Other parties

The dissolution of the Weimar Republic

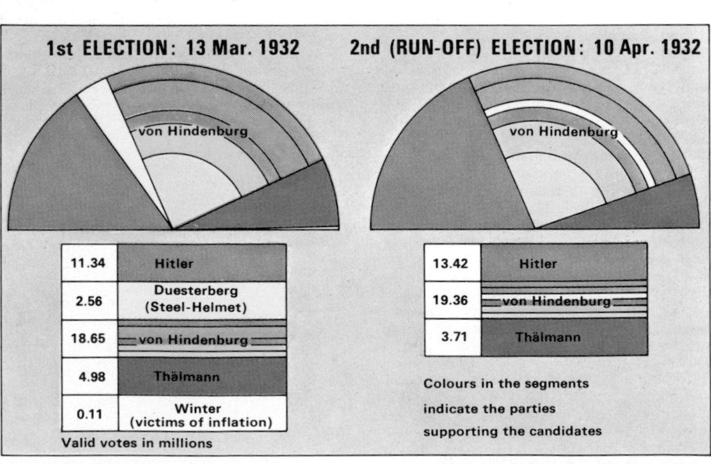

The presidential elections of 1932

The Brüning Gvt (1930–32)

After HERMANN MÜLLER, the last S.P.D. Chancellor, had fallen (p. 151) and the incapacity of the Reichstag to function had become increasingly evident, the Centre party politician **Heinrich Brüning** (1885–1970) formed a new

1930–32 gvt which, supported by HINDENBURG, resorted to Art. 48 of the constitution to carry on governing, opposed by the Left (K.P.D.) and the extreme Right (D.N.V.P. and N.S.D.A.P.). The S.P.D. did not at first oppose BRÜNING's policies. Measures to combat the intensifying (increasing unemployment, recall of short-term credits from abroad) econ. crisis. BRÜNING pursued a deflationary econ. policy ('emergency decrees to safeguard the economy and public finances': reduction of wages and salaries, lowering of prices, a cutback in spending and in unemployment compensation, an increase in taxes, etc.).

Sep. 1930 Elections to the Reichstag: the K.P.D. and N.S.D.A.P. gained votes. Domestic politics became increasingly radicalized.

1931 Formation of the 'Harzburg Front' (a 'nat. opposition' consisting of the N.S.D.A.P., D.N.V.P., and the 'Stahlhelm') and the 'Iron Front' (of the S.P.D., trade unions, and the 'Reichsbanner', a para-milit. organization serving as protection against violence from the S.A.).

1932 Re-election of Hindenburg (against the K.P.D. candidate, ERNST THÄLMANN (1886–1944 (murdered)) and the N.S.D.A.P. candidate, HITLER). In response to the rad. measures of the N.S.D.A.P., the S.A. and S.S. were banned. GRÖNER, the defence minister, resigned and was succeeded (in the PAPEN Cabinet) by General KURT VON SCHLEICHER (1882–1934 (murdered)), who was backed in his endeavour to support the radicals of the Right by the victs. of the N.S.D.A.P. in local elections in Prussia, Bavaria, Württemberg, Hamburg and Anhalt (Apr.). Even so, the motions of no-confidence proposed by the oppositions of the Left and the Right during the Reichstag session of 9–12 May 1932 were defeated.

The Gvts of Papen and Schleicher (1932–3)

30 May 1932 Brüning fell ('a 100 m from the finishing line') because of the intrigues of the clique around HINDENBURG (SCHLEICHER, HINDENBURG's son OSKAR, and the E. Elbian Junkers led by OLDENBURG-JANUSCHAU), which was suspicious of his policies of agrarian reform and settlement ('Bolshevik agrarian policies'). With the formation of the

Jun.–Dec. 1932 'Cabinet of Nat. Concentration', the transition to complete pres. gvt was made. FRANZ VON PAPEN (1879–1969) became Chancellor. After the dissolution of the Reichstag (4 Jun. 1932), the ban on the S.A. and S.S. was lifted. HITLER did not oppose the gvt. A situation approaching civil war provided the excuse for the

Jul. 1932 coup d'état in Prussia: the governing prime minister, BRAUN, was removed from office.

Jul. 1932 Elections to the Reichstag. The N.S.D.A.P. became the strongest individual party. HINDENBURG rejected HITLER as candidate for the chancellorship. The PAPEN gvt was voted down in the Reichstag because of its emergency decrees to carry through the 'Papen plan to stimulate the economy'. The Reichstag was dissolved and new elections were held in

Nov. 1932: the N.S.D.A.P. lost votes, the K.P.D. gained. The plan to create a 'New State', authoritarian and free from Reichstag influence, supported by the armed forces, failed. Chancellor PAPEN resigned.

1932–3 (28 Jan.) The SCHLEICHER Cabinet. The attempt to split the N.S.D.A.P. with the aid of its Socialist wing under GREGOR STRASSER (p. 183) resulted in failure. Negotiations with the Christ. and 'free' trade unions, the parties of the centre and the S.P.D. to rally support for the gvt remained fruitless.

Jan. 1933 Vict. of the N.S.D.A.P. in the local election of the small state of Lippe. The SCHLEICHER gvt resigned when the president refused to proclaim a nat. emergency, to dissolve the Reichstag, and to refrain from the call for new elections.

For. Policy (1930–33)

1930 The response of the Ger. gvt to BRIAND's plan for a 'United States of Europe' amounted, in fact, to a rejection because of the Ger. gvt's demand for full and equal rights for Germany.

1931 The plan for a Ger.-Aust. customs union failed because of Fr. opposition. The Int. Court of Justice in The Hague, which concerned itself with the case, denied its legitimacy. Germany and Austria did not therefore initial the agreement.

1932 Lausanne Conference: final settlement of the reparations question (Jun./Jul., p. 135).
Geneva 5-Power Agreement: recognition of equal rights for Germany in milit. matters (Dec.).

Hitler's Seizure of Power (1933)

4 Jan. Agreement of HITLER and PAPEN in the house of the banker SCHRÖDER to form a joint gvt.

22 Jan. Discussion between PAPEN, HITLER, OSKAR VON HINDENBURG and the secretary of state, MEISSNER. HITLER gained the support of OSKAR VON HINDENBURG. The President agreed to HITLER being cal. as chancellor as well as to new Reichstag elections.

The fate of the Weimar Republic was thereby sealed. Created after the defeat of 1918, it had been a stop-gap measure, not the product of a great revolution. The citizens lacked republican commitment and experience. The armed forces formed a 'state-within-the-state'. Constantly gaining in strength, the polit. Right reaped the benefits; for the people it created the illusion of a strong body politic that was to be the result of its work. It gave the *coup de grâce* to parliament: the N.S.D.A.P., often in concert with the K.P.D., made consistent parl. activity impossible until it had gained elect. vict. in 1932; then it proceeded to attain power by 'legal' means: the 'seizure of power' was followed by the 'legal revolution' (p. 195).

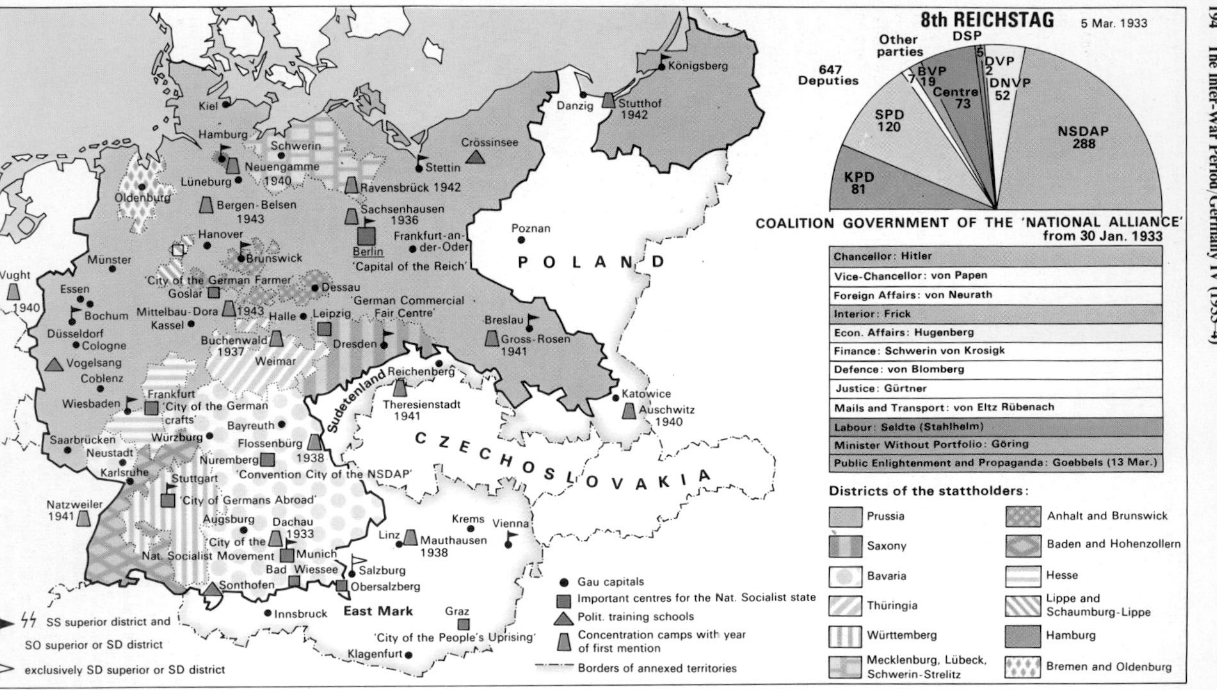
8th REICHSTAG
5 Mar. 1933
647
Deputies
Other
parties
7
BVP
19
DSP
5
Centre
73
DVP
2
DNVP
52
SPD
120
NSDAP
288
KPD
81
COALITION GOVERNMENT OF THE 'NATIONAL ALLIANCE'
from 30 Jan. 1933
Chancellor: Hitler
Vice-Chancellor: von Papen
Foreign Affairs: von Neurath
Interior: Frick
Econ. Affairs: Hugenberg
Finance: Schwerin von Krosigk
Defence: von Blomberg
Justice: Gürtner
Mails and Transport: von Eltz Rübenach
Labour: Seldte (Stahlhelm)
Minister Without Portfolio: Göring
Public Enlightenment and Propaganda: Goebbels (13 Mar.)
Districts of the stattholders:
Prussia
Saxony
Bavaria
Thüringia
Württemberg
Mecklenburg, Lübeck,
Schwerin-Strelitz
Anhalt and Brunswick
Baden and Hohenzollern
Hesse
Lippe and
Schaumburg-Lippe
Hamburg
Bremen and Oldenburg
Gau capitals
Important centres for the Nat. Socialist state
Polit. training schools
Concentration camps with year
of first mention
Borders of annexed territories
SS superior district and
SO superior or SD district
exclusively SD superior or SD district
Königsberg
Danzig
Stutthof
1942
Kiel
Hamburg
Schwerin
Crössinsee
Stettin
Neuengamme
1940
Lüneburg
Ravensbrück 1942
Oldenburg
Bergen-Belsen
1943
Sachsenhausen
1936
Hanover
Frankfurt-an-
der-Oder
Berlin
'Capital of the Reich'
Poznan
POLAND
Münster
Brunswick
Vught
1940
'City of the German Farmer'
Goslar
Dessau
Essen
Bochum
Mittelbau-Dora
1943
'German Commercial
Fair Centre'
Kassel
Halle
Leipzig
Breslau
Gross-Rosen
1941
Düsseldorf
Cologne
Buchenwald
1937
Weimar
Dresden
Vogelsang
Coblenz
Sudetenland
Reichenberg
Katowice
Auschwitz
1940
Frankfurt
'City of the German
crafts'
Wiesbaden
Theresienstadt
1941
Bayreuth
CZECHOSLOVAKIA
Saarbrücken
Würzburg
Flossenbürg
1938
Neustadt
Nuremberg
'Convention City of the NSDAP'
Karlsruhe
Stuttgart
'City of Germans Abroad'
Natzweiler
1941
Augsburg
Dachau
1933
Krems
Vienna
'City of the
Nat. Socialist Movement
Munich
Linz
Mauthausen
1938
Bad Wiessee
Salzburg
Sonthofen
Obersalzberg
Innsbruck
East Mark
Graz
'City of the People's Uprising'
Klagenfurt

The seizing of power and establishment of Hitler's dictatorship, 1930–45

The 'Nat. Revolution' and 'Gleichschaltung'

30 Jan. 1933 Hitler's gvt was sworn in; it drew its authority from pres. decrees–a 'pres. gvt'–and was a coalition of 'nat. accord'. The 'nat. revolution' was now followed by the 'lawful revolution', power was consolidated by invoking Art. 48, the 'emergency art.' of the constitution: total power of the N.S.D.A.P. and the 'Führer' principle were strengthened through the process of **'Gleichschaltung'**: basic const. rights were suspended by the decrees of the president 'to protect the Ger. people' (4 Feb. 1933) and (after the Reichstag fire of 27 Feb. 1933) 'for the protection of the people and the state' (proclamation of a state of nat. emergency on 28 Feb. 1933). Following elections to the Reichstag and the state ceremonial opening in the Garrison Church of Potsdam (21 Mar. 1933: the 'day of Potsdam'), **parliament was effectively deprived of its powers:**

23 Mar. 1933 passage of the 'Law for Removing the Distress of People and Reich' (the 'Enabling Act'). Legislative power was transferred to the executive; its functioning as executive organ was synchronized by the 'Law to Restore the Professional Bureaucracy' (7 Apr. 1933): politically undesirable and 'non-Aryan' civil servants were dismissed from office. The federalist structure of the state was dest.

31 Mar. 1933 'Preliminary Law to Harmonize [Gleichschaltung] the State Gvts and Nat. Authority' (the composition of the state parliaments was altered to conform to the outcome of the nat. elections to the Reichstag). After the passage of the

7 Apr. 1933 'Law to Harmonize the State Gvts and Nat. Authority', *'statthalters'* of the nat. gvt were appointed in the states, who in turn appointed the state gvts. The process of **'Gleichschaltung'** was completed with the **'Law for the Reconstruction of the Reich'**: the parliaments of the states were abolished (30 Jan. 1934) and the **Reichsrat** (Upper House of the nat. parliament) was dissolved (14 Feb. 1934).

The assumption of police powers affirmed Nat. Socialist authority. By 1936 the entire police force (the regular police force, detectives and polit. police (from 1934 the **Gestapo**)) were placed under the orders of the **Reichsführer of the S.S. and Chief of the Ger. Police, Heinrich Himmler** (p. 183). Following the RÖHM affair (see below), the S.S. took the place of the S.A.: **'the S.S. state was in the process of formation'**. The S.S. became the executive organ of the Führer. The judicial process came to be governed not by the classical democratic norms, but by the tenets of 'popular feeling': special courts (incl. the 'People's Court') were est. The will of the 'Führer' and Nat. Socialist ideology were the foundations of the Nat. Socialist conception of law; the principle of individual liberty under the law was denied. **The polit. police wielded arbitrary powers**: activities inimical to the interest of the state were searched out and prosecuted. Polit. opponents were punished by being deprived of their personal liberty and assignment to concentration camps 'to maintain and safeguard the community of the people'.

From May 1933 polit. parties and trade unions were liquidated and dissolved or proscribed: The D.A.F. (Ger. Workers' Front) was est. after the property of the trade unions had been confiscated. The D.V.P., B.V.P., D.St.P., D.N.V.P. and Centre party were dissolved. The S.P.D. and K.P.D. were proscribed. With the

1 Dec. 1933 'Law to Secure the Unity of Party and Reich', the N.S.D.A.P. became the state party.

The threat of a '2nd' Socialist 'revolution' and the merger of the armed forces and the S.A. to form 1 militia (the RÖHM plan) was overcome with by

Jun.–Jul. 1934 the murder of the chief-of-staff of the S.A., Ernst Röhm (p. 183) and the S.A. leadership devoted to him. Polit. opponents were liquidated at the same time (among them SCHLEICHER (p. 193), KAHR (p. 149), EDGAR JUNG). The murders were **legalized retroactively as public acts of self-defence.**

2 Aug. 1934 Death of President von Hindenburg. Hitler assumed the office of the president. The armed forces were from now on sworn in to the person of the **'Führer and Chancellor Adolf Hitler'**. All Germans were 'accounted for' through 'the organizations of the N.S.D.A.P.' and its 'associated groups' (p. 183).

Nat. Socialist Econ. Policy

To attain econ. autarchy, agriculture was supported: an **'estate of the tillers of the soil'** was proclaimed and a rigid law of entail **('Reichserbhofgesetz')**, protecting specified peasant holdings, was passed. **Unemployment was eliminated** through public works projects, the construction of the fed. highway system (**'Autobahnen'** initiated 27 May 1933), rearmament, and the mandatory **nat. workers' service** (26 Jun. 1935); job creation and rearmament were financed through the assumption of public debts **('Mefo bills'). By 1938 the state carried an internal debt of 42,000 mil. Marks.**

27 Feb. 1934 'Law for the Organic Reconstruction of the Economy' (the Enabling Act to account for and place under public control all organizations and individuals).

20 Jan. 1934 The 'Law Regulating Nat. Labour' was passed (factories were turned into 'communities of Labour' and 'trustees of labour' were created).

24 Oct. 1934 All workers were gathered into the Ger. Workers' Front (D.A.F.).

Policies Towards Ctr. and the Church

13 Mar. 1933 Establishment of the Ministry of Popular Enlightenment and Propaganda under Joseph Goebbels (p. 183). The entire process of *'Gleichschaltung'* was supported and justified by the unscrupulous methods of GOEBBELS's propaganda. The ministry also exerted strong pressure on sc. institutions (auton. university constitutions were abolished) and cult. life:

22 Sep. 1933 the Reich Chamber of Ctr. was founded.

Nat. Socialist Church policies ended in failure. Although a concordat was concluded (p. 197), the resistance of the Cath. Church (encyclical of Pope PIUS XI *Mit brennender Sorge* (*With Burning Sorrow*, 1937) increased.

May 1934 The Confessional Synod of the Ger. Prot. Churches opposed the establishment of an evangelical 'Nat. Church' by the Nazis: growing out of MARTIN NIEMÖLLER's (b. 1892) Pastors' Emergency League (1933), the **'Confessional Church'** was constituted.

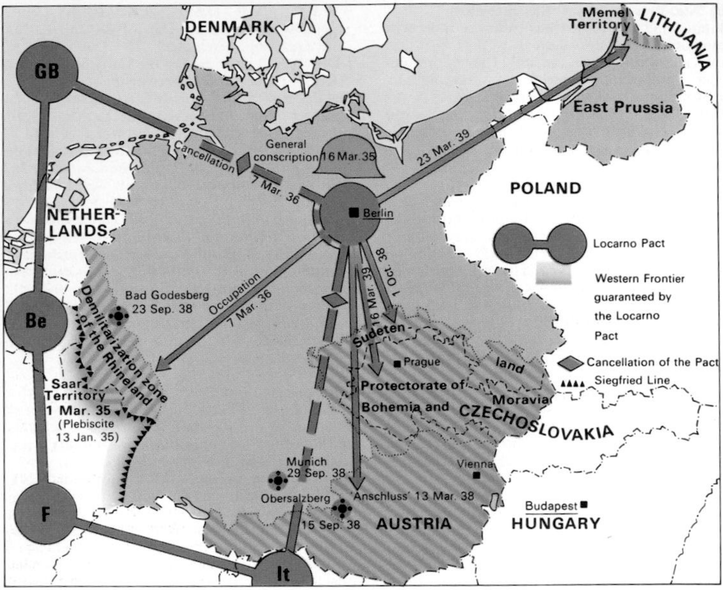

Expansion of German 'living-space' by Spring, 1939

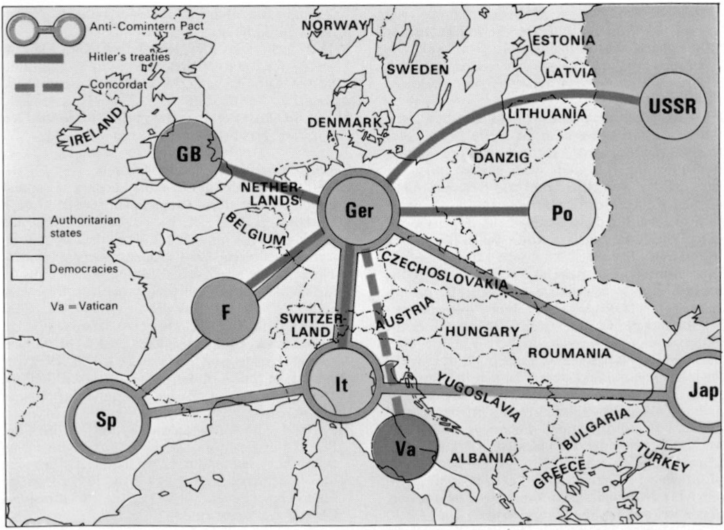

Hitler's alliances

Nat. Socialist For. Policy

Objective: revision of the Versailles Treaty as a preliminary to the 'conquest of additional living-space'. Though HITLER pledged the Ger. will to preserve peace, he rejected the policy of 'collective security' and advocated bilateral agreements.

1933 Conclusion of the concordat with the Vatican (Jul.). After Germany left the disarmament conference and the League of Nations (Oct.) it became increasingly isolated.

1934 Non-aggression Pact with Poland: the Fr. system of alliances was upset.
Following the abortive Nat. Socialist putsch in Vienna (p. 156) and the rejection of an 'Eastern Locarno', the result of the plebiscite in the Saarland and its reincorporation into the Ger. state were the first successes in for. policy (Jan. 1935).

Mar. 1935 Reintroduction of gen. conscription.

Jun. 1935 Ger.-Brit. naval agreement (the relative strength of the navies was to be 35:100). Unmoved by the advantage gained here,

Mar. 1936 Hitler cancelled the Locarno Pact (p. 135) and ordered the occupation of the demilitarized zone of the Rhineland: the order est. by the Treaty of Versailles had come to an end.

Jul. 1936 Agreement with Austria: rest. of friendly relations.

Aug. 1936 The Olympic Games were held in Berlin.

Aug. 1936 Introduction of the 2-yr milit. service obligation.

Nov. 1936 Anti-Comintern Pact: beginning of cooperation with **Japan** against mutual polit. opponents (U.S.S.R.). The pact was joined by **Italy** (Jan. 1937) after a Ger.-Ital. agreement had led to the proclamation of the 'Berlin–Rome Axis' (Oct./Nov. 1936); later on, **Spain** also joined (Mar. 1939).

The 'conquest of addit. living-space' ('Lebensraum') became an additional objective of Nat. Socialist for. policy on top of HITLER's preoccupation with gaining lands already settled by Germans. At the annual party convention in Nuremberg in Sep. 1936, the 4-yr plan to attain econ. autarchy was proclaimed. At the

Nov. 1937 'Führer' Conference, Hitler revealed his war aims ('Hossbach Memorandum'): 'addit. living-space' was to be obtained by the use of force.

1938 VON BLOMBERG (1878–1946), the war minister, was dismissed for having mar. below his station, while the commanding general of the army, Colonel-General VON FRITSCH (1880–1939), fell victim to an intrigue of HIMMLER and GÖRING. **A Supreme Command of the Armed Forces** (O.K.W.) was est.: the process of *Gleichschaltung* was thereby extended to the armed forces. **Joachim von Ribbentrop** (1893–1946 (executed)) assumed the For. Office. The president of the Reichsbank, HJALMAR SCHACHT (p. 149), was dismissed and the 'Ger. Reichsbank Law' was passed (Jun. 1939): HITLER assumed unrestricted direction and control of Germany's finan. affairs.

1938 Anschluss of Austria (p. 156). The 'reunification of Austria with the Ger. Reich' (13 Mar.) was affirmed by a plebiscite (Apr.).

In consequence of HITLER's secret directive to the armed forces to **destroy Czechoslovakia** (30 May 1938), the subsequent (Aug.) resignation of the chief of the Army General Staff, LUDWIG BECK (1880–1944 (suicide)), HITLER's talks with CHAMBERLAIN (p. 190) in Berchtesgaden and Bad Godesberg (Sep.) and Brit.-Ital. mediation led to the

29 Sep. 1938 Munich Conference of HITLER, MUSSOLINI, CHAMBERLAIN and DALADIER: **the Sudeten Ger. areas were ceded to Germany** (1–10 Oct. 1938). The Anglo-Ger. declaration of non-aggression (30 Sep.) and the Ger.-Fr. declaration (final recognition of the Ger.-Fr. borders) were intended, on the part of the Western Powers, to put an end to Ger. expansion. Despite HITLER's pledge, that the cession of the Sudetenland was his final demand (26 Sep.), he gave

21 Oct. 1938 secret orders to 'liquidate the rump of Czechoslovakia'. Following the visit of the Czechoslovak president, HACHA (p. 157), to Berlin (15 Mar. 1939) and the invasion by Ger. troops of Czechoslovakia (15–16 Mar. 1939),

16 Mar. 1939 the 'Ger. Protectorate of Bohemia and Moravia' was est.

23 Mar. 1939 The Memel territory was joined to the Ger. Reich. The econ. dependence of the Balk. and Danubian countries ('storehouse of Greater Germany') was initiated by the conclusion of a Ger.-Roum. trade agreement (p. 163).

The Outbreak of the War and the System of Alliances (1939–42)

21 Mar. 1939 Ger. demands on Poland: incorporation of Danzig into Germany, an extraterrit. avenue of communication between E. Prussia and Germany through the Pol. Corridor. The demands were rejected. The negotiations were broken off (26 Mar.) and, after the British and French had pledged guarantees for the territ. integrity of Poland (31 Mar.), the Ger.-Pol. Non-aggression Pact and the Anglo-Ger. Naval Agreement were cancelled by HITLER (28 Apr.). The Ger.

22 May 1939 Pact of Friendship and Mutual Aid with Italy ('Pact of Steel'), the

21 May–7 Jun. 1939 non-aggression treaties with Estonia, Latvia and Denmark, and the

23 Aug. 1939 Ger.-Soviet Non-aggression Pact, with its secret supplementary conditions (fixing the relative spheres of interest of the 2 powers in Eastern Europe), created the preconditions for the

1 Sep. 1939 Ger. attack on Poland; Poland had concluded a treaty of alliance with Britain (25 Aug.). Brit. attempts to mediate failed over the ultimative Ger. demand to Poland for the immediate dispatch of a plenipotentiary to Berlin.

1940 3-Power Pact of Germany, Italy and Japan. Objective: to reorder Europe and the Far East; the states were committed to aiding each other. Hungary, Roumania, Slovakia, Denmark, Finland, Nanking China, Bulgaria and Croatia joined the pact in 1942.

1942 Milit. alliance of Germany, Italy and Japan.

The campaigns in Poland, Denmark, Norway, Holland, Belgium, France, 1939–40

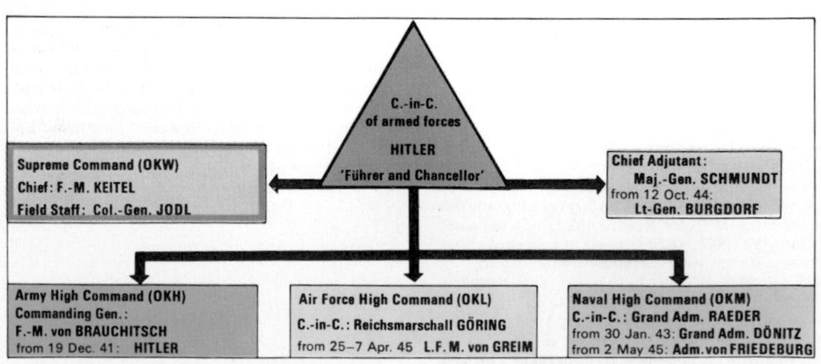

Leadership of the German armed forces

The Pol. Campaign ('Operation Case White', 1939)
Swift destruction of the Pol. army (1–18 Sep. 1939) by the superior Ger. tanks and air force. Warsaw continued to resist (27 Sep.), as did Modlin (28 Sep.).
Consequences of the attack: following fruitless attempts at mediation, MUSSOLINI proclaimed Italy a 'non-belligerent' power (2 Sep.). **Britain and France** ultimately demanded the withdrawal of the Ger. forces to behind the Ger. frontier and, **after the expiration of the deadline, declared war (3 Sep.).**
Prerequisites for the conduct of the war in the W.:
1. The 'reconstruction' of Poland (Oct. 1939): annexation of Danzig (1 Sep.) and the area ceded to Poland in 1918 (incorp. as the *Gau* (district) of Danzig–w. Prussia and the *Gau* of Wartaland; the district of Katowice and the Olsa region became part of the province of Silesia, the districts of Sudauen and Zichenau became part of the province of E. Prussia. Designated the *'Generalgouvernement'*, the rest of Poland was placed under the control of the Governor-General HANS FRANK (p. 183). **The objective of Nat. Socialist policy was the enslavement of the Poles**: secondary schools and universities were closed; the intelligentsia was eliminated; forced labour was introduced.
2. The relationship to the U.S.S.R.: invasion of Eastern Poland by the Red Army (17 Sep.) and conclusion of the
28 Sep. 1939 Ger.-Soviet Border and Friendship Treaty: the U.S.S.R. was given free sway over Lithuania in exchange for territ. concessions (the Bug Line, the Suwalki area).
7 Oct. 1939 Reichstag speech by HITLER: his peace offer (recognition of the status quo) was rejected by France and Britain.
11 Feb. 1940 Econ. agreement with the U.S.S.R., making the Brit. blockade ineffective.
3. Resettlement of people of Ger. origin (*'Volksdeutsche'*) on the basis of treaties with the Balt. states, Italy and the U.S.S.R. (Oct./Nov. 1939); the settlers became part of Germany's Eastern policy and were subject to the planning of the S.S. (HIMMLER (p. 183) was named 'Nat. Commissioner to safeguard Ger. nationality' (R.K.F.)): resettlement measures were taken.

The Fin.-Soviet 'Winter War' (1939–40)
Following the rejection of Rus. demands (for the granting of milit. bases)
30 Nov. 1939 the U.S.S.R. attacked Finland. The U.S.S.R. was expelled from the League of Nations (14 Dec.). After determined Fin. resistance, the Soviets broke through the 'Mannerheim Line'. To avert a conflict with the Western Powers, who planned to support Finland by a landing operation in Norway–and to cut off ore supplies from Sweden to Germany–the
12 Mar. 1940 Peace of Moscow was concluded: Finland ceded the Karelian Isthmus and Eastern Karelia and leased Hangö to the U.S.S.R. The U.S.S.R. received rights of transit in the Petsamo area.

Denmark, Norway ('Operation Weser', 1940)
To secure the supply route of Swedish ore and to broaden the base for the mercantile war against Britain, the **occupation of Denmark (9 Apr.)**, which surrendered without struggle, and the **occupation of Norway (9 Apr.–10 Jun.)**, which capitulated after the Allied troops left by sea (3–7 Jun.), was carried out by combined naval, land and aerial operations.
Denmark: the Dan. gvt continued in office, a 'Plenipotentiary of the Ger. Reich' was appointed. The Dan. gvt resigned on 28 Aug. 1943.
Norway: King HAAKON VII (1905–57) and his gvt fled to London and formed a gvt in exile (5 May 1940). TERBOVEN was appointed 'Commissar of the Ger. Reich'. He was supported by VIDKUN QUISLING (1887–1945 (executed)), leader of the Fascist 'Nasjonal Samling'.

The Campaign in the W. ('Operation Case Yellow', 1940)
10 May–4 Jun. 1940 1st phase ('the cut of the sickle'). Following the capitulation of the Netherlands (15 May) and Belgium (28 May), Ger. troops broke through to the coast of the Eng. Channel; but *c.* 335,000 Brit. and Fr. soldiers were rescued from the beaches of Dunkirk.
5–24 Jun. 1940 2nd phase ('the b. for France'). After the breakthrough of the 'Weygand Line', **Paris was occupied without struggle** (14 Jun.). The Germans reached the Atlantic coast (19 Jun.), and, by way of the Loire (16 Jun.), the Swiss border (17 Jun.).
10 Jun. 1940 Italy entered the war (p. 203).
22 Jun. 1940 The Armistice was concluded in the forest of Compiègne. France was partitioned into an occupied zone and an unoccupied zone (Vichy France). The Fr. army entered P.O.W. camps, the navy was not surrendered.

Polit. consequences: Britain: formation of a coalition Cabinet (10 May) under **Winston Churchill (1874–1965). The Netherlands**: flight of the royal family and gvt to London. ARTHUR SEYSS-INQUART (p. 156) became Reichkommissar for the Netherlands, supported by ANTON ADRIAN MUSSERT (1894–1946 (executed)), the leader of the Dutch Nat. Socialists. **Belgium**: King LEOPOLD III (1934–51) was interned. The Fascist 'Rexists' under LÉON DEGRELLE (b. 1906) supported the Germans. Return of Eupen-Malmédy and Moresnet (18 May). **Luxemburg**: Gauleiter SIMON became head of the civilian admin. (2 Aug.). **France**: after the fall of DALADIER (p. 191) and the resignation of REYNAUD, PÉTAIN (p. 129) formed the ('Vichy') gvt (16 Jun.).
3 Jul. 1940 The Fr. fleet, lying at anchor before Oran, dest. by the British.
10 Jul. 1940 Pétain became 'head-of-state'.
24 Oct. 1940 Meeting of Hitler and Pétain at Montoire: HITLER demanded Fr. entry into the war on the side of Germany; PÉTAIN refused.

Planned Ger. operations: the planned **landings in Britain ('Operation Sea-lion')** was postponed because Germany lost the **'b. of Britain'** in the air (p. 201). The plan for the **seizure of Gibraltar** ('Operation Felix') was given up after the fruitless meeting between HITLER and FRANCO (p. 161) at Hendaye (23 Oct.).

	1939	1940	1941	1942	1943	1944	1945
U-boat losses (Ger.)	9	22	35	85	287	241	153
Shipping losses (US, Brit.) in tons	810 000	4 407 000	4 398 000	8 245 000	3 611 000	1 422 000	458 000
New construction (US) in registered tons	101 000	439 000	1 169 000	5 339 000	12 384 000	11 639 000	3 551 000
New construction (Brit.) in registered tons	231 000	780 000	815 000	1 843 000	2 201 000	1 710 000	283 000
Total in registered tons	332 000	1 219 000	1 984 000	7 182 000	14 585 000	13 349 000	3 834 000

The war at sea, 1939–45

Total	1939	1940	1941	1942	1943	1944	-1945
Bombers 18 235	737	2852	3373	4337	4649	2287	
Fighter planes 53 729	605	2746	3744	5515	10 898	25 285	4936
Battle-support fighters 12 359	134	603	507	1249	3266	5496	1104
Reconnaissance planes 6299	163	971	1079	1067	1117	1686	216
Jet-propelled planes 1988						1041	947

German aircraft production, 1939–45

	1940	1941	1942	1943	1944	1945
Bombs (in tons) Dropped on Germany	10 000	30 000	40 000	120 000	650 000	500 000
Dropped on Britain	36 844	21 858	3260	2298	9151	761

Air bombardment during the war, 1940–45

The War at Sea (1939–45)

Attempting to cut off the enemy's routes of supply, the Ger. naval forces operated mostly in the Atlantic Ocean (the **'b. of the Atlantic'**). Despite heavy losses in tonnage by the British, Germany's attempt to blockade the Brit. Isles did not succeed. The Ger. navy played a decisive role in the occupation of Norway and Denmark, but suffered such heavy losses that it was only able to give limited support to operations in France in 1940 (Dunkirk, p. 199).

The surface fleet: following the self-destruction of the armoured cruiser *Graf Spee* in the mouth of the La Plata river (Dec. 1939) and the battleship *Bismarck* (May 1941), which had jointly with the heavy cruiser *Prince Eugen*, succeeded in destroying the Brit. battleship *Hood*,

1942 the battleships *Scharnhorst* and *Gneisenau* and the *Prince Eugen* broke through the Eng. Channel (both had operated in the Atlantic in 1940–41) to make their way to Norway. Further Atlantic operations were abandoned.

1943 Sinking of the *Scharnhorst* nr Murmansk (Dec.).

1944 Destruction of the battleship *Tirpitz* at Tromsö (Nov.).

1945 Loss of the *Admiral Scheer*, *Admiral Hipper*, *Lützow*, *Emden*, *Köln*, *Leipzig*, *Schlesien* and *Schleswig-Holstein*.

The U-Boat war: the war against trading vessels was at first waged in accordance with the int. rules of search and seizure.

1940 Proclamation of the Ger. 'sphere of operations' around Britain (17 Aug.) and intensification of the battle. At the beginning of the war, U-Boats were successful in missions undertaken by single vessels.

1942 Significant successes were achieved along the Amer. coast (absence of submarine defence). The high point of the period, that saw the employment of 'packs' of U-Boats, was reached

1942–3 in the operations against the convoys in the N. Atlantic. In Mar. 1943 851,000 gross registered tons of shipping were sunk. Owing to the dispute over the decommissioning of the large surface vessels, the c.-in-c. of the navy, RAEDER, resigned (1943, successor: DÖNITZ, p. 215). Attacks on the convoys in the Atlantic were broken off in 1943.

Developments in the U-Boat war turned to the advantage of the Allies due to their utilization of destroyers as convoy escorts, to the use of radar, to continued aerial surveillance and to deployment of 'support groups' to safeguard the convoys. The invention of the snorkel (1944) and the sound-sensitive torpedo did not improve the Ger. position.

The War in the Air (1939–45)

The Luftwaffe (under command of Reichsmarschall HERMANN GÖRING, p. 183) was at first superior to the opposing air forces, esp. in the support of operations on the ground (Stuka dive-bombers); it was therefore able to contribute to the success of the **Blitzkrieg** warfare. Despite its air superiority, however, the air force was unable to prevent the embarkation of the Brit. Expeditionary Force at Dunkirk (p.199) and was also defeated during the

1940–41 'b. of Britain'. The 'blitz' by the Luftwaffe on such cities as London, Coventry and Plymouth took a heavy toll of civilian lives and property without crushing the people's defiant mood. Neither were the Brit. fighter force, ground-support organization or war industry decisively disrupted, and aerial superiority over southern England was denied to the Germans (p. 199). The increasing superiority of the Allied air force (construction of long-distance bombers and fighters) and the development of radar technology brought the turning-point in the war in the air.

1942 Beginning of the Brit. and Amer. bombardment of war industries and urban pop. areas of Ger. cities with incendiary and high-explosive bombs (30–31 May, raid by 1,000 bombers on Cologne).

1943 Beginning of day-time raids by large groups of bombers.

1944 Raids on the Roum. oil region of Ploeşti (from Apr.), the Ger. hydroelectric plants (beginning in May) and the transport network. The pop. was not demoralized, and up to the middle of 1944 the armament industry was not decisively damaged. The climax of the Allied war in the air was the

1945 terror raid (firestorm) on the city of Dresden (13–14 Feb.), then crowded with fugitives. During the last months of the war, low-flying fighters attacked the civilian pop. and endeavoured to paralyse road traffic.

From mid 1944 the Allies controlled the air over Germany. Owing to the defective planning of Ger. aerial armaments (like the production of a jet-propelled light bomber, the ME 262, rather than a jet-fighter), the lack of petrol and trained crews, the Allies could not be beaten. The **production of the V (Vergeltung = revenge) weapons** was delayed by the R.A.F. raid on the experimental station at Peenemünde (Aug. 1943; the bombardment of Brit. targets (London) by V1 began on 13 Jun. 1944, by V2 on 6 Sep.). The bombardment by V weapons caused haphazard damage and contributed little. (For aerial warfare in the Pacific, see p. 217.)

The Ger. War Economy

No coherently planned and guided economy existed at the beginning of the war. After Stalingrad (p. 207) and the proclamation of 'total war' (18 Feb. 1943) by GOEBBELS (pp. 183, 195), the concentration of econ. life was implemented (2 Sep. 1943) under the Ministry of ALBERT SPEER (b. 1905). The productivity index reached its high point between Aug. and Dec. 1944. Shortages of raw materials were overcome because of pre-war planning (Buna, synthetic petrol, the mining of inferior ores, etc.) and by the exploitation of sources of raw materials in the occupied countries. The oil-fields of the Caucasus region were uncaptured (attempted at the end of 1942), the Roum. and Ukr. oil-fields were lost; Germany suffered a shortage of oil throughout the entire war. The indust. potential of the occupied countries was utilized.

Labour for the Ger. war industries, to take the place of the Ger. workers drafted into the armed forces, was provided by the recruitment of approx. 9 mil. for. workers, initially on a volunteer basis, but then increasingly subject to shipment by force (slave labour). After

30 Apr. 1942 all inmates of concentration camps were mobilized (in 1944 there were, besides the major camps, over 400 auxiliary camps).

The campaigns in North Africa and the Balkans, 1941/2

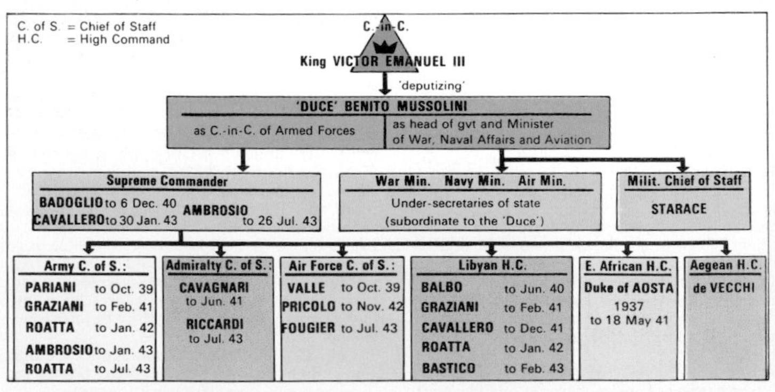

Leadership of the Italian armed forces

The War in N. Africa (1940–42)

1940 Italy declared war on France and Britain (10 Jun.). The Ital. offensive remained stuck on the Fr. Alp. front. The **armistice** did not bring satisfaction of Ital. aspirations (24 Jun.).

Sep. 1940 Ital. offensive from Libya in the direction of Egypt. Britain launched a

Dec. 1940 successful counter-offensive: Cyrenaica was lost (Tobruk and Benghazi were taken, Jan.–Feb. 1941). At Italy's request, the 10th Ger. Air Corps was transferred to Sicily (to serve in the fighting against Malta). Following talks between HITLER and MUSSOLINI (Jan. 1941), the **'Ger. Afrikakorps'** was est. (commanded by General ERWIN ROMMEL, 1891–1944 (suicide)).

1941 Reconquest of Cyrenaica (Mar./Apr.), exc. for Tobruk.

1942 Renewed Ger.-Ital. offensive: the Axis Powers took Benghazi (29 Jan.) and El Gazala (7 Feb.); Tobruk capitulated. Following the crossing of the Egypt. border (Mersa Matruh, 28 Jun.), the offensive stuck at El Alamein owing to shortages of supplies (30 Jun.).

Malta: the planned 'Operation Hercules' (Apr. 1942) was abandoned, although preparatory Ger. air-raids had been carried out on the island.

Oct. 1942 Counter-offensive by the British **8th Army** (under command of General MONTGOMERY led on 4 Nov. to the decisive Allied victory against ROMMEL's forces at **El Alamein**. The Axis Powers lost Cyrenaica.

Abyssinia: following the conquest of Brit. and Fr. Somaliland by Ital. troops, the British launched a counter-offensive: Ital. and Brit. Somaliland and Eritrea were lost (1941). Addis Ababa was taken (6 Apr.) and the Ital. forces capitulated (16 May 1941). Emperor HAILE SELASSIE I returned (p. 179).

The War in the Balkans (1940–41)

Personal (MUSSOLINI's prestige), historical (the failed occupation of Corfu, p. 159) and power-polit. motives (prevention of Nat. Socialist domination of the Balkans) led to the launching, from Albania, of the

1940 Ital. campaign against Greece (28 Oct.). In a counter-offensive, the Greeks occupied one third of Albania, and the Ital. fleet, attacked by Brit. carrier aircraft at Taranto, was weakened (11/12 Nov.). In consequence of Brit. guarantees (p. 165), Brit. milit. bases were est. on Crete; later on, Brit. forces (approx. 70,000 men) landed in Piraeus and Volos (from Mar. 1941).

Ger. Balk. policy: disregarding Balk. claims by the U.S.S.R. (p. 207), Germany broadened her sphere of infl. Balk. states joined the 3-Power Pact (1940, p. 197): Hungary (20 Nov.); Roumania (23 Nov.); it lost N. Bukovina and Bessarabia to the U.S.S.R. (28 Jun.), Northern Transylvania to Hungary, Southern Dobruja to Bulgaria (2nd Arbitration Award of Vienna, 30 Aug.); ION ANTONESCU, 1882–1946 (executed) became head of state (4 Sep.)); Slovakia (24 Nov.); Bulgaria (1 Mar. 1941); Yugoslavia (25 Mar. 1941). The Belgrade *coup d'état* (27 Mar. 1941) and the conclusion of a Treaty of Friendship of the new Yugoslav gvt with the U.S.S.R. (5 Apr. 1941) caused the broadening of the planned Balk. campaign. Turkey remained neutral.

The Balk. Campaign ('Marita'): because of the danger posed by the developing Allied Balk. front and the threat to the Roum. oil-fields by Brit. air-raids, HITLER decided on an offensive from Bulgaria to the Aegean Sea. Following the rejection of Ger. attempts at mediation by Greece (Feb.) and the transfer of the 12th Ger. Army to Bulgaria (Mar.),

1941 beginning of hostilities (6 Apr.).

Yugoslavia: the war, opened by an air-raid on Belgrade (6 Apr.), ended with the encirclement and capitulation of the Yugoslav army (17 Apr.). Ital., Hung. (11 Apr.) and Bulg. troops invaded Yugoslavia.

Greece: following the breakthrough of the Metaxas Line, the capture of Thessaloniki (9 Apr.) and the advance across the Pindus mts. the Gk campaign, coinciding with the attack on Yugoslavia, was concluded by the capitulation at Thessaloniki (21 Apr., formally repeated – on the urging of MUSSOLINI, to include the Italians – on 23 Apr.). After the breakthrough of the Brit. rearguard position at the Thermopylae Pass (24 Apr.), embarkation of the Brit. troops (by 30 Apr.). Occupation of Athens (27 Apr.), the Peloponnesus and the Gk islands (by 11 May) by Ger. forces.

20 May–1 Jun. 1941 Successful Ger. airborne occupation of Crete ('Merkur').

Consequences of the Balk. Campaign: Britain was shut off from the Continent, the Ger. SE. flank was secured in preparation for the attack on the U.S.S.R., the Roum. oil-fields were safeguarded.

'The New Order' in the Balkans – Yugoslavia: flight of King PETER II [1934–41]. Formation of gvt in exile in London. Establishment of a Ger. milit. gvt in **Serbia** and a puppet régime. Lower Styria and parts of Carinthia were annexed by Germany. Ljubljana (Laibach), the Dalmatian coastal region and Montenegro (officially 'ind.') came to Italy, the Drava 'corner' and Bačka to Hungary. Western Macedonia to Bulgaria. **Croatia** (the Ital. Duke AIMONE of Spoleto became king): Croatia became an ind. state, ruled by an authoritarian gvt (10 Apr. 1941) under the 'Poglavnik' ANTE PAVELIĆ (1889–1959), who based his power on the Fascist *'Ustaša'* movement.

Greece: establishment of a Ger., by mid 1941 of an Ital., milit. admin. (with Ger. reservations). Flight of King GEORGE II [1922–4, 1935–47] to London and establishment of a Gk gvt in exile.

Consequences: dissipation of Ger. forces in a multi-front war, strong engagement in the Mediterranean, postponement of the campaign against the U.S.S.R.

The Near East: for fear of further advances by the Axis Powers, the pro-Axis uprising of RASHID ALI EL-GAILANI in Iraq (May 1941) was beaten down and Britain occupied Syria, the Lebanon and Iran (p. 168): the Suez Canal remained secure.

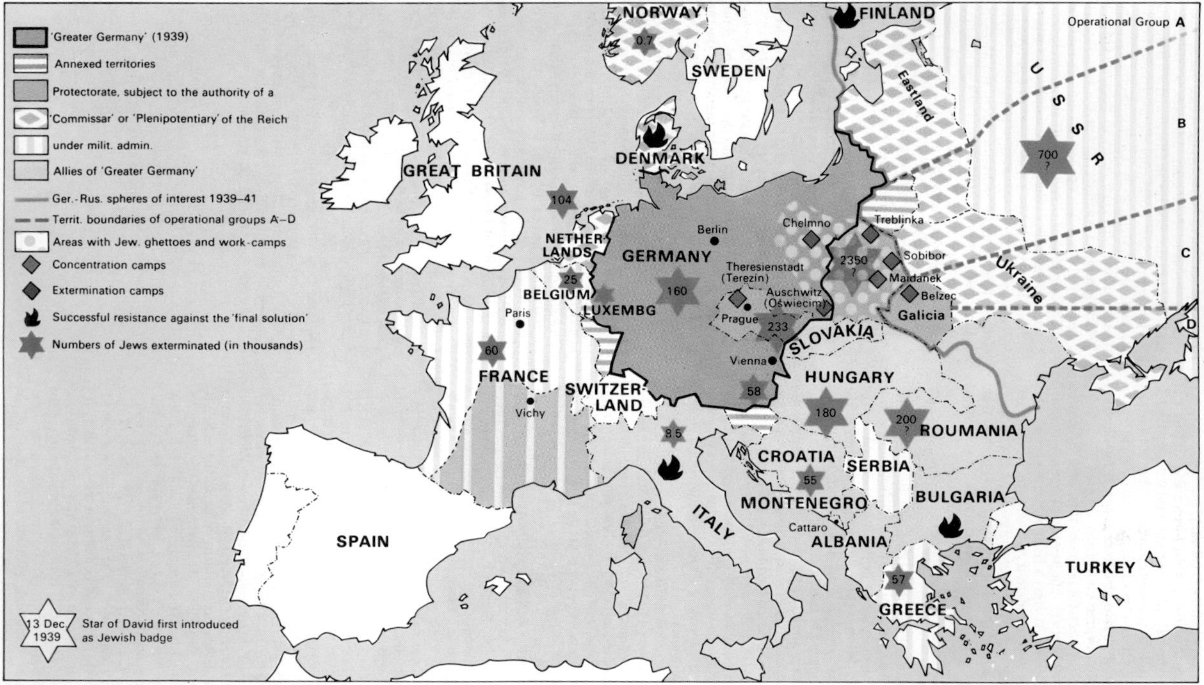
'Greater Germany' (1939)
Annexed territories
Protectorate, subject to the authority of a
'Commissar' or 'Plenipotentiary' of the Reich
under milit. admin.
Allies of 'Greater Germany'
Ger.-Rus. spheres of interest 1939–41
Territ. boundaries of operational groups A–D
Areas with Jew. ghettoes and work-camps
Concentration camps
Extermination camps
Successful resistance against the 'final solution'
Numbers of Jews exterminated (in thousands)
13 Dec 1939
Star of David first introduced as Jewish badge
Operational Group A
B
C
D
U S S R
700 ?
NORWAY
0.7
FINLAND
SWEDEN
Eastland
DENMARK
GREAT BRITAIN
104
NETHER-LANDS
BELGIUM
25
LUXEMBG
Paris
60
FRANCE
Vichy
SWITZER-LAND
GERMANY
160
Berlin
Chelmno
Treblinka
Sobibor
Maidanek
Belzec
2350 ?
Galicia
Ukraine
Theresienstadt (Terezin)
Auschwitz (Oświecim)
Prague
233
SLOVAKIA
Vienna
58
HUNGARY
180
ROUMANIA
200 ?
CROATIA
SERBIA
55
MONTENEGRO
BULGARIA
Cattaro
ALBANIA
8.5
ITALY
GREECE
57
TURKEY
SPAIN

The extermination of the Jews (the 'Final Solution'), 1939–44

The 'Jewish Question' and the 'Final Solution'

The basis for the racial policies of the **3rd Reich** was the **race ideology** (glorification of the 'Aryan', defamation of the 'subhuman jew'), the **desire to find a scapegoat to blame for the defeat of 1918** (the 'Jew.-Marxist Nov. criminals'), and **the singling out of an enemy**, a practice without which the totalitarian form of gvt cannot function (the Jew = the incarnation of evil *per se*). The restrained actions after the seizure of power were followed by the

1 Apr. 1933 Day of Boycott. The action was predominantly directed against Jew. businessmen, professors, teachers, students, pupils, lawyers and physicians. The demands specified in HITLER's *Mein Kampf* were realized systematically through the

15 Sep. 1935 Nuremberg Laws: 1. 'The Law of Citizenship': Jews lost legal equality once the pop. had been divided into 'subjects of the state' and 'citizens of the Reich or state'. 2. 'The Law to Protect the Ger. People and Ger. Honour': prohibition of 'racially mixed' marriages and 'extramarital relations between Jews and members of the nat. community of Ger. or kindred blood'. Jews were prohibited from raising the Ger. flag or employing non-Jew. female servants or staff below the age of 45 yrs. During the succeeding years, **13 supplementary decrees** to the 'Citizenship Law' were passed: Jews were excluded from the community of the state. Founded in 1933, the Reich Organization for all people of Jew. descent and Jew. associations, the **'Reich Representation of Ger. Jews'**, led by **Rabbi Dr Leo Baeck** (1873–1946), gave assistance to emigrants and those forced to change their professions, in the foundation of Jew. schools, and in soc. and cult. matters.

1938 High point of Ger. Jew. policy before the 2nd World War. Jew. cult. associations became 'registered associations' (28 Mar.), personal property amounting to more than 5,000 Marks had to be disclosed (26 Apr.), Jew. enterprises were marked (14 Jun.), the licences of all Jew. physicians were cancelled (25 Jul.), first names and surnames were altered (17 Aug.: Jews with non-Jew. first names had to add 'Sarah' and 'Israel' to their first names), Jew. lawyers were deprived of licences to practise law (27 Sep.), the passports of Jews were confiscated (5 Oct., new passports were issued, provided with the suffix 'J'), approx. 17,000 Pol. Jews living in Germany were expelled (28 Oct.). The

7 Nov. 1938 assassination of the 3rd secretary at the Ger. legation in Paris, Ernst von Rath, by HERSCHEL GRYNSPAN, the 17-yr-old son of a deportee, gave rise to

9–10 Nov. 1938 organized pogroms throughout Germany ('Crystal Night', or 'Night of the Broken Glass'): synagogues were set on fire, cemeteries violated, Jew. buildings dest., and approx. 26,000 male Jews arrested. On

12 Nov. 1938 the German Reich cal. for 1,000 mil. Marks in reparations, rest. of the damage done by the mob, repayment of the claims paid by the insurance companies. Jews were 'excluded' from Ger. econ. life ('mandatory Aryanization'), prohibited from visiting cult. sites or using public transport. Higher education was denied to Jews.

The 'Final Solution of the Jewish Question'

1939 Emigration increased because of the worsening of the position of Ger. Jews. Attempts to emigrate often failed, however, because of insufficient support from the potential host countries, the confiscation of Jew. property in Germany and the impossibility of transferring funds. After the outbreak of the war police powers in the occupied territories were in the hands of HIMMLER (p. 195) and his agents (S.S., S.D. 'security service'). **Extermination in Poland** proceeded in 3 stages:

1. **The establishment of ghettoes** (quartering of Jews in ghettoes and work camps), followed by liquidation on the site or transfer to extermination camps (from 1942).
2. **Mass arrests, shootings.**
3. **Searches, pogroms,** aided by local militia.

Extermination of the Jews in **Russia** was carried out by **'Action Groups'** (*Einsatzgruppen*).

31 Jul. 1941 GÖRING directed S.S. Obergruppenführer REINHARD HEYDRICH (1904–42 (assassinated)) to carry out the **'final solution of the Jew. question'**, the biological destruction of the Jews.

20 Jan. 1942 'Wannsee Conference'. The programme was fixed: work service in assigned groups (separation by sex; decimation through forced labour with insufficient nourishment; corresponding 'treatment' of the 'remnant'). Transportation of all Eur. Jews to the E. Jews severely wounded in the war or decorated for milit. service were brought to Theresienstadt.

Between 4,194,200 and 4,851,200 Eur. Jews were slaughtered or perished in the gas chambers of the extermination camps of Auschwitz, Chelmno, Belzec, Sobibor and Treblinka. Most of the powers allied to or friendly with Germany cooperated in the extermination of the Jews by antisemitic legislation. Successful resistance was put up by Finland, Italy, Bulgaria and Denmark.

'The Extermination of Unfit Life'

14 Jul. 1933 Introduction of a law to 'prevent coming generations from suffering from hered. diseases' (sterilization of carriers of certain hered. diseases). The **'Euthanasia programme'**, carried out during the war, was the final consequence of the law; it 'made merciful death possible for those suffering from incurable disease' (Oct. 1939). The execution of this arbitrary criminal action (killing 70,000 people by Aug. 1941) was also guided – apart from criteria based on the symptoms of disease – by the patient's 'capacity to work' and his 'race'.

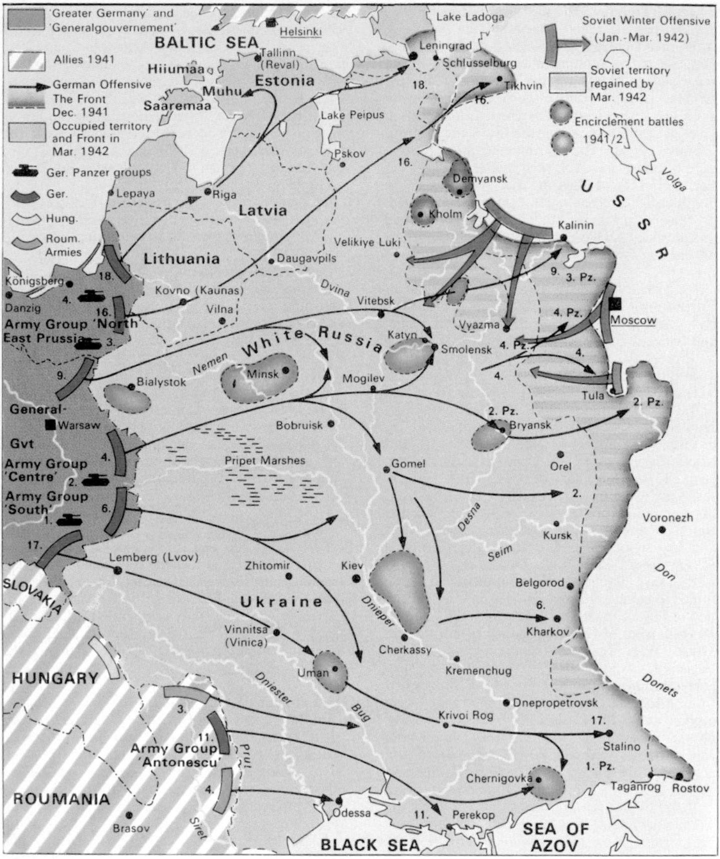

'Operation Barbarossa', 1941/2

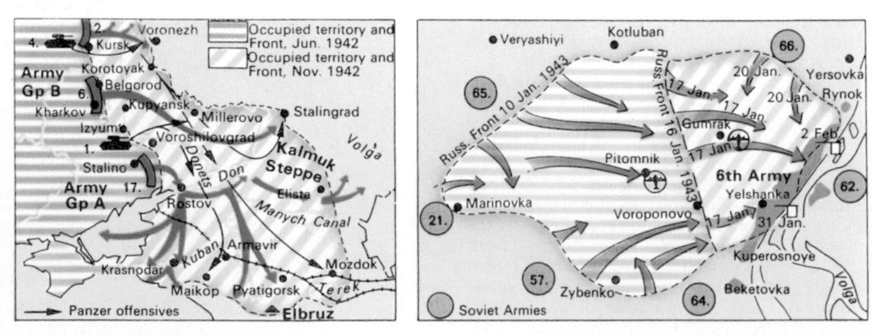

German summer offensive, 1942

Battle of Stalingrad, 1942/3

The War in Russia (1941–2)
To persuade the U.S.S.R. to join the 3-Power Pact, the Ger. for. minister, von Ribbentrop proposed – on the occasion of Molotov's visit to Berlin (Nov. 1940) – the partition of the Brit. Empire (Persia and India to become part of the Soviet sphere of infl.). Hitler disregarded the Rus. response to Ribbentrop's proposal, which, in a formal note, called for the inclusion of Finland, Bulgaria and Turkey in the Soviet sphere of interest in exchange for her joining the 3-Power Pact. He linked his aim, to gain 'living-space' in the E., to the plan to defeat Britain; after the subjugation of the U.S.S.R. he planned to defeat Britain by way of Rus. bases in Iran or the Near East. He issued **'Directive 21'** ('Operation Barbarossa', 18 Dec. 1940) to prepare the attack on the U.S.S.R.; meanwhile a Ger.-Soviet econ. agreement was concluded (10 Jan. 1941) and the U.S.S.R. recognized the newly created situation in the Balkans (p. 203, May 1941).

22 Jun. 1941 Ger. invasion of the U.S.S.R. without a declaration of war. Roumania, Italy, Slovakia and Hungary joined the war on the Ger. side, and Finland initiated an 'instalment' of her war against the U.S.S.R.

Defensive measures of the U.S.S.R.–Domestic politics: Stalin (Chairman of the Council of People's Commissars) proclaimed the **'Great Patriotic War'**. A public defence committee was formed to serve as the War Cabinet; it was composed of Stalin as both chairman and People's Commissar for Defence, Molotov, Voroshilov, Beria and Malenkov. All energies were mobilized and the country was defended by invoking the principle of 'scorched earth'; the partisan movement was organized (p. 208); the polit. commissars – who had been done away with after May 1940 – were reintroduced into the armed services; during the b. of Stalingrad, however, the unity of command was restored (see below).

For. policy: the Neutrality Pact with Japan (13 Apr. 1941) protected the U.S.S.R. from a 2-front war. Following the Ger. invasion

1941 a Brit.-Soviet alliance was concl. (12 Jul.), and the U.S.A. offered to provide war materials (30 Jul.). A milit. agreement was concl. between the U.S.S.R. and the Pol. gvt in exile in London (14 Aug.): Pol. P.O.W.s in the U.S.S.R. were to be organized in Pol. milit. formations and the Ger.-Soviet agreements relating to the partition of Poland were revoked. A Treaty of Friendship and Mutual Aid was concluded between the U.S.S.R. and the Pol. gvt in exile (4 Dec.).

The Course of the War
1st phase (to Aug. 1941): in the **N.** the Soviet lines were broken between Lake Peipus and Lake Ilmen; in the **Centre** and the **S.**, following the destruction of strong Soviet forces in the encirclement bs. of Minsk (by 9 Jul.), Orsha-Vitebsk (by 5 Aug.) and Uman (1–7 Aug.), the Desna and Dnieper rivers were reached. Fin. forces advanced to the Svir river and Lake Onega; Murmansk, Kandalakha and the Crimea were not reached.

2nd phase (to Dec. 1941): disregarding the operational conception of the Ger. General Staff, Hitler postponed the attack on Moscow and ordered the conquest of the Donets Basin and a link-up with the Finns in the northern sector. Following the b. of Kiev (21 Aug.–27 Sep.), the Donets Basin and the Crimea (exc. for Sebastopol) were occupied. The assault on Leningrad was broken off.

1941 The b. of Moscow (Oct.–Dec.). Following the twin-bs. of Vyazma–Bryansk, the Germans advanced to the vicinity of Moscow (16 Oct.: the Soviet gvt was transferred to Kuibyshev; Stalin, however, remained in Moscow, where martial law was proclaimed (19 Oct.)). Because of the onset of winter and the total exhaustion of the Ger. troops, forward operations were halted (8 Dec.).

The Soviet Winter Offensive (beginning 5 Dec. 1941) in the **N.** led to the retreat of the Ger. troops behind the Volkhov (Dec.); in the **Centre** the Germans retreated to the line Orel–Rzhev (Jan. 1942) and the Russians were able to break through into the area Vyazma–Smolensk–Vitebsk, encircling Ger. forces at Demyansk (Jan.–Apr.); in the **S.** the Kerch Peninsula was lost and the Ger. lines were broken at Izyum (Jan. 1942). From Jan. to Apr. the Eastern Front was stabilized. Following Hitler's 'no retreat' and 'fanatical resistance' order and the **dismissal of von Brauchitsch, the supreme commander of the army, Hitler's assumption of the supreme command of the army** rendered the milit. leadership impotent.

The Ger. Summer Offensive of 1942: the Kerch Peninsula was taken back (8–15 May); the b. of Kharkov (17–28 May); the conquest of the Crimea was completed with the seizure of Sebastopol (7 Jun.–4 Jul.); beginning in 28 Jun., the Summer Offensive aimed at the seizure of the oil-fields in the Caucasus and the capture of Stalingrad (a centre of the armament industry and transport network). Army Group 'A' advanced to the Elbrus (21 Aug.); but the southern border of Russia was not reached (the route of supplies from the U.S.A. was uninterrupted). The 6th Army and the 4th Panzer Army advanced into the outskirts of Stalingrad (1–15 Sep.) and captured *c.* 90% of the city (16 Sep.–18 Nov.). The Chief of the Ger. General Staff, Colonel-General Halder, was dismissed.

The Rus. Counter-Offensive (from 19 Nov. 1942): following the junction of the two advancing Rus. forces w. of Stalingrad, the Ger. troops were encircled in the city; an attempt to relieve them failed (12 Dec.). Hitler forbade attempts to break out (22–3 Dec.): the Russians demanded the city's capitulation (8 Jan. 1943). Following the Ger. refusal the Russians decided on 'liquidation by force' and ran a wedge between the encircled Ger. forces (25 Jan. 1943).

31 Jan. 1943 Capitulation of the southern contingent under Field Marshall Paulus and on

2 Feb. 1943 of the northern contingent (90,000 P.O.W.s).

The Ger. Resistance Movement

Causes: totalitarian demands of the Nat. Socialist state and consequences of the Nat. Socialist régime (p. 195): abolition of the 'const. state', persecution and extermination of the Jews (p. 205), party terror, 'liquidation' of polit. opponents, destruction of 'life unfit to live' (p. 205), opposition to the churches and HITLER's unrestricted dictatorship, which found its apogee in his assumption of the 'supreme judicial authority' (24 Feb. 1942, minister of justice: OTTO THIERACK; chief judge of the 'People's Court': ROLAND FREISLER); these developments prompted **the formation of active resistance cells** ('the arising of conscience'). **Milit. figures involved**: General LUDWIG BECK, General KARL-HEINRICH VON STÜLPNAGEL, Admiral WILHELM CANARIS, Major-General OSTER, and others; **politicians and diplomats**: CARL-FRIEDRICH GOERDELER, ULRICH VON HASSELL, FRIEDRICH WERNER Count VON DER SCHULENBURG; **Soc. Democrats and trade union figures:** WILHELM LEUSCHNER, JULIUS LEBER; the 'Kreisau Circle'; HELMUTH JAMES Count VON MOLTKE, PETER Count YORK VON WARTENBURG, Fr ALFRED DELP, ADAM VON TROTT ZU SOLZ, THEODOR HAUBACH, ADOLF REICHWEIN; the 'Solf Circle'; the 'White Rose': the brother-and-sister team, HANS and SOPHIE SCHOLL, Prof. HUBER; the 'Red Chapel' ('Rote Kapelle'): H. SCHULZE-BOYSEN, A. HARNACK. **Objectives of the resistance:** elimination of the Hitler régime, rest. of the 'const. state' with freedom of thought, belief, conscience and expression, the inviolability of person and property, 'rest. of honour' and 'punishment of those who violated the law'.

Following several **futile attempts at assassination and revolution** and the taking up of contacts by Ger. resistance groups with the Allies to learn what conditions of treatment Germany might expect following capitulation (which were rejected after the Allied demands of 'unconditional surrender' (p. 209)), the

20 Jul. 1944 assassination attempt by Colonel Claus Count von Stauffenberg in Hitler's H.Q. 'Wolfschanze' failed. The revolt in Berlin and Paris collapsed, the conspirators were hunted down: *c.* 5,000 people were executed, of whom *c.* 180–200 were involved in the 20 Jul. movement (trials before the 'People's Court' chaired by ROLAND FREISLER). Following the assassination attempt, HIMMLER (p. 195) was named commander of the Home Forces (*Ersatzheer*) (20 Jul.); HITLER decreed *'Sippenhaftung'* (1 Aug., 'liability of next of kin'): members of the families of the leading conspirators were also arrested.

Resistance in Occupied Countries

Active resistance movements were formed in **Denmark** ('Denmarks Frihedraad'), **Norway** ('Milorg'), and the **Netherlands** ('Het Verzet'). Nationalist and Com. resistance groups evolved in **Belgium**; in **Greece** (the 'Gk People's Liberation Army' (E.L.A.S.) of the Com. 'Gk Liberation Front' (E.A.M.) dest. the anti-Com. 'Gk Dem. Nat. Army' (E.D.E.S.)); and in **Poland** (the nat. 'Army within the country' ('Armia Krajowa') and the Com. 'People's Guard' (G.L.), later also the 'People's Army' (A.L.)). Establishment of centrally guided partisan formations, carrying on guerrilla warfare and tying down Ger. troops.

Yugoslavia: organization of a nat. resistance movement ('Četniks') in W. Serbia under Colonel DRAŽA MIHAJLOVIĆ and the S. Slav Communists under TITO (p. 231). Negotiations aiming at coordinating their activities failed (Oct. 1941). Each organization fought the other as well as the Germans, the Italians and the 'Ustaša' (p. 203). From autumn 1943, TITO dominated the mt areas of Bosnia, Croatia and Montenegro. Following the formation of a 'Nat. Committee of Free Yugoslavia' (Nov. 1943), the Allies supported only TITO, who had been given sole leadership of the resistance (Sep. 1944) by King PETER (p. 203).

France:

1940 Establishment of a 'Provisional Nat. Committee of the Free French' (18 Jun.) by **General Charles de Gaulle** (p. 246) in London; later (30 Jul. 1943) formation of a Cabinet. Apart from this, there were underground movements (the Resistance, the Maquis) in the occupied N. ('Libération Nord', 'Organization Civile et Militaire') and in the occupied S. ('Combat', 'Libération Sud'); the pro-Com. 'Front National' operated in both zones. Bases to aid fugitives and communications and an underground press were built up.

1941 Foundation of a cen. information and operations bureau in London to serve as a link between the Gaullists and the resistance movements; the troops of the resistance operating in the underground were organized as the 'Forces Françaises de l'Interieur' under the command of General PIERRE KOENIG (1944). Following the

1944 uprising of the resistance groups, the Ger. occupation troops of Paris surrendered (19 Aug.). DE GAULLE entered the cap.

The U.S.S.R.: one consequence of the brutal Ger. occupation policies was the formation of freebooting guerrilla fighters in partisan units; following the establishment of a cen. bureau of the partisan movement under Marshall VOROSHILOV, these were brought under control.

Italy: the resistance groups joined (esp. those in the N.) to form the 'Committee of Nat. Liberation'.

The fight against the partisans (who had directed their efforts against soldiers and officials, supply-lines and collaborators) was intensified by decrees and orders of HITLER (Oct. 1941: shooting of hostages; Dec. 1941: the 'night and fog order': arrests were to be carried out in such fashion that next-of-kin remained uncertain of the fate of arrested relatives) and the brutal methods of the S.S. and S.D.: after the assassination of HEYDRICH (p. 205), the Czech village of Lidice was razed and every adult murdered (10 Jun. 1942); the same fate befell the Fr. village of Oradour-sur-Glane (10 Jun. 1944).

The Cooperation of the Allies (1941–5)

War aims: from the beginning of the war, the U.S.A. supported Britain (p. 187) in Europe. Disregarding the issues (the Near and Middle East) that divided the U.S.S.R. and Britain, the 3 great powers joined (1941) with the aim of bringing down Nazi Germany. The U.S.A. in particular lacked concrete conceptions of the shape of Europe after the war; but the U.S.S.R. had a definite objective: expansion into Cen. Europe. Mistaken notions prevailed in the U.S.A. about STALIN's aims, and the public image of the U.S.S.R. was greatly improved. Britain acted cautiously and remained suspicious in her relations with Russia.

The 'unwritten alliance' between Britain and the U.S.A. brought about the formation of the 'Defence Advisory Commission' (p. 187): the process of re-armament was quickened. Following ROOSEVELT's speech describing the U.S. as the 'arsenal of democracy' (in response to CHURCHILL's account of the situation in the yr 1940 (Dec.)),

1941 proclamation of the '4 Freedoms (p. 187). The Lend-Lease Act became effective (p. 187): from Aug. 1941 deliveries of materials were made to the U.S.S.R. **The U.S.A. abandoned its neutrality**: beginning of Brit.-Amer. milit. staff talks. Ger. and Ital. ships in U.S. ports were confiscated; a base was est. in Greenland; U.S. forces landed in Iceland.

14 Aug. 1941 The 'Atlantic Charter', formulated by CHURCHILL and ROOSEVELT (p. 187) (an elaboration of the '4 Freedoms'): disavowal of any wish for territ. gain, territ. changes to be carried out only in agreement with those involved, the right of self-determination for all peoples, access to essential raw materials through int. trade between all nations, int. cooperation, freedom from fear and want, freedom of the seas, and the renunciation of armed force. These favourable conditions were not to benefit Germany. Following the entry of the U.S. into the war (p. 187), ROOSEVELT and CHURCHILL met at the

1941–2 1st Washington Conference ('Arcadia', 20 Dec.–14 Jan.). Convocation of the 'Allied War Council': a defensive posture in relation to Japan and a landing in N. Africa were decided upon.

1942 Washington Pact (1. Jan.): declaration by the 26 nations at war with the Axis Powers not to conclude any separate armistice. The pact became the nucleus of the United Nations (p. 223). Following the conclusion of the Soviet-Brit. alliance treaty (26 May), the Rus. for. minister, MOLOTOV (p. 189), visiting Washington (May), urged milit. assistance for the U.S.S.R. and cal. for econ. aid. The **2nd Washington Conference** (18–26 Jun.) decided on the establishment of a 2nd front and the intensification of atomic research. **Talks** regarding mutual measures against Germany **were held between Stalin, Churchill and Harriman** (as ROOSEVELT's representative) in Moscow (Aug.). STALIN was informed about a landing in N. Africa ('Operation Torch').

1943 Casablanca Conference (14–24 Jan.): ROOSEVELT and CHURCHILL decided on the landing in Sicily. ROOSEVELT cal. for Germany's 'unconditional surrender'. Principles regarding the systematic bombing of Germany were worked out.

5th Washington Conference ('Trident', 12–25 May): deliberations concerning the invasion of France, the reconquest of Burma, the use of atomic weapons and naval construction. Recognition of Soviet annexations.

Quebec Conference ('Quadrant', 14–24 Aug.) concerning global strategy.

Talks between the Allied for. ministers in Moscow (19–30 Oct.) regarding continued cooperation until vict., the entry of the U.S.S.R. into the war against Japan, the foundation of a supranational organization and general disarmament after the war. Ger. war criminals were to be put on trial, and democracy was to be re-established in Italy and Austria.

1st Cairo Conference (ROOSEVELT, CHURCHILL, CHIANG KAI-SHEK, 22–6 Nov.) concerning the operations against Japan, the independence of Korea and the territories occupied since 1894 or 1914.

Teheran Conference (ROOSEVELT, CHURCHILL, STALIN, 28 Nov.–1 Dec.): the decision was made to invade Northern France and not the Po valley. The Curzon Line (pp. 154f.) was to form the future eastern border of Poland. Poland was to expand westward to the Oder at the expense of Germany.

1944 Dumbarton Oaks Conference (U.S.S.R., U.S.A., Britain, China, 21 Aug.–7 Oct., p. 223): ROOSEVELT withdrew his signature from the **Morgenthau Plan** (partition of Germany and transformation into an agrarian society), which had already been signed. **Moscow meeting** (CHURCHILL, EDEN, STALIN, 9–18 Oct.): fixing of the spheres of interest in the Balkans: Roumania, Bulgaria and Hungary were to be under Rus. infl., Greece under Brit. infl., and Yugoslavia under joint infl.

1945 Yalta Conference (CHURCHILL, ROOSEVELT, STALIN, 4–11 Feb.): **a declaration was made regarding 'liberated Europe'. Poland**: admission of the members of the gvt in exile to the Lublin Committee (the Com. gvt); the western border was to be fixed in a peace treaty, the Curzon Line became Poland's eastern border. **Post-war Ger. policy**: elimination of Nat. Socialism, partition of Germany into occupation zones acc. to the 1st and 2nd protocols of the 'Eur. Advisory Commission', formation of the Allied Control Council (p. 249), dismantling of factories, reparations, territ. cessions. **Yugoslavia**: formation of a coalition gvt (p. 231). **Non-Eur. affairs**: declaration of war against Japan by the U.S.S.R. (within 3 months of the end of the war in Europe) in exchange for concessions (preservation of the status quo in Outer Mongolia, the granting of rights in Inner Mongolia and to Pacific ports, possession of the Kurile Islands and Southern Sakhalin). Agreement was reached on proportions of votes in the Security Council of the U.N. (p. 223).

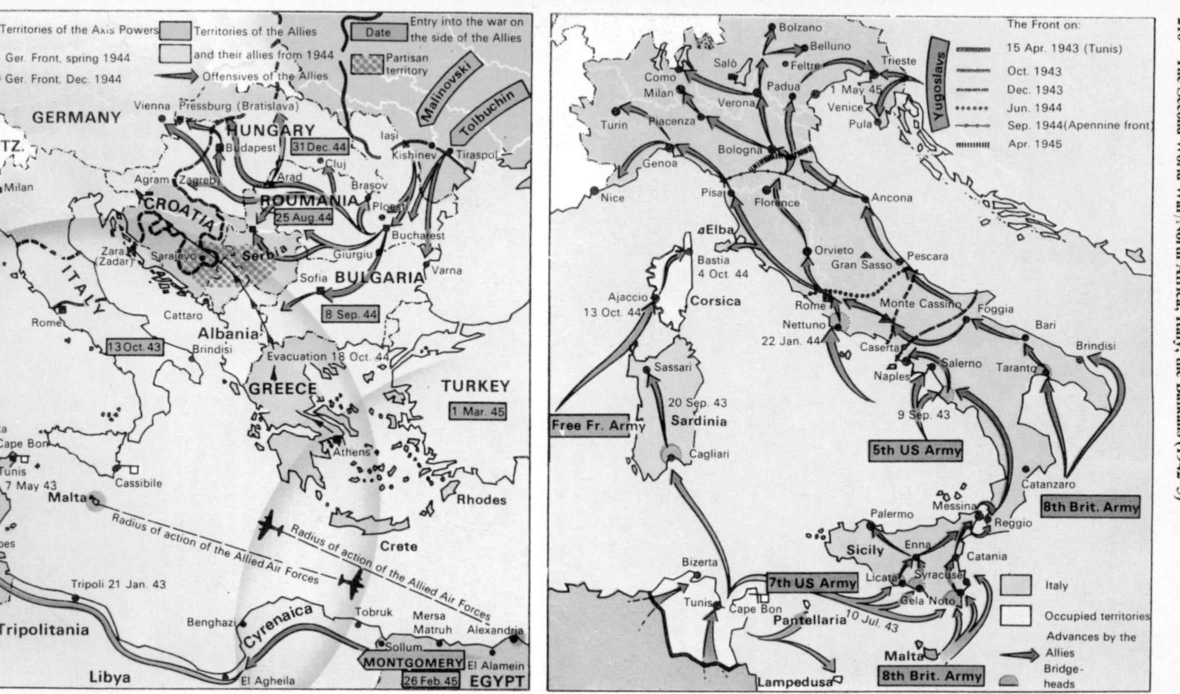

Theatres of war in North Africa and the Balkans, 1943/4

Allied advance in Italy, 1943/5

North Africa

1942 Beginning of the Brit. counter-offensive (Oct., 'Operation Lightfoot') under **Lieutenant-General Bernard L. Montgomery** (1887–1976), leading to the loss of Cyrenaica (Nov.) by the Axis powers. A 2nd Allied front in North Africa was est. through the **landing of Amer.-Brit. forces (Nov., 'Operation Torch',** p. 209) in Morocco and Algeria under **General Eisenhower**.

Milit. and polit. consequences: after initial resistance, the Fr. troops of the Vichy gvt went over to the Allies. Admiral DARLAN concluded an armistice with the Allies (12 Nov. 1942). He formed a gvt, but was assassinated. General GIRAUD became High Commissioner for Fr. Africa. Since a proposed Ger.-Fr. milit. alliance was rejected by the prime minister, LAVAL, Ger. and Ital. forces landed in Tunisia; the rest of France was occupied ('Operation Attila'). The PÉTAIN gvt protested, but was powerless. On 27 Nov. Ger. troops occupied the Fr. naval base of Toulon ('Operation Anton'): self-destruction of the Fr. Fleet.

The Axis defeat in Africa: following the loss of Tripolitania and the defensive operations in the Mareth Line s. of Gabes and in Western Tunisia, the 2-front war was terminated by the

13 May 1943 capitulation of the 'Army Group Africa': 252,000 Ger. and Ital. soldiers became P.O.W.s. N. Africa and the Mediterranean were lost to the Allies, the southern flank opened for the assault on 'Fortress Europe'.

Italy:

1943 Seizure of Sicily by the Allies (10 Jul.–17 Aug.). Following the landing of Brit. troops at Taranto and American forces at Salerno, the Germans retreated to a line that stretched across the peninsula N. of Naples.

The fall of Mussolini: following the talks between MUSSOLINI and HITLER at Feltre (19 Jul. 1943), King VICTOR EMANUEL, at the request of the Fascist Great Council, assumed the supreme command. MUSSOLINI was dismissed from office and arrested (25 Jul.). A gvt without Fascist members was formed (26 Jul.) by Marshal BADOGLIO (1871–1956): the Fascist party was dissolved (28 Jul.). Assurances of loyalty to Germany notwithstanding, secret negotiations with the Allies were begun in Lisbon (3 Aug.). Following the publication of the **armistice agreement** (8 Sep.) by EISENHOWER (signed 3 Sep.), **Ger. counter-measures** began ('Operation Axis'): Rome was occupied and Ital. troops were disarmed, discharged from service, or placed in P.O.W. camps. The BADOGLIO gvt and the royal family fled to the Allies. **Italy declared war on Germany** (13 Oct.). A Ger. surprise *coup* freed MUSSOLINI (12 Sep.). He assumed the leadership of the counter-gvt (formed on 9 Sep.): **foundation of the Repubblica Sociale Italiana** (the Republic of Salò).

1944 Landing of Amer. troops behind the Ger. front at Nettuno. The Germans put up determined resistance at Monte Cassino (15 Feb., destruction of the monastery); their lines were broken by the end of May and they were unable to prevent the occupation of Rome (4 Jun.), Pisa (26 Jul.) and Florence (4 Aug.). The Apennines front (the 'Goth Line') was held against the

1945 Allied offensive (9–14 Apr.): Amer. breakthrough at Bologna (19 Apr.).

28 Apr. 1945 Capitulation of the Ger. forces in Italy (made public on 2 May). **Fleeing to Switzerland, Mussolini was shot en route by partisans.**

The Balkans

Roumania: following the Soviet advance into the Balkans (Aug. 1944), Marshal ANTONESCU (p. 203) was arrested (23 Aug.). The Cabinet of General SANATESCU discontinued the war against the U.S.S.R. and allowed the Ger. troops to withdraw freely. Following the Ger. bombardment of Bucharest, **Roumania declared war on Germany**. The Russians occupied the oil-fields of Ploeşti (30 Aug.) and Bucharest (31 Aug.).

12 Sep. 1944 Moscow armistice.

Bulgaria:

1944 Declaration of war by the U.S.S.R. against Bulgaria (5 Sep.), which up to this point was in a state of war with Britain and the U.S.A. On 8 Sep. **Bulgaria declared war on Germany**. Following the *coup d'état* by the pro-Soviet Bulg. forces removing GEORGIEFF (9 Sep.), the Red Army occupied the country without meeting resistance.

28 Oct. 1944 Moscow armistice.

Greece: on HITLER's orders (25 Aug.) Ger. troops (Army Group 'E') evacuated Greece (completed by 2 Nov. 1944), withdrawing in continuous engagements with partisans and Bulgarians to their new positions (see map). **Civil war between monarchists and Communists broke out in Greece.** Following fruitless mediation attempts in Athens by CHURCHILL and EDEN (25–7 Dec.), King GEORGE appointed Archbp DAMASCINOS of Athens regent (31 Dec. 1945).

Albania: following the evacuation of Ger. troops, Colonel ENVER HOXHA (p. 232) formed a pro-Soviet gvt.

Yugoslavia:

1944 Occupation of Belgrade (18 Oct.) by TITO's (p. 231) partisans, who (from 9 Sep.) had made contact with the Red Army.

Hungary:

After the occupation of Hungary by Ger. troops (19 Mar., 'Operation Margaret'),

1944 a secret armistice was concluded with the U.S.S.R. (11 Oct.). When it was made public (15 Oct.), Admiral HORTHY (p. 157) was, under heavy Ger. pressure, forced to rescind it. HORTHY was taken to Germany and replaced by FERENC SZÁLASI (p. 157). A counter-government under Colonel-General BÉLA MIKLÓS-DÁLNOKI (23 Dec.) **declared war on Germany**.

20 Jan. 1945 Moscow armistice.

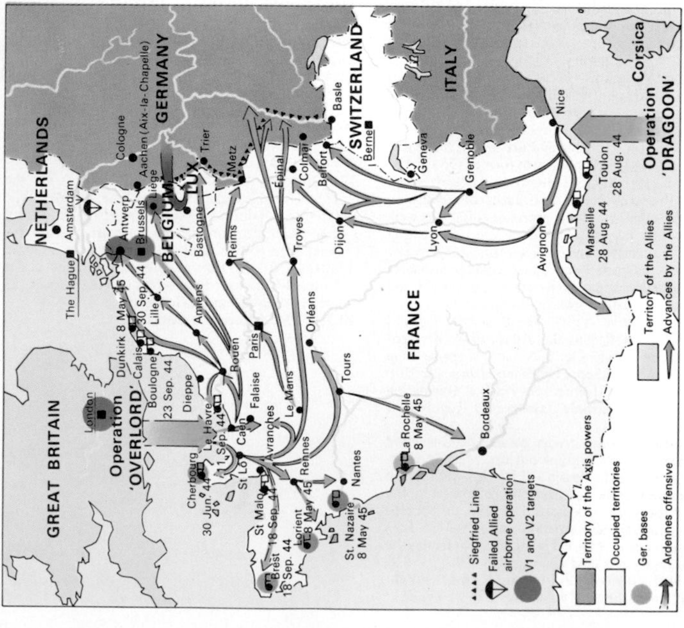

'Greater Germany'
Allies
Soviet border 1940
Soviet offensives
Territories regained by Soviet troops by Mar. 1943
Ger. Front
Mar. 1943
Oct. 1943
Dec. 1943
Apr. 1944
Sep. 1944
Encircled Ger. contingents
Partisan areas

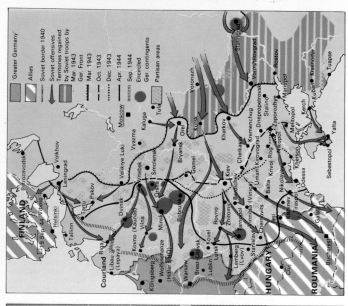

The war in the East, 1943–4

Siegfried Line
Failed Allied airborne operation
V1 and V2 targets
Territory of the Axis powers
Occupied territories
Ger. bases
Ardennes offensive
Territory of the Allies
Advances by the Allies

The Allied invasion of France, 1944

Ger. Rule in the E. (1941–4)

1941 Hitler's decree determining the admin. of the occupied territories in the E., which were placed under the authority of a Ministry of the E. headed by ROSENBERG. The 'Reich protectorates' of 'Ostland' and the Ukraine were est. A rigorous policy of exploitation was pursued.

1942 The 'General Plan for the E.', approved by HIMMLER, provided for the resettlement of 80–85% of the Poles, 65% of the Ukrainians, 75% of the White Russians and 50% of the Czechs in Siberia. **A decree regulating the 'treatment of the inhabitants of enemy countries'** (6 May 1941) and the **'Commissar Order'** (13 May 1941), providing for the liquidation without trial of commissars in Ger. hands, were meant to 'legalize' a conduct of warfare which was in violation of int. law.

Rus. volunteer contingents: almost 1 mil. Rus. volunteers (*'Hiwis'* = willing to help) served the Ger. side. The 'Gen. of the Eastern Troops', ANDREY A. VLASOV (1900–46 (executed)) raised (1943) armed contingents of volunteers.

1944 The Himmler–Vlasov agreement (providing for the establishment of a Rus. Liberation Army) and the Conference founding the Committee to Liberate the Peoples of Russia came too late.

Reactions to the Ger. measures by the U.S.S.R.: a return to tradition roused the energies of nat. resistance: reintroduction of (élite) guard units, STALIN's appointment as 'Marshal', restructuring of the milit. in categories of enlisted men, subordinate officers (non-commissioned), commissioned officers and generals. The election of the Metropolitan SERGIUS as Patriarch **amounted to a truce between party and Church**; this, and the **dissolution of the Comintern**, had a strong impact on for. relations.

1943 The Germans **discovered mass graves at Katyn**, containing the bodies of *c.* 4,000 Pol. officers who had been shot. The Pol. gvt in exile demanded an investigation by the Red Cross. **The U.S.S.R. thereupon cancelled the Pol.-Soviet Agreement of 1941** and est. diplomatic relations with the **Pol. Committee of Nat. Liberation** (the 'Lublin Committee'). **The Nat. Committee 'Free Germany' and the 'League of Ger. Officers' were founded by Ger. Communists and Ger. soldiers and officers who were Rus. P.O.W.s.** BENEŠ concluded a **Treaty of Friendship and Mutual Assistance with the U.S.S.R.** which regulated questions of cooperation after the war and was supplemented by the

1944 agreement relating to the occupation of Czechoslovakia by the Red Army.

The Defence of 'Fortress Europe' (1943–4)

The East: shaken by the Soviet breakthrough, the Southern Front (p. 207) was stabilized after the defensive bs. of the Don and the Mius (Jan.–Mar. 1943). The Ger. Caucasus army retreated to the Ukraine (via Rostov) and to the Kuban bridgehead; it was ordered to evacuate and the withdrawal was complete by 7 Oct.

1943 The last Ger. offensive in the basin of Kursk ('Operation Citadel', 5–13 Jul.) was broken off. The initiative was now with the Soviets, whose superiority became ever more apparent. Ger. forces were senselessly sacrificed because of HITLER's rigid adherence to fronts once est. and to 'fortified positions'. The **Soviet offensives** in the **N.** led to the defence of the Narva region (from 6 Oct.), in the **Centre** to the seizure of Bryansk (17 Sep.), Smolensk (24 Sep.) and Gomel (25 Nov.), and in the **S.** to the loss of the Donets Basin (Sep.) and the breakthrough to the Dnieper – resulting in the isolation of the Crimea (1 Nov.).

1944 Initial advances of the Soviets in the S.: the Southern Ukraine was regained and an advance was made to Galicia (Mar.); the Ger. troops evacuated the Crimea (by May). Defensive bs. were fought in the Baltic countries (Jan.–Apr.). The **Soviet summer offensives** began on 6 Jun.: destruction of 25 divisions of the Army Group 'Centre' (Minsk, 2 Jul.); penetration of the Balk. front; advance into the Vistula region. The **Warsaw uprising** of the Pol. underground army (Aug.–Oct.) failed: the Pol. underground army capitulated; the Army Group 'N.' was encircled and E. Prussia was reached (Oct.). **Finland**: the breakthrough of the front on the Karelian Isthmus (10 Jun.) led to the **Moscow Armistice** (19 Sep.). The Ger. Lapland army retreated to northern Norway.

The West:

Northern France: to establish the 2nd Front (p. 209), which had also been cal. for by the U.S.S.R., the **Western Allies** staged the

6 Jun. 1944 invasion of Northern France ('Operation Overlord') between Cherbourg and Caen under command of General EISENHOWER. They obtained the Cotentin Peninsula (14 Jun.), took Cherbourg (30 Jun.), Caen (9 Jul.) and St-Lô (18 Jul.), and broke through the Ger. positions at Avranches (25 Jul.): transition to mobile warfare. The destruction of the Ger. Panzer units in the 'hell of Falaise' (16 Aug.) opened the road to Paris, where an uprising of the resistance movement broke out (19 Aug.). The Ger. troops capitulated and Gen. DE GAULLE entered Paris (25 Aug.). The Allies reached the Ger. border between Trier and Aachen and the southern border of the Netherlands in Sep./Oct.

Southern France:

15 Aug. 1944 Landing of Allied troops in southern France ('Operation Dragoon'). The Americans reached the Swiss border via Grenoble (23 Aug.). Fr. troops captured Toulon and Marseille. Advances were made to the N., and Metz, Belfort, Mulhouse and Strasbourg were taken (Nov.): the Americans broke into the Siegfried Line (3 Dec.).

The Ger. Ardennes offensive ('b. of the Bulge'), **beginning 16 Dec.** and aiming at Antwerp, failed because of Allied counter-attacks.

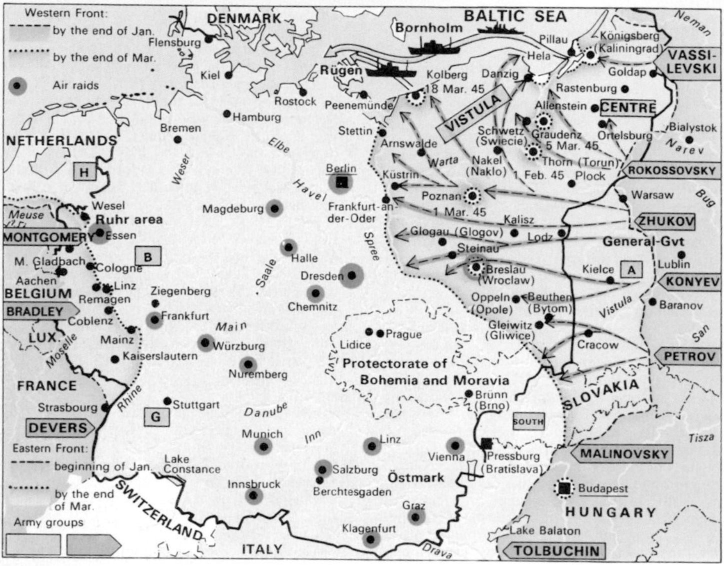

Collapse of the German Eastern Front, Jan.–Mar. 1945

End of 'Greater Germany', May 1945

Germany's Last-Ditch Stand

1944 Draft of all men able to bear arms, from the ages of 16 to 60, to serve in the *Volkssturm* ('People's storm', 25 Sep.);

1945 reduction of the rations of foodstuffs; draft of those b. in 1929 (5 Mar.).

19 Mar. HITLER ordered the destruction of all installations serving milit. purposes, transport, communication, industry and supply (the 'Nero Decree') and the defence of Ger. cities (under threat of the death penalty for those disobeying his orders).

The establishment of special courts martial was intended to drive the troops to the most extreme, reckless resistance. The news announcing the existence of a *'Werewolf'* organization, which was to continue resistance behind the enemy lines, prompted Allied defensive measures.

The Conquest of Eastern Germany

12 Jan. Beginning of the major Soviet offensive from the Baranov bridgehead, demolishing the Ger. front of the Centre sector; the Pol. territories that had remained under occupation were lost, as was Upper Silesia with its undamaged indust. area and Lower Silesia E. of the Oder. E. Prussia was cut off.

26 Feb. Breakthrough of the Soviets from Bromberg to the Baltic at Kolberg (18 Mar.), to the Lagoon of Stettin and the Bay of Danzig (30 Mar.). Enduring incredible difficulties (sub-zero temperatures), the Ger. pop. attempted to escape the violence of the aroused Rus. soldiers by fleeing to the W. Actions of the navy and defensive engagements by Ger. troops made the rescue of many civilians and wounded soldiers possible. Proclaimed 'fortresses', the cities of Thorn, Posen, Graudenz, Königsberg, Breslau and others had to be defended.

16 Apr. Beginning of a major Soviet offensive advancing from the Oder and Neisse rivers. The leading Soviet columns joined at Nauen and encircled Berlin (24 Apr.).

25 Apr. Meeting of Amer. and Soviet troops at Torgau on the Elbe river.

2 May Capitulation of Berlin.

Soviet attacks in Courland were repulsed until the day of capitulation.

The SE.: following the seizure of Budapest (13 Feb.), the Soviets advanced to Vienna, which fell after street fighting (13 Apr.), and met with Amer. and Brit. units on the Enns and in Styria. The advance of the Red Army from Pressburg to Prague led to the

5 May Czech uprising against the Ger. occupation in Prague.

20 Mar. Offensive by TITO's partisans against the Ger. troops (p. 211).

The Conquest of the W.

Following the Allied counter-offensive in the Ardennes (3 Jan.) and the junction of Amer. and Brit. troops at Houffalize (16 Jan.), the territories on the left bank of the Rhine were lost by the Germans (Feb.) and the Americans est. a bridgehead at Remagen (7 Mar.). With that **the Ger. front in the W. collapsed.**

The North: the British crossed the Rhine at Wesel (24 Mar.) and advanced into Emsland (cutting off the Ger. troops stationed in 'Fortress Holland') and through Westphalia to the Elbe (19 Apr.), Holstein and Mecklenburg (2 May).

The Centre: following the encirclement of 21 Ger. divisions in the Ruhr area and their capitulation (after their pocket of resistance had been split), the Americans reached the Elbe (see above).

The South: the Americans advanced from Mainz to the Erzgebirge and the line of demarcation agreed on with the Russians, which ran Karlsbad–Budweis–Linz. The 7th U.S. Army advanced with its left flank into the Salzkammergut; its right flank advanced to the Brenner Pass, where it encountered Amer. troops coming from Italy (4 May). The French crossed the Rhine N. of Karlsruhe (1 Apr.) and at Strasbourg (15 Apr.) and advanced to Voralberg.

Total Defeat

HITLER, who had returned to the bunker in the Chancellery in Berlin (16 Jan.), decided to remain there (21 Apr.). **Contacts with the Allies** to terminate the war were sought by HIMMLER and GÖRING; HIMMLER, unknown to HITLER, offered the Western Powers partial capitulation (23 Apr.), through the mediation of the Swed. Count BERNADOTTE, which was rejected; the offer was announced over the radio nevertheless (28 Apr.). GÖRING inquired of HITLER whether he should assume the leadership of the Reich (23 Apr.). In drawing up his polit. testament, HITLER had GÖRING and HIMMLER expelled from the party and their offices; **Grand Admiral Karl Dönitz (b. 1891) was appointed president of the Reich and c.-in-c. of the armed forces; Goebbels was made chancellor.**

30 Apr. 1945 Hitler committed suicide.

2 May Dönitz called on the minister of finance, Count SCHWERIN VON KROSIGK, to form a **'provis. caretaker gvt'** (it resided in Plön, from 3 May in Mürwick nr Flensburg). The N.S.D.A.P. was dissolved, HIMMLER was removed from all his offices (5 May). Following the capitulation of Berlin, of the army in Italy (p. 211), and of Army Group SW. (4 May),

4 May capitulation of the Ger. forces in Holland, NW. Germany, Denmark and Norway was signed by General-Admiral VON FRIEDEBURG in MONTGOMERY's H.Q. in Lüneburg.

7 May Signature of 'unconditional surrender' of the Ger. armed forces by Colonel-General JODL in EISENHOWER's H.Q. in Reims.

8 May Repetition of the act of capitulation in the Soviet H.Q. in Berlin-Karlshorst in the presence of Marshal ZHUKOV by Field-Marshal KEITEL, General-Admiral VON FRIEDEBURG, and Colonel-General STUMPFF. The capitulation of all forces became effective on 9 May.

23 May Dismissal and arrest of the Dönitz gvt.

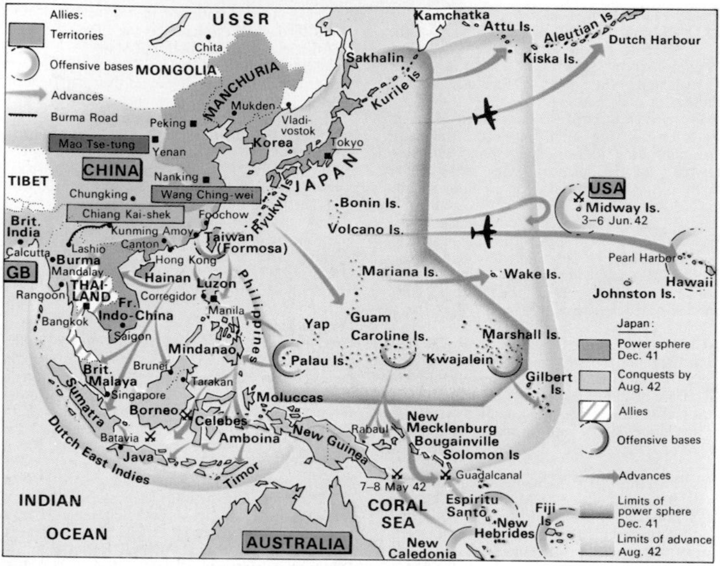

Japanese offensive operations, 1941/2

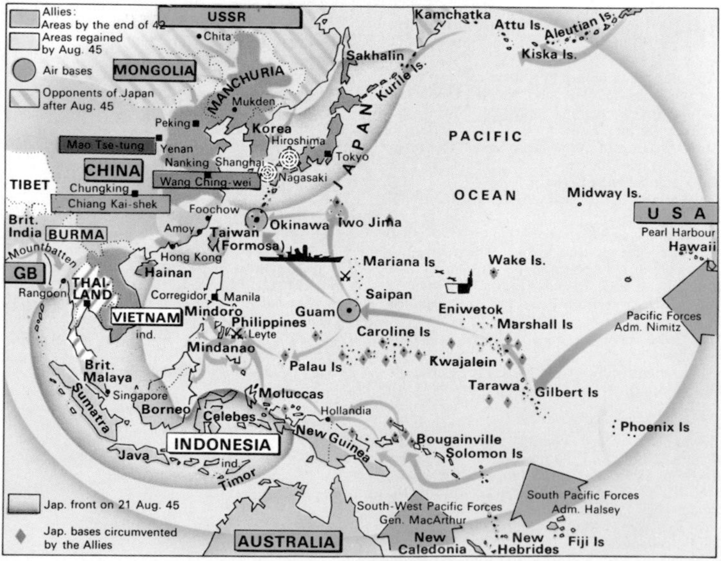

Allied counter-offensives from 1942

Jap. Expansion (1941–2)
Polit. backing for their 'New Order' in the Pacific (p. 175) was provided for the Japanese through the Anti-Comintern Pact, the 3-Power Pact (p. 197)–intended to prevent the intervention of the U.S.A. in the war–and the Pact with the U.S.S.R. (p. 175). Following the establishment of the Nanking gvt (p. 173), Japan turned to the s. The Allies were unable to prevent the blocking of the Burma Road (1940). The northern part of Indo-China was occupied (Sep. 1940).
Consequences: CHIANG KAI-SHEK's China was isolated and the sources of raw materials in Malaya and Indonesia were threatened.
The U.S.A. reacted to Jap. expansion by 'imposing quarantine' (p. 187) and cancelling the trade agreement (p. 175). An embargo on oil and scrap metals weakened the Jap. armament industry and Jap. accounts were blocked by the U.S.A., Britain and the Dutch E. Indies. Jap.-Amer. negotiations (the U.S.A. calling for Jap. withdrawal from China and Indo-China) failed.
1941 Attack on Pearl Harbor (p. 187): the Amer. Pacific Fleet was paralysed, but docks and shipyards were not dest. Three Amer. aircraft carriers escaped destruction because they were at sea. The U.S.A. and Britain declared war on Japan (8 Dec., p. 187); Germany and Italy declared war on the U.S.A. (11 Dec.).
1941–2 Jap. offensives (simultaneous advances in 3 directions). The **main thrust** ('Operation South') in the Centre was directed against the Philippines and the Dutch E. Indies (with the aim of attaining econ. autarchy).
1942 Seizure of the Philippines (for MACARTHUR, see p. 237): the occupation of the Philippines was completed with Jap. landings on Luzon and Mindanao and the taking of Manila (2 Jan.) and the capitulation of the island fortress of Corregidor (6 May).
The **struggle for the Dutch E. Indies** (11 Jan.–8 Mar.): occupation of Celebes, Borneo and Amboina (Jan.). The Japanese landed on the coast of Sumatra. Following Jap. naval victs. in the Macassar Strait (24–7 Jan.), Timor (threatening Australia), Java and the Sunda Islands were occupied (27 Feb.–1 Mar.) and the Dutch capitulated (8 Mar.).
The right flank of the main Jap. thrust was located on the continent of Asia. Following the
1941 sinking of the Brit. battleships *Prince of Wales* and *Repulse* (12 Dec.), Japan concluded an alliance with Thailand. The Brit. bases of Hongkong (25 Dec.) and Singapore (15 Feb. 1942) fell; Burma was occupied (cutting off Nationalist China from Allied supplies, Apr. 1942). **India was threatened.** A Nat. Ind. Army, commanded by the former president of the Nat. Congress, SUBHAS CHANDRA BOSE (p. 169), was raised in Burma.
The left flank of the Jap. main thrust was sustained by 'multiple advances radiating into Oceania'. Guam and Wake were taken (10 and 20 Dec. 1941), the Bismarck Archipelago, New Guinea and the Solomon Islands were attacked (Jan.–Mar. 1942), and a landing was carried out in the Aleutian Islands (Jun. 1942). The **conquest of this gigantic area** within the span of 6 months was made possible by the masterful coordination of the Jap. army, navy and air force and the utilization of tactical surprise.
Econ. and polit. consequences: by 1942 Japan dominated territories with a pop. of *c.* 450 mil. and ample riches of natural resources (95% of the world production of raw rubber, 90% of quinine, 70% each of tin and rice). There were sufficient oil resources and important ores (bauxite, chromium ore and others). The Japanese supported the nationalist movements directed against the Eur. colon. powers (formation of a pro-Jap. gvt in the Philippines, recognition of the independence of Burma (1943), Vietnam and Indonesia.

The Allied Offensive (1942–5)
1942 The b. of the Coral Sea: termination of Jap. advance to the S. (7–8 May). **The naval b. of the Midway Islands** (3–7 Jun., weakening the Jap. navy through the loss of 4 aircraft carriers) and the **Amer. landing on Guadalcanal** (7 Aug.) signified the beginning of the Amer.-Aust. counter-offensive. The island was taken after months of fighting (8 Feb. 1943).
1943 Major Allied offensive in the SW. Pacific ('island-hopping': C.-in-C. General MACARTHUR). Landings in New Georgia (1 Jul.), Vella-Lavella (15 Aug.), New Guinea (4 Sep.), Bougainville (1 Nov.) and New Britain (15 Dec.). Rabaul was rendered useless (Jap. naval forces withdrew from there in Mar. 1944).
1944 Advance of Amer. forces in the Cen. Pacific (under command of Admiral NIMITZ), following the regaining of the Aleutians (May–Aug. 1943): occupation of the Gilbert and Marshall Islands (Nov. 1943–Mar. 1944), the Marianas, Saipan and Guam (Jun./Jul.). Following the joining of forces with those of MACARTHUR and the naval b. of Leyte Gulf (Oct.),
1944–5 the Philippines were retaken (Oct.–Feb.): Manila (4 Feb.) and all of Luzon (24 Feb.) were occupied.
1944–5 Burma was regained by Brit., Amer. and Chin. troops. Three Jap. armies were dest. and the Burma Road was opened.
1945 Landing of the Americans in Japan (Iwo Jima, 19 Feb.).
The war in the air: the Amer. offensive was supported by Amer. air raids on Jap. cities. Proceeding from Chin. and Pacific air bases and aircraft carriers, the U.S. Air Force bombarded Jap. indust. centres and gained superiority in the air from 1943.
1945 Dropping of the 1st atomic bomb on Hiroshima (6 Aug.; the 2nd atomic bomb was dropped on Nagasaki, 9 Aug. (p. 272)). **Declaration of war on Japan by the U.S.S.R.** (8 Aug.): the Red Army invaded Manchuria and Korea; it occupied the Kurile Islands and Sakhalin.
2 Sep. 1945 Capitulation of Japan.

The Consequences of the War

Human casualties: the greatest war in history–on land, in the air and at sea–also caused the largest number of casualties: acc. to estimates there were approx. **55 mil. dead, 35 mil. wounded and 3 mil. missing persons**. Never before had civilian casualties been so high: air raids took the lives of 1·5 mil, partisan fighting, mass-exterminations (4–5 mil. Jews, p. 205), labour and concentration camps, acts of vengeance, dispossession and flight, deportations and expulsions (p. 221) prob. of another **20–30 mil. civilians**, among them 7 mil. Russians, 5·4 mil. Chinese, 4·2 mil. Poles, 3·8 mil. Germans. In terms of **combatants**, the U.S.S.R. lost 13·6 mil., China 6·4 mil., Germany 4 mil., Japan 1·2 mil. Lesser losses were incurred by the U.S.A. with 259,000 dead and Britain with 326,000.

Costs of the war: the total cost has been figured at $1,500 bil. (U.S.), of which the U.S.A. spent 21%, Britain 20%, Germany 18%, the U.S.S.R. 13%.

Econ. life: war damages were relatively quickly balanced out by general tech. and indust. progress. By 1948 world production and trade had reached the pre-war level and expanded after the Kor. crisis. **Europe** lost its leading position: the destruction of areas of habitation and industry (esp. in Cen. and Eastern Europe) slowed the process of reconstruction. **Western Europe** caught up with the help of Amer. capital (Marshall Plan, p. 245); using measures of econ. liberalization and **integration** (p. 245), it recovered by 1950. Indust. expansion was forced through by strict planning in the **countries of the Eastern Bloc**: heavy industry was given precedence at the expense of agricult. production and the general standard of living. Only after the death of STALIN was a loosening of econ. centralism introduced in the 'New Course' (p. 228), raising the production of consumer goods.

Politics: to secure world peace, the **United Nations Organization** (U.N.O., U.N. (p. 223)) was chartered; however, the unconditional surrender of the defeated had radically altered the polit. situation in the world. Stretching to the borders of the Brit.-Amer. occupation zones, a **Soviet satellite system** developed (p. 231); the borders of **Poland** were moved westward (p. 232), the **Ger. question** remained unsolved. Despite its immense losses, **the U.S.S.R.**, freed in the W. of Ger., in the E. of Jap. pressure, rose to the rank of world power (p. 227). Com. successes (China, p. 235) seemed to confirm LENIN's teaching of their own superiority and the inevitability of conflict between Communism and capitalism. Soviet self-confidence and power consciousness sought absolute leadership in the Eastern Bloc and the world. The **U.S.A.**, placed to lead the W. less by its own aspirations than by the lack of any alternative power, lacked a clear programme. Only gradually–and simultaneously with the waning of its own sense of security (among other things, the loss of the monopoly of atomic energy, p. 272)–did America became aware of the dangers on the int. polit. horizon. The **East–West conflict**, carried out in terms of power politics and ideology as the **'Cold War'** between Eastern Bolshevism and Western ideals of freedom, manifested itself in the politics of prestige and propaganda, rearmament, supranational alliances (p. 239), tech. and econ. rivalry (space exploration, p. 272; aid to developing nations, p. 261), and crises in divided nations (p. 237). The E.–W. split encouraged the feeling of polit. self-confidence and the aspirations for independence of the **peoples of the 3rd World** (p. 261). Newly established states (Israel, p. 259; the Congo, p. 269) intensified the gen. crisis situation. The solidarity of the economically underdeveloped **(uncommitted) nations** presented new problems in int. affairs. The **necessity for coexistence** under the **'balance of fear'** (p. 272) seemed to initiate a **lessening of tensions** between the world powers, accompanied by tendencies towards polit. decentralization (polycentrism) in the Western camp (the NATO crisis, p. 239), in the Eastern camp (the Moscow–Peking conflict, p. 235; Titoism, p. 231f.) and among the neutral powers (breakdown of the policies of solidarity).

Peace treaties: to prepare them, the Potsdam Conference (p. 249) decided on the convocation of a **council of for. ministers** in London, with Fr. and Chin. participation. The

1945 2nd (Moscow) Conference of For. Ministers agreed, among other things, on the withdrawal of Soviet and Amer. troops from China and the polit. reorganization of Japan and Korea. It invited all Allied states to be represented at the

1946 Paris Peace Conference (Jul.–Oct.). Following the 3rd Conference of For. Ministers in New York (Nov.–Dec.), the

1947 Paris Peace Treaties were concluded (Feb.). **Finland** lost Karelia (p. 231); **Italy** was obliged to pay reparations and lost her colonies and Trieste; **Hungary** was cut back to the borders of 1937; Roumania had to cede Bessarabia and Bukovina; **Bulgaria** incurred no territ. losses. **Trieste** became a Free State under U.N. supervision (p. 231). **Japan** was demilitarized and democratic reforms were introduced under the Amer. milit. admin. (General MACARTHUR, p. 237). The Com. seizure of power in China hastened the conclusion of the

1951 Peace of San Francisco with Japan (signed by 49 states, but not by the U.S.S.R. and India): the Jap. borders were fixed in accordance with the status of possessions in the yr 1854.

Austria: the question of a treaty was vainly discussed at int. conferences, until Chancellor RAAB (p. 243) was able to bring about the

1955 conclusion of the Aust. State Treaty.

The Soviet-Jap. state-of-war was terminated by the

1956 Moscow Declaration (Prime Minister HATOYAMA and BULGANIN).

The Ger. Question after 1945

A basic problem of int. affairs, the **Ger. question** (division of the country, its reunification, polit. status, borders) mirrored the E.–W. conflict. In the

1945 Potsdam Agreement (p. 249) the 3 occupying powers committed themselves to concluding a peace treaty with the whole of Germany; however, the agreement lacked specific instructions regarding the Ger. right of self-determination. Agreement on Germany could not be reached at the

1947 (4th) Conference of For. Ministers in Moscow which followed the Paris Peace Treaties; the Truman Doctrine (p. 241) and the Marshall Plan (p. 245) increased existing tensions. The (5th) Conference of For. Ministers in London (Nov.–Dec.) postponed a settlement of the Ger. question; the (*continues*)

1948 London 6-Power Conference (p. 249) therefore decided to tie the western zones of Germany economically to Western Europe. The Eastern Bloc, formed in the meantime (p. 231), objected at the Warsaw Conference of For. Ministers (Jun.). During the Berlin Blockade (p. 253), the **Western Powers**, meeting at the

1949 Washington Conference of For. Ministers (Apr.) signed the occupation statute for W. Germany. At the (6th) Conference of For. Ministers at Paris the West rejected a proposal for a cen. gvt formed without free elections (proposed by VISHINSKY as Rus. for. minister). The division of Germany was intensified. New considerations of the w. resulting from the

1950 London 3-Power Conference were made obsolete by the **Kor. Crisis** (p. 237). The New York Conference of For. Ministers (Sep.) decided on the defence of the Free World, guaranteeing the Fed. Republic of Germany and w. Berlin, Ger. rearmament and the exclusive right of polit. representation of the Fed. Republic of Germany for all Germany. The development of NATO was accelerated.

1951 Washington Conference of For. Ministers (Sep.): formation of a Eur. army under participation of the Fed. Republic of Germany. Soviet notes relating to a peace treaty did not prevent the conclusion of the

1952 Germany and Eur. Defence Community Treaty (E.D.C.) (May, p. 251) with the Fed. Republic of Germany. Following the death of STALIN, the

1954 (7th) Conference of For. Ministers in Berlin (Jan.–Feb.) again failed over the question of gen. elections (**Eden plan**: elections to an all-Ger. nat. assembly, to be followed by the drafting of a constitution, the formation of a gvt and the conclusion of the peace treaty; **Molotov plan**: a peace treaty with delegates from the Fed. Republic of Germany and the Ger. Dem. Republic, thereafter general elections). The sovereignty of the Ger. Dem. Republic was extended (Mar.). Following the Fr. rejection of the E.D.C., the Fed. Republic of Germany joined the **W.E.U.** (Western Eur. Union) **and NATO** in the

Oct. 1954 Paris Treaties (p. 251). The Moscow Conference of the Eastern Bloc (Nov.–Dec.) thereupon declared reunification to be impossible. Although the signing of the

1955 Warsaw Pact (p. 239) seemed to indicate otherwise, the conclusion of the Aust. State Treaty (p. 218) gave rise to new hopes for the easing of tensions. Convoked in a spirit of reconciliation, the

Jul. 1955 Geneva Summit Conference (EISENHOWER, EDEN, FAURE, BULGANIN) emphasized the responsibility of the 4 Powers and gave **directives** to the for. ministers to continue deliberations on the questions of Eur. security and Germany. The

Oct.–Nov. 1955 (8th) Conference of For. Ministers at Geneva yielded no results as **For. Minister Molotov** subordinated the Ger. question to the problem of Eur. security, whereas the U.S. secretary of state, **Dulles**, referring to the Geneva directives, insisted on considering both questions jointly. Subs. the U.S.S.R. hardened its position on the

2-State Theory (reunification only through an understanding between the 2 Ger. states, without alteration of the Socialist achievements of the Ger. Dem. Republic), first espoused by **Khrushchev** in E. Berlin (Jul.). The Hung. crisis (p. 233) revealed the Rus. campaign of easing tensions as a tactical manoeuvre; the w. also suffered a severe defeat during the Suez crisis (p. 257).

1958 The Berlin Ultimatum (Nov., p. 253): KHRUSHCHEV cancelled the 4-Power Statute and called for a demilitarized **'Free City of W. Berlin'**. The Western Powers, NATO and the Fed. Republic of Germany rejected the

3-State Theory and demanded the observation of int. agreements; however, they declared their readiness to negotiate. A

1959 Soviet draft for a peace treaty (Jan.) cal., among other things, for neutralization, recognition of the Oder–Neisse Line and a 'free city of w. Berlin'. KHRUSHCHEV extended the deadline for the settlement of the Berlin question (Mar.), but threatened a separate peace with the Ger. Dem. Republic in the event of a Western rejection of the draft. With the participation of advisers from the Ger. Fed. Republic and the Ger. Dem. Republic the

May–Aug. 1959 (9th) Conference of For. Ministers took place at Geneva: a graduated Western **peace plan** (Secretary of State **Herter**): (a) unification of Berlin on the basis of free elections; (b) an elect. committee for all Germany (with 25 representatives from the Fed. Republic and 10 from the G.D.R.) and a plebiscite regarding elect. law; (c) elections to a nat. assembly (a constitution), formation of a gvt; (d) conclusion of peace. As Rus. for. minister, **Gromyko** again put forward the Soviet peace draft. State visit of KHRUSHCHEV to the U.S.A. (Sep.): agreement on renewed negotiations was reached at Camp David. A Western meeting of heads of state (EISENHOWER, DE GAULLE, MACMILLAN, ADENAUER) in Paris (Dec.) invited KHRUSHCHEV to a conference. KHRUSHCHEV sabotaged the

1960 Paris Summit Conference (May, the U-2 affair, p. 228); but, returning via E. Berlin, issued a moderate declaration on the Berlin question. In his

1961 meeting with President KENNEDY in Vienna (Jun.), KHRUSHCHEV repeated the Soviet demands. The renewed Berlin crisis, aggravated by ULBRICHT (Aug., p. 253), again increased int. tensions. Vice-President JOHNSON, visiting w. Berlin, reiterated the **3 basic freedoms** ('essentials') proclaimed by President KENNEDY: milit. protection, free access and a free and viable life for the w. Berliners. From 1962 the U.S.S.R. and the U.S.A. exercised restraint on the Ger. question. No further mention was made of a 'separate peace' in the

1964 Soviet Treaty of Friendship with the Ger. Dem. Republic, to which the 3 Western powers responded with a 'Ger. declaration' (4-Power responsibility and self-determination).

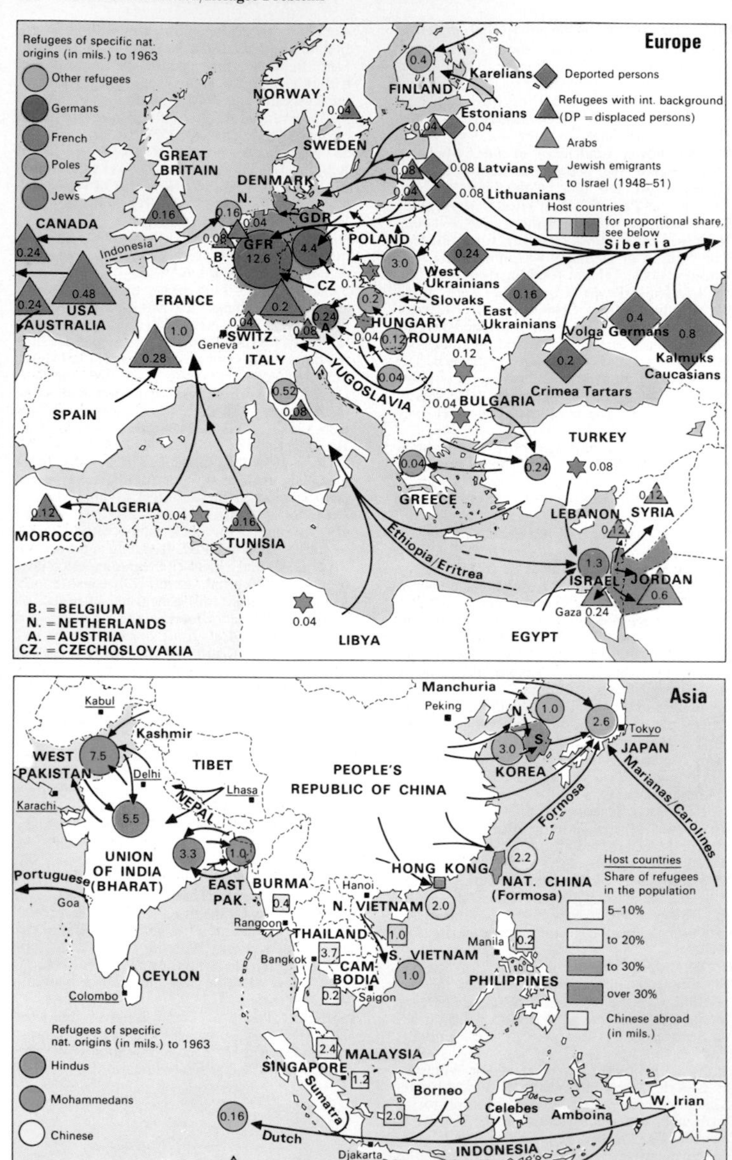

Refugees and displaced persons after 1945

The 'Century of the Refugees'

Catastrophes, wars and relig. struggles have at all times caused people to flee or to be expelled from their countries. **Intensified ideological attitudes** (racism, nationalism, Communism) brought about a frightening increase in refugee problems from the beginning of the 20th cent.

Germany: to attain the Nat. Socialist objective of 'living-space' (p. 197),

1939–44 people of Ger. origin were resettled.

1940–41 Forced migration of Poles into the 'General Gouvernement'. Shortage of labour made the 'importation' of *c.* 9 mil. foreign labourers necessary. The extermination of the Jews was nevertheless continued (p. 205).

SE. Europe: changes in the borders brought about resettlement in Transylvania (Hungarians, Roumanians) and in Dobruja (Roumanians, Bulgarians). Serbs fled from Croatia and Slovenia in 1941.

Finland: following the 'Winter War' (p. 199).

1940 Karelia was evacuated. After the 1944 armistice with the U.S.S.R., those who had returned were forced to leave permanently.

U.S.S.R.:

1940–41 Resettlement of 2 mil. eastern Poles to northern Russia.

1941 Deportation of Germans and 'unreliable' peoples (Estonians, Lithuanians, Kalmuks, Caucasians) to Siberia. To strengthen the 'Soviet peoples', the deportations were continued after the war.

Refugee movements at the time of the end of the war:

1944–5 Fleeing from partisans and the advancing troops of the Red Army, ethnic Germans escaped from the Danubian area into Austria.

1944 Following the collapse of the Eastern Front, refugees of int. background sought asylum in the w. and overseas.

1945 Flight of the E. Germans before the advancing Red Army.

Expulsions in consequence of the war:

1945 The Potsdam Conference (p. 249) sanctioned the expulsion of almost all Germans from the Ger. territories in the E., Czechoslovakia (the Sudetenland) and Hungary. More than 3 mil. perished in the process.

1945–7 Resettlement of the depopulated areas. Notwithstanding repatriation and the exchange of nat. minorities, pop. density decreased (e.g. in the Sudetenland).

1946–7 Expulsion of nat. minorities from Yugoslavia (Italians), 1950–52 from Bulgaria and Greece (Turks).

1948–52 Emigration of Jews from Eastern Europe.

Consequences: *c.* 30 mil. Europeans (60% of them Germans) lost their homeland. Almost all ethnic and nat. borders coincide since that time, also in Eastern Cen. Europe. To care for the **displaced persons** (D.P.s: for. labourers, refugees of int. background, the deported), the U.N. took over the

1945 UNRRA organization (founded 1943 in the U.S.A.) and transformed it into the

1947 Int. Refugee Organization **(IRO)**. From

1951 a High Commissioner for Refugees was attached to the U.N. (**UNHCR**, p. 222).

Refugee Problems (after 1945):

1. Owing to Com. expansion of power.

China: following the collapse of the Kuomintang,

1949 flight of the Nationalist Chinese to Formosa; however, employment was found for them there relatively quickly. The Brit. enclave of

Hongkong, on the other hand, grew from 1 mil. to 3·7 mil. inhabitants (1964), and no efforts could ease the misery of the refugees.

1962 Massive exodus from China (p. 235) and remigration of unwanted Chinese from SE. Asia.

Korea: flight of millions of people during the

1950–53 Kor. War (p. 237). The U.N. and the U.S.A. helped agricultural, politically unstable s. Korea to develop new industries.

Vietnam: the Cath. peasants migrating

1954 to the s. were integrated through the expansion of rice-cultivating areas.

Tibet: following the

1959 uprising against China, 200,000 Tibetans fled with the Dalai Lama to India.

Hungary: following the

1956 revolution (p. 233), 200,000 refugees fled into all parts of the world; however, 30% of them returned after being assured of immunity from punishment.

Germany: there was a continuous stream of refugees from the Ger. Dem. Republic (p. 250). This 'voting with their feet' ('abandonment of the Republic') was obstructed by the closing of the borders and the construction of the

1961 Berlin Wall.

2. Owing to the end of colon. rule.

1945 Defeat of Japan: resettlement of people from Korea, Sakhalin, Manchuria and Polynesia. They were able to find employment only after econ. recovery set in, dating from the Kor. crisis (p. 235). Apprehensive of nationalist excesses, the Dutch left

1952–3 Indonesia and

1962 New Guinea.

1954–62 The Algerian crisis (p. 269): refugees awaited repatriation in Moroccan and Tunisian emergency camps.

1962 Massive return of Algerians of Fr. extraction to France. Following the granting of

1960 independence to the Congo (p. 269), Europeans (Belgians) were forced by excesses to flee, leaving their property behind.

3. Owing to relig. fanaticism in India: the

1947 granting of independence (p. 265) unleashed the hatred between Hindus and Moslems. Those caring for the varying streams of fugitives encountered the greatest difficulties because of the already prevailing over-pop. The

1950 agreement between India and Pakistan governing the treatment of minorities did not prevent further relig. unrest.

Israel (p. 259) occupied an exceptional position. Idealism and energy, together with for. aid, made the settlement of the heterogeneous pop. possible (see Ger. reparations, p. 251). One consequence of the

1948 struggle for Palestine, the **problem of the Arab refugees,** remains unresolved. The refugees, housed in emergency camps and cared for by the U.N., are together with the host countries uninterested in integration, since they consider the Jew. state to be only provis.

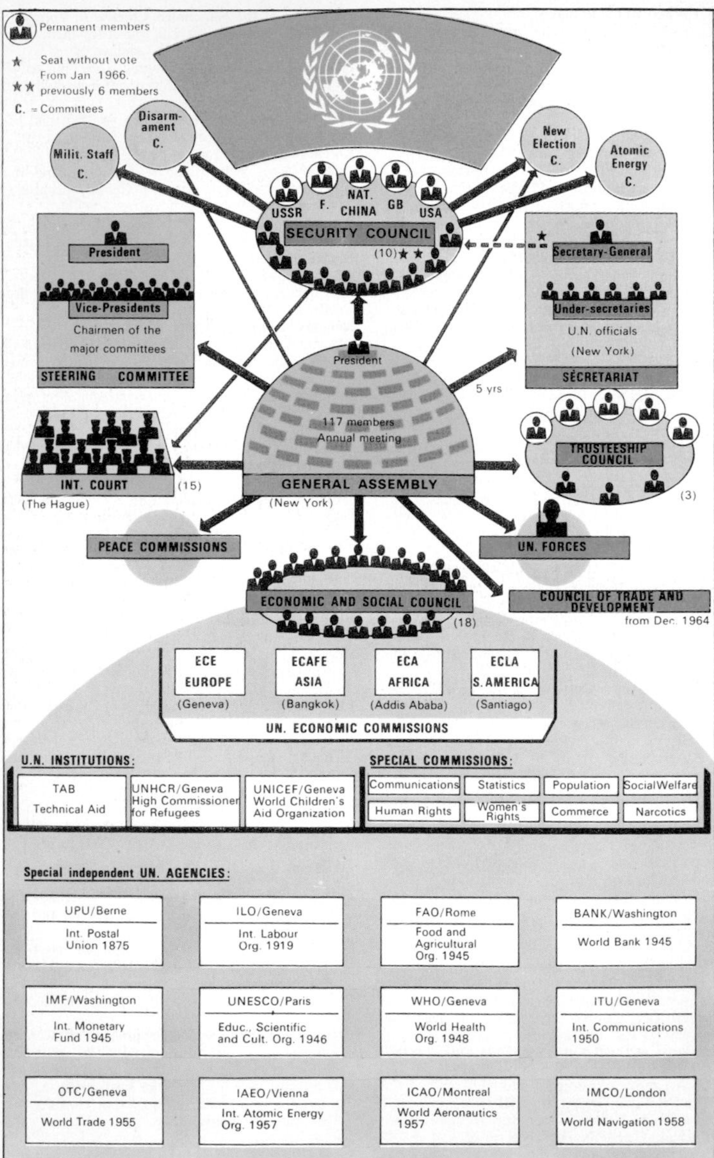

Organization of the United Nations, as at the end of 1965

The United Nations (U.N.)

Development: President ROOSEVELT proclaimed the **4 Freedoms** (p. 187) in his

1941 message to the U.S. Congress. They were incorporated into the **Atlantic Charter** (p. 209). In the

1942 Washington 'Declaration of the 26 Nations' (p. 209), the Allies for the first time referred to themselves as the **United Nations**. The

1943 Moscow Conference of For. Ministers decided to create an int. organization to 'safeguard peace and security'. The basic principles of the future organization were worked out by the U.S.A., the U.S.S.R., Britain and China at the

Aug.–Oct. 1944 Dumbarton Oaks Conference, and later supplemented at the Yalta Conference (p. 209): the permanent members of the Security Council received the veto right. Following negotiations at the San Francisco Conference (Apr.–Jun. 1945),

26 Jun. 1945 foundation of the United Nations (U.N., also U.N.O.): representatives of 50 nations signed the **Charter of the United Nations** (consisting of 111 articles). Following ratification (by Poland as 51st founder nation on 15 Oct.), the Charter became effective on

24 Oct. 1945 ('United Nations Day').

1946 Final meeting of the League of Nations for the purpose of dissolution (p. 137).

Objectives: safeguarding of world peace, protection of human rights, equal rights for all peoples, improvement of the general living standards in the world (Art. 1).

Principles: the sovereign members committed themselves:

1. To actively safeguard peace by non-violent means (recommendations, investigations, mediation, arbitration–Art. 35), by polit. or econ. sanctions (Art. 45), or by the use of armed forces (Art. 42) which were to be delegated by the members (Art. 43; milit. agreements governing the U.N. forces, the milit. staff committee, and world-wide disarmament have not so far been concluded).
2. To acknowledge the right of nat. self-defence (Art. 51), also with the aid of regional security treaties (Art. 53).
3. To non-interference in domestic affairs (which meant abandonment of the protection of human rights in authoritarian and totalitarian states; the Proclamation of the General Declaration of Human Rights in Dec. 1948 remained unbinding).
4. Loyal fulfilment of the U.N. obligations 'in good faith' (Art. 2), esp. the pledge not to threaten or use force (for all practical purposes ineffective). As a matter of principle, all states recognizing the Charter of the U.N. and willing to abide by its charter were eligible to become members of the organization.

Organs: as the most important organ, permanently in session, the

Security Council was made responsible for safeguarding peace. Its decisions (with 7 of 11 votes) were to be binding; polit. actions, changes in the Charter and the admission of new members needed its approval. Notwithstanding the presence of special committees to advise it, the Security Council was hampered in its work by the veto power of the 5 permanent members (in the period from 1946 to 1964 it was used by the U.S.S.R. 103 times, by Britain 4, France 3, and Nationalist China once). Apart from special meetings, the

General Assembly was to meet once a yr (as a rule, from Sep. to Dec.), beginning in 1952 in New York; its decisions (in part requiring two-thirds majorities) were to be binding only on those members voting affirmatively. Each member was allowed to send up to 5 delegates, but had only 1 vote (with the votes of the Ukraine and White Russia, the U.S.S.R. had for all practical purposes 3 votes). The General Assembly elects the non-permanent members of the Security Council for 2-yr terms, the Secretary-General and the members of all councils and the Int. Court of Justice. Committees and commissions (for observing the maintenance of peace and collective measures) were coordinated by the steering committee. The **budget** of the U.N. and the contributions of the members (and also of the non-members, as in the case of the Fed. Republic of Germany) were fixed annually (the largest share was paid by the U.S.A. with approx. 32% (to 1973), the U.S.S.R. with 15%, Britain 7%, France and Nationalist China 5% each). After the Kor. War (p. 237) the General Assembly, through the

1950 Uniting for Peace Resolution, assumed the right to decide over the raising of troops and materials to defend against an aggressor, in case the Security Council was blocked by a veto. Elected on the recommendation of the Security Council, the

Secretary-General–as the head of the secretariat (with approx. 4,500 officials)–assumed the leadership of the admin.; he takes part in the meetings of the Security Council without voting. The

Econ. and Soc. Council (with subordinate regional commissions) concerns itself with raising the general standard of living, making use of other U.N. agencies and special commissions. The former mandates of the League of Nations (in so far as they had not become ind., as in the case of Togoland, the Cameroons, Somaliland, Tanganyika) were administered by the

Trusteeship Council; the ind.

Int. Court of Justice (with 15 justices elected for 9-yr terms) gives, on request, legal opinions regarding int. disputes. Auton.

special organizations, est. by int. agreement, closely cooperate with U.N. organs and committees. Of great importance are the

1945 Int. Bank for Reconstruction and Development (the World Bank) and the Int. Monetary Fund (I.M.F.) in Washington.

Int. organizations outside of the U.N.:

1945 the World Federation of Trade Unions, which came under Com. influence. At the

1948 World Conference of Churches in Amsterdam the Christ. churches jointly formed the **Ecumenical Council** (without the Cath. Church).

1949 Int. Confederation of Free Trade Unions.

1 = GER. FED. REPUBLIC
2 = RUS. OCCUPATION ZONE
3 = SWITZERLAND
L. = LAOS
P.G. = PALESTINE (Gaza)
B. = Berne
G. = Geneva
H. = The Hague
Lo. = London
P. = Paris
R. = Rome
V. = Vienna
Dan.
USA
San Francisco
Montreal
New York
Washington
Dumbarton Oaks
Chapultepec
Santiago
GB
Moscow
Yalta
USSR
Cyprus
Kashmir
PEOPLE'S REPUBLIC OF CHINA
N. KOREA S.
NAT. CHINA
Bangkok
VIETNAM
Addis Ababa
CONGO
SOUTH-WEST AFRICA
INDONESIA
W. NEW GUINEA
Australia
EUROPE 14 26 28
ASIA 9 21 26
AMERICA 22 22 24
AFRICA 4 5 37
AUSTRALIA/OCEANIA 2 2 2
Founder states 1945
Admitted by 1955
Admitted by 1965
Left the org. 1965
Non-members
Trusteeship territories
Colon. territories
Permanent seat on the Security Council
Seat on a UN agency
Milit. intervention by UN
UN peace actions
1945 43% 27% 18% 4% 8%
1955 29% 34% 27% 3% 7%
1965 20% 24% 22% 2% 32%
Votes in the General Assembly

The United Nations, as at the end of 1965

The Attempt at World Gvt

Initially some progress was made in the Security Council in the maintainance of the status quo, which in 1945 had not yet been clearly defined: 1946 **Iran** was evacuated by Rus. troops (p. 229); 1947 the **Trieste question** was settled (p. 231); 1947–8 the conflicts in **Palestine** (p. 259), **Indonesia** (p. 263) and **Kashmir** (p. 265) were contained; econ. commissions for Europe, Lat. America, Asia and the Near East (Africa 1958) were est. U.S. hopes for loyal cooperation with the U.S.S.R. were disappointed: constant **Soviet vetoes** (p. 227) paralysed policies aimed at peace. **The U.N. General Assembly** under

1946–53 Secretary-General Trygve Lie/Norway (1896–1968) was a moral factor only; its resolutions mirrored world opinion:

1946 1st General Assembly meeting (London/New York): control of atomic energy, refugee problems (I.R.O., p. 221), condemnation of Fascism and boycott of Spain (to 1950).

1947 2nd General Assembly meeting (New York): U.N. commissions for **Korea** (general elections), the **Balkans** (border conflicts) and **Palestine** (UNSCOP).

1948–49 3rd General Assembly meeting (Paris/New York): condemnation of genocide; Declaration of Human Rights.

1949 4th General Assembly (New York): acceleration of the process providing for colon. self-admin., esp. in the U.N. trusteeship territories.

Stagnation of U.N. Efforts

1950 The Kor. crisis (p. 237): in the absence of the Soviet representative, MALIK (who was protesting against the rejection of the admission of the People's Republic of China), the Security Council declared N. Korea the aggressor; a **U.N. force** was raised and sent into action under command of General MACARTHUR. The U.S.S.R. protested and vetoed the condemnation of Chin. volunteer units in Korea.

The U.N. Security Council: int. conflicts and problems (disarmament, p. 272f.) remained unresolved: 1951 the Brit.–Iran. dispute over oil concessions (p. 229), 1957 Kashmir, 1958 **Lebanon** (U.N. observers), 1959 **Laos** (a U.N. investigation commission was appointed over Rus. protest), 1959 **S. Tirol**, and others.

The U.N. General Assembly meetings moved into the centre of U.N. politics following the **Uniting for Peace Resolution** (p. 223), but they were only able to make recommendations. The U.S.A. sought to make them the instrument of anti-Soviet policies (repeated rejection of the admission of **Red China** into the U.N., beginning in 1953); the Eastern Bloc (the Ger. Dem. Republic, Hungary) refused to grant entry permits to U.N. commissions; France declared the **conflict in Algeria** (p. 269) a domestic affair (1955); because of the condemnation of its racial policies (Apartheid, p. 267), the Union of s. Africa repeatedly withdrew its delegates.

1950–51 5th General Assembly meeting: support of underdeveloped areas; discharge of Jap. and Ger. P.O.W.s.

1951–2 6th General Assembly meeting: U.N. disarmament commissions (p. 272).

1953 Secretary-General Dag Hammarskjöld/Sweden (1905–61) introduced the U.N. as the driving force in the process of decolonization; his personal successes raised the prestige of the **office of the Secretary-General:**

1956 Geneva convention to fight slavery; special meeting of the General Assembly during the Suez and Hung. crises (Oct.–Nov.); termination of fighting in Egypt (p. 257), aid for Hung. refugees (p. 233); raising of a **U.N. police force** (under General BURNS, Canada) to maintain peace and order in the **Suez Canal Zone**, 1957 in the **Gaza Strip** (p. 258); settlement of Syr.-Israeli border conflicts.

1958 Int. Conference on Maritime Law in Geneva.

The U.N. as a Forum for Young Nations

The composition of the U.N. was altered by the admission of new members; next to the Eastern and Western Blocs, they gained a third position of power, supported the strengthening of U.N. policies, and forced the major powers to pay attention to U.N. resolutions and also to the problem of their development (p. 261). The result was a revaluation of the **Neutral Bloc** by the U.S.A. (KENNEDY) and the U.S.S.R. (KHRUSHCHEV). At the request of the **Congo** (LUMUMBA), the Security Council authorized HAMMARSKJÖLD to

1960 pacify the Congo with the aid of a U.N. milit. unit (Jul.), but refraining from the use of force. Overriding Rus. accusations, the U.N. General Assembly gave the Secretary-General a vote of confidence at a special meeting (Sep.).

1960–61 15th General Assembly meeting: admission of 17 new states (the 'Magna Charta of decolonization'); in vain KHRUSHCHEV demanded a revision of the U.N. statutes (**the Troika system**: replacement of the Secretary-General by one representative each from the E., the W. and the neutral powers, to weaken the office).

1961 Secretary-General U Thant/Burma (1909–74) continued the policies of his predecessor and gained added prestige for the office. The U.S.A. supported the

1962–3 milit. U.N. action against Katanga (TSHOMBE); a special meeting was held to discuss the finan. crisis of the U.N. (caused by the unpaid contributions of members disagreeing with its Congo policies); sanctions were levied against the Union of s. Africa (embargo on armaments, oil).

1964 Intervention of a U.N. force in Cyprus (p. 246); the U.N. action in the Congo (Jun.) was suspended for lack of funds.

1964–5 19th Gen. Assembly meeting: postponement of all votes until the settlement of the finan. crisis. **Indonesia** left the U.N. when Malaysia was elected to the Security Council (Jan.).

1965 20th General Assembly meeting: **Pope Paul VI** [from 1963] visited the U.N. in New York and delivered an appeal for world peace.

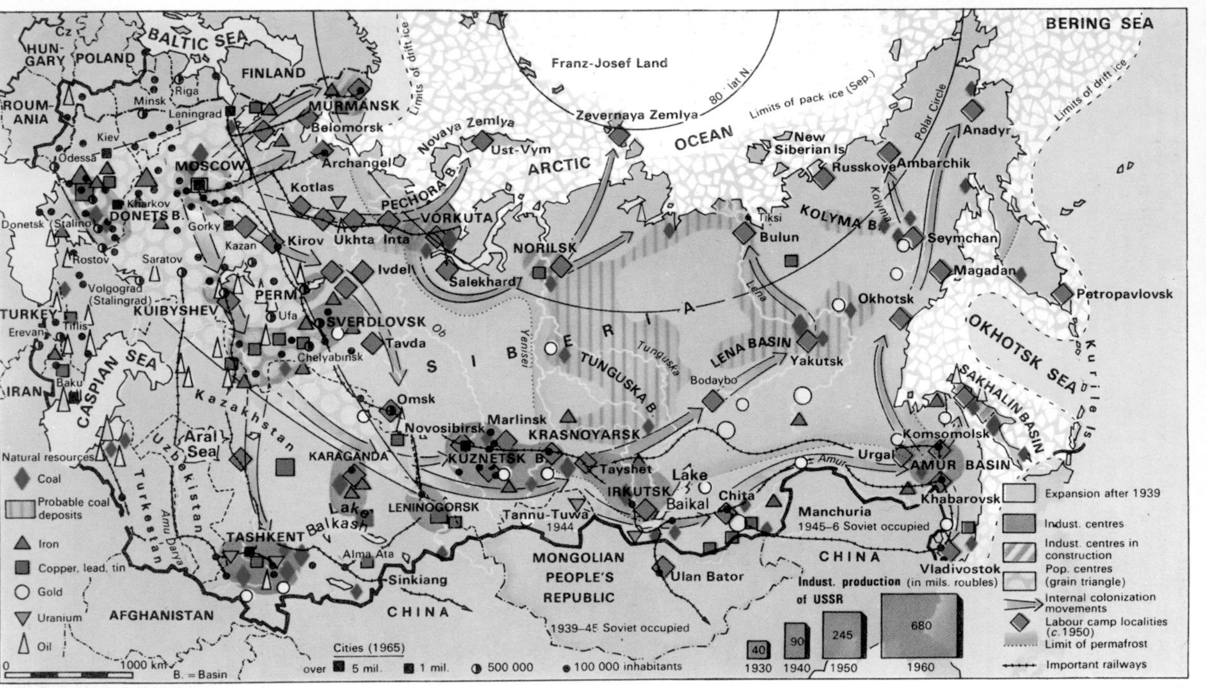

U.S.S.R. as a major industrial power after 1945

The Late Stalinist Period (1945–53)

Celebrated and feared as the 'leader and genius of humanity', Generalissimo **Stalin** (p. 189) ruled absolutely after Russia's hard-fought vict. (over 20 mil. dead; 25 mil. homeless). His personal régime and secret police (N.K.V.D. (from 1946 the M.V.D.) under **Beria**, 1899–1953 (liquidated)) supervised the admin. and party bureaucracy. Terror was used against those suspected of deviating from the official party line. (The Com. party of the Soviet Union had become the mass party of the officials; by 1952 it had almost 7 mil. members, of whom 60% were in the bureacracy.) The supreme organs of the party were deprived of power by the increasing of their membership; ZHDANOV (p. 189) shaped the course of cult. policy so as to create a trend to glorifying STALIN **(personality cult)** while fostering 'Soviet patriotism' (p. 207) and 'Socialist Realism'; 'objectivism', 'formalism' and 'cosmopolitanism' were eradicated.

1946 Changes in constitution and gvt: as prime minister, min. of defence (1947 BULGANIN) and 1st secretary of the Cen. Committee, STALIN combined in his person the power of the party, the admin. and the armed forces. Following the death of ZHDANOV, the 'Troika' (MALENKOV, BERIA, KHRUSHCHEV) was able

1949 to deprive the 'reactionary' ZHDANOV group (KUZNETSOV, KOSYGIN (p. 228) and ANDREYEV) of power, to engineer the fall of VOZNESSENSKY (1903–50 (liquidated)) and to change the for. ministers from MOLOTOV to **Andrei J. Vyshinsky** (1883–1954).

Econ. life: bureaucratic planning and achievement control (norms), the use of P.O.W.s and (*c.* 20 mil.) forced labourers, exploitation of the satellite states (reparations, forced exports, forced labour); the production of consumer goods was slowed down in favour of heavy industry.

1946–50 4th 5-Yr Plan (MALENKOV) to overcome the damage caused by the war (a housing construction programme), armaments and increased productivity: reconstruction of industry in the W.; expansion of the industries that had been transferred to the E. during the war; opening of the Arctic zone; extension of the areas of agric. cultivation.

1950 Introduction of the gold rouble. The establishment of large collective farms and the planning of major agricult. settlements (KHRUSHCHEV) did not eliminate the crises of food supply. Notwithstanding these shortcomings,

1951 the transition to Communism was proclaimed.

1951–5 5th 5-Yr Plan: major construction (the Volga and Dnieper projects) of irrigation projects and hydroelectric plants to provide energy for the construction of mod. weapons (atomic bombs, rockets).

For. policy: by the use of Soviet advisers, polit. parties devoted to Moscow, bilateral alliances, the Cominform and Comecon (p. 231), the states occupied during the war were transformed into satellite people's democracies. The **Eastern Bloc** was secured by the lowering of the **'Iron Curtain'**. Com. parties elsewhere (Syria, Lebanon, p. 257) and uprisings (Greece, p. 229) were supported. A severe setback was suffered through the

1948 defection of Yugoslavia (p. 231). **Titoism** was sharply opposed; it contradicted the **'2-camp theory'** (ZHDANOV, VOZNESSENSKY), which justified the polit. offensive against the capitalist camp. It was carried out on 3 levels:

1. **By paralysing U.N. policies** (p. 225) by utilizing veto power.
2. **By the 'Peace Offensive'** (also utilizing the Rus. Orth. Church):

1948 Moscow Church assembly;

1949 1st World Peace Congress (Paris, Prague);

1950 foundation of the World Peace Council: meetings resulting in resolutions on disarmament, the atomic threat and the Ger. question, among other issues, always corresponding to Soviet policy;

1952 'People's Congress for the Maintenance of Peace' in Vienna.

3. **By the 'Cold War'** against the W.: from

1946 tensions over Poland and Hungary, reparations policies and the Ger. question (p. 249). Attempt at intervention in Iran (Azerbaijan, p. 256); pressure on Turkey (p. 167). Suspension of co-operation with the W. began after the

1947 Paris Marshall Plan Conference (p. 245) and the

1948–9 1st Berlin Crisis (p. 253); however, the taking of milit. risks was avoided and polit. activity was directed to the E.:

1949 Trade and cult. agreement with N. Korea; first visit of MAO TSE-TUNG to Moscow, agreements for econ. aid and a

1950 Mutual Assistance Pact with China were signed (p. 235). During the

1950–51 Kor. crisis (p. 237), N. Korea was indirectly supported (weapons, advisors).

Results: (a) Expansion of Rus. power in Europe (satellites), but loss of Communist unity (Yugoslavia); isolation in for. affairs (polit. and milit. union of the W., p. 245). **(b) Structural crisis in econ. life:** notwithstanding the extensive increase in productivity and war potential, there was a decrease in the rate of growth, an exhaustion of labour and capital reserves, a lack of skilled labour and incidents of malinvestments resulting from faulty planning. **(c) The improvement in the standard of living did not match prevailing theory**, causing isolation from the W., low morale and productivity of labour.

1952 19th Party Congress of the Com. party of the Soviet Union. As heir presumptive to STALIN, **Malenkov** announced the revaluation of polit. policies (defensive strategy, the primacy of ecomics over politics). A renewed purge (a supposed plot of Jew. physicians in the Kremlin, antisemitic agitation) was cut short by the

Mar. 1953 death of Stalin. Gvt control was assumed in collective leadership by the party presidium (Presidium of the Cen. Committee): president, **Voroshilov** (1881–1969); prime minister, **Malenkov** (b. 1902); 1st deputy prime minister, **Kaganovich** (p. 189); for. minister, **Molotov** (p. 189); minister of the interior, **Beria**; minister of trade, **Mikoyan** (b. 1895); minister of defence **Bulganin** (b. 1895); 1st secretary of the Cen. Committee (from Sep.) **Nikita S. Khrushchev** (1894–1971).

The U.S.S.R. (1953–65)

A power struggle over STALIN's inheritance developed between MALENKOV (the state) and KHRUSHCHEV (the party), accompanied by intellectual liberalization (**'The Thaw'**, so-called after ILYA EHRENBURG's novel of that title).

1953 Fall of Beria (Jul.): the secret police were subordinated to the party. **As prime minister, Malenkov proclaimed the New Course**: improvements in the supply of consumer goods and the life of peasants on collective farms; amnesties and moderation of penal justice: dissolution of penal labour camps, discontinuation of banishment and liability of next-of-kin. KHRUSHCHEV emphasized the preferred position of heavy industry. His

1954 actions, bringing about the cultivation of new lands (Western Siberia, Kazakhstan), eased MALENKOV from power. Promises of consumer goods were withdrawn under

1955 Prime Minister Bulganin (minister of defence, ZHUKOV, from 1957 MALINOVSKY, who d. in 1967).

1. Destalinization: unofficial address of KHRUSHCHEV at the

1956 20th Party Congress of the Com. party of the Soviet Union concerning the personality cult and dogmatism of STALIN, whose books, monuments, etc., were placed under a ban. Unrest in Georgia (Tbilisi); revolutions aiming at liberation in the Eastern Bloc (p. 233). KHRUSHCHEV achieved the

1957 expulsion of the group opposed to the party (**Malenkov**, **Molotov**, KAGANOVICH, SHEPILOV) from the Cen. Committee, admitting in turn, among others, the ideologue **Frol Koslov** (1908–65), BREZHNEV (president from 1960) and KOSYGIN (from 1960). Following the resignation of

1958 Bulganin (Mar.), **Nikita Khrushchev**, serving as prime minister and 1st secretary of the party, was undisputed head of state and party.

1957–8 Reforms aiming at improvements in the general standard of living. The following changes were introduced: **(a) Econ. admin.**: de-emphasis of specific bureaucratic ministries in favour of decentralized econ. councils (104). **(b) Agriculture**: dissolution of tractor stations (M.T.S.), establishment of large collective farms (*Kolkhoz*) and state farms (*Sovkhoz*); intensification of agriculture and animal husbandry (cultivation of corn (maize)). **(c) Education**: development of professional schools and polytechnics (coordination of intellectual and physical endeavours).

1959 21st Party Congress: 7-Yr Plan to overtake the U.S.A. in per capita production. Chin. people's communes (p. 235) and the claim of the Com. party of China to int. leadership were rejected. **The conflict with Peking deepened**. At the

1960 Moscow Conference of 81 Com. parties (the 'Red Council'), the ideologue of the Com. party of China, TENG HSIA-PING, denounced KHRUSHCHEV's **coexistence theses** and defended STALIN's '2-camp theory'. The conflict was sharpened by the process of

2. destalinization: public denunciation of STALIN at the

1961 22nd Party Congress: a new programme for the 'development of Communism' (by 1980) was announced. Agrarian crises caused

1962–3 rises in prices, reforms in the cen. admin., the revision of planning and puchases of grain (from Canada and Australia).

The Policy of 'Peaceful Coexistence'

1953–6 The relaxation of tensions to overcome isolation in for. affairs (p. 227): settlement of the Kor. crisis; participation in int. conferences on Germany (p. 219) and Indo-China (p. 237); surrender of unimportant bases abroad:

1955 Porkkala/Finland; Port Arthur/China; **Austria** (p. 218). Compromise with **Yugoslavia**–its special brand of Socialism was accepted. Good-will demonstrations: proposals for disarmament and discharge of 1·2 mil. soldiers.

1955 s. Asia trip of KHRUSHCHEV and BULGANIN and promise of econ. aid.

1956 20th Party Congress of the Com. Party of the Soviet Union: strategy of **coexistence** to adapt the world revolution to the atomic age.

1. Avoidance of int. conflict, but support of limited 'wars of liberation' or popular risings.
2. Intensification of the econ. struggle.
3. Coordination of activities with the 'coloured' nations, which were recognized as an auton. '3rd force' (*pro tempore*);
4. The taking up of contacts with the w. under strict rejection of any kind of ideological coexistence

Overestimating Rus. power (Soviet successes in space, p. 273) and the revolutionary force of the new nations, KHRUSHCHEV believed in the coming of a 'Com. floodtide' (atomic stalemate, Amer. inferiority in rockets, the structural crisis in the econ. life of the w. due to decolonization). The **3rd crisis of world imperialism** (following the two world wars) was to be intensified decisively (in terms of the world revolution) by a

1957–62 phase of dynamic offensives: intervention in the Near East (Suez Canal crisis, p. 257) and

1958 Berlin ultimatum: cancellation of the 4-power status, the '3-state theory' (p. 253). Simultaneously, the diplomacy of summits and **for. travel**:

1959 state visit to the U.S.A.; 1960 to Austria, France, India, Indonesia, among other countries. Threats and **provocations**:

1960 Failure of the Paris summit (p. 219) under pretext of the U-2 incident (the shooting down of a U.S. spy plane over Sverdlovsk); the 'shoe incident' staged by KHRUSHCHEV at the U.N., when it rejected any change in the constitution to the 'Troika' system (p. 225);

1961 testing of the super bombs (p. 273);

1962 disruption of the access routes to Berlin; though KHRUSHCHEV, under pressure of agricult. problems and the conflict with Peking, turned to conciliation after the

Oct. 1962 Cuban adventure (p. 271). The

1963 agreement limiting atomic testing led to the

1964 break with China, who accused KHRUSHCHEV of ideological treason.

Oct. 1964 Fall of Khrushchev and change in leadership: Mikoyan became President (from 1965 **Podgorny**), **Kosygin** prime minister, and **Brezhnev** 1st secretary of the Cen. Committee. The split in world Communism was not overcome.

Greece, Turkey, Iran (1945–65)

Relieved from Soviet pressure (p. 227) by the

1947 Truman Doctrine (p. 241), the south-western neighbours of the U.S.S.R. joined the Western alliance system (p. 239).

Greece: following the withdrawal of Ger. troops
1944 return of the gvt from exile **(Archbp Damaskinos)**; actions of Brit. troops against the Com. E.A.M. units (p. 208) were terminated by the
1945 armistice (Feb.).
1947–64 PAUL I. The Com. E.A.M. Republic in the N. was fought by the gvt army, newly formed with U.S. aid.
1949 Termination of the Civil War by the for. minister, **Papagos** (1883–1955). Following the
1952 elect. vict. of PAPAGOS (prime minister), the country was reconstructed and agrarian reform was introduced.
1955–64 Prime Minister KARAMANLIS. The Cyprus question (p. 246) increased tensions with Turkey to the point of threatened open conflict.
1964 CONSTANTINE II (b. 1940). The Centre Union **(Prime Minister Papandreou)** won the majority.
1965 Anti-monarchist gvtl crisis: demonstrations; conspiracy of left-wing officers (Aspida); resignation of PAPANDREOU.
Turkey: in 1946 the U.S.S.R. demanded border revisions (Kars, Ardahan) and changes in the Straits agreements (p. 167).
1947 U.S. aid treaty (armaments, credits); an active Eur. policy was pursued (p. 245). Association with the U.S.A. and participation in the Kor. War (p. 237). Following the vict. of the Dem. party, founded in 1946,
1950 **Celal Bayar** (b. 1884) became president. As prime minister, **Menderes** (1894–1961 (executed)) gave in to reactionary relig. tendencies and re-Ottomanized the state, which incurred heavy debts by its generous support for agriculture.
1955 Anti-Gk excesses resulted from the struggle over Cyprus (Istanbul, Izmir). There was a general increase in the level of prices and struggles with the opposition (censorship); also student unrest and a
1960 milit. revolt: the 'Committee of the Nat. Front' under
1961 President General Gürsel (1895–1966) proclaimed the return to 'Kemalism' and death penalties for the members of the MENDERES gvt. A popular referendum **on the New Constitution of the 2nd Republic** was carried out (providing for special protection of the laws of ATATÜRK (p. 167) concerning the Europeanization of Turkey).
1961–5 Coalition gvt under the prime minister Inönü (p. 167); an amnesty was granted to the followers of BAYAR; the polit. situation remained unstable.
1962–3 Unsuccessful putsches; 1963 5-Yr Plan to restore public finances, increase exports and cover debts.
1964 Milit. intervention in the Cyprus conflict (p. 246). Disappointment over the Western position on this question led to a rapprochement with the U.S.S.R. without, however, any abandonment of existing treaty obligations.
Iran: (map, p. 260): protected by Rus. occupation troops, the Com. **Tudeh party** formed an auton. gvt in Azerbaijan and Kurdistan (Mahabad).
1946 Withdrawal of Brit. troops; but of Rus. units only after an appeal to the U.N. and in exchange for oil concessions (refused by parliament). The auton. territories were reintegrated.
1949 Com. assassination attempt on Mohammed Reza Pahlavi (Shah from 1941). Reforms were made difficult by corruption, Isl. sects, the soc. gap separating the uneducated, the restless intelligentsia and the reactionary property-owning class of the '200 families'.
1951 Nationalization of the oil industry, enforced by the prime minister **Mussadeq** (*c.* 1880–1967).
1952 Brit. oil blockade (the Anglo-Iran. Oil Co.); rad. course of the Nat. Front, bankruptcy of the state and
1953 const. conflict: MUSSADEQ had an unauthorized vote taken determining the removal of the Shah from power and then dissolved parliament; he was toppled by the army.
1954 Oil agreement with an int. consortium in exchange for compensation for the Anglo-Iran. Oil Co. ($U.S. 700 mil.). Notwithstanding creeping inflation, illegal agitation by the Tudeh party and
1960–61 student unrest, the U.S.A. gave development aid. Large landowners obstructed soc. and polit. reforms supported by the Shah.
1963 Popular referendum on land reform.

Scandinavia (1945–65)
1951 The Scand. Council for cult. and soc.-polit. cooperation was founded (joined 1955 by Finland).
Denmark: the Faroes (1948) and Greenland (1953) were granted domestic autonomy. Soc. Dem. gvt under HANSEN (1955–60) as prime minister, from 1962 under KRAG. After 1953 there was a 1-chamber legislature (Folketing).
1955 Agreement regarding minorities with the Fed. Republic of Germany.
Iceland: following the dissolution of the personal union with Denmark
1944 Iceland became a **republic**.
1951 A milit. agreement was concluded with the U.S.A. within the framework of NATO. The broadening of sovereignty over surrounding waters (12-mi. zone) led to the
1958–61 fisheries conflict with Britain.
Norway: the policy of neutrality was abandoned under the prime minister GERHARDSEN (from 1945), but atomic weapons were strictly rejected.
1957 OLAV V (b. 1903).
1965 1st middle-class gvt since 1935.
Sweden: during the war Sweden was the preferred country for polit. emigrants; the Soviet Union, however, forced the surrender of Ger. and Balt. refugees. Soc. Dem. policies (from 1946 prime minister, ERLANDER) aimed at the development of a Welfare State.
Finland: during the
1946–55 presidencies of Paasikivi (1870–1955) and **Kekkonen** (b. 1900, 1956–), Sovietization was not achieved, despite Rus. pressure and Com. infiltration.
1948 Mutual Assistance Pact; 1950 Trade agreement with the U.S.S.R.
1952 Fulfilment of all reparations obligations. From
1958 the Com. party was the strongest party. Tensions with the U.S.S.R. were resolved (the Soviets gave up the plan for a common defence proposed in 1961 by KHRUSHCHEV).

Soviet satellite system in Europe after 1945

The Soviet Satellite System

By armistice treaties, reparations and milit. occupation, the U.S.S.R. gained infl. over Eastern Europe. STALIN used it for the expansion of power **(Soviet imperialism):**

1945 Northern E. Prussia, Carpatho-Ukraine and the eastern regions of Poland were incorp. into the U.S.S.R.

1947 The Paris Peace Treaties (p. 218): the U.S.S.R. received Karelia from Finland, Bessarabia from Roumania.

The 'Sovietization' of the satellites was carried out in 6 phases:

1. Com. minorities gathered nationalist resistance groups in 'patriotic fronts', which after the occupation were supported by the Red Army.
2. 'Provis. gvts' were est.; exiled Communists, schooled in Moscow, received key positions in state and Com. party.
3. Following relatively free elections, coalition gvts with bourgeois heads were formed: the Com. party secured the Ministry of the Interior and thereby obtained the disposal of police power. Beginning of reconstruction: popular land reforms and nationalization of industry.
4. Bourgeois parl. majorities were eliminated by terror, denunciation, compulsion and the indictment of bourgeois politicians; Socialist **unity parties** under Com. leadership were formed, 'bloc politics' were practised and new coalition gvts were formed with 'fellow-travelling' parties, leaders of the opposition were eliminated (some of them fleeing to the W.).
5. Formation of Com. gvts, confirmed in controlled popular elections based on **unity lists**. Persecution of the Church and internal **purges** of the Com. party: show trials of 'deviators' (Titoists and others).
6. Conforming of the people's democracies to the Soviet example: collectivization of agriculture, supra-regional econ. planning and milit. commands. To coordinate joint cooperation,

1947 an information bureau was founded (the **Cominform**); by

1948 treaties of friendship and mutual assistance with the U.S.S.R. had been concluded; the satellites concluded treaties between themselves; there was also cooperation in the

1949 Council for Mutual Econ. Assistance (Comecon, p. 244) and in the

1955 Warsaw Pact: a joint supreme command under the Soviet Marshal KONYEV (from 1960 GRETCHKO). During

'The Thaw' period, which introduced the process of de-Stalinization, esp. after the

1956 20th Party Congress of the Com. party of the Soviet Union (p. 228), the satellites were allowed to 'pursue their own paths to Socialism', condemned politicians were rehabilitated and contacts with Yugoslavia were sought. The Cominform was dissolved, the cult of personality was denounced, the economy decentralized. Following the

1956 uprisings in Poland and Hungary (p. 232), the U.S.S.R. restricted the new freedoms; however, since that time, Poland and Roumania above all have pursued relatively independent domestic and econ. policies. Solidarity in ideology and for. policy with Moscow was maintained (exc. for Albania, p. 232).

Yugoslavia

Marshal Josip Broz, cal. Tito (b. 1892), prime minister in 1945, president in 1953, brought about the early withdrawal of Rus. troops (Mar. 1945). He formed a coalition gvt with politicians returning from exile and concluded a Mutual Assistance Pact with the U.S.S.R. (cancelled 1949). **Elections to the Nat. Assembly**: the unity list of the 'Popular Liberation Front' received 90% of the votes.

1945 Proclamation of the Federative People's Republic of Yugoslavia (a multinat. state consisting of 6 countries and 2 auton. regions).

1946–7 Internal 'sovietization' with the aid of the polit. police (under RANKOVIĆ) and the secret services: execution of polit. opponents. Nationalization of trade, industry, banks and soc. insurance; collectivization. Regimentation and econ. blackmail led to the

1948 break with Moscow, which prevented the realization of the Yugoslav plan for a Balk. federation with Bulgaria and Albania. An econ. blockade forced TITO to conclude

1949 trade agreements with Western countries. Moscow reacted to this 'auton. road to Socialism' with the persecution of 'revisionist **Titoism**'.

1950 Introduction of self-admin. by soviets of workers in factories.

1952 U.S. finan. and milit. assistance.

1953 10-Yr Plan to develop agriculture; suspension of forced collectivization. Official toleration of small private enterprises.

1954 Removal from office and 1957 conviction of TITO's compatriot **Milovan Djilas** (b. 1911). His writings (*The New Class*) criticized the dictatorship of the party and the personality cult (*Conversations with Stalin*).

1955 Visit of KHRUSHCHEV and BULGANIN to improve polit. relations; however, tensions increased after the

1958 Party Congress of the 'Yugoslavian Com. League' in Ljubljana: rejection of all for. interference. Econ. cooperation with O.E.E.C., E.E.C., EFTA (p. 245); from 1964 also with Comecon.

For policy: the major objective was the annexation of Istria and **Trieste**.

1947 Paris Peace Treaty: Istria fell to Yugoslavia, Trieste became a Free State under a U.N. High Commissioner.

1954 Partition agreement between Italy (Zone A: the harbour and city of Trieste) and Yugoslavia (Zone B: all of Istria).

1954 Balk. Pact (p. 244) with Greece and Turkey. Tension with Bulgaria over Macedonia, with Albania over the auton. border province Kosovo-Metohija. After the

1956 meetings with NASSER (p. 257) in Cairo and NEHRU (p. 265) on Brioni, TITO pursued a **policy of peaceful coexistence and neutralism to consolidate the power of the '3rd World'**: congresses of bloc-free states were held in Belgrade.

1962 Amer. credits were granted. Moscow was supported in the conflict with Peking (p. 228).

The States of the Eur. Eastern Bloc (1945–65)

Albania

1945 A Popular Front gvt under Com. party chief Enver Hoxha (b. 1908) was est. Following the break with TITO (p. 231), the former Yugoslav satellite orientated itself towards STALIN's policies. There was no de-Stalinization. Albania received Rus. econ. aid.

1959 KHRUSHCHEV's state visit and polit. attacks by other Com. parties did not disrupt the polit. cooperation with China.

1961 Break of relations with the U.S.S.R.

Bulgaria

The 'Fatherland Front', led by the former secretary-general of the Comintern, **Georgi Dimitrov** (1882–1949), effected the

1946 abolition of the monarchy through a popular referendum. The new gvt, with DIMITROV as prime minister, shattered

1947 the opposition of the Peasant party (execution of its leader PETKOV). By

1951 17 of the 40 members of the Cen. Committee had fallen victim to purges within the Com. party, incl. the deputy prime minister KOSTOV (1897–1949 (rehabilitated 1956)). The Stalinist VULKO CHERVENKOV (prime minister, 1950–56) was able to maintain his position in the Politburo until 1961.

1965 'Titoist' putsch attempt against CHIVKOV, the head of the gvt.

Poland

Despite the protests of the London gvt in exile, the **1945 Lublin Committee**–supported by the U.S.S.R. –proclaimed itself the **'provis. gvt'** and assumed the admin. of the Ger. eastern territories. Recognized by the Western Powers, the 'Gvt of Nat. Unity' agreed to the cession of the Pol. eastern territories to the U.S.S.R. The **shifting of the borders to the W.** caused profound problems of resettlement and expulsion (p. 221). Up to

1947 there was fighting with nat. resistance groups (W.I.N. and N.S.Z. units). To deprive the opposition of power, the Com. party chiefs **Wladyslaw Gomulka** (b. 1905) and **Josef Cyrankiewicz** (b. 1911, prime minister in 1947), pursued a policy of bloc politics.

1947 Rigged elect. vict. for the dem. bloc. (80%): the 'Pol. Stalin' **Boleslaw Bierut** (1892–1956) became president. Arrests of bourgeois politicians: MIKOLAJCZYK, leader of the strong agrarian People's party, fled to London (Oct.). The nat. Com. group around GOMULKA (arrested 1949) was forced to conform.

1948 The Com. party and the Socialists formed the United Workers' Party (P.Z.P.R.). Next to it, the Peasants' party (Z.S.L.) and the Dem. party (S.D.) continued a perfunctory existence.

1949 Conformity was imposed on the army: the Soviet Marshal CONSTANTIN ROKOSSOVSKI, a native Pole, became minister of defence. The people rejected sovietization; anti-Rus. nat. feeling was strengthened by the Cath. Church. Although the state recognized eccles. authority, it demanded loyal observance of its own interests. Following the

1953 Cracow show trial a struggle set in with the Church. The people reacted with an attitude of passive resistance to the arrests of priests (among them **Stephan Cardinal Wyszynski**, b. 1901): productivity and the standard of living, incl. that of the party leaders, declined. For these reasons, the

1954 2nd Congress of the United Workers' party, in the presence of KHRUSHCHEV, decided on a 'course of half-way measures' (Mar.). Dissolution of the Ministry of Security (Dec.). Strikes and protests because of excessive norms of productivity and the high cost of living culminated in the

1956 Jun. uprising of Poznan; which was quelled with the aid of Rus. troops, but had an effect on domestic policies.

The 'Pol. Spring in Oct.': re-election of GOMULKA to the Cent. Committee of the United Workers' party (notwithstanding a spontaneous state visit by KHRUSHCHEV, MOLOTOV, MIKOYAN and others); purges of party and admin.; dissolution of collective farms, formation of workers' soviets. Cardinal WYSZYNSKI was rehabilitated. ROKOSSOVSKY resigned.

1957 Elect. vict. of Gomulka and exclusion of the Stalinists. Econ. aid by the U.S.A. (renewed 1959). GOMULKA was able to steer a relatively ind. polit. and econ. course; indust. production rose; there were setbacks in agriculture.

1962 Renewed tensions with the Church; an exchange of notes with the Ger. episcopate regarding Ger.-Pol. reconciliation was sharply criticized (1965–6).

Roumania

The process of 'Sovietization' began under Rus. pressure, though there were hardly any Communists. The

1944 Popular Front Agreement of the Com. party under **Gheorghe Gheorghiu-Dej** (1901–65) with the Peasants' party (MANIU) and the Lib. party (BRATIANU) fell apart; a Nat. Dem. Front (F.N.D.), composed of Socialists, the Com. party and the Peasant Workers' Front, was formed under **Petru Groza** (1884–1958), whose F.N.D. cabinet initiated agrarian reforms.

1946 The F.N.D. received 89% of the votes. The opposition was dest. when it questioned the election results; BRATIANU was able to escape.

1947 Prohibition of the Peasants' party: MANIU was convicted, the lib. for. minister TARTARESCU was replaced by 'STALIN's stattholder' **Ana Pauker** (b. 1897) (to 1952); King MICHAEL abdicated (Dec.).

1948 Foundation of the Unity party (P.M.R.) (Secretary-General GHEORGHIU-DEJ. In

1951 the 1st 5-Yr Plan, with the objective of Socialist industrialization (steel, coal, oil), was introduced. The régime was stabilized under

1952–8 President GROZA and the prime minister, GHEORGHIU-DEJ (head-of-state to 1965). As prime minister, (from 1958) **Ion Gheorghe Maurer** (b. 1902) strove for greater polit. independence; he mediated in the dispute between Moscow and Peking (p. 228).

1962 Completion of collectivization. Significant expansion of trade with Western countries (the U.S.A. and the Fed. Republic of Germany). From

1964 closer relations between France and Roumania developed: state visit of MAURER to Paris; conclusion of a Franco-Roumanian cult. agreement.

Czechoslovakia

Following the 1943 alliance with the U.S.S.R., the London gvt in exile, represented by BENEŠ (p. 157), concluded negotiations in Moscow concerning the rest. of the state. The Carpatho-Ukraine was ceded (p. 231); Slovakia received limited autonomy.

1945 The gvt in exile returned to assume its functions in Prague (Prime Minister ZDENEK FIERLINGER, Socialist). **Beneš became president, Jan Masaryk** (1888–1948 (suicide?)) for. minister, the exiled Communist **Klemens Gottwald** (1896–1953) deputy premier. Beginning of the expulsion of the **Sudeten Germans** (completed by the end of 1946). Landed property and 'enemy holdings' of Germans, Hungarians and collaborators fell to the state. Socialization of mining and industry. Withdrawal of Rus. and Amer. troops (Dec.).

1946 Elect. vict. of the Com. party (38%). BENEŠ and MASARYK hoped for a dem. gvt of the Nat. Front under GOTTWALD as prime minister. Following the settlement of border conflicts, a

1947 Mutual Aid Pact with Poland was concluded. The decision of all parties to take part in the Paris Marshall Plan Conference (p. 245) was rescinded under pressure of an ultimatum from Moscow (p. 245). The Socialists declined a fusion with the Com. party (Nov.). Arrests and trials successfully deprived the Slovak. Dem. party of power.

Feb. 1948 Com. coup d'état, triggered by the resignation of 12 gvt minis. who protested against the infiltration of the police by Communists (minister of the interior, NOSEK, Com. party). Calling for strikes and demonstrations against the 'conspiracy', the trade-union leader **Antonin Zapotocky** (1884–1957) put pressure on BENEŠ. At the President's request GOTTWALD formed a new gvt. The press, radio and the admin. were forced to conform; rigged elections on the basis of unity lists were conducted; BENEŠ refused to sign the new constitution, modelled after those of the 'people's democracy', and resigned. **Gottwald** became his successor. **Zapotocky** became the new head of the gvt. After the U.S.S.R. and the Ger. Dem. Republic, the C.S.S.R. was the strongest indust. nation of the Eastern Bloc; it unconditionally followed the instructions of Moscow. Resistance by the Cath. Church to state interference was broken by the

1949 anti-clerical measures: priests placed under arrest.

1951–2 Purges within the Com. party.

1953 Separation of state and party; denunciation of the personality cult. From

1957 Antonin Novotný (b. 1904) was president.

1962–3 Elimination of Stalinists; amnesty for polit. prisoners.

1965 A new econ. system provided for improvements in econ. life (price policies and market orientation). Trade agreements were concluded.

Hungary

The armistice with the U.S.S.R. cal. for the purge of the state from fascists and war criminals. Communists returning from exile used this condition to eliminate undesirable dem. forces.

1945 Land reform: Church property, and that of Fascists and ethnic Germans, was expropriated. The existence of unprofitable small peasant holdings created the basis for the collectivization of agriculture. Elect. vict. of the **Small Landholders' party** in Nov.: it gained 245 of 409 seats in the parliament. With only 70 seats, the small Com. party occupied 4 ministries: minister of the interior, **Imre Nagy** (1896–1958 (prob. executed)), minister of transport, **Ernö Gerö** (b. 1899), minister without portfolio **Mátyás Rákosi** (1892–1971). A wave of terror was directed against 'Fascist remnants'.

1947 Shattering of the Small Landholders' party through the revelation of 'conspiracies': show trials of 220 members; the prime minister, FERENC NAGY (b. 1903), fled to Switzerland. A new election gave the desired majority to the Com. party. Alongside the

1948 Socialist Workers' party, other parties of the Popular Front suffered a perfunctory existence. The Church resisted the 4-Point Programme to place schools under state control. Priests were persecuted under the minister of the interior, **János Kádár** (b. 1912). **Joseph Cardinal Mindszenty** (b. 1892) was condemned to death, but his sentence was commuted to life imprisonment. Rigorous industrialization and collectivization. Trials of 'Titoists': KÁDÁR, among others, was incarcerated (1950–53).

1953 Proclamation of the New Course by Imre Nagy: he was unable to assert himself against the Stalinists surrounding RÁKOSI and fell from power. Among the party intelligentsia and students unrest increased ('Petöfi Circle').

1956 RÁKOSI was forced to turn over the party leadership to GERÖ. Demonstrations were followed by the

Oct. 1956 nat. popular uprising: students demanded the unconditional withdrawal of Rus. troops, the dissolution of the secret police, free elections, freedom of the press, etc. The gvt requested Rus. aid. After bloody clashes with workers, students and Hung. troops under Colonel MALETER, the Red Army retreated. As prime minister, **Nagy** formed a Cabinet incl. several parties and announced Hungary's withdrawal from the Warsaw Pact (p. 231). New Soviet tank units intervened and protected the counter-gvt of **Kádár**, placed in office by the U.S.S.R. Hoped-for Western aid did not materialize; *c.* 200,000 people fled the country. NAGY and MALETER fell into Rus. hands. Cardinal MINDSZENTY found asylum in the U.S. embassy.

1957 Special courts were est. to counteract renewed strikes and unrest: death penalties, terror and deportations to the U.S.S.R. The U.N. condemned the actions of the U.S.S.R. and confirmed the legitimacy of the NAGY gvt (Jun.). A U.N. Commission was refused entry (p. 225). Dissolution and reconstruction of the army; reorganization of the Socialist Workers' party. Slow transition to a more moderate course.

1961 Completion of collectivization, support for heavy industry through the 2nd 5-Yr Plan.

1962 Party trial of RÁKOSI and GERÖ.

Chinese Civil War, 1945/50

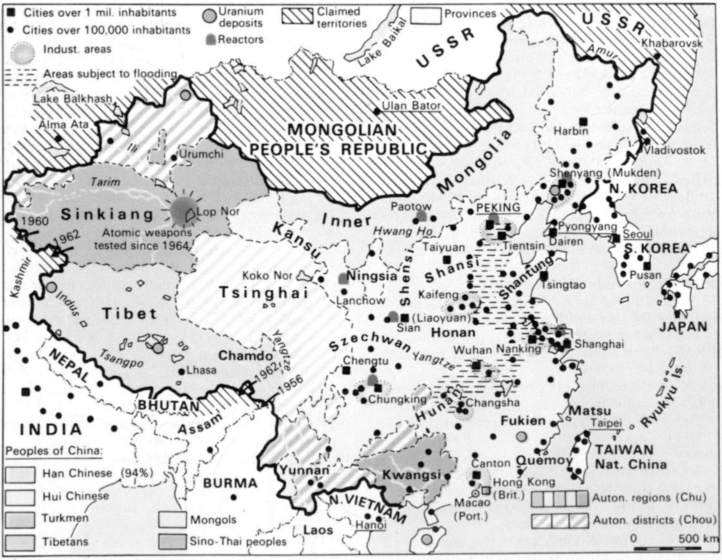

People's Republic of China, 1965

China (1945–65)

The assumption of power by the Com. party: after the Jap. occupation (p. 173), China was impoverished and demoralized. Kuomintang troops occupied the major cities with Amer. assistance, but were unable to establish order (corruption). Milit. dictatorship of CHIANG KAI-SHEK.

1945 Treaty with the U.S.S.R., which received concessions incl. Port Arthur (till 1955). Initial hostilities between the Kuomintang and the Com. party of China. After an unsuccessful Amer. attempt to mediate (General MARSHALL, p. 245), Amer. aid to the Kuomintang was cut.

1947 Intensification of the civil war. The U.S. China Aid Bill did nothing to stem the Red Chin. advance.

1949 Major offensive in Southern China; reconquest of Nanking. Proclamation of the People's Republic of China (Sep.). The gvt and army of the Kuomintang fled to Formosa.

1950 Seizure of Hainan. Prestige was gained through the intervention in Korea and Indo-China (p. 237). The U.S.A. blocked the admission of the People's Republic of China into the U.N. (p. 225); introduced a **'no-trade policy'**; and guaranteed the protection of **Nationalist China**, which was under the rule of President CHIANG KAI-SHEK.

1950 Conclusion of a Mutual Assistance Pact with the U.S.S.R.

The Domestic New Order: pressure was exerted on private industries and for. enterprises until they 'volunteered' for nationalization.

1950–56 Land reform was carried out in 4 stages: (a) distribution of the landed property, (b) the obligation of mutual aid, (c) cooperatives, (d) collective farms. Currency reform (1955). **Re-education of the people**. Training of party cadres and functionaries. Introduction of the Lat. alphabet (1956). The

1953 1st 5-Yr Plan, aiming at industrialization, failed because of the shortage of specialists.

1954 New Constitution: organization of the state acc. to the principle of 'dem. centralism': 5 auton. regions, 21 provinces, *c.* 175 municipal admins. and 2,000 districts. **A Cen. Council** (56 members), under the chairmanship of MAO TSE-TUNG (p. 173), was given absolute power; there was also an Administrative Council, on which the premier and for minister, **Chou En-lai** (1898–1976), served. MAO's lib.

1957 '100-Flowers Speech' evoked criticism of the system; this criticism was suppressed by campaigns against 'deviators of the right' and the rad. policy of **'transition to Communism'**:

1958 Establishment of people's communes: workers' combines (shared meals, living quarters: 'each peasant a soldier'); increase of steel production through the use of mini-furnaces. The **'Great Leap Forward'** ended in econ. catastrophe; nevertheless, beginning in

1959 an atomic energy programme was initiated. Changes in leadership: **Liu Shao-ch'i** (b. 1898) assumed the leadership of the state, MAO remained party chairman; CH'EN YI became for. minister.

1960 As a consequence of the **ideological conflict with Moscow** (p. 228), Rus. technicians were withdrawn: 178 indust. projects were halted.

1961–3 Famines, accompanied by plunder, the spread of contagious diseases, counter-revolutionary unrest (with Nationalist China providing arms and sending agents); streams of refugees to Hong Kong (p. 221); taxation of private aid funds supplied by Chinese abroad provided for. currency for the purchase of grains.

Open break with the Com. party of the Soviet Union in consequence of the Cuban crisis (p. 271): KHRUSHCHEV was accused of having betrayed the world revolution.

1963 '25-Point Programme' of the Com. party of China; attempts to bring about splits in other Com. parties.

1964 Detonation of China's 1st atomic bomb. KHRUSHCHEV's fall leads to no ideological reconciliation.

For. policy: claims were raised on territories which had belonged to China before the conclusion of the 'Unequal Treaties' (p. 91).

1950 Occupation of Tibet (1951: dom. autonomy). Chin. policies were consciously orientated towards Asia: rapprochement with India (p. 265). China initiated the Bandung Conference (p. 261) and compromised with Japan. World-wide conflict threatened because of the

1957 offensive against Formosa: bombardment of Quemoy (1958). The U.S.A. considered intervention. The crisis was alleviated under Rus. pressure.

1959 Uprising in Tibet: flight of the Dalai Lama. Border conflict with India (p. 265).

1962 Attack on Assam (MacMahon Line) and Kashmir (Ladakh); improved relations with Pakistan; increased activity and successes in for. policy following the

1963–4 travels in Africa and Asia of the prime minister, CHOU EN-LAI, and the for. minister CH'EN YI. Loosening of the trade embargo (initiated by Britain in 1957).

1964 Recognition of the People's Republic of China by France. From

1965 there were setbacks in for. policy (anti-Chin. revolts in, among other places, Indonesia, Ghana.

Japan (1945–65)

1945–50 Amer. milit. gvt under General **MacArthur** (p. 237): trials of war criminals; resettlement problems (p. 221); reparations; distribution of landed property; democratization.

1946 A constitution was introduced based on the Amer. model. Japan's situation improved under the

1949–54 2nd Yoshida Cabinet: E.-W. tensions (Korea, p. 237) forced the U.S.A. to win Japan as an ally.

1951 Peace of San Francisco: Japan lost all her aquisitions since 1854, concluded a milit. treaty with the U.S.A. and received back her sovereignty (1952).

1954 Rearmament was begun. Despite overpop. and a shortage of raw materials, Japan increased her exports.

1955 The prime minister Itshivo Hatoyama (1883–1959) proclaimed a policy of peace and introduced administrative and tax reforms.

1956 Termination of the state of war with the U.S.S.R. The

1960 Security Pact with the U.S.A. evoked strong anti-Amer. reactions. The Kishi Cabinet resigned (in office since 1957).

1960–64 Prime Minister Hayato Ikeda (b. 1899): settlement of polit. difficulties; favourable development of trade and industry.

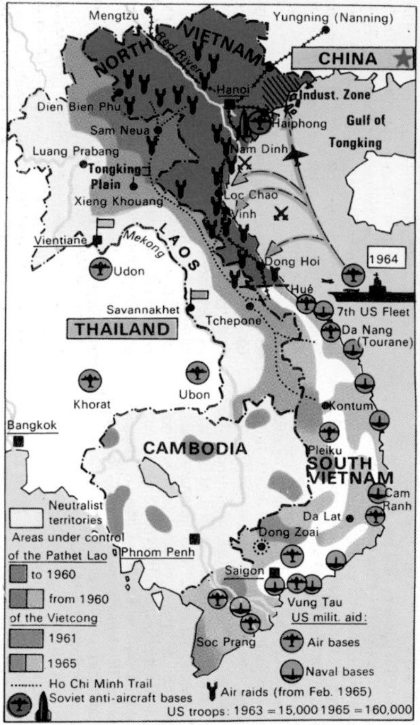

Second Indo-China War, from 1957 (as at 1965)

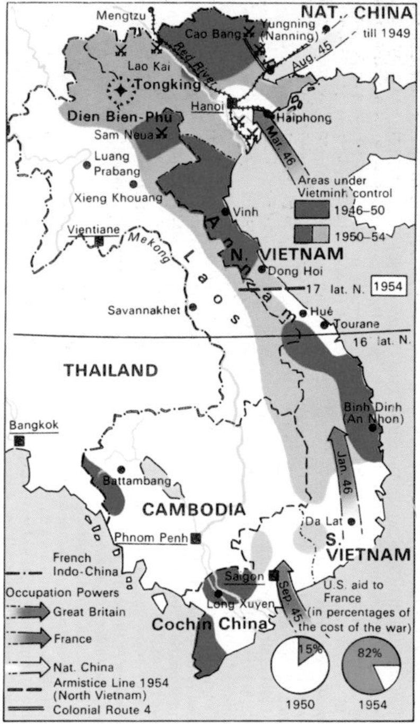

First Indo-China War, 1945–54

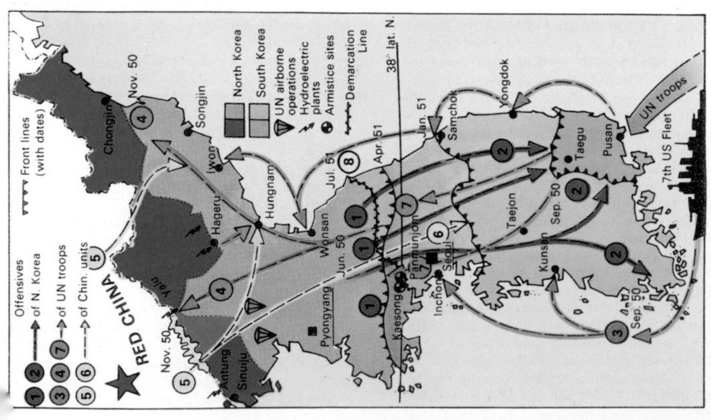

Korean War, 1950–53

Crisis Areas of the E.–W. Conflict in Asia

Korea:

1945 Rus.-Amer. occupation, based on Allied agreements. In the N. (with its mining and industry), Popular Front committees were est., led by Com. Koreans returned from exile; in the S. (primarily agricult.) the establishment of a U.S. milit. gvt. At the Conference of For. Ministers in Moscow (Dec.) arrangements were made for the establishment of a gvt for all Korea. Following disagreements with the U.S.S.R., the U.S.A. proposed the establishment of a

1947 U.N. Commission to supervise free elections; but the commission was refused permission to enter N. Korea. In the S.

1948 elections were held to a Nat. Assembly; **Syngman Rhee** (1875–1965) became president of the **Republic of S. Korea** (Aug.); proclamation of the People's Republic of N. Korea (Sep.) under Kim Il Sung (b. 1912) as prime minister. Both gvts claimed jurisdiction over all Korea; a U.N. resolution decided in favour of S. Korea. Withdrawal of Rus. and Amer. troops.

1950–53 The Kor. War was unleashed by an attack by N. Korea on S. Korea, who requested aid: President Truman (p. 241) gave orders for U.S. troops to intervene. The U.N. Security Council (p. 225) declared N. Korea the aggressor and cal. on U.N. members to support the S. The U.N. army (with contingents from 15 nations), commanded by General **Douglas MacArthur** (1880–1964) was pushed back to the bridgehead of Pusan. In Sep. U.N. troops advanced to the Chin. border, leading to the intervention of Chin. 'volunteers' (Nov.). The war stagnated along the 38th Parallel. Prices in the world market boomed (the **'Korea boom'**).

1951 MacArthur demanded authorization for the destruction of Chin. air and supply bases. President Truman, fearful of another world war, replaced MacArthur with General Ridgeway.

1953 Armistice of Panmunjom: partition of Korea. The Conference of For. Ministers at Geneva was unable to find a solution for the reunification of the country.

N. Korea: reconstruction with the aid of Rus. credits; the country was dependent on the People's Republic of China.

1961 Treaties of friendship with the U.S.S.R. and China; from 1962 accommodation to the polit. course of the Chin. party.

S. Korea: reconstruction with U.S. aid.

1953 A Mutual Security Treaty was concluded with the U.S.A., which supported the authoritarian régime of the S. Kor. president. Domestic unrest also continued after the

1960 resignation of Syngman Rhee.

1963 General Chung Hee Park became president; he endeavoured to restore domestic order and bring about accommodation with Japan.

Indo-China: following preparations for an uprising

1945 troops of the Fr. Vichy gvt were disarmed by the Japanese (Mar.); Vietnam and Cambodia became ind. The Brit.-Chin. zones of operations were fixed at the Potsdam Conference (p. 249). Jap. capitulation was followed by the Chin. occupation of the northern zone. The Com. party leader **Ho Chi Minh** (1894–1969), head of the **Vietminh** (liberation movement, est. 1941), proclaimed the establishment of the **Dem. Republic of Vietnam** in Hanoi. Brit. occupation of the southern zone with Saigon. A Fr. expeditionary force fought against Buddhist sects and the Vietminh.

1946 Brit. transfer of admin. to Fr. colon. authorities. Chin. withdrawal was purchased with the Fr. abandonment of all claims on China (the S. China railway). Ho Chi Minh allowed the return of Fr. troops (Mar.). Negotiations of Ho Chi Minh in Paris were sabotaged by the High Commissioner for Vietnam, Admiral d'Argenlieu, who est. the Republic of Chochin China without consultation (Jun.). Fr. 'Ultras' pressed for a milit. solution of the Vietnam problem.

1946–54 1st Indo-China War: Fr. élite troops (For. Legion, 'Paras') occupied the delta of the Red River, but were unsuccessful in fighting the Vietminh partisans of General **Giap**.

1948 The counter-gvt of the former emperor Bao Dai (b. 1913) was powerless.

1953 The Vietminh invaded Laos and split Indo-China. Hopes for a Fr. victory dwindled; President Eisenhower refused U.S. intervention.

1954 Capitulation of the fortress of Dien Bien Phu.

1954 Geneva Conference of Foreign Ministers (the People's Republic of China represented by Chou En-lai, p. 235): **partition of Indo-China** with guarantees for the sovereign states of **Laos, Cambodia** and **Vietnam**, which was partitioned.

Laos: fighting between the Com. **Pathet Lao** and gvt troops (General Novasan). An attempt at mediation by the U.N. was without success.

1962 The Geneva 14-Power Conference decided to **neutralize** Laos; renewed fighting of rival groups nevertheless erupted.

1964 Conquest of the strategically important Plain of Jars by the Pathet Lao.

1965 Unsuccessful right-wing putsch.

N. Vietnam: industry was developed with the aid of the Eastern Bloc countries; polit. orientation towards Red China; support of the Vietcong with the aim of 'liberating Vietnam from the U.S. imperialists'.

S. Vietnam: following the

1955 deposition of Bao Dai, the prime minister **Ngo Dinh Diem** (1901–63)–with Amer. help–stabilized the state by using dictatorial methods. He fought with Buddhist sects and Com. agents and refused to accept the decision of the Geneva Conference calling for a popular referendum. At this point the **Vietcong partisans** initiated the

1957 2nd Indo-China War, employing disruptive and terroristic methods. Their expanding operations were counteracted by the gvt through the establishment of

1961 fortified villages. Buddhist demonstrations (self-immolations) led to the

1963 milit. putsch. Diem was killed. Direct U.S. intervention began with the

1964 naval encounter in the Gulf of Tongking: supply bases in N. Vietnam were bombarded from th air and shelled from off-shore vessels. Troops we reinforced (also by contingents from SEA states and S. Korea).

1965 Milit. gvt under Marshal Ky; the uncert of the dom. polit. situation continued. The **lation of the war** added to the danger of a g world-wide conflict.

OAS ('Rio Pact' 1947/8)
OAS Protective Zone
NATO (North Atlantic Pact, 1949)
ANZUS ('Pacific Pact' 1951)
SEATO (South-East Asia Pact, 1954)
States under SEATO protection
CENTO ('Near East Pact' 1955)
Assoc. by USA
Warsaw Pact 1955
Communist States
Arab League 1945
Defensive Pact of the League 1950
Members of Balkan Pact 1953
Defensive treaties or treaties establishing bases
of US (outside NATO)
of USSR
of Britain
Bases
US (former)
Rus. (former)
Brit.
Colonies

World population 1965: Communist states 26%; Western states 24%, of them NATO 12%; 7% of them Warsaw Pact; Arab League 2%; 50% Neutral states

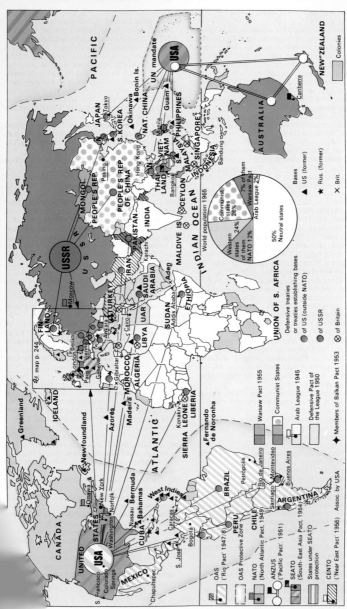

International alliance systems (as at 1965)

The alliance policies of Washington and Moscow differed from each other and reflected the bi-polarity of the world: a multiplicity of alliances (the principle of dem. freedom) in the W., and bloc politics with the claim for absolute leadership (the principle of centralism) in the E.

The Alliance Systems of the W.

The Organization of American States (O.A.S.). Intended as an expression of Pan-Amer. policies, its principles were formulated in the

1945 Act of Chapultepec, agreed on at the

1947 Pan-Amer. Conference of Petrópolis (the Rio Pact), and signed at the

1948 Pan-Amer. Conference of Bogotá: commitment to mutual assistance in the event of aggression; peaceful arbitration of conflicts among O.A.S. members or sanctions. **Organs**: Inter-Amer. Conference; Conference of For. Ministers for consultation; Council of Defense.

1954 Pan-Amer. Conference of Caracas: anti-Com. resolution.

1959 Declaration of Santiago: a dem. public order as prerequisite for peace.

1962 Conference of Punta del Este: condemnation of Marxism-Leninism; exclusion of Cuba.

Actions of the O.A.S. were carried out against Nicaragua, Honduras, Cuba, the Domin. Republic, among others.

The N. Atlantic Treaty Organization (**NATO**, see also p. 244f.); it was founded in Washington in 1949 for a period of 20 yrs, in response to E.–W. tensions. **Objectives**: the preservation of dem. freedoms through collective defence measures, polit. and econ. cooperation.

Civil organs: a secretariat and permanent Council of Representatives (Paris) to carry out the decisions of the N. Atlantic Council (the ministers of finance, defence and for. affairs). **Milit. organs**: a committee of chiefs of staff and a standing committee (Washington).

Bilateral agreement of the U.S.A. and Britain, within the framework of NATO, regarding naval, air and missile bases.

NATO policies:

1950 Establishment of a Eur. army (p. 245);

1952 Greece and Turkey joined, 1955 the Fed. Republic of Germany;

1958 Eur. 'shield forces' (30 divisions) and provisions for nuclear defence weapons to be used in the event of an attack; France refused to subordinate its Medit. fleet to NATO command. To bolster defence

1961 atomic submarines equipped with Polaris missiles were introduced.

1962 Expansion of conventional forces to make 'graduated response' possible.

1963 Brit.-Amer. disagreement over the establishment of a multilateral atomic force (M.L.F.) equipped with Polaris missiles. France cal. for

1965 structural changes in NATO and threatened to leave the organization.

1966 Fr. ultimatum: withdrawal of NATO troops or their subordination to Fr. command; removal of the Eur. H.Q. (SHAPE) by 1967.

The ANZUS Pact (Australia, New Zealand, U.S.A.), est. in San Francisco in 1951, was intended to serve as protection against attacks by Japan or other aggressors. **Organ**: Consultative Council (one meeting a yr).

The SE. Asia Treaty Organization (SEATO) was founded in Manila in 1954 and was intended also to serve the defence of states not belonging to SEATO (e.g. s. Vietnam). Consultation in the event of Com. infiltration and joint milit. manoeuvres were provided for. **Organs**: a permanent Council of Ministers with an executive secretariat (Bangkok); a milit. planning staff; research services were provided to monitor Com. subversion. From

1958 contacts were taken up with NATO and CENTO (see below). In 1965 Fr. officers were recalled from all staffs.

Cen. Treaty Organization (CENTO); it developed 1955 out of the 'Baghdad Pact' of Turkey and Iraq (which left the organization in 1959, p. 256). There was no mandatory mutual assistance, but cooperation in milit. and polit. questions was provided for. **Organs**: a permanent Council of Ministers;

1958 a milit. planning staff was est.; the U.S.A. joined the organization indirectly in 1959 by concluding bilateral mutual security treaties; 1961 an Amer. chief of the milit. staff was named.

Bilateral pacts of the U.S.A. in the Pacific: 1953 with s. Korea (mandatory mutual assistance); 1954 with Nationalist China (which undertook not to attack the mainland without consultation with the U.S.A.), 1961 with Japan.

Alliance Systems of the E.

To supplement bilateral milit. treaties, and in reaction against the Paris treaties (p. 251), the

Warsaw Pact (p. 244) was est. in 1955 for a period of 20 yrs. **Purpose**: automatic mutual assistance in the event of armed attacks in Europe; consultation on questions relating to security and polit. cooperation. **Organs**: a committee of polit. advisers (2 meetings a yr), a secretariat and supranational supreme command in Moscow.

1956 Admission of the Ger. Dem. Republic. Treaties allowing the stationing of Rus. troops were concluded with Poland in 1956, with Hungary, Roumania, and the Ger. Dem. Republic in 1957.

Soviet alliance treaties were concluded with the Mongol. People's Republic in 1946 (followed by association with the Warsaw Pact as an observer), Red China in 1950, Afghanistan and Finland in 1955.

Alliance Systems of the Neutral Powers

The Balkan Pact (p. 244) developed out of the

1953 Treaty of Friendship of Ankara and was supplemented by the

1954 Mutual Assistance Pact of Bled (limited to 20 yrs); inactive since 1955.

The Arab League (p. 257) was founded 1945 in Cairo as a treaty of non-aggression and consultation, providing for close cooperation. Decisions were t[illegible] be binding for those powers voting affirmativel[illegible] there were frequent conflicts of interest. **Orga**[illegible] a Council of Heads of State (from 1964[illegible] Council of For. Ministers to coordinate [illegible] policy. Libya joined in 1953, the Sudan i[illegible] Tunisia and Morocco in 1958, Kuwait in [illegible]

A **collective Treaty of Defence** exists within t[illegible] work of the League since 1950; it is [illegible] above all, against Israel.

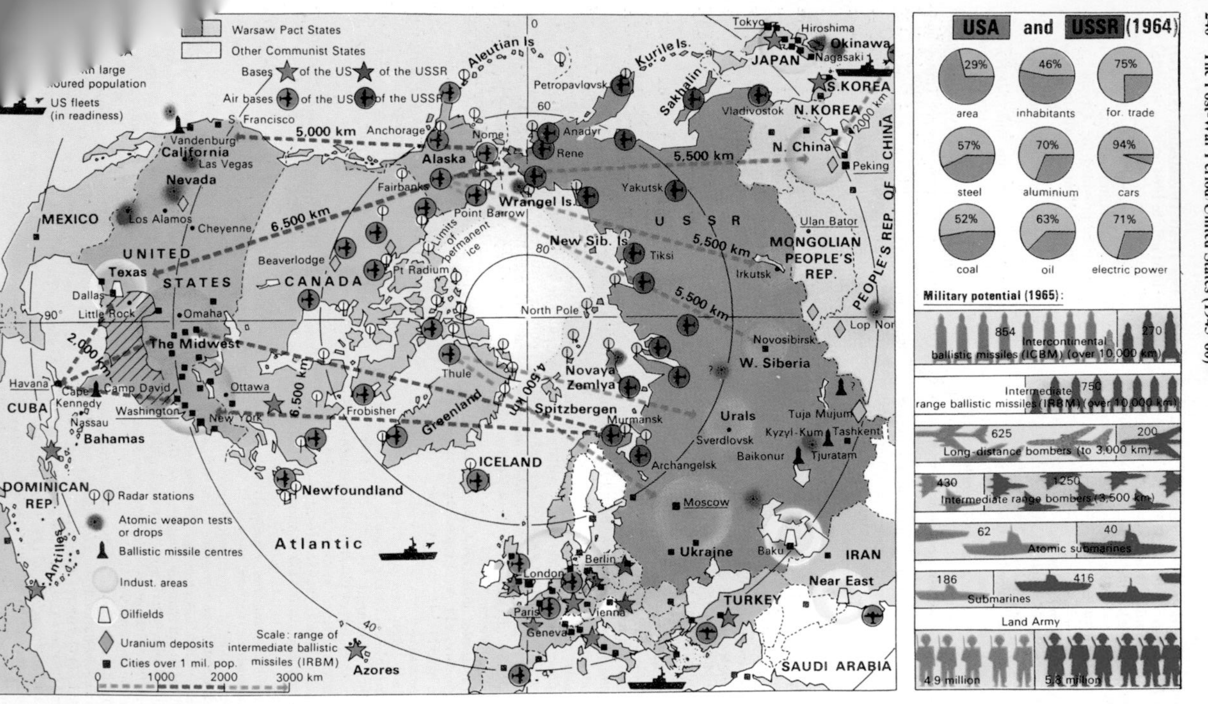

U.S.A. and U.S.S.R.: the two major powers, *c.* 1960

The U.S.A. after 1945

1945–53 President Harry S. Truman (1884–1973), who succeeded the deceased F. D. ROOSEVELT (p. 187) after serving as his vice-president. Possessing the atomic monopoly (p. 272), the U.S.A. became the leading nation after the vict.; she sought to shape int. affairs – in conjunction with the U.N. (p. 223) – on the basis of the Atlantic Charter.

For. policy: with the beginning of the E.–W. conflict (p. 219) the policy of the 'containment' of Communism replaced cooperation with the U.S.S.R. The

1947 Truman Doctrine (p. 229), proclaimed by the president in a message to Congress, deliberately turning from isolationism and the Monroe Doctrine (p. 95), promised all countries milit. and econ. assistance to preserve their independence.

Consequences: support for Greece and Turkey (p. 229), the Marshall Plan (p. 245), the Berlin Airlift (p. 253), the Nat. Security Council, the establishment of NATO. To ward off Communism in Asia

1946 the Philippines were given their independence (p. 263) and a programme of econ. stabilization of Japan (beginning in 1949) was carried through. Following his election in 1948, TRUMAN affirmed the global responsibility of the U.S. in the

1949 4-Point Programme (p. 261), endorsing it by taking the initiative in implementing U.N. measures against the N. Korean aggressors during the

1950–53 Kor. crisis (p. 237); but, in the

1950 8-Point Programme (Sep.), moderate objectives of U.S. policy in Korea were announced, later supplemented by EISENHOWER's radio address, which opened the 'Crusade for Freedom'. In Dec. President TRUMAN proclaimed a state of nat. emergency: reconstruction and expansion of the armed services, which had been demobilized after 1945. The ANZUS Pact (p. 239) and the

1951 peace treaty with Japan (p. 235) strengthened the Amer. position in Asia. A new programme for the Near East was introduced (Mar. 1950), which provided for tech. assistance, capital investments, help to refugees and improved trade and cult. relations.

Domestic policies:

1947 The Taft-Hartley Act was passed (overriding the veto of the president): prohibition of the 'closed shop' and the use of union funds to support polit. parties; the president was given the right to suspend strikes for limited periods ('cooling-off periods'). Notwithstanding the opposition of conservative Republicans and southern Democrats, the president – to extend econ. and soc. democracy – introduced the

1949 'Fair Deal', intended to consolidate the achievements of the New Deal (p. 187).

1951 22nd Amendment: the president's term of office – in case of re-election – was limited to 2 terms.

The collapse of Nationalist China (p. 235) and the realization that the U.S.S.R. possessed atomic weapons precipitated a fear psychosis: trials of leading Communists in the U.S.A. and leftist intellectuals (the ALGER HISS case), espionage trials (JULIUS and ETHEL ROSENBERG). Senator **Joseph McCarthy** (Wisconsin) initiated his struggle against anti-Amer. subversion. Against the opposition of the president, Congress passed the McCarran–Nixon Act ('McCarran Internal Security Act') (1950: registration of all Com. and Com.-front organizations) and the McCarran–Walter Act (1952: revision of immigration quotas). A Senate Investigation Committee (ESTES KEFAUVER) est. that trade unions were in underworld control: expulsion of the Int. Longshoremen's Association (1954) and the Teamsters Union from the A.F.L. (1955 fusion of A.F.L. and C.I.O.).

1953–61 President Dwight D. Eisenhower/Republican (1890–1969).

A 'New Positive For. Policy' was introduced under **Secretary of State John Foster Dulles** (1888–1959), succeeded in 1959 by CHRISTIAN HERTER (1895–1966). Proceeding from the premise of a permanent conflict between Communism and Amer. power in the world, the 'long-range policy' envisaged the 'roll-back' of Communism by means of milit. alliances (p. 239) and for. aid. Following the

1953 Kor. armistice the U.S.A. moderated the crises over Formosa (p. 235), Hungary (p. 233) and the Suez Canal (p. 257). Formulated in response to a request by states of the Near East, the

1957 Eisenhower Doctrine (p. 257) gave assurance of milit. assistance in the event of Com. attacks. Responding to Russia's call for coexistence, DULLES switched to a policy more friendly to the U.S.S.R.

1959 Vice-President NIXON's trip to the U.S.S.R. and Poland. **Khrushchev's visit** (Sep.): talks between the heads of state at **Camp David** regarding the possibilities of solving int. problems.

1960 EISENHOWER's tours in Lat. America and the Far East revealed the existence of anti-Amer. feelings in these areas. The relationship of the U.S. with Cuba (p. 271) worsened.

Domestic policies: McCARTHY, as chairman of the Permanent Senate Committee on Investigations, intimidated officials of the State Department and intellectuals (the OPPENHEIMER case). Official censure by the Senate terminated his activity.

The question of the blacks: good experiences with integrated units in the Kor. War and the negative impression made on coloured nations by the unresolved racial question in the U.S. made racial integration, esp. in schools, desirable. The unanimous

1954 decision of the Supreme Court holding public school segregation to be unconst. (and, among other rulings, bringing judgements against the segregation of public means of transport) was boycotted in the S. Racial unrest (in, among other places, **Little Rock**, Ark.) led to the intervention of Fed. troops.

1957 By a vote of 72:18 the U.S. Senate passed the **Civil Rights Bill** (safeguarding the voting rights of Negroes).

The U.S.A. (1961–5)

1961–63 President John F. Kennedy/Democrat (1917–63 (assassinated)), elected with 50·1% of the votes over RICHARD M. NIXON/Republican (b. 1913).

The new polit. style of the Kennedy era: the presid. office was transformed into a planning staff of advisers (among others MCGEORGE BUNDY), chaired by the president; scientists were employed and experienced specialists became part of the admin., among them Secretary of State **Dean Rusk** (b. 1909), Secretary of Defense **Robert S. McNamara** (b. 1916), Ambassador to the U.N., ADLAI E. STEVENSON. The budget was increased (which again made the furtherance of the indust. rates of growth necessary) to finance development aid, missile, space and armament programmes.

For. policy: Soviet offensives (p. 228) were met by

1. Strengthening milit. striking power: combination of nuclear and mobile conventional weapons ('strike command').
2. Eliminating rivalries between America's alliance partners by acknowledging their right to participate in decision-making:
   1962 offer of an Atlantic partnership to a united Europe.
3. Extensive development aid, with precedence given to milit. aid, coordinated by an Office of Int. Development:

1961 Establishment of the **'Peace Corps'**, consisting of trained volunteers. To promote the 'peaceful revolution' of Lat. America the **Alliance for Progress** was formed (p. 271). During the

1962 Congo crisis (p. 269) the U.S. declared that they would not permit unilateral attempts at intervention. On the basis of pressure exerted under the Truman Doctrine (p. 241) and SEATO armament aid, an armistice was concluded in Laos (May). A comprehensive **Berlin declaration** was issued (Jun.: '3 essentials', p. 219). Milit. advisers were sent to **S. Vietnam.** Following the break in diplomatic relations with **Cuba** by the EISENHOWER admin. (Jan. 1961) an invasion was attempted; the **Cuban crisis** (Oct., p. 271) was ended by a relaxation of tensions (p. 228): Washington–Moscow 'hot line' and the **Atomic Test-Ban Treaty** (p. 273).

Econ. life: presid. messages proposed measures to improve the competitive position. Tariffs were lowered on goods coming from EEC states (Kennedy Round, p. 245); measures were taken to improve the econ. position of agriculture. Strikes and the rise of steel prices were prevented.

Domestic policies: increasing racial discrimination and, beginning in 1962, unrest owing to resistance by governors of Southern states, who believed that states' rights had been violated by the decisions of the Supreme Court (p. 241). The

1963 Civil Rights programme of the president was supported by a Washington mass demonstration (200,000 Negroes and whites) and the Nat. Association for the Advancement of Colored People (N.A.A.C.P.) and the Southern Christian Leadership Conference under **Martin Luther King**. Visiting Dallas, Texas,

22 Nov. 1963 President Kennedy was assassinated. KENNEDY's course in for. policy was continued by

1963–9 President Lyndon B. Johnson (1908–73).

1964 Speech espousing the principles for the preservation of a lasting peace (Apr.). Resistance to Com. aggression. Support for allies. There followed increased milit. aid to Vietnam (p. 237). Intervention in the

1965 civil war in the Domin. Republic (p. 271): the declaration by the U.S. (Johnson Doctrine) that it would intervene only in case of the threat of Com. takeover remained controversial among the O.A.S. states and in the U.N.

Domestic politics: to eliminate racial discrimination, the

1964 Civil Rights Bill was passed; it has been called the most important measure intended to bring about equality for black people since the emancipation of the Negroes under LINCOLN (p. 95); it was supplemented by the

1965 Voting Rights Act. In the **'War against Poverty'** the

1964 Econ. Opportunity Act (initiated by President KENNEDY) was passed. From

1965 the 'Great Society' programme endeavoured to bring justice, freedom and cooperation to all men.

Canada (1945–65)

Essentially an agrarian country, Canada developed its industry during the 2nd World War. Owing to a world-wide demand for raw materials and foodstuffs, waves of immigrants and the discovery of oil-fields, uranium and other ore deposits, Canada experienced an econ. upswing in the post-war period. Soc. welfare measures were introduced. The Liberals under **Mackenzie King** (1874–1950) and LOUIS STEPHEN ST LAURENT worked for the decentralization of the Commonwealth.

1949 Newfoundland (p. 171) became the 10th province. As a reaction to the close cooperation of the Liberals with the U.S., in

1957 the Conservatives won an elect. vict. **The John G. Diefenbaker** (b. 1895) Cabinet aspired to assert Canad. independence and neutrality.

1963 Differences with the U.S.A. over the equipping of Canad. forces with atomic weapons, which was endorsed by the Lib. opposition. The conflict brought about the dissolution of parliament and new elections (Apr.): the Liberals won an absolute majority. As prime minister, **Lester Bowles Pearson** (1897–1972) pressed for equal rights for Fr.-Canadians, the lessening of direct U.S. investments and Canad. participation in nuclear defence.

1964 Visit of Queen ELIZABETH II on the occasion of the 100th aniversary of the Dominion: there were demonstrations by Fr.-Canadians for autonomy, or secession of the areas inhabited by them. These demonstrations intensified the general feeling that the constitution should be revised.

Southern Europe (1945–65)

Spain: polit. isolation of the **Franco régime** (p. 161);

1947 A popular referendum decided in favour of monarchy. The E.–W. conflict moved the U.S.A. to revise its anti-Sp. policies:

1953 An **agreement was concluded** between the U.S.A. and Spain, providing for Amer. milit. bases to be est. on Sp. soil in exchange for econ. and milit. aid. Spain gave up some N. Afr. possessions to Morocco (1956). Student unrest was directed against censorship and the lack of polit. freedom; from 1962 there was also soc. unrest: strikes (in part condoned by the Church) accompanied econ. recovery.

Portugal: maintaining friendly relations with Spain, the prime minister, **Salazar** (p. 161), governed with almost absolute powers; 1951 a treaty for the establishment of bases was concluded with the U.S.A. Beginning in

1961 Portugal lost its possessions in India (Goa, p. 265) and experienced unrest in Angola and Mozambique; the U.N. condemned Portugal's colon. policy.

Italy: at the end of the war liberation committees (resistance groups) and internally divided polit. parties had wrestled for power. The use of force and 'purgative legislation' against Fascists disqualified whole segments of the pop. Repatriated people (p. 221) and occupants of internment camps increased the general misery and danger of civil war.

1945–53 Prime Minister Alcide de Gasperi/D.C.I. (1881–1954). Following elections to the Nat. Assembly and a popular referendum

18 Jun. 1946 proclamation of the Republic.

1947 Peace Treaty (p. 218): reparations, the loss of Istria, the colonies and the surrender of the fleet were the result. A currency reform (under Minister of Finance EINAUDI) curtailed inflation.

1948 President Einaudi (1874–1961); the **Christ. Democrats (D.C.I.)** obtained an absolute majority in parliament. Notwithstanding strikes and Popular Front opposition, the prime minister, DE GASPERI, carried out his Eur. policies (p. 245): his opposition was composed of **Communists (P.C.I.)** under **Togliatti** (1893–1964) and left-wing **Socialists (P.S.I.)** under **Nenni** (b. 1891).

1949 Agrarian crisis in Southern Italy (uprisings in Calabria): partial expropriation of large landed properties. The export business (film industry, fashions) and tourism recovered.

1951–2 Consolidation of the moderate **Socialists/P.S.D.I.** under **Saragat**. Elect. gains of the Left (P.C.I., P.S.I.), the **Neo-Fascists/M.S.I.** and the **Monarchists/P.N.M.** weakened the D.C.I. coalitions, leading, from

1953, to frequent changes of gvt.

1955 President Gronchi/D.C.I. (b. 1887), **from 1962 Segni**. The

1960 state crisis (unrest, strikes), over the planned M.S.I. congress in Genoa, was overcome by Prime Minister **Fanfani**/D.C.I. (b. 1908), who introduced

1962 the **'Opening to the Left'** (a D.C.I. coalition with the P.S.D.I. (SARAGAT)).

1963 Communist elect. gains (25% of the votes). Prime Minister **Aldo Moro**/D.C.I. formed a coalition gvt of the Left (with the P.S.I., P.S.D.I. and P.R.I.=republicans); it stabilized the currency, the balance of payments and improved the tourist trade. There was interior migration from S. to N. and a flow of labour abroad. From

1964 President Saragat/P.S.D.I. (b. 1898).

S. Tirol: the peace treaty confirmed the

1946 Ital.-Aust. autonomy agreement; but the Ital.

1948 Statute of Autonomy applied not to Bolzano, but to the Bolzano-Trentino region. The **People's party/S.V.P.** protested against Italianization.

1960 Austria brought the question of S. Tirol before the U.N.

1961 Negotiations failed (Milan, Zürich); **acts of terrorism**, arrests, severe sentences in, among others, the

1964 Milan explosives trial, followed. The foreign ministers KREISKY and SARAGAT decided on the formation of a mixed commission of experts to alleviate the conflict.

The Alpine States (1945–65)

Austria (map, p. 248):

1945 Provis. gvt (Apr.) under KARL RENNER (p. 156), supervised by the occupying powers: Vienna was divided into four zones (Jul.) and was the seat of the **Allied Control Council**. Following the elections to the Nat. Council, the Ö.V.P., S.P.Ö. and K.P.Ö. formed a coalition under Fed. Chancellor **Leopold Figl**/Ö.V.P. (1902–65). **Karl Renner** became Fed. President (1951 **Theodor Körner**/S.P.Ö., 1873–1957; 1957 **Adolf Schärf**/S.P.Ö., 1890–1965; from 1965 **Franz Jonas**/S.P.Ö., b. 1899). The

1946 Allied law requiring their unanimity to reject Aust. legislation gave a measure of flexibility to Aust. politics.

Heavy industry, mining, banking and other major enterprises were nationalized. The

1947 law to protect the currency caused the Com. party to leave the gvt. Domestic polit. stability on the basis of **Grand Coalitions of the Ö.V.P. S.P.Ö.** (the proportional system, to 1965) and Rus. concessions following STALIN's death made it easier for

1953–61 Fed. Chancellor Julius Raab/Ö.V.P. (1871–1964) to conclude the

15 May 1955 Treaty of State (p. 218): suspension of occupation in exchange for material obligations (to 1964) and voluntary neutrality (Oct.). After that the economy turned upwards, from 1962 in conjunction with price rises and wage demands by trade unions (FRANZ OLAH).

1961–4 Fed. Chancellor ALFONS GORBACH/Ö.V.P., Vice-Chancellor BRUNO PITTERMANN/S.P.Ö.

Tensions within the coalition were caused by the return of the heir to the throne, OTTO VON HABSBURG (who received permission to enter the country in 1966). The

1966 elect. vict. of the Ö.V.P. terminated the era of the Grand Coalition (1966: Ö.V.P. gvt under JOSEF KLAUS, Fed. Chancellor from 1964).

Switzerland: strictly observing the principles of neutrality, the country participated in charitable undertakings (the Swiss Fund for Refugees, the Pestalozzi children's villages), and cult. and econ. agencies (UNESCO, O.E.E.C., E.Z.U.).

1955 The research centre for Atomic Energy in Geneva (CERN). While indust. development was on a sound basis (employment of 'guest', i.e. migrant, workers), agriculture was subsidized; intense efforts to strengthen the defence of the country, incl. (from 1958) plans for atomic weapons, were made.

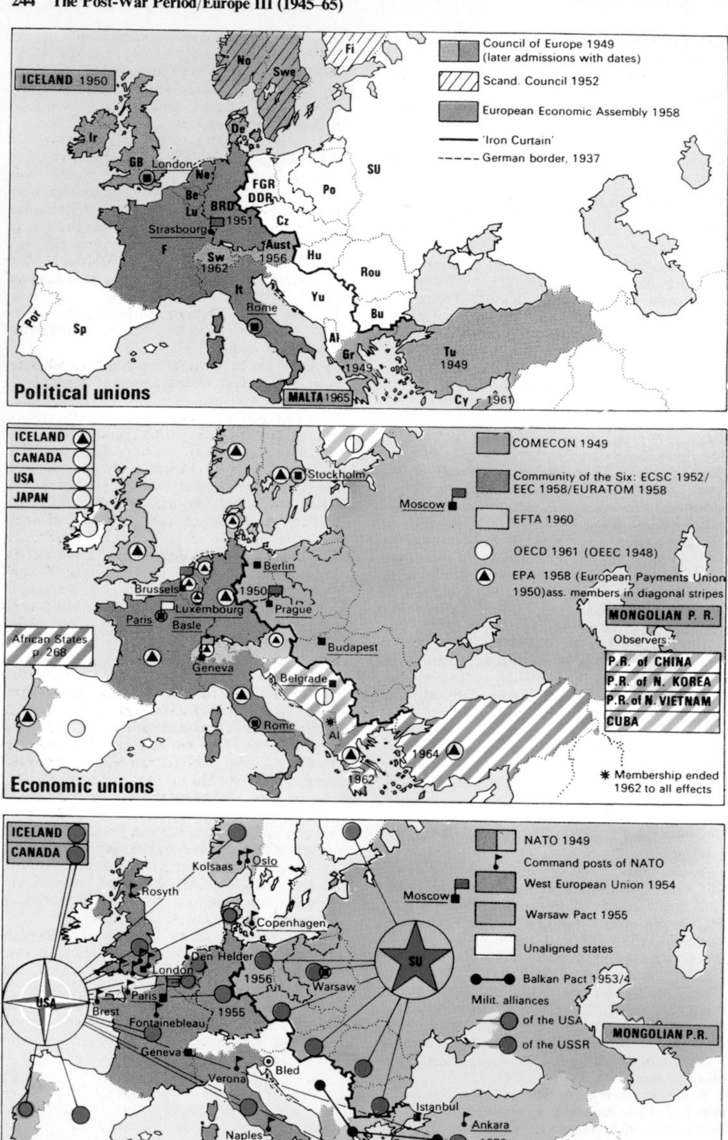
Council of Europe 1949 (later admissions with dates)
Scand. Council 1952
European Economic Assembly 1958
'Iron Curtain'
German border, 1937
ICELAND 1950
MALTA 1965
Political unions
COMECON 1949
Community of the Six: ECSC 1952/ EEC 1958/EURATOM 1958
EFTA 1960
OECD 1961 (OEEC 1948)
EPA 1958 (European Payments Union 1950) ass. members in diagonal stripes
MONGOLIAN P. R.
Observers:
P.R. of CHINA
P.R. of N. KOREA
P.R. of N. VIETNAM
CUBA
Membership ended 1962 to all effects
African States p. 268
ICELAND
CANADA
USA
JAPAN
Economic unions
NATO 1949
Command posts of NATO
West European Union 1954
Warsaw Pact 1955
Unaligned states
Balkan Pact 1953/4
Milit. alliances
of the USA
of the USSR
MONGOLIAN P.R.
Military alliances

The politics of European integration after 1945

The Polit. Integration of Europe

After 1945, the conceptions of a Eur. Union (incl. Germany), given voice by CHURCHILL (in the Zürich speech of 1946), Prof. H. BRUGMANS, former resistance groups, and others, gained adherents (esp. among the young). Brussels became the centre of the

1948 Europe movement (PAUL-HENRI SPAAK). The Congress of The Hague (presided over by CHURCHILL) and the Fr. gvt gave impetus to the

1949 Council of Europe (founded in London) to safeguard the Eur. heritage and soc. progress. **Organs**: the Secretariat (Strasbourg), the Consultative Assembly (composed of delegates from the parliaments of the countries), the **Committee of Ministers**. Reservations by individual nations (Britain) caused

1950–51 the failure of the project for a Eur. Union, planned by the 'Federalists'.

1953 Convention on Human Rights. Agreement on universities (Eur. Conference of Rectors), medical aid, passports, a 'soc. charter' (1962).

Milit. Integration

1948 Mutual Assistance Pact of Brussels ('Brussels Treaty') between the Benelux states, Britain and France. Its standing Milit. Committee was absorbed by

1949 NATO (p. 239). Following suggestions by CHURCHILL and Fr. prime minister, **Pleven**, the NATO Council, during the course of the Kor. crisis (p. 237), decided to form a Eur. Defence Community (E.D.C.) with Ger. participation; Fed. Chancellor ADENAUER used this opportunity to raise the prestige of the B.R.D. (p. 251).

1952 Paris Eur. Defence Community Treaty, providing for the raising of a supranat. w. Eur. army with ties to NATO (Pleven Plan). Following Fr. rejection, the

1954 Paris Treaties (p. 251) transformed the Brussels Treaty into the **Western Eur. Union** (W.E.U.) providing for nat. troop contingents under NATO supreme command). **Organs**: the Council of Ministers, the Permanent Committee, committees on armaments and armament control; a W.E.U. parliament within the framework of the Council of Europe.

1955 The Warsaw Pact (p. 231).

Econ. Integration

The Marshall Plan: planning within the overall context of the Truman Doctrine (p. 241), U.S. Secretary of State **George C. Marshall** (1880–1959) proposed a

1947 Eur. Recovery Programme (E.R.P.): the U.S.A. was to supply raw materials, goods and capital, partly in form of credits, partly as outright subsidies. The U.S.S.R. rejected this 'instrument of dollar imperialism' (p. 227), while Poland and Czechoslovakia recanted their affirmative replies to the **Paris Marshall Plan Conference** (Jul.–Sep.).

1948 Organization for Eur. Econ. Cooperation (O.E.E.C.), in Paris, for the distribution of E.R.P. funds (by 1952 *c.* $14,000 mil. U.S.)

Consequences in the E.: Russia reacted with the

1949 Council for Mutual Economic Assistance (**COMECON**, p. 231): adjustment of nat. econ. planning to conform to overall Rus. interests.

Consequences in the W.: the opportunity for polit. unification was passed over, but the achievements of O.E.E.C. and E.R.P. gave impetus to the establishment of addit. institutions:

1947 General Agreement on Tariffs and Trade at Geneva **(G.A.T.T.).**

1950 Eur. Payments Union (E.P.U.): convertibility of Eur. Payments Union currencies through the **Bank for the Int. Balance of Payments** in Basle.

1958–9 O.E.E.C. deliberations concerning the establishment of a Eur. free trade area failed because of Brit.-Fr. differences. Following Brit. initiative, and as a protective measure directed against the E.E.C., a

1959–60 limited Eur. Free Trade Association (EFTA) was est. The Eur. Payments Union was expanded in the

1959 Eur. Payments Agreements (E.P.A.): free convertibility also in the int. transfer of payments and capital.

1961 Organization for Econ. Cooperation and Development (O.E.C.D.). Termination of the O.E.E.C., expansion of world trade, and coordination of Western development aid.

The Community of the 6: to maintain harmony (control of the Ruhr area, p. 251), the for. minister, **Schuman** (p. 247) proposed a

1950 Common Market for Coal, Iron and Steel for a period of 50 yrs (Schuman Plan). Formation of the

1951 'Montan Union' (Eur. Coal and Steel Community, E.C.S.C.) in Luxemburg. **Organs**: the High Authority (9 members) with immediate authority, appointed for 6-yr terms by the **Council of Ministers** (veto power). The

1952–3 plan for a polit. union failed, but the success of the E.C.S.C. encouraged the

1955 Conference of For. Ministers in Messina to expand the Community.

1957 The Treaties of Rome concerning the **utilization of atomic energy (EURATOM)** and the establishment of the **Eur. Econ. Community (E.E.C.),** including as its core a customs union (to be completed by 1970). **Organs**: the **Council of Ministers** (authority over guidelines and budget, from 1967 on the basis of majority decision) appoints the **E.E.C. Commission** in Brussels (consisting of 9 members, under the presidency of **Hallstein** of the Fed. Republic of Germany) for 4-yr terms; provisions for diplomatic relations were made. Control by the

1958 Eur. Parliament (Strasbourg); Econ. and Soc. Council (consisting of 101 employers and employees); a Eur. Court of Justice.

Associated states: exports were to be free of customs, as standard customs were levied on E.E.C. goods.

1961–3 Negotiations over the entry of Britain into the Community failed because of the Fr. veto (DE GAULLE). Econ. development proceeded on favourable lines, but there were difficult structural adjustments to be made for agric. products under

1962 the E.E.C. market regulations.

1964 The reduction of tariffs was discussed with the U.S.A. under the General Agreement on Tariffs and Trade (G.A.T.T.) ('Kennedy Round'). Liberalization of the grain market encountered resistance from the Fed. Republic of Germany.

1965 E.E.C. Crisis: France rejected a compromise proposal (to postpone price adjustments to Jul. 1967), demanded const. changes and broke off negotiations (Jul.).

Britain (1945–65)

Although among the victors, Britain lost its position as a major world power: indebtedness ($14,000 mil. (U.S.)), losses of capital, devaluation of the currency.

1945–51 Lab. gvt under Clement Attlee (1883–1967). In **for. policy** (for. secretary, **Bevin** (p. 146), from 1950 **Morrison**, 1888–1965) close ties to the U.S.A. with regard to Ger. policy and alliance systems (p. 239); agreement on milit. bases, 1948, participation in the Kor. War, mediation in the Indo-China War (p. 237); restraint in Eur. politics (p. 245).

Austerity programmes (chancellor of the Exchequer, **Sir Stafford Cripps**, 1889–1952) provided for economy measures to aid recovery: rationing continued to 1950, imports were curtailed, capital was raised (U.S. loan) to increase exports and amortize the debt.

1947 A restrictive econ. programme and

1949 devaluation of the pound (from $4 to $2·80 (U.S.)).

Welfare policies: the Bank of England (1945), aviation, coal mining (1947), railways, energy production, the iron and steel industry (returned to private hands in 1953) were nationalized; soc. insurance systems (1946) were made **mandatory** (1948, in accordance with the 1942 Beveridge Plan) for, among other things, public health care, family and child-care assistance; low incomes were raised.

The Commonwealth: transition to a community of sovereign partners from

1947 in India (p. 265), SE. Asia (p. 263), Africa (p. 267).

1948 The Palestine Mandate was given up (p. 259).

Ireland: officially left the Commonwealth; the Ireland Bill guaranteed the polit. status of Northern Ireland.

1949 Republic of Eire, from 1959 under President **de Valera** (p. 170).

1951–64 The Con. Era:

1951–3 3rd Churchill Cabinet (for. secretary, **Eden**). Econ. stagnation eased, income and gold reserves increased.

1952 Elizabeth II (b. 1926).

1954 The Suez Canal zone and the Sudan were given up (p. 257).

Cyprus (p. 256): led by Archbp **Makarios** (banished 1956), the Gk Orth. majority (80%) sought union with Greece (ENOSIS); the Turk. minority sought partition for the island. From

1954 there was guerrilla fighting with the Gk EOKA movement (Colonel GRIVAS). The Greeks rejected Brit. and Turk. plans to introduce self-admin.

1959 London Agreement on Brit. milit. bases and 3-power guarantee of independence.

1960 The Republic of Cyprus (President MAKARIOS). Following the revision of the constitution

1963–4 civil war: intervention of Gk and Turk. nationalists, Turk. bombing raids; engagement of a U.N. peace-keeping force. The Cyprus conflict and the Suez crisis (p. 257) brought down the

1955–7 Eden gvt (for. secretary, SELWYN LLOYD (to 1960)). EDEN was replaced by

1957–63 Harold Macmillan (b. 1894).

1957 Ending of general conscription (Nat. Service). The testing of Britain's H-bomb gave the country its ind. nuclear deterrent, a fact opposed by the **Campaign for Nuclear Disarmament** (C.N.D.).

1959 Con. elect. vict. (365:265 seats). At the Blackpool Lab. Party Conference the opposition leader **Hugh Gaitskell** (1906–63), clashing with HAROLD WILSON (b. 1916), cal. for party reform (the state is neither capitalist nor regulator, but only the biggest 'shareholder').

1960 Scarborough Conference: split of the Lab. Party over questions of nuclear armament and use of Brit. bases for U.S. Polaris submarines.

Econ. life: large imports and capital exports, halting investment, decreasing rates of productivity; lulls in shipping construction and the motor-car industry (shortening of the working week and dismissals of workers).

1963 The attempt to join the E.E.C. failed because of the Fr. veto. The scandal over the secretary of state for war, JOHN PROFUMO, shook the gvt. Then the illness of MACMILLAN led to a change to the gvt of a new prime minister, **Sir Alec Douglas-Home** (b. 1903). Following a narrow elec. vict. (by 5 seats), formation of the

1964 Lab. Cabinet of Harold Wilson: rigorous measures to improve the balance of payments (tariffs on imports, a nat. price and income commission, for. support for the pound, etc.).

France (1944–6)

Following the liberation of Paris (p. 213), the Resistance and General **Charles de Gaulle** (1890–1970) formed a 'gvt of concord' (Aug. 1944). A Treaty of Alliance and Mutual Security was concluded with the U.S.S.R. (Dec.). France received a seat in the U.N. Security Council and a Ger. and Aust. zone of occupation (p. 248).

1944–5 Persecution and (sometimes arbitrary) conviction of **'collaborators'** and 'followers of Vichy': **Pétain** (p. 129) and **Laval** (p. 191) among others were condemned to death; PÉTAIN's sentence was commuted to life imprisonment.

Econ. life: public indebtedness rose from 1939 by 300%, the index of indust. production fell to 20%. To eliminate inflation, banknotes in circulation had to be exchanged and a capital tax was levied.

1945–6 Nationalization of the **Banc de France**, insurance companies, coal mines and sources of energy. A nat. reconstruction programme was introduced. The course of **domestic politics** was determined by the outcome of the

1945 election to the Nat. Assembly (Oct.): the Communists obtained 25%, the Socialists (S.F.) and the Dem. People's Movement (M.R.P.) 23% each of the vote. Disgruntled over the const. plans of the polit. parties, in

1946 de Gaulle resigned (Jan.). A popular referendum decided against the 1st draft of the constitution. Fresh elections in Jun. brought a small majority for the M.R.P.; the parties concluded a 'domestic peace' under **Georges Bidault** (b. 1899) as prime minister and the 2nd draft of the constitution was accepted.

France (1946–58)

The Constitution of the 4th Republic: a bi-cameral system (**Nat. Assembly** and Council of the Republic); the executive (prime minister and Cabinet) were dependent on the confidence of the Nat. Assembly; the president (elected for a 7-yr term by both chambers of parliament) carried no polit. responsibility; a const. committee for normative control of legislation; a **Fr. Union** of the mother country, overseas departments, associated territories (Togo, the Cameroons) and states (Tunisia, Morocco, Indo-China).

1947–54 PRESIDENT VINCENT AURIOL/S.F. †1884–1966). Because of their opposition to a wages freeze and milit. spending for Indo-China,

1947 the Communists left the gvt of **Ramadier**/S.F. The Com. party (**Thorez**, p. 191) and the nationalistic **R.P.F.** (Rassemblement du Peuple Français, a polit. union movement aspiring to a presid. régime by DE GAULLE) prevented the dem. **'3rd Force'** from attaining stable gvtl majorities; the '3rd Force' was a coalition of S.F. (**Ramadier**, 1888–1961; GUY MOLLET, b. 1905), **M.R.P.** (**Bidault**, **Robert Schuman**, 1886–1963) and Radicals (**R.S.: René Pleven**, b. 1901; **Pierre Mendès-France**, b. 1907). The

1947–8 econ. crisis (increased prices, strikes) was overcome with U.S. credits, E.R.P. funds, selective investments to increase the production of energy, coal, iron, and steel (**Monnet**), Eur. integration (the Schuman Plan, p. 245), and the devaluation of the franc.

1950 Conscription extended to 18 months. Notwithstanding the

1951 elect. reform (joint lists and majority vote at department level), the '3rd Force' split into opposing groups over questions of educ. policy (infl. of the Church), socialization and Eur. integration (E.E.C. Treaty, p. 245).

1953 Amnesty proclaimed for former Vichy civil servants and politicians.

1954 President **René Coty** (1882–1962) elected after 13 ballots. The 4th Republic fell because of its

Colon. policy: 1954–5 Indo-China and Tunisia were given up under Prime Minister MENDÉS-FRANCE; Morocco under Prime Minister **Edgar Faure** (b. 1908). Prime Minister GUY MOLLET endeavoured to bring about a federalist solution to the **Alger. crisis** (p. 269); he recalled Governor-General JACQUES COUSTELLE/Gaullist (b. 1912) and made contact with the Alger. rebels. The

1956 Suez conflict (p. 257) was followed by continual gvtl crises; in Algeria, Gaullists and the army (Generals MASSU, SALAN) assumed power.

1958 Coup in Algiers (May); a state of nat. emergency was proclaimed; Prime Minister PIERRE PFLIMLIN resigned (May); **President Coty summoned General de Gaulle to become prime minister with special powers**; the Nat. Assembly adjourned.

Sep. 1958 A popular referendum decided in favour of the new presid. constitution (79·25% of favourable votes): the president was to appoint the prime minister. A Fr. Community (*Communauté*) was formed, consisting of auton. members enjoying the right to leave (p. 265), and DE GAULLE was given special authorities to carry out the reorganization of the state.

The 5th Republic (1958–65)

1958 Elections to the Nat. Assembly (Nov.): vict. of the 'Union for the New Republic' (U.N.R.); as the new president, **de Gaulle** appointed the

1959 Michel Debré gvt (for. minister **Couve de Murville** (b. 1907)). From

1960 establishment of a Fr. nuclear deterrent (p. 273). The **Alger. crisis** continued (coup attempts, O.A.S. terror) until Algeria was granted independence (Agreement of Evian, 1962). From then on the strong-willed policies of DE GAULLE, 'leader of the nation', aimed at strengthening France and freedom from 'Amer. tutelage'.

1962 Const. reform: direct election of the president; DEBRÉ resigned as prime minister over Eur. plans for confederation ('the Europe of fatherlands'); President DE GAULLE appointed **Pompidou** (1911–74) as prime minister.

1963 A Franco-Ger. treaty of cooperation was signed; rejection of Brit.-Amer. NATO planning (M.L.F., p. 239), of the ban on atomic testing (p. 273), and of Brit. entry into the E.E.C.; demand for NATO reform.

1964 Diplomatic relations taken up with Com. China.

1965 NATO and SEATO manoeuvres without Fr. participation; criticism of the structure of the E.E.C. (p. 245).

The Benelux States after 1945

Planned by the 3 gvts in exile in 1944, a

1948 Benelux customs union was est.; an econ. union followed in 1958, a passport union in 1960, a joint court of justice in 1964. Active policies for Eur. integration were pursued; the post-war period saw rapid econ. recovery.

Belgium: a crisis (general strike) was caused by LEOPOLD III's resumption of the throne; LEOPOLD abdicated in favour of his son

1951 Baudouin I (b. 1930). As for. minister, **Paul-Henri Spaak** (b. 1899) worked for border revisions with the Fed. Republic of Germany (return of territories occupied in 1949).

1958 World Exhibition in Brussels. A general strike against the

1960 econ. programme, introduced to cushion econ. setbacks incurred during the Congo crisis (p. 269), was unsuccessful. The Flemish question ('Frenchification') and the structural crisis of the Walloon indust. area remained unresolved.

The Netherlands: despite severe war damage having dest. harbours, ships and homes, plunder, and the burden of people repatriated from Indonesia (p. 263), rapid econ. recovery (balance of payments from 1951 on); heavy urbanization (construction of new suburbs) and industrialization; emphasis on soc. policies (aid for the poor).

1948 Queen Juliana (b. 1909) ascended the throne.

1953 Catastrophic flooding. Following negotiations, Ger. border territories were returned in 1960.

Luxemburg: a centre of the coal, iron, and steel industry (the ARBED Corporation), Luxemburg in 1948 abandoned its policy of 'eternal neutrality'.

1964 Grandduke Jean (b. 1921) ascended the throne.

Germany after the collapse, 1945

ivision of Germany, 1945

Germany after the Capitulation

Notwithstanding the discussions of the subject at the conferences of Teheran and Yalta, there was no unified conception of the **occupation forces** regarding the treatment of Germany.

1945 Berlin 4-Power Declaration: gvtl powers were assumed by the commanders of the occupation zones: General EISENHOWER/U.S.A. (from 1947 General CLAY); Marshal ZHUKOV/U.S.S.R. (from 1946 General SOKOLOVSKY); Field Marshal MONTGOMERY/Britain (from 1947 General ROBERTSON); General KOENIG/France.

Formation of the **Allied Control Council**; withdrawal of Brit. and Amer. troops from Mecklenburg, Saxony and Thuringia; joint occupation and admin. of Berlin (p. 253).

The **Potsdam Conference (Stalin, Truman, Churchill/Attlee** and the for. ministers) resulted in the **Potsdam Agreement** (Jul./Aug.):

1. Elimination of nationalism and militarism.
2. **Partition of Germany** (pending conclusion of a peace treaty) into 4 occupation zones: 2 territories to be under Rus. or Pol. admin., with a special status for Berlin; resettlement of Germans from Poland, Hungary and Czechoslovakia.
3. Appointment of local admins. and Ger. cen. authorities under the supervision of a Control Council (unanimous decision).
4. Control of industry – a unified economy to be preserved; dissolution of cartels, syndicates, trusts; **reparations** and **dismantling** of indust. plants.

The Fr. gvt, uninvited to the Conference (p. 246), rejected Ger. cen. authorities and pressed for control of the Ruhr area.

Separation of the Saar territory (Jul.): auton. admin. under a Fr. protectorate; econ. ties with France.

Denazification: prohibition of the N.S.D.A.P. Nat. Socialist leaders were interned and removed from public office; *c.* 6 mil. former members of Nat. Socialist organizations had to fill out questionnaires and subject themselves to investigative tribunals. At the

1945–6 Nuremberg Trials 24 major war criminals were tried by Allied judges. The **Nat. Socialist leadership corps, the Gestapo, S.D., and S.S. were declared criminal organizations**; trials of lawyers, S.S. doctors, concentration camp commandants and guards, diplomats, senior army officers, industrialists and leading officials followed.

Admission of polit. parties: the following parties were est. in 1945: K.P.D. (Com. party of Germany), S.P.D. (Soc. Dem. party of Germany), C.D.U. (Christ. Dem. Union; in Bavaria, the C.S.U. (Christ. Soc. Union)), F.D.P. (Free Dem. party; in the Rus. Zone, the L.D.P.D. (Lib. Dem. party of Germany)). In the Rus. Zone, the S.P.D. and K.P.D. combined to form the **Socialist Unity party** (S.E.D.).

Formation of new Ger. states was effected in all zones by 1946; also, in

1945 11 cen. administrative bodies were est. in the Rus. zone; in Stuttgart a **Council of States** for the U.S. zone was created; and in 1946, a Zone Advisory Council for the Brit. zone was set up.

Allied econ. policy: to increase production

1945 mandatory work for men and women was introduced. Germany's merchant navy was confiscated, as were patents, property abroad, mines and large corporations (Krupp, I.G. Farben); skilled workers and scientists were assigned to forced labour. **Land reform** in the Rus. zone (Oct.): expropriation and redistribution without compensation of landed properties over 100 hectares.

1946 Indust. planning of the Control Council: reduction of industry to 50% of the pre-war period. In the Rus. zone, 213 companies (25% of total capacity) came into the possession of the U.S.S.R. as joint-stock companies.

The failure of the Control Council to establish a cen. admin. (Fr. veto) and fear of econ. chaos forced a **change in the course of Brit.–Amer. policy**: in his Stuttgart speech (Sep.), the U.S. secretary of state, JAMES F. BYRNES (1879–1972), cal. for a unified economy and election of a Ger. gvt.

1947 The 'Bizone' (Brit. and U.S. zones combined) est. (Jan.) in the face of Franco-Rus. protests. A conference of Ger. chiefs of state in Munich (Jun.) failed over the demand of the heads of state of the Rus. zone that the question of econ. union be subordinated to that of polit. union. Development of bizonal admin. through the Frankfurt **Econ. Council**. Mining was nationalized in the Rus. zone and a Ger. Econ. Commission was est. there (May). The S.E.D. convoked the Ger. **People's Congress** for 'Unity and a Just Peace' (the C.D.U. in the E. and the polit. parties of the W., exc. the K.P.D., rejected it).

Union of the Western Zones: a Fr. approximation to Brit.-Amer. policy resulted from increasing E.–W. tension (p. 219).

1948 London 6-Power Conference with recommendations for W. Germany: econ. integration into Western Europe, development of a constitution, int. control of the Ruhr. As a consequence, the Allied Control Council was dissolved; the U.S.S.R. no longer participated in its meetings. The 2nd People's Congress of the S.E.D. decided on the formation of an **'All-Ger. People's Council'**.

Jun. 1948 Reform of the currency in the Western zones: (10 RM = 1 DM-West). The Rus. milit. gvt responded with the exchange of currency in the same proportion (DM-East) and the Berlin Blockade (p. 253).

Jul. 1948 Frankfurt Documents of the occupation powers regarding the convocation of a constituent assembly and announcement of an occupation statute.

Sep. 1948 Convocation of the Parl. Council (65 members elected by the states) in Bonn. **Konrad Adenauer** (1876–1967), a former mayor of Cologne, and chairman of the C.D.U., became president.

1949 Washington Agreement (Apr.): high commissioners were to replace the milit. gvt.

May 1949 Passage of the 'Bonn Basic Laws', ratified by all states, exc. Bavaria.

Soviet zone: transformation of the S.E.D. into a cadre 'party of the new type'. The Trade Union League (F.D.G.B. = Free Ger. Trade Union League) became the controlling organ of production planning and work performance norms.

1949 Elections to the 3rd People's Congress (May), manipulated on the basis of 'unity lists'. The Congress confirmed the draft of the constitution (Mar.) presented by the People's Council.

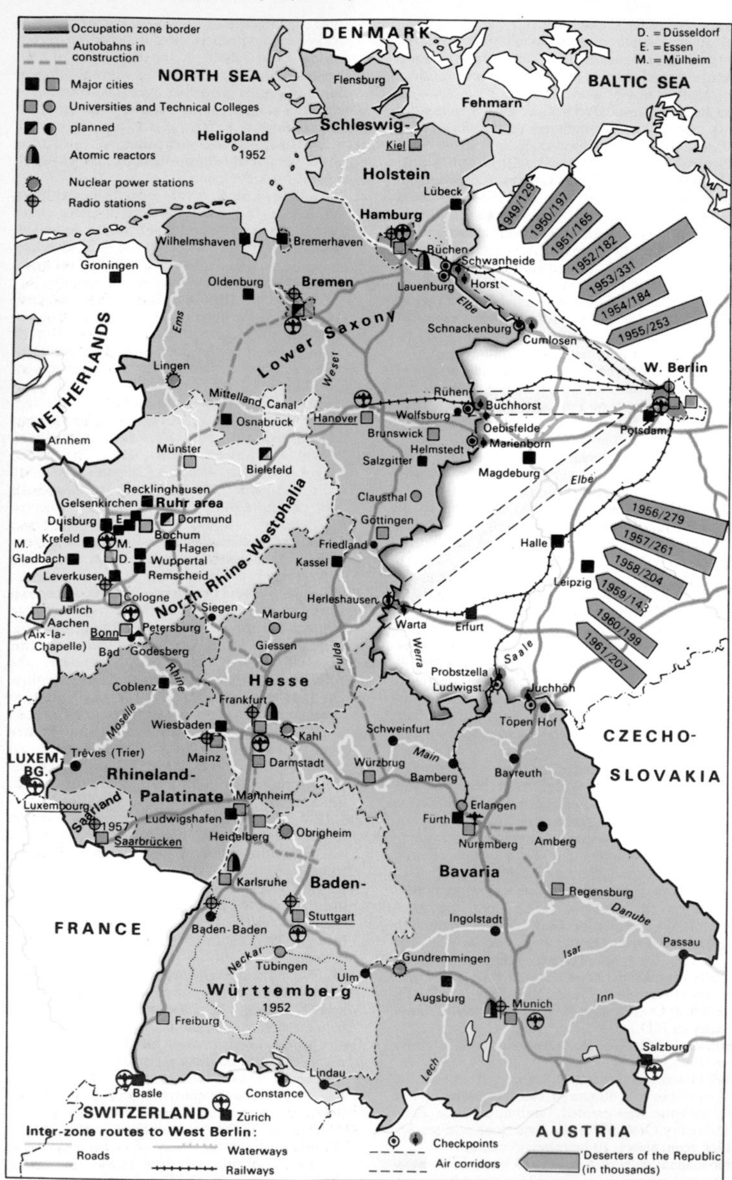

Occupation zone border
Autobahns in construction
Major cities
Universities and Technical Colleges
planned
Atomic reactors
Nuclear power stations
Radio stations
D. = Düsseldorf
E. = Essen
M. = Mülheim
DENMARK
NORTH SEA
BALTIC SEA
Heligoland 1952
Schleswig-Holstein
Flensburg
Fehmarn
Kiel
Lübeck
Hamburg
Büchen
Schwanheide
Lauenburg
Horst
Elbe
Schnackenburg
Cumlosen
1949/129
1950/197
1951/165
1952/182
1953/331
1954/184
1955/253
W. Berlin
Potsdam
Wilhelmshaven
Bremerhaven
Groningen
Oldenburg
Bremen
Lower Saxony
NETHERLANDS
Ems
Weser
Lingen
Mittelland Canal
Osnabrück
Hanover
Rühen
Buchhorst
Wolfsburg
Oebisfelde
Brunswick
Marienborn
Helmstedt
Magdeburg
Salzgitter
Arnhem
Münster
Bielefeld
Recklinghausen
Gelsenkirchen
Ruhr area
Dortmund
Duisburg
Bochum
Krefeld
Hagen
M. Gladbach
Wuppertal
Remscheid
Leverkusen
Cologne
Jülich
Aachen (Aix-la-Chapelle)
Bonn
Petersburg
Bad Godesberg
North Rhine-Westphalia
Siegen
Clausthal
Göttingen
Friedland
Kassel
Herleshausen
Warta
Erfurt
Werra
Halle
Leipzig
1956/279
1957/261
1958/204
1959/143
1960/199
1961/207
Marburg
Giessen
Fulda
Hesse
Saale
Probstzella
Ludwigst.
Juchhöh
Töpen
Hof
Coblenz
Rhine
Moselle
Frankfurt
Wiesbaden
Kahl
Schweinfurt
CZECHO-SLOVAKIA
LUXEM-BG.
Trèves (Trier)
Mainz
Darmstadt
Würzbrug
Main
Bamberg
Bayreuth
Rhineland-Palatinate
Luxembourg
Saarland 1957
Mannheim
Ludwigshafen
Erlangen
Furth
Nuremberg
Amberg
Saarbrücken
Heidelberg
Obrigheim
Karlsruhe
Baden-
Bavaria
Regensburg
Danube
Stuttgart
FRANCE
Baden-Baden
Ingolstadt
Passau
Neckar
Tübingen
Gundremmingen
Isar
Ulm
Württemberg 1952
Augsburg
Munich
Inn
Freiburg
Lech
Salzburg
Lindau
Basle
Constance
SWITZERLAND
Zürich
AUSTRIA
Inter-zone routes to West Berlin:
Roads
Waterways
Railways
Checkpoints
Air corridors
Deserters of the Republic (in thousands)

The Federal Republic of Germany

The Fed. Republic of Germany (B.R.D.)

23 May 1949 Proclamation of the 'Basic Law' (p. 253). Control of the B.R.D. through the **Ruhr Authority** and the **occupation statute**.

Aug. 1949 Elections to the 1st Bundestag (lower house of the Fed. Assembly): C.D.U. 139, S.P.D. 131 seats. **Theodor Heuss** F.D.P. (1884–1963) became fed. president.

1949–63 Fed. Chancellor Adenauer (p. 249) formed a coalition gvt (C.D.U./C.S.U., F.D.P., D.P. = Ger. party).

The occupation statute was gradually phased out as Germany became integrated into the Western alliance system. The S.P.D. opposition under **Kurt Schumacher** (1895–1952) and **Erich Ollenhauer** (1901–63) feared a delay of reunification.

Nov. 1949 Petersberg Agreement: participation of the B.R.D. in Western organizations.

1950 Law against rearmament. Following the Kor. crisis (p. 237), a **defence contribution** of the B.R.D. within the framework of a Eur. army was given consideration. Establishment of the 'Office to Safeguard the Constitution' (Aug.). The Conference of For. Ministers in New York issued a guarantee for the B.R.D. and w. Berlin.

Oct. 1950 The 'Office Blank': the minister of the interior, GUSTAV HEINEMANN (b. 1899), resigned in protest over the policy of remilitarization. Development of the fed. border police force.

1951 Revision of the occupation statute (Mar.): termination or suspension of the state of war (by the Eastern Bloc in 1955), discontinuation of the dismantling of industries and curtailment of indust. production; the B.R.D. assumed Germany's for. debt. ADENAUER was for. minister until 1955.

1952 'Germany Treaty' (May): abrogation of the occupation statute. Admission of the B.R.D. to the E.D.C. (p. 245). Sharp domestic polit. struggles (S.P.D.) over Germany's milit. contribution.

1954 Paris Treaties (Oct.): agreement on troop contingents for mutual defence; admission of the B.R.D. to W.E.U. and NATO (p. 245); denial of ABC weapons; **Franco-Ger. Saar agreement**: autonomy of the Saar under control of the W.E.U., which was rejected in

1955 by popular referendum.

1957–9 Integration of the Saar territory.

Parties/Trade Unions:

1949 association of 16 trade unions in the Ger. Trade Union Federation (D.G.B.). The newly founded polit. party of the refugees was at first successful (B.H.E., 1950). The newly founded parties did not halt the trend towards the 2-party system by the C.D.U. and S.P.D.

1956 Prohibition of the K.P.D. (1952 that of the rad. right-wing S.R.P.). In the

1959 Godesberg Programme the S.P.D. abandoned Marxist ideology.

Econ. and Soc. policy: under the minister of economics, **Ludwig Erhard** (b. 1897), the 'open market economy' developed favourably. Following the 'Korea boom', the yield of taxation and prices rose while unemployment declined.

1950 Termination of the rationing of foodstuffs; gvtl support of public housing construction; legislation providing for the victims of the war.

1950 Charter of the refugees and displaced persons (no revenge, just distribution of the war debt). The D.G.B. worked for a share for employees in the 'econ. miracle' (expansive wage demands: contracts to be adjusted acc. to the growth rate of the soc. product): full employment, shortening of the working week. From

1955 subsidies were given to agriculture.

1957 Reform of pension laws. **Marketing crisis in the coal industry** (which received subsidies from 1962). Measures were taken to prevent an **'overheating' of the economy**:

1959 Issue of 'people's shares' in the stock market; legislation governing the accumulation of property; gvt appeals for moderation; upward valuation of the DM.

1963 Lessening of the growth rate of the soc. product; increase of imports, wages, prices and public spending. For. migrant workers (1964: over 1 mil.) did not offset the shortage of labour. Gradual discontinuation of rent control.

Domestic affairs: many refugees from the Rus. zone.

1952 Formation of the sw. state of **Baden-Württemberg**. Amendments to the Basic Law and milit. legislation to bring about the

1956 establishment of the Bundeswehr (fed. armed forces) within the framework of NATO; Minister of Defence **Franz Josef Strauss**/C.S.U. (b. 1915). General conscription (for 12, from 1962 18 months). Controversies over atomic weapons and fall-out shelters.

1958 Appeal by Ger. academics to forgo atomic armaments. The Bundestag decided on equipping the Ger. Bundeswehr with the latest weapons, but at the same time cal. for general disarmament.

1958 trials began of those responsible for antisemitic excesses and concentration camp crimes. Resignation of the cabinet members OBERLÄNDER (1960) and KRÜGER (1964) because of their former Nat. Socialist activities.

1959 Fed. President Heinrich Lübke/C.D.U.

1962 Gvt crisis over the 'Spiegel Affair' (arrest of journalists under suspicion of treason): resignation of F.D.P. Cabinet members and the minister of defence, FRANZ JOSEF STRAUSS.

1963 1st Erhard Cabinet (C.D.U./C.S.U., F.D.P.).

1964 The Bundeswehr reached its planned strength of 12 divisions as required by NATO. The deputy of the Bundestag for milit. questions, HEYE (C.D.U.), criticized the morale of the troops.

1965 Debates over planned emergency decrees; prolongation of the statute of limitations for Nat. Socialist crimes.

2nd Erhard Cabinet (C.D.U./C.S.U., F.D.P.).

For. policy: in **reparation** for Nat. Socialist crimes

1953 Treaty with Israel, from 1959 also with Eur. states.

1955 State visit of ADENAUER to Moscow: discharge of Ger. P.O.W.s; resumption of diplomatic relations. The **Hallstein Doctrine** (break of diplomatic relations with states that recognized the D.D.R.: 1957 Yugoslavia). (For Eur. policies, see p. 245; for the 'Ger. question', p. 219.)

1958 Trade agreement with the U.S.S.R.

1963 Franco-Ger. Treaty of Friendship. Also trade agreements with countries of the Eastern Bloc.

1965 Near E. crisis (secret deliveries of arms to Israel, visit of ULBRICHT to Egypt). Establishment of diplomatic relations with Israel (p. 257) Cooling-off of Franco-Ger. relations because c the E.E.C. and NATO crises (p. 239).

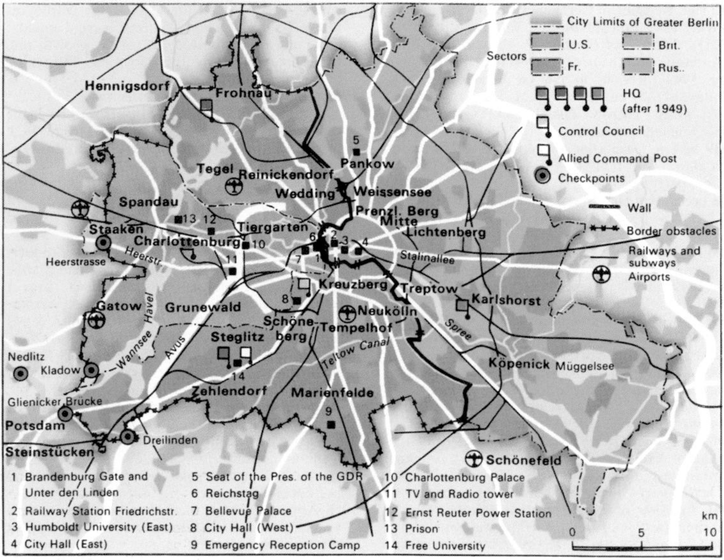
City Limits of Greater Berlin
Sectors
U.S.
Brit.
Fr.
Rus..
HQ (after 1949)
Control Council
Allied Command Post
Checkpoints
Wall
Border obstacles
Railways and subways
Airports
Hennigsdorf
Frohnau
Pankow
Tegel
Reinickendorf
Wedding
Weissensee
Spandau
Prenzl. Berg
Mitte
Lichtenberg
Staaken
Tiergarten
Charlottenburg
Heerstrasse
Heerstr.
Stalinallee
Kreuzberg
Treptow
Karlshorst
Gatow
Havel
Grunewald
Neukölln
Schöne-berg
Tempelhof
Spree
Wannsee
Avus
Steglitz
Teltow Canal
Nedlitz
Kladow
Köpenick
Müggelsee
Zehlendorf
Marienfelde
Glienicker Brücke
Potsdam
Dreilinden
Steinstücken
Schönefeld
1 Brandenburg Gate and Unter den Linden
2 Railway Station Friedrichstr.
3 Humboldt University (East)
4 City Hall (East)
5 Seat of the Pres. of the GDR
6 Reichstag
7 Bellevue Palace
8 City Hall (West)
9 Emergency Reception Camp
10 Charlottenburg Palace
11 TV and Radio tower
12 Ernst Reuter Power Station
13 Prison
14 Free University
km
0
5
10

Berlin after 1945

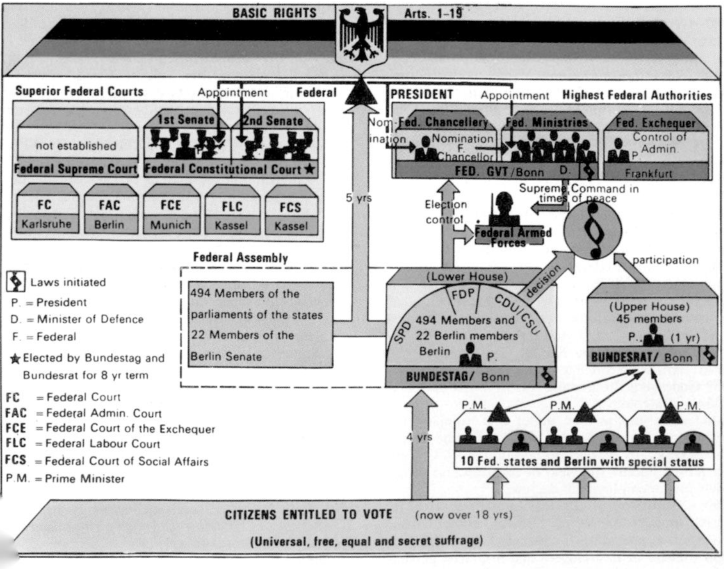
BASIC RIGHTS
Arts. 1–19
Superior Federal Courts
Appointment
Federal
PRESIDENT
Appointment
Highest Federal Authorities
1st Senate
2nd Senate
not established
Federal Supreme Court
Federal Constitutional Court ★
Nom-ination
Fed. Chancellery
Nomination F. Chancellor
Fed. Ministries
Fed. Exchequer
Control of Admin.
P.
FED. GVT/Bonn
D.
Frankfurt
FC Karlsruhe
FAC Berlin
FCE Munich
FLC Kassel
FCS Kassel
5 yrs
Election control
Supreme Command in times of peace
Federal Armed Forces
participation
decision
Federal Assembly
494 Members of the parliaments of the states
22 Members of the Berlin Senate
(Lower House)
FDP
SPD
CDU/CSU
494 Members and 22 Berlin members
Berlin
P.
BUNDESTAG/ Bonn
(Upper House) 45 members
P. (1 yr)
BUNDESRAT/ Bonn
Laws initiated
P. = President
D. = Minister of Defence
F. = Federal
★ Elected by Bundestag and Bundesrat for 8 yr term
FC = Federal Court
FAC = Federal Admin. Court
FCE = Federal Court of the Exchequer
FLC = Federal Labour Court
FCS = Federal Court of Social Affairs
P.M. = Prime Minister
P.M.
P.M.
P.M.
4 yrs
10 Fed. states and Berlin with special status
CITIZENS ENTITLED TO VOTE (now over 18 yrs)
(Universal, free, equal and secret suffrage)

Constitution of the German Federal Republic (B.R.D.)

Berlin (1945–65)

At the time of the capitulation (p. 215) Berlin was a field of rubble: its pop. had been reduced from 4·3 mil. (1939) to 2·8 mil.; 600,000 housing units had been dest.; there was no water, gas or electricity, and 75% of industry was out of commission. The Rus. commandant of the city, Colonel-General BERSARIN, appointed the first magistrate (Mayor WERNER); Moscow-trained cadres of polit. activists (Ulbricht Group) began their work; anti-Fascist parties were est. (Jun.): K.P.D., S.P.D., C.D.U., L.D.P.D.; the trade union federation (F.D.G.B.) came under Com. infl. (in 1948 the Independent Trade Union Organization (U.G.O.) split away). Because of the Allied agreement on '4-Power Status'

1945 Amer., Brit. and Fr. troops entered Berlin (Jul.); admin. of the **4 sectors** through the **Allied Command**.

1946 Permission to the S.E.D. to operate throughout Berlin. The only free district and magistracy election took place in Oct.: S.P.D. 48%, C.D.U. 22%, S.E.D. 20%. In May 1947 the place of Mayor OSTROWSKI/S.P.D. was taken by LOUISE SCHROEDER/S.P.D. (1887–1957).

Soviet war of nerves: controls, restriction on the mails and transportation of goods; paralysing of the operation of the Allied Control Council (p. 249) and the Joint Command.

1st Berlin crisis (Russia's reaction to the currency reform in the West) led to the

1948–9 Berlin Blockade: all access routes blocked and deliveries from the Rus. zone (foodstuffs, coal) to W. Berlin halted. General **Lucius D. Clay** (b. 1897) initiated the organization of the **'airlift'** (up to 927 flights transporting 6,393 tons of goods daily). Maintaining solidarity with the occupation troops, the W. Berliners stood up to the test under great sacrifices. Massive Com. pressure forced the transfer of the city council to W. Berlin (Sep.). An 'East Municipality' was formed under Mayor **Friedrich Ebert**/S.E.D. (b. 1894), resulting in the

1948 partition of Berlin (Nov.). Establishment of the Free University (F.U.). New W. Berlin magistracy elections; **Ernst Reuter**/S.P.D. (1889–1953) became Mayor. He obtained the help of the free world for the 'front-line city of the Cold War'.

1949 Suspension of the blockade (May). The supply and transportation networks remained disrupted (exc. for the subway system). **E. Berlin became cap. of the D.D.R.** (Oct.).

Development of W. Berlin: included in the E.R.P. programme (p. 245), Berlin received, beginning in

1950, finan. aid from the B.R.D. (the *Notopfer* (= 'sacrifice to need') Berlin).

The Berlin Constitution (applying, in fact, to W. Berlin, Oct.): a fed. state with special status (under 4-Power gvt), a Senate (chaired by the governing mayor), and a House of Representatives.

17 Jun. 1953 E. Berlin uprising against the S.E.D. régime. Started by construction workers in the Stalinallee, it spread to the Rus. zone (p. 255), but was crushed by forces including tank units of the Soviet Army.

1954 Conference of For. Ministers at Berlin (p. 219). It brought no solution to the Ger. question. The London guarantee for W. Berlin by the Western powers was kept to by NATO.

1955 A Grand Coalition (S.P.D./C.D.U.) under Mayor OTTO SUHR/S.P.D. (1894–1957), from 1957 **Willy Brandt**/S.P.D. (b. 1913).

2nd Berlin crisis, caused by the

1958 Khrushchev ultimatum (Nov., p. 219): withdrawal of all troops within 6 months and establishment of a **'Free City of W. Berlin'**; the alternative was to surrender control over the access routes to the D.D.R. In the face of the firm position taken by the Western powers and West Berlin, Moscow relented. The head of the D.D.R., WALTER ULBRICHT, provided the

3rd Berlin crisis so as to curtail the 'desertions from the Republic'. After the approval of the Warsaw Pact states had been obtained, on

13 Aug. 1961 the Berlin Wall was erected, ostensibly to 'prevent a milit. attack'. W. Berliners were prohibited from entering the Eastern Sector, border areas were evacuated by force, and the order was given to shoot on sight. The freedom of W. Berlin was guaranteed by the U.S.A. (Vice-President JOHNSON, Special Ambassador CLAY).

1962 Dissolution of the Rus. Command in E. Berlin.

1963 State visit of U.S. President Kennedy (Jun.). Interference with Brit. and Amer. convoys on the Autobahn by Rus. troops. Following extended negotiations, the **1st entry-permit agreement** was concluded between representatives of the Senate of W. Berlin and the D.D.R. gvt (Dec.): West Berliners (over 1 mil.) were allowed to visit their relatives in E. Berlin on the occasion of the New Year holidays. Addit. agreements were reached in Sep. 1964 and Nov. 1965.

1965 Manoeuvres by the U.S.S.R. and D.D.R. to disrupt the sessions of the Bundestag in W. Berlin.

The Constitution of the Ger. Fed. Republic (B.R.D.).

The Bonn Basic Law (p. 249) was considered a **prov. constitution**, awaiting the proclamation of an all-Ger. constitution (Art. 146). The state created on the basis of this constitution was a state of laws with polit. parties, basic civil rights, the separation of powers and representative gvt **(Bundestag)**; however, there was no provision for **'emergency decrees'**.

Differences from the Weimar Constitution (p. 149): (a) a mixture of proportional representation and single-member districts, no provision for plebiscites, indirect election of the **Fed. President** (whose powers were limited to representative functions); (b) only parties receiving more than 5% of the total popular vote were represented in the Bundestag (the 5% clause); (c) the **Fed. Chancellor** was given a strong position through the limitation of parl. control over the gvt (the 'constructive vote of no-confidence' was effective only if the Bundestag simultaneously presented a new chancellor with a majority vote); (d) a **Const. Court**, holding the power of decision over and supplying opinions (on request) on questions of const. conflicts; the court also interprets the Basic Law and rules on the unconstitutionality of parties or associations.

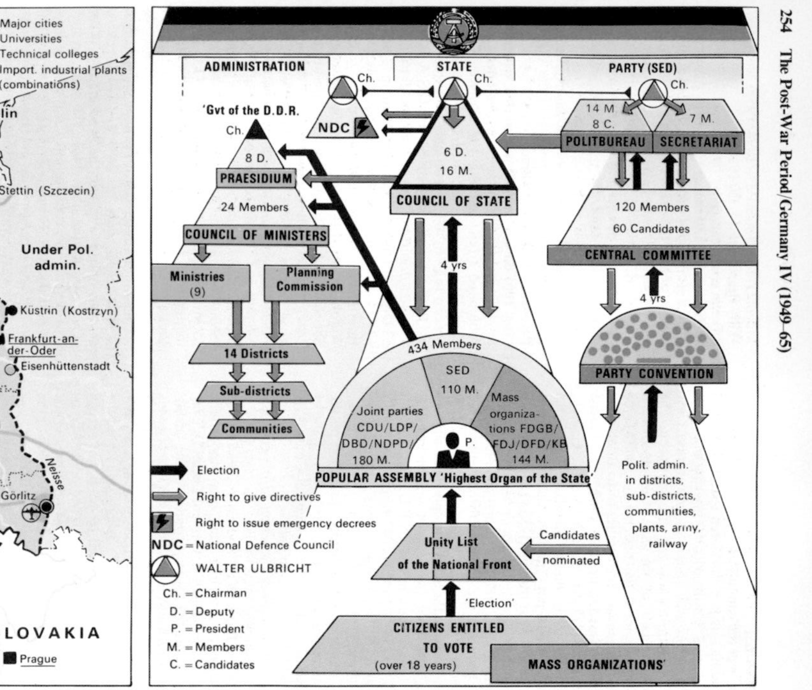

The Russian Zone of Occupation (D.D.R.) after 1952

The political structure of the German Democratic Republic (D.D.R.)

The Ger. Dem. Republic (D.D.R.)

Oct. 1949 Proclamation of the D.D.R. by the People's Council (p. 249). **Wilhelm Pieck** (1876–1960) became **president, Otto Grotewohl** (1894–1964) prime minister. The Rus. milit. gvt transferred administrative tasks to the new gvt.

The **constitution** was drawn up to shape the form of democracy; incl. basic rights such as the right to work, recreation and welfare; the constitution also obliged the citizen to help to maintain socialist achievements (collective ownership of certain properties, a state-guided economy) and prohibited the promotion of **boycotts** (Art. 6).

People's Republic after the Soviet model: the party (S.E.D.), admin. and state were organized acc. to the principle of dem. centralism. After 1960 the place of the president was taken by the

Council of State, which was given the right to decree laws, also without the approval of the **Popular Assembly** (elected acc. to a fixed ratio = the Unity List).

S.E.D. organs (Cen. Committee, Politburo and Secretariat) wield absolute control and the right to issue directives.

Walter Ulbricht (1893–1973), co-founder of the K.P.D., in exile in the U.S.S.R. 1938–45, and a representative of an uncompromising 'Moscow course', concentrated the largest amount of power in his own hands.

Domestic affairs: reorganization of the People's Congress into the **Nat. Front** (N.F.), led by S.E.D. functionaries, structured in residential and occupational communities. Objectives: nomination of candidates for the election of judges, jurors and members of the popular assembly (from 1950); polit. enlightenment, 'struggle for peace and Ger. unity', infiltration of K.P. agents and propaganda material into the B.R.D. Decisions of the N.F. were considered to be the 'general will of the people' and as such to be binding on all parties of the 'bloc' and all **mass organizations**: the Free Ger. Trade Union Federation (F.D.G.B.), the Free Ger. Youth (F.D.J.), the League of Ger. Women (D.F.B.), the Ctr League (D.K.), among others.

1950 Establishment of the Ministry for Public Security (polit. secret police, S.S.D.) under Zaisser (to 1953 Wollenweber, from 1957 General Mielke). Establishment of the **People's Police** (D.V.P.), 1952 of the milit. People's Police (housed in barracks, K.V.P.), and paramilitary organizations: combat groups of the S.E.D., associations dedicated to sports and technology (G.S.T.). The

1952 2nd S.E.D. Party Conference cal. for 'the development of Socialism'; transformation of the 5 component states of the D.D.R. into 14 administrative districts; construction of obstacles at the borders of the occupation zone, constantly reinforced by addit. minefields, watchtowers and barbed wire. Following

1953 Stalin's death, the 'New Course' was proclaimed, aiming at an improvement in living conditions. Protest demonstrations in E. Berlin (p. 253) mushroomed into the

17 Jun. 1953 popular uprising: demonstrations, freeing of polit. prisoners. Rus. troops suppressed the uprising. Mass arrests, court martials, executions, a stream of refugees into the B.R.D.

1954 Recognition of sovereignty of the D.D.R. by the U.S.S.R. Organization of the 'special police force' ('the domestic army') and the

1956 Nat. People's Army, to function within the framework of the Warsaw Pact (p. 245).

1957 Passport Law, which included penalties for assistance to 'desertion of the Republic' (leaving the country without permission). Attacks on the Evangelical Prot. Church (*Junge Gemeinde*), propagation of the atheistic *Jugendweihe* ('celebration of youth'). To cut off the increasing stream of refugees into the B.R.D. (from 1949 2·7 mil. people, i.e. 15% of the pop., among them many skilled specialists),

Aug. 1961 the Berlin Wall was erected (p. 253), and security along the borders of the occupation zone was intensified (shoot-on-sight order).

1962 Introduction of general conscription.

1964 Pensioners were allowed to visit the B.R.D.; amnesty for 'deserters of the Republic'. **Willi Stoph** (b. 1914) became prime minister,

Econ. life: heavy industry was expanded through the

1951 1st 5-Yr Plan (indust. combinations); from

1952 collectivization through the establishment of agricult. producers' cooperatives (L.P.G.) followed the Soviet model. Under the impact of the 'New Course'

1953 the Rus.-owned joint-stock companies (S.A.G., p. 249) were transferred to public control (V.E.B. = people-owned enterprises); the Russians gave up further claims to reparations; norms of work performance were lowered, and the rationing of textiles and shoes was suspended. Nevertheless, inflationary pressure continued without respite.

1958 The 5th S.E.D. Party Convention proclaimed the transition to a period of the 'Consummation of Socialism' and called for the overtaking of the standard of living of the B.R.D. by 1961. The rationing of foodstuffs was discontinued.

1959 7-Yr Plan providing for intensified socialization and

1960 compulsory collectivization.

1963 6th S.E.D. Party Convention: proclamation of the 'New Econ. System' (N.Ö.S.). Profit incentives brought about a rise in productivity and the soc. product.

1965 Trade agreement with the U.S.S.R.

For. policy (dependence on the U.S.S.R., esp. on the Ger. question, p. 219): polit. and econ. integration into the Eastern Bloc (p. 245).

1950 Görlitz Treaty with Poland: recognition of the Oder–Neisse 'peace border'.

1955 Treaty of Moscow: dissolution of the Rus. High Commission.

1957 Establishment of diplomatic relations with Yugoslavia. Constant efforts to obtain int. recognition outside the Eastern Bloc; progress made in the establishment of trade missions.

1959 State visit of Khrushchev. He emphasized that the rejection of a peace treaty with both Ger. states would lead to the conclusion of a separate peace between the U.S.S.R. and the D.D.R.

1963 Condemnation of the polit. course of the Com. party of Czechoslovakia.

1964 Treaty of Friendship with the U.S.S.R.: the status of W. Berlin was interpreted as that of an ind. polit. unit (the '3-State Theory').

1965 State visit by Ulbricht to Egypt.

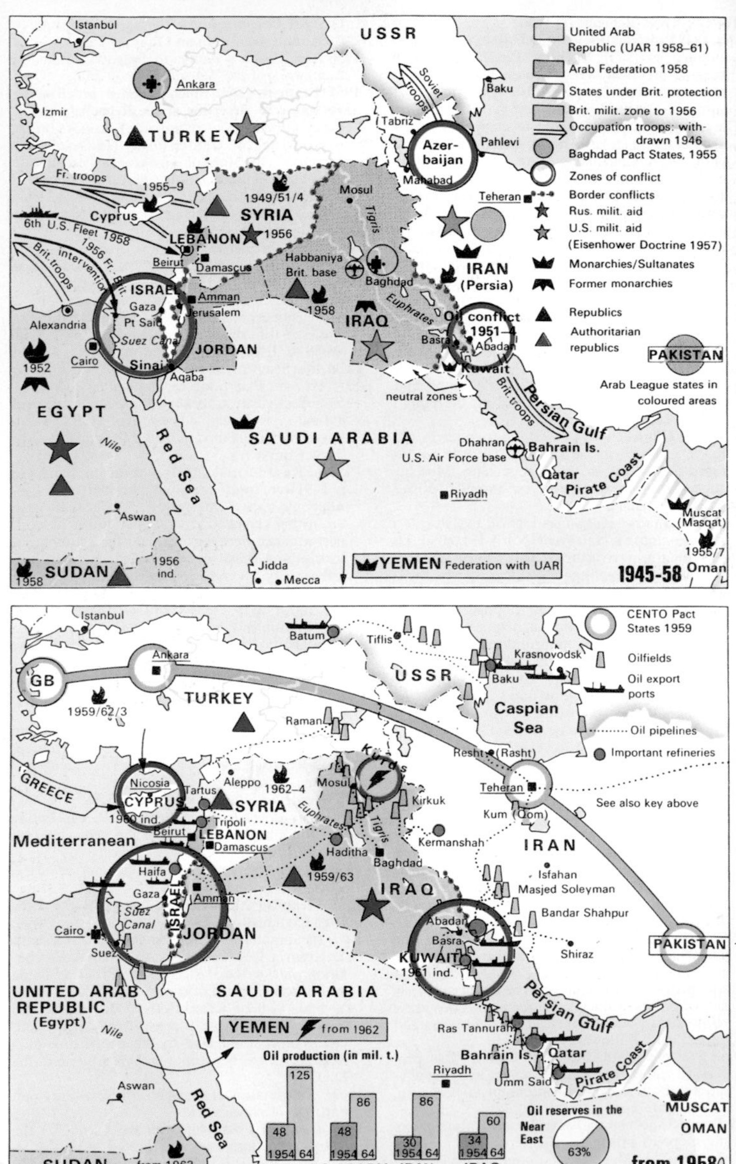

	1954	64
KUWAIT	48	125
S. ARABIA	48	86
IRAN	30	86
IRAQ	34	60

The Near East after the Second World War

The Crisis Area of the Near East (1945–65)
Even before the Brit. and Fr. occupation troops withdrew and the British gave up Palestine (p. 259), the states of the Near East had joined in the **Arab League** (p. 239), united by common religion, language, traditions (see the Isl.-Arab. Empire, I. p. 134f.), and anti-Jew, sentiments. The **Pan-Arab. movement** and plans for unification could not conceal rivalries among the leadership, nor the tensions between the old aristocracy (the monarchistic feudal nobility) and the new leadership groups (repub. intellectuals (army officers)); between oil-rich states (Kuwait, Saudi Arabia) and poor, desert countries (Egypt, Syria, Jordan); between con. movements (the Moslem brotherhood) and movements aiming at soc. revolution (the Baath party). The **instability** of the area was aggravated by (a) the **oil interests of the W.**; (b) the polit. and ideological struggle between E. (U.S.S.R.) and W. (U.S.A.) to gain infl. and power in the area; (c) the **undeclared state of war with Israel** following the Arab failure in 1948–9 (p. 259). No decision was reached concerning the policy of Arab neutralism as part of the '3rd World' (NASSER), or orientation towards the W. or the E.

Egypt: spurred on by the Wafd party (p. 179), the urban masses were the main source of unrest, calling for the Brit. evacuation of the Canal Zone (agreed on by treaty in 1954).

1952 Milit. revolt against the corrupt monarchy and Wafd gvt: King Farouk I (1920–65) abdicated. Proclamation of the

1953 republic by General NEGUIB, who was removed by the revolutionary council. The parties were forced to conform (Moslem brotherhood) and join the Nat. Union. Power was assumed by

1954 the prime minister, Colonel Gamal Abdel el Nasser (1919–70 (president from 1956)): reforms (distribution of land, industrialization) to overcome widespread misery were introduced (Arab Socialism). Egypt's Pan-Arab policy was directed against Israel and linked with that of Syria and Saudi Arabia among others;

1955 purchases of arms from Czechoslovakia. Western mistrust led to the

1956 Suez Crisis: the U.S. (secretary of state, DULLES) denied Egypt finan. aid for the construction of the **Aswan Dam**; to finance this major construction project

1956 Jul. Nationalization of the Suez Canal with provision for compensation for the (mostly Brit. and Fr.) stockholders and guarantees for the freedom of shipping. At the 3 fruitless London conferences of the Suez Canal users, India and the U.S.S.R. approved the Egypt. step.

Israeli attack (Oct., p. 259); Brit.-Fr. milit. action to protect the canal, condemned by the U.S. and the U.N. (Nov.). Withdrawal of the troops because of a massive Rus. threat; U.N. troops occupied the Canal Zone.

Consequences: a severe polit. defeat for France and Britain. Increased prestige for the **U.S.S.R., which now entered the politics of the Near E.** and provided milit. and econ. aid for Egypt (the Aswan Dam) and Syria.

1957 Eisenhower Doctrine: offer of aid by the U.S. to counteract Com. aggression.

NASSER's leading position in the Arab world was strengthened:

1958 Establishment of the United Arab Republic (U.A.R.), incl. Syria (President KUWATLI) and federative association of **Yemen**. Egypt advanced claims against the Sudan, where N.–S. tensions (Arabs *v.* Negroes) were brought under control 1958 by a milit. gvt.

1958 Lebanon crisis: the polit. stability of this 'Arabian Switzerland' was endangered by Pan-Arabic uprisings. On the request of the Christ. President, CHAMOUN (1952–8), and against Rus. protests, U.S. troops landed. They withdrew from Beirut after General FUAD CHEBAB, a Mohammedan, had been elected president (to 1964): CHEBAB restored Christ.-Moslem parity.

Iraq: the pro-Western monarchy was overthrown

1958 by **milit. putsch:** murder of FEISAL II. Disintegration of Arab unity because of Jordan; cancellation of the Baghdad Pact (p. 239). Prime Minister **Kassem** beat down the counter-revolution (Colonel AREF), accepted Rus. aid and laid claim to the oil-rich state of

1961 Kuwait (which was under Brit. protection and enjoyed the guarantee of the Arab League).

1962–4 Kurd uprising: MUSTAFA BARZANI demanded autonomy.

1963 Milit. uprising (army and Baath party): KASSEM was liquidated; unrest continued.

1964 A dem. Socialist republic, the state was inclined to join the U.A.R.

Jordan: under pressure from Arab circles, King **Hussein I** (from 1952) dismissed the Brit. commander of the Arab Legion, General GLUBB PASHA (p. 168), and cancelled the Brit. aid treaty of 1946; however, during the

1958 Pan-Arab. uprising in Jordan he asked for Brit. milit. assistance.

Syria: from 1944 constant unrest and border conflicts.

1961 Milit. revolt aimed at dissolution of the U.A.R. (to escape Egypt. tutelage); the Baath party and NASSER's followers temporarily again gained the upper hand in a

1963 *coup d'état*.

The U.A.R.–Egypt: President NASSER steered a neutral course between E. and W. (cf. p. 231); he supported the revolutionary gvt of ABDULLAH AL-SALAL (b. *c.* 1920) during the

1962–5 civil war in the Yemen by supplying arms and troops; but the followers of the Imam held their position. They received aid from **Saudi Arabia**, which was ruled more or less autocratically by the kings SAUD [1953–64] and FEISAL [1964–75]. After 1957, relations with NASSER cooled and

Saudi Arabia cooperated with the W., esp. the U.S.A. (bases), necessitated by the predominantly Amer. production of oil.

Notwithstanding its setbacks, the

Pan-Arab policy of NASSER retained its appeal, so long as it was directed against **Israel.** In

1963 the U.A.R. made plans for a federation with Syria and Iraq; Israel was threatened because of its plans to divert the course of the Jordan river (p. 259).

1965 Invitation to the head of the D.D.R. gv[illegible] WALTER ULBRICHT, in protest against B.R.[illegible] assistance to Israel. Following the discontinuat[illegible] of econ. aid to the Arab states and establishn[illegible] of diplomatic relations between the B.R.D [illegible] Israel, the 10 Arab states, urged by Egypt, [illegible] off relations with the Fed. Republic of Ge[illegible]

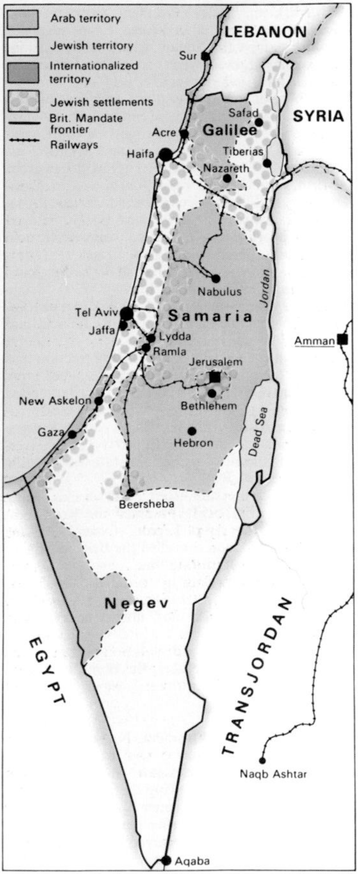

Partition plan of the U.N., 1947

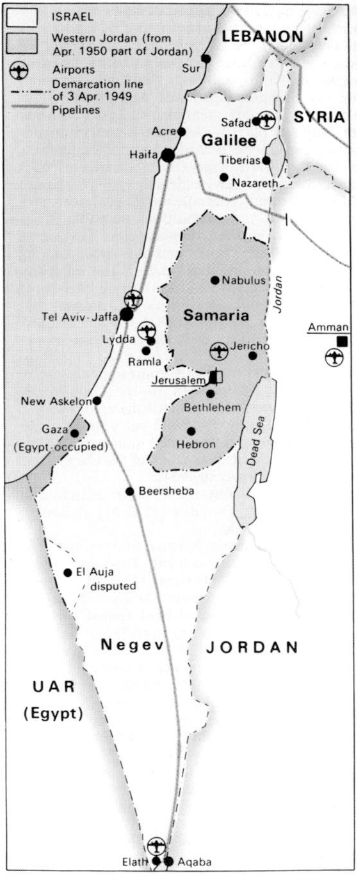

Israel after 1949

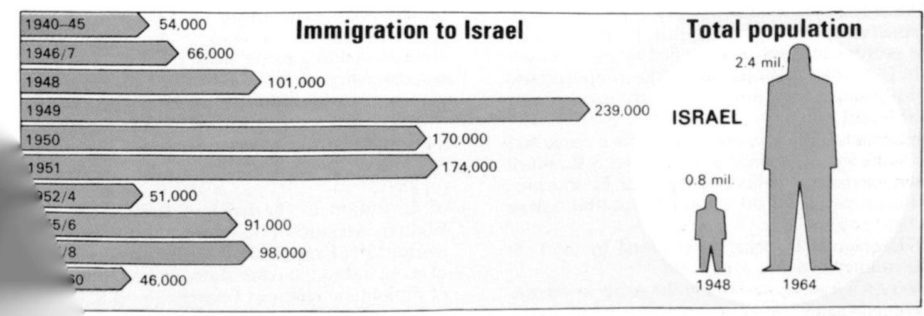

on growth in Israel to 1964

The Palestine Problem (1933–48)

Organized by the **Jew. Agency** (the unofficial gvt), the **Histadrut** (General Federation of Labour with its own enterprises, settlements and schools), and the **Nat. Fund** (for the acquisition of land), Jew. immigration increased from 1933. By 1939 one third of the pop. and 12% of the soil of Palestine were Jewish. The resistance of the Arabs, who were economically backward and politically split into two camps (that of the Grand Mufti HUSEINI of Jerusalem (b. 1895) and that of the supporters of King ABDULLAH of Jordan (p. 168)) intensified.

1936–9 Civil war: the Brit. admin. of the Mandate by turns supported the Arab partisans and the Jew. **Haganah** (milit. self-defence organization). Both parties rejected such compromise proposals as the

1937 Peel partition plan.

In its

1939 Brit. plan (the White Paper), the Brit. gvt gave in to Arab pressure (the 'New Munich'): limitation of Jew. immigration and purchases of land to maintain an Arab majority; the policy was fought by Jew. terrorists (Irgun Zwai Leumi). Faced with indirect Brit. and direct Ger. antisemitism, the Jew. Agency during the 2nd World War took the side of the Allies and developed Palestine into a centre of Allied supplies, while the Arabs (the Grand Mufti of Jerusalem) leaned towards the Axis powers. Beginning in

1942 a Jew. Brigade of volunteers became part of the Brit. army. Nevertheless, after the end of the war, the British continued their 'White Paper' policy: blockade of illegal Jew. immigrant ships (the *Exodus* tragedy); concentration of Jews in camps (Cyprus) and repatriation. Jew. terror alternated with Arab counter-terror. A Brit.-Amer. commission

1946 urged the opening of the borders to 100,000 Jew. immigrants. At the London Palestine Conference (with the participation of the Arab League, which was determined to go to war, p. 239), the Brit. for. secretary BEVIN found no solution for the problem; he passed it to the U.N.

1947 U.N. Special Commission on Palestine (UNSCOP) recommended the partition of Palestine, approved by the U.N. General Assembly and the Jew. Agency, but rejected by the Arabs. The Arab 'Liberation Army' occupied Galilee and attacked the Jew. Old City of Jerusalem.

1948 The British gave up the Mandate (May). Withdrawal of the Brit. army and admin. plunged the country into anarchy.

The New Israel (1948–65)

14 May 1948 Proclamation of the state of Israel by the Jew. Nat. Council (under the chairmanship of **Ben Gurion**); the attack by the Arab League – interrupted by U.N. mediation efforts (Jun.–Jul.) – was repulsed (Israeli air superiority); flight by sections of the Arab pop. (p. 221); Jew. terrorists murdered the U.N. emissary Count BERNADOTTE. Following fighting in the Negev desert (conquest of Elath), a joint

1949 armistice treaty was concl. (Feb.–Jun.): partition of Jerusalem, the w. bank of the Jordan fell to Jordan, the Gaza Strip came under Egypt. admin.; the lines of the front stabilized and became the states' borders.

Development of the state: the elections to the parliament (Knesset) brought a majority for the (Socialist) **Mapei** party and confirmed

1948–63 David Ben Gurion (1886–1974) in office as prime minister (1953–5 prime minister, MOSHE SHARETT).

1949–52 President Chaim Weizman (p. 63).

Inflow and integration of Jews from all over the world; development of the New Hebraic official language (Iwrith); development of the country through cooperative villages (*moshavot*) and voluntary collectives (**kibutzim** with property held in common): 'conquest of the desert', forestry, irrigation and drainage projects with the aid of for. capital and econ. aid.

1952 Reparations treaty with the B.R.D. (3,500 mil. DM.). To protect the borders a modern army was maintained; general conscription and mandatory labour service for men and women.

1952 President Isaac Ben Zwi (1884–1963), from 1963 SALMAN SHAZAR (b. 1889).

1954 Establishment of Hebrew University in Jerusalem.

1956 Meeting of the Zionist World Congress (President **Nahum Goldmann**, b. 1894): appeal to the Eastern Bloc to suspend the prohibition of Jew. emigration. To counteract Arab boycotts (blockade of the Suez Canal and the port of Elath), the incursions of Egypt. sabotage units (*Feddayin*), and Rus. milit. aid,

1956 attack on Egypt (Oct.): disarming of Egypt. troops, opening of the port of Elath. (The relationship between the Israeli attack and the Suez Canal conflict (p. 257) has never been fully explained.) In observance of a U.N. resolution

1957 the occupied territories (Sinai, the Gaza Strip) were turned over to U.N. forces. Econ. and milit. aid from the B.R.D. was promised by ADENAUER during his

1960 meeting with BEN GURION in New York. The former head of the S.S. department in charge of the 'Jew. question' in the Ger. 'Office for Jew. Emigration', **Adolf Eichmann**, was kidnapped in Argentina and brought to Israel; following the

1961 Eichmann trial in Jerusalem, he was executed (1962). Beginning in

1962, to counteract the unfavourable balance of trade, a new econ. policy was pursued: protective tariffs were decreased, and an agreement with the E.E.C. concluded (1964). The Arabs threatened war because of Israeli **use of the waters of the Jordan**, border incidents and the milit. alliance with Iran. The prime minister was from

1963 Levi Eshkol (1895–1969); the for. minister GOLDA MEIR (1956–65).

1964 Pilgrimage of the Pope to the Holy Land: **Paul VI** met the Patriarch ATHENAGORAS, head of the Gk-Orth. Church.

1965 The establishment of diplomatic relations wi the B.R.D. (p. 251) was rejected by sections of pop. The Arab countries rejected a prop peace with Israel offered by the Tunisian BOURGUIBA.

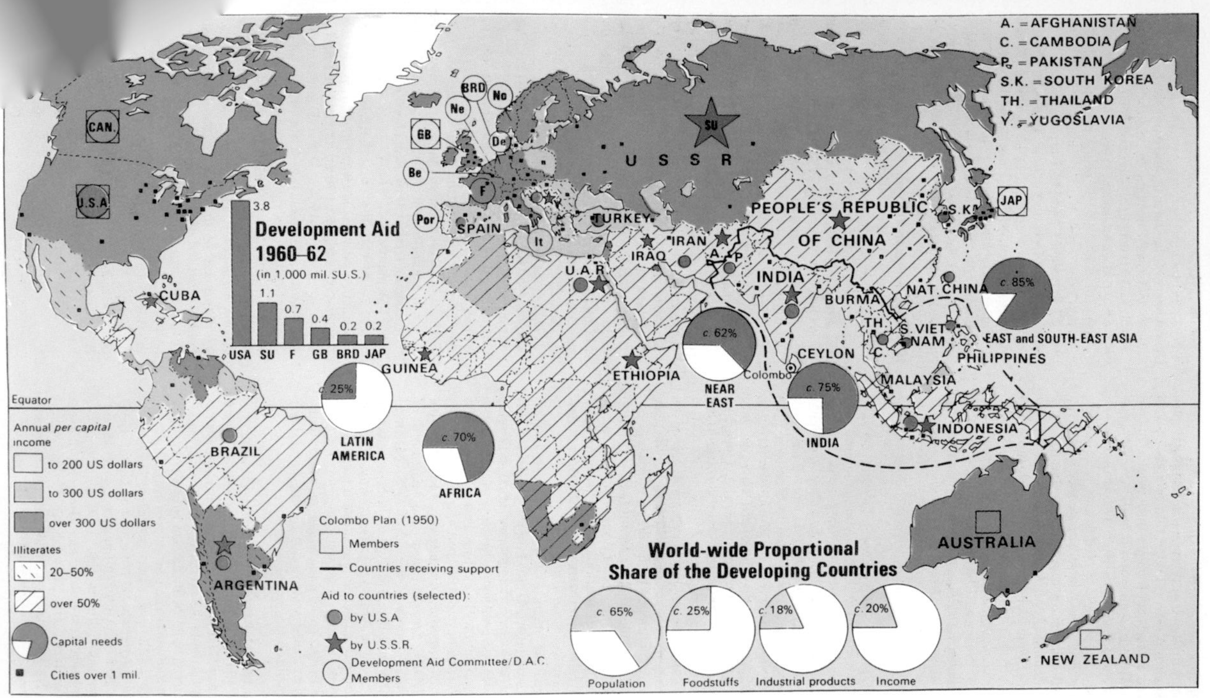
A. = AFGHANISTAN
C. = CAMBODIA
P. = PAKISTAN
S.K. = SOUTH KOREA
TH. = THAILAND
Y. = YUGOSLAVIA
Development Aid 1960–62
(in 1,000 mil. $U.S.)
3.8
1.1
0.7
0.4
0.2
0.2
USA
SU
F
GB
BRD
JAP
World-wide Proportional Share of the Developing Countries
c. 65%
Population
c. 25%
Foodstuffs
c. 18%
Industrial products
c. 20%
Income
Annual per capital income
to 200 US dollars
to 300 US dollars
over 300 US dollars
Illiterates
20–50%
over 50%
Capital needs
Cities over 1 mil.
Colombo Plan (1950)
Members
Countries receiving support
Aid to countries (selected):
by U.S.A
by U.S.S.R.
Development Aid Committee/D.A.C.
Members
Equator
CAN.
U.S.A
CUBA
BRAZIL
ARGENTINA
LATIN AMERICA
c. 25%
GUINEA
AFRICA
c. 70%
GB
Be
Ne
BRD
No
De
F
Por
SPAIN
It
TURKEY
U.A.R.
ETHIOPIA
IRAQ
IRAN
NEAR EAST
c. 62%
U S S R
SU
A.
P.
INDIA
Colombo
CEYLON
c. 75%
INDIA
PEOPLE'S REPUBLIC OF CHINA
BURMA
TH.
C.
S. VIET NAM
MALAYSIA
INDONESIA
NAT. CHINA
S.K.
JAP
c. 85%
EAST and SOUTH-EAST ASIA
PHILIPPINES
AUSTRALIA
NEW ZEALAND

The developing nations. *c.* 1960

The Emancipation of the Coloured Peoples

Polit. emancipation (from colon. tutelage): it was attained after 1945 with the polit. independence of almost all colon. peoples, by means of

- the spread of Eur. theories of freedom and equality (human rights and the right of self-determination, the Marxist idea of the class struggle);
- transition of colon. policy to a sort of 'ethical imperialism': participation of coloured élites in tasks of leadership;
- weakening of the major Eur. powers (the world wars);
- the Anglo-Saxon conception of dem. cooperation between all peoples (the Atlantic Charter, p. 209), realized in the U.N., which became the polit. forum of the new nations (p. 225).

Notwithstanding their polit. differences, the coloured nations conceived of themselves as united in the struggle against 'white colonialism' and sought a distinctive '3rd alternative' between E. and W., influenced by Socialism.

1955 Bandung Conference: 29 Afro-Asian states condemned colonialism, racial discrimination and atomic weapons.

1957 The 1st Solidarity Conference at Cairo (43 states, among them the U.S.S.R.) proclaimed the principle of peaceful coexistence. Resolutions opposing interventionist and racist policies (Conakry Conference, 1960), **neo-colonialism** (indirect econ. domination) and soc. debasement (Bandung Conference, 1961) were passed.

1961 Belgrade Conference: differences between moderate and anti-Western states were aired.

Internal emancipation: the adjustment of pre-indust. living conditions to the modern world became the major task of the new nations.

Polit. and soc. problems: public institutions adapted their forms from the Eur. models (constitutions, parliaments, admins., armies). But, in the background, trad. indigenous ctrs. continued to exert their infl.: secret societies, sects, tribal units. **Tensions** arose from the contrasts between large modern urban centres and the villages, from ethnic, relig. and linguistic differences, and from the contrast between an educated upper class and an **illiterate** mass. The tensions manifested themselves in **polit. instability**: revolutions, a lack of law and order, racial discrimination (cf. p. 233), relig. hatred (Hindu v. Mohammedan), interventions (China in Tibet), wars (India v. Pakistan). The **nat. states**, developing within the (often accidental) colon. boundaries (cf. the 'Balkanization of Africa', p. 266), were held together by nat. pride, polit. parties and trade unions, and had the army as a mainstay. The new states tended towards **authoritarian forms of gvt** (milit. dictatorship, 'guided democracy') under trad. leadership (Ethiopia, Arabia), **Western-educated politicians**, officers, nationalistic **popular leaders**, and trained **Communists**. Alongside these developments were indications of tendencies towards regional federation.

Socio-econ. problems: characteristics of the predominantly agricultural **'developing nations'**:

- a **feudalistic** soc. order with a rich upper class and impoverished agricultural labourers, whose soc. security depended on a large family unit. The dissolution of the old order led to polit. radicalization in urban squalor;
- **technological-indust. backwardness** (a high input of labour and low yields). Profits from mining, refineries and plantations benefited for. corporations as well as an upper class which hoarded its wealth (land and precious metals) while resisting soc. change and **land reform** and was consequently often deprived of power through revolutionary action.
- pop. explosion, poverty, famine and diseases (40 mil. p.a. dead from starvation). Econ. progress did not halt increasing squalor; there was no development of capital stock within the countries;
- **insufficient econ. and work incentive:** conceptions of econ. success and their associated prestige were alien to the uneducated masses; the specific material needs, sense of economy and work discipline necessary to a new type of econ. life were lacking.

Development aid: the 'soc. question' (p. 67), hitherto limited to the indust. nations, became a worldwide problem affecting both rich and poor nations. Overlaid by the E.–W. conflict, it endangered general security and world peace. 'Aid with the aim of encouraging self-help' encompassed:

1. **Capital aid** through gifts, loss compensation (e.g. in the event of natural catastrophes), private investments stimulated by tax exemptions, and long-term credits, usually arranged by multilateral institutions: the World Bank (1945) and other U.N. organizations (p. 222); the **Colombo Plan** within the framework of the Brit. Commonwealth (1950, expanded 1955); the Int. Finance Corporation (I.F.C., 1956), the E.E.C. and the O.E.C.D. (p. 245).
2. **Manpower aid:** provision for expert consultants; training of students, trainees, teachers; scholarships, etc.
3. **Tech. aid** for the development of industries, transport and communications facilities, public utilities, schools, etc.
4. **Price stabilization** by means of long-term trade agreements.

Initially concerned with milit. assistance (bases), the U.S. later provided the impetus for econ. assistance through the

1949 4-Point Programme (President TRUMAN). The U.S.S.R. began to intensify its aid efforts only with the ascendancy of KHRUSHCHEV. From

1955, in the context of the policy of peaceful coexistence, Russia initiated the 'diplomacy of state visits' with deliberate polit. programmes, bilateral agreements, and provisions for manpower and tech. aid. Owing to a lack of coordination ('watering-can principle'), faulty investments (through ignorance of local problems) and racial resentments, the effect of the much larger Western capital aid was less positive; moreover, the Com. method of total econ. planning and guidance promised more rapid results. Beginning in

1960–61, the People's Republic of China entered the field with interest-free credits, notwithstanding its own econ. difficulties (p. 235). Only with the presidency of JOHN F. KENNEDY (p. 242) did a fresh Western approach become apparent.

1961 Establishment of the **U.S. Peace Corps** providing for trained volunteers to aid development.

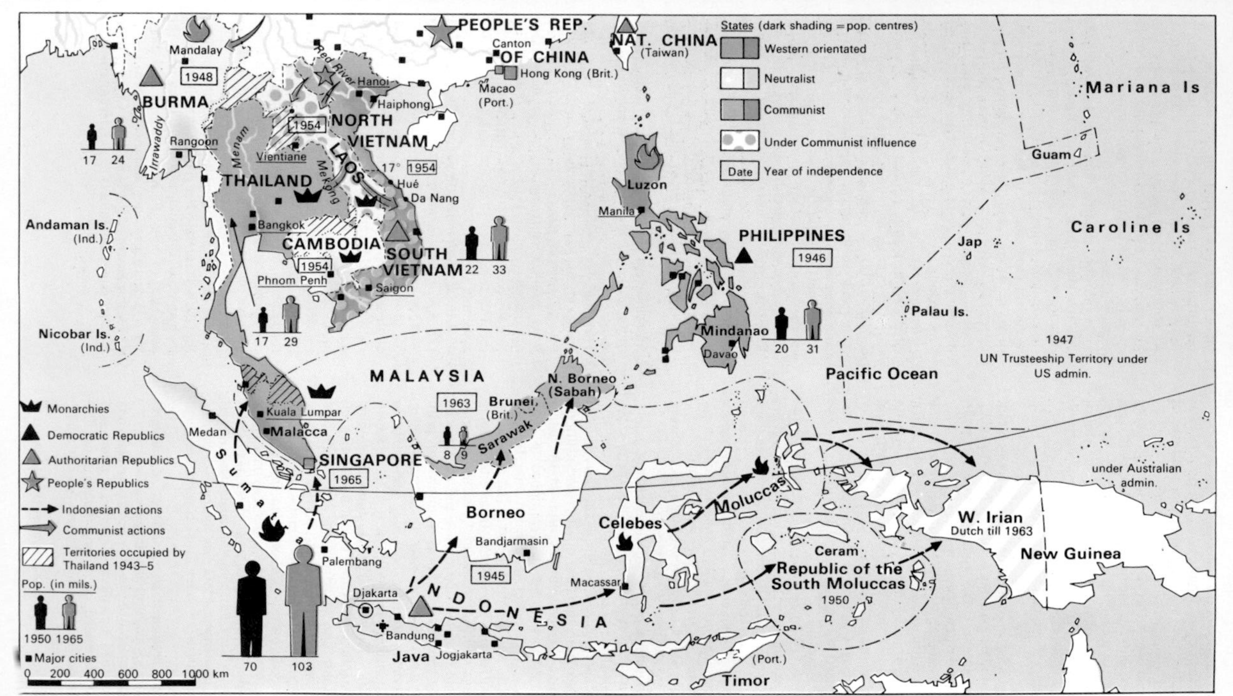

South-East Asia, 1945–65

The End of Colonialism

The Japanese had in many cases been welcomed as liberators; during their occupation they promoted nationalistic movements and granted local autonomy. Their withdrawal marked the beginning of revolutionary changes. Western-educated élites drafted liberation programmes (containing a mixture of democratic and Socialist conceptions). They became the leaders in the struggle of the masses against colon. feudalism and, after having achieved independence, were confronted with difficult polit. and econ. problems, often on the defensive against Com. subversion. The rise and accomplishments of China became an example.

Indonesia

Guerrilla warfare against Dutch troops under Governor-General VAN MOOK (1942–8). **Achmed Sukarno** (1901–70) proclaimed the **'5 Principles'** of the nat. struggle: faith in God, humanitarianism, nationalism, democracy, soc. justice.

1945 Proclamation of the Indonesian Republic by SUKARNO and **Mohammed Hatta** (b. 1902). While under a Dutch protectorate,

1946 the Treaty of Linggadjati led to the formation of a union with the Republic of E. Indonesia. Following U.N. pressure (p. 225),

1947–8 Dutch police actions on Java were discontinued and negotiations initiated.

1949 Round-Table Conference in The Hague: foundation of the United States of Indonesia under President SUKARNO (made life president 1963), with HATTA as prime minister, to function within the framework of a Union of the Netherlands.

1950–52 The Republic of the Southern Moluccas split away.

1954 Dissolution of the Union of the Netherlands (completed 1956). Aspirations to autonomy manifested themselves in the outer provinces of the culturally and religiously heterogeneous Isl. state of 13,600 islands.

1957–8 Rebellions (in Sumatra and other places) against the centralist gvt and 'guided democracy' of SUKARNO; with the aid of the army – utilizing its tensions with the Chin.-orientated Com. party of AIDIT (b. 1923) – SUKARNO est. a

1959 dictatorship. Internal unrest was to be concealed by the proclamation of nat. aims:

1961–2 Conflict with the Netherlands over W. Irian which, as a result of U.N. mediation (New York Agreement), came under Indonesian admin. in 1963 (to the 1969 plebiscite).

1964 Threat of war to destroy Malaysia; partisan campaigns in Malacca and Northern Borneo.

1965 Indonesia left the U.N.; milit. *coup* depriving SUKARNO of power and destroying the Com party: anti-Com. demonstrations resulted in more than 87,000 dead.

1966 General SUHARTO became prime minister.

The Philippines

In fulfilment of U.S. promises dating from 1934

1946 declaration of independence. Continued strong infl. by the U.S.A. (finan. aid, milit. treaties, 1946/51), but corrupt and authoritarian misconduct of gvt under 2 successive presidents,

1946–53 ROXAS and QUIRINO.

1949–52 Insurrection by the Com. HUKS (1942 against the people's army founded by the Japanese): plunder of cities on Luzon. The U.S.A. promised aid on condition of reforms, which were introduced by

1953–57 President MAGSAYSAY and continued by

1961 President MACAPAGAL (b. 1910).

Malaya

Differences among the pop. (50% Malay, 40% Chinese, 10% Indian) made the establishment of a state difficult. 9 sultanates and Brit. crown colonies

1948 formed the Malay League as a Brit. protectorate.

1954 Guerrilla warfare was waged with the aid of Brit. troops against Com. partisans (Chin.).

1957 The Federation of Malaysia was formed; it included Northern Borneo, Brunei and Sarawak, (prime minister, Prince TUNKU ABDUL RAHMAN, b. 1903). The federation joined the Brit. Commonwealth; Singapore was given domestic autonomy and remained a Brit. base.

1963 Proclamation of the Fed. State of Malaysia; the state was burdened by actions of Com. Chin. and Indonesian 'irregulars' (N. Borneo). Following Chin.-Malay clashes

1965 Singapore left the federation. LEE KUAN YEW became prime minister.

Thailand

Return of the territories occupied in 1943–5. An authoritarian milit. gvt suppressed dem. opposition and Com. guerrilla units. In for. policy, Thailand leaned towards the U.S. (treaties providing for bases).

1947 Dictatorship under Marshal PHIBUL SONGGRAM (1897–1964), whose rule was approved by

1950 King BHUMIDOL ADULYADEJ (b. 1927).

1957 *Coup d'état* by Marshal SARIT THANARAT (1908–63): suspension of the constitution, prohibition of polit. parties, intensive struggle against Com. units; tensions with Cambodia. From

1959 a transitional constitution with extensive authority for the head of the gvt, THANARAT.

Burma

The post-war Brit. Labour admin. promised self-gvt to the Freedom League (A.F.P.F.L.), founded in 1944 during the struggle against the Japanese. Nationalists murdered AUNG SAN and other A.F.P.F.L. leaders.

1947 Independence Treaty of London. The Socialist

1948 Union Republic of Burma, led by U NU as prime minister,

1948–54 was engaged in a civil war with the Christ. Karens, Communists and Nationalist Chin. soldiers who had fled from China.

1958 Anti-Com. milit. dictatorship of General NE WIN (b. 1911?). Following an elect. vict. of A.F.P.F.L.

1960 a new Cabinet was formed under U NU (b. 1907); a border treaty with China was concluded.

1962 Milit. *coup d'état* under General NE WIN to safeguard the status quo. As chairman of the revolutionary council, he conducted an authoritarian régime without a parliament. Banks were nationalized.

1964 Prohibition of all polit. parties.

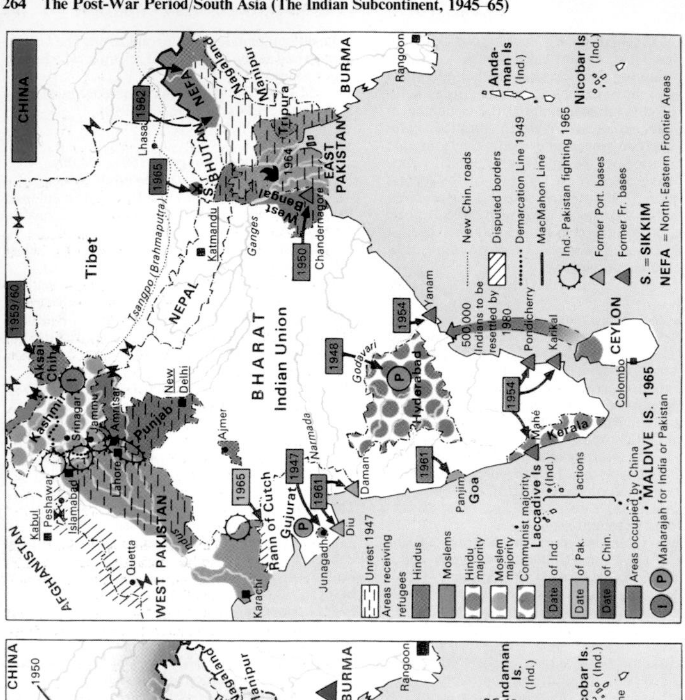

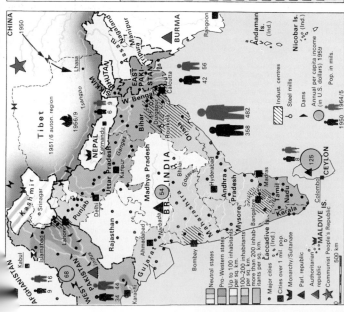

India–Pakistan partition and border conflicts

The Indian Sub-continent, 1965

The Ind. Subcontinent in the Post-colonial Era (1945–65)

The Lab. gvt of CLEMENT ATTLEE (p. 246) honoured the Brit. commitments made during the war (p. 169). A constituent assembly and an interim

1946 Ind. gvt prepared the country for independence, which was proclaimed in the

1947 Ind. Independence Act. Severe crises followed: Hindu and Moslem massacres, flight and resettlement of relig. minorities (p. 221). India was partitioned, **Pakistan** (divided into separate E. and W. regions), becoming the state of the Moslem minority.

1948 Assassination of Gandhi.

The Ind. Union (Bharat):

1947–64 As prime minister and for. minister, Jawaharal Nehru (p. 169) reorganized the admin. The princes were made to abdicate their polit. authority.

1948 The Moslem principalities of Junagadh and **Hyderabad** were incorp. into the Union.

1950 Constitution of the Ind. Fed. Republic: 27 (from 1956, 14) fed. states with separate gvts and parliaments, 6 territories and Sikkim with the status of a protectorate. **Rajendra Prasad** (1884–1963) became the 1st president, succeeded in 1962 by **S. Radhakrishnan** (b. 1888).

1951/2 Elect. vict. of the Congress party (75% of the vote).

The most difficult problem of India was **over-pop.**: the state introduced programmes to combat famine, poverty and increasing squalor.

1951 1st 5-Yr Plan to aid and develop agriculture. By

1955 land reforms were carried out, in part as a result of the efforts of the itinerant preacher VINOBE BHAVE and his appeal for the voluntary surrender of landed property.

1946 2nd 5-Yr Plan to open up raw-material resources, develop industries (with for. aid; the steel mills of Rourkela, Bhilai and others), schools and the educ. system. Despite all efforts, the nat. income decreased (the pop. increasing annually by about 15 mil.). Efforts were made to combat relig. tabus (sacred cows), prejudices (caste system), ignorance (birth control). Relig. unrest (1964), language conflicts (1965), and natural catastrophes aggravated the situation. Assam, Nagaland and the Sikhs demanded autonomy.

1958 The first Com. gvt in Kerala was dispersed.

For. policy: owing to NEHRU's policy of 'dynamic neutrality', India, as the leading nation of the 'bloc-free states', was able to play a mediating role in leading world crises.

1954 Chin. state visit (by the prime minister, CHOU EN-LAI); proclamation of the '5 principles of co-existence': sovereignty, equality, peaceful aspirations, rejection of aggression, non-intervention.

1955 On NEHRU's state visit to Moscow, these principles were acknowledged; they secured **econ. aid** for India from the E. and the W.

1959 Border conflicts with China, which did not recognize the McMahon Line and occupied northern border territories (p. 235). India lost prestige because of her use of force in the

1961 annexation of the remaining Port. colonies in India (Goa).

1962 Chin. offensive in the North-eastern Province. The weaknesses of the Ind. army were revealed.

The dispute over

Kashmir strained the relationship with Pakistan: Hindu volunteers and Afghan tribes intervened

1947 in the revolt against the feudal princely gvt in Kashmir, joined by India and Pakistan after massacres had occurred. Mediated by the U.N.,

1948 the armistice sealed the **partition** of the area. Ind. initiative led to the

1953 arrest of Sheikh ABDULLAH, the prime minister who sought autonomy for Kashmir.

In disregard of a U.N. resolution,

1957 the Ind.-occupied portion was annexed to India. The Chin. occupation of the Aksai-Chih Plateau aggravated the conflict.

Pakistan: owing to the actions of cliques of large landowners and relig. fanatics, and a shortage of educated leaders, the bi-furcated 'land of the pure' was in a state of permanent gvtl crisis. **E. Pakistan** resisted tutelage by the western part of the state (Urdu as the official language). Following the

1954 elect. defeat of the Moslem League, an emergency gvt introduced const. reforms; but the army supported Governor-General GHULOM MOHAMMED (from 1951). **For. policy** remained unchanged, holding to the Western alliance (p. 239).

1956 Proclamation of the Isl. Republic (as a full Commonwealth member); meanwhile, the conflicts between the eastern and western parts of Pakistan deepened.

1958 Assumption of power by the for. minister Ayub Khan (b. 1908), who stabilized the admin., domestic politics, the economy and the communities (the 'basic units of democracy').

1960 The utilization of the Indus waters was settled with India and the project to **irrigate the Indus Basin** was begun.

1963 Border Treaty with China. Tensions with India following the dispute over the Rann of Kutch were defused through an agreement; but, the actions of Isl. irregulars in Kashmir led to the

1965 India-Pakistan War. Following U.N. mediation and an initiative by the U.S.S.R., the conflict was brought to an end through the

1966 Tashkent Conference.

Ceylon: a Brit. crown colony, Ceylon

1948 received **dominion status** under its prime minister, D. S. SENANAYAKE (1884–1952).

1954 The Colombo Conference of Asian States aimed at coordinating polit. cooperation. The rad. left-wing

1956 Popular Front gvt of the prime minister, **S. Bandaranaike** (1899–1959 (assassinated)), neutralist in for. policy, demanded the withdrawal of Brit. troops. His widow

1960–65 Sirimawo Bandaranaike, assuming the premiership, continued the policies of the Freedom party. There was unrest among the Tamil minority, followed in

1962 by a nat. officers' revolt. The U.S. blocked credits until

1965 a coalition gvt was formed.

Afghanistan: modernization proceeded slowly under King MOHAMMED SAHIR (p. 169). Border revisions were agreed with the U.S.S.R. (1946–8), and following tensions, also with Pakistan.

1955 Treaty of Mutual Assistance with the U.S.S.R. and provisions for milit. aid. Neutrality and 'bloc-free' policies earned Afghanistan econ. aid from both E. and W.

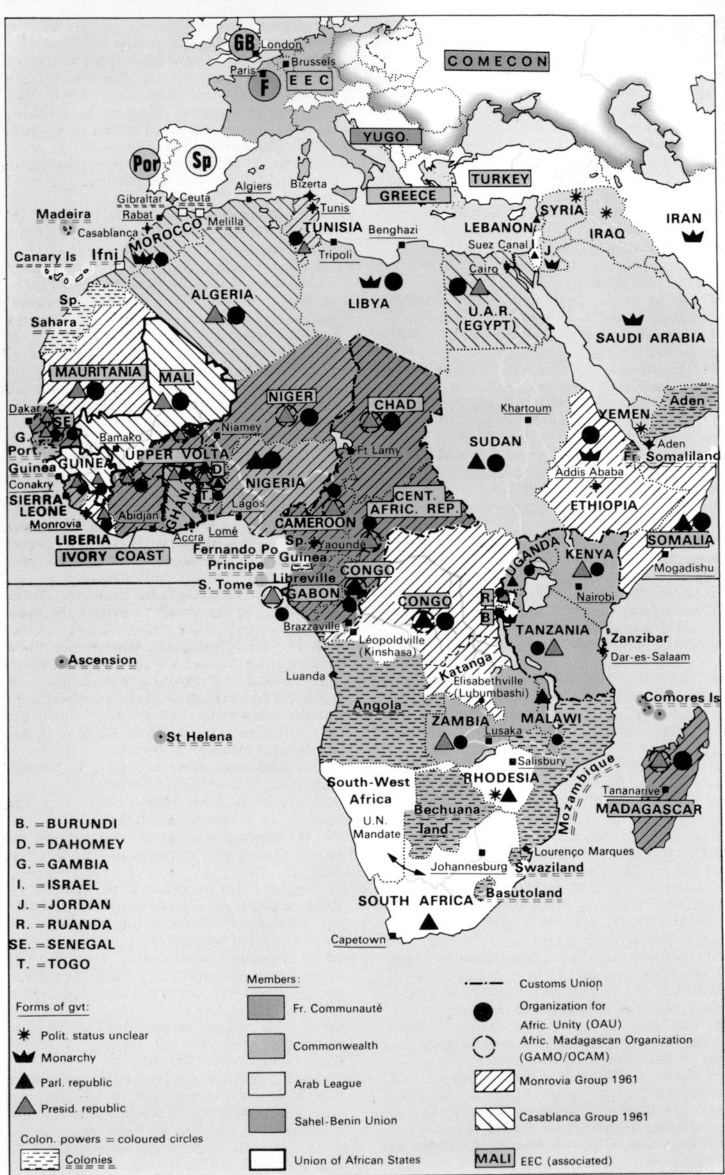
London
Brussels
Paris
E E C
COMECON
YUGO.
TURKEY
GREECE
Algiers
Bizerta
Tunis
Gibraltar
Ceuta
Rabat
Madeira
Casablanca
Melilla
MOROCCO
TUNISIA
Benghazi
LEBANON
SYRIA
IRAQ
IRAN
Canary Is
Ifni
Tripoli
Suez Canal
Cairo
Sp. Sahara
ALGERIA
LIBYA
U.A.R. (EGYPT)
SAUDI ARABIA
MAURITANIA
MALI
NIGER
CHAD
Aden
Khartoum
YEMEN
Dakar
SE
G.
Port. Guinea
Bamako
Niamey
Ft Lamy
SUDAN
Aden
Fr. Somaliland
GUINEA
UPPER VOLTA
D
Conakry
SIERRA LEONE
NIGERIA
Addis Ababa
GHANA
T.
CENT. AFRIC. REP.
ETHIOPIA
Monrovia
Abidjan
Lagos
CAMEROON
LIBERIA
Accra
Lomé
SOMALIA
IVORY COAST
Fernando Po
Sp. Guinea
Yaoundé
UGANDA
KENYA
Principe
Mogadishu
S. Tome
Libreville
CONGO
GABON
CONGO
Nairobi
R
B
Brazzaville
TANZANIA
Zanzibar
Léopoldville (Kinshasa)
Dar-es-Salaam
Ascension
Luanda
Katanga
Elisabethville (Lubumbashi)
Angola
Comores Is
ZAMBIA
MALAWI
Lusaka
St Helena
Salisbury
South-West Africa
RHODESIA
Mozambique
Tananarive
MADAGASCAR
Bechuana-land
U.N. Mandate
Lourenço Marques
Johannesburg
Swaziland
Basutoland
SOUTH AFRICA
Capetown
B. = BURUNDI
D. = DAHOMEY
G. = GAMBIA
I. = ISRAEL
J. = JORDAN
R. = RUANDA
SE. = SENEGAL
T. = TOGO
Forms of gvt:
Polit. status unclear
Monarchy
Parl. republic
Presid. republic
Colon. powers = coloured circles
Colonies
Members:
Fr. Communauté
Commonwealth
Arab League
Sahel-Benin Union
Union of African States
Customs Union
Organization for Afric. Unity (OAU)
Afric. Madagascan Organization (GAMO/OCAM)
Monrovia Group 1961
Casablanca Group 1961
MALI
EEC (associated)

Africa, 1965

The New Africa

The 2nd World War raised Afr. self-awareness (cf. p. 261). Commitments to polit. changes were fulfilled in part only after 1945. The **Fr. Union** (1946) guaranteed 'equality of rights and obligations' of the mother country and the former colonies (Art. 107). The Brit. Lab. gvt (p. 246) also initiated const. reforms; as a consequence, Afr. **nat. movements** developed.

Parties: FÉLIX HOUPHOUET-BOIGNY (b. 1905) founded the

1946 'Rassemblement Démocratique Africain' (R.D.A.), headed in Guinea by **Sekou Touré** (b. 1922), in Mali by **Modibo Keita** (b. 1915); **Léopold Sédar Senghor** (b. 1906) led the Democratic Bloc of Senegal;

1949 The Convention People's party (C.C.P.): Kwame Nkrumah (1909–72);

1954 Tanganyika Afr. Nat. Union (TANU): **Julius K. Nyerere** (b. 1918).

Trade unions: the Afr. branches of Eur. or int. unions drew on civil servants and white-collar employees. The formation of Afr. unions was initiated in

1956 with the establishment of the Union of Afr. Workers (UGTAN) in Conakry by SEKOU TOURÉ; it was an organization under Com. influence, which was expanded through the establishment of the

1961 Pan-Afr. Trade Union of Casablanca (USPA).

Secret societies: harking back to ancient Afr. tribal traditions (rites), these sought to attain their objective of liberation through the use of terror.

1952–4 The Mau-Mau campaigns of the Kikuyu in Kenya forced Brit. police to make mass arrests.

Federations: semi-auton. transitional federations gave Africans the opportunity to prepare for later polit. tasks.

1953 Establishment of the federations of Brit. W. Africa and Nigeria (1954). The

1953 Cen. Afr. Federation failed because of the privileges given to whites, opposed by **Banda** (b. 1906).

1964 **Malawi** (Nyasaland), under BANDA as prime minister, and **Zambia** (prime minister, KAUNDA, b. 1924) left the federation. In defiance of the then Lab. gvt (p. 246), the Rhodesian prime minister, IAN SMITH (b. 1919), proclaimed

1965 U.D.I. for Rhodesia. (U.D.I. = Unilateral Declaration of Independence.) The new constitution secured polit. power exclusively to Whites. Since then Rhodesia has been condemned and boycotted by the U.N., the O.A.U. (see below), the Commonwealth and others.

1958 The Fr. Communauté, planned by DE GAULLE, did not satisfy the aspirations of Guinea and other Afr. states. The

1959 Mali Federation broke up in 1960.

New States:

1957 Ghana became the first ind. black Afr. state. As prime minister, **Nkrumah** pursued a policy of 'active neutralism' and Pan-Afr. objectives. A dictatorial régime and his orientation to the left (U.S.S.R., China) led to his fall in 1966. Another preferred object of Com. contacts was

1958 Guinea under the prime minister, SEKOU TOURÉ. During the

1960 'Afr. Yr', Cameroun, Congo-Brazzaville, Gabon, Chad and the Cen. Afr. Republic became ind.; their trade and econ. policies were coordinated in the

Union of Cen. Afr. Republics; Togo, Ivory Coast, Dahomey, Upper Volta and Niger formed the

Union of Sahel-Benin. Also Nigeria, Senegal, Mali, Madagascar, Somalia, Mauretania, Congo-Léopoldville (p. 269). They in turn were joined by

1961 Sierra Leone and Tanganyika, which united with Zanzibar to become **Tanzania** (1964); 1962 Uganda, Ruanda, Burundi; 1963 Kenya. 1965/6 Gambia.

Problems of internal emancipation (p. 261), Afr. leadership of admin. and army, and a relatively low level of education led in most of the states to the development of **'enlightened dictatorship'**: gvtl guidance of polit., econ. and soc. life. Instead of lawful polit. opposition, leadership and tribal rivalries were generated, marked by conspiracies, assassinations, unrest and mutinies.

The Pan-Afr. Movement: the movement developed during the 1920s in the U.S.A. After 1945, Afr. intellectuals (AZIKIWE, KENYATTA, NKRUMAH) assumed leadership, their aim being the polit. emancipation of Africa.

1958 1st Conference of Ind. Afr. States in Accra.

1958 Conference of the peoples of Africa in Accra (1960 in Tunis, 1961 in Cairo). Revolutionary parties and extremist minorities dominated these conferences. Beginning in 1961 there were 2 groups: the revolutionary-neutralist **Casablanca states** (7), and the moderate **Monrovia states** (21). On the initiative of Emperor HAILE SELASSIE I (p. 179).

1963 Summit Conference of Addis Ababa: foundation of an **Organization for Afr. Unity** (O.A.U.), providing for commissions of arbitration for the solution of conflicts and a **'freedom committee'** to serve the still dependent areas (Dar-es-Salaam 1964); boycott of the Union of s. Africa.

1964 Conference of the O.A.U. in Cairo: resolution in support of the Congo rebels (p. 269). The extreme course followed by the O.A.U. prompted the moderate states to form the

1965 Afr. Madagascan Organization (G.A.M.O./O.C.A.M.).

S. Africa: following the elect. vict. of the 'Nat. Front', to protect the interest of 3 mil. Whites (faced by 11 mil. Bantus),

1948 the prime minister, Daniel F. Malan (1874–1954) introduced the policy of racial separation. As prime minister, STRIJDOM [1951–8] and subs.

1958 Hendrik F. Verwoerd (1901–66 (assassinated)) continued this policy of **Apartheid** against the opposition of the Progressive party and the Bantus. The opposition was united in the **Afr. Nat. Congress'** (A.N.C.), an organization headed by

Albert J. Luthuli (1899–1967) until its prohibition in 1960. In

1959 the 'Pan-Afr. Congress' (P.A.C.) was est., radically led by **Robert M. Sobukwe** (b. 1924). The

1960 introduction of identity cards for blacks and the suspension of their parl. representation was followed by bloody suppressions (Sharpeville). Despite the effects of boycott measures, U.N. protests and the condemnation of the world press,

1961 s. Africa left the Commonwealth and in

1963 est. the Bantu state of **Transkei**.

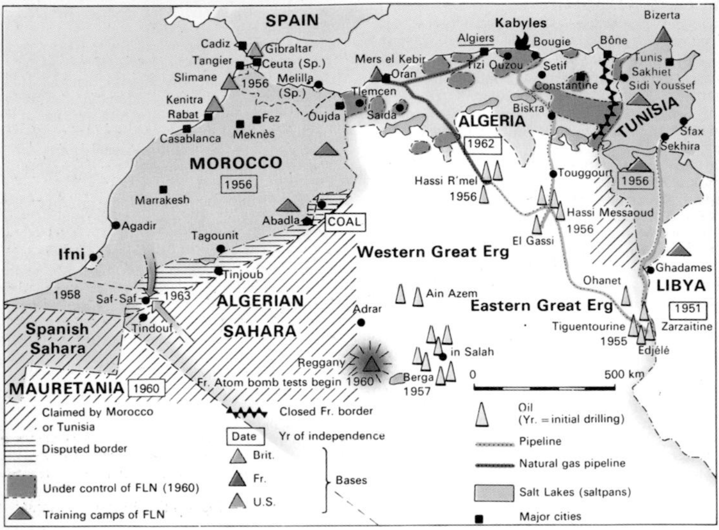

North-West Africa, 1960

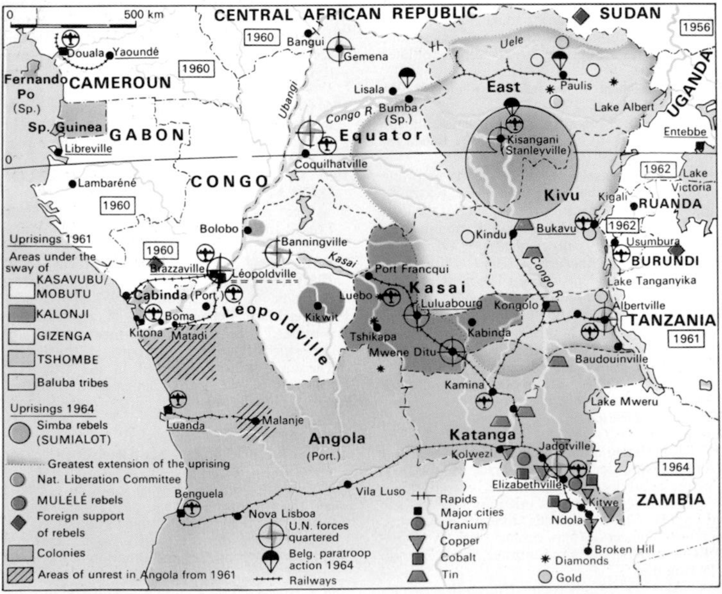

The Congo crisis, 1960–65

The Arabian W. (Maghreb)

Morocco: in the exploitation of the phosphate, managanese, and lead-ore deposits, Morocco was given finan. assistance by the U.S.A. and

1927–61 Sultan BEN JUSSUF was promised independence. Founded in 1944, the **Istiqlal party** cal. for it. France granted the U.S.A.

1951 bases (to 1963), played off Berber against Arab and sent the Sultan into banishment to Madagascar (1953). His successor, BEN ARAFA, was not recognized.

1955 Return of BEN JUSSUF. With Fr. approval, assuming the name of

1956 Mohammed V, he proclaimed the independence of Morocco. Tangiers and Sp. Morocco were joined to the state. The Istiqlal party split: the Union Nationale (U.N.F.P.) under **Ben Barka** rejected the monarchy and urged dem. reforms (constitution).

1960 MOHAMMED V assumed the powers of gvt and raised claims to Ifni, the Sp. Sahara and Mauretania.

1961 HASSAN II (b. 1930) worked for the establishment of a Federation of the Maghreb. In the

1963 border conflict with Algeria, Emperor HAILE SELASSIE (p. 179) functioned as mediator. Following the

1965 dissolution of parliament, the country suffered an econ. crisis and was governed by the personal régime of the king.

Tunisia: the Fr. gvt gave in to the pressure of the **Neo-Destour party**, founded in 1934 by HABIB BOURGUIBA (b. 1903).

1954 Autonomy Treaty. The opposition (SALAL BEN JUSSUF, assassinated 1961) accused BOURGUIBA of pro-Western policies; BOURGUIBA was able to overcome the opposition with trade union help.

1956 Independence. The nat. assembly proclaimed a

1957 republic (authoritarian) under President BOURGUIBA.

1961 Conflict over the Fr. base of Bizerta: France agreed to evacuate it.

1964 Expropriation of for.-owned landed property. In for. policy, BOURGUIBA, as NASSER's opposite number, represented a moderate course in the Pan-Arab movement.

Algeria: autonomy was demanded by the

1946 Liberation Movement (M.T.L.D.) (MESSALI HADJ; **Ferhat Abbas**, b. 1899); however, the 'Algerian French', resorting to elect. fraud, sabotaged the

1947 Algeria Statute (providing for parl. self-admin.) **Achmed Ben Bella** (b. 1916), KRIM BELKASSEM (1912–70), BEN KHIDER, and others organized the **Front de Libération Nationale (F.L.N.)**; it opposed the Algerian Nat. movement (M.N.A.) and began the

1954–62 struggle for liberation. The For. Legion and paratroopers responded to terror with counter-terror. Fr. nationalists and officers **(Ultras)** agitated for an *'Algérie française'*. Their

1958 Algiers coup (Generals SALAN and MASSU) caused the fall of the 4th Republic and brought **Charles de Gaulle** to power (p. 246).

1958 The Algerian exile gvt (G.P.R.A.) in Cairo under **Ferhat Abbas** as prime minister est. diplomatic contacts. DE GAULLE granted the Algerians

1959 self-determination, a measure ratified by the Fr. people in 1961 by a majority of 75%. Within the G.P.R.A. the representatives of the 'hard course' under

1961 the prime minister, Ben Khedda (b. 1920), carried the day. Terror actions by the F.L.N. and the **O.A.S. secret army** under General SALAN continued. Initial Fr. negotiations with the G.P.R.A. failed because of the **Sahara question** (exploitation of oilfields discovered after 1945).

1962 Armistice of Evian: guarantees for the 'Algeria French' in exchange for a commitment to full independence for Algeria on the part of France. Following elections on the basis of F.L.N. 'unity lists', the **'Popular Dem. Republic of Algeria' was proclaimed**. Over the opposition of polit. enemies and uprisings among the Kabyles (AIT ACHMED), President **Ben Bella** est. a 1-party Socialist state.

1965 Coup d'état of the Revolutionary Council under Colonel Boumedienne (b. 1925); fall of BEN BELLA.

Libya: placed under U.N. trusteeship, the desert state received its

1951 independence under **King Mohammed Idris I** (b. 1890).

The Congo Crisis (1960–65)

Supported by the M.N.C. party under the leadership of **Patrice Lumumba** (1925–61 (murdered)), the Afr. liberation movement spread to the area of the Belg. Congo.

1959 Uprising in Léopoldville. Precipitate surrender of the colony.

1960 Transfer of the gvt to President **Rasawubu** (1917–69) and Prime Minister **Lumumba** (Jun.). Mutinies of Congo troops (Jul.). The flight of Belg. officers, officials and technicians plunged the country into chaos. The mining province of **Katanga**, which had been spared disruption, declared its independence under **Moise Tshombe** (1919–69) as prime minister. LUMUMBA protested against the intervention of Belg. paratroops and requested U.N. aid (p. 225). He was driven from power (Sep.) by Colonel **Mobutu** (b. 1930).

1961 Fleeing to join the counter-gvt of his follower **Gizenga** (b. 1925) in Stanleyville, LUMUMBA was murdered *en route*. Upheavals continued without cease. U.N. troops, predominantly Afr., and the new cen. gvt under its prime minister **Adoula** (b. 1923), were unable to assert themselves (Aug.). Under pressure of the Western powers, TSHOMBE agreed to the

1962 U.N. peace plan, but did not attend a const. assembly (Oct.).

1963 U.N. action against Katanga. TSHOMBE left the country. Finan. reasons

1964 forced the withdrawal of U.N. troops. President KASAVUBU named **Tshombe** prime minister of the cen. gvt. He fought against the uprisings of **Simba** and **Mulélé rebels** (partly influenced by Communism, partly by mystical tribal ideas), utilizing U.S. aid and white mercenaries (p. 267). Belg. paratroopers were able to free white hostages (Nov.). (White) gvt troops quashed the uprisings, carrying on

1965 brutally conducted bush warfare. In a *coup d'état*, **Mobutu** removed KASAVUBU, declared himself president, appointed Colonel BOBOZO c.-in-c. of the armed forces, and entrusted Colonel **Mulamba** with the powers of gvt.

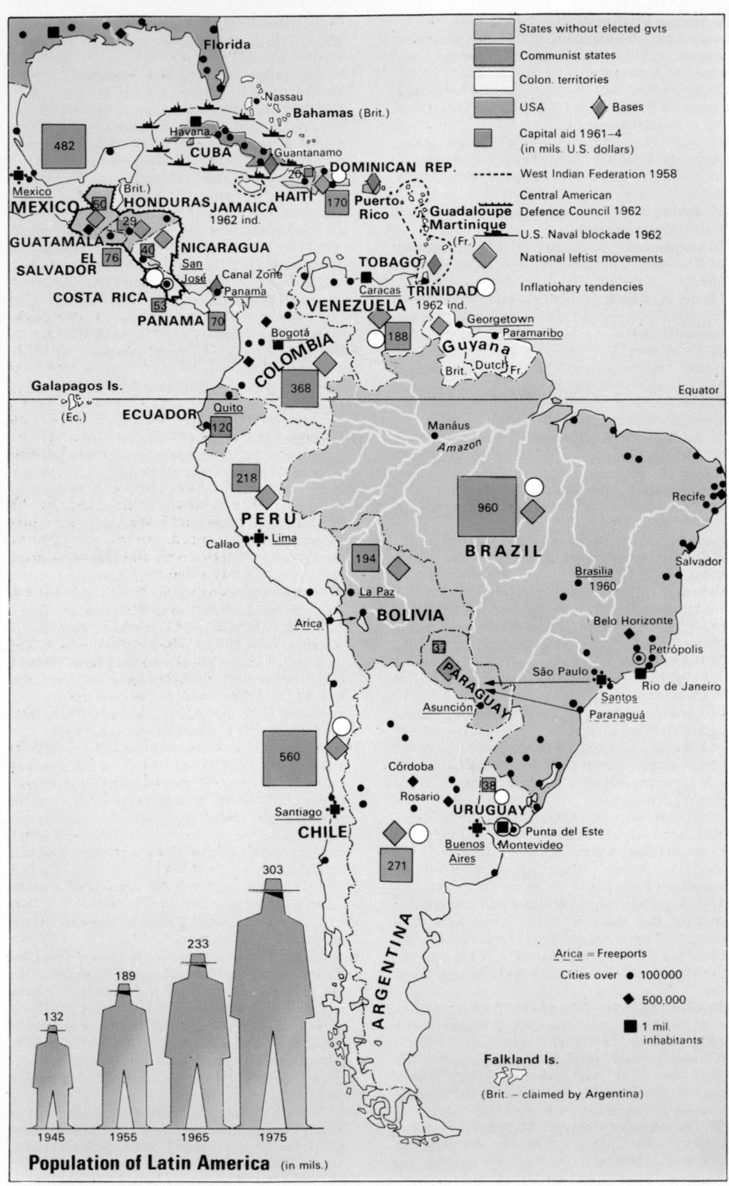
States without elected gvts
Communist states
Colon. territories
USA
Bases
Capital aid 1961–4 (in mils. U.S. dollars)
West Indian Federation 1958
Central American Defence Council 1962
U.S. Naval blockade 1962
National leftist movements
Inflationary tendencies
Florida
Nassau
Bahamas (Brit.)
Havana
CUBA
Guantanamo
DOMINICAN REP.
HAITI
Puerto Rico
Guadaloupe
Martinique
(Fr.)
JAMAICA
1962 ind.
(Brit.)
HONDURAS
MEXICO
Mexico
GUATAMALA
EL SALVADOR
NICARAGUA
San José
COSTA RICA
Canal Zone
Panama
PANAMA
TOBAGO
TRINIDAD
1962 ind.
Caracas
VENEZUELA
Georgetown
Paramaribo
Guyana
Brit.
Dutch
Fr.
Bogotá
COLOMBIA
Galapagos Is.
(Ec.)
ECUADOR
Quito
Equator
Manáus
Amazon
PERU
Callao
Lima
BRAZIL
Recife
Salvador
Brasilia
1960
La Paz
BOLIVIA
Arica
Belo Horizonte
Petrópolis
São Paulo
Rio de Janeiro
Santos
Paranaguá
PARAGUAY
Asunción
Córdoba
Rosario
URUGUAY
Santiago
CHILE
Punta del Este
Buenos Aires
Montevideo
ARGENTINA
482
60
129
76
40
53
70
170
188
368
120
218
960
194
37
560
38
271
Arica = Freeports
Cities over 100 000
500,000
1 mil. inhabitants
Falkland Is.
(Brit. – claimed by Argentina)
132
189
233
303
1945
1955
1965
1975
Population of Latin America (in mils.)

Latin America, 1965

The continent was dependent on the world market (U.S.A.) (export of raw materials, import of finished products); polit. crises, tied to soc. and econ. factors, increased again as the market turned downward: **pop. explosion**, massive migration from the countryside into the deteriorating sections of urban centres (*favelas*), inflation, a low standard of living and education, accompanied by blatant soc. inequality. Gvtl soc. programmes, carried out with insufficient funds by an overblown bureaucracy, 'standardized' misery. Alongside the old forces of order (the military, oligarchic parties, pres. dictatorships), popular leaders (PERÓN, CASTRO), active Com. cadres and nat. revolutionary movements of the left asserted themselves. Attempts were made to alleviate crises and unrest by:

1. **Milit. and polit. integration** (O.A.S., p. 239).
2. **Agrarian reforms.**
3. **Industrialization;** however, there was a shortage of skilled labour (owing to the educ. problem) and capital. Private capital was invested in fixed properties (real estate), speculative ventures, or abroad; for. capital could be attracted only against sufficient security, but for. control and the drain of profits abroad were considered to be exploitation (anti-Amer. mood).
4. **The establishment of markets transcending nat. frontiers** to stimulate for. trade.

1951 O.D.E.C.A. Charter for Cen. America (San Salvador). 'Operation Pan-America': integration of the O.A.S. states in the

1958 'Committee of 21'.

Following the **Revolution in Cuba**, the U.S.A. intervened to counteract Com. subversion in Lat. America.

1959 Inter-Amer. Development Bank;

1960 Lat. Amer. Free Trade Association/LAFTA (Treaty of Montevideo). President KENNEDY announced the establishment of the

1961 Alliance for Progress (Charter of Punta del Este): U.S. cap. aid for nat. development projects.

Crises in Cen. America

Leftist policies in **Guatemala**; President ARBENZ GUZMAN (1949–54) expropriated the holdings of the U.S. Fruit Co.; he was overthrown with U.S. help (secretary of state, DULLES) by Colonel C. ARMAS (assassinated 1957). There was also a movement to force the U.S. to abandon the Canal Zone in **Panama**: unrest and a flag dispute began in 1956. Overthrow of the TRUJILLO régime (p. 177) in the **Domin. Republic**. U.S. intervention in the **civil war of 1965** that erupted during the presidency of JUAN BOSCH (in office since 1962); the O.A.S. and U.N. intervened.

Brit. colonies: Jamaica and **Trinidad/Tobago** left the auton. w. Ind. Federation (est. 1958) in 1962.

Cuba: under the leadership of **Fidel Castro** (b. 1927)

1956–9 guerrilla warfare was carried on against the BATISTA dictatorship (p. 177).

1959 Nat. and soc. revolution: expropriations included for. (U.S.) refineries and land reform. The CASTRO régime came under Com. influence: a Socialist 1-party state was est. The U.S.A. responded with an embargo on Cuban sugar.

1961 Bombing raids and landing attempts by exiled Cubans. Following the

1962 expulsion of Cuba from the O.A.S. (p. 239) increased aid from the U.S.S.R. (advisers, technicians, weapons); establishment of **rocket bases**.

Oct. 1962 The Cuban missile crisis: U.S. blockade; KHRUSHCHEV consented to dismantle the rocket installations; in Moscow, CASTRO was fêted as a 'Hero of the U.S.S.R.'.

1964 O.A.S. sanctions (break in trade relations).

1965 An agreement was reached with the U.S.A. concerning the emigration of Cubans.

States Experiencing Revolutionary Unrest

Following the fall of the JIMENÉZ dictatorship (1952–58) in **Venezuela**, the country experienced finan. crises, assassinations and revolts. The establishment of the dictatorship of General ROJAS PINILLA in **Colombia** (1953–57) was preceded by civil war; since then, coalition of the Nat. Front. **Bolivia**: 1952 Revolution of the Workers' party (M.N.R.): the army and landowners were deprived of power, for.-owned tin mines were expropriated without bringing about an improvement of econ. life; a milit. uprising occurred in 1960.

Argentina: rising to power in Fascist manner in 1946, Colonel **Juan Domingo Perón** (1895–1974) proclaimed the establishment of a welfare state; his régime, however, drove the country into inflation and conflicts with the Church.

1955 Milit. revolt of General ARAMBURU.

1958–62 President FRONDIZI: a programme of economies to restore public finances; elect. gains of the *Peronistas*, unrest, strikes and putsches. Polit. instability continued under President ILLIA (driven from power 1966).

Brazil: notwithstanding his promotion of trade and industry, the army was opposed to the gvt of

1950–54 President Vargas (p. 177). The army

1955–60 overthrew **President Kubitschek,** whose régime had been marked by inflation resulting from increased public spending. The ill-effects of corruption and bureaucracy were fought by

1960 President QUADROS; rad. reforms were carried out under

1961–4 President Goulard, until he was removed by **milit. coup d'état** (General **Castello Branco**). Communists were persecuted, yet retained infl.

Relatively Stable States

Under the presidency of DÍAZ ORDAZ (from 1964), **Mexico** was marked by a balanced economy, stable currency and finances. **Ecuador**: President IBARRA (1944–61), from 1963 milit. gvt. **Peru**: following the régime of President PRADO (1956–63), a moderate left-wing gvt was est. **Uruguay**: beginning in 1952, a Nat. Council modelled after that of Switzerland was est. From 1954, **Paraguay** was under the dictatorial régime of General ALFREDO STROESSNER.

Chile:

1952 President IBANEZ rose to power as a candidate of the Agricult. Workers' party. Inflation and

1956 a gen. strike against a law freezing wages led to a nat. crisis (upheavals, martial law); but

1958–64 President RODRÍGUEZ was able to stabilize prices and wages.

1960 Currency reform. Raising of the standard of living through industrialization. However, there was no increase of agricult. production and therefore an increased danger of revolution.

1965 President FREI MONTALVA (Christ. Democrat) planned the redistribution of land.

Disarmament: Baruch plan (U.S.): destruction of all atomic weapons and int. control of nuclear energy (rejected by the U.S.S.R.).

1950 Disarmament: appeal of the (Com.) World Peace Council calling for the prohibition of all atomic weapons.

Disarmament: formation of a U.N. disarmament commission.

Disarmament: the U.S.S.R. rejected the Brit.-Fr. proposal for phased disarmament (rejection of any controls).

Disarmament: the U.S.S.R. did not agree to the U.S. 'Open Skies' plan for mutual control by aerial inspection.

Disarmament: London 5-Power Conference, requested by the U.N.: discussion of the reduction of armament, armed forces and nuclear testing. The U.S.S.R. agreed to aerial inspections. **The movements of those opposing nuclear weapons** (e.g. C.N.D., p. 246) grew: protest ('Easter') marches in Western countries (prohibited in the E.).

Disarmament: London 5-Power Conference: the U.S.A. (Stassen) urged the suspension of all nuclear testing for 2 yrs to facilitate the creation of a control system; the U.S.S.R. (Sorin) insisted on aerial inspection.

In an effort to ease tensions, the Pol.

Oct. Rapacki Plan proposed the exclusion of all nuclear weapons from Cen. Europe.

Oct. Geneva Conference on the suspension of nuclear testing. The 3 atomic powers suspended their nuclear testing.

Disarmament: 14th U.N. Gen. Assembly: a Brit. 3-stage plan. Khrushchev cal. for immediate and total disarmament within 4 yrs.

Disarmament: Geneva 10-Power Conference: as the Western powers demanded the establishment of an int. control commission and rejected the proposal calling for an immediate removal of for. bases, the states of the Eastern Bloc withdrew their cooperation.

Disarmament: resumption of the Geneva Conference (Mar.). The daily expenditure on armaments throughout the world came to *c.* U.S. $330 mil.

Disarmament: 18-Power Conference in Geneva (8 neutral, 5 Western and 5 Eastern states; France did not participate): the problem of controls remained unsolved.

Disarmament: Amer.-Rus. agreement to establish the Moscow–Washington 'hot-line'.

Aug. Agreement suspending nuclear testing: prohibition of nuclear testing in space, in the atmosphere and under water; France and China did not join the treaty.

Disarmament: the Pol. Gomulka Plan proposed the 'freezing' of nuclear weapons in Cen. Europe, with parity in enforcement control.

Feb. 1967 Signature of a treaty by 14 countries, prohibiting nuclear weapons in Latin America.

Oct. 1967 Treaty on the peaceful use of space became effective (France and the People's Republic of China refused to sign).

1 Jul. 1968 The Nuclear Non-Proliferation Treaty was signed by the U.S.S.R., the U.S.A., Britain and 59 other countries. Some states were reluctant, incl. the Fed. Republic of Germany (B.R.D.), because they feared interference with research and development of the peaceful uses of atomic energy. Beginning of negotiations between representatives of the U.S.S.R. and the U.S.A. concerning the limitation of strategic armaments (Strategic Arms Limitation Talks/SALT):

Nov.–Dec. 1969 **1st SALT round** in Helsinki.

Mar. 1970 Signed by 98 states, the Nuclear Non-Proliferation Treaty became effective (it was not signed by France, the People's Republic of China, Israel, India or Pakistan, among others).

Feb. 1971 Signature of the Ocean Floor Treaty by the U.S.A., the U.S.S.R. and Britain.

Apr. 1972 A U.N. Convention concerning the prohibition of bacteriological weapons was signed by 73 countries (not by France and the People's Republic of China).

Nixon's visit to Moscow.

May 1972 the Interim Agreement on the Limitation of Strategic Offensive Arms was signed.

Nov. 1972–Mar. 1973 Beginning of the 2nd SALT talks in Geneva.

Jun. 1973 Brezhnev's visit to the U.S.A. Amer.-Rus. agreement on the prevention of nuclear war.

Mar.–Jun. 1973 Consultation talks (NATO–Warsaw Pact) about reduction of armaments and troops in Cen. Europe (C.F.E.) began.

1974 Geneva Conference on disarmament: joined by B.R.D. and D.D.R.

Conclusion of SALT II at the meeting.

Dec. 1974 Ford–Brezhnev in Vladivostok: agreement on numbers.

1976 Geneva Conference on disarmament: no concrete results. SALT: problem of cruise missiles.

1977 Renewal of SALT I.

1978 U.N. convention prohibited military use of technology that changes the environment.

1979 Signature of SALT II agreement; because of Afghanistan crisis, not ratified. Beginning of

1982 START negotiations about reduction of intercontinental rockets.

1984 Conference on Confidence and Security-building Measures and Disarmament in Europe (C.S.M.D.) began in Stockholm. New round of negotiations in Geneva

1985 about nuclear and space weapons. In Washington Gorbachev and Reagan signed the

1987 I.N.F. Treaty about the complete dismantling of intermediate-range nuclear weapons; ratification in Moscow (1988).

1988 Amer.–Rus. disarmament negotiations (N.S.T., START, S.D.I.). Before the U.N. Gen. Assembly

Dec. 1988 Gorbachev announced unilateral troops reduction of 50,000 men.

Feb. 1990 U.N. Conference on disarmament in Geneva. At C.S.C.E. summit in Paris

Nov. 1990 conclusion of C.F.E. Treaty about disarmament in Europe.

Jul. 1991 START Treaty about restriction of strategic nuclear weapons: U.S.A. and U.S.S.R. made a commitment to reduce their strategic nuclear weapons (launch systems equipped with intercontinental rockets) by approx. a third.

Warsaw Pact (p. 239)

Oct. 1966 The Moscow Conference (the 'Red Council') was unable to reach joint decisions on the question of Vietnam and the conflict with Peking.

Mar. 1968 At the meeting of the Advisory Polit. Committee in Sofia, all participants, exc. Roumania, cal. for the acceptance of the Nuclear Non-Proliferation Treaty. Beginning in Jun. with numerous manoeuvres, preparations were made for the

20/21 Aug. 1968 milit. intervention in Czechoslovakia by 5 member states of the Warsaw Pact (Bulgaria, D.D.R., Poland, Hungary, U.S.S.R.) under Rus. leadership.

Sep. 1968 **Albania** formally left the Warsaw Pact.

Feb. 1971 The Conference of For. Ministers in Bucharest cal. for the convocation of a general Eur. Conference without preconditions; it also cal. for equal rights in the relationshp with the D.D.R.

1974 Defence Minister GRETCHKO supported further reinforcement of fighting power for the defence against the imperialist threat.

1975 World-wide manoeuvres of Soviet fleet.

1976 Unofficial NATO study established superiority of Warsaw Pact forces which could reach the river Rhine in 48 hrs.

1979 BREZHNEV offered unilateral withdrawal of troops from the D.D.R. in return for not stationing new rocket weapons in Europe (Oct.).
GROMYKO warned against stationing U.S. intermediate-range rockets in the B.R.D. (Nov.–Dec.).

1983 Proposal for a treaty to avoid the use of force (Jan.).

1984 100 Soviet SS-20 rockets positioned in D.D.R. and Czechoslovakia as a reaction to the Pershing stationing (Oct.).

1990 Summit in Moscow: GORBACHEV called for a radical change of W.P.O. and for closer links with NATO (Jun.).

1991 Disbanding of the Warsaw Pact military structure (31 Mar.).
At the last session of the Advising Committee in Prague the

1 Jul. 1991 Warsaw Pact was officially dissolved.

NATO (p. 239)
Fr. disengagement from milit. integration:

1967 Transfer of NATO headquarters (SHAPE) to Casteau/Belgium, of the permanent NATO Council to Brussels.

1968 The Czechoslovakian crisis (p. 281) led to a re-examination of the defence-readiness of the alliance.

1969 Establishment of a communications satellite system (SATCOM).

Mar. 1970 Following a suggestion of the B.R.D., the NATO Council meeting in Rome **proposed the mutual reduction of troop strength to ease tensions.**

Oct. 1971 The NATO Conference requested the former secretary-general, BROSIO, to undertake exploratory negotiations with the Warsaw Pact states concerning the mutual, balanced reduction of troop strengths.

May 1972 The NATO Council of Ministers agreed to conversations in preparation for a general Eur. Security Conference.

Jun. 1974 NATO summit conference in Brussels: 'Declaration about Atlantic Relations'.

Apr.–Aug. 1974 First milit. confrontation of two NATO partners (Greece, Turkey): Cyprus conflict.

Aug. 1974 Withdrawal of Greece from the milit. alliance.

1975 Council of Ministers established increase in milit. armament in the Warsaw Pact, compared with NATO.

1976 Unofficial NATO study feared that Warsaw Pact forces could cross the river Rhine within 48 hrs.

Jun. 1976 Indirect integration of Spain through treaty with the U.S.A.

1977–8 Discussions around the neutron bomb.

1979 NATO double resolution.

1980 Greece returned to the milit. alliance.

1981 In Rome the Council of Ministers confirmed the NATO double resolution from 1979.

1982 Spain became 16th NATO member (May).

1988 Summit meeting of NATO nations in Brussels: modernization of atomic short-range weapons (Mar.).

1990 Session of Council of Ministers (Jun.) in Scottish Turnberry: 9-point offer to the U.S.S.R.; C.S.C.E. in future forum for solving mutual problems of the Eur. nations.

Conference on Security and Cooperation in Europe (C.S.C.E.). After introductory ambassador talks the

Jul. 1973 C.S.C.E. was opened in Helsinki, continued in Geneva (1973–5) and concluded at a summit conference with the

1975 Final Document of Helsinki: inviolability of borders, non-interference in internal affairs, but foremost, the respect for human rights and fundamental liberties.

1977 Report of U.S. President CARTER about violation of human rights in Eastern Europe (infringement of C.S.C.E. Final Document).

1980–83 C.S.C.E. follow-up conference in Madrid.

1986–9 3rd C.S.C.E. follow-up conference in Vienna. Final Document: negotiations about disarmament and steps to build trust.

Oct.–Nov. 1989 C.S.C.E. environment conference in Sofia.

Mar.–Apr. 1990 C.S.C.E. economy conference in Bonn.

Jun. 1990 C.S.C.E. human rights conference in Copenhagen. After successful conclusion of C.F.E. negotiations (p. 272) in Vienna

Nov. 1990 C.S.C.E. summit meeting and 'Charter of Paris': **end to a divided Europe.**

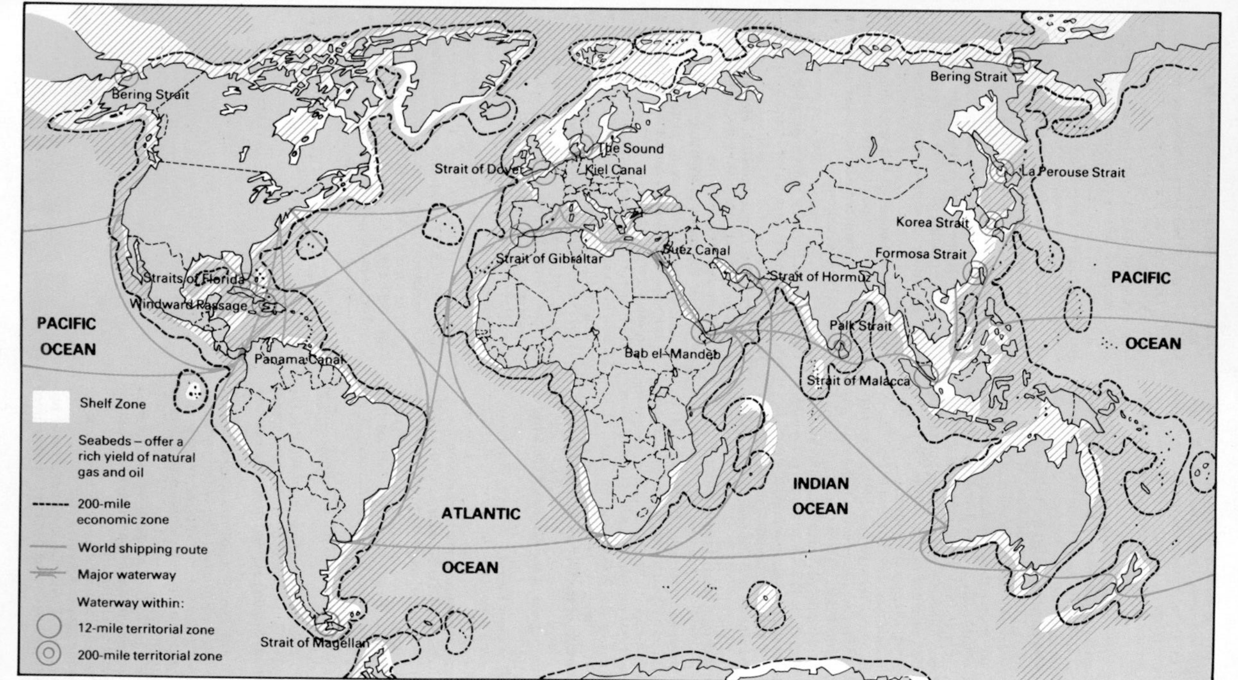
Bering Strait
Bering Strait
The Sound
Strait of Dover
Kiel Canal
La Perouse Strait
Korea Strait
Suez Canal
Strait of Gibraltar
Formosa Strait
Straits of Florida
Strait of Hormuz
PACIFIC
Windward Passage
PACIFIC OCEAN
Palk Strait
OCEAN
Panama Canal
Bab el-Mandeb
Strait of Malacca
Shelf Zone
Seabeds – offer a rich yield of natural gas and oil
INDIAN OCEAN
200-mile economic zone
ATLANTIC
World shipping route
OCEAN
Major waterway
Waterway within:
12-mile territorial zone
200-mile territorial zone
Strait of Magellan

World maritime law

The United Nations (p. 225)

1966 Security Council: the stationing of U.N. troops on **Cyprus** was extended to the end of the yr (further extensions to 1972).
Condemnation of Israeli actions against **Jordan** (Nov.).
Econ. sanctions against **Rhodesia** (Dec.).

Sep.–Dec. 1966 21st Gen. Assembly: decision to suspend the s. Afr. Mandate over **South-West Africa** and re-election of

Dec. 1966 **U Thant** Burma as U.N. secretary-general. The

May 1967 withdrawal of U.N. troops from the Gaza Strip was followed by the Israeli–Arab War:

Jun.–Jul. 1967 5th Extraordinary Meeting of the U.N. Gen. Assembly (requested by the U.S.S.R.). Proposed resolutions to settle the conflict remained unsuccessful.

Sep.–Dec. 1967 (adjourned) 22nd Gen. Assembly: denunciation of s. Afr. policies of Apartheid. Efforts to settle the conflicts in the Near East and Vietnam remained unsuccessful.

Apr.–Jun. 1968 Resumption of the 22nd General Assembly: deliberations concerning the **prevention of the spread of nuclear armaments** and the **South-West Africa Resolution** were completed (s. Africa was requested to surrender control over Namibia, as South-West Africa was called). Because of the disagreement on the Near-East conflict, the General Assembly was adjourned for an indeterminate period and formally terminated in Sep.

Jun. 1968 Security Council: a resolution was passed, guaranteeing the security of the signatory states of the treaty limiting nuclear armaments.

Sep.–Dec. 1968 23rd General Assembly: convention concerning the extension of the Statute of Limitations on War Crimes for an unlimited period.

Jan. 1969 The convention concerning the elimination of all forms of racial discrimination became effective.

Sep.–Dec. 1969 24th General Assembly: GROMYKO presented the draft of an 'appeal to all states of the world' and a draft proposal concerning the prohibition of the development, production and storage of C- and B-weapons.

Sep.–Dec. 1970 Gen. Assembly: the U.S.S.R. and 7 Socialist states presented the draft of a 'declaration concerning the strengthening of int. security'; a Near East resolution and a resolution on the treaty governing the use of the sea bed were passed.

Dec. 1970 The Security Council condemned the Port. invasion of Guinea.

Sep.–Dec. 1971 26th General Assembly. With a two-thirds majority and against the vote of the U.S.A., the **General Assembly on 26 Oct. admitted the People's Republic of China** (refused admission continuously since 1950) **as the representative of China**, and simultaneously expelled Taiwan from the U.N.

Dec. 1971 Security Council: the resolution concerning the India–Pakistan War failed over the veto of the U.S.S.R.

Dec. 1971 The Aust. chief delegate **Kurt Waldheim was elected secretary-general.**

Jan.–Feb. 1972 Special meeting of the Security Council in Addis Ababa: resolution concerning Namibia, the policy of Apartheid in s. Africa, and the Afr. territories under Port. admin.

Jun. 1972 U.N. Conference concerning the human environment in Stockholm (boycotted by the countries of the Eastern Bloc because of the non-admission of the D.D.R.): passage of a 'declaration concerning the human environment'.

Sep.–Dec. 1972 27th Gen. Assembly: disarmament and decolonization problems.

Sep.–Dec. 1973 28th Gen. Assembly: admission of the B.R.D. and the D.D.R.

Dec. 1973 3rd U.N. maritime law conference (1st session); further sessions in Caracas (1974), Geneva (1975), New York (1976) and New York (1976).

Apr.–May 1974 U.N. raw material conference.

Sep.–Dec. 1974 29th Gen. Assembly: admission of the Palestinians to Near East debate (Nov.): P.L.O chief YASSIR ARAFAT demanded a democratic Palestinian state without discrimination against any section of the population.

Nov. 1974 UNESCO conference in Paris: Israel was reproached; resolution in support of revolutionary movements and the Arabs in regions occupied by Israel.

Nov. 1974 U.N. world nutrition conference in Rome, prompted by declining world grain production in 1972 (for the first time since 2nd World War) and natural disasters (droughts, floods and others): creation of an

Dec. 1976 international fund for agricultural development.

Sep.–Dec. 1976 31st Gen. Assembly: resolution for disarmament and peace security, U.S.A. again vetoes the admission of Vietnam.

Jul. 1979 Condemnation of Israeli settler policy in the occupied Arab regions.

1980 Condemnation of South Africa's apartheid politics (Jun.).

1981 Perez de Cuellar new secretary-general (Dec.).

1982 Special session for the 'International Year of the Implementation of Sanctions against South Africa' (Nov.). With the signature (of 119 nations) of a

Dec. 1982 convention, the 3rd U.N. maritime law conference concluded: maximum width of territorial waters of 12 nautical mi., economic zone of 200 nautical mi., exploitation rights for the coastal nations of the continental shelf, administration of the sea bed by international sea-bed office as the 'natural heritage of mankind'.

1987 'International Year of the Homeless'.

1990 Resolution of the Security Council (No. 660 ff.) against the annexation of Kuwait by Iraq (from Aug.).
World Children Summit about the improvement of children's living conditions (Sep.).
On behalf of the U.N., Allied Troops led (under U.S. General SCHWARZKOPF)

Jan.–Feb. 1991 the Gulf War against Iraq to free Kuwait.
Allied Troops guard a security zone for protection of the Kurds in northern Iraq.

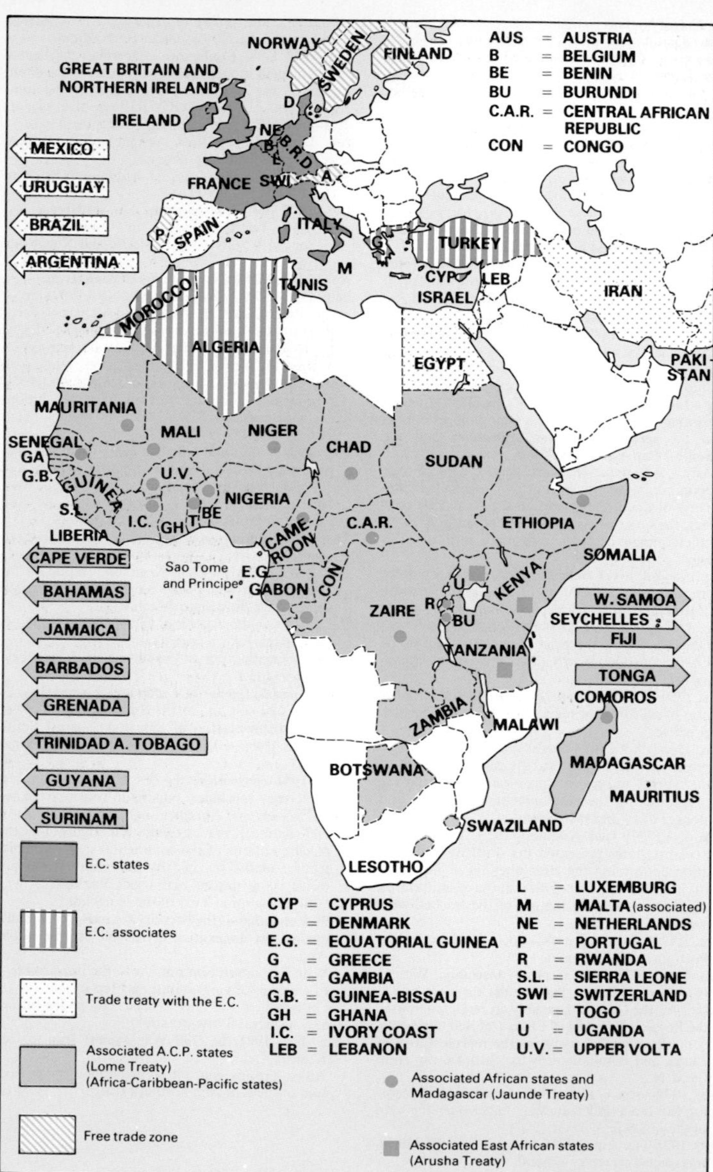
AUS = AUSTRIA
B = BELGIUM
BE = BENIN
BU = BURUNDI
C.A.R. = CENTRAL AFRICAN REPUBLIC
CON = CONGO
NORWAY
SWEDEN
FINLAND
GREAT BRITAIN AND NORTHERN IRELAND
IRELAND
D
NE
B.R.D
B
L
A
FRANCE
SWI
ITALY
MEXICO
URUGUAY
BRAZIL
ARGENTINA
P
SPAIN
G
TURKEY
M
CYP
LEB
ISRAEL
TUNIS
IRAN
MOROCCO
ALGERIA
EGYPT
PAKI-STAN
MAURITANIA
MALI
NIGER
CHAD
SUDAN
SENEGAL
GA
G.B.
GUINEA
U.V.
NIGERIA
S.L.
I.C.
GH
T
BE
LIBERIA
CAMEROON
C.A.R.
ETHIOPIA
SOMALIA
CAPE VERDE
Sao Tome and Principe
E.G.
GABON
CON
U
KENYA
BAHAMAS
R
BU
ZAIRE
W. SAMOA
SEYCHELLES
FIJI
JAMAICA
TANZANIA
BARBADOS
TONGA
COMOROS
GRENADA
ZAMBIA
MALAWI
TRINIDAD A. TOBAGO
MADAGASCAR
BOTSWANA
GUYANA
MAURITIUS
SURINAM
SWAZILAND
LESOTHO
E.C. states
E.C. associates
Trade treaty with the E.C.
Associated A.C.P. states (Lome Treaty) (Africa-Caribbean-Pacific states)
Free trade zone
CYP = CYPRUS
D = DENMARK
E.G. = EQUATORIAL GUINEA
G = GREECE
GA = GAMBIA
G.B. = GUINEA-BISSAU
GH = GHANA
I.C. = IVORY COAST
LEB = LEBANON
L = LUXEMBURG
M = MALTA (associated)
NE = NETHERLANDS
P = PORTUGAL
R = RWANDA
S.L. = SIERRA LEONE
SWI = SWITZERLAND
T = TOGO
U = UGANDA
U.V. = UPPER VOLTA
Associated African states and Madagascar (Jaunde Treaty)
Associated East African states (Arusha Treaty)

E.C. economic power 1975

E.E.C. (p. 245)

1966 Following the return of the Fr. representative, the E.E.C. crisis was overcome. The B.R.D. (Fed. chancellor, ERHARD) worked for the admission of Britain and the Brit. gvt announced negotiations to that end.

1967 E.E.C. Currency Conference (Jan./Apr.) with the aim of reforming the Int. Monetary Fund (I.M.F.) and of coordinating tax policies. The Belgian JEAN REY (b. 1902) became president of the newly formed

1 Jul. 1967 Commission on Europe of the **Eur. Community of the 6** (the E.E.C., the Eur. Coal and Steel Community (E.C.S.C., or Montan Union), and EURATOM). Repeated efforts by Britain for admission failed owing to Fr. resistance.

1968 Passage of the market regulations governing milk, dairy products and beef. Association Agreement with the countries of the E. Afr. Community (Kenya, Tanzania, Uganda). Vice-President SICCO L. MANSHOLT presented the

Dec. 1968 Agrarian Reform Plan (**Mansholt Plan**).

1969 Association Agreement with Tunisia, Morocco, 18 Afr. states and Madagascar. A summit conference of the 6 E.E.C. states in The Hague prepared negotiations for the admission of Britain.

Jul. 1970 Start of negotiations concerning the admission of Britain; in Sep. those with Ireland, Denmark and Norway.
Beginning of negotiations concerning cooperation with the neutral EFTA states, Austria, Switzerland and Sweden.
Association Agreement with Malta.

Feb. 1971 The E.E.C. Council decided on the gradual implementation of the plans for econ. union and a common currency.

Mar. 1971 During the Council Meeting in Brussels, E.E.C. farmers demonstrated for better prices for agricult. products.

May 1971 Finan. crisis in Western Europe resulting from the inflow of U.S. dollars; the B.R.D. and the Netherlands temporarily floated the exchange rate of their currency to the U.S. dollar.

Jun. 1971 Resolution of all open questions of principle relating to the admission of Britain to the Common Market.

Jan. 1972 The members of the Community and **Britain, Denmark, Ireland and Norway** signed the treaty forming the Community of the 10.

Mar. 1972 Following the premature resignation of the Italian FRANCO MARIA MALFATTI (1970–72), SICCO L. MANSHOLT became new president of the E.E.C.

Sep. 1972 Norway: plebiscite against entry into the E.E.C.

Jan. 1973 E.E.C. of 9 comes into force.
F.-X. ORTOLI (France) becomes new president of the E.E.C. Commission.
After free trade agreement with Finland, the E.E.C. came to an agreement with all 7 states of EFTA (Oct.).

Nov. 1973 Near East declaration of foreign ministers in the E.E.C. which supported Arab position in 4th Near East war (p. 297). In recognition, OPEC refrains from a cut in production.

1975 Agreement of Lomé with the A.C.P. states (cf. p. 276).

1977 Free trade area with EFTA came into force (Jul.).

1978 Foundation of the **European Monetary System** (E.M.S.) with the **European Currency Unit** (ECU). Great Britain postponed entry (Dec.).

1979 **The E.M.S. came into force** (Mar.). **First direct election for the European Parliament** (Jun.). 2nd convention of Lomé: regulation of the relations between E.E.C. and A.C.P. states (Oct.).

1981 Greece became 10th E.E.C. member (Jan.). 12.8 mil. unemployed (excluding Greece).

1984 Direct election for the European Parliament (Jun.).

1986 Admission of Spain and Portugal forming **Europe of the 12** (Jan.).

1987 Delors package: reform of mutual agrarian policy, structure fund and household regulation.

1987 Consistent European File (C.E.F.) extended powers of the European Parliament, also contained basis for the 'Home Market 1992'.

1989 Elections for the European Parliament (Jun.). Signature of the agreement of Lomé IV (Dec.).

1990 Cyprus and Malta applied for admission to the E.E.C. (Jul.). Great Britain joined the E.M.S. (Oct.).

COMECON (p. 245)

Efforts to intensify the cooperation of member states progressed only slowly. Special efforts were made to establish a currency that would be convertible in terms of int. currencies (or the convertibility of the currencies of the member states).

1970 Establishment of an int. investment bank, exclusive of Roumania; however, Roumania joined Jan. 1971.

1971 CEAUSESCU cal. for admission of non-Socialist states. Chile indicated its intention to join. At the 25th Meeting of COMECON, a multi-faceted **20-yr programme** was launched. In the context of changes in parity in the int. money market, currencies were revalued upward.

Feb. 1972 Establishment of the atomic energy organization 'Interatominstrument' (excel. Roumania).

Apr. 1972 The investment bank accepted a 60 mil. Euro-dollar loan, the first loan taken up by this bank in the int. money market.

Jul. 1972 Cuba was admitted to membership.

1978 Vietnam 10th member. Despite positive objectives, increasingly in debt to the West and weakening of the economy.

1990 Decision regarding the transition of the accounting of trade to a freely convertible currency.
The shift of most member states away from the communist centrally planned economies led to the

1991 disintegration of the COMECON at the last plenary session in Budapest (28 Jun.).

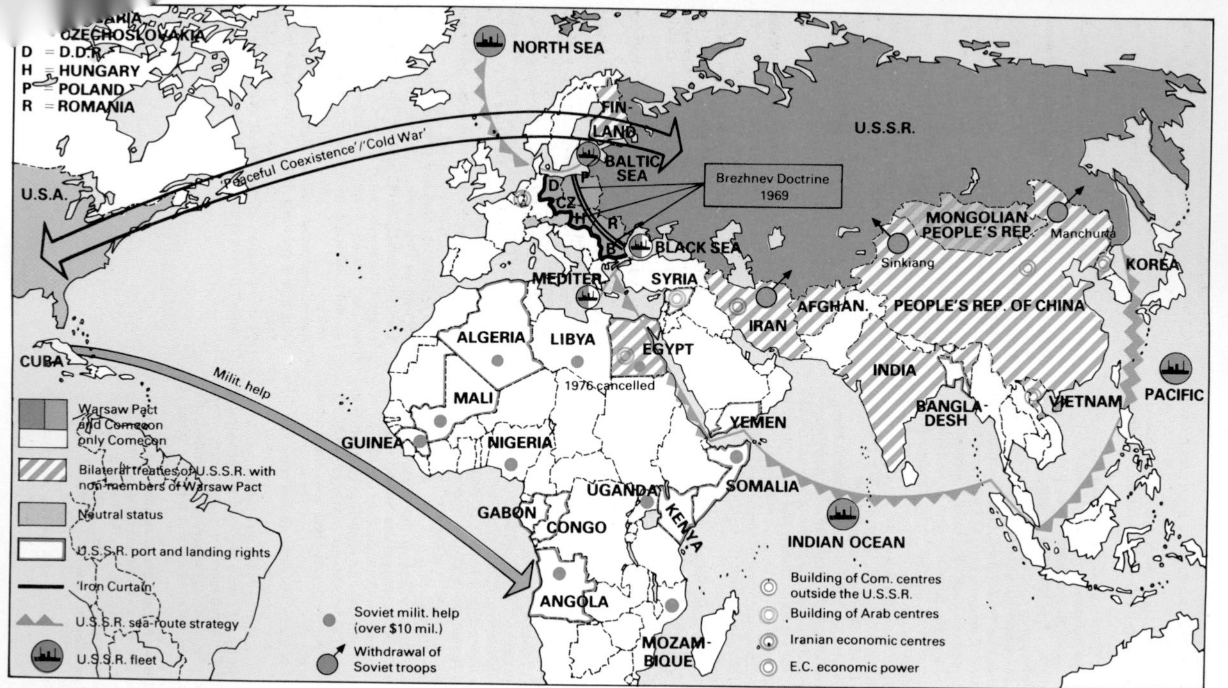
D = D.D.R.
H = HUNGARY
P = POLAND
R = ROMANIA
NORTH SEA
U.S.S.R.
FIN-LAND
BALTIC SEA
'Peaceful Coexistence'/'Cold War'
U.S.A.
D
CZ
H
R
B
Brezhnev Doctrine 1969
BLACK SEA
MONGOLIAN PEOPLE'S REP.
Manchuria
Sinkiang
KOREA
MEDITER.
SYRIA
AFGHAN.
PEOPLE'S REP. OF CHINA
IRAN
ALGERIA
LIBYA
EGYPT
CUBA
Milit. help
INDIA
PACIFIC
1976 cancelled
MALI
VIETNAM
BANGLA-DESH
YEMEN
GUINEA
NIGERIA
UGANDA
SOMALIA
GABON
CONGO
KENYA
INDIAN OCEAN
ANGOLA
MOZAM-BIQUE
Warsaw Pact and Comecon
only Comecon
Bilateral treaties of U.S.S.R. with non-members of Warsaw Pact
Neutral status
U.S.S.R. port and landing rights
'Iron Curtain'
U.S.S.R. sea-route strategy
U.S.S.R. fleet
Soviet milit. help (over $10 mil.)
Withdrawal of Soviet troops
Building of Com. centres outside the U.S.S.R.
Building of Arab centres
Iranian economic centres
E.C. economic power

U.S.S.R. foreign policy 1967–75

The U.S.S.R. (p. 228)

Mar.–Apr. 1966 23rd Party Congress of the Com. party of the U.S.S.R.; representatives of the People's Republic of China were not present: the party chief, BREZHNEV (b. 1906), criticized the U.S.A. (Vietnam policy) and the B.R.D. (for upsetting Eur. security); the prime minister, KOSYGIN (b. 1904), discussed the new 5-Yr Plan, which provided for 'increased incentives to material interests'.

1967 During the Israel conflict, the U.S.S.R. took the Arab side.
Opposition to reform measures in Czechoslovakia increased after

Jul. 1968 announcement of the **Brezhnev Doctrine** (main thesis: the sovereignty of the single communist state finds its boundaries at the interests of the socialist community) until

20–21 Aug. 1968 Warsaw Pact troops invaded Czechoslovakia.

Mar. 1969 Serious border incident at the Ussuri.

Aug. 1970 Signature of the treaty with the B.R.D. renouncing the use of force.

1970 Ambassador talks in Berlin (from Mar.). Signature of the treaty with the B.R.D. to avoid violence (Aug.).

Mar.–Apr. 1971 24th Congress of the Com. party of the Soviet Union: discussion about the 9th 5-Yr Plan (1971–5).

Sep. 1971 **Crimea meeting:** Fed. Chancellor BRANDT (B.R.D.) was the guest of BREZHNEV.

May 1972 NIXON became the 1st U.S. president to visit the U.S.S.R.: several agreements were signed.

31 May 1972 Ratification of the treaty between the U.S.S.R. and the B.R.D.

1974 Deportation of SOLZHENITSYN (Feb.). NIXON's 2nd visit (Jun.–Jul.).

Nov. 1974 BREZHNEV met President FORD in Vladivostok.

1976 Egypt cancelled Treaty of Friendship: deportation of Soviet adviser and termination of harbour rights in Egypt.

1977 President PODGORNY visited Africa, military help for 10 African states. Dissidents were hospitalized in psychiatric institutions. Pres. PODGORNY was excluded from the Politburo (Jun.). A new constitution was passed (Oct.).

1978 State visit of BREZHNEV to the B.R.D. (May): no threat through the U.S.S.R., cooperation in economy and industry.

1976–88 Human rights movements were fought with arrests and convictions (SAKHAROV sent into exile).

Dec. 1980 Soviet troops marched into Afghanistan.

1981 BREZHNEV travelled to Bonn on a working visit (Nov.).

1982 Death of Brezhnev (10 Nov.); ANDROPOV became new secretary-general, from 17 Jun. 1983 also head of state.

Nov. 1983 Dispute between U.S.A. and U.S.S.R. over the shooting down of a s. Korean airliner.

1984 Death of Andropov (9 Feb.). CHERNENKO became new secretary-general, from 13 Apr. also head of state.

1985 Death of Chernenko (10 Mar.); **Michail Gorbachev** became new secretary-general, since 1980 full member of the Politburo, fought the corruption, criticized deplorable state of affairs and announced at the

Feb. 1986 27th Congress of the Com. party of the Soviet Union the 'conversion' (**Perestroika**) of Soviet affairs and 'openness' (**Glasnost**).

26 Apr. 1986 Reactor accident in Chernobyl: strong international reaction.

11–12 Oct. 1986 GORBACHEV and President REAGAN met in Reykjavik. After signature of the Afghanistan Treaty in Geneva (14 Apr. 1988) start of the

15 May 1988 Soviet withdrawal of troops from Afghanistan (completed Feb. 1989).

29 May–2nd Jun. 1988 Summit meeting of REAGAN and GORBACHEV in Moscow: ratification of the I.N.F. Treaty.
Disturbances in Armenia, Azerbaijan, Nagorno Karabakh and the Baltic States.

As A. GROMYKO's successor (1985–8)

Oct. 1988 GORBACHEV also became head of state.

7 Dec. 1988 GORBACHEV announced before the U.N. Gen. Assembly unilateral steps of disarmament: decrease in armed troops of 500,000 men and withdrawal of 6 tank divisions from the D.D.R., Czechoslovakia and Hungary.

2–3 Dec. 1989 GORBACHEV and President BUSH met before Malta.

1990 Declarations of independence of the Baltic States
Lithuania (1 Mar. after election victory of Sajudis), Estonia (30 Mar.) and Latvia (4 May) were not recognized by the U.S.S.R.
Further nationality conflicts with Uzbekistan and Kirghiz in Armenia, the Ukraine, Georgia, Vlatava.

15 Mar. 1990 Gorbachev became president of the U.S.S.R., his opponent in domestic politics

29 May 1990 Boris Yeltsin was elected president of the Russian S.F.S.R.

Jul. 1990 28th Congress of the Com. party of the Soviet Union: despite strong criticism re-election of Secretary-General GORBACHEV and continuation of *Perestroika.*
Treaty with the B.R.D. about avoidance of violence and cooperation (Sep.).
Supreme Soviet decided to introduce market economy (Oct.).

15 Oct. 1990 GORBACHEV received Nobel Prize for Peace.

1991 Bloody milit. actions against the endeavours to obtain independence by the Baltic states (Jan.).

Apr. 1991 Georgia declared its independence, changed the constitution (Georgian Democratic Republic) and elected a president.

Jun. 1991 YELTSIN elected president of the Russian Soviet Federal Soc. Rep. (S.F.S.R.) in a direct election. Draft agreement for renewal of the U.S.S.R.

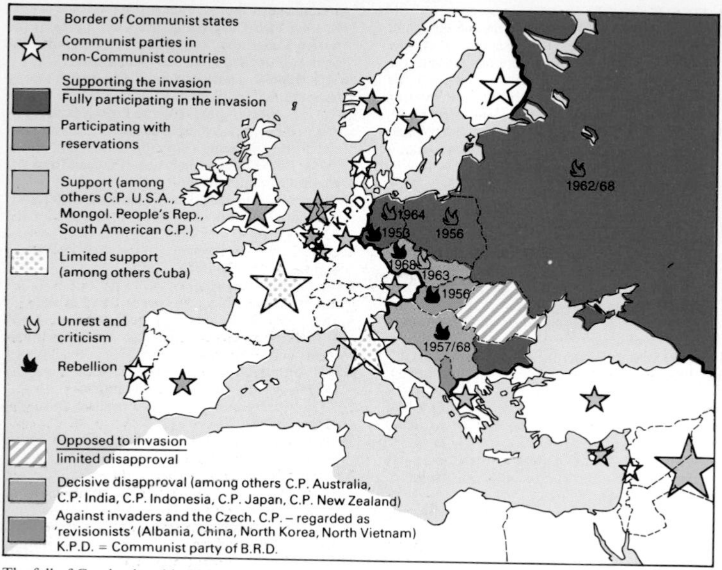

Border of Communist states

Communist parties in non-Communist countries

Supporting the invasion

Fully participating in the invasion

Participating with reservations

Support (among others C.P. U.S.A., Mongol. People's Rep., South American C.P.)

Limited support (among others Cuba)

Unrest and criticism

Rebellion

Opposed to invasion

limited disapproval

Decisive disapproval (among others C.P. Australia, C.P. India, C.P. Indonesia, C.P. Japan, C.P. New Zealand)

Against invaders and the Czech. C.P. – regarded as 'revisionists' (Albania, China, North Korea, North Vietnam)

K.P.D. = Communist party of B.R.D.

K.P.D.

1962/68

1964

1953

1956

1968

1963

1956

1957/68

The fall of Czechoslovakia 1968

ROMANIA

Bucharest

Belgrade

Danube

YUGOSLAVIA

BULGARIA

Serbia

Sofia

Kosmet

Skopje

Macedonia

Present state borders

Tirana

ALBANIA

Saloniki

Istanbul

TURKEY

GREECE

Diocesan border of Bulgarian exarchate

Border of 'Greater Bulgaria' after San Stefano Treaty 1878

People's Rep. of Macedonia 1945

Greater Macedonia, from Yugoslav perspective

Dissemination of Macedonians

Macedonia – the unsolved problem

Poland (p. 232)

Dec. 1970 Visit of Chancellor Brandt and signing of the Ger.–Pol. treaty in Warsaw.
Bloody unrest in Northern Poland, owing to sharp price increases.

Dec. 1970 Resignation of Gomulka, Edward Gierek (b. 1913) became the new party chief.

Jan. 1971 Lowering of food prices, increase of wages and improved soc. services.

Mar. 1971 The prime minister, JAROSZEWICZ, received Cardinal WYSZYNSKI.

26 May 1972 The Council of State ratified the treaty with the B.R.D. while rejecting the resolution of the Ger. Bundestag which had accompanied it.

1975 Treaty about pension payments with the B.R.D.

1976 Constitutional reform: stand against church and intellectuals was tightened.
KAROL WOJTYLA, Cardinal of Krakow, became

1978 Pope John Paul II.

1979 Pope JOHN PAUL II visited his home country.

1980 Resignation of Prime Minister JAROSZEWICZ. His successor, Prime Minister E. BABIUCH (Feb.–Aug. 1980) tried to alleviate economic difficulties by, among other things, cutting subsidies. Esp. the increased prices for meat led to a

Jul.–Sep. 1980 strike wave in Warsaw, Danzig and Silesia. Agreement between the gvt and industry-wide strike committees led by LECH WAŁĘSA. S. KANIA replaced GIEREK as party chief.

Oct. 1980 Registration of 'Solidarity' (Solidarność) as free trade union association.

1981 General W. JARUZELSKI became prime minister (Feb.). Continuing liberalization. Foundation of a 'Farmers' Solidarity'.

Oct. 1981 Gen. Jaruzelski became party leader (1st secretary of the Cen. Committee) of the Polish Workers' Party (P.W.P.). Imposition of state of war (Dec.).

1982 Prohibition of Solidarity (Oct.).

1983 Cancellation of state of war (Jul.).

1984 Abduction and murder of priest POPIELUSZKO (Oct.–Nov.).

1985 JARUZELSKI became chairman of the Council of State, Prime Minister MESSNER (1985–8).

1988 Prime Minister M. RAKOWSKI, admission of private enterprise and opposition.

1989 Talks at the 'Round Table' (Feb.–Apr.) led to free elections with 65% compulsion quota for the gvt (Jun.), Solidarity won all free seats in the Sejm.

JARUZELSKI was elected state president (Jul.). Solidarność member T. MAZOWIECKI became prime minister (Aug.). Abolition of the term 'People's Republic':

Dec. 1989 Republic of Poland.
At the party Congress the Com.

Jan. 1990 P.W.P. decided on dissolving into several social-democratic parties. Privatization of state enterprises (Jul.).
After election victory (25 Nov.–9 Dec.)

Dec. 1990 Lech Wałęsa became state president.

Jan. 1991 Prime Minister J. K. BIELECKI.

Czechoslovakia (p. 233)

1968 **Alexander Dubček** (b. 1921), a Slovak, was elected 1st secretary of the party; head-of-state ANTONÍN NOVOTNÝ (p. 233) resigned (22 Mar.). OLDRICH CERNIK became prime minister, General LUDVÍK SVOBODA (b. 1895) became president (30 Mar.). JOSEF SMRKOVSKY (1911–74) became president of the Nat. Assembly (18 Apr.).
The course of reform, introduced by the Czechoslovak Com. party at the beginning of the yr, was watched by the members of the Warsaw Pact with increasing suspicion.

Jun. 1968 Warsaw meeting (U.S.S.R., D.D.R., Poland, Hungary, Bulgaria): a letter of warning was sent to the Cen. Committee of the Com. party of Czechoslovakia. Conferences in Cierna and Tisou (29 Jul.–1 Aug.) with the Politburo of the Com. party of the Soviet Union and in Bratislavia with representatives of the 'Warsaw 5' appeared to have defused the situation.

21–2 Aug. 1968 Invasion of Czechoslovakia by troops of the 5 Warsaw Pact states. Tough negotiations by a Czech delegation led by President SVOBODA in Moscow gained 'normalization'. Reintroduction of censorship.

Oct. 1968 Conclusion of a treaty regulating the stationing of Rus. troops in Czechoslovakia.

Apr. 1969 DUBČEK's position as chief of the Com. party was taken over by HUSÁK. Following the resignation of CERNIK

Jan. 1970 STROUGAL became prime minister.

May 1971 Party Convention of the Com. party of Czechoslovakia: the statutes were changed to make it into a cadre party.

Jul. 1974 The treaty of normalization with w. Germany comes into force.

1975 HUSÁK also became president.
Position worsened for dissident intellectuals:

1977 foundation of the civil rights group Charta 77.

1979 Expulsion of the dissident writer PAVEL KOHOUT (Oct.).

1988 Prime Minister L. ADAMEC. After mass demonstrations against the Com. regime, foundation of the opposition alliance Citizens' Forum, resignation of the Com. party leadership and renunciation of the power monopoly by the Com. party of Czechoslovakia (CPC):

1989 'Gvt of national understanding' (10 Dec.) under Prime Minister M. ČALFA.
The Fed. Assembly elected **Alexander Dubček** as president and the writer

29 Dec. 1989 Vaclav Havel (Charta 77) as state president. The Fed. Assembly decides on the state name (Apr.)

1990 Czech and Slovak Fed. Republic (C.S.F.R.).
At the first free parliamentary elections

Jun. 1990 victory of the democratic parties in the Czech (Citizens' Forum) and Slovak (Public against Violence) Republic.
Coalition government, ČALFA.
The last of the

1991 Soviet troops stationed in the C.S.F.R. since 1968 left the country.

Bulgaria (p. 232)

1971 The new constitution entrusted the leadership of society and state jointly to the Com. party and the Agrarian Union. ZHIVKOV became chairman of the newly formed Council of State; TODOROV the new chief of the gvt.

1975 Treaty with the B.R.D. about industrial cooperation.

1981 Prime Minister G. FILIPOV.

1986 Prime Minister G. ATANASOV.

After harassment by the authorities in 1989 exodus of the Turkish minority into Turkey.

After the C.S.C.E. environment conference in Sofiá

10 Nov. 1989 fall of Zhivkov. Creation of opposition groups and

Jan. 1990 talks at the 'Round Table'. Com. party Congress approved reforms (Jan.–Feb.).

Feb. 1990 A. LUKANOV becomes new prime minister. Change of name from Com. party to Bulgarian Socialist party (B.S.P.), which won the first free elections (Jun.).

Roumania (p. 232)

1966 The prime minister, MAURER, and the for. minister, MANESCU, strove to loosen Roumania's ties to the Eastern Bloc.

1967 Party chief CEAUSESCU proposed cooperation between all Balk. states; he became chairman of the Council of State (9 Dec.) and introduced reforms.

1968 Roumania took an affirmative position to the reform course in Czechoslovakia.

Roumania condemned the intervention of Warsaw Pact troops in Czechoslovakia.

Aug. 1969 NIXON visit.

Jul. 1970 Treaty of Friendship with the U.S.S.R.

Mar. 1971 The nat. assembly passed a lib. for. trade law.

At the 24th Conference of the Com. party of the Soviet Union, CEAUSESCU defended Roumania's right to an independent course.

Jul. 1971 A 17-point programme aimed at the intensification of an orth. ideological orientation of the people.

Mar. 1974 CEAUSESCU became president after change of constitution, MANESCU prime minister.

Nov. 1974 11th Congress of the Com. party: programme established until the year 2000; codex of work.

1975 CEAUSESCU against uniting families and emigration.

1986 Limitation of religious freedom. Destruction of churches.

1988 Destruction of villages.

16 Dec. 1989 Rebellion of Timisoara, fall, arrest (22 Dec.) and **execution of Ceausescu (25 Dec.).**

New leadership under I. ILIESCU (26 Dec.).

1990 Free elections (20 May): victory of the 'Front for the Rescue of the Nation'. President ILIESCU.

Hungary (p. 233)

Admission of private initiatives led to some economic success.

1987 Prime Minister K. GROSZ succeeded Prime Minister G. LAZAR (1975–87).

After resignation of party chief KADAR

1988 GROSZ became new party chief of the Hungarian Socialist Workers' Party (H.S.W.P.) (May). Radical economic reform (Jul.). The People's Republic became

1989 Republic of Hungary. Central Committee of the H.S.W.P. decided to introduce a multi-party system (Feb.). Rehabilitation and funeral of IMRE NAGYS. Dismantling of frontier barriers (Jun.).

Sep. 1989 Opening of the border to Austria: the beginning of the end of the 'Iron Curtain'.

1990 Agreement on withdrawal of Soviet troops (10 Mar.).

Mar.–Apr. 1990 Free elections; victory of the Civil Democratic Forum; failure for the H.S.W.P. Coalition gvt under J. ANTALL (May).

Yugoslavia (p. 231)

1966 Monetary reform (1 Jan.) and econ. liberalization.

1967 Admission of for. capital to strengthen the economy.

1968 Student unrest was suppressed and reforms were announced (Jun.). The occupation of Czechoslovakia was condemned.

Dec. 1969–Apr. 1970 Disputes between Croatia and Belgrade.

Sep.–Oct. 1970 NIXON visit.

Jun. 1971 A const. change transferred rights of autonomy to republics and provinces.

Sep. 1971 BREZHNEV visit: recognition of Yugoslavia's independence.

1971–2 An intensification of the nationalities conflict between the Belgrade cen. gvt and the Croatian party and gvt leadership led to changes in gvt personnel, arrests, expulsions from the party and trials.

1974 First state visit of TITO to the B.R.D.

1975 Final settlement of the Trieste question.

1980 Illness and **death of Tito** (May). Collective state presidency.

1988 Conflict between the autonomous provinces and Serbia (from Aug.), unrest in Kosovo.

1990 Constitutional question and efforts towards independence (Slovenia, Croatia).

After official

Jun. 1991 declaration of independence by the republics of Slovenia and Croatia, there were fights between the Slovenian and the Croatian civil forces and the Yugoslav People's Army.

Jul. 1991 Decision of the state presidency: federal army evacuated Slovenia.

Albania (p. 232)

1968 Resignation from the Warsaw Pact.

1985 Death of Enver Hoxha; successor as party leader became state president (since 1982) RAMIZ ALIA (Apr.).

1990 Beginning of democratization: admission of political parties (Dec.).

Jun. 1991 Joined the C.S.C.E.

Finland (p. 229)
After the Soc. Democrats won the elections of
1966, the prime minister, PAASIO (b. 1903), formed a popular front gvt.
1968 President KEKKONEN (p. 229) was re-elected; a coalition gvt was formed under the Soc. Democratic premier MAUNO KOIVISTO (b. 1924).
1970 Coalition Cabinet of KARJALAINEN (b. 1923).
1971 Communists left the gvt.
Feb.–Sep. 1972 A Soc. Democratic minority gvt under PAASIO; succeeded by a coalition gvt under KALEVI SORSA/Soc. Democrat.
1975 People's Front gvt under MIETTUNEN.
1978 Re-election of KEKKONEN as president.
1982 Koivisto new president.
1987 Civil coalition gvt H. HOLKERI.

Sweden (p. 229)
Sep. 1968 the Soc. Democrats gained an absolute majority.
The chairman of the Soc. Democratic party,
Oct. 1969 Prime Minister Olof Palme (1927–86, assassinated) continued policies aimed at the growth of a welfare state. New king
1973 CARL XVI GUSTAV, due to change in constitution, without any real powers.
Victory of the non-socialist coalition parties:
1976 Prime Minister TH. FÄLLDIN/Centre Party, after resignation (1978), Prime Minister O. ULLSTEN.
1979 Prime Minister FÄLLDIN again. After election victory of the Soc. Democrats again
1982 Prime Minister PALME.
Feb. 1986 Prime Minister Palme was assassinated. Successor was I. CARLSSON/Soc. Democrat (Mar.).

Norway (p. 229)
Following the resignation of BORTEN's Cabinet, a middle-class coalition,
1971 the Soc. Democratic minority gvt of BRATTELI continued E.E.C. negotiations.
Sep. 1972 Referendum rejected E.E.C. membership. BRATELLI resigned.
Oct. 1972 Middle-class minority gvt of KORVALD.
Oct. 1973 New BRATELLI gvt.
1974 Announcement of big oil and natural gas find in the North Sea.
1976 Prime Minister O. NORDLI of the Soc. Democratic gvt, followed by the Conservative
1981 K. WILLOCH (1983–5 coalition gvt). As she had been once before (Feb.–Oct. 1981)
1986 Mrs GRO HARLEM BRUNDTLAND became prime minister of a Soc. Democratic minority gvt.
1989 Civil gvt under Prime Minister J. SYSE (Oct.).
1990 BRUNDTLAND minority gvt (Nov.).
Death of King Olav (p. 229), new
1991 King HARALD V (Jan.).

Switzerland (p. 243)
1971 Introduction of female suffrage in matters relating to the Swiss Confederation.
1974 Population of the Jura voted for their own canton.
1 Jan. 1979 New canton of Jura.
1989 Referendum rejected abolition of the army.

Austria (p. 243)
1969 Approval of the 's. Tirol package'.
Apr. 1970 an S.P.Ö. minority gvt under Fed. Chancellor **Bruno Kreisky** (b. 1911) was formed.
Apr. 1971 President JONAS was re-elected.
Premature new elections led to an absolute majority for the S.P.Ö.
Oct. 1971 S.P.Ö. gvt under Chancellor KREISKY.
1974 President of the Republic, KIRCHSCHLÄGER.
A referendum
1978 Rejected the commissioning of the nuclear power station Zwentendorf. After the S.P.Ö. lost the absolute majority
1983 Kreisky resigned. Coalition gvt with the F.P.Ö. under
Apr. 1983 Chancellor F. SINOWATZ, who resigned because of the election of
1986 K. Waldheim as president (Jun.).
There followed a coalition between the S.P.Ö. with Chancellor **F. Vranitzky** and the F.P.Ö. (N. STEGER). The change in chairmanship in the F.P.Ö. to J. HAIDER led to a
1987 **S.P.Ö./Ö.V.P. coalition** (Jan.). F. VRANITZKY remained chancellor. After election victory of the S.P.Ö. new
1990 S.P.Ö./Ö.V.P. gvt under VRANITZKY (Dec.).

Belgium (p. 247)
The coalition gvt (Christ. Socialists/Liberals), formed by the prime minister, VAN DEN BOEYNANTS (b. 1919), in Mar. 1966, resigned over the language controversy.
Jun. 1968 A coalition gvt (Christ. Socialists/Socialists) was formed under GASTON EYSKENS as prime minister.
1970 Const. reform provided for decentralization of the admin. and the granting of cult. autonomy for Flemings, Walloons and Germans.
Jan.–Nov. 1972 Another EYSKENS coalition gvt.
Jan. 1973 Coalition gvt under LEBURTON.
May 1974 Coalition gvt (Christ. Socialist/Liberals) under TINDEMANNS.
1978 Transitional gvt under VAN DEN BOEYNANTS.
1979 Christ. Socialist Prime Minister W. MARTENS with changing coalitions; since
1988 centre-right gvt under MARTENS.

The Netherlands (p. 247)
Nov. 1966 Fall of the CALS gvt. Despite losses incurred by the governing parties,
Apr. 1967 the Christ. Lib. DE JONG gvt was formed.
1971 A treaty was signed with the B.R.D. settling the partition of the Continental Shelf in the North Sea.
Jun. 1971–Jul. 1972 Coalition gvt of BIESHEUVEL. Socialists win the election (Nov. 1972).
May 1973 UYL gvt.
1975 Surinam became independent.
1977 Prime Minister A. V. AGT of the newly formed Christ. Democrat Appeal (C.D.A.).
1980 Abdication of Queen JULIANA. **Queen Beatrix I** became successor.
1982 Coalition gvt (C.D.A./People's party) under **R. Lubbers**, which was also renewed in 1986 and 1989.

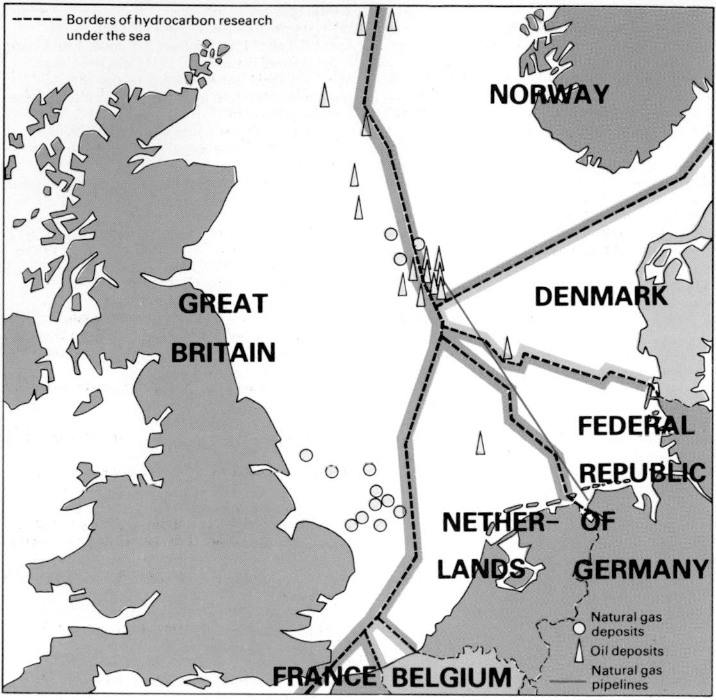

Borders of hydrocarbon research under the sea
NORWAY
GREAT BRITAIN
DENMARK
FEDERAL REPUBLIC OF GERMANY
NETHER- LANDS
FRANCE
BELGIUM
Natural gas deposits
Oil deposits
Natural gas pipelines

Division of the continental shelf in the North Sea

Coleraine
Londonderry
LONDONDERRY
ANTRIM
Ballymena
Larne
Strabane
L. Neagh
Belfast
Omagh
TYRONE
Dungannon
Enniskillen
FERMANAGH
Armagh
ARMAGH
Newry
DOWN
Downpatrick
Proportion of population with Roman Catholic belief
in rural regions
under 50%
25–50%
under 25%
in towns
under 50%
25–50%
under 25%

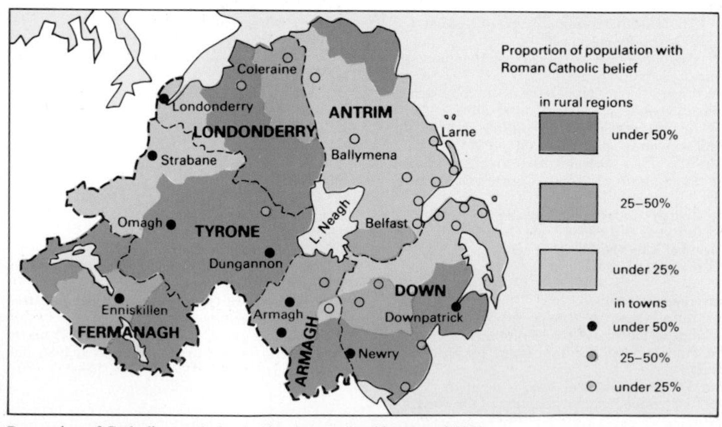

Proportion of Catholic population in Northern Ireland in around 1970

Britain (p. 246)
Following Labour's election victory.
1966 the 2nd Wilson Cabinet was formed.
1967 Renationalization of the steel industry.
Jan. 1968 WILSON announced an extensive programme of economies; evacuation of all milit. bases E. of Suez by 1971 spelled the **abandonment of Britain's role as world power**.
Mar. 1968 Restrictions on numbers of Commonwealth immigrants.
1969 Restrictions of the right to strike were successfully campaigned against by the trade unions. A Con. vict. in the general election led
Jun. 1970 to the cabinet of Edward Heath (b. 1916).
Feb. 1971 Changeover of the currency to the decimal system.
Econ. difficulties: increasing unemployment, strikes.
Jan. 1972 Signature of the E.E.C. membership treaties.
1 Jan. 1973 Entry into the E.E.C.
Following an early election
1975 Labour gvt, Wilson.
1975 Referendum: 2/3 majority for remaining in the E.E.C. (Jun.)
Opening of the 1st oil pipeline from the North Sea (Nov.).
1976 New prime minister, CALLAGHAN.
1976 Settlement of the fishing war with Iceland (since 1973).
After election victory of the Conservatives (May)
1979 cabinet of Margaret Thatcher.
1981 Foundation of a Soc. Democratic party (S.D.P.; disintegrated 1990).
Wedding of Crown Prince CHARLES and Lady DIANA (Jul.).
Argentina occupied the Brit. Falkland Islands (Apr.).
1982 Falklands War ended with a victory over the Argentine troops (Jun.).
Victory for Conservatives at the parl. elections:
1983 new THATCHER cabinet.
Election results gave the Conservative party an absolute majority:
1987 again THATCHER cabinet.
22 Nov. 1990 Resignation of Prime Minister Margeret Thatcher. JOHN MAJOR became successor.

Northern Ireland
1969 Clashes between Cath. civil rights advocates and Prot. right-wing extremists. Attempts at reform by
1969–71 the prime minister, CHICHESTER-CLARK, did not quieten the situation.
Aug. 1969 The situation in Belfast and Londonderry bordered on civil war. The deployment of Brit. troops produced no lasting solution to the tension.
1970–74 Street fighting, bombings and sniper attacks led to fatalities, casualties and considerable damage. There were also acts of terror by the illegal Provisional I.R.A. (Irish Repub. Army).
Mar. 1971 The prime minister, BRIAN FAULKNER, reacted to a new wave of terror by rounding up suspected individuals into
Aug. 1971 internment camps.
Mar. 1972 The Brit. gvt assumed direct rule in Northern Ireland.
Mar. 1973 Referendum in favour of remaining united with Britain.
1974 Prevention of terrorism act was extended. Up to 1976 approx. 1,500 deaths.
1976 Peace demonstrations by women of both denominations: MAIREAD CORRIGAN and BETTY WILLIAMS receive the Nobel Prize for Peace.
1979 Assassination of Lord MOUNTBATTEN.
1982 New Northern Ireland law; further terrorist attacks.
1988 Severe unrest (from May).

Ireland (p. 246)
1966 President DE VALERA was re-elected.
1967 Prime Minister JACK LYNCH. Policy of non-intervention in the
1969 unrest in Northern Ireland.
1 Jan. 1973 Entry into the E.E.C.
1973 LIAM COSGRAVE became prime minister, following elect. vict. of a Nat. Coalition (Fine Gael and Labour); a Protestant, ERSKINE CHILDERS (1906–74), became president (Jun.).
1974 CEARBHALL O'DALAIGH became president (Dec.).
1976 President P. HILLERY.
1987 Prime Minister C. HAUGHEY/Fianna Fáil (Mar.).
1990 President MARY ROBINSON (Independent).

Denmark (p. 229)
1968 Middle-class coalition gvt under HILMAR BAUNSGAARD (Rad. Lib. party) as prime minister.
Jun. 1970 Beginning of negotiations for admission to the E.E.C.
1971 A treaty was signed with the B.R.D. settling the partition of the Continental Shelf in the N. Sea.
Oct. 1971 Soc. Dem. KRAG Cabinet.
King FREDERICK IX (1947–72) was succeeded by his daughter
Jan 1972 Margrethe II (b. 1940).
After a referendum in favour of E.E.C. entry.
Oct. 1972 Soc. Dem. gvt of JÖRGENSEN;
1 Jan. 1973 entry into the E.E.C.
Dec. 1973 Lib. minority gvt of HARTLING.
1975 Soc. Democratic minority cabinet under JÖRGENSEN.
1979 Greenland received autonomous gvt.
1982 Minority gvt of the Conservatives under Prime Minister P. SCHLÜTER.
After referendum
1985 Greenland resigned from the E.E.C.
1988 Again minority gvt under SCHLÜTER.

Iceland
1973 Fishing-zone suit brought before the International Court of Justice by Great Britain and the B.R.D.; sentence in favour of the plaintiffs, rejected by Iceland.
Dec. 1973 Fishing war with Great Britain.
1975 Extension of the fishing zone to 200 nautical mi.
1976 3rd cod war with Great Britain.
1980 Mrs VIGDIS FINNBOGADOTTIR became state president.

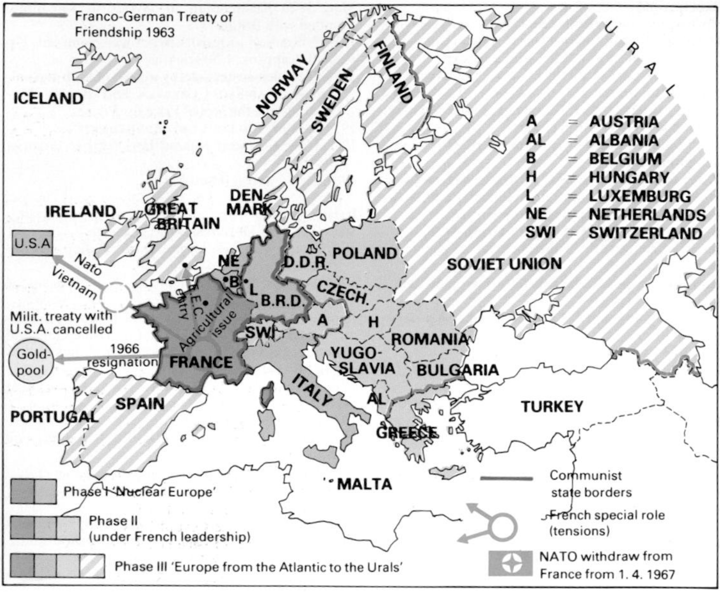

De Gaulle's European policies and European model

Elections in Italy 1976

France (p. 247)
Following his re-election as president
Jun. 1966 DE GAULLE made a state visit to the U.S.S.R. and travelled around the world.
Apr. 1967 A new gvt was formed under POMPIDOU. Student unrest in Nanterre and
May 1968 in **Paris**, suppressed by police brutality: general strike. POMPIDOU's gvt made concessions. Bordering on **civil war** (street fighting), the atmosphere caused DE GAULLE to **dissolve the Nat. Assembly** and concentrate troops around Paris. Conditions of normality returned only slowly and the strike was settled after sharp increases in wages had been granted. Parl. elections
Jun. 1968 brought an absolute Gaullist majority. Following the resignation of POMPIDOU's gvt
Jul. 1968 COUVE DE MURVILLE became prime minister (p. 247).
Aug. 1968 Detonation of the 1st Fr. H-bomb.
Jun. 1969 President Georges Pompidou (p. 247).
Jun. 1969–Jul. 1972 Prime Minister CHABAN-DELMAS.
1972 Testing of nuclear armaments in the Pacific.
Jul. 1972 Prime Minister PIERRE MESSMER.
Following POMPIDOU's death, the candidate of the con. parties,
May 1974 Giscard d'Estaing became **president**; the new prime minister was CHIRAC.
Feb. 1976 22nd Congress of the Com. party: MARCHAIS supported abolition of the term 'dictatorship of the proletariat'.
Aug. 1976 Prime Minister RAYMOND BARRE presented plan to fight inflation.
1979 Left-wing union (MITTERRAND/MARCHAIS) gained at regional elections.
May 1981 President François Mitterrand (born 1916). Socialist gvt with 4 Com. ministers under
Jun. 1981 Prime Minister PIERRE MAUROY. Nationalization of important industrial enterprises and big banks (Dec.).
At the elections for the European Parliament the radical right under
Jun. 1984 M. LE PEN won 10.9 % of votes.
Because of failed attemt to reform schools, new
Jul. 1984 Prime Minister L. FABIUS.
After election victory of the civil parties
Apr. 1986 J. CHIRAC again became prime minister of a 'cohabitation' government (president and prime minister come from opposite polit. directions).
Reprivatization of the nationalized industrial enterprises and banks. Re-elected with a big majority:
May 1988 2nd Mitterrand presidency.
New gvt under M. ROCARD.
1989 Celebrations for the 200th anniversary of the French Revolution.
May 1991 Prime Minister EDITH CRESSON.

The Vatican
Dec. 1965 The **2nd Vatican Council**, convoked by Pope JOHN XXIII (1958–63) in 1962, ended. Main topics of discussion: reform of the liturgy, the position of the laity within the Church, the relationship of the Church to the modern world. The Index of Forbidden Books (I. p. 239) was abolished.
Mar. 1967 In the soc. encyclical *Populorum progressio* Pope PAUL VI (from 1963) called for efforts to fight hunger, poverty and soc. injustice.
Mar. 1968 The reform of the Curia became effective.
Jul. 1968 The encyclical **Humanae vitae** prohibited artificial birth control.
Aug. 1968 The 39th Eucharistic World Congress, to which Pope PAUL VI contributed, concerned itself with the responsibility of the Church on questions of soc. justice.
After the death of PAUL VI
26 Aug.–28 Sep. 1978 Pope JOHN PAUL I was chosen. After his sudden death the Pole KAROL WOJTYLA, Archbishop of Krakow, became
16 Oct. 1978 Pope John Paul II (born 1920); he travelled abroad frequently. In
13 May 1981 an attempted assassination in St Peter's Square in Rome JOHN PAUL II was badly injured.

Italy (p. 243)
The econ. disparity of the underdeveloped s. was made more obvious by the indust. growth of northern Italy. There was a danger of radicalization on the Right and on the Left.
The Centre-Left gvt of MORO (1963–8) was replaced by the
May 1968 D.C.I. transition gvt of LEONE.
Dec. 1968 Centre-Left gvt of RUMOR D.C.I.
1969 Passage of the 's. Tirol package'.
Aug. 1970 Centre-Left gvt of COLOMBO D.C.I.
Dec. 1971 President Leone D.C.I. (b. 1908).
Jul. 1972 Centre gvt of ANDREOTTI/D.C.I.
Jul. 1973 Centre-Left gvt of RUMOR.
Nov. 1974 Two-party cabinet under MORO.
Jun. 1975 Strong gains for the Com. party at regional, provincial and communal elections.
Oct. 1975 Final settlement of the Trieste question.
1976 D.C.I. minority gvt under ANDREOTTI (until 1979) which depended on the Com. party (P.C.I.) but didn't agree to the offer of a 'historical compromise'.
9 May 1978 Assassination of A. MORO (born 1916) by the Red Brigades.
1978 Socialist Sandro Pertini became state president (1896–1990).
1980 Explosives attack on the Bologna railway station by right-wing radicals.
1981 Secret lodge 'P2' affair shook the country.
The first (since 1946)
Jun. 1981 prime minister not to be put forward by the D.C.I. was G. SPADOLINI (Republican), followed by
1983–7 Prime Minister B. CRAXI (Socialist). New
1984 Concordat with the Vatican.
Jun. 1985 State President F. Cossiga (D.C.I.).
Oct. 1985 Hijack of the Ital. cruiser *Achille Lauro* (state crisis).
1988 Approval of the 's. Tyrol package'.
Jul. 1989 Prime Minister G. ANDREOTTI again (born 1919).

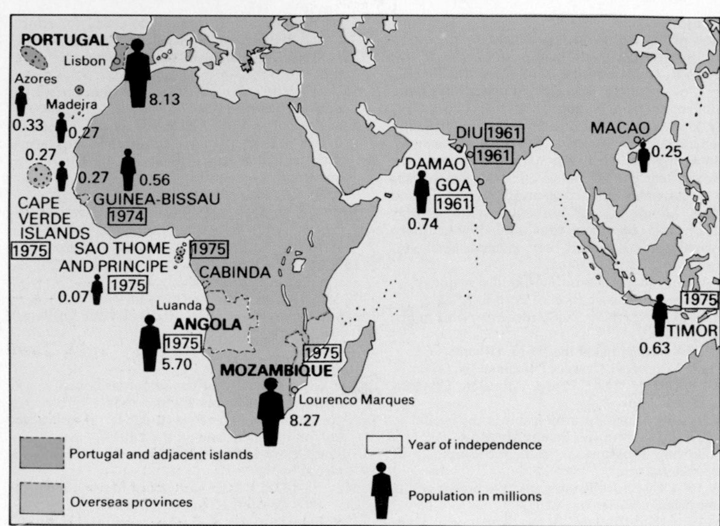

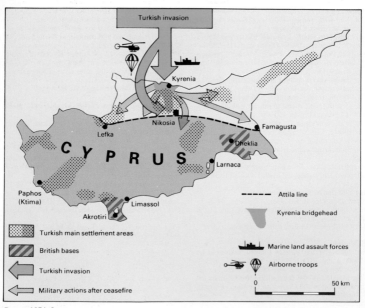

The disintegration of the Portuguese colonial empire 1974–5

Turkish invasion
Kyrenia
Nikosia
Lefka
Famagusta
CYPRUS
Dheklia
Larnaca
Paphos (Ktima)
Limassol
Akrotiri
Attila line
Kyrenia bridgehead
Turkish main settlement areas
British bases
Turkish invasion
Military actions after ceasefire
Marine land assault forces
Airborne troops
0
50 km

Cyprus 1974–5

Spain (p. 242)

1966–8 Students and priests demonstrated for liberalization and democratization.

1968 Introduction of national service.

1969 Cession of the **Ifni** enclave to Morocco.

Jul. 1969 JUAN CARLOS was nominated as future king and successor to FRANCO.

1970 The Falange was deprived of power and renamed the Movimiento Nacional.

Jun. 1973 Prime Minister CARRERO BLANCO, who was assassinated by Basque terrorists (Dec.).

Jan. 1974 Prime Minister ARIAS NAVARRO. Increasing terrorism and anti-terrorist laws (incl. death sentences).

Nov. 1975 Death of Franco. JUAN CARLOS I became king. Beginning of liberalization and democratization.

Dec. 1975 Spanish Sahara: treaty between Spain, Morocco, Mauritania; end of Spanish rule (Jan. 1976). Through

Jun. 1976 Treaty of Friendship with the U.S.A. Spain was virtually integrated in the defence system of NATO.

Jul. 1976 Prime Minister SUAREZ GONZALES.

1977 Disintegration of the Movimiento Nacional; admission of the Com. party. Election of an assembly to establish constitution. The new

29 Dec. 1978 constitution came into force: Spain became a parliamentary hereditary monarchy.

1981 Coup attempt by TEJERO (Feb.).

1982 Spain became NATO member.
After parliamentary elections

Oct. 1982 the Socialists gained a majority. GONZALES MARQUEZ became new Prime Minister (1986 and 1989 re-elected).

1986 Spain joined the E.E.C.

Gibraltar

Continued tensions between Britain and Spain over the possession of Gibraltar.

1967 By popular referendum. Gibraltar's inhabitants in favour of remaining with Britain (95%).

1969 Border to Spain was closed; only

1985 opened again.

Portugal (p. 243)

Sep. 1968 The prime minister, MARCELO CAETANO (b. 1906), became the successor of SALAZAR, incapacitated by a stroke.

Apr. 1974 Caetano toppled by milit. putsch; General SPINOLA became president but was replaced after supposed *coup* by COSTA GOMES. Left-wing gvt under GONCALVES.

Aug. 1974 Overseas provinces were granted self-determination (p. 311).

Sep. 1975 Prime Minister AZEVEDO; unrest, demonstrations.

Apr. 1976 Elections: victory of Socialists; Prime Minister M. SOARES (until 1978 and again 1983–5).

1976 State president General A. R. EANES.

1982 New constitution came into effect (Oct.).

1985 Prime Minister A. CAVACO SILVA (Soc. Democrat).

1986 Portugal became E.E.C. member. General EANES is succeeded

Mar. 1986 as state President by M. SOARES.

Greece (p. 229)

21 Apr. 1967 Coup d'état by the army (General SPANDIDAKIS). King CONSTANTINE II (p. 229) was forced to recognize the milit. regime (prime minister, KOLLIAS). Dem. politicians were arrested.

13 Dec. 1967 An attempt by King CONSTANTINE to regain power was unsuccessful and he went into exile in Rome. Colonel GEORGIOS PAPADOPOULOS became the new prime minister.

Sep. 1968 Popular referendum on a new constitution (94.9% affirmative votes).

Dec. 1968 A degree gave **Papadopoulos virtual dictatorial powers.**

Aug. 1973 Abolition of the monarchy.
The PAPADOPOULOS regime was in

Nov. 1973 toppled and replaced by a milit. gvt led by General GIZIKIS. Meanwhile, as a result of the Cyprus crisis, there was a rest. of democracy in Greece:

Aug. 1974 Prime Minister Karamanlis. Withdrawal from the NATO military alliance.

1975 State President K. TSATSOS.

1980 State President K. KARAMANLIS.

1981 Greece became E.E.C. member. After election victory of the PASOK.

Oct. 1981 Prime Minister A. PAPANDREOU.

1985 State President C. SARTZETAKIS.

1989 Transitional gvt examined corruption accusations against PASOK.

1990 State president K. KARAMANLIS (N.D.) again.

Cyprus (p. 246)

From 1964 U.N. troops were stationed on Cyprus.

Jul. 1974 The Gk Cypriot Nat. Guard of President Makarios rebelled; in consequence, Turkey invaded and occupied the N. of the island.

Dec. 1974 Return of MAKARIOS to the Greek-Cypriot S. In the N.

1975 proclamation of the Federal Turk.–Cypriot State under President R. DENKTASCH (until 1990) and independence as

1983 Turk. Republic of N. Cyprus.
In the S. after the death of MAKARIOS:

1977 President S. KYPRIANU.

1988 G. WASSILIU (Independent) became president.

Turkey (p. 229)

1965–71 DEMIREL as prime minister.

1966 General SUNAY became president.
Unstable domestic polit. situation: student unrest and activities of left-wing army officers.

1971 The coalition gvt of the prime minister, NIHAT ERIM, was replaced by

May 1972 the coalition gvt of FERET MELEN.

Apr. 1973 President KORUTURK; coalition gvt of TALÛ.

Jul.–Aug. 1974 Armed invasion of Cyprus.

Mar. 1975 Coalition gvt under DEMIREL.

Dec. 1975 Visit of KOSSYGIN: Turkey rejected no-attack treaty.

Sep. 1980 Military coup: National Security Council under General K. EVREN; political trials, tortures, executions.

1982 New constitution (Nov.): EVREN became state president. The Motherland party won

Nov. 1983 parliamentary elections: Prime Minister **T. Özal**.

Nov. 1989 ÖZAL elected president, Y. AKBULUT became prime minister.

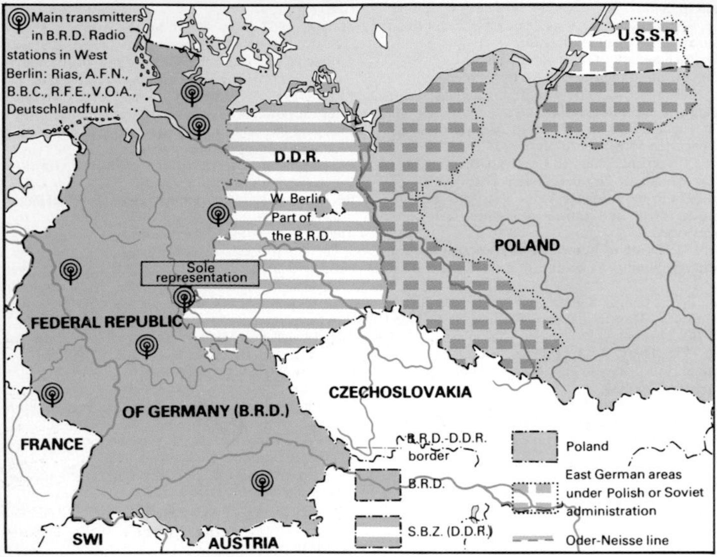

Ideological separation from the B.R.D. perspective

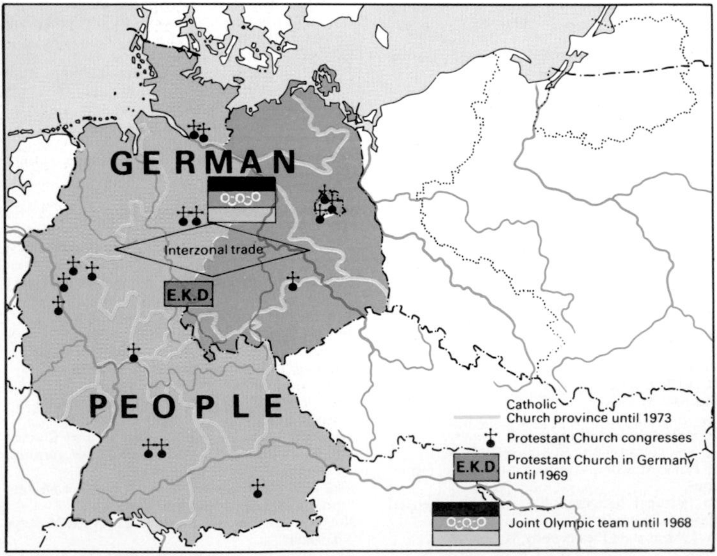

Remnants of the German union

The Fed. Republic of Germany (B.R.D.) (p. 251)

1966 Econ. recession: rising prices and a structural crisis in the mining industry of the Ruhr.

26 Oct. 1966 Resignation of the 4 ministers of the Fed. Dem. party. Gains by the Nat. Dem. party (N.P.D. 'neo-Fascist'), formed in 1964, in regional elections.

1 Dec. 1966 A 'Grand Coalition' gvt under Chancellor KURT GEORG KIESINGER C.D.U. (b. 1904) and the for. minister, WILLY BRANDT/S.P.D. (p. 253) was formed. Principal task: the rest. of finances.

1967 Following the balancing of the budget through cuts in spending, a budget was presented to stimulate investments (19 Jan.): 'concerted actions' by the partners in the productive process and the lowering of bank rates were aimed at stimulating the economy.

May–Jun. 1967 Public unrest on the occasion of the state visit of the Shah of Iran.

Summer/autumn 1967 Formation of an 'extra-parl. opposition' (A.P.O.) in reaction to the Grand Coalition and the increasing inflexibility of the Bundestag.

1968 Introduction of 'value-added' tax (V.A.T.).

Easter 1968 Assassination attempt on and wounding of RUDI DUTSCHKE (b. 1940), an S.D.S. leader, unleashed student unrest. Despite vehement protests

30 May 1968 passage of emergency articles to the constitution: once these laws became effective, the Allied legal privileges established in the Germany Treaty were terminated. Continued unrest at the universities over questions of university reform.

1969 Following the early retirement of President HEINRICH LÜBKE, **Gustav Heinemann S.P.D.** (p. 251) **was elected president.** A change of gvt followed the elections to the

Sep 1969 6th Bundestag (C.D.U./C.S.U. 242 seats, S.P.D. 224 seats, F.D.P. 30 seats):

Oct. 1969 Fed. Chancellor Willy Brandt/S.P.D. formed a coalition gvt (S.P.D./F.D.P.); WALTER SCHEEL/F.D.P. (b. 1919) became vice-chancellor and for. minister. The fed. gvt signed the **Nuclear Non-Proliferation Treaty**.

Dec. 1969 Beginning of conversations with the gvt of the U.S.S.R. in Moscow, and that of Poland in Warsaw, concerning the renunciation of the use of force (state secretary, EGON BAHR).

Aug. 1970 Signing of the Moscow Treaty: treaty renouncing force between the U.S.S.R. and the B.R.D., recognizing the inviolability of all existing Eur. borders, incl. the Oder–Neisse Line and the borders of the B.R.D. and the D.D.R.

Dec. 1970 Signing of the Warsaw Treaty: normalization of relations between Poland and the B.R.D., renunciation of the use of force and recognition of the Oder–Neisse Line as Poland's western frontier.

May 1971 Monetary crisis because of the increased inflow of U.S. Dollars: the Ger. Mark was floated (minister of economics and finance, KARL SCHILLER/S.P.D.).

Sep. 1971 Crimea: meeting between the fed. chancellor, BRANDT, and the Rus. party secretary, BREZHNEV.

Nov. 1971 BRANDT received the Nobel Peace Prize. Negative attitude of the C.D.U./C.S.U. opposition to the **treaties with the East.** The gvt's parl. majority was reduced by a desertion of deputies.

28 Apr. 1972 A 'constructive vote of no-confidence' by the opposition, proposed by RAINER BARZEL (b. 1924) against Chancellor BRANDT, only just failed.

In a final vote.

17 May 1972 ratifying the treaties with the E., most of the opposition abstained and few C.D.U./C.S.U. votes were cast in opposition.

3 Jun. 1972 The treaties with the E. and the transit agreement with the D.D.R. became effective.

On account of a decreasing majority, vote of no confidence in the chancellor and

Sept. 1972 dissolution of the Bundestag.

Nov. 1972 7th Bundestag (S.P.D. 230, C.D.U./C.S.U. 255, F.D.P. 41 seats); continuation

Dec. 1972 of the BRANDT/SCHEEL coalition.

1973 Rising prices. Stability programme (Feb./May). to slow down inflation. A 3% (Mar.) and a 5.5% (Jun.) revaluation of the DM.

May 1973 BREZHNEV's visit to Bonn. On

21 Jun. 1973 Basic Treaty with E. Germany came into operation.

Following BRANDT's resignation as chancellor over the 'Guillaume affair'

May 1974 Fed. Chancellor Helmut Schmidt S.P.D. continued to lead the soc. democrat-lib. coalition.

Jul. 1974 President Walter Scheel.

Jan. 1975 Cooperation Treaty with Czechoslovakia.

Oct. 1975 Foreign Minister GENSCHER signed four treaties with Poland about pension and accident insurance in Warsaw.

Nov. 1975 Chancellor SCHMIDT in Peking.

Dec. 1975 Traffic negotiations with the D.D.R. about Berlin traffic, transit package regulations and motorway extension (plan for a new motorway from Berlin to Hamburg).

Mar. 1976 New treaties with Poland came into effect, Aug. 1975 initialled (pension payments to prevent return of approx. 125,000 people of German origin), rejected by the Upper House for 11 reasons (Nov. 1975). Feb. 1976 agreement of the Lower House. After improvements, the Upper House also agreed (Mar.).

Jul.–Aug. 1976 Border incidents with the D.D.R. Disruption of the transit traffic.

3 Oct. 1976 Elections for the Lower House: growth of the C.D.U./C.S.U., however S.P.D./F.D.P. coalition remained in power. After lengthy negotiations (and cancellation by the C.S.U.) C.D.U. and C.S.U. again formed a party alliance.

Dec. 1976 B.R.D. proclaimed a 200-nautical-mile fishing zone.

1977 Murder of Chief Federal Prosecutor BUBACK, JÜRGEN PONTO and H. M. SCHLEYER by terrorists. Liberation of hijacked Lufthansa Boeing in Somalia. State visit by BREZHNEV (Oct.).

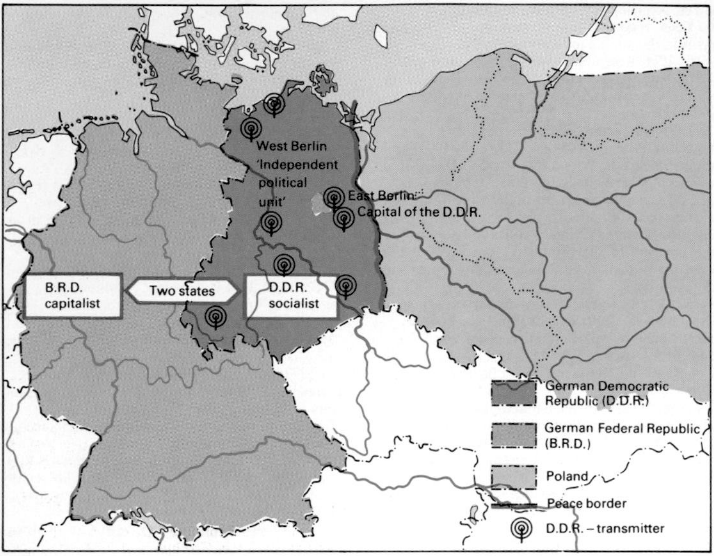

Ideological separation from the D.D.R. perspective

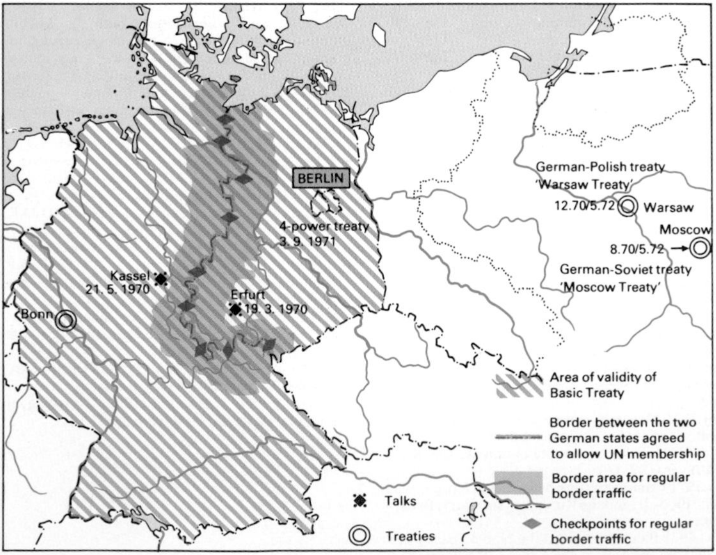

The Basic Treaty

The Ger. Problem (p. 219)

1966 Negotiations aiming at an exchange of polit. speakers failed.

1967 HERBERT WEHNER (b. 1906), the B.R.D. Minister of All-Ger. Affairs, proposed a 4-power conference on Germany (1 Feb.), also hinted at by ULBRICHT in a 10-point programme outlining steps towards the confederation of the 2 Ger. states.
An exchange of letters between Fed. Chancellor KIESINGER and the D.D.R. prime minister, STOPH, yielded no results (May/Jun./Sep.).

1968 Introduction of mandatory passports and visas for W. Germans (11 Jun.) travelling between the D.D.R. and W. Berlin.
The U.S.S.R. insisted on its continued prerogative to intervene against the B.R.D. (5 Jul.).

1969 Negotiation offer by ULBRICHT: draft of a treaty concerning the establishment of **relations between 2 states on the basis of int. law**; W. Berlin was to have the status of an ind. polit. entity. HEINEMANN's response emphasized the unity of the nation and the **special nature of the relationship** between the B.R.D. and the D.D.R.

19 Mar. 1970 Erfurt: 1st meeting between Fed. Chancellor BRANDT and the D.D.R. prime minister, WILLI STOPH (p. 255).

21 May 1970 Kassel: 2nd meeting of the 2 Ger. chiefs of gvt.

Nov. 1970 Beginning of the negotiations between the 2 state secretaries, BAHR/B.R.D. and KOHL/D.D.R.

Sep. 1971 Signing of the protocol regulating mail and telephone service.

Dec. 1971 Transit agreement.

Feb. 1972 The D.D.R. made the transit agreement to apply at Easter and Whitsun. The 1st state treaty between the 2 German states.

26 May 1972 The Transit Treaty was signed.
After negotiations (beginning in Aug.) between BAHR/W. Germany and KOHL/E. Germany

Dec. 1972 signing of the Basic Treaty dealing with the relationship between W. and E. Germany.

21 Jun. 1973 Basic Treaty comes into force.

Jun. 1974 Exchange of permanent representatives of both German states.

1974 Escape-helper trials, disruption to the transit traffic.

Dec. 1974 New Swing Agreement between the B.R.D. and the D.D.R. (850 Mil. clearing units).

1975 Further increase in automatic firing devices on the internal German border.

Berlin (p. 253)

1966 4th entrance-permit agreement.

Dec. 1966 H. ALBERTZ/S.P.D. took BRANDT's place as Mayor of W. Berlin.

Mar. 1967 Following elections, the gvt coalition S.P.D./F.D.P. was carried on. Following the unrest on the occasion of the Shah's visit. ALBERTZ resigned.

Sep. 1967 Mayor of Berlin KLAUS SCHÜTZ/S.P.D.

1968 Disputes between the 'extra-parl. opposition' (APO) and the Senate: student demonstrations.

Mar. 1970 Beginning of **4-power negotiations** (France, Britain, U.S.A. and U.S.S.R.) at ambassadorial level in West Berlin.

Sep. 1971 Signing of the Berlin Agreement.

Dec. 1971 Agreement regulating visits and the exchange of territories to solve the question of enclaves.

3 Jun. 1972 The 4-Power Berlin Agreement became effective.

Jun.–Jul. 1974 Building of a Federal Environment Office in Berlin. U.S.S.R. and D.D.R. protests were rejected by the Western powers.

Apr. 1975 The Western powers confirmed in a note to the U.N. the 4-powers' general responsibility for all of Berlin, whilst the U.S.S.R. stated (May) that E. Berlin was an integral part of the D.D.R. and not under the 4-powers' responsibility.

May 1975 Berlin declaration by Western foreign ministers: U.S.S.R. declared that the 4-power status no longer existed.

Dec. 1975 Agreements between the B.R.D. and the D.D.R. about Berlin traffic.

The Ger. Democratic Republic (D.D.R.) (p. 255)

1966 Trade agreements with the states of the Eastern Bloc, Italy and Austria (15 Mar.).

13 Oct. 1967 The 'Law to protect citizens of the D.D.R.' was passed.

1967 D.D.R. Citizenship Law (20 Feb.).
Conclusion of Treaties of Friendship with Poland (13 Mar.), and Czechoslovakia (17 Mar.). Parl. elections (2 Jul.): 99.98% of the votes were cast for the 1-party list.

1968 Acceptance of a new constitution by popular referendum (6 Apr.).
Participation of units of the People's Army in the intervention in Czechoslovakia (20–21 Aug.).

1969 Recognition of the D.D.R. by states outside the Eastern Bloc (Iraq, Cambodia and others).

Sep. 1969 Ratification of the Nuclear Non-Proliferation Treaty.

1970 A new law governing civil defence became effective.

3 May 1971 Resignation of Ulbricht (1893–1973) as 1st Secretary of the Cen. Committee of the S.E.D.; ERICH HONECKER (b. 1912) became his successor.

1 Jan. 1972 Opening of the borders with Poland and Czechoslovakia.

21 Jun. 1973 Basic Treaty with W. Germany.

Oct. 1973 W. STOPH became privy chancellor; H. SINDERMANN prime minister.

Oct. 1974 A constitutional revision came into effect in which the term 'German nation' was left out.

Sept. 1975 HONECKER opposes unlimited freedom of information.

Oct. 1975 New Treaty of Friendship with the U.S.S.R. on the 26th anniversary of the foundation of the D.D.R. (integration continues).

May 1976 9th Congress of the S.E.D.: Discussion relations with the B.R.D. about territorial demarcation in accordance with international law. Intensive integration in the socialist camp and the socialist economy.

Oct. 1976 HONECKER also became chairman of the state council; Prime Minister STOPH.

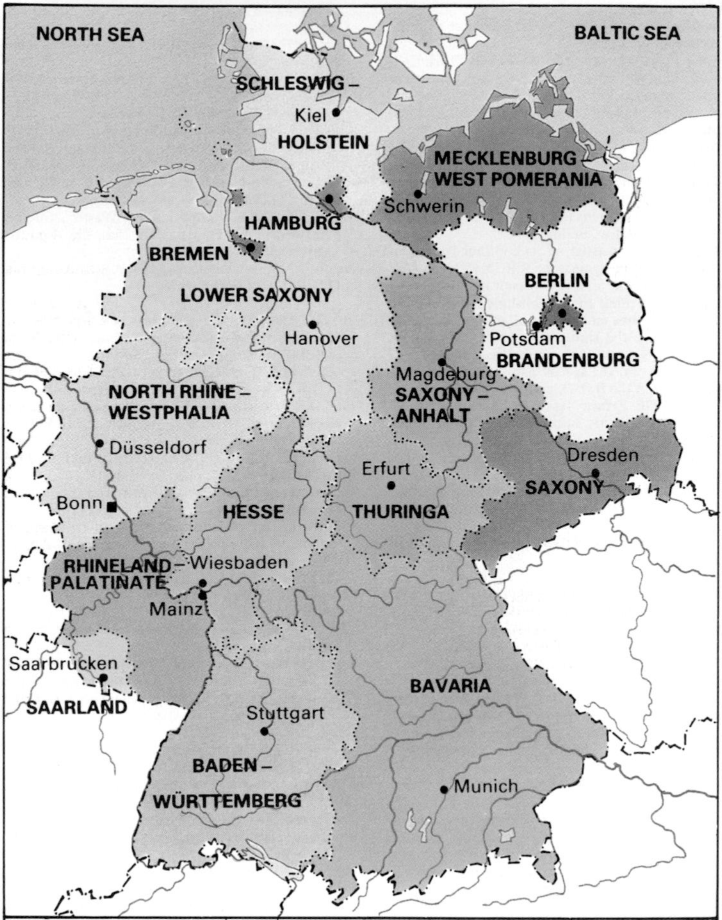

State	Area km^2	Population 1000
Schleswig-Holstein	15,730	2,594
Hamburg	755	1,626
Lower Saxony	47,349	7,283
Bremen	404	673
North Rhine – Westphalia	34,068	17,103
Hesse	21,114	5,660
Rhineland – Palatinate	19,849	3,701
Baden – Württemberg	35,751	9,618
Bavaria	70,554	11,220
Saarland	2,570	1,064
Berlin	883	3,409

State	Area km^2	Population 1000
Brandenburg	29,060	2,641
Mecklenburg – West Pomerania	23,835	1,963
Saxony	18,338	4,900
Saxony – Anhalt	20,444	2,964
Thuringa	16,251	2,683
B.R.D. the above in total	356,957	79,112
B.R.D. with N. Berlin	248,626	62,679
D.D.R. with E. Berlin	108,332	16,433

The Federal Republic of Germany at the end of 1990

Berlin (p. 293)
1977 London–Berlin declaration of the 4 Western powers (including the B.R.D.).
1977 Governing Mayor D. STOBBE/S.P.D.
Jan. 1981 H.-J. VOGEL/S.P.D. Victory of the C.D.U.:
Jun. 1981 R. v. Weizsäcker/C.D.U. governing mayor, from 1983 C.D.U./F.D.P. coalition. Because of the election of V. WEIZSÄCKER as president
1984 E. DIEPGEN/C.D.U. became governing mayor.
Mar. 1989 Coalition gvt S.P.D./Alternative List (A.L.) with 8 women (of 14 senate members). Governing Mayor W. MOMPER/S.P.D.
9 Nov. 1989 Breaching of the wall between W. and E. Berlin.
For pedestrians
22 Dec. 1989 Brandenburg Gate was opened.
1990 Demolition of the wall.
3 Oct. 1990 All of Berlin became part of the B.R.D.

D.D.R. (p. 293)
1980 Increase of the minimum obligatory exchange.
1982 New military service and border laws.
1986 5-Yr Plan for 1986–90: expansion of key technologies, solution of the housing problem.
1987 Abolition of capital punishment (Jul.). Unauthorized peace demonstration in E. Berlin (Sep.). HONECKER visited the B.R.D. (Sep.).
1988 Arrest of members of independent human rights groups (Jan.). Services to display solidarity. Growing number of exit applications to the B.R.D.
1989 Travel law made visits to the B.R.D. easier (from Apr.). Fraud suspected in communal elections (May). Occupation of B.R.D. embassies in E. Berlin, Budapest, Prague and Warsaw by D.D.R. citizens (Jul.–Sep.). Mass demonstrations, foundation of opposition groups.
18 Oct. 1989 Fall of Honecker. New secretary-general and State Council chairman, EGON KRENZ. Resignation of the STOPH government (7 Nov.).
9 Nov. 1989 Opening of the border to the B.R.D., fall of the Berlin wall.
Prime Minister HANS MODROW (13 Nov.). Politburo and Central Committee resigned (3 Dec.), GREGOR GYSI became secretary-general of the S.E.D./P.D.S.
'Round Table' (from 7 Dec.) decided on
18 Mar. 1990 free parliamentary elections: victory of the C.D.U. in the 'Alliance for Germany' for 'Freedom and Welfare – never again Socialism'. Prime Minister LOTHAR DE MAIZIERE/C.D.U. of a 'Grand Coalition' (Apr.).
Signature (18 May) of the state treaty about
1 Jul. 1990 monetary, economic and social union with the B.R.D.
After conclusion of the agreement, treaty about joining the B.R.D.:
3 Oct. 1990 end of the D.D.R.

Federal Republic of Germany (p. 289)
1978 FILBINGER affair (Aug.).
Jul. 1979 President KARL CARSTENS.
1980 Elections for the Lower House (Oct.). Strengthening of the S.P.D./F.D.P. coalition. H. SCHMIDT remained chancellor.
Nov. 1980 Krefeld appeal demanded renouncement of the deployment of new arms. Growth of the peace movement up to the
10 Oct. 1981 peace demonstration in Bonn with approx. 250,000 participants. Increasing state debts and unemployment led to the
1982 end of the Social/Liberal coalition (17 Sep.). Fall of the SCHMIDT government through a constructive vote of no confidence:
1 Oct. 1982 Chancellor Helmut Kohl/C.D.U. of the C.D.U./C.S.U./F.D.P. gvt. GENSCHER remained vice-chancellor and foreign minister. Because of vote of no confidence in KOHL (17 Feb.) new elections brought forward.
1983 Election success of the C.D.U./F.D.P. coalition with Chancellor KOHL (Mar.).
Stationing of new U.S. rockets agreed by the Lower House (Nov.).
Jul. 1984 President Richard v. Weizsäcker/C.D.U.
Nov. 1984 The French president, MITTERRAND, and Chancellor KOHL visited milit. cemeteries of Verdun.
May 1985 State visit of U.S. President REAGAN.
1986 Discussion about stream of refugees.
1987 Elections for the Lower House: confirmation of the gvt coalition (Jan.).
BARSCHEL affair (Sep.–Nov.).
1988 Over 200,000 resettlers from Eastern Europe came into the B.R.D. Withdrawal of U.S. intermediate-range rockets (from Sep.).
Death of F. J. STRAUSS (3 Oct.).
1989 Visit of U.S. President BUSH (May). Visit of GORBACHEV (Jun.). Occupation of B.R.D. embassies by D.D.R. citizens (Jul.–Sep.).
9 Nov. 1989 Opening of the internal German border by the D.D.R.
10-point plan of Chancellor KOHL for overcoming Germany's division (28 Nov.).
1990 Signature of the state treaty (18 May), approved by the German Lower House and the parliament of the D.D.R. (21 Jun.), about
1 Jul. 1990 monetary, economic and social union with the D.D.R.
After conclusion of the 2 + 4 talks (since May) in Moscow signature of the
12 Sep. 1990 German Treaty: end of the Allies' rights and sovereignty in Germany. State unification completed:
3 Oct. 1990 joining of the D.D.R. to the B.R.D.
GORBACHEV visit (9–10 Nov.): German–Soviet Basic Treaty. German–Polish Border Treaty (14 Nov.). Elections for the 1st all-German Lower House:
2 Dec. 1990 victory of the gvt coalition under Chancellor Kohl (C.D.U./C.S.U. 319, S.P.D. 239, F.D.P. 79, P.D.S. 17 seats).

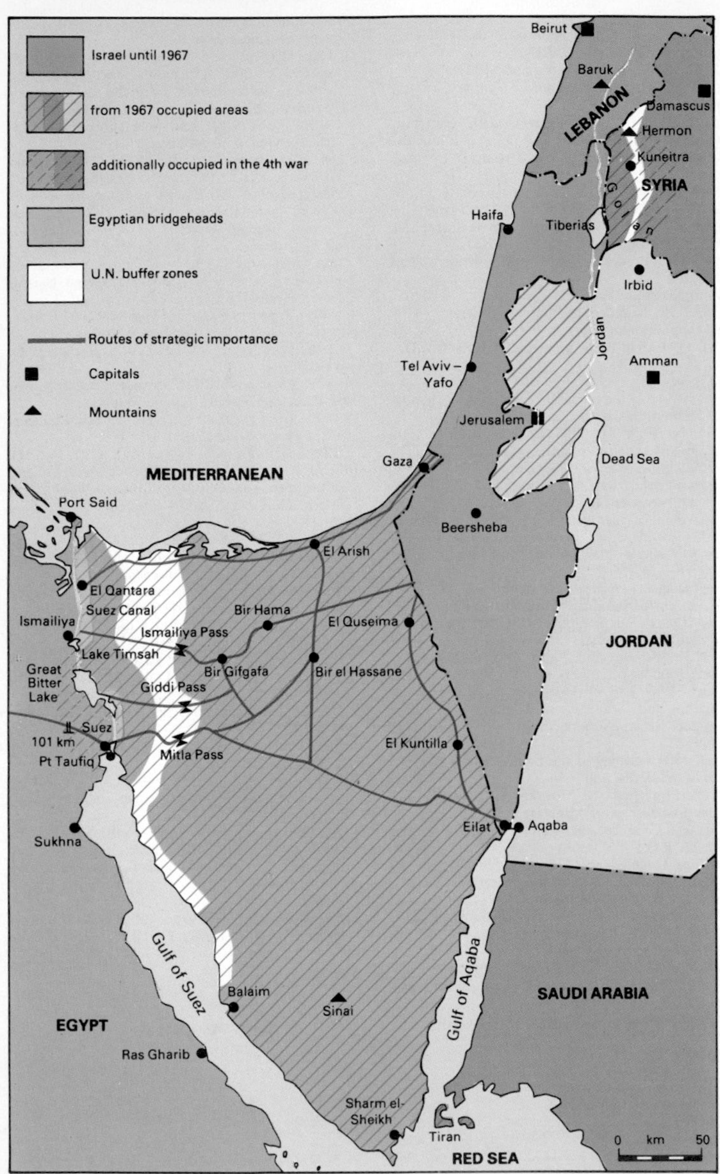
Israel until 1967
from 1967 occupied areas
additionally occupied in the 4th war
Egyptian bridgeheads
U.N. buffer zones
Routes of strategic importance
Capitals
Mountains
Beirut
Baruk
LEBANON
Damascus
Hermon
Kuneitra
SYRIA
Golan
Haifa
Tiberias
Irbid
Jordan
Amman
Tel Aviv – Yafo
Jerusalem
Dead Sea
Gaza
MEDITERRANEAN
Port Said
Beersheba
El Arish
El Qantara
Suez Canal
Ismailiya
Bir Hama
El Quseima
Ismailiya Pass
JORDAN
Lake Timsah
Bir Gifgafa
Bir el Hassane
Great Bitter Lake
Giddi Pass
Suez
101 km
Pt Taufiq
Mitla Pass
El Kuntilla
Eilat
Aqaba
Sukhna
Gulf of Suez
Gulf of Aqaba
SAUDI ARABIA
Balaim
Sinai
EGYPT
Ras Gharib
Sharm el-Sheikh
Tiran
RED SEA
0 km 50

The state of Israel 1967–76

Israel (p. 259)

1966–7 Border incidents with Arab neighbours; acts of sabotage by Al Fatah. Following the withdrawal of U.N. troops from the Gaza Strip, the U.A.R. announced the blockade of the Gulf of Aqaba (Elath); concentration of Arab troops. **Moshe Dayan** (b. 1915) was appointed minister of defence.

5–10 Jun. 1967 3rd Arab–Israeli war (6-Day War: Israel *v.* the U.A.R., Syria and Jordan).
Following an armistice, the conquered territories remained occupied (Gaza Strip, Sinai Peninsula, Western Jordan, The Syr. Golan Heights).

1968 Border incidents; acts of sabotage by Al Fatah, reprisals by Israel. Following the death of ESHKOL

Mar. 1969 GOLDA MEIR (b. 1898) became prime minister; from 1966 ABBA EBAN was for. minister. Skyjackings and assaults were carried out by the Palestine Liberation Organization (P.L.O.) under YASSIR ARAFAT.
Increase in the number of border skirmishes, esp. along the Suez Canal. A U.S. peace plan

Aug. 1970 led to **cease-fire.**

1971 Isolated actions by Palestinians and Israeli reprisals continued.

Oct. 1973 4th Arab–Israeli War. During the world **oil crisis** the Arab states placed embargoes on supplies to the developed countries. Negotiations at the initiative of the U.S.A. (Secretary of State KISSINGER) and the U.S.S.R. guided event towards

1974 an agreement of disengagement with Egypt (Jan.) and Syria (May), U.N. forces occupying the buffer zone.

Dec. 1973 Geneva Near East conference soon adjourned in favour of KISSINGER's personal diplomacy.

1974–77 Prime Minister RABIN.

Oct. 1975 Sinai Treaty with Egypt and an implementing protocol: obligation to solve conflict peacefully.

Nov. 1975 U.S.S.R. demanded reopening of Geneva Near East conference, as separate treaties didn't lead to solution.

Jun.–Jul. 1976 Israeli plane taken by P.L.O. terrorists to Entebbe (Uganda) and liberation of the hostages by Israeli commandos.
After victory of the Likud block

1977 cabinet of Menachem Begin.
After mediation by U.S. President CARTER (Camp David)

1979 Peace treaty with Egypt: evacuation of Sinai (until 1982).

1981 Destruction of the Iraqi nuclear reactor near Baghdad (Jun.).
Annexation of the Golan Heights (Dec.).

1982 Invasion of the Lebanon (until 1985).

1983 Prime Minister I. SCHAMIR (Oct.). From

1984 coalition gvt Likud/Workers' party under Prime Minister S. PEREZ, from

1986 SCHAMIR became prime minister again.
Rebellion of the Arab population in the occupied areas: from

Dec. 1987 'Intifada'.

1990 Massacre of Palestinians on the Temple Mount (8 Oct.).
Neutral in the Gulf War, in spite of which

1991 Scud missile attacks by Iraq (Jan.–Feb.).

Lebanon (p. 257)

1973 Fights between army and Palestinians.

1974 Attacks by Palestinian terrorists on Israeli settlements.

1975–76 Civil war between Christians and Muslims. SAKRIS elected state president. Invasion by Syrian troops. Despite the bringing in of Multinational Peace Troops (M.P.T.)

1978–81 unrest and milit. action, interrupted by short cease-fires.

1982 Invasion by Israeli troops (from Jun.). President B. GEMAYEL (Aug.) was murdered (Sep.), succeeded by his brother, A. GEMAYEL. Massacre in the P.L.O. camps Sabra and Chatila.

1983 Bomb attacks on M.P.T. quarters in Beirut (death of 230 U.S. marines and 58 French paratroopers).

1985 Withdrawal of Israeli troops (by Jun.).

1987 Invasion by the Syrians (Jan.–Feb.).

1988 The milit. gvt of AOUN is brought in by President A. GEMAYEL (Sep.).

1989 Cease-fire (Sep.). Document for national peace (Oct.).

1990 After murder of the elected President MUAWAD (Nov.), President E. HRAWI.

1990 Bloody power struggle between Christian groups.

1991 Army advances also against the militia in s. Lebanon.

Jordan (p. 257)

1966 Border incidents with Israel. During the

Jun. 1967 6-Day War, the territory on the western bank of the Jordan was occupied by Israel.

1970 Civil war. Following intensive fighting, gvt troops

1971 dispersed the guerilla units.

1974 Relinquishing of western bank of Jordan in favour of the Palestinians.

1975 Agreements on cooperation with Syria.

1988 King HUSSEIN confirms relinquishing of w. Jordanian territory.

1989 Parliamentary elections (Nov.).

1990 Support for Iraq over U.N. blockades.

Syria (p. 257)

Jun. 1967 6-Day War with Israel.
After power struggles the

1970 right wing of the Baath party asserted itself:

1971 General Assad became president.

Oct. 1973 War against Israel.

1974 Treaty with Israel withdrawing troops from the Golan Heights.

1975–6 Intervention in the Lebanon forced a cease-fire.

1981 Annexation of the Golan Heights by Israel.

1987 Syrian troops entered Beirut.

Southern Yemen
Following severe unrest, the Brit. protectorate, the Southern Arab Federation (Aden and the Aden protectorate) became ind. as the
Dec. 1967 People's Republic of Southern Yemen.
Nov. 1970 The state was renamed the Dem. People's Republic of Yemen.
After *coup* and civil war
1986 revolutionary council took over gvt.
1990 Alliance with the Republic of Yemen.

Yemen (p. 257)
1966–70 Fighting between the royalists, supported by Saudi Arabia, and republicans, supported by Egypt. troops (to Dec. 1967).
Dec. 1970 constitution of the **Republic of Yemen.**
1970–73 Armed clashes with the People's Republic of Yemen.
1974 Milit. junta took over presidency.
1978 President SALEH.
Union of both Yemeni states into the
22 May 1990 Republic of Yemen.

Iraq (p. 257)
A bloodless
Jul. 1968 milit. coup led to the fall of President AREF: the right wing of the Baath party assumed the gvt under President AL-BAKR. Agreement with the
1970 Kurds: involvement in the gvt.
1973 Involvement of the Com. party in the gvt.
1974–5 Kurdish War; the Kurdish liberation struggle ended by the Iraq–Iran normalization treaty, but further persecution and forced resettlements. Com. party resigned from the gvt and Pesident AL-BAKR resigned,
Jul. 1979 General Saddam Hussein became new president.
1980 Start of the Gulf War with Iran.
1981 Destruction of the nuclear reactor Osirak by Israeli fighter-bombers (Jun.).
1982 Iraq was taken off the U.S. list of 'terrorist countries' (Feb.).
1988 Use of toxic gas against the Kurds (Apr.–May), who fled to Turkey.
20 Aug. 1988 Cease-fire with Iran, peace negotiations.
2 Aug. 1990 Attack on Kuwait: the Emirate was occupied and declared Iraqi province. Foreigners were taken hostage. Condemnation by the U.N. Security Council. After expiry of the U.N. ultimatum
17 Jan.–28 Feb. 1991 (2nd) Gulf War which ended with a bloody defeat of SADDAM HUSSEIN and his loss of Kuwait. Bloody oppression of Iraqi opposition, esp. **persecution of the Kurds.**

Kuwait (p. 257)
1977 Agreement with Iraq on disputed border areas.
2 Aug. 1990 Occupation by Iraqi troops. The U.N. resolutions 660ff. were forcibly implemented by multinational troops:
Feb. 1991 liberation of Kuwait. Threat of an **environmental disaster** from the oil that the Iraqis released into the gulf and from the oil wells which they set on fire.

Saudi Arabia (p. 257)
1973 King FEISAL declared his intention to use oil as an Arab weapon against Israel.
Mar. 1975 Assassination of FEISAL, new King KHALED: FAHD became crown prince.
1979 Occupation of the Great Mosque in Mecca (Nov.) by a group of revolutionary Muslims was broken up by milit. force (Dec.).
1983 Death of KHALED, new King FAHD.
1987 Massacre of Iranian pilgrims by Saudi security forces in the Great Mosque in Mecca.
Involvement in
1991 Gulf War for the liberation of Kuwait. Acted as deployment area for Allied troops.

The Emirates of the Pers. Gulf
1968 Establishment of the Federation of the Emirates of the Pers. Gulf (the former Pirate Coast, Bahrain and Qatar). When Bahrain and Qatar left the federation
1971–2 the Federation of Arab Emirates.

Islamic Summit Conferences
Sep. 1969 in Rabat: close cooperation and mutual help.
Feb. 1974 in Lahore: basic problems with the world economy.
Sep. 1968 Foundation of OPEC (Organization of Arab Oil Exporting Countries): cooperation in all areas of oil management.

Iran (p. 229)
1978 Bloody unrest, demonstrations, strikes; social-revolutionary fundamentalists demanded the fall of the Shah.
Jan. 1979 Shah Pehlewi left the country.
Return of the Shiite leader
1 Feb. 1979 Ayatollah Khomeini from exile in France, who proclaimed the Islamic Republic.
Nov. 1979 In the U.S. embassy in Tehran hostages were taken by 'students' who demanded the extradition of the Shah and his foreign fortune.
Apr. 1980 The U.S. forces rescue operation failed. With the attack by Iraqi troops, the border conflict at the Schatt el-Arab developed into the
Sep. 1980 Gulf War with Iraq. After the death of the Shah (27 Feb.) and mediation by Algeria
Jan. 1981 hostages were set free.
Oct. 1981 State President ALI KHAMENEI.
After 8 yrs of heavy losses due to war a
Aug. 1988 cease-fire in the Gulf War was agreed on with Iraq, to be supervised by U.N. troops.
4 Jun. 1989 Death of Khomeini. Successor as religious and political leader was the current President,
Jul. 1989 revolution leader Khamenei, new state president, RAFSANJANI.

Afghanistan (p. 265)
Fall of King Sahir (since 1933) through
1973 milit. *coup* under General Daud, who proclaimed a republic. Brought down by
1978 Com. party gvt under Taraki. After his fall brought about by Amin,
Dec. 1979 invasion by Soviet troops.
Karmal became president. Civil war between the Soviet and gvt troops and the mujahedin. Mass flight to Pakistan.
Dec. 1986 Najibullah became party chief and head of state. Negotiations in Geneva:
Apr. 1988 Afghanistan Treaty with agreement on **Soviet troop withdrawal**, by
Feb. 1989. Despite this the fights between gvt troops and the Mujahedin continued.
Mar. 1990 *coup* attempt against the Najibullah gvt failed.

India (p. 265)
Jan. 1966 Indira Gandhi (b. 1917) became prime minister in succession to Shastri.
Famine, unrest, relig. demonstrations by Hindus.
Sep. 1967 Sino-Ind. conflict in the border area of Sikkim.
Sep. 1969 Bloody conflicts between Hindus and Moslems in Ahmadabad.
Split of the Congress party and
Mar. 1971 clear elect. vict. of the left wing under Prime Minister Indira Gandhi.
A refugee problem was created in Bengal by the civil war in E. Pakistan (see below). India was victorious in the
Dec. 1971 3rd India–Pakistan War.
May 1974 Atomic weapons test; India becomes 6th nuclear power.
Sep. 1974 Sikkim became an associated, then a federated state (1975). After judicial revocation of Mrs Gandhi's election into parliament:
Jun. 1975–Mar. 1977 Indira Gandhi declared a state of emergency: arrests, prohibition of the opposition, press censorship.
Mar. 1977 Election victory for the opposition, M. Desai/Janata became the new prime minister.
1979 Prime Minister C. Singh/Janata.
After election victory of the Indira Congress
Jan. 1980 Indira Gandhi became prime minister again. Sikh action against the governing Hindus (since Apr.) in the Punjab.
Jan. 1982 National general strike. After attacks by militant Sikhs
Oct. 1983 state of emergency in the Punjab.
Jun. 1984 Assault on the Golden Temple of Amritsar with thousands of Sikhs dead.
31 Oct. 1984 Assassination of Indira Gandhi by Sikh bodyguard; her son Rajiv Gandhi became new prime minister.
1985 Toxic gas disaster in Bhopal (Dec.).
1989 Election victory for the opposition (Nov.). Gvt under V. P. Singh/Janata. The former prime minister,
21 May 1991 R. Gandhi was murdered. After election victory of the Congress party
Jun. 1991 Prime Minister N. Rao/Congress.

Pakistan (p. 265)
Unrest in E. Pakistan led to the
Mar. 1969 resignation of Ayub Khan and the transfer of power to President Yahya Khan.
Dec. 1970 Elections to the nat. assembly brought vict. for the 'Awami League' under Mujibur Rahman, who strove for the autonomy of E. Pakistan. Victorious in w. Pakistan, the centralistic People's party under Ali Bhutto prevented the convocation of the nat. assembly. There were severe and bloody uprisings in E. Pakistan and the ind. state of
Apr. 1971 **Bangladesh** was proclaimed. Civil War: millions fled to India. The
3–17 Dec. 1971 3rd India–Pakistan War ended with the defeat of Pakistan and the vict. of E. Pakistan, which became the ind. state of **Bangladesh**.
Yahya Khan resigned; Ali Bhutto became president.
New constitution:
1973 Prime Minister Ali Bhutto. Because of fraudulent elections
1977 the army took over power: General Zia ul-Haq (Jul.) became president from 1978. Islamization of the judicial system.
1979 Execution of Bhutto (Apr.).
1980 Stream of Afghans, support for the Mujahedin.
1985 State of war was lifted for the first time in 8 yrs.
1988 Death of Zia in a plane crash (Aug.). G. Ishaq Khan became president. In free elections the daughter of the former prime minister won:
Dec. 1988 Prime Minister Benazir Bhutto.
Dec. 1990 President Ishaq dimissed the Bhutto gvt. New elections resulted in a majority for Islamic Democratic Alliance, Prime Minister N. Sharif (Nov.).

Bangladesh
Feb. 1974 Recognition by Pakistan.
Jan. 1975 Positions of state president and prime minister amalgamated by Mujibur Rahman.
Aug. 1975 Milit. *coup.* Mujibur Rahman murdered. Power struggles.
Nov. 1975 Milit. *coup.*
1977 Zia ur-Rahman became state president.
1981 *Coup* attempt: murder of ur-Rahman (May), A. Sattar became new president (Nov.).
1982 Milit. *coup* (Mar.) under **General H. M. Ershad**, from Dec. 1983 president. After continuing unrest
Dec. 1990 President Ershad announced his resignation. The widow of Rahman won free elections:
Mar. 1991 Prime Minister Khaleda Zia.

Sri Lanka
1972 Ceylon (p. 265) became Republic of Sri Lanka.
1970–77 S. Bandaranaike became prime minister again.
After introduction of the pres. system
1978 President J. R. Jayawardene.
Since 1980 racial unrest between Sinhalese and Tamils: civil war.
1987 Landing of Indian peace troops (Jul.).
1988 President R. Premadasa.
1990 Withdrawal of the (unsuccessful) peace troops.

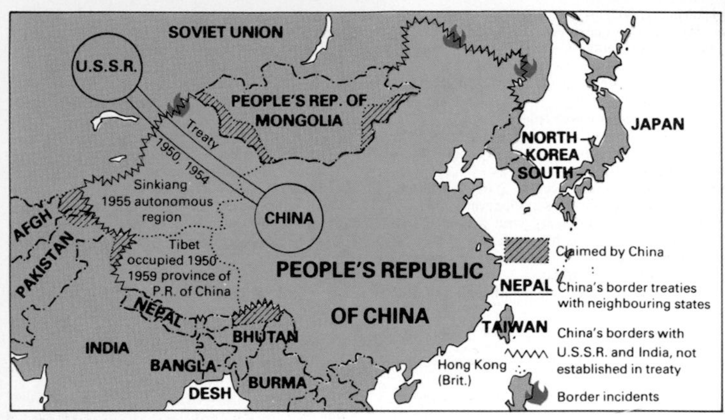

China and the 'unjust treaties'

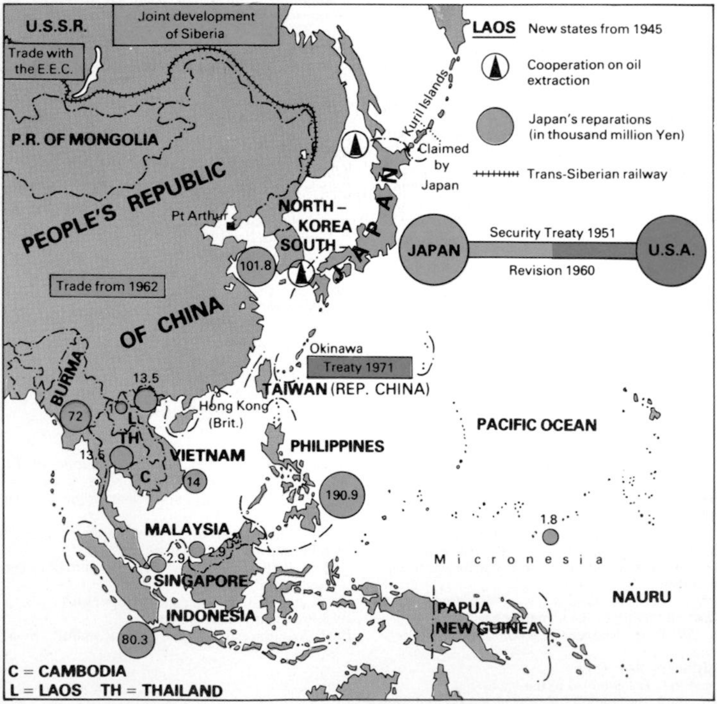

Japan's foreign policies

The People's Republic of China (p. 235)

1966 The 'Great Proletarian Cult. Revolution' (beginning in Sep. 1965). Purges in party, army and econ. life. Minister of defence, LIN PIAO (1907–71) called for struggle against the reactionaries.
In Peking and other cities students formed **'Red Guards'**, supported by MAO TSE-TUNG, to eliminate party opposition that had gathered around President LIU SHAO-CH'I (p. 235). Terror was directed against the bourgeois needs of the élite class, against everything 'for.' and the '4 Ancients' (ideas, culture, customs and traditions).

Feb. 1967 The 'Red Guards' were dissolved. Followers of MAO assumed the supreme powers of gvt.

Jun. 1967 Detonation of the 1st Chin. H-bomb.

Oct. 1968 End of the 1st phase of the cult. revolution; expulsion of LIU SHAO-CH'I from the party and all his offices.

Mar. 1969 Border incidents with the U.S.S.R. at the Ussuri river border.
Invitation of a U.S. table-tennis team to Peking:

Apr. 1971 'ping-pong diplomacy'.

Jul. 1971 Secret visit of NIXON's adviser KISSINGER to Peking.

Oct. 1971 Admission of the People's Republic of China into the U.N. as the representative of China, and expulsion of Taiwan.

Feb. 1972 Visit of President NIXON.

1975 New constitution: DENG XIAOPING (born 1904) became deputy chairman of the Central Committee.

Jan. 1976 Death of Chou En-lai. Prime Minister HUA GUOFENG in office (Feb.). DENG XIAOPING was dismissed (Apr.).

9 Sep. 1976 Death of Mao. After disputes HUA GUOFENG became successor. Condemnation of MAO's widow, JIANG QING, and her adherents (Gang of Four).

1977 Rehabilitation of Deng, who rose to become the most powerful man and replaced HUA GUOFENG (prime minister until 1980, party leader until 1981) with his own supporters.

1978 Normalization Treaty with the U.S.A.

End of 1980 Conviction of the Gang of Four; the death sentences, amongst others of MAO TSE-TUNG's widow, were not carried out.

1980 Prime Minister ZHAO ZIYANG.

1981 HU YAOBANG became party chairman, from 1982 secretary-general. Reform course led to economic boom.

1987 Student demonstrations for more freedom. LI PENG became prime minister (Nov.).

1989 Student unrest; mass demonstrations in the 'Square of Heavenly Peace' (Tiananmen Square) in Peking, ending in a

4 Jun. massacre by the army, arrests and executions. Dismissal of ZHAO (secretary-general since Jan. 1987), JIANG ZEMIN became party chief.

Nov. 1989 Resignation of DENG XIAOPING as chairman of the Central Military Commission.
Party chief JIANG became his successor (1990).

Taiwan (p. 234)

5 Apr. 1975 Death of CHIANG KAI-SHEK. His son

1978 CHIANG CHING-KUO elected president; successful reform programme.

1988 President LI TENG-KUI. Continuation of the cautious *rapprochement* with the People's Republic of China.

Korea (p. 237)

Since 1972 negotiations and attempts at reunification have failed.

Republic of Korea:

1979 President PARK CHUNG HEE murdered. Violent measures against the opposition.

1987 Severe unrest forced gvt to elect the president directly, the split opposition failed:

1988 ROH TAE WOO became president.

Japan (p. 235)

Lib.–Dem. Cabinets under

1964–72 Eisaku Sato as prime minister brought Japan to the rank of

1968 3rd largest indust. nation in the world.

Sep.–Oct. 1971 The 1st journey abroad by a Jap. emperor when HIROHITO visited Eur. countries.

May 1972 Return of Okinawa to Japan, but U.S. bases retained on the island.

Jul. 1972 Prime Minister KAKEUI TANAKA resigned because of corruption accusations (Nov.).

1975 Visit of Emperor HIROHITO to the U.S.A.

1978 Peace Treaty with the People's Republic of China.

1982 Dispute about 'revised' school history textbooks (2nd World War).

1982–7 Prime Minister Y. Nakasone; Japan remained one of the leading industrial nations.

1987–9 Prime Minister N. TAKESHITA.

1989 Death of Hirohito (7 Jan.), AKIHITO became new emperor.
Blackmail scandal led to gvt resignation. Prime Minister S. UNO was followed by

Aug. 1989 Prime Minister TOSHIKI KAIFU.

Philippines (p. 263)

After pres. elections

1986 fall of President Marcos. CORAZON AQUINO, widow of murdered opposition leader, became president (Feb.); several *coup* attempts failed.

Nauru

1968 This Pacific island became an ind. republic within the framework of the Brit. Commonwealth.

Niue

1974 Self-gvt in association with New Zealand.

Fiji

1970 Independent within the Commonwealth.

Papua New Guinea

1975 Independent within the Commonwealth.

Australia

Jan. 1966 HAROLD HOLT succeeded ROBERT GORDON MENZIES (1949–66) as prime minister.

Jan. 1968 Prime Minister JOHN GORTON.

Mar. 1971 Prime Minister WILLIAM MCMAHON.

1972 Labour gvt under GOUGH WHITLAM who wanted to give up the 'White Australia Policy'.

1975 Election victory of the Liberals under MALCOLM FRASER who again formed a cabinet in 1980.

1983 Labour gvt under Prime Minister BOB HAWKE.

1990 4th HAWKE cabinet.

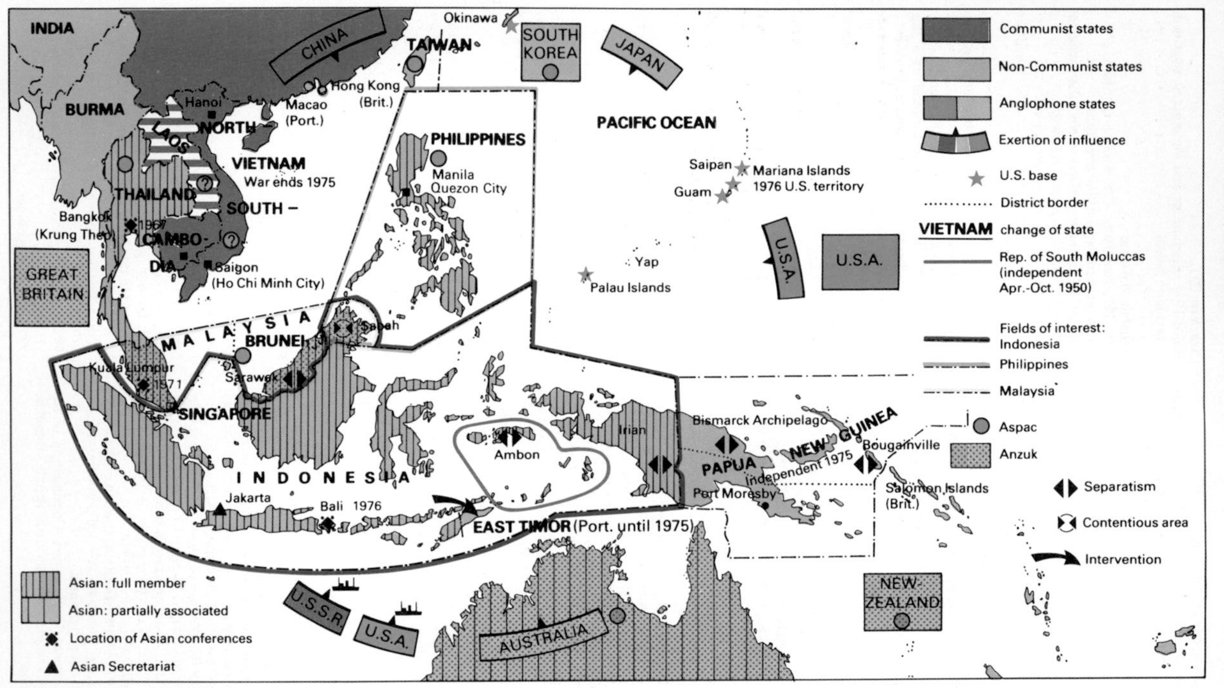

South Pacific area of conflict: Alliances in the Pacific

Thailand (p. 263)
1968–70 Com. guerrilla activity.
1971 Military gvt revoked the constitution.
1976 Withdrawal of U.S. troops; again milit. gvt.
1978 New constitution.
1980–88 Prime Minister General PREM.
1988 Prime Minister C. CHOONHAVEN.

Laos (p. 237)
1966–72 Continued fighting between gvt troops and units of the Com. **Pathet Lao**, who occupied the larger part of the country.
U.S. air-raids on Vietcong supply routes (the **'Ho Chi Minh Trail'**).
Feb. 1973 Peace treaty between the gvt and the Pathet Lao.
1975 Pathet Lao takes over power, proclamation of a Democratic People's Republic; chairman of the revolutionary council, SOUVANNA VONG.

Khmer (Cambodia)
1966–9 Com. guerrillas; Prince SIHANOUK, the head of state, attempted to steer a neutralist course.
Mar. 1970 Fall of SIHANOUK, who formed a gvt-in-exile in Peking.
May 1970 Invasion by S. Vietnamese and U.S. troops. Abolition of the monarchy and renaming to
Oct. 1970 Republic of Khmer.
Mar. 1972 President LON NOL.
1973 The 'Khmer Rouge' advance to besiege the capital Phnom Penh.
Apr. 1975 Occupation of Phnom Penh: terror in the territory isolated under the regime of
1976 Prime Minister POL POT/Khmer Rouge. With Vietnam's milit. help the oppositional
1978–9 Com. National Union Front won under President HENG SAMRIN (since 1981): proclamation of the **People's Republic of Cambodia.** POL POT engaged in guerrilla war.
1989 Withdrawal of the Vietnamese troops (Sep.). The 'Democratic Kampuchea' gvt in exile, supported by China and the U.N., led a guerrilla war, since Feb.
1990 'National gvt of Cambodia' with President SIHANOUK.
Jun. 1991 Agreement on a permanent cease-fire between the gvt and the 3 competing civil war parties.

S. Vietnam (p. 237)
Mar. 1966 Demonstrations by anti-gvt Buddhists under THICH TRI QUANG forced the milit. gvt under KY as prime minister to call for elections.
Ground fighting around Da Nang and Hue.
U.S. air-raids on Hanoi and Haiphong. U.S. troop strengths were increased to 42,000.
Encouraged by milit. successes, U.S. President JOHNSON and KY, meeting
Mar. 1967 on Guam, decided on domestic reforms and positive measures against Com. infiltration.
Sep. 1967 President NGUYEN VAN THIEU was re-elected; KY became vice-president.
Jan. 1968 'Tet Offensive': fighting in Saigon, Hué and around the U.S. base of Khe Sanh.
May 1968 Beginning of negotiations between the U.S.A. and N. Vietnam in Paris.
Nov. 1968 Termination of bombing of N. Vietnamese territory.
Jan. 1969 Paris Peace Talks.
Sep. 1969 President NIXON announced a phased withdrawal of U.S. troops (at this point there were 550,000 Amer. soldiers in Vietnam): **'Vietnamization'** of the war.
Mar. 1970 Extension of the fighting to Cambodia.
Feb. 1971 A S. Vietnamese advance into Laos.
Mar. 1972 Massive N. Vietnamese offensive against Quang Tri, Kontum and An Loc could be stopped by the gvt troops only with the aid of large-scale U.S. air support and an offshore bombardment of N. Vietnam.
U.S. ground forces (still 69,000 men) did not interfere in the fighting.
Jan. 1973 Cease-fire agreement. Release of all P.O.W.s; complete withdrawal of U.S. troops.
Feb.–Mar. 1973 Paris Vietnam Conference.
30 Apr. 1975 **Unconditional surrender** and reunification with N. Vietnam to form the Socialist Republic of Vietnam (Jul. 1976).

North Vietnam (p. 237)
After death of HO CHI MINH (p. 237)
Sep. 1969 TON DUC THANG became state president.
After capitulation of S. Vietnam:
Nov. 1975 political consultative conference about reunification. After the elections in the all-Vietnam National Assembly
2 Jul. 1976 reunification and proclamation of the Socialist Republic of Vietnam.

Vietnam
1978 Member of COMECON.
Treaty of Friendship with the U.S.S.R.
1979 Invasion of Cambodia (withdrawal in 1989).

Malaysia (p. 263)
1966 Indonesian 'confrontation' ended with the Treaty of Jakarta.
After Malay–Chinese unrest
1969–71 state of emergency.

Indonesia (p. 263)
1966 General Suharto (b. 1921) assumed power; SUKARNO gradually eased out. Massacres of Communists and those suspected of being Communist.
Sep. 1966 Resumption of U.N. membership.
May 1967 SUKARNO formally deposed.
Mar. 1968 SUHARTO becomes president.
Aug. 1969 Following a plebiscite, W. Irian annexed.
1976 Annexation of former Portuguese Timor.
1989 President SUHARTO visited Moscow.
1990 Approx. 170 mil. inhabitants in Indonesia.

Pacts
SEATO (p. 239), 1977 disintegration.
ASEAN, founded 1967 by Thailand, Malaysia, Indonesia, Singapore and the Philippines for the advancement of economic stability.
ANZUK, founded 1971: defence treaty between Great Britain, Australia, New Zealand, Malaysia and Singapore.

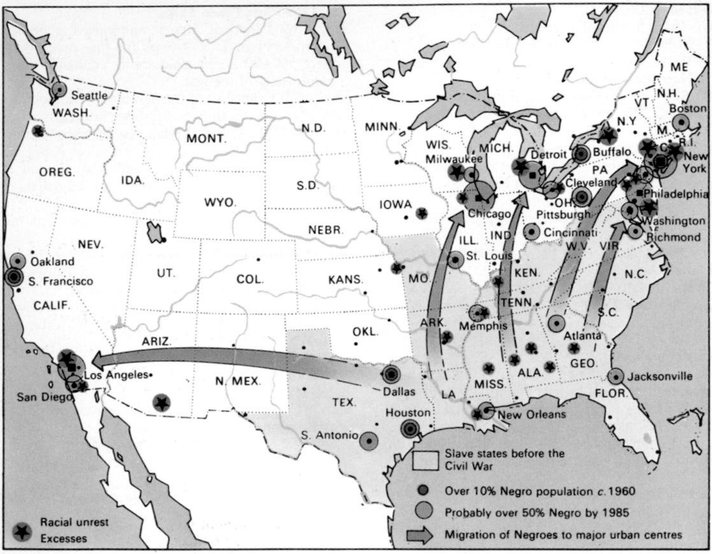

The United States: the Negro question

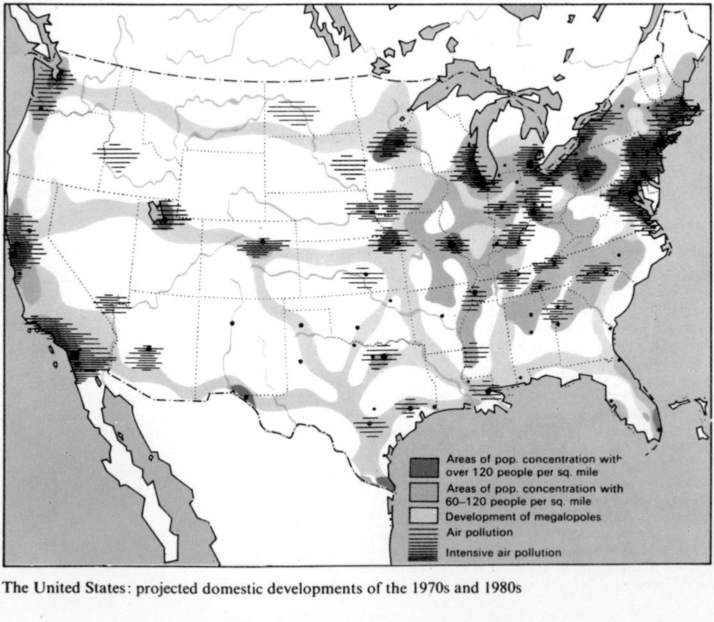

The United States: projected domestic developments of the 1970s and 1980s

Canada (p. 242)
After resignation of PEARSON (p. 242)
1968 Prime Minister Pierre E. Trudeau/Liberal (born 1921).
1972 Minority gvt under TRUDEAU.
1974 Liberals had absolute majority again; Prime Minister TRUDEAU.
1976 and 1981 French separatists won the local elections in Quebec, tensions between French- and English-speaking Canadians.
1982 Queen ELIZABETH II proclaimed the constitution in Ottawa.
1984 Election victory of the Conservatives: Prime Minister B. MULRONEY (Sep.). The
1990 Canadian navy formed part of the multinational troops against Iraq.

The United States (p. 242)
1966 Racial unrest: besides those who protested without resort to force (e.g. MARTIN LUTHER KING), militant groups ('Black Muslims', advocates of 'black power') gained adherents.
Jun. 1967 Summit Meeting in Glassboro, N.J.: conversations between President JOHNSON and the Rus. prime minister, KOSYGIN, brought no solutions to the Vietnam and Israel questions.
1968 President JOHNSON announced the initiation of peace negotiations with N. Vietnam.
1969 Richard M. Nixon/Republican (p. 242) became president, having defeated HUBERT H. HUMPHREY/Democrat by a small majority.
Sep. 1969 NIXON announced the gradual withdrawal of U.S. troops from Vietnam.
Jun. 1971 Publication of the *Pentagon Papers* on the history of the Vietnam War.
Jul. 1971 Nixon's adviser Kissinger went to Peking.
Feb. 1972 President Nixon visited the People's Republic of China.
Nov. 1972 Re-election of NIXON (61%) against GEORGE MCGOVERN/Democrat. Serious domestic crisis as a result of the
1973 Watergate scandal. Following **Nixon's resignation**
Aug. 1974 Gerald R. Ford succeeded to the presidency.
BREZHNEV in Vladivostok (Nov.): declaration about SALT.
Mar. 1976 FORD supported 'politics for peace through strength' and opposed the term *'détente'*.
200th anniversary of the foundation of the U.S.A. (4 Jul.).
1977 President James E. Carter/Democrat; he mediated the Egypt–Israeli
1978 Camp David Treaty.
1980 The milit. rescue operation of hostages, taken during the *coup* in Iran at the U.S. embassy in Teheran, failed (freed on 20 Jan. 1981). Economic sanctions and
1980 withdrawal from the Olympics in Moscow because of Soviet invasion of Afghanistan.
1981 President Ronald W. Reagan/Republican.
Aug. 1981 Libyan fighter planes were shot down over the Gulf of Sirte.
Oct. 1983 Milit. action in Grenada. Aid for Contras in Nicaragua. Radical lowering of tax and cut of social payments led to economic growth: with a big majority
Nov. 1984 Reagan is re-elected; research programme for the defence of rocket weapons in space for the 21st century (Star Wars):
Jan. 1985 Strategic Defence Initiative (S.D.I.).
1986 Arms affair: weapons supplied to Iran by the C.I.A.
1988 Intermediate-range rockets were withdrawn from Europe and destroyed.
After victory over the Democrat M. DUKAKIS:
1989 President George Bush/Republican. By way of executing the resolutions which were unanimously agreed upon (no. 660ff) by the U.N.,
1990 U.S.A. participated in the deployment against Iraq; after expiry of an ultimatum, milit. victory of the Allies in the
18 Jan.–28 Feb. 1991 Gulf War for the liberation of Kuwait.

Caribbean
1973 Signature of the Foundation Treaty of the Caribbean Economic Alliance (C.E.A.).
1975 Convention of Lomé: Barbados, Grenada, Bahamas, Jamaica and Trinidad and Tobago became associated states of the E.E.C.

Bahamas
Jul. 1973 The Brit. colony achieved independence.

Barbados
Nov. 1966 The Brit. colony became independent.

The Domin. Republic (p. 271)
Following unrest bordering on civil war,
Jun. 1966 President BALAGUER; O.A.S. troops withdrawn.
Since 1974 President BALAGUER, re-elected (also in 1990).

Grenada
Feb. 1974 Independence.
1979 *Coup* under M. BISHOP. After left-wing *coup* by the milit. and murder of BISHOP
1983 intervention of Amer. and Caribbean troops (Oct.).

Haiti
1986 Fall of DUVALIER who fled to France (Jan.–Feb.).

Cuba
Mar. 1971 Decree which made regular work a soc. duty for all.
Jul. 1972 Admission of Cuba to COMECON.
1975 O.A.S. lifted sanctions.
Intervention in Angola and
1977 also in Ethiopia (withdrawal in 1989).
1988 Angola–Namibia Treaty: beginning of the
1989 troops withdrawal from Angola. Conviction of high-ranking officers for corruption and drug dealing.
1990 Refugees try to force exit by flight to Western embassies.

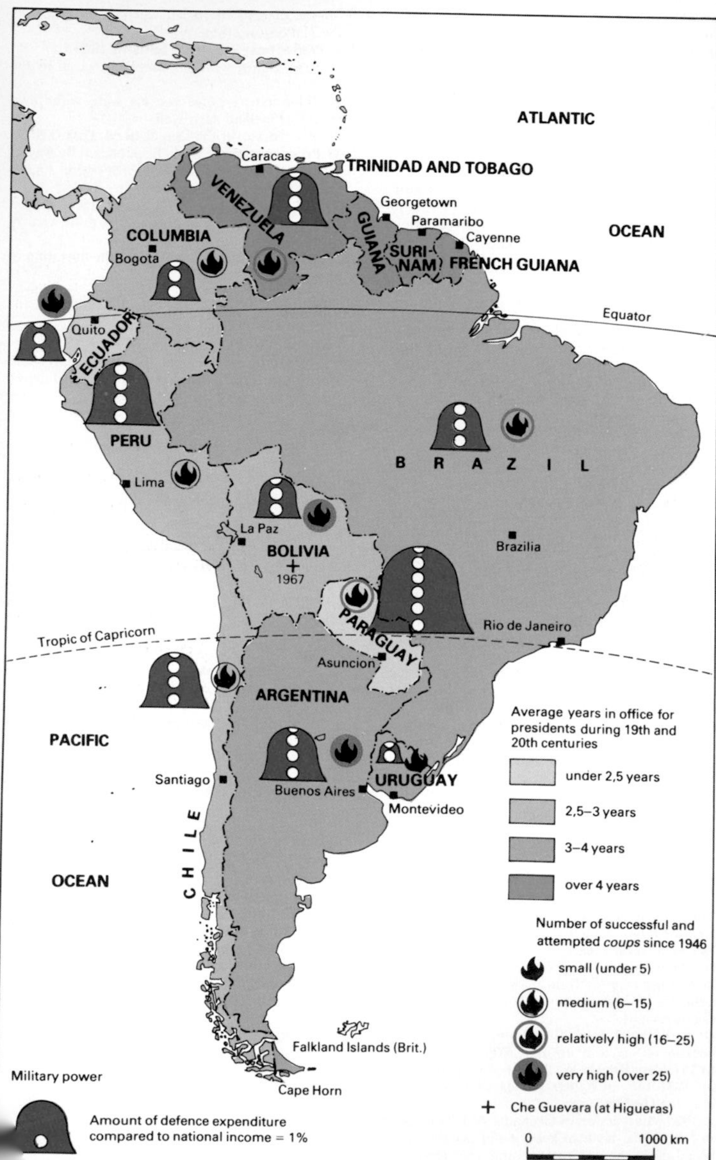
ATLANTIC
OCEAN
Caracas
TRINIDAD AND TOBAGO
VENEZUELA
Georgetown
Paramaribo
Cayenne
GUIANA
SURI-NAM
FRENCH GUIANA
COLUMBIA
Bogota
Quito
ECUADOR
Equator
PERU
Lima
B R A Z I L
La Paz
BOLIVIA
1967
Brazilia
PARAGUAY
Rio de Janeiro
Tropic of Capricorn
Asuncion
ARGENTINA
PACIFIC
OCEAN
Santiago
Buenos Aires
URUGUAY
Montevideo
CHILE
Falkland Islands (Brit.)
Cape Horn
Average years in office for presidents during 19th and 20th centuries
under 2,5 years
2,5–3 years
3–4 years
over 4 years
Number of successful and attempted coups since 1946
small (under 5)
medium (6–15)
relatively high (16–25)
very high (over 25)
+ Che Guevara (at Higueras)
0
1000 km
Military power
Amount of defence expenditure compared to national income = 1%

…estic relations in South America

Mexico (p. 271)

1970 President L. ECHEVERRIA ALVAREZ; undertook two journeys around the world (1973, 1975) to show solidarity with Third World.

1976 President LOPEZ PORTILLO. Oil findings relieved the state budget.

1982 President M. DE LA MADRID.

1985 Earthquake in the capital took several thousand lives.

1988 President C. SALINAS.

Guatemala

1974 LAUGERUD after disputed pres. elections. Milit. regime and guerrilla activities. Elections (Dec.) won by

1986 President V. CEREZO/Christ. Democrat.

British Honduras

1973 Renamed **Belize**.

1981 Belize gained independence.

El Salvador

1969 Football War: border disputes with Honduras ended only in

1976 with a cease-fire treaty.

1979 Milit. *coup*, civil warlike conditions.

Dec. 1980 Junta chief DUARTE declared himself

1984 President. After election new

1989 President A. CRISTIANI/ARENA.

1989–90 Negotiations with the guerrilla organization Farabundo Martí National Liberation Front (F.M.L.N.) failed.

Honduras

1969 Football War with El Salvador (see above).

Sep. 1974 Hurricane Fifi destroyed the economy of Honduras. After milit. junta, from

1980–82 civil gvts were once more established; refugees from El Salvador and Nicaragua strained the domestic political situation; supply bases of the Nicaraguan **Contras**.

1990 President R. LEONARDO CALLEJAS.

Nicaragua

Dec. 1972 Earthquake destroyed the capital, Managua.

1978 Murder of the oppositional P. J. CHAMORRO. Rebellion of the Sandinistas (F.S.L.N.) led to the

1979 fall of the Somoza regime.

Junta took over the gvt under the leadership of the Sandinista, D. ORTEGA.

1983 Fights between Sandinistas and rebels (Contras).

1984 Nicaraguan ports were mined with the help of the C.I.A. (U.S.A.).

Pres. and parliamentary elections:

Nov. 1984 President Ortega F.S.L.N. Guerrilla war against the Contras, who were supported by the U.S.A., continued.

1987 10-point suggestion by ARIAS, the president of Costa Rica, for the domestic democratization of Nicaragua (Feb.). Dialogue between the gvt and 11 opposition parties (Oct.).

1988 Cease-fire treaty of Sapoa (Mar.).

1990 Free elections won by the centre-right coalition: victory of the opposition over the Sandinistas (Feb.). Power was handed over to the new

Apr. 1990 President VIOLETA CHAMORRO: demobilization of the Contras.

Panama

1972–8 TORRIJO, 'Leader of the new revolution'.

1977 Treaties with the U.S.A. signed: after returning approx. 55% of the area to Panama, mutual administration of canal and canal zone until end of 1990.

1989 Annulment of the pres. elections of 7 May (May). *Coup* attempt against supreme commander General NORIEGA (Oct.) failed.

20 Dec. 1989 U.S. milit. intervention ended with fall and

Jan. 1990 arrest of NORIEGA; in the U.S.A. charged with drug dealing.

Colombia (p. 271)

1974 President LOPEZ MICHELSEN/Liberal: nationalization of all oilfields. Guerrilla fights against the revolutionary liberation movements; death troops used against the right.

1986 President V. BARCO VARGAS/Liberal. From

1989 intensified fights against the drug mafia (Cartel of Medellin).

1990 President C. GAVIRIA/Liberal.

Ecuador

1968 President VELASCO IBARRA cancelled the

1970 constitution. Milit. *coup*

1972; junta under RODRIGUEZ LARA. Power struggles in the milit. leadership:

1976 top gvt council under POVEDA BURBANO. After elections, from

1979 a civilian became president again.

1988 President RODRIGO BORJA.

Peru (p. 271)

Following increasing tensions in domestic politics

1963–8 President Belaúnde Terry was overthrown.

Oct. 1968 General VELASCO ALVARADO became president: continuation of policies aiming at the development of state Socialism.

Jun. 1971 Introduction of land reform.

1973 Nationalization of the fish meal industry and of the biggest U.S. mining company.

1974 'Inka': schedule of the revolution.

1975 President was overthrown by the milit. New President General MORALES BERMUDEZ, but further unrest and *coup* attempts.

1978 Assembly to establish constitution. From the 1980s terrorist attacks by the Maoist guerrilla movement Shining Path.

1980 F. BELAÚNDE TERRY became president again.

1985 President GARCIA PEREZ.

1990 President A. FUJIMORI, after election victory over the writer M. VARGOS LLOSA, announced savings programme.

Bolivia

1967 **Ernesto 'Che' Guevara**, the leader of the guerrillas, was killed.

President BARRIENTOS (1919–69) proclaimed martial law and appointed a

Jul. 1968 milit. gvt. A left-wing milit. *coup*

Sep. 1969 led to the presidency of General OVANDO CANDIDA: nat. revolution and nationalization.

Oct. 1970 President JOSÉ TORRES.

Aug. 1971 A right-wing *coup* brought Colonel BANZER SUARES to the presidency; several unsuccessful, then successful

1978–82 *coups* in quick succession. After elections

1982 President H. SILES ZUAZO.

1983 Extradition of the German war criminal KLAUS BARBIE to France.

1985 President N. PAZ ESTENSSORO.

1986 Use of U.S. troops to fight drugs.

1989 President J. PAZ ZAMORA, offensive against drug dealing.

Paraguay

1989 President STROESSNER (p. 271) was overthrown by milit. *coup* (Feb.) under General A. RODRIGUEZ, who became president (May).

Chile (p. 271)

With the assistance of the Christ. Democrats, the **Popular Front candidate**

Oct. 1970 **Salvador Allende** became the new (Marxist) president: nationalization of industry and landed property.

Sep. 1973 Fall and death of Allende caused by the milit. junta.

Jun. 1974 General A. Pinochet became chief of state, in Dec. president of the Republic. Violation of human rights, arrest of political enemies.

Sep. 1975 Still 8,000 political prisoners.

1975 Foundation of a State Council (Dec.).

1981 New constitution: PINOCHET 1st president, from 1981 unrest, torture, violation of human rights.

1988 Referendum against extension of PINOCHET's time in office (exceeding 1990).

1989 Free elections won by the opposition candidate (Dec.):

1990 President P. AYLWIN/Christ. Democrat.

Argentina (p. 271)

Following a bloodless *coup* by the army

Jun. 1966 President ONGANIA: dissolution of parliament, prohibition of polit. parties.

Coup by the milit. leadership:

Jun. 1970 President LEVINGSTON.

Mar. 1971 General LANUSSE became the new president: polit. parties were allowed to resume activities; cooperation with Peronist unions.

Mar.–Apr. 1973 Election victory for the Peronists;

Sep. 1973 JUAN PERÓN became president again. Death of PERÓN, his wife

1974 'ISABELLA' PERÓN became president. Terrorism, state of emergency programmes.

1976 Milit. junta took over power; state President General VIDELA who was followed by the

1981–2 General VIOLA and GALTIERI as president. After occupation of the Malvinas:

1982 war over the Falkland Islands (Mar.–Jun.) with Great Britain ended in defeat.

General BIGNONE new president, disintegration of the milit. junta.

1983 Elections: President R. ALFONSIN (Dec.).

1984 Commission examined the cases of the 'missing'. Quick trials against junta leaders.

1986 Statute of Limitation for crimes committed during the military dictatorship.

1989 Peronist C. S. MENEM became president.

Uruguay

1968 A state of siege was declared because of the activities of the 'urban guerrillas' (Tupamaros).

Feb. 1972 President J. M. BORDABERRY.

1976 President was overthrown by the milit. because of undemocratic ideas.

General A. MENDEZ became new president.

1981 General G. ALVAREZ. After elections, a civilian

1985 J. M. SANGUENETTI/Colorado became president.

1990 President L. LACALLE/Blanco.

Brazil (p. 277)

1967 President General COSTA E. SILVA.

Commission report about the murder of Indians by the Ind. Protection Agency.

Dec. 1968 Milit. dictatorship under General COSTA E. SILVA: wave of arrests, terrorist attacks.

1969 General MEDICI became new president.

1974 General GEISEL became new president.

1976 Nuclear power station: treaty with the B.R.D.

1979 General FIGUEIREDO became new president.

1983 Brazil had to stop debt servicing. After elections:

1985 President J. SARNEY. Extremely high inflation rates. After direct pres. elections:

1990 President F. COLLOR DE MELLO with radical financial redevelopment programme.

Surinam

Nov. 1975 Independence.

1980 Milit. junta on a socialist course.

1987 New constitution, election victory for the opposition.

Guyana

May 1966 Brit. Guyana obtained independence.

Venezuela

1973 Border with Brazil established.

1974 C. A. PEREZ/Democratic Action (A.D.).

Mar. 1975 Coffee association with Mexico, Costa Rica and El Salvador.

Aug. 1975 Nationalization of the oil economy as the basis of the plan for a new economic structure (Guayana project).

1979 President L. HERRERA CAMPINS/COPEI.

1984 President J. LUSINCHI/A.D.

1988 C. A. PEREZ became president again.

1989 Bloody unrest over the PEREZ gvt's drastic savings programme.

Morocco

Nov. 1975 Green March opposing the independence of Sp. Sahara.
1976 Occupation of the northern part,
1979 also the s. Conflicts with the independence movement, Polisario.

Mauritania

1975–6 Occupation of the southern part of Sp. Sahara. OULD DADDAH lost power through
1978 milit. *coup* which was followed by others.
1984 President TAYA.

Algeria

1978 Death of BOUMEDIENNE (p. 269).
1979 Colonel CHADLI became president.
1980 Congress of the F.L.N.: end of the BOUMEDIENNE era. Release of BEN BELLA (Oct.).
1984–5 Unrest and terrorism caused by Muslim fundamentalists.
1988 Bloody unrest over increase in food prices.
1991 Unrest provoked by Muslim fundamentalists (Jun.).

Tunisia

1970 Treaty with Algeria.
1974 Merger with Libya agreed, postponed by Tunisia. BOURGUIBA (p. 269) president for life (Dec.).
1978 Social tensions, general strike.
1987 Replacement of BOURGUIBA (because of incompetence) by BEN ALI, who became president and party chief.

The Federation of Arab Republics

1 Jan. 1972 The union, agreed on by Egypt, Libya and Syria, became effective.

Libya

1969 Milit. coup by young officers: revolutionary council under GADAFFI proclaimed republic.
1973 GADAFFI proclaimed Islam to be a social-revolutionary way (3rd International Theory).
1975 Armament treaties with the U.S.S.R.
1976 People's republic on the basis of the Koran. After resignation as state chief
1979 GADAFFI remained 'leader of the revolution'.
1980 Interference by Libyan troops in the Chad. After incidents during U.S. manoeuvres (Feb.) and military clashes (Mar.)
1986 U.S. air attack on Tripoli and Bengasi (Apr.).
Since 1988 affair of the chemical weapons factory in Rabta.

Egypt (p. 257)

5–10 Jun. 1967 Arab–Israeli war (6-Day War).
1968–69 Fighting along the Suez Canal; establishment of Rus. rocket bases.
Oct. 1970 **President Anwar El-Sadat** became the successor of NASSER.
Sep. 1971 Renaming of the United Arab Republic as the **Arab Republic of Egypt**; new constitution adopted.
1972 Deportation of the Soviet counsellors.
Oct. 1973 War against Israel.
Jun. 1975 Suez Canal reopened.
1976 Cancellation of the Friendship Treaty with the U.S.S.R.; withdrawal of all Soviet battleships. Defence pact with the Sudan, esp. against Libya.
1977 SADAT visited Israel.
1979 Friendship Treaty with Israel (Mar.).
1980 SADAT became president for life (May). Domestic opposition and religious unrest.
1981 Assassination of Sadat (6 Oct.).
M. H. MUBARAK became new president.
1982 Return of the Sinai (Apr.)
1987 President MUBARAK re-elected.

Sudan

Struggle of the Afr. s. against the domination of the Arab. N., especially the introduction of Islamic law.
1969 Milit. *coup* under General NUMEYRI.
1971 Following an abortive left-wing *coup*, persecution of Communists.
1972 Peace agreement with s. Sudan.
1985 Fall of Numeiri.
1989 State of war and civil war. *Coup* under General AL-BASHIR.

Ethiopia (p. 203)

1974–5 The emperor was deprived of power by the army. Nationalization of land, abolition of the monarchy.
Aug. 1975 HAILE SELASSIE I died.
1977 MENGISTU HAILE MARIAM new head of state and leader of the gvt of a Socialist Ethiopia. With the help of Soviet weapons and Cuban troops
1978 victory over western Somalia (Ogaden) and over the Eritrean Liberation Front.
1984 Foundation of the Marxist Ethiopian Workers' Party (Feb.). Famine (Oct.–Nov.).
1984–5 Operation Moses: air-bridge for Ethiopian Jews to Israel.
1987 New constitution: Democratic People's Republic of Ethiopia; MENGISTU elected president.
1990 Setting up of private companies allowed. Victory of the various liberation movements and
May 1991 fall of MENGISTU.

Fr. Somaliland

1967 A popular referendum decided in favour of remaining with France; severe unrest. Change of name to **'Territory of the Afar and Issas'**.
1977 Independence as the Republic of Djibouti.

Somalia

1967–9 President SCHERMARKE (murdered).
1969 Milit. *coup* under General BARRE.
1974 Treaty with the U.S.S.R. (1977 cancelled).
1976 Socialist one-party state. General BARRE became state president.
1977 German GSG 9 freed a German plane in Mogadishu abducted by terrorists.
1977–8 Conflict with Ethiopia over Ogaden.
1979 New constitution.
1986 President BARRE confirmed by direct election. Civil war and
Jan. 1991 fall of President BARRE.

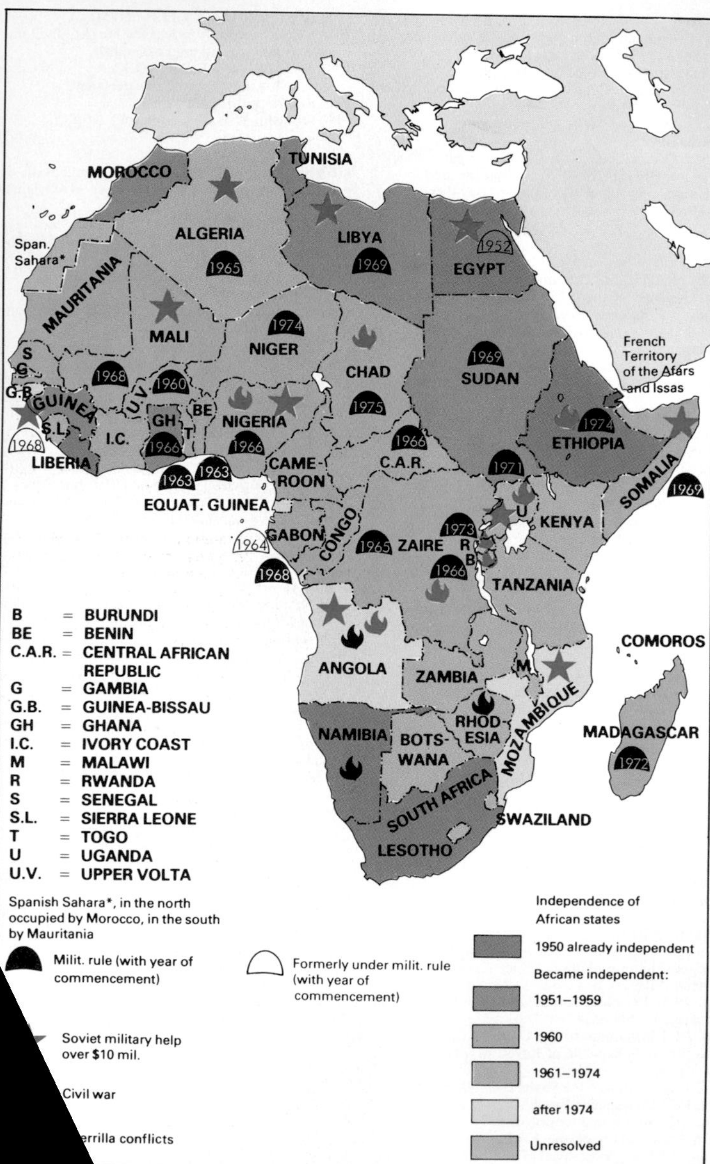
MOROCCO
ALGERIA
TUNISIA
LIBYA
EGYPT
1952
Span. Sahara*
MAURITANIA
1965
1969
MALI
NIGER
1974
CHAD
SUDAN
1969
French Territory of the Afars and Issas
S
G
G.B.
GUINEA
S.L.
1968
1968
U.V.
1960
GH
BE
NIGERIA
1975
1974
ETHIOPIA
I.C.
T
1966
1966
1966
LIBERIA
1963
1963
CAME-ROON
C.A.R.
1971
SOMALIA
1969
EQUAT. GUINEA
U
KENYA
GABON
1964
CONGO
1965
ZAIRE
1973
R
B
1966
1968
TANZANIA
B = BURUNDI
BE = BENIN
C.A.R. = CENTRAL AFRICAN REPUBLIC
G = GAMBIA
G.B. = GUINEA-BISSAU
GH = GHANA
I.C. = IVORY COAST
M = MALAWI
R = RWANDA
S = SENEGAL
S.L. = SIERRA LEONE
T = TOGO
U = UGANDA
U.V. = UPPER VOLTA
ANGOLA
ZAMBIA
M
COMOROS
MOZAMBIQUE
RHOD-ESIA
NAMIBIA
BOTS-WANA
MADAGASCAR
1972
SOUTH AFRICA
SWAZILAND
LESOTHO
Spanish Sahara*, in the north occupied by Morocco, in the south by Mauritania
Milit. rule (with year of commencement)
Formerly under milit. rule (with year of commencement)
Soviet military help over $10 mil.
Civil war
errilla conflicts
Independence of African states
1950 already independent
Became independent:
1951–1959
1960
1961–1974
after 1974
Unresolved

rica 1976

Kenya

President Jomo Kenyatta (1891–1978) governed with his KANU party. After KENYATTA's death
1978 D. A. MOI became state president.

Uganda

1966–71 President M. OBOTE.
1971 Milit. *coup* under Major General IDI AMIN, who established a reign of terror.
Invasion by Tanzanian troops and
1979 fall of the dictator Idi Amin.
1980 MILTON OBOTE became president again.
1983–4 Massacre of hundreds of thousands of Ugandans by the milit.
1985 Milit. *coup* under T. OKELLO.
1986 Milit. *coup* under Y. MUSEVENI.

Ruanda

1973 Milit. *coup* under J. HABYALIMANA (president since 1978); one-party system, the Tutsi deprived by force.

Burundi

1966 King NTARE V was dismissed by Prime Minister MICOMBERO, republic under
1966 President MICOMBERO.
1972 Bloody tribal feuds between the Hutu and the governing Tutsi.
1974 First constitution.
1976 *Coup* under Colonel J.-B. BAGAZA.
1987 *Coup* under Major P. BUYOYA.

Tanzania

President Nyerere governed with the united party (TANU); principles stated in the
1967 Charter of Arusha.
1985 Resignation of NYERERE; succeeded by A. H. MWINYI.

Zambia

President Kenneth Kaunda (since 1964) tried to overcome tribalism (72 tribes) with the help of his gvt party U.N.I.P.

Malawi

1966 New constitution: the prime minister, BANDA, became president of the republic.

Madagascar

President TSIRANANA deprived of power:
1972 Milit. gvt under RAMANANTSOA.
1975 Milit. junta, President RATSIRAKA.
1976 New constitution (Democratic Republic), RATSIRAKA president of the gvt council.

Mauritius

1966 The Brit. island became ind.

Seychelles

1976 Independent as a republic within the Commonwealth.

Botswana

Bechuanaland became independent as
1966 Republic of Botswana; S. KHAMA (1966–80) became first president.

Lesotho

1966 The Brit. protectorate of Basutoland became ind. as the kdm of Lesotho.
1970 *Coup*: Prime Minister L. JONATHAN (1965–86).
1986 Milit. *coup*.

Swaziland (Ngwane)

1968 The Brit. protectorate became ind.
1973 King SOBHUZAS II.
1986 King MSWATI III.

Independence of the former Portuguese overseas provinces (p. 283): 1974 **Guinea-Bissau.** 1975 **Mozambique; Sao Tomé/Pricipe; Cape Verde; Angola.**

Mozambique

1975 President S. MACHEL/FRELIMO: Socialist People's Republic, economic difficulties. Civil war with the anti-Marxist RENAMO which controlled wide parts of the country.
1984 Treaty of Mkomati with South Africa: renounced support for the A.N.C.
1986 Death of MACHEL in a plane crash. J. A. CHISSANO became new president.
1990 New constitution: republic with multi-party system, free market economy.

Angola

Nov. 1975 Constitution: People's Republic with single Marxist party (M.P.L.A.). Conflicts between the liberation movements.
Mar. 1976 M.P.L.A. under A. NETO won with the help of U.S.S.R. and Cuban troops, but UNITA continued civil war. After NETO's death
1979 President J. E. DOS SANTIOS. Support for the Namibian SWAPO.
1988 Decision about Cuban troop withdrawal and cease-fire; withdrawal of South African troops. Despite
1989 cease-fire, fighting did not end.
1991 Peace treaty with UNITA.

Rhodesia (p. 267)

U.N. condemnation, trade embargoes did not cause the SMITH gvt to back down.
1970 New constitution: independent republic. From
1975 guerrilla conflict.
1976 Geneva Rhodesian conference failed.
1978 Prime Minister A. MUZOREWA/A.N.C. of an initially mixed-race gvt.
1979 London Rhodesia conference decided on independence as **Zimbabwe**.

Zimbabwe

The ZANU/P.F. won parliamentary elections:
Apr. 1980 Prime Minister R. MUGABE/ZANU, tribal rivalries led to
1982 civil war with ZAPU under J. NKOMO.
1987 Union of ZANU and ZAPU: pres. system, President R. MUGABE.
1990 Re-election of President MUGABE (Mar.); NKOMO became vice-president (Aug.).

S. Africa (p. 267)

Sep. 1966 Prime Minister BALTHAZAR J. VORSTER (b. 1915); no changes in apartheid policy (p. 267).

Cancellation of the U.N. mandate over s.w. **Africa** was not complied with.

Jun. 1971 An opinion by the Int. Court of Justice in The Hague declared the presence of s. Africa in **Namibia** (s.w. Africa) to be illegal.

1974–7 Moderation of apartheid policies.

1976 Severe unrest in Soweto. The Transkei homeland became independent, others followed.

1978 Prime Minister P. W. BOTHA.

Milit. action against SWAPO in s. Angola. Economic recession in the 1980s.

1981 Invasion of s. Angola (Aug.–Sep.).

1984 New constitution, again did not include the black majority; parliament of 3 chambers (Whites, Coloureds, Indians), pres. system. P. W. BOTHA became state president.

1986 State of emergency (Jun.). Economic sanctions imposed by Western states. After resignation of BOTHA

1989 President F. W. DE KLERK (Sep.). Release of A.N.C. leaders.

1990 Release of the A.N.C. leader Nelson Mandela after 27 yrs of imprisonment (11 Feb.). Direct negotiations between DE KLERK and MANDELA (May).

State of emergency ended (Jun.). Conflict between A.N.C. and Zulu organization, Inkatha.

Return of A.N.C. President TAMBO (Dec.).

1991 President DE KLERK announced **end of apartheid policies** (Apr.).

Jun. 1991 Cancellation of the law which classified s. Africans according to race as: Whites, Blacks, Asians and Coloureds.

Namibia

At elections, not recognized by the U.N.,

1978 The Turnhalle Alliance won.

1988 Signature of Peace Treaty in New York (Dec.).

1989 Parl. elections: success for SWAPO.

Mar. 1990 Independence of the Republic of Namibia; President S. NUJOMA/SWAPO.

Senegal

President SENGHOR (1960–80) was replaced by

1981 President A. DIOUF (Jan.).

1982 Union with Gambia (until 1989).

1990 Border conflict with Mauritania.

Gambia

1970 Republic within the Commonwealth.

President D. K. JAWARA, also

1987 re-elected.

Guinea

1974 Bases for Soviet long-range planes.

1984 Death of Sékou Tourés and seizure of power by the milit.

Sierra Leone

1967 Milit. *coup* under General JUXON-SMITH.

1968 Milit. *coup*: Prime Minister STEVENS/A.P.C. Change to

1971 Republic under President STEVENS.

1978 New constitution: one-party state (A.P.C.).

1985 President J. MOMOH.

Liberia

1971 Death of President TUBMAN (since 1943). M. R. TOLBERT became successor, but was

1980 murdered during milit. *coup* under S. K. DOE.

1984 New constitution.

1985 Parl. elections.

1986 DOE became 20th president.

1990 Death of President DOE (10 Sep.), civil war.

Feb. 1991 Cease-fire treaty of the civil war parties.

Upper Volta

President M. YAMEOGO (1960–66) overthrown by

1966 milit. *coup* under Colonel LAMIZANA.

1974 'Gvt of National Restoration'.

1975–8 United party U.D.V.

President LAMIZANA (1966–80) overthrown by a

1980 milit. *coup*. Like his successors, S. ZERBO overthrown by

1982 President QUEDRAOGO and he in turn by

1983 President T. SANKARA.

1984 Change of name to **Burkina Faso**.

Burkina Faso

President SANKARA also overthrown by

1987 milit. *coup*: B. CAMPAORE became president.

Ghana

1979 Milit. *coup* under Lieutenant RAWLINGS (Jun.). After elections J. LIMANN became president.

1981–2 *Coup* under RAWLINGS again. National Defence Council.

Togo

1967 Milit. *coup* under Lieutenant Colonel EYADÉMA.

1969 Sole legal party R.P.T. under President EYADÉMA.

1990 Unrest of the opposition against the dictator EYADÉMA.

Dahomey

1965 and 1967 Milit. *coup*.

1968 Prime Minister ZINSOU.

Again milit. *coup*.

1969 Pres. Council led the gvt.

1972 Milit. *coup*: President Major KEREKOU.

1974 Marxism–Leninism became state doctrine.

1975 Failed *coup* attempts.

Nov. 1975 Change of name to People's Republic of Benin.

Benin

Nationalization of the banks. After departure from Marxism

1990 Prime Minister M. SOGLO.

Nigeria
Jan. 1966 Milit. *coup* under General IRONSI: a centralized and united state was the aim. A counter-*coup* aiming at confederation was staged under
Jul. 1966 Colonel GOWON. The eastern region demanded autonomy.
May 1967 Proclamation of the Republic of Biafra under Colonel OJUKWU.
1967–70 Civil War, ending with the unconditional surrender of Biafra.
1975 *Coup*: President General R. MOHAMMED,
1976 murdered during *coup*. President General OBASANJO. After elections
1979 President A. S. SHAGARI.
1983 Milit. *coup* under General BUHARI.
1985 Milit. *coup* under General BABANGIDA.

Sahel States
1980–81 Famine disaster.

Mali
President KEITA (since 1960) overthrown by
1968 milit. *coup* under M. TRAORÉ.
1974 New Constitution: pres. system. Single party (U.D.P.M.).
1979 TRAORÉ confirmed with first election.
1985 Border disputes with Burkina Faso.
1991 TRAORÉ overthrown by *coup*.

Niger
President H. DIORI (since 1960) overthrown by
1974 *coup* under Colonel S. KOUNTIE; after his death
1987 President A. SEIBU.

Chad
1975 Milit. *coup*, death of President TOMBALABAYE (since 1960).
Supreme milit. council under F. MALLOUM.
1979 Civil war; transitional gvt under President G. QUEDDEI.
1980 Libya interfered in the civil war.
1982 Withdrawal of Libyan troops, President QUEDDEI went into exile, formed oppositional gvt. HARRE became president. Help from France and Zaire against
1983 further attacks by QUEDDEI's troops.
1987 Peace with Libya. Fall of HARRE:
Dec. 1990 President IDRISS DEBY.

Cent. Afr. Republic
President DACKO (1960–66) was overthrown by the
1966 milit. *coup* under Colonel BOKASSA.
1972 President for life; terror
Dec. 1976 Proclamation of empire.
1979 Fall of Emperor BOKASSA I; again republic; President DACKO again.
1981 President General A. KOLINGBA through a *coup* without bloodshed.
1987 Ex-Emperor BOKASSA sentenced to death for multiple murder.

Equatorial Guinea
Sp. Guinea (Rio Muni), joined by the islands of Fernando Po and Annobón, became ind. as the
1968 Republic of Equatorial Africa.
1969 MACIAS reigned after death or assassination of leading opposition politicians.
1979 Fall of the MACIA NGUEMA dictatorship. Colonel T. OBIANG NGUEMA MBASOGO became president.

Cameroon
1972 Became a centralized state.
1975 President AHIDJO re-elected.
After resignation of AHIDJO
1982 P. BIYA became president.

Congo/Brazzaville
1968 Milit. *coup* by left-wing officers under Captain NGOUABI (murdered Mar. 1977), who became state president).
Dec. 1969 Proclamation of the **People's Republic of Congo**.
1977 President J. YHOMBI-OPANGO.
1979 President D. SASSOU NGUESSO.

Congo-Léopoldville/Kinshasa (p. 269)
1966 President MOBUTU, also prime minister.
1971 Change of name to **Republic of Zaire**.

Zaire
1977–8 Conflict in Shaba province (formerly Katanga) with Katangese exiles.
1978 New constitution; presidential system. MOBUTU remained as president.

Organization of African Unity (O.A.U.)
Conference in Lusaka passed
1970 resolution about southern Africa: against racial discrimination.
1988 (25th) Conference in Addis Ababa ascertained failure of African union.
The presidents of 51 O.U.A. states signed a
1991 treaty about the African Economic Community to be realized by the yr 2025 after the model of the E.C.

Econ. unions
1965 The Joint Afr. Madagascan Organization (Dahomey, Ivory Coast, Gabon, Cameroon Republic, Republic of Congo, Republic of Madagascar, Mauritius, Niger, Upper Volta, Ruanda, Senegal, Togo, Chad, Zaire, the Cen. Afr. Rep.).
1967 E. Afr. Common Market (Kenya, Uganda, Tanzania); 1970 association treaty with the E.E.C.
1964 Central African Customs and Economic Union (UDEAC): Gabon, Cameroon, Republic of Congo, Central African Republic, (since 1983) Equatorial Guinea.
1975 Convention of Lomé with the E.C. (p. 276).
1975 Economic Community of West African States (CEDEAO): the 6 CEAO states: Burkina Faso, Ivory Coast, Mali, Mauritania, Niger, Senegal and (since 1984) Benin as well as Gambia, Ghana, Guinea, Guinea-Bissau, (since 1977) Cape Verde, Liberia, Nigeria, Sierra Leone and Togo.

Index

Roman figures indicate an entry to be found in volume 1.
Italic figures indicate an entry to be found in volume 2.
Bold figures indicate an entry of central importance to be found in volume 1.
Bold italic figures indicate an entry of central importance to be found in volume 2.